S0-BFB-384

The CIA & the Security Debate: 1975-1976

The CIA & the Security Debate: 1975-1976

Editor: Judith F. Buncher

Contributing Writers: Joseph Fickes, Bob Hollingsworth, and Chris Larson

FACTS ON FILE
119 West 57th Street
New York, New York

The CIA & the Security Debate: 1975-1976

 Published by Facts on File, Inc., 119 West 57th Street, New York, N.Y. 10019.

Library of Congress Cataloging in Publication Data

Main entry under title:

The CIA & the security debate, 1975–1976.

Includes index.

1. United States. Central Intelligence Agency. 2. United States—Politics and government—1969–1974. 3. United States—Politics and government—1974. I. Buncher, Judith F. II. Fickes, Joseph. III. Hollingsworth, Bob. IV. Larson, Chris.

JK468.I6C283 327'.12'0973 75-18070

ISBN 0-87196-364-7

9 8 7 6 5 4 3 2 1

PRINTED IN THE UNITED STATES OF AMERICA

Contents

The CIA and the Presidency

Ford fires Schlesinger, Colby. Major changes were reported in the Ford Administration Nov. 2, 1975 and confirmed by the President at a news conference Nov. 3. Vice President Nelson A. Rockefeller withdrew Nov. 3 from consideration as Ford's running mate in 1976. The other changes:

- James R. Schlesinger was ousted as defense secretary. Ford said he would nominate Donald H. Rumsfeld, currently White House chief of staff.
- William E. Colby was dropped as director of the Central Intelligence Agency. George Bush, head of the U. S. liaison office in China and former Republican Party chairman, was Ford's choice to fill the job.

Could he say why Schlesinger and Colby "did not fit on your new team?" A. They were kept on when he assumed office "because I wanted continuity. But any president to do the job that's needed and necessary has to have his own team in the area of foreign policy. I believe the team that I have assembled . . . will do a first-class job."

Bush nomination opposed—The nomination of George Bush to be director of the Central Intelligence Agency attracted some prominent opposition. Sen. Frank Church (D, Idaho), chairman of a Senate probe of the U.S. intelligence operations, made known his opposition Nov. 4. He said he knew "of no particular reason" why Bush was qualified to head an agency that was "the least political and most sensitive in government."

In a Senate speech Nov. 11, Church urged his colleagues to "stand up and oppose this nomination" and "insist upon a Central Intelligence Agency which is politically neutral and totally professional."

Another critic Nov. 4 was Sen. William Proxmire (D, Wis.), who, noting that Bush was a former Republican national chairman, said the appointment violated "the cardinal rule of the intelligence business—separation of all political influences from the intelligence process."

Senate Democratic Leader Mike Mansfield (Mont.) said Nov. 12 he would support the Bush nomination but suggested Bush renounce any vice presidential inclinations before accepting the intelligence post.

At the White House, Press Secretary Ron Nessen said Nov. 5 President Ford had asked William E. Colby to stay on as Director of the CIA until Bush returned from his diplomatic post in Peking and was confirmed by the Senate into the new post. A carryover of the confirmation proceedings into 1976 was possible in view of Ford's scheduled visit to Peking in early December and probable adjournment by Congress shortly afterwards.

Nessen defended Bush Nov. 5 with the observation that if the agency were headed by a man who had run for public office it could make it more "responsive" to the public interest. Bush had served two terms in the House of Representatives and had run unsuccessfully for the Senate.

Bush confirmed—The Senate Jan. 27, 1976 confirmed George Bush as CIA director. He was approved 64–27. The Senate had blocked his confirmation until President Ford excluded Bush as a potential vice presidential running mate.

Ford comments on CIA, FBI. President Ford held a televised news conference Nov. 26, 1975. He said that he hoped he was "fully aware of everything the CIA" was doing. He noted his recent "specific instructions" to the CIA "that under no circumstances should any agency in this government, while I'm President, participate in or plan for any assassination of a foreign leader."

"Equally emphatic instructions," he said, "have gone to any domestic agency of the federal government and/or the CIA or intelligence agency that they should not violate the law involving the right of privacy of any individual in the United States."

As for the reports about FBI attempts to discredit Dr. Martin Luther King before his assassination, the President said: "I certainly condemn those actions which were taken regarding Martin Luther King. I think it abhorrent to all Americans, including myself. Whether or not we can identify the individuals, if they are still alive, is difficult, but I certainly will consult with the attorney general regarding that matter." A reporter asked did he think an effort should be made to identify the people responsible? "I think so," Ford replied.

What about reopening the investigation of the assassination of President Kennedy? There were "some new developments—not evidence," Ford replied. If these could be fully investigated "without C
reopening the whole matter," he said, he thought "some responsible group or organization ought to do so." "But not to reopen all of the other aspects," he continued, "because I think they were thoroughly covered by the Warren Commission."

In light of his membership on the Warren Commission, he said, he thought an investigation of any new developments "might be better done by somebody other D
than I appoint."

In response to another query, Ford affirmed the necessity on national security grounds to undertake foreign covert intelligence operations, but he said he was not going to discuss details. Would he "allow the country to involve itself in situations which could potentially be dangerous to other leaders?" he was asked. "The people in the intelligence agencies know what my instructions are," he replied. "If they violate them, proper action E
will be taken."

Ford addresses Congress. President Ford told the nation Jan. 19, 1976 that it was time "for a fundamentally different approach for a new realism that is true to the great principles upon which this nation was founded."

His approach, as outlined in his second State of the Union message, delivered F
before a joint evening session of Congress, was to reduce taxes and federal spending; secure the financial base of the Social Security system; consolidate federal education, health and social-services programs for more flexible application by the state and local governments.

On the foreign front, the President cautioned Congress not to curb his conduct of foreign policy nor to hobble the U.S. intelligence capabilities. He also stressed G
the necessity of a strong defense.

> As conflict and rivalry persist in the world, our United States intelligence capabilities must be the best in the world.
>
> The crippling of our foreign intelligence services increases the danger of American involvement in direct armed conflict. Our adversaries are encouraged

> to adopt or attempt new adventures, while our own ability to monitor them, and to influence events short of military action, is undermined.
>
> Without effective intelligence capabilities, the United States stands blindfolded and hobbled.
>
> A In the near future, I will take actions to reform and strengthen our intelligence community. I ask for your positive cooperation. It is time to go beyond sensationalism and insure an effective, responsible and responsive intelligence capability.

He promised steps in the near future to reform and strengthen the intelligence community and asked for "positive cooperation" from Congress. It was time, he said, "to go beyond sensationalism and insure an effective, responsible and responsive intelligence capability."

B

Muskie gives Democratic rebuttal—A Congressional Democratic rebuttal to President Ford's State of the Union message deplored the Administration's "jobless policies" at home and questionable entanglements abroad without public consultation. It was delivered by Sen. Edmund S. Muskie (D, Me.) in a national telecast Jan. 21 during evening time made C available by the three major commercial networks and the Public Broadcasting System.

As for the Congressional investigations of the U.S. intelligence operations, he asked: "How else is the American public to get hold of its foreign policy again? How else can we guarantee that interventions in other countries are an appropriate expression of deliberate United States policy, not the making of some faceless bureaucrat?"

D

Intelligence structure revised. President Ford announced at a televised news conference Feb. 17 his plans for revision of the command structure of U.S. foreign intelligence operations and establishment of guidelines for such operations. He also planned to request special legislation to safeguard "critical intelligence secrets."

The President said he was acting be- E cause, "As Americans, we must not and will not tolerate actions by our government which will abridge the rights of our citizens. At the same time, we must maintain a strong effective intelligence capability . . . . I will not be a party to the dismantling of the CIA [Central Intelligence Agency] or other intelligence agencies."

"We must have a comprehensive in- F telligence capability," Ford emphasized.

The President proposed a three-part plan:

■ He was establishing by executive order a "new command structure for foreign intelligence." All policy direction would come from the National Security Council, consisting of the President, the Vice President and the secretaries of state and defense. Management of the policy would be conducted by a new committee G that would be headed by the CIA director, George Bush.

A new independent oversight board made up of private citizens would be established "to monitor the performance of our intelligence operations." The members of that board were former undersecretary of state Robert D. Murphy, 81, chairman; Washington lawyer Stephen Ailes, 63, a former secretary of the Army and currently president of the Association of American Railroads; and New York economist Leo Cherne, 63, a member of the existing President's Foreign Intelligence Board since 1973.

■ "A comprehensive set of public guidelines" was being issued "to improve the performance of the intelligence agencies and to restore public confidence in them." These were to "serve as legally binding charters for our intelligence activities." The charters were to "provide stringent protections for the rights of American citizens."

Ford said he would meet with Congressional leaders "to map out legislation to provide judicial safeguards against electronic surveillance and mail openings" and he would also "support legislation that would prohibit attempts on the lives of foreign leaders in peacetime."

■ "Special legislation to safeguard critical intelligence secrets" would be proposed to Congress. The legislation "would make it a crime for a government employe who has access to certain highly classified information to reveal that information improperly."

The President said that intelligence must not be confined to a warning of "an imminent military attack," that it also must provide information about the world's economy, political and social trends, food supplies, population growth and terrorism, among other things.

The intelligence operation was a "great pillar" of American strength, Ford said, and "the overriding task now is to rebuild the confidence as well as the capability of our intelligence services so that we can live securely in peace and freedom."

During the news conference following his announcement, the President was asked why the CIA was being put more under control of the presidency since "we know that office has abused the CIA in the past." Ford said a president "ought to be accountable" and his proposals were an attempt "to make the process and the decision-making fall on the shoulders of the President and he will be held accountable by the American people."

As for the possibility of abuse, Ford said, "it shouldn't happen." "I would hope that the American people will elect a president who will not abuse that responsibility. I certainly don't intend to."

On his proposed legislation, he was asked whether it would not prevent in the future the kind of disclosures which had brought out the CIA abuses in the past. Ford replied that under his reorganization and proposed legislation, "There won't be any abuses and the people, if there are any abuses, will be held accountable. So I don't feel at all apprehensive that what happened in the past will be repeated in the future."

Asked what steps would be taken to prevent misuse of the classification system "or the secrecy label" to cover up policy mistakes, Ford cited the inspector general system within the intelligence services.

Also in reply to queries, Ford explained that the new oversight board would not supersede the 40 Committee, which would be given a new name (Operations Advisory Group) and "some change in personnel." It would consist in the future, he said, of the president's national security aide, the secretaries of state and defense, the CIA director and the chairman of the Joint Chiefs of Staff and it would have two observers—the attorney general and the director of the office of management and budget.

The President expressed concern about Congressional leaking of intelligence secrets. Congress should "address itself" to this problem, he said, which could be "a very serious matter."

He urged Congress to establish a joint committee for oversight of the "program and the performance" of intelligence activities.

As for the Federal Bureau of Investigation, in light of past abuses in the intelligence-gathering area, Ford said the attorney general was developing "very strict guidelines" on this.

Executive order effective March 1—An executive order on the government's foreign intelligence activities was issued Feb. 18, to be effective March 1. It proscribed, in general, spying on Americans or testing drugs on them, infiltrating domestic groups or intercepting mail for any other reason than counterespionage or security checks on government employes.

On covert operations abroad, the order stipulated that no federal employe "shall engage in, or conspire to engage in, political assassination."

The ban against drug experimentation on human subjects contained an exception permitting such activity with "the informed consent, in writing and witnessed by a disinterested third party, of each such human subject."

Language in the other provisions also would permit the CIA: (a) to infiltrate within the U.S. organizations "composed primarily of non-United States persons . . . reasonably believed to be acting on behalf of a foreign power"; (b) to collect information within the U.S. on "corporations or other commercial organizations which constitutes foreign intelligence or counterintelligence"; (c) to gather domestic intelligence against U.S. citizens, corporations or resident aliens who were "reasonably believed to be acting on behalf of a foreign power or engaging in international terrorist or narcotics activities"; (d) to enter into arrangements with academic institutions for research and other services.

The President's draft legislation barring federal employes from disclosing sources and methods of American foreign intelligence operations also was submitted to Congress Feb. 18. An exemption from criminal prosecution was provided for journalists or others receiving such secrets, but Attorney General Edward H. Levi, explaining the draft bill Feb. 18, said that grand juries could question reporters under the law about their sources.

FORD FIRES SCHLESINGER, COLBY; KISSINGER LOSES SECURITY POST

President Ford shifted his staff in several key governmental posts. The following were among the major changes, widely reported in news leaks Nov. 2 and confirmed by Ford at a news conference Nov. 3:

- James R. Schlesinger was ousted as defense secretary. Ford said he would nominate Donald H. Rumsfeld, currently White House chief of staff.
- William E. Colby was dropped as director of the Central Intelligence Agency. George Bush, head of the U.S. liaison office in China and former Republican Party chairman, was Ford's choice to fill the job.
- Secretary of State Henry A. Kissinger was relieved as director of the National Security Council. The post was to go to Air Force Lieut. Gen. Brent Scowcroft, currently deputy director of the National Security Council.

Ford confirmed reports of the changes, and announced a new one:

- Elliot L. Richardson would be nominated as commerce secretary to replace Rogers C. B. Morton, who, Ford said, desired to return to the private sector. Richardson currently was ambassador to Britain.
- The President said he had selected Richard B. Cheney to succeed Rumsfeld as chief of the White House staff, formally known as assistant to the President. Cheney currently was a deputy assistant to the President.

There was much speculation about the reasons for the shake-up, such as—friction between Kissinger and Schlesinger, and, with the departure of Schlesinger, a compensatory lessening of influence for Kissinger by removal from the security position. However, Scowcroft, moving into the post, was considered a loyal Kissinger aide. But most observers attributed the shake-up primarily to Ford's desire to assert more positive leadership and stem an apparently growing threat from Ronald Reagan against Ford's nomination as the GOP candidate for 1976.

The Dispatch

Columbus, Ohio, November 6, 1975

SPECULATION attendant to recent changes in President Ford's cabinet tends to obscure an important point — the Chief Executive has not acted with undue haste in selecting members of his own team of administrators.

That any president is entitled to surround himself with advisers of his own choosing is an unquestioned right.

That Mr. Ford is chiefly concerned with maintaining continuity during the selection process is commendable evidence he is acting without disrupting influence.

UPON confirmation of the most recent nominations for cabinet posts, the President will be retaining only three secretaries who were on deck when Mr. Ford assumed the presidency in August of 1974.

They are Secretary of State Henry Kissinger, Treasury Secretary William Simon and Secretary of Agriculture Earl Butz.

IT IS unfortunate that questioners at the press conference where the cabinet changes were made official were so enamored with the personalities of Mr. Ford's cabinet.

There was a dearth of inquiries regarding problems and issues bothering the nation and which cabinet secretaries must play major roles in solving.

Vice President Nelson Rockefeller's announcement he does not wish to be considered as a running-mate with Mr. Ford during the 1976 presidential campaign helps to clear the political air.

THE PRESIDENT, as well as his Republican party, each now is free to contemplate all alternatives in shaping a team of candidates to be placed before the electorate.

This development, along with the President's attitude about cabinet selections, emphasizes a need for deliberateness, an absence of haste and more importantly a realization by Mr. Ford he must establish himself as his own man.

In essence, that is what President Ford's press conference announcement was all about.

St. Petersburg Times

St. Petersburg, Fla., November 4, 1975

In a major shakeup of his Administration, President Ford has prepared his personnel as well as his issues for the 1976 political campaign. His actions will place a Ford stamp on both the Defense Department and the Central Intelligence Agency. He will choose a new running mate. But the manner in which the changes took place raises serious questions about Mr. Ford's White House.

IT HAS BEEN apparent for months that time had run out for CIA Director William E. Colby. His firing evidently was linked with that of Defense Secretary James R. Schlesinger on the theory that departures are cheaper by the dozen.

Despite Ford's denials last night, Schlesinger's ouster was caused by his dispute over dentente with Secretary of State Henry Kissinger and his insistence on an inflated military budget. It will be denied often that all this had anything to do with Vice President Nelson A. Rockefeller's removal from the 1970 ticket. But if Schlesinger's dismissal had come separately, Mr. Ford certainly would have been attacked by the right wing of his party, which he is wooing so fervently. With Rockefeller off the ticket at the same time, the Reagans and Buckleys are likely to be so delighted that there won't be much appetite for criticizing the President.

The removal of Kissinger as head of the National Security Council was a cosmetic half-measure that failed to bring about needed change. The foreign-policymaking machinery functions best when the President has the advantage of independent advice from both his national security adviser and his secretary of state. Kissinger no longer will hold both jobs, but the new adviser is Kissinger's chief military aide, Air Force Lt. Gen. Brent Scowcroft.

Donald Rumsfeld, the new defense chief, seems to have the intellectual toughness and political skills needed for that job. He has served in Congress, as head of the poverty program, as ambassador to NATO and as White House staff chief. George Bush, shifted from the U.S. liaison office in China to the CIA, has an indistinct record as a personally attractive Texas congressman and U.N. ambassador. Eliot Richardson is well qualified to become commerce secretary.

THE POLICY implications of the shakeup are considerable. The Schlesinger firing was a triumph for Kissinger and his foreign policies. In recent weeks, Kissinger's top aides have been describing the Strategic Arms Limitations Talks with the Soviet Union as being in serious trouble, caught between conflicting demands from the Pentagon and the Kremlin. Schlesinger's ouster should raise the likelihood of successful arms limitations, a large plus for the country and the world.

Except for one sour note, the shakeup leaves Mr. Ford stronger politically for the 1976 campaign. More than 24 hours before the White House acknowledged them, the personnel changes were revealed by Sen. Henry M. "Scoop" Jackson, a Democratic candidate for the presidency. Is that any way to run the White House?

Arkansas Gazette.

Little Rock, Ark., November 5, 1975

President Ford presided Monday over the most dramatic administrative upheaval since the famous "Saturday night massacre" in the Nixon administration. There has been much ensuing excitement in Washington and around the country — possibly more excitement, we might add, than is warranted in basic policy consideration.

Mr. Ford replaced the Secretary of Defense and the director of the CIA, even as he took away Henry Kissinger's long-disputed portfolio on the National Security Council. For good measure, heightening the general effect, he announced that he was bringing back Elliot Richardson from the Court of St. James to make him Secretary of Commerce. The whole scene was climaxed, as it happened, with Nelson Rockefeller's announcement that he was withdrawing from contention as a candidate to succeed himself as Vice President.

It was a day of startling developments, all right, and with so much coming and going in places of power it might be unwise, we suppose, to discount heavily such events. Certainly the dismissal of James R. Schlesinger as Secretary of Defense appears to connote a strengthening of the detente policy as advocated by Secretary of State Kissinger, who was often at odds with Schlesinger, himself something of a hard-liner in the context of detente. The departure of Schlesinger is certainly the most important of the announcements that Ford made, and it set off an angry buzzing on the Republican right.

As for the dismissal of CIA Director William F. Colby, it may be said that he was one of the most eminently expendable figures in the U. S. government, given the dimensions of the trouble that the CIA has been in and continues in. Whether his successor, George Bush, U. S. representative to the Peking government, will perform better is a question to be determined.

The return of Elliot Richardson, out of exile in the Scepter'd Isle, in its turn, is intriguing politically, for Richardson is one of the most respected of Republicans, even if he happens to be one who was instrumental in bringing down former President Richard Nixon. The GOP has a certain ambivalence in its view of Richardson but Ford, in any case, can do his administration no harm by putting Richardson on public view. At the same time, Commerce is just about the safest place that Richardson could be installed.

As for poor Nelson Rockefeller, his humiliation at the hands of his fellow Republicans and at the hands of the Ford administration could hardly have been more complete after the President harshly dismissed the pleas of the city and of the state of New York for help in their financial crisis. Rockefeller, as governor of New York, had helped preside over the buildup toward bankruptcy and he had recommended to Ford that aid be granted. In any event the coup de grace to the political career of Nelson Rockefeller was administered by Ford in the "final answer" to New York which was summed up so admirably by the New York Daily News, in the imperishable headline: "FORD TO CITY: DROP DEAD!"

There is one more factor in interpreting the President's reshuffling of top executive positions. He said with emphasis that he was putting his own men, Donald Rumsfeld and Bush, into the positions at Defense and in the CIA, replacing two men who were not his own close associates. As much as anything else, the great upheaval in Washington may have been an exercise in presidential machismo, with Ford simply telling the world that he was President and meant to run the country's affairs with his own men in his own way.

Minneapolis Tribune

Minneapolis, Minn., November 4, 1975

Domestic politics and foreign policy are cause as well as effect in the shakeup of top positions in the Ford administration. Without slighting the significance of the changes in terms of politics — internal White House politics as well as the presidential-election variety — we think it important to pay at least equal attention to the foreign-policy consequences.

Vice President Rockefeller's decision to remove himself from consideration as President Ford's running mate next year, if Ford wins the Republican nomination, opens the presidential campaign to a variety of new considerations. As last night's press conference indicated, they will be the subject of lively discussion in the coming weeks, but deserve at least this initial observation:

Rockefeller's duties in Washington and his earlier responsibilities as governor of New York have focused primary attention on his domestic political views. In particular, his past role inevitably gave him a share of the burden for New York City's current fiscal crisis. But this tends to eclipse the fact that Rockefeller brought to the vice presidency unusual experience and understanding in foreign affairs. That aspect of qualifications is something to keep in mind during the speculation about Republican vice-presidential candidates.

The foreign-policy consequences of the shifts in leading figures in the national-security establishment are more evident. George Bush, named to succeed William Colby as head of the CIA, seems to have performed competently heading U.S. missions to the United Nations and to China. There's no reason to think he would do otherwise as director of central intelligence. Also, in view of the changes coming in the intelligence establishment, there's much to be said for replacing an intelligence insider like Colby with an outsider like Bush.

A secretary of commerce is as much concerned with domestic as with foreign economic policy, and Elliot Richardson brings to Ford's new team impressive experience in both. Replacing Rogers Morton, who is leaving government, Richardson in the past seven years has held senior or top positions at State; Health, Education and Welfare; Defense, and Justice Departments before his present post as ambassador to Britain. He should be a valuable addition to the Cabinet.

The change involving the State Department and the National Security Council is overdue. Until the advent of Henry Kissinger, the job of secretary of state was not considered a condition of underemployment that required additional duties as national-security adviser to the president. It makes sense to limit Kissinger's assignment to that of secretary of state. We are less sure about the wisdom of naming Kissinger's security-council deputy, Gen. Brent Scowcroft, the new security adviser. Our reservation is not because of doubts about Scowcroft's abilities, but because of questions about the independence he will have from Kissinger. Those questions remain despite the president's praise last night for Scowcroft's "independent mind;" they can be answered only by observing what happens in the months ahead.

The president's firing of James Schlesinger was unexpected, even though Ford as vice president had once indicated he might look for a new defense secretary if he became president. We agree with Sen. Jackson's characterization of Schlesinger as "a man of courage, integrity and honor." But none of those qualities is at issue. The defense secretary has demonstrated an unusual grasp of his subject and has presented his case well; no one questions his dedication. Interestingly, his arguments against cuts in military expenditures are consistent with Ford's views — and, as the president said at his press conference, are consistent with the views of White House chief of staff Donald Rumsfeld, Ford's choice for a replacement.

But Schlesinger's position on negotiations with the Soviet Union is at variance with Kissinger's. The secretary of state sees an urgent need to bring the current phase of strategic-arms talks to fruition; the secretary of defense wants more concessions from the Russians than Kissinger believes are possible or essential. In that situation the president may have felt he had to make a choice between his two leading advisers on security and defense matters. It is no slight to Schlesinger to say that we hope the president's choice was sound and a limit on nuclear weapons will be the result.

Post-Tribune

Guarding Your Interests Daily

Gary, Ind., November 5, 1975

OK, we accept the premise that a President, any President, is entitled to his "own team."

But acceptance of that premise carries with it the further premise that it then becomes the responsibility of that President to make that "team" work.

So it is with President Ford and his further heavily reshuffled Cabinet.

As an aside, it's worth noting that the President has once more proved one of his original statements—that he is a "Ford and not a Lincoln." Abraham Lincoln had several strong willed Cabinet members—notably William Seward at State and Edwin Stanton at War (the latter a replacement for the briefly tenured Simon Cameron)—frequently at odds with each other and generally convinced that they knew more than the President, yet he kept them. Ford has had the same sort of thing in Henry Kissinger at State and James Schlesinger at Defense, but he has decided to keep the former, drop the latter for a man closer to him personally than either—a former fellow House member, Donald Rumsfeld.

The situations are not, of course, identical. Ford had inherited his Cabinet and now says he went along with the foreign affairs aspects of it as long as he did in order to give proof of a continuity of foreign policy. Lincoln made up his own, and yet he was guided more by political realities of a newly rising party than by personal preference.

But the fact remains that it will now be up to Ford—as it was up to Lincoln—to make the new "team" work. Kissinger and Schlesinger were obviously often at odds. Will a Kissinger who remains "dominant," as the President says he will be, in foreign affairs be able to work with Rumsfeld once the latter gets hold of the Pentagon? If they clash will Ford be able to prove he's the boss as he says he will be? Will Gen. Brent Scowcroft as chairman of the National Security Council as a replacement for Kissinger continue only as a Kissinger agent, or will he show independence?

On the surface, it is difficult to find fault with the Rumsfeld and Scowcroft appointments or with those of George Bush to head the Central Intelligence Agency or Elliot Richardson in his fourth Cabinet position at Commerce in place of Rogers C. B. Morton.

But in each case there is a lack of experience to be overcome.

Bush has been able on the ambassadorial and political level, but working with the intelligence apparatus is something different, particularly an intelligence apparatus under fire. His appointment may be designed to quench that fire, but that won't come without further probes.

Richardson has proved enough ability in the past to seem able in any Cabinet post, but working out the Commerce Department's part of the energy crisis requires new skills.

Rumsfeld is a great team member and has shown leadership qualities, but fitting Pentagon policies into both spending debates and foreign policy will require real wizardry.

Which all gets back to the point that, except possibly for the Treasury, Ford would now seem to have his own team, and now it's up to him to make it work.

The Morning Star

Rockford, Ill., November 5, 1975

In an action startling mostly because it was so unexpected, President Ford has realigned his Cabinet and made other changes in top leadership posts.

The President said he made the changes, to use his words, to put "my guys" on the team.

Most certainly, that is what they are. Don Rumsfeld (the new secretary of defense) and George Bush (the new director of the Central Intelligence Agency) clearly bear the Ford team stamp.

It is obvious, going into a political campaign, that Ford wants just this: An administration that has his label and now that of the man he succeeded in the Oval Office.

In that sense the change is political and in readiness for an upcoming campaign.

But we also view the changes as a classic example of a President of the United States acting like a president. It is not only the right of a President to select a Cabinet of his personal choosing, it is the duty of a President to place in posts of top leadership persons he knows and trusts as men who will contribute to a team effort that has as its aim the good of the country.

In announcing the changes Monday night, Ford did an adequate job of explaining himself. With good grace, he warded off news conference questions suggesting that the changes were prompted by political considerations.

Everyone knows, of course, that the big election is just one year away, and that President Ford is in the running for election to the presidency he now holds via the appointment route.

And it's also pretty clear that the changes are likely to help Mr. Ford in November, 1976.

But, first and foremost, the President is improving his administration leadership team.

Chicago Sun-Times

Chicago, Ill., November 5, 1975

In his press conference Monday night, President Ford went to great lengths to dismiss any suggestion that his Cabinet-level changes were motivated by political forces, within the administration or without it. He insisted repeatedly that he made the changes only because he wanted his own team. He would have made the changes earlier, he said, except that he wanted to assure continuity between the Nixon administration and his own.

But Ford failed to answer when reporters pressed him to answer the question: Why did it takes 15 months to make the change? It doesn't take 15 months to make a smooth transition of power and to develop new priorities.

What has taken 15 months to develop, however, is a persistent difference of opinion between Sec. of State Henry A. Kissinger and outgoing Defense Sec. James R. Schlesinger. These differences of opinion — Ford insisted only that they were not "basic" — relate to the Strategic Arms Limitation Talks and to other aspects of U.S.-Soviet detente. However much Ford wanted to minimize them, the disagreements are matters of public record.

These internal policy disputes finally compelled Ford to choose between Schlesinger and Kissinger. William E. Colby, fired as director of the Central Intelligence Agency, had become a political liability. Such liabilities are dangerous at a time when Ford faces nagging economic problems (in the form of high unemployment) and nagging political problems (in the person of former California Gov. Ronald Reagan).

The ouster of Schlesinger has cost Ford the support of some conservatives in both parties. But his decision to replace Colby with GOP loyalist George W. Bush was politically advantageous. And the decision of Vice President Nelson A. Rockefeller not to seek re-election gives Ford a flexible hand in meeting the conservative challenge. Whether the appointments are good for the country is another matter.

The Chattanooga Times

Chattanooga, Tenn., November 5, 1975

The substantive reasons behind the fast breaking series of top level changes in the Ford Administration are for the moment at least buried beneath the President's repetitive defense of a need to have "my guys" closest at hand.

Secretary of Defense James Schlesinger is out, summarily dismissed. Donald Rumsfeld, White House chief of staff with long running ambitions for a cabinet post, is to be nominated.

Secretary of State Henry Kissinger will give up his second — though scarcely secondary — position as chief White House adviser on national security matters as well as foreign affairs. Lt. Gen. Brent Scowcroft will assume the post. Since he is a Kissinger protege, the secretary's influence is not likely to be diminished.

Commerce Secretary Rogers Morton wants out at year's end. Seemingly the least likely choice, Elliott Richardson will replace him. Mr. Richardson held a handful of Cabinet level jobs under Richard Nixon and is now ambassador to Great Britain.

CIA Director William E. Colby, target of heavy fire as the current head of an agency in deep trouble for apparent abuse of its assigned authority, is leaving. George Bush, chief of the U.S. diplomatic mission in China, will take over.

And, in a coincidental but apparently self-initiated action, Vice President Nelson Rockefeller said he would not take a place on the 1976 GOP ticket with Mr. Ford.

The President was repeatedly asked: "Why? Who did what to warrant these sweeping changes after 13 months of apparent satisfaction with those now leaving with warm words of praise?" Mr. Ford had one answer: The President has the right, even the duty, to bring together the people he wants to carry out national policies. He and he alone "fit the pieces together" to form this team which will "affirmatively" act for the public interest.

As for Mr. Rockefeller, the President said, the Vice President made his own choice "and I accepted it."

The public saw a new Gerald Ford in the news conference exchanges, not necessarily a more effective President or even a more attractive personality. But this was not the man who, shortly after entering the White House, said simply: "I don't like to hurt people's feelings . . . It's the hardest thing for me to tell somebody they ought to leave. . . . That's my nature and I guess you're not going to change it."

For right reasons or wrong, he appeared out to prove he could indeed move appointees around by his own authority, and without acknowledgement of advice from others.

He was uneasy in the exercise of power, visibly bristling when pressed for reasons of inaction over the past year. But he has wielded power in a display of abnormal energy which Henry Brooks Adams called "the most serious of facts," and it should be noted.

At the same time, it wouldn't hurt for the President to recall another of Adams' points: "Those who seek education in the paths of duty are always deceived by the illusion that power in the hands of friends is an advantage to them."

Herald-Journal

Syracuse, N.Y., November 9, 1975

President Ford possesses every right in the world to fire Secretary of Defense James Schlesinger and CIA Director William Colby to put his own people in their jobs.

That's a sound canon of management.

Without engaging in debate over the new appointees' qualifications, whether they are interested primarily in their own political careers, or whether Ford is more comfortable with former House colleagues, the President applied a right that we must grant to all presidents.

But the way the changes came about isn't in accord with what we had been accustomed to seeing.

Ford, from the start, built a refreshing reputation for candor, an earnest frankness that has been his No. 1 asset.

We felt comfortable with a president who practiced what he preached about conducting an "open" administration.

He cracked the mirror presenting that image only once: when he pardoned former President Nixon.

During the energy crisis, for example, we received more down-to-earth estimates and explanations than we had seen since the first Apollo was launched. For once, we felt Uncle Sam trusted the good sense of the people.

Along with most Americans, we were fed up with government by shock and surprise. We appreciated Ford for being steady and candid from the day he took the oath of office.

But he drew down that capital account with his overnight Halloween blitz, executed almost with stealth.

From now until next November, we'll be dealing with Ford, the presidential politician. Too bad. We thought he had the strength to resist and, by keeping the people's trust, serve his own best political interest.

Herald News

Fall River, Mass., November 6, 1975

The shakeup within President Ford's cabinet has confused the nation. It is reported the President was trying to strengthen his position with Republican conservatives to offset the threat of Ronald Reagan's candidacy. But if so, the dismissal of James Schlesinger is incomprehensible. Schlesinger is generally admired by the Republican right wing.

The assumption is that Nelson Rockefeller's decision not to be the President's running mate next year was based on Ford's desire to placate the GOP conservatives. And in this case, that may have been the real motivation. But then, the decision to retain Secretary Kissinger and uphold Kissinger's detente policy is bound to put off the conservatives who lump Kissinger and Rockefeller together.

The replacement of Interior Secretary Rogers Morton with Elliot Richardson is gratifying only in the sense that Richardson will be more influential than he could possibly be in London. The cabinet post is really less important than those Richardson has already successfully filled.

The truth is that the "Sunday night massacre", as it has already been termed, was at best ineptly handled. And from a sheerly political standpoint, the President's actions can be assailed both by GOP conservatives and moderates. He himself claims he will now have his own team. This is presumably true, but will it be a better team?

The question can only be satisfactorily answered after some lapse of time, but the way the shakeup happened and the ambiguity surrounding the President's motives are not encouraging.

The Evening Gazette

Worcester, Mass., November 4, 1975

Not since those stormy Watergate days when power was frequently shifted within the White House has there been such an abrupt change of faces within the presidential circle of advisers as there was Sunday night.

In one move, President Ford dumped Defense Secretary James R. Schlesinger and CIA Director William E. Colby. Hours later, Vice President Nelson Rockefeller announced he would not seek re-election as Ford's running mate.

Then, Monday night Ford pulled another surprise by announcing his intention to nominate Elliot Richardson to replace Commerce Secretary Rogers C. B. Morton, who apparently is voluntarily resigning.

Although the personnel changes may seem unrelated, they bear one thing in common: politics. When it comes time for writing a history of the 1976 presidential election, it might fairly be said that Ford really launched his campaign when he swept Schlesinger, Colby and Rockefeller out.

Schlesinger goes because he and Secretary of State Henry Kissinger couldn't agree on military might and foreign policy. Kissinger pushed detente with the Communists, both in the Soviet Union and Red China, while Schlesinger warned of the need to go slow in relations with those countries. Kissinger pushed for trade deals, technology exchanges and SALT treaties, while Schlesinger pushed for increased defense spending and a larger Pentagon budget. The two were incompatible and in their struggle for the President's ear, Kissinger clearly won. His victory could have broad implications far beyond the White House.

Colby goes because the CIA, once the pride of America, has become an embarassment for the administration. Although Colby is a career intelligence officer who hasn't been tied to any of the much-publicized excesses of the CIA, he is the easy target as the agency's current administrator. A change of face may only be cosmetic, but politically is imperative.

Finally, Rockefeller has bowed out because he is a liberal liability to the President. Challenged by the conservative element of the Republican party, Ford now won't have Rockefeller, a man many Republicans refuse to trust, at his heels. And, by bringing Richardson into his cabinet, he appears to be trying to mollify GOP liberals at the same time.

Heads are rolling as the President gears up for an election still a year away, but the impact of the changes, especially the decision to dump Schlesinger, will undoubtedly extend well past the election itself. They tell a lot about the man in the White House and potentially a lot about the future of this country and free men everywhere. With Kissinger clearly in control, Ford is committing the country, election or no election, to a continued policy of detente that has thus far proved largely one-sided.

The Standard-Times

New Bedford, Mass., November 5, 1975

The upheaval in the Ford administration would appear to represent part Fordian policy, part Henry Kissinger and part Ronald Reagan.

Mostly, we would say, the White House eye was on former Governor Reagan. This is regrettable. It forced Vice President Rockefeller, who should have had a chance (as Ford had pledged him) to survive or fall on his own, to put a time limit on his services.

And the threat of a Reagan candidacy seems to have cost the director of the Central Intelligence Agency, William E. Colby, his job. Admittedly Colby has been smeared with the CIA "spying" image. But he had nothing to do with the agency during the period of its alleged transgressions. He has been forthright in his testimony. And rendering him a sacrifice can have been only a politically-based easy way out.

The dismissal of Secretary of Defense James Schlesinger is ironical in that it is probably the least defensible of the high-level changes and yet represented more White House policy than political intrigue. Secretary of State Kissinger reportedly wanted Schlesinger out as a price of Kissinger's giving up the National Security Council chairmanship, but the likelier explanation is the administration's increasing hard-line on spending.

In recent weeks, Schlesinger has not hesitated to challenge Congress, inferentially Kissinger and the presidential office in defending his defense outlay program. Last week, even as the White House Office of Management and Budget was suggesting he could survive on less, Schlesinger reiterated he was making a "cause" of his stand because it "is the responsiblity of my position.

"If we are to maintain a position of power, the public must be informed about the trends. Some years from now, somebody will raise the question, 'Why were we not warned' and I want to be able to say, 'Indeed you were warned."

This is collision course stuff. But the nation wants a semi-independent chief of defense. Mr. Ford could, and should, have found a way to get along with Schlesinger. As it is, by replacing him with the White House chief of staff, Donald Rumsfeld, the President is reducing the office to satellite status.

Whether political motives or sound policy removed Kissinger from the council chairmanship is immaterial. He should not wear both hats. Kissinger is so sold on detente he cannot concede it's debatable, and the immense influence he wielded as handler of policy, and its administrator as council chairman, should be curtailed.

In the over-all, however, these changes raise a note of uneasiness. The President cannot be blamed for wanting to be an elected chief of state, and for getting a fast start on the "art of politics" in achieving it. But he and his advisers seem to be practicing the art like foundry workers.

Vice President Rockefeller got the heavy-handed treatment. Mr. Ford's refusal to go along with a federal bailout of New York City, a proper and courageous stand to take, put Rocky on the spot somewhat. But he could have survived—except that immediately after his announcement the President went to Reagan's California to reframe the stand from one of principle to partisan politics.

As for the selection of Elliot L. Richardson to assume the secretary of commerce post, we continue to share — with many others, undoubtedly — a feeling of confidence in Mr. Richardson's many abilities. Assuming his confirmation, this will be his fourth Cabinet post, certainly an outstanding and historic achievement. His return from the Court of St. James's to this side of the Atlantic is bound to start speculation that he could be Mr. Ford's running-mate in '76, now that the field is wide open.

However, we do not believe the electorate has in mind electing a "Gerry Reagan" to the White House next year. But that idea seems to be motivating recent Ford administration developments more than what is best for the national interest.

The Wichita Eagle

Wichita, Kans., November 5, 1975

One conclusion that seems inescapable in the wake of Sunday's upheaval in Washington is that President Ford has made his own assessment of the political climate of the country and found it to be conservative.

Whether this is an accurate estimate cannot be known until the results of some of the presidential primaries are in, and may not be known until November of next year.

But if this is Ford's premise it would suggest that he fears Reagan's challenge more than he fears that of any Democrat. It would also suggest that George Wallace will figure largely in the political strategy the Ford people will construct between now and the beginning of his campaign in earnest.

It is not yet known, of course, whether Rockefeller departed of his own free will or at the invitation of the President, but it may safely be assumed that he would not have ruled himself out of the vice presidential running if Ford had actively encouraged him to remain.

As yet there has been little speculation about who may replace Rockefeller on the ticket. Ford is said to regard himself as a moderate, though most of the country doubtless sees him as tending more to the conservative side than otherwise.

If this is true, it would seem that Rockefeller would have been more help than hindrance to the Ford chances next year. For if the President chooses a conservative to replace Rockefeller, there will be nowhere for those Republicans of moderate to liberal leanings to go. Some will vote for him out of party loyalty. Others doubtless will defect.

It may be that the nation's mood is indeed more conservative than it once was, though the only real indication there is is the voting in the 1974 congressional elections. In those the people sent an unusually large number of Democrats to Congress, and of them a substantial number are liberals.

And the liberal leaders in Congress may have helped to blunt the thrust of the conservatives by joining them in their protests that government is getting too big; that the bureaucracy is failing to do its job effectively. If this becomes the liberal line it could prevent what otherwise might be a sizeable defection of waverers to the conservative cause in November of next year.

Moreover, the sudden Sunday firing of the Defense secretary and the head of the CIA does not appear to the public to reflect the actions of a well-ordered and decisive President. And if Rockefeller's action was really taken on his own initiative, this may have been the compelling reason for it.

In any case, it doesn't look as if President Ford's Sunday night massacre has forwarded his political chances any more than did that other notable Sunday accomplishment of his, the pardon of Richard Nixon.

The Virginian-Pilot

Norfolk, Va., November 11, 1975

Having said six days before at his news conference that his firing of James R. Schlesinger as Secretary of Defense did not grow out of a rivalry within his Cabinet, President Ford was hard put in his "Meet the Press" interview Sunday to adjust his words to what clearly was so. First he insisted that on Monday he had told "the simple truth"—a truth so simple that it had not been fully grasped. Then he conceded that he had sacked Mr. Schlesinger to eliminate tension—"For me to do the job as well as I possibly can, I need a feeling of comfort within an organization—no tension, complete cohesion."

It was not necessary for Mr. Ford to elaborate much. Washington commentators in the preceding days had reported in detail the differences between Mr. Schlesinger and Secretary of State Henry A. Kissinger on defense spending, the wisdom of strategic arms limitations agreements, the intentions of the Soviet Union, and the prospect of detente. And these journalists had not needed to speculate; Mr. Kissinger over the months had sought them out in a campaign to undermine his adversary (although once the job was complete, he put out word that he had tried to save Mr. Schlesinger's skin).

Nobody—hardly anybody—likes tension. President Ford's desire for "complete cohesion" may be compared to President Eisenhower's demand for consensus reports from the Joint Chiefs of Staff. To find it intolerable, though, to choose a position from conflicting advice offered by professionally competent officials whose ultimate objective is the same is hardly the mark of a strong leader.

Even as he changed his story about the Schlesinger firing, Mr. Ford claimed that among the accomplishments of his 15-month-old Presidency was "a restoration of credibility and confidence in the White House." His success there lately has suffered from a preoccupation with being nominated and elected to continue in office. Surely politics dictated Mr. Ford's sacrifice of Mr. Schlesinger to his reliance on Mr. Kissinger's foreign-policy direction. If he knew that the Schlesinger notion of an ample arms budget was closer than the Kissinger philosophy to Republican thinking, he knew also that Mr. Schlesinger was on the verge of resigning over the Administration's failure to support him totally in his blunt criticism of Congressional cuts; the President appears to have concluded that it was politically safer to abandon the Secretary of Defense than be abandoned by him.

Mr. Ford relied on his dismissal also of William E. Colby from the directorship of the Central Intelligence Agency (which, on second thought, he had to put in abeyance) and the withdrawal of Vice President Rockefeller from consideration for the 1976 ticket to soften the impact of Mr. Schlesinger's ouster. His plan was flimsy, and will be further exposed as such when his Defense and CIA nominees, the ubiquitous Donald Rumsfeld and George Bush, undergo confirmation questioning by Democratic Senators. For the significant truth of Mr. Ford's Sunday-night Massacre is that he weakened his Government and in the process pointed up his shallowness. He now has had two shots at persuading the nation that he moved correctly and reported candidly, and twice has failed.

WINSTON-SALEM JOURNAL

Winston-Salem, N.C., November 5, 1975

It is possible that President Ford, at his Monday evening press conference, fully explained the circumstances of his Cabinet shakeup and his vice president's bailout. It is also possible, despite evidence supplied by astronauts, that the moon is made of green cheese. Certainties are few in a difficult world, and discretion demands that at least some room be left available for the discovery that obvious conclusions — whether on the subject of the President's candor or the moon's composition — may not be entirely accurate.

That having been said, the President's performance seemed an inglorious exercise in obfuscation. He dodged questions like the football player he once was, substituting rah-rah rhetoric for any serious effort to clarify the events of the preceding two days. Everything is just fine, the President insisted, acting in a manner more appropriate to the selection of a homecoming queen than to the aftermath of high-level purge and defection.

Make no mistake: However the President may wish to downplay the situation, purge and defection is precisely what has taken place. Defense Secretary James Schlesinger has been fired in favor of White House Chief of Staff Donald Rumsfeld; CIA Director William Colby has been fired in favor of Ambassador to China George Bush; Secretary of State Henry Kissinger has given up his role as head of the National Security Council in favor of . . . himself, cleverly disguised as a Kissingerian factotum named Lt. Gen. Brent Scowcroft; and Kissinger's former boss, Nelson Rockefeller, has given up any 1976 vice presidential aspirations in favor of Heaven only knows who.

All that shuffling led the President to make the following "clarifications": (1) Schlesinger and Colby bit the dust because "I wanted a team that was my team"; Rumsfeld and Bush were chosen because "these are my guys, and the ones I wanted"; Kissinger was replaced by Scowcroft at NSC because — well, just because; and Rockefeller bailed out because he wanted to, not because of any presidential pressure: "Under no circumstances was it a request by me," said the President.

To accept as complete those explanations is, of course, to believe that with a sufficient supply of ham, rye and mustard, one could survive forever on the moon. Not that the President lied directly to the nation; he probably managed to avoid doing that. But he also managed to avoid telling the whole truth — managed to avoid demonstrating that candor upon which he originally based his presidency.

For there are numerous tentative conclusions that can be drawn about the purge and defection that are far more pertinent than the President's mush about "my guys" and a vice president acting on "his own." Indeed, it is immediately clear that in the Cabinet shakeup, Kissinger and the policies he represents are the clear winners. The switchover at NSC is merely a diversion: Through Scowcroft, Kissinger will control the council as effectively as ever.

But the appearance of a power loss is important for Kissinger, as a trade-off for the gains he has made at Defense and the CIA. Both Schlesinger and Colby were, from Kissinger's viewpoint, threats to his present well-being and to the policy of detente that is to be his future monument. Both men refused to knuckle under to the Kissinger mystique, refused to serve Kissinger's policies unthinkingly. They were in the way.

So they have now been removed, to be replaced by Ford factotums who will better know their place in the scheme of things. And their place will be wherever Kissinger chooses, working through the President. In turn, the President will continue to lean on Kissinger, having done so from the beginning of his tenure and now having acquiesced in what must be seen as a Kissinger-guided defenestration of top-level resisters.

And what of Rockefeller? Only he and his ambition can answer why he chose the moment he did to reject a vice presidential nomination. But it is true that Rockefeller tends to pursue what he feels are his own best interests; it is true that his timing added to the impression, however transient, of turmoil at the top of the Ford administration; and it is true that Rockefeller and his old friend Kissinger continue to see eye-to-eye on a number of things, including, perhaps, the growing vulnerability of the President to defeat next year. With all things possible, Rockefeller and Kissinger may perceive a shared destiny down a road beside which lies a cast-off Ford, buried in his own green cheese.

DAILY NEWS

New York, N.Y., November 5, 1975

President Gerald Ford professes to see no reason for concern over whether his cabinet shake-up will be misread by leaders of the Soviet Union as a sign that the U.S. will weaken its defense posture or soften its position in the current Strategic Arms Limitation Talks.

Donald Rumsfeld

We find it difficult to share his confidence. The Kremlin has a sharp ear and a keen nose when it comes to detecting shifts, even subtle ones, in opponents' policies. It almost certainly will regard the removal of Defense Secretary James Schlesinger as a plus for the USSR.

Donald Rumsfeld, the designated successor, is a former congressman who no doubt has many talents and endearing qualities. There is nothing to indicate, however, that he is in Schlesinger's league when it comes to vision, analytical powers and independence of mind.

Nor is he, as the kind of "team" player Mr. Ford values, likely to make waves about the course of detente even if he feels personal misgivings.

The timing and nature of the changeover virtually invited Russian chiefs to conclude that the administration is awfully eager for a SALT II understanding soon, and can be pressured into making substantial concessions on site inspections, warhead numbers and the like to get one.

It is going to take some tall, hard talking on Mr. Ford's part to convince them—and a sizeable number of domestic skeptics—that such is not the case.

THE INDIANAPOLIS NEWS

Indianapolis, Ind., November 4, 1975

President Ford's decision to dismiss Defense Secretary James R. Schlesinger appears to clinch Secretary of State Kissinger's control of both foreign relations and defense policy.

The Schlesinger-Kissinger conflict has existed ever since Schlesinger entered the Cabinet. Known as a "hard-liner" on Soviet relations, Schlesinger has made no secret of his concern that under the Kissinger detente policy, the U.S. is becoming a second-rate military power.

Schlesinger grudgingly "went along" with the President's acceptance of the Vladivostock agreement which, he said, offered some hope of "stability" in the U.S.-Soviet arms race, but at the same time called for "restructured strategic forces." To Schlesinger, this meant more arms, and he has consistently contested with Kissinger and others who favored giving the Russians the benefit of the doubt about their peaceful intentions. Schlesinger's rebuttals have called the Soviet arms effort "staggering in size and build up."

The behind-the-scenes maneuvering against Schlesinger was climaxed recently with the President's refusal to name a Pentagon representatve to the new board created by Congress to monitor trade with Communist nations. This was a singular victory for Kissinger who is determined to keep the Pentagon out of strategic arms limitation talks (SALT) and military negotiations with Egypt and Israel.

There are doubtless other elements in the internal controversy, but it is clear that Secretary of State Kissinger has won this round.

Americans are not much impressed by such power struggles, and, whatever is the final resolution of this continuing debate, President Ford has not strengthened his party or the nation by the sudden dismissal of a man whose abilities or objectives have never been questioned.

THE SACRAMENTO BEE

Sacramento, Calif., November 4, 1975

While the precise facts surrounding President Ford's administrative shakeup over the weekend have yet to emerge, the implications for American foreign policy are clear enough: Secretary of State Kissinger and his policy of detente — which have come under increasing attack — are more entrenched than ever.

The firing of James Schlesinger as Secretary of Defense has eliminated the administration's most articulate and forceful skeptic about detente with the Soviet Union. Apparently Schlesinger's all-too-public criticism of Kissinger's eagerness to conclude another strategic arms treaty and Schlesinger's pique over reports that that the Secretary of State had promised Pershing missiles to Israel antagonized Kissinger beyond the tolerance level. Schlesinger had to go.

The unfortunate spin-off of this clash of egos, however, has been to squelch some of the legitimate criticism of detente which had been taking place. The whole effectiveness of detente as a means to restrain Soviet aggressiveness while liberalizing Communist societies through expanded relations with the west had begun to be re-evaluated in the light of recent events.

For example, while the U.S. had entered into an increasing number of trade agreements beneficial to the Russians — primarily in the area of farm produce and computer technology — Soviet efforts in the direction of offensive strategic superiority have been increasing. Moreover the Soviet Union has stepped-up its campaign to aggravate the volatile situations in Portugal and the Middle East, while Soviet Jews find it just as difficult to emigrate as before the Helsinki Conference and freedom of travel for East Europeans is still dismissed as "bourgeois propaganda."

While President Ford's administrative shakeup may limit skepticism over detente, it does little to satisfy recent congressional complaints that Kissinger has become too powerful.

A House Intelligence Committee hearing last week into the conduct of CIA operations heard testimony that Kissinger had acquired a near monopoly of authority in the conduct of covert intelligence operations because of his triple role as presidential security adviser and chairman of the "Forty Committee" in addition to his post as Secretary of State.

In an apparent effort to calm growing congressional concern, President Ford has made the rather faint-hearted and primarily cosmetic move of replacing Kissinger as presidential security adviser with one of Kissinger's own administrative assistants, Lt. Gen. Brent Scowcroft.

While the after shocks of the president's administrative shakeup are still to make themselves felt, initial seismic indications are that Secretary of State Kissinger and his policy of detente predominate American foreign policy more than ever.

THE LOUISVILLE TIMES

Louisville, Ky., November 4, 1975

And now there is one.

Henry A. Kissinger, secretary of state, has for years been a one-man team, charging tirelessly around the globe on diplomatic missions, and, wearing his other hat, serving as chief adviser to the President on national-security matters.

President Ford's "Sunday morning massacre" apparently took away that second hat, but in the wake of the firing of Defense Secretary James R. Schlesinger, it seems that Mr. Kissinger is more firmly in command than ever.

The situation is clouded by other factors. The director of the CIA, William E. Colby, was also fired, Commerce Secretary Rogers Morton is returning to private life, and Vice-President Rockefeller chose this particular moment to announce that he would not seek the vice-presidency again.

The obvious questions are running rampant despite the President's press conference last night: Is Mr. Ford trying to appease the right wing of his party in this election year? Has Mr. Kissinger emerged the victor in a telling power struggle, or has Mr. Schlesinger been made the victim of his own political ineptitude?

One thing seems obvious: The President will hear one less voice on issues of foreign affairs.

Mr. Schlesinger is a bluff, pipe-smoking man with a reputation for intellectual capacity and honesty. His insistence on what he considered an adequate defense budget has made him few friends in either Congress or the other branches of the Executive. Last week he found himself in opposition to the White House Office of Management and Budget over next year's defense budget, even while opposing what he has called "savage" and "arbitrary" cuts in this year's allocation.

Mr. Schlesinger's hawkishness has not been popular in an administration enamoured of detente. Still, he had been outspoken in advancing his views, which had made him an anomaly in a Cabinet marked by its anonymity rather than the quality of its advice to the President.

Detente, moreover, is one of the two proudest achievements of Henry Kissinger (the other is currently the Mid-East settlement — no one is talking much about the Vietnam peace agreement anymore). Detente and the SALT agreement were among the more publicized points of disagreement between Mr. Kissinger and Mr. Schlesinger. The rest of the list is long and tails off into what columnists Rowland Evans and Robert Novak last week characterized as "a deeply personal feud."

Author John Hersey spent a week in the Oval Office early this year. In the resulting article in *The New York Times Magazine* the writer concluded that the President is insulated from diversity of opinion on foreign affairs. Mr. Ford relied almost totally on Secretary Kissinger said the piece, or, when he is unavailable, a Kissinger deputy with occasional recourse to Secretary Schlesinger. With Mr. Schlesinger gone, where will even this small varying viewpoint come from?

The new head of the National Security Council will be Lt. Gen. Brent Scowcroft, formerly the deputy director of that group and a man described as Mr. Kissinger's "alter ego." Can we look for diversity there?

The new secretary of defense will be Donald Rumsfield, currently the President's chief of staff and a man whose most outstanding characteristic seems to be ambition. Can he play in Mr. Kissinger's league?

The candidate for the CIA directorship is George Bush, currently envoy to China and a former chairman of the Republican National Committee. The same questions apply.

The one-man team, it seems, at last has the field to himself.

St. Louis Globe-Democrat

St. Louis, Mo., November 4, 1975

The political earthquake triggered by President Ford's dismissal of Defense Secretary Schlesinger and CIA Director Colby had not been felt fully before Vice President Rockefeller announced he was withdrawing from consideration for the second spot on the Republican ticket next year.

Rockefeller's departure can be considered as addition by subtraction. President Ford is spared the embarrassment of having to maneuver into position to dump Rockefeller in an effort to appease conservative Republicans. While Mr. Ford had maintained that he was satisfied with Rockefeller, the President's campaign manager long ago had put out the word that Rocky was a handicap.

Far more important than political futures is the state of the nation's security. In sacking Schlesinger to satisfy Secretary of State Kissinger, the President has committed a grave disservice to the nation. Colby's dismissal, while anticipated, is unwarranted. He has been made the scapegoat for any real or imagined sins committed by his predecessors in the CIA.

AS SECRETARY OF DEFENSE, Schlesinger has been more than competent. He has been a bastion of strength against the coalition in Congress that has set the country on a course of weakness through injudicious spending for unessentials, at the expense of national defense. It is distressing that President Ford appears willing to accommodate Congress in this misdirection.

CIA Director Colby's assessments of Soviet military expenditures and forces have been the same as Schlesinger's.

Schlesinger has taken his duties seriously and with patriotic fervor. He has not been timid about speaking out against the policy of detente pursued by Secretary Kissinger, nor has he hesitated to oppose the concessions for Soviet superiority being made by Kissinger in the SALT talks.

It could be calamitous for the country that Kissinger has had his way. The Secretary of State has a reputation for being a negotiator of consummate skill but there is ample evidence that in dealings with the Soviets he is vastly over-rated. It is easy to be regarded as a great negotiator by the other side if one gives everything away.

PRESIDENT FORD'S CHOICE of Donald H. Rumsfeld to succeed Schlesinger cannot excite enthusiasm. Rumsfeld, a confidante of the President who has been serving as his chief of staff, is a former Illinois congressman who served as head of the Office of Economic Opportunity. His performance in that role showed he was an opportunist. Rumsfeld twice overruled former Gov. Warren E. Hearnes' vetoes of funding for improper Legal Aid services. Rumsfeld's brief tenure as Ambassador to NATO does not especially qualify him to be Defense Secretary. His claim to the appointment is purely political because of his closeness to Ford.

George H. Bush, who will be nominated to succeed Colby at CIA, is also a former congressman. A wealthy New Englander who became a transplanted Texan, he headed the United States delegation to the United Nations and served as chairman of the Republican National Committee before being assigned to Peking as American liaison officer to Communist China. Bush appears to have the knowledge, ability and integrity to serve as CIA director, though Colby should have been retained in fairness to a man who has performed admirably under great stress.

The cabinet shakeup should widen the opening for Ronald Reagan to make his anticipated move against Ford. But Reagan expressed shock and surprise at Rockefeller's withdrawal and there is speculation the former California governor's position may be weakened now that the New Yorker is out of the picture as a target of conservative criticism.

Time will be needed to assess the impact in all its ramifications. For now it is appalling that a man of Secretary Schlesinger's character and ability should be sacrificed to satisfy Kissinger's thirst for power. The nation is the loser in this unsavory bloodletting.

The Ann Arbor News

Ann Arbor, Mich., November 14, 1975

IT IS a time-honored principle that a president has a right to determine the makeup of his administration. But that doesn't mean George Bush's nomination to the CIA will go uncontested.

On its face, Bush does not seem to be one of President Ford's better appointments. Bush has held some important-sounding jobs at the UN and in Peking, but these jobs have chiefly been "visibility" posts rather than policy-making positions.

Bush is an unusual case study. He is a politician who seems to get stronger with every defeat. His appointment is being criticized as being too political, yet even his track record in politics is flawed.

He twice ran for the Senate and lost both times. After defeat number two, President Nixon named him ambassador to the UN. In 1973 and 1974, Bush was chairman of the Republican National Committee during a near disastrous decline in the party's fortunes and the disgrace of a Republican president to whom he remained scrupulously loyal.

The New York Times reported Nov. 5 that Bush could come under fire for the financial practices of his campaign committee when he ran for the Senate in Texas in 1970. This may be grist for senators such as Frank Church of Idaho, who opposes Bush's nomination.

Church, who heads the Senate intelligence committee, says Bush is not qualified because of his lack of experience in the intelligence field and his political background.

* * *

MORE to the point, a politician such as Bush in such a sensitive position is seen as unlikely to stand up to the White House and Pentagon. Ford's refusal to rule out Bush as a possible vice presidential running mate in 1976 probably does not help Bush's cause. Says Church: "We just can't have a director of the CIA who is under active consideration for higher political office."

The first CIA director William Colby is thought to have been sacked because he "cooperated" too closely with congressional investigators of the agency's operations. By contrast, will Bush be under orders to clam up and stonewall?

The CIA needs a professional person to head its operations and carry out its reforms, but it also needs a director with a feel for permanence. Bush doesn't look like either one of these.

Ford has made some good appointments, notably Edward Levi to Justice and Carla Hills to HUD. Some not-so-good ones have been Hathaway and Kleppe to Interior. Bush also qualifies in the latter category.

CHICAGO DAILY NEWS

Chicago, Ill., November 7, 1975

Chairman Frank Church of the Senate Intelligence Committee is trying to make the nomination of George Bush as chief of the Central Intelligence Agency look like a political ploy by President Ford. We would doubt, at this stage, that any President including Richard Nixon would have the gall to try to re-politicize the CIA, and there just might be a tincture of politics in Democrat Church's tirade.

Nevertheless, we welcome the assurance that the Senate will put Bush through an intensive examination on the way to confirmation. In this anxious post-Watergate season the public needs the strongest assurance that the chief of the CIA understands and respects that agency's role.

Contrary to Church's criticism, we do not think Bush's shortage of specific intelligence experience disqualifies him. True, he has been chairman of the Republican National Committee and will be the first CIA director with a really partisan political background. But he has also been through the mill as a congressman, as ambassador to the United Nations and as informal ambassador to the People's Republic of China, and has earned praise from administration adversary Sen. William Proxmire as "capable," "intelligent," and "hard-working." The CIA is full of careerists who can handle the professional end. The director has other responsibilities.

What needs to be examined is Bush's attitude toward his new command, and his understanding of what it should and should not be.

"I believe in the importance of a sound and strong intelligence capability," he says.

But to do his job for the American people he will also have to believe that an intelligence agency wholly insulated from public control is a menace to the republic; that an intelligence agency that can be converted into the personal instrument of a President is unaffordable; and that an intelligence agency that exceeds its lawful mission by engaging in domestic espionage has acquired some of the habits of a Gestapo.

In the execution of its mission of foreign intelligence the CIA is bound to face some close and delicate decisions. And that is exactly why the new head of the CIA must be established, to the Senate's satisfaction, as a man of judgment and integrity, beyond any taint of political leaning that could sway a professional decision. By the same token we trust that the Senate will subordinate its own political instincts and make an honest appraisal.

THE RICHMOND NEWS LEADER

Richmond, Va., November 6, 1975

President Ford's summary firing of Defense Secretary James Schlesinger — evidently because the Secretary refused to share in Henry Kissinger's enthusiasm for detente — suggests a crippling unwillingness of the President to tolerate vigorous dissent among his top advisers. If the firing of Schlesinger by our friendliest of Presidents was inexcusable, the firing of CIA Director William Colby was inevitable; for the better part of a year, now, it has been clear that sooner or later, Colby would have to go. But for other reasons, Colby's departure is equally troubling.

The fault is hardly his. It is true that he has exhibited too much alacrity in his dealings with the politicians who are riding the CIA issue in frenzied pretense. For that alacrity alone, he probably should have been replaced. But perhaps more than that, it was his peculiar misfortune to be directing the CIA when the CIA became an explicitly political issue. Most of the "revelations" about the CIA have concerned alleged misdeeds that occurred prior to Colby's tenure. Yet scapegoat hunters never lack prey, and most of the hunting politicians sent their dogs after Colby.

That the dogs have returned with his skin says less about the diligence of the dogs or the failings of Colby, than it says about where the nation currently stands on the hysteria index. The CIA now is the favorite and fashionable target of polemical opportunists. And a large part of the public has submitted to the opportunists' seductions about the menacing dangers posed by the CIA.

Yet in our opinion — and, we believe, in the opinion of a larger part of the public — the CIA remains essentially a suppositional enemy. It remains so particularly when compared with the threats posed by the nation's declared enemy, the Soviet Union — and the Soviet Union's massive intelligence activity here and throughout the Free World. Congress currently has heaven-knows-how-many committees investigating this country's several intelligence agencies. But as far as we know, Congress has not a single committee investigating the intelligence activities of the Soviet Union.

Indeed, Congress has just dismantled the two committees which heretofore have done precisely that — the House Committee on Internal Security and the Senate Internal Security Subcommittee. Moreover, the dismantling of those committees — coincident with the attack on the American intelligence community — came at about the same time as astounding reports of (1) Soviet penetration of congressional staffs, and (2) Soviet monitoring of White House telephone calls. Yet few of our politicians have shown much interest in pursuing those reports, so determined are they to pursue the CIA.

If we have our guess, most of the public subscribes to the proposition that it is the legitimate and primary function of government to protect us from others; less justifiable tend to be those government endeavors to protect us from ourselves. Reasoning from that proposition, it follows that the public is more concerned about the depredations of the Soviet Union than about the supposed espionage excesses of the CIA. Oversee the CIA, of course. But in doing so, do not undermine its efforts to counter the intelligence activities of the Soviets. For against the malignant damage the Soviets seek to do to us, the alleged misdeeds of the CIA are like after-school mischief.

It has become one of the largest myths in the American garden of mythical cabbage that our intelligence agencies must be pure. Americans should keep in mind that government learned long ago to be shameless; we should be satisfied with knowing that our government is vastly less shameless than any other. Perhaps the most shameful spectacle on Capitol Hill today is the continuing attack on this nation's intelligence community. The attack has claimed William Colby as a casualty; before it is over, the attack may claim his successor, George Bush, as well. And those who worry about the Free World's rapid disintegration, worry that in the attack on the American intelligence community, a good deal more may be at stake than a few personal reputations.

The Washington Star
and Daily News

Washington, D.C., November 6, 1975

Of all the battered players thumbed to the showers last weekend in President Ford's search for a new "team," the most badly bruised is the ousted director of the Central Intelligence Agency, William Colby. The timing of his ouster falls somewhere between terrible and awful. It is welcome news that Mr. Ford has asked him to stay on for a while longer.

Mr. Colby, one of the original American intelligence professionals who came out of General Donovan's OSS during World War II, had manfully taken on (and certainly not completed) the thankless job of cleaning the skeletons out of the CIA's closet. He took over the agency just as its misjudgments, excesses, and its dangerous vulnerability to White House tampering were being paraded through the headlines.

He promptly made what seems to us an entirely correct and plucky — and professional — judgment: that if the nation's intelligence professionals could be salvaged in the current witchhunting mood, they would not be salvaged by the concealment of past mistakes. Mr. Colby co-operated more closely with the relevant congressional committees than on certain fashionable theories of the separation of powers and executive confidentiality he needed to do.

How welcome Mr. Colby's candor has been to the Ford White House is a matter of speculation But the President's letter of this week to Senator Church about the Church Committee's approaching report on intelligence shows that Mr. Ford is jittery about certain parts of it — especially the parts that may impute collaboration in foreign assassination plots to past administrations.

Unfortunately, the President's unceremonious sacking of Mr. Colby amidst the purgative process gives the impression, which we hope is false, that the White House would prefer buttoned lips at the top of the CIA. That impression is reinforced by the essentially political identity of Director Colby's designated replacement, Ambassador George Bush.

The presidential press secretary, in announcing a somewhat more leisurely and civilized transition from Colby to Bush, described Mr. Bush yesterday as "more sensitive to public interests and public desires" in the agency's management than his immediate predecessors. What Mr. Nessen neglected to mention is that Mr. Bush's political sensitivity may be keener too.

After all, it could hardly be otherwise with an able and personable young man who only two years ago headed the Republican National Committee, who has no past in professional intelligence work, and who has natural political ambitions. President Ford said of Donald Rumsfeld's qualifications to head the defense establishment that he had, after all, been a naval aviator; but so far as anyone knows Mr. Bush hasn't even had part-time summer employment as a spook.

One of the CIA's problems is that it appears, in past years, to have lacked the independence and stature to resist White House tampering — which may, by the way, be easily distinguished from White House policy direction. On this account, Mr. Bush could be in serious trouble when his nomination to head the agency comes before the Senate. It is even imaginable that the delay suddenly announced yesterday will lengthen into a full-dress reconsideration of the wisdom of appointing Mr. Bush at all.

Last summer the Rockefeller Commission did say, after all, that an "individual of stature, independence and integrity" is needed to head the CIA — an individual, one might add, who will stay around for more than a refrain or two of the musical chairs game. Mr. Bush has stature and integrity; but does he, in the nature of his case, have the independence?

At least, the President has moved to cut his losses by giving Mr. Colby more time to finish his cleanup of the closets. To have jerked him out of the job on the schedule indicated only two days ago would have seemed a gratuitous slap at the congressional committees he has been working with. They have come to depend on Mr. Colby's candor and co-operation in setting the intelligence community back on an acceptable footing with the American public. And that is more important than an election.

BUSH CONFIRMED AS CIA DIRECTOR; SENATE HAD CONTESTED NOMINATION

The Senate Jan. 27 confirmed George Bush, 51, as director of the Central Intelligence Agency. Bush was approved 64–27 to succeed William E. Colby. Although Bush was nominated Nov. 3, 1975, the Senate blocked his confirmation until Ford excluded Bush as a potential vice presidential running mate.

Sen. Frank Church (D, Idaho), chairman of a Senate probe of the U.S. intelligence operations, made known his opposition Nov. 4. He said he knew "of no particular reason" why Bush was qualified to head an agency that was "the least political and most sensitive in government." In a Senate speech Nov. 11, Church urged his colleagues to "stand up and oppose this nomination" and "insist upon a Central Intelligence Agency which is politically neutral and totally professional." Another critic Nov. 4 was Sen. William Proxmire (D, Wis.), who, noting that Bush was a former Republican national chairman, said the appointment violated "the cardinal rule of the intelligence business—separation of all political influences from the intelligence process."

Senate Democratic Leader Mike Mansfield (Mont.) said Nov. 12 he would support the Bush nomination but suggested Bush renounce any vice presidential inclinations before accepting the intelligence post. At the White House, Press Secretary Ron Nessen defended Bush Nov. 5 with the observation that if the agency were headed by a man who had run for public office it could make it more "responsive" to the public interest. Bush had served two terms in the U.S. House and had run for the Senate twice, unsuccessfully.

THE DALLAS TIMES HERALD

Dallas, Tex., February 3, 1976

FINALLY, after the most incomprehensible of Washington's many political productions, Texan George Bush has been installed as the new Director of the Central Intelligence Agency.

President Ford formally swore him in Friday and history's notebook a few years hence will prove that it was a good day for the country.

George Bush is competent, impeccably honest and a leader. He will learn the intelligence business and he will devote 24 hours a day solely to his assignment.

Odd, indeed, was the debate concerning Bush's appointment. In the final vote of confirmation — 64-to-27— there were two hours of speechmaking and most of it was laudatory. Even the 27 who voted against Bush spent most of their time praising his ability and integrity.

But, they contended, it was improper to name a former national chairman of a political party to the sensitive post as Director of CIA during the present hassle over the agency's past sins.

It didn't figure. If George Bush is possessed of all the integrity that even his opponents conceded to be quite true, why wasn't he just the man to step in and untangle an operation that has been lacking in that same integrity?

No one should expect miracles of George Bush in the first days, or months, of his CIA leadership.

But if anyone can restore total confidence in the CIA, he can. He is a thorough, painstaking man who is not afraid to assume leadership.

It should not only be a better, but a far improved CIA because of his presence.

FORT WORTH STAR-TELEGRAM

Fort Worth, Tex., November 25, 1975

This 94th Congress seems to have more than the quota of arm-wavers and shriekers among its leaders who profess to see evil where there is none and devils instead of public servants.

Two of these questionable actors who come to mind are Rep. Otis Pike of New York and Sen. Frank Church of Idaho.

In his insistence that Secretary of State Henry Kissinger be drawn and quartered (or was it merely cited for contempt of Congress?) for refusing to give Mr. Pike some documents the secrecy of which both the state secretary and the president judged to be in the national interest, the New York congressman raised eyebrows of disbelief the world over.

The House Intelligence Committee chairman appeared to be conducting an incredible, unjustifiable orgy of governmental self-flagellation. Some qualified observers, however, have put Mr. Pike's performance down merely as an exercise in delusions of grandeur—a trait shared by a distressingly large group of the 94th's members.

Senator Church, over on the other side of the Capitol, has been occupying a larger stage as he conducts, whip in hand, the Senate Intelligence Committee's search-and-publicize march through the Central Intelligsnce Agency's past.

But it is not Mr. Church's exertions in that arena alone that catch the eye. We were dismayed the other day by his illogical attack on President Ford's nomination of George Bush to head the CIA.

Senator Church, himself a politician of apparently boundless ambition, said Mr. Bush should not be director of the CIA because he is a "politician" and therefore not to be trusted to perform with independence and objectivity.

If the senator's charge were valid as stated it would be damning equally to Mr. Bush and to Senator Church as well—and to every other public servant who has toiled in the fields of politics because that was where the work was. But the charge of course, is not valid. It is hogwash.

If Senator Church could argue a truly valid case against the personal and professional qualifications of Mr. Bush for the office to which the president has nominated him, his case would be worth examination.

But it is nonsense to say that this former Texas congressman and son of a former U. S. senator from Connecticut, who has served his nation well as U. S. ambassador to the United Nations and chief emissary to China, cannot make a good CIA boss because he is a "politician."

It won't do. The decision should be made on the basis of whether Mr. Bush is a good, qualified man for the job— on the criteria of character, experience, ability and dedication to public service. The question of whether he is a politician (in whatever sense that abused word is taken), diplomat, lawyer, businessman or farmer is not paramount. It is even irrelevant except as it bears on the criteria we mentioned earlier.

Senator Church does the nation a disservice with his misguided protests of Mr. Bush's nomination, citing primarily the fact that the Texan is a former national chairman of his political party.

San Jose Mercury

San Jose, Calif., January 29, 1976

Confirmation of former Republican party Chairman George Bush as the director of the Central Intelligence Agency came with only token Senate opposition. The 64-27 approval may be read as a recognition of the personal qualities and ability of George Bush.

Nevertheless, there is considerable merit to the minority argument that there are inherent dangers to the politicizing of our nation's intelligence apparatus.

The Des Moines Register

Des Moines, Iowa, January 30, 1976

The Senate approved the nomination of George Bush as director of the Central Intelligency Agency (CIA) by a vote of 64 to 27.

Bush served as Republican national chairman in the closing months of the Nixon administration, and that caused the relatively large vote against him. He was viewed as an able person but a partisan politician — not the type calculated to restore confidence in the badly shaken CIA.

The compelling need to rebuild and restore confidence in the CIA called for a nominee not merely competent but outstanding — a nonpartisan person of such stature that he could survive a change of party in the White House, which Bush almost certainly could not.

Ford's failure to make such a nomination is regrettable. So is the Senate's decision to ride along with the President and settle for likeable George Bush.

THE MILWAUKEE JOURNAL

Milwaukee, Wisc., February 3, 1976

George Bush, President Ford's choice for CIA director, who became controversial because of his past political ties, has been confirmed and is in office. Ford is entitled to select his chief of the nation's civilian intelligence agency. There was nothing unsavory revealed about Bush's background. He has served competently as US ambassador to the United Nations and has been America's chief diplomat in China.

What stirred controversy in Congress was Bush's past title of national chairman of the Republican Party. Critics feared that Bush would bring a political taint to the CIA at a time when the agency was already under fire for its past missteps into domestic politics. Bush has promised to keep poltics and the intelligence agency separate. He has also promised to resign if he intends to run for political office. He has been mentioned as a potential Republican vice presidential candidate. There is no reason to believe that Bush will not keep his word, but, nevertheless, Congress should keep a wary eye open.

Keeping the CIA out of politics should be a long range concern. One safeguard is to recruit competent leaders of integrity for the top intelligence post. But the best way of insuring the insulation of the CIA is to provide the institutional safeguards and oversight necessary to keep politics out. That Congress and the White House have yet to accomplish.

The Cleveland Press

Cleveland, Ohio, November 25, 1975

When President Ford recently nominated George Bush to head the CIA, it didn't take long for both well meaning and political opposition to surface.

Several major newspapers and at least two senators, Democrats Frank Church and William Proxmire, came out against Bush, now U.S. envoy to China, long before he could come home and testify on his own behalf.

The objections to Bush boil down to two: He is a former chairman of the Republican National Committee, and he has no professional background in intelligence work.

To be facetious for a moment, one could say that a head of the national committee under Richard Nixon who didn't get indicted must be very honorable or very stealthy, both useful qualities in a CIA boss.

More seriously, however, Bush's detractors assume that because of his GOP background he would "politicize" the CIA and would not refuse if a Republican president asked him to do something dirty on behalf of the party.

Such suspicions are most unfair to Bush, who has a record of integrity, and to the trade of politician, which is often followed by decent people.

As to Bush's not being an intelligence insider, all one can say is bravo. For most of its history the CIA was led by professionals, such as Allen Dulles and Richard Helms, and the country is still reeling about disclosures about the agency's illegal domestic snooping and its bizarre plots to kill foreign leaders.

If the CIA is to be reformed, live under its charter and give up stunts like trying to make Fidel Castro's beard fall out, it will take the efforts of a talented outsider, not one with close links to the spook network which brought the agency into disrepute.

Busn has been a naval aviator, successful businessman, two-term congressman from Texas, U.S. ambassador to the United Nations, head of the U.S. mission in Peking, as well as chairman of the GOP's national committee.

That varied background should entitle him to a fair hearing on his qualifications to head the CIA — not the premature cloak and dagger job some are trying to do on his nomination.

Press Herald

Portland, Me., November 29, 1975

President Ford, without looking very hard, can find someone much better equipped to head the Central Intelligence Agency than George Bush.

No intelligence agency is enjoying any popularity right now. The rating of the CIA is particularly low. We're inclined to agree with Secretary of State Henry Kissinger that little is to be gained by further public discussion of grave errors made several years ago but since corrected. And we cannot entirely blot out the thought that some of this probing may be related to the presidential aspirations of some of the probers.

But it is important that confidence in the agencies be restored. The work for which they were created must still be done. And it cannot be accomplished in a continuing atmosphere of doubt and suspicion or downright hostility.

Months ago the Rockefeller CIA Commission filed its report. However that report may be evaluated as a whole, it included one section that is beyond dispute. It read:

"In the final analysis, the proper functioning of the agency must depend in large part on the character of the director of Central Intelligence. The best assurance against misuse of the agency lies in the appointment to that position of persons with the judgment, courage, and independence to resist improper pressure and importuning, whether from the White House, within the agency, or elsewhere."

Bush appears to be able to qualify as a "nice guy." He has been ambassador in Peking. Prior to that he was chairman of the Republican National Committee.

Despite all the admirable qualities he undoubtedly possesses, his name does not come quickly to mind when one searches for a person "with the judgment, courage and independence to resist improper pressure and importuning."

The CIA may be a necessary evil, but necessary it is and it urgently needs leadership of a stronger caliber than it is likely to receive from Ambassador Bush. As we said, President Ford can do better.

Long Island Press

Jamaica, N.Y., November 13, 1975

After exposure of the CIA's links with the Watergate scandal, we had good reason to expect that President Ford would nominate a highly qualified administrator to be the new director of the agency. The new CIA chief should not only be experienced in intelligence gathering, but should also be free from undue political influence and acutely aware of how easily spy agencies can infringe on civil liberties.

Sadly, President Ford's nominee, George Bush, doesn't meet these standards. If he is dedicated to anything, it is to partisan politics. Mr. Bush is a former chairman of the Republican National Committee, and it is hard to be more partisan than that.

Mr. Bush presently this country's representative in China. That's an important assignment, but we doubt if he has learned espionage techniques or much about citizens' rights from Chairman Mao.

That's why the Senate Intelligence Committee acted responsibly in subjecting Mr. Bush's qualifications to close scrutiny. As argued by the committee's chairman, Sen. Frank Church, D-Idaho, Mr. Bush's confirmation by the Senate for such a sensitive position would make a "travesty" of agency reform.

President Ford should withdraw Mr. Bush's name.

THE SPRINGFIELD UNION

Springfield, Mass., November 11, 1975

In nominating former GOP National Chairman George Bush as director of the Central Intelligence Agency, President Ford was moving politics into a job where it least belongs.

The hand that controls the CIA should be free of political character. That much is basic to the responsibilities of the agency — whose political involvements in recent years almost destroyed it.

It might be said that an appointment by any President implies a political obligation. But Bush's background is strongly political, and that by itself casts doubt on his fitness for the CIA post.

Ford's answer, in Springfield last Friday, to a question as to Bush's qualifications, stressed the nominee's "nonpartisan" service as U.S. ambassador to the UN, and as this country's envoy to Peking.

True as that may be, it's not enough to justify the nomination of Bush as CIA director — a post that requires specialized abilities and independence of partisan pressures.

Thus, while the President takes pride in bringing "credibility, candor and frankness" to the White House, he would cast a deep shadow of doubt over the sensitive CIA directorship.

Far better for the agency — also for the appointee and the Ford administration itself — would be the nomination of a person experienced in the intelligence mission and not a member of the White House "family."

Certainly the CIA — target of probes that have uncovered its involvement in activities outside its jurisdiction — needs leadership that will restore public confidence in the agency.

THE BLADE

Toledo, Ohio, November 10, 1975

AMONG the sweeping changes ordered by President Ford in his sudden shake-up of top-level administration personnel, none is more dubious than the selection of George Bush, U. S. representative to China, as director of the Central Intelligence Agency.

The inescapable fact is that, as a two-term congressman from Texas and former national Republican chairman, Mr. Bush is a political animal with no background whatever in intelligence gathering and, as such, has no credentials for heading the CIA. One of the obvious problems brought out by the current congressional investigations of past CIA misdeeds is that it became overly involved in political machinations, both domestic and foreign, even under directors who were not primarily politicians as Mr. Bush unquestionably is.

The basic incompatibility of the candidate and the job was trenchantly underlined by Sen. Frank Church of Idaho. In announcing his probable opposition to the Bush appointment, the senator noted that he knew "of no particular reason why he (Mr. Bush) is qualified" for a post that was "the least political and most sensitive in government."

Mr. Bush, by his own description in 1973 after a two-year stint as U.S. ambassador to the United Nations, was "enamored of elective politics" and admitted to little experience or interest in foreign affairs. And his U.N. tenure and his subsequent cloistered year in the U. S. liasion office in Peking can hardly be regarded as having corrected that deficiency to the point where he is prepared to direct the nation's vital foreign intelligence apparatus.

Whatever Mr. Ford's reason might be for firing CIA Director Willam Colby — and the best speculaton is that the agency chief is being made a scapegoat for CIA activities that took place well before he became director — there is no credible rationale for replacing him with someone of Mr. Bush's stripe. Indeed, there is every reason for the Senate to reject the appointment when it comes before that body for confirmation. It will be difficult enough to keep the agency within its legislative bounds and free from political taint in the future, even under the best of leadership.

New York Post

New York, N.Y., November 13, 1975

It is dismaying enough that the Central Intelligence Agency has been deeply engaged over the years in trying to manipulate governments abroad. It could be even more damaging if the agency were openly exposed to further charges of meddling in American domestic politics.

That prospect has rapidly become a matter of intense concern to Chairman Church (D-Idaho) of the Senate Select Committee on Intelligence since President Ford's designation of George Bush to be head of the CIA. Bush, a former Republican National Chairman, is one of his party's most prominent national figures.

Church, who regards Bush as a "personal friend," has nevertheless appealed to the Senate to withhold support for the nomination on the ground that "we need a CIA that can resist all the partisan pressures which may be brought to bear by various groups in and out of government." But it is by no means clear that this argument will prevail.

The nomination of the able, appealing Bush, now special U. S. representative to Peking, has been endorsed by such conservatives as Sens. Buckley (RC-N.Y.), Goldwater (R-Ariz.) and Tower (R-Tex.), and Majority Leader Mansfield (D-Mont.), long an admirer, has added his warm endorsement.

In Mansfield's opinion, all concern would be allayed if Bush would renounce any ambition for the GOP's 1976 Vice Presidential nomination—for which he has been mentioned since the Rockefeller withdrawal. But that is not the principal point. The issue is whether a man who has been so actively steeped in partisan politics should serve as head of an agency that demands a strictly nonpartisan, independent, objective and professionally skilled administration. On the evidence, the answer must be negative.

Bush's abilities are many. They surely warrant further federal employment in a responsible post. They do not embody the essential qualifications of detachment required in the office of Director of Central Intelligence.

San Francisco Chronicle

San Francisco, Calif., November 13, 1975

THE PRESIDENT'S NOMINATION of George Bush as director of the Central Intelligence Agency has elicited the criticism of Senator Frank Church, who heads the Senate Select Committee on Intelligence, and the criticism is appropriate.

As investigations by the Church committee and others have shown, the CIA needs an independent director who can run the agency as an intelligence-gathering operation without being subject to external pressure or the appearance of outside interference.

Bush, who is now U.S. representative to Peking, served as chairman of the Republican National Committee in 1973 and 1974. He is an able and dedicated public servant who, as Senator Church points out, could hold many public offices with distinction.

AS A PRACTICAL matter, however, it would be ill-advised to put into such a sensitive position a man who has so recently held such a highly partisan post.

The CIA is suffering from a crisis of public confidence these days, and for good reason. Bush's appointment as head of the agency can do nothing to ease the crisis, and might hinder efforts to rebuild the agency along less suspect lines.

President Ford should consider withdrawing the nomination for the good of the man, the country, and the CIA itself.

FORD PROPOSES CIA REORGANIZATION, END TO SURVEILLANCE OF AMERICANS

President Ford announced at a televised news conference Feb. 17 his plans for revision of the command structure of U.S. foreign intelligence operations and establishment of guidelines for such operations. He also planned to request special legislation to safeguard "critical intelligence secrets." The President said he was acting because, "As Americans, we must not and will not tolerate actions by our government which will abridge the rights of our citizens. At the same time, we must maintain a strong effective intelligence capability.... I will not be a party to the dismantling of the CIA [Central Intelligence Agency] or other intelligence agencies."

The President proposed a three-part plan:

■ He was establishing by executive order a "new command structure for foreign intelligence." All policy direction would come from the National Security Council, consisting of the President, the Vice President and the secretaries of state and defense. Management of the policy would be conducted by a new committee that would be headed by the CIA director, George Bush. A new independent oversight board made up of private citizens would be established "to monitor the performance of our intelligence operations."

■ "A comprehensive set of public guidelines" was being issued "to improve the performance of the intelligence agencies and to restore public confidence in them." These were to "serve as legally binding charters for our intelligence activities." The charters were to "provide stringent protections for the rights of American citizens." Ford said he would meet with Congressional leaders "to map out legislation to provide judicial safeguards against electronic surveillance and mail openings" and he would also "support legislation that would prohibit attempts on the lives of foreign leaders in peacetime."

■ "Special legislation to safeguard critical intelligence secrets" would be proposed to Congress, to "make it a crime for a government employe who has access to certain highly classified information to reveal that information improperly."

During the news conference following his announcement, the President was asked why the CIA was being put more under control of the presidency since "we know that office has abused the CIA in the past." Ford said a president "ought to be accountable" and his proposals were an attempt "to make the process and the decision-making fall on the shoulders of the President and he will be held accountable by the American people."

An executive order on the government's foreign intelligence activities was issued Feb. 18, to be effective March 1. It proscribed, in general, spying on Americans or testing drugs on them, infiltrating domestic groups or intercepting mail for any other reason than counterespionage or security checks on government employes. On covert operations abroad, the order stipulated that no federal employe "shall engage in, or conspire to engage in, political assassination."

The President's draft legislation barring federal employes from disclosing sources and methods of American foreign intelligence operations also was submitted to Congress Feb. 18. An exemption from criminal prosecution was provided for journalists or others receiving such secrets, but Attorney General Edward H. Levi said that grand juries could question reporters about their sources under the proposed law.

CHICAGO DAILY NEWS

Chicago, Ill., February 19, 1976

President Ford's executive orders reorganizing the nation's intelligence agencies will do much to clarify the responsibility for the work those agencies do. The head of the Central Intelligence Agency, now George Bush, is given a broader role. A three-member panel appointed by the President comes into being to guard against a repetition of the shocking abuses that have come to light.

The reorganization plan at least clears up any question as to where the ultimate authority lies. It rests squarely on the shoulders of the President. If there had been any doubt about that before — and in the murky area of foreign intelligence, passing the buck seemed a part of the game — there is none now. The necessary but unpleasant business of spying will go as far as the President commands, and if that is too far, the blame is his.

What this boils down to is a plea to trust the President, whoever he may be. Given the pattern of recent history, that's not a wholly satisfactory situation. Yet foreign intelligence is a function of the executive department and there is no higher repository of trust than the President.

Welcome as some of the President's assurances are that the CIA and other intelligence agencies will be brought under better control, a further step needs to be taken. There is a role for Congress in overseeing the intelligence agencies, and it is one the Congress should not shrink from. A joint committee of Congress — small, bipartisan, trustworthy and known to the public — should also be set up as an additional watchdog over the agencies. Ford indicated he would welcome such a committee, and establishing it should now become a congressional goal of high priority.

The new guidelines, some to be imposed by executive order and some to be proposed to Congress, aim at the most serious flaws in the CIA operations turned up by congressional investigations. The CIA would be more severely limited to overseas operations, for example, and barred from spying on American citizens at home. And in a proposal that almost makes the skin crawl, a flat ban will be sought on plots to assassinate foreign leaders "in peacetime." Who could have thought, just a short time ago, that such a prohibition would be needed? It confirms the worst allegations that there were such assassination plots.

While the President's actions and proposals may put some fears to rest, they raise further questions. His request for a law to punish any who "leak" secrets brings up the possibility that a cover-up attempt might have a better chance to succeed the next time around. And would an oversight committee appointed by and responsible to the President dare to "blow the whistle" if that time came again?

It's safe to say that the argument over the intelligence function and how to handle it is not yet over.

The Virginian-Pilot

Norfolk, Va., February 19, 1976

President Ford's proposal for the reform and reorganization of American intelligence operations is cosmetic, iffy, and political. It also may be the best that can be expected.

It boils down to the proposition that George Bush, as director of the Central Intelligence Agency and as chairman of the committee Mr. Ford wants to charge with the "management of intelligence," is going to do a better job than his predecessors. And the corollary that Mr. Ford is going to do a better job than his predecessors in the White House. (Cynics may note that the President commandeered the networks to announce his program just prior to the New Hampshire primary.)

Mr. Ford's managerial reforms seek to centralize the direction of our intelligence efforts and to give the necessary public reassurance that all's well.

Henceforth, the President promised, the National Security Council will be directing intelligence policy and Mr. Bush's committee will be managing the day-to-day operations. Both will be monitored by "a new independent oversight board to be made up of private citizens."

Former Ambassador Robert D. Murphy will be chairman of the new oversight board, with former Secretary of the Army Stephen Ailes and Leo Cherne, the economist and publisher, as board members. All are distinguished men. But Mr. Murphy is 81. And it is doubtful that civilian oversight will be any more prophylactic than Congressional oversight was.

Which is to say that Mr. Murphy and Company serve a cosmetic function. The basic responsibility for seeing that the intelligence agencies don't go off half-cocked is — and must be — the day-to-day responsibility of the man running the show: George Bush.

It is also an executive responsibility — Mr. Bush's and Mr. Ford's — to deal with the intelligence sprawl in Washington. Given a generation of Cold War and a climate of secrecy in which growth was largely unchecked, the intelligence agencies have naturally proliferated. There is no reason to think that they are immune to the workings of Parkinson's Law and every reason to think that there is overlap, redundancy, and wastefulness in them today. But Mr. Bush, sitting on top of the bureaucratic heap, isn't the man to do much about that. The Church Committee's forthcoming recommendations should be useful.

Mr. Ford's guidelines issued yesterday and the FBI guidelines that Attorney General Levi is preparing are also useful. But they are designed mostly to reassure us that it won't happen again. The abuses didn't occur in the past because there wasn't any executive guideline about drug experiments on unsuspecting victims, to cite an example from Mr. Ford's list. They occurred in a climate where anything went in the name of national security. That climate has changed dramatically. The abuses of the past are the best protection against abuses in the future; the guidelines just lock the barn door.

Lastly, there is the paradox of secrecy. The government's intelligence operations cannot be conducted in the daylight. But the abuses dominating the news not only occurred in secret, but occurred as the result of secrecy.

In the Pike report Secretary of State Henry Kissinger is criticized for his "passion for secrecy." That is a common mania in officialdom. It encourages error, and the compounding of error. It is one thing to defend a dubious policy in the light of pitiless publicity, and another to defend it in cozy executive session.

But Mr. Ford is proposing stiff new laws to prevent the leakage of official secrets and to enhance the government's power to block the publication of secrets. The paradox probably shouldn't be resolved. On the one hand, the Executive Branch must try to keep its guard up. On the other hand, Congress leaks like a sieve and always will. The leak is a way of life in official Washington and not without its public uses. In short, there are secrets and then there are secrets: the political sort should and will be leaked.

It is not guidelines and laws and oversight boards that are going to protect us ultimately, but the men who hold power. There is no substitute for character, in the old-fashioned sense, and no guarding against bad men, such as John Mitchell or Richard Nixon, by devising pristine structures. We have lost the presumption of trust to Vietnam and Watergate. Mr. Bush and Mr. Ford operate in a climate of suspicion. Restoring the presumption of trust is not only their task, but the nation's.

DESERET NEWS

Salt Lake City, Utah, February 19, 1976

Anything as sensitive and far-reaching as the White House's new plan for reshuffling U.S. intelligence operations almost inevitably becomes a target for professional nit-pickers.

But there's no justification for much of the flak that is being directed at the comprehensive package of reforms outlined this week by President Ford.

Some of the criticism is based on the simple pretense that the White House is preoccupied exclusively with tightening its own control over the Central Intelligence Agency without any concern for improving congressional oversight.

Some of it ignores the way Congress has become prone to spring leaks involving important national security matters, and seems to assume that the legislative rather than the executive branch should bear final responsibility for intelligence operations.

And some of the criticism is founded on the apparently attractive but risky belief that the U.S. should confine its intelligence operations to gathering information even though this could amount to letting other nations have a corner on the "dirty tricks" of the spy business.

Though some of the administration's new bans on intelligence activities do little more than elaborate on the restriction on domestic spying already in the CIA's charter, it's certainly safer to reaffirm and spell out those limitations than to rely on them in their present form.

Likewise, the new Oversight Board of three distinguished citizens looks like window-dressing that shouldn't be necessary if the White House and Congress were doing an adequate job of monitoring all U.S. intelligence activities abroad. But when other monitors break down, it could be vital to have this back-up system in place.

By extending the authority of the CIA's director to cover not just that agency but all nine of the nation's intelligence operations, the White House provided machinery that should help pinpoint responsibility and provide needed coordination.

Congress could also pinpoint its part of the same responsibility by following the White House's advice to form a joint congressional committee on intelligence oversight. It's a suggestion that seems to be ignored by critics who insist the administration is interested in more secrecy rather than more supervision.

As it is now, the intelligence agencies must brief at least six separate congressional committees, each with separate staffs. This fragmentation of effort contributes to the leaking of intelligence information for the simple reason that the more widely any secret is shared the harder it is to keep. Yet Congress has been thinking seriously of continuing this fragmentation by maintaining separate intelligence committees for both the House and Senate, possibly in addition to the existing committees.

When President Ford recommended a single joint committee on intelligence, it's no accident that he suggested that it be patterned after the Joint Atomic Energy Committee. The atomic energy committee has demonstrated it's possible for Congress to oversee another sensitive field without exposing vital secrets.

To make sure intelligence secrets aren't exposed, the White House is seeking a law making it a federal crime for anyone in government to leak security matters. Such a law should have been put on the books long ago for reasons that shouldn't require elaboration. Yet some of the legislation Congress has been pushing skirts this vital problem by providing no penalties at all for unauthorized leaks of classified intelligence information.

This failure on the part of Congress strengthens President Ford's contention that the lawmakers should be told about specific intelligence activities after they have been carried out but not beforehand. Advance notification would, in effect, give the lawmakers a veto over intelligence operations. At times that procedure might spare the cloak-and-dagger boys some red faces by thwarting ill-advised intelligence operations. But those occasions seem likely to be only the rare exception rather than the rule.

Congress has no monopoly on wisdom regarding intelligence operations or anything else. Besides, that body is too unwieldy to become involved in day-to-day administration of intelligence activities. That's the job of the executive branch.

By this or just about any other standard of sound management, the White House rates high marks for its intelligence reforms. Congress can best serve the public by seeking to build on those plans rather than trying to shoot them down.

Portland Press Herald

Portland, Me., February 19, 1976

President Ford's new command structure for the intelligence community has much that is good, some that is questionable, and admits that it is vulnerable to abuse by means over which it has little control.

Unifying foreign intelligence under one management committee appears to be a good approach but it is weakened somewhat by the fact that the head of the committee will be CIA Director George Bush. Bush's qualifications for that job were marginal at best and when questioned in that area at his news conference Tuesday evening, the best the President could do was to insist that Bush had served well in the House and had experience in foreign diplomacy as an ambassador.

The President could not say that Bush is an expert in the area of intelligence. And that weakness on the part of the Ford appointee weakens the whole management arrangement.

The President also is naming a three-person committee of overseers to watch over the intelligence operation. Here again, the basic approach can be applauded but to that committee Ford has named another former ambassador, Robert D. Murphy, who is 81 years old.

The President said he would ask for legislation which would provide criminal penalties against government employes who leak classified material. Ford acknowledged he was deeply disturbed that classified information developed by the House Intelligence Committee was leaked to the press even after the House had voted by a substantial margin not to release the report containing the information.

Something can, and should, be done to prevent leaks by committee staff members or other employes. As for leaks by congressmen themselves, the President urged the Congress to clean up its own House.

The President's program also contains provisions to further safeguard the public against intrusion by intelligence agencies either by electronic surveillance or by opening of mail. The President said intelligence agencies would be prohibited from any plot to assassinate foreign leaders in peace time and later, in response to probing by reporters, said he had always been on record as opposed to assassination and would not order it.

The new setup proposed by the Chief Executive will leave primary responsibility and accountability for intelligence operations with the President. In our view, that is where it belongs. As the last several presidents have demonstrated, it can be abused by a president. But it is also quite evident that classified material is not safe if entrusted to congressional sources. With the new command structure it is to be hoped that should any future president attempt to misuse the intelligence services, he would be halted or exposed by some one or more of those committees.

What is missing in the new plan is one of the elements which has been missing all along and that is something which may be impossible to counter by policy or general standards. There is still the opportunity for government personnel to be excessive in the classification of information. There has been an abundance of that in the past. The President's plan does not cope with it, leaving it to the discretion of people he hopes will be honorable and fair.

The House committee betrayed the confidence of the White House in leaking the classified information. It violated the vote of the House itself. Who did it may not be known, but the committee must bear the responsibility. And it would be good if the House would be more energetic in fixing responsibility for those leaks.

The President's new command structure has weaknesses and flaws, but it seems to us an earnest attempt to tighten up the intelligence operation while assuring its continued effectiveness in its vital role in the nation's defense.

The Seattle Times

Seattle, Wash., February 19, 1976

THE necessary task of reforming and reorganizing United States intelligence activities ought to be a matter of cooperation, not competition, between the White House and Congress.

In the aftermath of President Ford's report on his intelligence-overhaul plans, there are encouraging signs of just the sort of cooperation that is needed — even in an election year.

True, there has been grumbling on Capitol Hill to the effect that Mr. Ford is trying to carry out most of his reforms through executive order, rather than legislation.

But the President is, in fact, proposing substantial legislation in the intelligence field, including that which would require judicial warrants for national-security wiretaps and mail openings, and which would restrict the use of electronic surveillance by the Federal Bureau of Investigation.

A welcome reaction was that of Mike Mansfield, majority leader of the Senate. He said he thought Mr. Ford's proposals for revamping the structure of intelligence-agency management were "a good step in the right direction."

A number of members of the Senate intelligence committee offered similar positive views.

A PREDICTABLY sour reaction was offered by Representative Otis Pike, chairman of the House intelligence committee. Pike complained that the President was "much more interested in secrecy than oversight."

Pike's leaky committee, which spilled closed-door testimony all over town, of course did more than any other individual or group to make the point that secrecy safeguards are essential, particularly in the relationship between intelligence activities and Congress.

The Pike committee's example should persuade a majority of congressmen to vote for Mr. Ford's proposed legislation to make it a federal crime for government employes to leak secret information.

After 29 years without a major reorganization, the intelligence establishment would need an overhaul even if there had not been the recent round of Watergate-inspired probes and disclosures.

IN our view, the presidential move concentrating overall control over intelligence activities in the hands of one man — the Central Intelligence Agency director — makes just as good sense as having a single secretary of defense.

This country's intelligence operations have for many years been not only too fragmented but unnecessarily competitive, resulting in the waste of millions of dollars.

We hope Congress — at the urging of Senator Mansfield, as well as that of Mr. Ford and George Bush, the new C.I.A. director — will create a joint intelligence committee capable of exercising strong oversight of intelligence operations with suitable security safeguards.

Congress of course has a necessary role to play. But the final and ultimate responsibility must, as Mr. Ford says, lie with the President, who is accountable to the American people.

Intelligence activities, in that respect, are no different than any other executive-branch activity. Nor should they be.

The Dallas Morning News

Dallas, Tex., February 19, 1976

PRESIDENT FORD seems to us to have struck about the right balance in his organizational reform of the U.S. intelligence establishment.

The President, in his Tuesday night press conference, affirmed that abuses of power by agencies like the CIA will not be tolerated. Yet likewise he made plain that national security will not be sacrificed on the altar of "public accountability."

In fine, the intelligence agencies will receive better supervision—through the upgrading of CIA director George Bush's authority; through the creation of a blue-ribbon oversight committee; through the creation, if Congress sees fit, of a joint intelligence committee. At the same time, it will be the President, not Congress, who sets overall intelligence policy.

The President's goal is to "rebuild the confidence and capability of our intelligence services." That is just what the goal ought to be.

Not that the President's reforms—many of which he has already implemented by executive order—end the controversy over what to do about intelligence. The Pike committee, in the House, has weighed in with recommendations for, among other things, curbing domestic intelligence activities. The Church committee, in the Senate, will be heard from in due course. The debate will go on for a long time.

What the President has done is very properly to bear down on the need for effective and reliable intelligence gathering. Such an emphasis is almost wholly missing from the Pike committee recommendations, which have to do mainly with ways we can hedge in the CIA, the FBI and the rest in the performance of their duties.

Lamentably, the committee seems oblivious to the effect of its proposed restrictions upon the task of amassing information about the outside world. It is well to fret about presumable violations of civil liberties committed by the CIA. But it is not well at all to forget that the CIA has an urgent and vital job to perform.

That is where the matter of balance comes in, with regard to Ford's proposals.

The CIA, says Ford, cannot be allowed to plot peacetime assassination of foreign leaders. Very well; but he does not say wartime assassination. Neither does he say that government employes should henceforth feel free to leak secret information that embarrasses or discredits the government. On the contrary, Ford urges that the leaking of such secret information be made a federal crime.

As to this, it is only fair to say that there must be safeguards for a free press. Leaking information is a fine old tradition that cannot be brought to a jarring halt. Yet it is fair to say also that information injurious, if released, to domestic security cannot be spread casually across the front pages of every newspaper in the land. That is not freedom of the press; that is almost-suicidal naivete.

There may be shortcomings in the President's reform proposals, but at least they do not spring up out of naivete. If only the same could be said of other proposals—proposals whose authors plainly do not grasp the difference between reform and manslaughter.

The Dispatch

Columbus, Ohio, February 19, 1976

CONGRESS NOW has before it a proposal designed to provide this nation with what it must have — a reliable and respected foreign intelligence service buoyed with both the cloak of secrecy and the discipline of oversight.

President Ford's proposal will receive early study by appropriate congressional committees and it should for what cannot be ignored is the reality that other nations, both friend and foe, have not abandoned their intelligence gatherings with reference to their relations with this country.

THE FORD proposal tends to winnow much of the controversy which served to dilute the effectiveness of this country's vital intelligence community.

On the one hand, it rejects the idea America must abolish completely its Central Intelligence Agency.

On the other, it places vital supervision of both covert and open intelligence operations in the hands of known and proven civilian authorities.

IT SHOULD be candidly admitted there is no escape from covert operations whether they involve economic, political and military matters or even social trends, food supplies and population growths abroad.

At the same time, there is an obvious need to separate domestic operations from foreign intelligence gathering and to forthrightly eschew such solutions as assassination of individual leaders abroad.

IT IS EQUALLY obvious that a strong element of trust must be embodied in this nation's intelligence gathering supervision and that such an organization be accepted as a truly secret secret service, protected in that respect from erosion caused by leakage of classified information.

Mr. Ford's proposition attempts to hew away the parts of America's intelligence operation which have been negative and counterproductive. At the same time, the plan seeks to retain those essentials which the nation's leadership must have to assure vital protection for the country.

CONGRESS now has an opportunity to evaluate this fresh suggestion and in light of the needs would do well to approach the proposal promptly and efficiently.

The San Diego Union

San Diego, Calif., February 19, 1976

In all probability the intelligence agencies of the United States of America have been exposed and shaken enough so that a self correcting mechanism already is engaged in Washington.

We don't think, for example, that the CIA is going to participate in domestic spying activities for the foreseeable future, or in plots to assassinate heads of state.

The reason is plain. The officials in Congress and in the executive branch responsible for the direction and oversight of the intelligence community have been shaken awake by the political uproar of the last year.

However, political realities being what they are, it is not likely that the status quo will prevail. Before the dust settles, the intelligence agencies will feel firm new hands on the reins. If that is the case, the mature, constructive approach is to find a balance—to be certain that the pull on the reins is not so strong as to bring the team to a halt.

President Ford's program for the intelligence community, which he presented to Congress yesterday, appears to strike that balance. He will give the CIA director and the attorney general broader powers, create a new White House agency to monitor day-to-day intelligence activities, define and limit covert activities abroad and urge Congress to live up to its responsibilities by stopping leaks of classified data. A new civilian group of three people will help to prevent abuses.

The executive plan understandably has opposition because it is not without dangers. For example, additional power for the CIA director means less for the Secretary of Defense. It is conceivable that security could be weakened if wrong judgments are made.

By the same token, a White House panel keeping a strict account of clandestine activities does dilute the powers of the individual intelligence agency directors. It could weaken their missions.

And even the limited publicity that the President suggests for the tasks and roles of the intelligence groups might create headaches for the State Department. If a mission in a foreign country is publicized, the department fears, it will have to speak out automatically against the United States involvement.

In the last analysis, however, fears that the executive tightening up could be counterproductive put the burden on effectiveness and performance squarely where it belongs—on the President himself. What Mr. Ford is proposing is nothing more than an old fashioned vertical chain of command with enough checks and balances on the President to keep him from abusing his office.

His is a well researched, thoughtful and moderate approach to the problem which should go a long way toward ending the power struggle that has marked our intelligence activities since the inception of the CIA nearly 30 years ago.

THE STATES-ITEM

New Orleans, La., February 21, 1976

President Ford's proposals to bring the Central Intelligence Agency (CIA) and the National Security Agency (NSA) more directly under presidential control is appropriate.

The President should be thoroughly accountable for all agencies of the Executive Branch. But greater presidential accountability alone is not enough. The best safeguard against abuse of federal police powers is to subject them regularly to the checks and balances inherent in the separation of powers of the branches of government.

Congress and the Judicial Branch should share the responsibility of supervising and controlling the CIA, the NSA and the Federal Bureau of Investigation. This does not mean individual congressmen should be informed routinely of clandestine intelligence operations. It means Congress should periodically review the operations of the agencies without waiting for scandals to provoke review. Never again should an agency director be allowed to operate in a vacuum for decades as was the late FBI Director J. Edgar Hoover.

At his press conference Tuesday night, the President responded to the suggestion that greater presidential control of the CIA might increase a president's temptation to abuse its powers. "It should not happen," said Mr. Ford, "and I would hope that the American people will elect a president who will not abuse that responsibility."

The important point, of course, is that not all presidents can be counted on to share Mr. Ford's sense of responsibility. A tripartite system of checks and balances, with Congress conducting periodic reviews and court authorization required for unusual surveillance operations, would make it more difficult for the exceptional president to abuse the police powers.

Meanwhile, stricter guidelines for day-to-day intelligence operations, such as those Mr. Ford has proposed, are in order. Agency directors and, ultimately, the president would be accountable for their enforcement.

FORT WORTH STAR-TELEGRAM

Fort Worth, Tex., February 21, 1976

One aspect of President Ford's proposal to impose tighter control on U.S. intelligence operations bears watching closely. It's the part designed to prevent leaks of secret information which, in the hands of the enemy, could be dangerous to the nation's security.

The proposal calls primarily for fines and prison sentences for government employes convicted of leaking classified information.

But some provisions of the law would apply to thousands of other Americans whose jobs may give them access to classified information. They also could apply to news media and their employes, a fact which brings the First Amendment guarantee of a free press into potential jeopardy.

Penalties in the bill would cover "a contractor of the United States government" or any employ of such a contractor, as well as government employes.

Legal experts also say there is nothing in the proposal to prevent a reporter from being hauled before a grand jury and demanded to reveal his sources when federal prosecutors are tracking down the source of a leak.

The reporter, under the bill, would become the witness to a crime by receiving leaked classified information. A reporter refusing to disclose his sources under such circumstances would be subject to indefinite imprisonment for contempt.

Knowing this, as one Civil Liberties Union Lawyer points out, a government employe would be forced to consider "that the newsman he's talking to may end up as the prime witness against him."

Thus, the bill intended to prevent abuses by intelligence agencies could turn up with provisions that would:

— Greatly expand the scope of persons subject to legal entanglements with vague "national security" statutes, which calls to mind the use of such devices in totalitarian countries to suppress individual liberties and conceal government activities from the people.

— Tend to further choke off—by intimidation, if nothing else—the flow of information on which the people of a democracy depend in their decision making as citizens.

Congress, and the people, should be diligent to see that this doesn't happen.

And with all of our cherished liberties at stake, that's an understatement.

The Philadelphia Inquirer

Philadelphia, Pa., February 20, 1976

It is lamentable, if inevitable, that America's international intelligence and national security requirements and democracy's dependence on open dissent must draw together in conflict. Lamentation aside, though, it is encouraging that the debate is moving forward.

President Ford, with impressively more decisiveness than shown by either house of the Congress, has offered a set of fundamental reforms of the intelligence structure. It is unfortunate that his plan puts its most dramatic public emphasis directly where it does not belong: On penalizing breaches of secrecy.

Ultimately, it must be up to the Congress to fashion the most significant intelligence reforms. Among the lexicon of catch-phrases which have attached themselves to the broad debate, "oversight" represents the most centrally critical concept.

Oversight, that is, in the manner of overseeing—or monitoring and controlling—not overlooking, which has been the sorry recent history both of the internal watchdogs of the executive branch and of the Congress itself.

In that, Mr. Ford chose with political sensitivity in his Tuesday evening news conference to leave to the legislative branch what it must anyway face. "The Congress," the President said, "I hope, will establish a joint committee (with) an oversight responsibility as to the program and the performance of the intelligence communities in the federal government."

Some headway has been made in that important area, especially with the Hughes-Ryan amendment, which now is law, requiring "timely" executive notice to six Congressional committees of all covert action intelligence operations.

A great deal more needs to be done, however, before it will be possible to begin to assume with any rational confidence that U. S. intelligence operations are free from the excesses and illegalities which have brought them to such dismaying ill repute in the last half-dozen years.

There is much to be examined in Mr. Ford's internal, executive branch restructuring of the intelligence machinery. On first blush, his proposals seem constructive and responsible —tighter central coordination of resources and decisions, and thus a far greater degree of accountability for intelligence operations on the President himself than has been past practice.

The idea, however, that the executive branch can police the executive branch is not a plausible one when it comes to the gross violations of both law and fundamental morality which have been traced to the Central Intelligence Agency and its surrounding clumps.

The Congress must proceed to meet that responsibility, first by establishment of one or more committee responsibilities on the lines suggested by Mr. Ford and then by giving that committee or committees the statutory teeth to detect breaches of the law and of good judgment and to prevent or punish such breaches.

Meanwhile, however, neither Mr. Ford nor those in the Congress who are of a mind to cooperate with his secrecy proposals will add dignity or plausibility to their cause by pressing for draconian measures to prevent "leaks" of information.

The President's ill-conceived executive order on secrecy, while not enforceable by criminal sanctions, would impose on officials within the executive branch stronger-than-ever discouragements from internal dissent. Far more threatening, the President's secrecy proposal to the Congress would seek to make it a crime for government officials or former officials to disclose intelligence "sources and methods."

There is perilous danger to the entire concept of democracy in any proposal to restrict the free flow of information or ideas. One of the most instructive lessons of the last decade has been that without the surfacing of internal dissent, without breaches of secrecy, the American government is susceptible to intolerable manipulations—as witness the horrors of the Watergate scandals and the endless web of government-sponsored lies about the war in Indochina.

Putting into practice the lessons of those national traumas does not promise to be easy or without earnest dispute. But it is a clear principle that the most constructive response to bad news is *not* to cut out the tongue of the messenger.

The Chattanooga Times

Chattanooga, Tenn., February 20, 1976

Intelligent Reform

The key to President Ford's plan to reform and reorganize the nation's intelligence agencies lies in his statement that "the overriding task now is to rebuild the confidence and capability of our intelligence services . . . " so that they can perform the vital job for which they were established.

Mr. Ford's action is regarded as the most extensive of its kind in nearly 30 years, in itself a measure of the lack of oversight that contributed to shocking abuses the reform is expected to curtail, if not eliminate. Added details of what the Administration has in mind will be made available shortly but on balance, we would have to say the President has made a good beginning.

Basically, he announced that the Director of Central Intelligence — George Bush, at this point — will be given strong new powers for "management of intelligence," that covert operations abroad be curtailed, and that a three-man "independent oversight board" be created to monitor the operation of intelligence operations.

Most important, Mr. Ford said that he would issue a comprehensive set of public guidelines that would serve as legally binding charters for intelligence agencies. By providing "stringent protections for the rights of American citizens," the President said the guidelines would improve the agencies' performance and "restore public confidence in them."

If, as has been reported, the guidelines include strong proscriptions against domestic surveillance operations by the CIA, limitations on foreign covert operations and regulation to prohibit civil rights violations by any federal intelligence agency, a major step forward will have been taken in restricting the agencies to their primary responsibility: gathering intelligence that is needed for the nation's security.

An important element in the President's plan is that it could lower the decibel level of the debate over CIA activities, which on each side has at times bordered on hysteria.

We have not been impressed with arguments that the months-long investigation of the CIA has somehow "exposed" the United States to mortal danger from outside enemies; neither have we agreed with the more radical demands that the CIA be so drastically regulated that its usefulness would be impaired.

By pledging to maintain a strong intelligence agency that is, nevertheless, subject to strict oversight to prevent abuses, President Ford has staked out a position that should enable the intelligence community to perform its job effectively — and constitutionally.

. . . And a Caution

President Ford reacted with some heat at his press conference the other day when asked if his proposal that Congress make it a crime to reveal government secrets might not be comparable with the British Official Secrets Act. Nevertheless, we believe it imperative that Congress consider the Ford proposal warily. For one reason, it is possible it could erode the First Amendment by subjecting reporters to prosecution under conspiracy laws for publishing classified information. The Administration contends the law would apply only to government employes releasing intelligence "sources and methods," not other secrets. But it is easy to see the CIA could stretch the term to cover a wide range of subjects — as it has done in the past — and to hide mistakes. Secrets vital to national security obviously must be protected. But we should not negate the move toward reform by acts that could allow future abuses.

The State

Columbia, S.C., February 20, 1976

DISPLAYING a fine sense of political timing, President Ford has taken the offensive in the raging controversy over the U.S. intelligence community.

Obviously sensing that Congress has blundered in the eyes of the public by leaking American secrets all over the place, Mr. Ford moved to tighten security and improve administrative control over the activities of the CIA and other U.S. agencies that gather foreign intelligence.

He placed policy direction of these activities where it should be: at the top. The buck will stop at the National Security Council, consisting of the President, the Vice President, and the Secretaries of State and Defense.

And he gave administrative control to one man, new CIA Director George Bush. Some have questioned the qualifications of politician-diplomat Bush for this role. But it might not be a bad idea to have a man who understands the potential political implications of questionable covert activities.

We are not quite sure we understand the precise role of the independent Oversight Board created in the President's executive order, but he named an experienced trio of private citizens to man it.

Mr. Ford banned, or asked legislation to ban, a number of covert practices and dirty tricks that drew heavy criticism during the months of congressional hearings on the CIA, hearings which seriously crippled this vital, protective arm.

His suggestion that Congress create one joint oversight committee on intelligence is a meritorious one. Currently six committees are demanding information on covert activities. That is one reason they don't remain "covert" very long. Many such actions become useless once the cover is blown.

Mr. Ford got on tricky ground when he moved to plug leaks in the executive department. He wants every federal employe with access to classified documents to sign statements that they will not divulge the information therein and that they expect punishment if they do. Furthermore, he wants legislation making such unauthorized release a criminal offense.

The government, to say nothing of every American citizen, has an obvious interest in protecting legitimate national security secrets. But the public, particularly, has an equal interest in knowing of blundering and wrongdoing inside its government. The classification system (marking a document "Confidential," "Secret," or "Top Secret") has been and can be used to hide matters of public interest and concern.

It is difficult to plug leaks in the manner suggested by the President (and the revised Criminal Code now being considered by Congress) without abusing important protections under the First Amendment's right-to-know provision. If releasing classified information is made a crime, not only the giver (a government employe) but the receiver (a news reporter) might be subject to prosecution.

The answer, perhaps, lies in restricting regulations and criminal sanctions to release of the most sensitive material. Another idea that might be useful would be the establishment of an independent classification appeals panel. Government employes, reporters or others who had reason to believe a document is over-classified could appeal to this quasi-judicial body, made up of individuals with the highest security clearance.

Regardless of our qualms about his secrecy provisions, Mr. Ford has shown leadership and good sense in this effort to restore the credibility and effectiveness of America's intelligence community.

Minneapolis Tribune

Minneapolis, Minn., February 19, 1976

The shortcomings in President Ford's proposed overhaul of the intelligence community are stunning. In an attempt to strengthen government secrecy, he has proposed legislation that would make it a criminal act to disclose such matters as the criminal acts by government agencies that prompted investigations of the CIA and FBI in the first place. His executive orders to prevent such abuses by the federal government lack the legislative safeguards without which those orders could be changed arbitrarily. Despite his emphasis on the "new command structure," nothing suggests that this is a change in any important way from what now exists. Finally, he gave scarcely a nod to the new and essential role that Congress must play in intelligence oversight.

It is well to remember that the impetus behind more than a year of examination of intelligence operations was a New York Times report, gathered from a number of sources and confirmed by subsequent investigation, that the CIA had violated its charter by conducting domestic surveillance. That disclosures of assassination attempts on foreign leaders arose during the administration's own Rockefeller Commission investigation. And that a strong incentive for executive secrecy is the wish to prevent public knowledge of illegal or foolish acts by intelligence agencies.

Disclosure of such acts is indeed embarrassing to the United States. But the way to prevent the embarrassment is to prevent them from occurring in the future, not to cover up what has happened in the past; a successful cover-up removes the pressure for correction.

Implicitly acknowledging past infringements on American civil rights, the president has published executive orders which, he said, will provide "stringent protection." The better way to do that would be to incorporate those protections into law, which is not subject to arbitrary change by the executive.

The centerpiece of Ford's intelligence reorganization plan is a new committee in the National Security Council accompanied by a new "Oversight Board" made up of private citizens. The security council committee, chaired by CIA Director George Bush, would manage all foreign intelligence. But that is what the CIA director was supposed to do all along. If the president means to give Bush authority over those substantial parts of the Defense and State Department budgets devoted to intelligence, he should say so. That has never happened before. Ford's failure to spell this out suggests that the change is more likely to be on paper than in fact.

Little need be said about the Oversight Board, which is to be a subcommittee of the present Foreign Intelligence Advisory Board. If the present board had been effective, intelligence abuses would not have occurred. But even if these organizational changes work better than they now seem likely to, they would not obviate the need for constitutional balance. No single lesson of the past year stands out more sharply than the importance of congressional oversight in intelligence.

Thus we were dismayed to hear the president dismiss the suggestion of congressional review of FBI intelligence activities. The attorney general is writing guidelines for the FBI, he said, "and those guidelines will take care of the problems." This illustrates the familiar presidential penchant, certainly not unique to Ford, for decision-making without Congress; it also suggests that Ford considers corrective measures a one-time event rather than a continuing process of review within and outside the executive branch.

Congress, we trust, will take a longer view. Evidence that it will is already in hand in the Senate bill establishing a strong oversight committee with such powers as annual authorization and appropriation of intelligence funds. The administration worries about congressional leaks, with some justification. Congress worries, with greater justification, that executive secrecy is an invitation to the abuse of power. Hearings to be held soon on the Ford intelligence plan should suggest ways to change it into one that will serve the public interest as well as that of the intelligence community.

The Courier-Journal

Louisville, Ky., February 20, 1976

THE OUTLINE that President Ford has sketched for his proposed reorganization of the Central Intelligence Agency shows that the executive branch is on the right compass heading. Congressional proposals have yet to be fully disclosed, but first indications are encouraging. Between them, they offer the prospect of reshaping U.S. intelligence activities to provide firmer control and oversight without jeopardizing legitimate security needs.

It would be impossible, of course, to eliminate entirely the possibility of future misdeeds. The secrecy inherent in intelligence work makes watertight control impossible. But memories of the trauma caused by recent disclosures should keep the intelligence agencies on the straight and narrow path for a few years at least. As memories fade, however, the danger of an agent, or an official, or even the President himself, misusing an agency's authority could always recur. The caliber and integrity of the persons involved will always have to be the ultimate safeguard.

But at least the possibilities would be limited by the proposed reforms. Mr. Ford's expressed intention, for instance, to strengthen the chain of command, putting more emphasis on the president's responsibility for foreign intelligence operations, should be a useful tightening. So is the plan to bring all the intelligence agencies, including the FBI, into a single command structure.

The pledge to issue public guidelines for these agencies should be reassuring to the American people, and presumably this could be done without being detailed enough to be, at the same time, informative to potential enemies. Equally reassuring should be the promised legislation to provide judicial safeguards for American citizens against wiretapping and mail openings by the federal government. Letting the courts, rather than the Attorney General, decide whether such surveillance is necessary, even in national security matters, is a long overdue protection.

The new apparatus to improve oversight of intelligence activities also is valuable, though much may depend on how effectively the committees are allowed to operate. The revamping of the 40 Committee, for example, doesn't guarantee that covert operations will be more closely directed and supervised than before. Committees can be bypassed. But the addition to this body of two outsiders — the Attorney General and the director of the Office of Management and Budget — offers added checks while holding out the prospect of a welcome broadening of viewpoints.

Nor does the establishment of a new citizen oversight panel at the White House to watch for and report abuses automatically ensure that there will be no more cover-ups. But it does offer a back-up mechanism through which additional checks can be maintained on intelligence operations, and thus increases the likelihood that improprieties would be disclosed. If Congress also can come up with a more competent way to exercise its constitutional oversight responsibility, then these agencies would be subject to as much outside supervision as is consistent with an intelligence gathering operation.

Congress will have to decide for itself, of course, how best to overhaul its oversight committees. But President's Ford's suggestion of a joint congressional committee makes the most sense, even though Congress appears to be resisting this. Duplication of effort in the past failed to provide the extra measure of control that might have been expected; multiple watchdogs were not better than one. As a few legislators are beginning to realize, a better way to encourage vigilance is to keep the committee membership rotating so that it isn't lulled into a cozy, unquestioning relationship with the agencies it is supposed to be policing.

But whether Congress sets up a joint committee or two separate ones, it will have to guarantee better security against indiscriminate leaks. Successful experience with the joint atomic energy committee shows this to be possible.

President Ford's proposal to make it a crime for any government employe to reveal highly classified information, however, seems heavy-handed. Ways already exist to prosecute unauthorized disclosures — Daniel Ellsberg, for instance, was charged with espionage, conspiracy and theft of government property for his role in the publication of the Pentagon Papers. So the purpose of such legislation would appear to be intimidation rather than closing a loophole. If the control mechanisms are working properly, an employe disturbed that an agency's power was being misused would not need to take his story to the press; he could report it to the new citizens panel or to the congressional committee, confident that appropriate action would be taken. But if these watchdogs become as compliant and acquiescent as their predecessors, someone with evidence of wrongdoing would have no alternative but to go public.

The best hope for effective safeguards, since memories of recent abuses will grow dim with the passage of time, is a tighter control structure and greater accountability at the top. It's hard to see how much tighter controls could be instituted than the President is now proposing without seriously endangering the nation's ability to remain accurately informed of what is happening around the world.

DAYTON DAILY NEWS

Dayton, Ohio, February 19, 1976

The machinery President Ford has set in motion to oversee the CIA and other U.S. intelligence operations has some value, but as a response to the unnerving intelligence-agency abuses revealed over the last year, his program is woefully incomplete.

It is obviously good that the President wants to increase the accountability of his office for the operations and policies of the agencies, and his new oversight arrangements show promise of accomplishing that. And it is good he is placing the CIA director in policy command of other intelligence branches. That, too, will sharpen accountability.

But there are three major flaws in the President's program.

ONE — The proposed law against leaks by government officials is terrifying to contemplate. Remember, it was thanks only to leaks that the nation learned in the first place of the need for the reforms Mr. Ford now has initiated.

If leaks were effectively forbidden by the threat of prison, a president's accountability for intelligence abuses would be meaningless because the public could not learn that any abuses had occurred.

Certainly leaks can be a problem, potentially even tragic in their consequences. But in the main they have been effectively restrained by existing threats, including the loss of the leaker's job. That has tended to confine leaks to matters of serious and legitimate public concern.

Any proposal for attempting to stop leaks totally, by resort to felony law, is also a proposal for hiding abuses totally.

TWO — Mr. Ford made little provision for congressional involvement in the supervision of U.S. intelligence agencies. Congress is going to want in on the process and ought to be in.

Fairly broad congressional supervision should be established over intelligence gathering and analysis. Congress needn't get into the details of who is spying on whom for what. But it should set the emphases in intelligence, review the budget for the appropriateness of the agencies' priorities and establish and police basic policy guidelines.

Further, a joint committee should be responsible for overseeing covert operations, adding another judgment to the executive branch's about whether specific operations are essential for national purposes. If the committee were small, the probable responsibility for any security compromises usually would be clear, a strong check against casual leaks.

THREE- — Mr. Ford did not propose splitting covert operations away from general intellignece gathering and analysis. Congress should insist on that reform.

Spying and data analysis get the nation into little trouble, and just about everyone agrees with the necessity for them. The inevitable exposures of covert operations undermine morale and efficiency in those activities, however — which is exactly what is happening now.

If covert operations were clearly separated from the other activities, they could be more intimately supervised both by the executive branch and the joint committee, more carefully reviewed for necessity and appropriateness and more effectively secured.

The Pittsburgh Press

Pittsburgh, Pa., February 20, 1976

For all its good features, President Ford's plan to reorganize the U.S. intelligence community leaves the uneasy, and perhaps misleading, impression that he cares more about plugging information leaks than about correcting the past abuses of the CIA and other intelligence agencies.

Certainly the activities and identities of American agents must be protected. As Mr. Ford says, the United States needs — and must have — foreign intelligence if it hopes to survive in a world of plots, counterplots and revolutions.

But the President may be treading on thin ice when he proposes that government employes be fined $5,000 or sent to jail for up to five years for disclosing "information relating to intelligence sources and methods" — because that phrase is so loose it could cover even the disclosure of operations which themselves are in violation of U.S. laws.

And requiring thousands of additional workers to sign a secrecy agreement — backed up by a threat to prosecute — could also work against the best interests of the public's right to know what its government is doing.

Not even the three-member "oversight board" of distinguished private citizens would be able to uncork improperly classified information with sanctions like that in effect.

What makes this overemphasis on secrecy so unfortunate is that much of what the President is doing to restructure the intelligence apparatus deserves public and congressional support.

Mr. Ford, for example, has tightened the lines of command so that the CIA and other intelligence agencies will be more responsive to supervision.

By executive order, he has forbidden the CIA to harass individuals, to infiltrate domestic groups or otherwise to violate the civil liberties of American citizens.

He also has asked Congress to specifically outlaw assassination attempts on foreign officials and to require warrants both for wiretapping in this country and for opening of private mail from abroad.

His suggestion that Congress set up a single joint committee to oversee the CIA makes sense because, unfortunately, legitmate security suffers when too many congressmen — and their staff members —have access to secret documents.

Congress will continue to insist, no doubt, that its oversight committee or committees should be notified of intelligence operations in advance.

In some cases, that might be possible. But the President is right in insisting that the CIA — or any other intelligence agency — be free to act swiftly in crisis situations and without prenotification, so long as the appropriate congressional overseers are properly briefed after the operation has begun.

No intelligence agency can operate with one arm tied.

ALBUQUERQUE JOURNAL

Albuquerque, N.M., February 19, 1976

President Ford's proposals for reorganization and sweeping reforms of the nation's intelligence-gathering agencies should go far in forestalling the past abuses that have been brought to the public's attention in recent months.

But it is apparent the President has closed his eyes to the political reality which dictates that Congress must have an oversight role in the intelligence program. It is acknowledged that Congress has failed miserably to demonstrate the sense of responsibility that qualifies it for such a role. Nevertheless, no intelligence effort can succeed without congressional assent, and now, in view of recent humiliating disclosures, Congress will insist on increased oversight.

The President's creation of a three-member executive oversight board, publicly oriented, is a step in the right direction although a larger, broader-based board could assure greater response to the sensibilities of the American people, who are now deeply concerned.

Most disturbing is the adamant insistence of both the President and his newly designated intelligence czar, George Bush, for tighter security over "classified" intelligence data. The danger in their position is strongly implied by recent over-reaction within the administration and in certain congressional quarters over the recent "leaking" of intelligence to the press — data which should not have been kept secret in the first place. Now, as always, there is a chronic inability of administrators to distinguish between that which could be officially embarrassing and that which is genuinely security-sensitive.

In this respect we suggest another public-oriented panel of citizens, similar to that which operated within the U.S. Office of Censorship in wartime. The wartime panel operated superbly to draw the thin lines between the public's right to know and the nation's need to survive whenever the two concerns came into conflict.

All reforms outlined by the President for the nation's intelligence-gathering bodies are justified by the glaring abuses so recently impressed on the public mind. Whether they become hard, fast rules or merely advisory guidelines will depend largely on the character of those in charge of the agencies. Conscientious administrators sensitive to the rights, the privacy and the immunities of their fellow citizens and the internal integrity of foreign governments will be the determining factor.

Because of — and not in spite of — his partisan political background, George Bush is extremely well qualified to read the pulse of the American people and recognize the practical boundaries.

We believe that, for some years to come, the nation's intelligence efforts will be held within those boundaries — with or without the limitations enunciated by the President. The American people and their outraged sense of decency will demand it. Our disillusioned allies and collaborators abroad, whose continued cooperation is vital, will have to be assured and reassured.

Los Angeles Times

Los Angeles, Calif., February 20, 1976

After the long series of disclosures of domestic spying and other abuses of power by the Central Intelligence Agency, President Ford proposes to protect the huge intelligence community from future exposure by laws that place heavy emphasis on secrecy.

That, in effect, is the thrust of his appeal to Congress to adopt civil and criminal penalties against government employes who divulge classified information. And in an accompanying 36-page executive order, he decreed that all federal agencies and all federal contractors require their employes to sign agreements not to disclose classified data to unauthorized persons.

Before the order, only CIA employes and some employes in other agencies were required to commit themselves to such secrecy. But thousands of other federal employes and additional thousands of employes of government contractors are now included.

With thousands of government documents routinely classified, the order gives the executive branch of government unprecedented control of information, a vast amount of which has no rational bearing on security.

The President's proposal for a stringent secrecy act includes "only those who improperly disclose secrets, not those to whom secrets are disclosed," but the law would lay harsh restraints on the gathering and dissemination of news. Atty. Gen. Edward H. Levi acknowledged that, in the enforcement of the law, news reporters could be subpoenaed to disclose their sources, and could be jailed if they refused to comply.

Ford insisted that the law would not be an "official secrets act," and he said it "could not be used to cover up abuses and improprieties" because it "could in no way prevent people from reporting questionable activities to appropriate authorities in the executive and legislative branches of the government." The history of recent years refutes that hope.

The restrictions that Ford put into effect to control the domestic activities of intelligence agencies —in contrast to his call for more secrecy—are welcome, if long overdue. His executive order limits infiltration of domestic groups, prohibits the illegal use of tax-return information, bars such practices as burglaries and drug tests without consent, and limits the physical and electronic surveillance of Americans. The order requires court approval of electronic surveillance or the opening of mail.

The President's decision to make operative the CIA director's theoretical authority over all intelligence agencies is sound, as is his decision to place control of covert operations at a higher level in the executive branch than before. We share his view that a joint House-Senate committee is the proper vehicle for congressional oversight.

But overshadowing these substantial improvements in the control of intelligence agencies is the proposed secrecy act with its powers to suppress information under the guise of protecting national security.

WINSTON-SALEM JOURNAL

Winston- Salem, N.C. February 19, 1976

It will take some time to unravel the intelligence reforms that President Ford offered the nation during a press conference Tuesday night. He spoke of many things — of shoes and ships and civil rights, of monitors and crimes. He did not, however, put forward more than the "bare bones" of his proposals, preferring instead to promise an end to abuses now, and the details of how that is to be accomplished later.

But the skeleton key of his program is already apparent: the elevation of the CIA director to the role of U. S. intelligence czar. It is the President's plan to create a Committee on Foreign Intelligence, led by George Bush, that would be charged with the "management of intelligence." The committee would be given overall control of the CIA, the Defense Intelligence Agency, the National Security Agency, and all other organizations involved in the gathering of foreign intelligence. Such centralization would supposedly increase accountability within the intelligence community, while decreasing opportunities for mischief.

The idea is wholly consistent with the President's position, stated during his press conference, that he "will not be a party to the dismantling of the CIA . . ." It is so consistent, in fact, and so obviously a building up rather than a dismantling of the CIA, that one must wonder precisely where the President has been the past year or two.

For the CIA is the epicenter of the very scandals to which the President's reforms are presumably directed. Had a Cabinet member or distinguished private citizen been chosen to lead the Committee on Foreign Intelligence, that would have been one thing; but to give the CIA director such unprecedented power is to ignore totally the revelations of the recent past, and to cast severe doubts on the President's entire reform package.

Indeed, the President's proposal comes perilously close to mocking those many Americans who wish to see a strong but properly controlled intelligence community. Saying that does not impugn the President's integrity, or that of George Bush: Under those particular men, the plan might be eminently workable. But true reform can never be based on present circumstances or present personalities; it must look to the future while learning from the past. The President's plan does neither, and should be altered, if not scrapped completely, as soon as possible.

THE ATLANTA CONSTITUTION

Atlanta, Ga., February 20, 1976

President Ford has now outlined the administration's plan to "reorganize" the intelligence community. That means, mostly, the CIA, which has been catching most of the flak lately, but also our other intelligence agencies run by the Army and Navy and other government bodies.

The plan curbs domestic spying, calls for new guidelines on covert operations, new powers for the head of the CIA, stronger inspectors general in each of the intelligence agencies, a "secrecy law" making it a crime for past or present members of the executive branch to disclose intelligence secrets, and an expanded Foreign Intelligence Advisory Board.

Two basic problems have come out of the long congressional probe into the activities of our intelligence agencies. One is that they have sometimes grossly overstepped the limits on what they are supposed to do. Few Americans want our government to sanction murder plots in peacetime against foreign leaders or police state-type activities against our own citizens. The CIA has been involved in this sort of thing.

The other problem is, as George Bush, the new CIA director, puts it, that we live in a very tough world where the other side plays hardball. If our intelligence operations are subjected to periodic exposure by disaffected former agents or by others who have axes to grind, we might as well get out of the business.

President Ford's reorganization plans apparently try to hit a balance. The emphasis is on stricter "oversight." That is an obvious need. A basic problem has been that nobody has been accountable for what these agencies do, or so it appears. Congressional and executive "oversight" bodies have not rushed forward in the recent investigations and accepted responsibility for assassination plots, payment of huge sums of money to neo-fascists against the advice of the CIA agents on the spot, and a host of other abuses.

There are some items in Ford's proposals that ought to be very carefully considered. The proposed secrecy law, for instance. There are, of course, already laws in this area. But if new laws made it impossible for anyone to criticize intelligence agencies and back their criticism with facts, we might be asking for trouble.

"The organization is streamlined, people are held accountable," an administration official said in explaining the President's proposals. "From now on, everybody that does foreign intelligence is going to have to do it under presidential direction." That seems reasonable. But the Watergate episode should suggest that even the President can abuse the functions of intelligence agencies.

President Ford's proposals basically call for two things: that the intelligence agencies police themselves more stringently and that the executive branch assures that they do so. Where does this leave the congressional "oversight" bodies—what are they supposed to oversee? The President's plans don't provide for much control over intelligence operations outside the intelligence agencies themselves and the executive. Maybe, considering the fact that "leaks" from the congressional investigations often reached tidal wave proportions, that's the way it has to be. But all conscientious citizens of one of the world's last open and democratic societies ought to think about these questions carefully.

THE BLADE

Toledo, Ohio, February 22, 1976

THE President's intelligence-reorganization plan, so long awaited, is a disappointment. It falls short on the crucial point, repeatedly emphasized in recent weeks by Mr. Ford himself, of the need to rebuild confidence that U.S. foreign-intelligence operations will be conducted properly and effectively. And the essential weakness of his design lies not so much in the mechanical details — a few of which do have merit — as in the all-too-habitual attitude lurking behind the overall blueprint.

It was not to be expected, given the President's political orientation and the cold-war background of his public career, that he would come in with a radically overhauled approach to the work of the CIA and related agencies. But it was reasonable to hope that he would suggest more change than he did, if only as a signal to a disillusioned citizenry that their Chief Executive recognized the grave import of recent revelations. Instead, the principal message Mr. Ford seems to be conveying is that he wants the old intelligence establishment to get back as soon as possible to business as usual.

He is narrowing policy responsibility but leaving it basically in the hands of the same National Security Council infrastructure where it has been lodged all along. He is bestowing more sweeping managerial powers than ever on the CIA chief, a move the more dismaying because the individual tapped for the job is George Bush — all-around political handyman whose principal qualification is his ability to slip quickly into the in-group groove. Supposedly keeping a watchdog's skeptical eye on the activities of those worthies will be a new "citizens" committee composed of three men whose roots in the federal/intelligence/military milieu reach back to World War II or beyond. And hovering over the whole mechanism is the familiar, self-justifying preoccupation with secrecy for secrecy's sake. That was dramatically symbolized by the fact that even part of the follow-up executive order — presumably aimed at assuring the public a new day had arrived — was censored.

It is as if Mr. Ford has missed entirely the most fundamental lesson that has come out of the investigations of the CIA: It was primarily the lack of genuine accountability which eventually led the agency beyond the bounds of legality, propriety, and morality — indeed, into operations that sometimes proved to be actually inimical to the nation's own interests.

Through such misdeeds, the CIA ultimately sabotaged a good deal of its standing in this country and much of its effectiveness abroad. Mr. Ford seems well on the way to similarly subverting his opportunity to restore the integrity and credibility the intelligence apparatus must have if it is going to be able to do the job it is supposed to do.

Senate CIA Investigation and Reports

Assassination Report

Church bars secret report on CIA plots. en. Frank Church (D, Ida.), chairman of he Senate Select Committee on Intelligence, in a letter to the White House, ov. 4, 1975 rejected a request by President Ford that the committee keep secret forthcoming report on Central Intelligence Agency involvement in assassination lots against foreign chiefs of state.

In a letter to Church, released Nov. 4, he President asked that the panel not nake its assassination report public because it would "do grevious damage to ur country . . . likely be exploited by oreign nations and groups hostile to the Jnited States . . . [and] seriously impair ur ability to exercise a positive leading ole in world affairs." He also feared, ord said, that publication might ndanger individuals named in the report r who otherwise might be identified by oreign agents carefully studying the eport.

Responding to Ford, Church said that he committee's intention to make the eport public had "long been clear." Moreover, Church said he felt the naional interest would be "better served by etting the American people know the true nd complete story" behind the alleged leath plots. Church, whose remarks were ontained in a letter to the President, said he committee had voted to submit the 00-page report to the full Senate and ntended to go ahead with publication if he Senate did not object.

Assassination report issued. The Senate elect Committee on Intelligence Nov. 20 nade public a report that said U.S. government officials had ordered the assassiation of two foreign leaders and had een involved in assassination plots gainst three other foreign officials. Although four of the five leaders were ssassinated, none of them died as the lirect result of the assassination plans nitiated by U.S. officials, the report conluded. [See text, pp. 33–35]

According to the committee's 347-page eport, which was released over the opposition of the Ford Administration, Fidel Castro of Cuba and Patrice Lumumba of he Congo (now Zaire) were the targets of leath plots originated in Washington. The others—Rafael Leonidas Trujillo of the Dominican Republic, Ngo Dinh Diem of South Vietnam and Gen. Rene Schneider of Chile—died as the result of coup plots, which U.S. officials had encouraged or were at least privy to.

The committee said it was unable to determine if any president had explicitly ordered the death of a foreign leader, but it indicated that available evidence strongly suggested that President Eisenhower had "authorized" the assassination of Lumumba.

The report concluded with the recommendation that Congress adopt legislation making it illegal to kill or conspire to kill a foreign leader or politician.

Authorization—The committee acknowledged in its report that it had encountered difficulties in determining if any U.S. president had authorized a plot to assassinate a foreign leader. President Nixon had explicitly authorized the CIA to foment a military coup against Allende, an assignment the CIA undertook and failed at. There was no evidence to implicate Nixon in the bungled kidnapping attempt that resulted in Schneider's death, the report said.

Available evidence permitted the "reasonable inference that the plot to assassinate Lumumba was authorized by President Eisenhower," but this was not certain.

With regard to Castro, Diem and Trujillo, the committee report said it was impossible on the basis of the evidence uncovered to conclude that any incumbent president was involved in their deaths.

However, the report did conclude that Allen Dulles, director of the CIA during the Eisenhower Administration, had taken part in the plots against Castro and Lumumba. Moreover, the report quoted a cable Dulles sent to the head of the CIA station in Leopoldville Sept. 24, 1960: "We wish every possible support in eliminating Lumumba from any possibility resuming governmental position or if he fails in Leopoldville, setting himself in Stanleyville or elsewhere." The committee's report also noted that Dulles had expressed a similar view three days before in Eisenhower's presence at a meeting of the National Security Council.

John A. McCone, who succeeded Dulles as CIA director, might not have known of the plots against Castro and Lumumba, the report said. But Richard Helms, director of plans under McCone and later CIA director, took part in the plots, according to the report. The committee found that in some cases officials withheld information about the assassination plots from CIA superiors and other government officials. C
The report specifically criticized Helms and Deputy Director for Plans Richard Bissell.

Helms withheld information from President Johnson and Attorney General Robert F. Kennedy on the plots against Castro. Helms did not tell McCone of the CIA's use of underworld figures in the plots against Castro.

Bissell on several occasions "had the opportunity to inform his superiors about D
the assassination effort against Castro." Yet "he either failed to inform them, failed to do so clearly or misled them."

The report said that attempts to pinpoint responsibility for various assassination plots often foundered because of bureaucratic techniques that diffused or disguised individual responsibility. "Plausible denial" insulated high officials from the covert activities of subordinates in order that these senior officials would be E
able to deny culpibility in case the activities were discovered. To establish "plausible deniability," officials frequently resorted to "circumlocution and euphemism."

These latter techniques, the report said, were used by senior officials to deliver instructions indirectly, or by subordinates to report indirectly on their activities. The committee also found that senior officials issued "generalized instructions" that F
were vague enough that they could be interpreted in several ways. An example, the report said, was the order to "get rid of the Castro regime."

"The system of executive command and control was so ambiguous that it is difficult to be certain at what level assassination activity was known and authorized. This situation creates the disturbing prospect that government officials might have G
undertaken the assassination plots without it having been incontrovertibly clear that there was explicit authorization from Presidents."

Schneider—Evidence obtained by the committee indicated that U.S. officials

had supplied arms to and otherwise encouraged Chilean dissidents, who plotted the kidnapping of Gen. Rene Schneider,
A commander-in-chief of the Chilean army. Schneider, a constitutionalist, opposed military intervention in Chilean politics.

In a Sept. 15, 1970 White House meeting attended by President Nixon, CIA Director Richard Helms, Attorney General John N. Mitchell and National Security Council Director Henry A. Kissinger, Nixon stated that the Marxist regime of Salvador Allende—who had won a plurality in a presidential election 11 days before—would be unacceptable to
B the U.S. Nixon then instructed the CIA to work actively to see that Allende did not take office.

After making 21 contacts with key police and military officials in Chile during the period Oct. 5-Oct. 20, 1970 and assuring U.S. support for a coup against Allende, the CIA singled out Schneider for removal in preparation for the coup.

Following two unsuccessful kidnap attempts by Chilean officers using CIA-sup-
C plied arms, conspirators intercepted Schneider's car Oct. 22, 1970 and mortally wounded him during an ensuing gunfight. The conspirators involved were not those using CIA weapons.

Castro—As early as March 1960, Central Intelligence Agency officials had begun scheming against Cuban Premier
D Castro. Among the suggested schemes: impregnating his cigars with a disorienting agent before a speech and dusting his boots with a substance that would make his beard fall out.

Between 1960 and 1965, the CIA instigated at least eight separate plots against Castro, but none was successful. A box of the Cuban leader's favorite cigars contaminated with botulism toxin was delivered by the CIA to an unidentified
E person in Cuba in February 1961, but there was apparently no attempt to pass them on to Castro.

Robert Maheu, a former Federal Bureau of Investigation agent and later an aide to millionaire industrialist Howard R. Hughes, was contacted in August 1960 by Col. Sheffield Edwards, director of the CIA office of security, who had proposed that a member of the crime syndicate that formerly ran gambling operations in Cuba
F be used to kill Castro. Maheu in turn contacted racketeer John Roselli,* who was told by Maheu that "high government officials" wanted to eliminate Castro.

Accepting the proposal, Roselli travelled to Miami, where he recruited exiled Cubans for the job and also met with CIA agents, who supplied poisoned pills, money and electronic gear for the assassination. A Cuban working in Castro's favorite restaurant was to administer the poison when he received the word. However, the signal did not come and the waiter returned the pills and money.

The poisoning plan was reactivated in April 1962 by CIA agent William Harvey, who turned the poisoned pills and $5,000 worth of arms and radio equipment over to a Cuban contact. (No evidence that an attempt on Castro's life occurred was uncovered, however.)

In early 1963, "Task Force W," a covert CIA group assigned to covert operations in Cuba, studied and rejected a plan to place an exploding seashell in an area in which Castro was known to skin dive.

In January 1963, a skin diving suit contaminated with a poisonous fungus was prepared as a gift to Castro from James Donovan, U.S. negotiator for the release of Cuban prisoners. This plan failed because Donovan decided to give Castro an uncontaminated suit.

An unidentified highly placed Cuban leader met with Desmond Fitzgerald, chief of the CIA special affairs staff, in August 1963 and offered to kill Castro with a high powered rifle. Fitzgerald later told in-house CIA investigators that he had rejected the offer.

In a meeting in Paris November 22, 1963, the day President Kennedy was assassinated, Fitzgerald offered a Cuban agent a poison ball point pen with a hypodermic needle too small to be felt. The agent rejected the device as amateurish.

From 1963 until early 1965, the CIA arranged for the delivery of arms and explosives for use against Castro. (The committee's report did not contain specifics on these attempts.)

Lumumba—CIA action against Congolese leader Patrice Lumumba began in the late spring of 1960 with the discussion of killing an unnamed African leader. In September 1960, Sidney Gottlieb, a CIA scientist, acting on orders from Deputy Director for Plans Richard Bissell, obtained poison and hypodermic needles from Army stockpiles and flew to Leopoldville (Kinshasha) with instructions for CIA station officer Victor Hedgman to kill Lumumba, who had been dismissed as Congolese premier Sept. 5.

In the following month, Bissell asked senior CIA official Michael Mulroney to go to the Congo and kill Lumumba. Mulroney refused but agreed to go to the Congo. Once in the Congo, Mulroney sent for two other CIA agents, one of them described as "a foreign citizen with a criminal background" as a smuggler and the other, a former forger and bank robber.

The CIA's operatives were unable to kill Lumumba, who was captured by members of a rival Congolese faction Jan. 17, 1961 and subsequently executed. CIA authorities in Africa later disclaimed any involvement. (According to the report, cable traffic showed no CIA link to Lumumba's death.)

Trujillo—President Eisenhower in April 1960 approved a contingency plan for the Dominican dictator's removal. The following June, Joseph Farland, U.S. ambassador to the Dominican Republic, agreed to be a link between Dominican dissidents and the CIA. A CIA memorandum dated Oct. 3, 1960 indicated that arms and explosives would be delivered to the dissidents. In March 1961, three .38 caliber pistols were delivered to the U.S. embassy in Santo Domingo in a diplomatic pouch and then passed to the dissidents through an American intermediary. Trujillo was gunned down May 30, 1961 near San Cristobel by handguns and shotguns used by the dissident group.

Diem—South Vietnamese President Ngo Dinh Diem and his brother, Ngo Dinh Nhu, were killed Nov. 2, 1963 during a coup led by South Vietnamese generals. Lucien Conein, then a CIA operative in South Vietnam, was told of the planned coup as early as Oct. 3, 1963 and informed U.S. officials. Cables from John A. McCone, then director of the CIA, indicated that McCone at first neither supported nor opposed the planned coup, but that he opposed it later.

Recommendations—The committee recommended Congressional passage of a law making it a federal offense to assassinate or plot to assassinate foreign leaders. Directives, issued by directors of the CIA in 1972 and 1974, that prohibited assassination as an intelligence tool were not enough, the report said.

---

*Roselli was found dead Aug. 7, 1976. His body was discovered inside a floating oil drum in Florida, "a true gangland-style killing," according to a police doctor. Police sought a link between Roselli's death and that of Sam Giancana, who was murdered in 1975. [See Vol. I, p. 24] Both men had testified before the congressional committees on CIA-Mafia contacts.

Excerpts From Senate Select Intelligence Committee Report on Assassination

Summary of Findings and Conclusions

The Questions Presented

The committee sought to answer four broad questions:

Assassination plots. Did United States officials instigate, attempt, aid and abet, or acquiesce in plots to assassinate foreign leaders?

Involvement in other killings. Did United States officials assist foreign dissidents in a way which significantly contributed to the killing of foreign leaders?

Authorization. Where there was involvement by United States officials in assassination plots or other killings, were such activities authorized and if so, at what levels of our government?

Communication and control. Even if not authorized in fact, were the assassination activities perceived by those involved to be within the scope of their lawful authority? If they were so perceived, was there inadequate control exercised by higher authorities over the agencies to prevent such misinterpretation?

Summary of Findings and Conclusions on the Plots

The committee investigated alleged United States involvement in assassination plots in five foreign countries:[1]

Country	Individual involved[2]
CUBA	FIDEL CASTRO
CONGO (ZAIRE)	PATRICE LUMUMBA
DOMINICAN REPUBLIC	RAFAEL TRUJILLO
CHILE	GENERAL RENE SCHNEIDER
SOUTH VIETNAM	NGO DINH DIEM

The evidence concerning each alleged assassination can be summarized as follows:

Patrice Lumumba (Congo/Zaire). In the fall of 1960, two CIA officials were asked by superiors to assassinate Lumumba. Poisons were sent to the Congo and some exploratory steps were taken toward gaining access to Lumumba. Subsequently, in early 1961, Lumumba was killed by Congolese rivals. It does not appear from the evidence that the United States was in any way involved in the killing.

Fidel Castro (Cuba). United States government personnel plotted to kill Castro from 1960 to 1965. American underworld figures and Cubans hostile to Castro were used in these plots, and were provided encouragement and material support by the United States.

Rafael Trujillo (Dominican Republic). Trujillo was shot by Dominican dissidents on May 31, 1961. From early in 1960 and continuing to the time of the assassination, the United States government generally supported these dissidents. Some government personnel were aware that the dissidents intended to kill Trujillo. Three pistols and three carbines were furnished by American officials, although a request for machine guns was later refused. There is conflicting evidence concerning whether the weapons were knowingly supplied for use in the assassination and whether any of them were present at the scene.

Ngo Dinh Diem (South Vietnam) Diem and his brother, Nhu, were killed on November 2, 1963, in the course of a South Vietnamese generals' coup. Although the United States government supported the coup, there is no evidence that American officials favored the assassination. Indeed, it appears that the assassination of Diem was not part of the generals' pre-coup planning but was instead a spontaneous act which occurred during the coup and was carried out without United States involvement or support.

General Rene Schneider (Chile). On October 25, 1970, General Schneider died of gunshot wounds inflicted three days earlier while resisting a kidnap attempt. Schneider, as commander-in-chief of the army and a constitutionalist opposed to military coups, was considered an obstacle in efforts to prevent Salvador Allende from assuming the office of president of Chile. The United States government supported, and sought to instigate a military coup to block Allende. U.S. officials supplied financial aid, machine guns and other equipment to various military figures who opposed Allende. Although the CIA continued to support coup plotters up to Schneider's shooting, the record indicates that the CIA had withdrawn active support of the group which carried out the actual kidnap attempt on October 22, which resulted in Schneider's death. Further, it does not appear that any of the equipment supplied by the CIA to coup plotters in Chile was used in the kidnapping. There is no evidence of a plan to kill Schneider or that United States officials specifically anticipated that Schneider would be shot during the abduction.

Assassination capability (Executive action). In addition to these five cases, the committee has received evidence that ranking government officials discussed, and may have authorized, the establishment within the CIA of a generalized assassination capability. During these discussions, the concept of assassination was not affirmatively disavowed.

Similarities and differences among the plots. The assassination plots all involved "third world" countries, most of which were relatively small and none of which possessed great political or military strength. Apart from that similarity, there were significant differences among the plots:

(1) Whether United States officials initiated the plot, or were responding to requests of local dissidents for aid.

(2) Whether the plot was specifically intended to kill a foreign leader, or whether the leader's death was a reasonably foreseeable consequence of an attempt to overthrow the government.

The Castro and Lumumba cases are examples of plots conceived by United States officials to kill foreign leaders.

In the Trujillo case, although the United States government certainly opposed his regime, it did not initiate the plot. Rather, United States officials responded to requests for aid from local dissidents whose aim clearly was to assassinate Trujillo. By aiding them, this country was implicated in the assassination, regardless of whether the weapons actually supplied were meant to kill Trujillo or were only intended as symbols of support for the dissidents.

The Schneider case differs from the Castro and Trujillo cases. The United States government, with full knowledge that Chilean dissidents considered General Schneider an obstacle to their plans, sought a coup and provided support to the dissidents. However, even though the support included weapons, it appears that the intention of both the dissidents and the United States officials was to abduct General Schneider, not to kill him. Similarly, in the Diem case, some United States officials wanted Diem removed and supported a coup to accomplish his removal, but there is no evidence that any of those officials sought the death of Diem himself.

[1] In addition to the plots discussed in the body of this report, the committee received some evidence of CIA involvement in plans to assassinate President Sukarno of Indonesia and "Papa Doc" Duvalier of Haiti. Former Deputy Director for Plans Richard Bissell testified that the assassination of Sukarno had been "contemplated" by the CIA, but that planning had proceeded no farther than identifying an "asset" whom it was believed might be recruited to kill Sukarno. Arms were supplied to dissident groups in Indonesia, but according to Bissell, those arms were not intended for assassination.

Walter Elder, executive assistant to CIA Director John McCone, testified that the director authorized the CIA to furnish arms to dissidents planning the overthrow of Haiti's dictator, Duvalier. Elder told the committee that while the assassination of Duvalier was not contemplated by the CIA, the arms were furnished "to help [the dissidents] take what measures were deemed necessary to replace the government" and it was realized that Duvalier might be killed in the course of the overthrow.

[2] Assassination plots against the Cuban leadership sometimes contemplated action against Raul Castro and Che Guevarra. In South Vietnam Diem's brother Ngo Dinh Nhu was killed at the same time as Diem.

Summary of Findings and Conclusions on the Issues of Authority and Control

To put the inquiry into assassination allegations in context, two points must be made clear. First, there is no doubt that the United States government opposed the various leaders in question. Officials at the highest levels objected to the Castro and Trujillo regimes, believed the accession of Allende to power in Chile would be harmful to American interests and thought of Lumumba as a dangerous force in the heart of Africa. Second, the evidence on assassinations has to be viewed in the context of other, more massive activities against the regimes in question. For example, the plots against Fidel Castro personally cannot be understood without considering the fully authorized comprehensive assaults upon his regime, such as the Bay of Pigs invasion in 1961 and Operation Mongoose in 1962.

Once methods of coercion and violence are chosen, the probability of loss of life is always present. There is, however, a significant difference between a cold-blooded, targeted, intentional killing of an individual foreign leader and other forms of intervening in the affairs of foreign nations. Therefore, the committee has endeavored to explore as fully as possible the questions of how and why the plots happened, whether they were authorized, and if so, at what level.

The picture that emerges from the evidence is not a clear one. This may be due to the system of deniability and the consequent state of the evidence which, even after our long investigation, remains conflicting and inconclusive. Or it may be that there were in fact serious shortcomings in the system of authorization so that an activity such as assassination could have been undertaken by an agency of the United States government without express authority.

The committee finds that the system of executive command and control was so ambiguous that it is difficult to be certain at what levels assassination activity was known and authorized. This situation creates the disturbing prospect that government officials might have undertaken the assassination plots without its having been incontrovertibly clear that there was explicit authorization from the Presidents. It is also possible that there might have been a successful "plausible denial" in which Presidential authorization was issued but is now obscured. Whether or not the respective Presidents knew of or authorized the plots, as chief executive officer of the United States, each must bear the ultimate responsibility for the activities of his subordinates.

The committee makes four other major findings. The first relates to the committee's inability to make a finding that the assassination plots were authorized by the Presidents or other persons above the governmental agency or agencies involved. The second explains why certain officials may have perceived that, according to their judgment and experience, assassination was an acceptable course of action. The third criticizes agency officials for failing on several occasions to disclose their plans and activities to superior authorities or for failing to do so with sufficient detail and clarity. The fourth criticizes Administration officials for not ruling out assassination, particularly after certain Administration officials had become aware of prior assassination plans and the establishment of a general assassination capability.

There is admittedly a tension among the findings. This tension reflects a basic conflict in the evidence. While there are some conflicts over facts, it may be more important that there appeared to have been two differing perceptions of the same facts. This distinction may be the result of the differing backgrounds of those persons experienced in covert operations as distinguished from those who were not. Words of urgency which may have meant killing to the former, may have meant nothing of the sort to the latter.

While we are critical of certain individual actions, the committee is also mindful of the inherent problems in a system which relies on secrecy, compartmentation, circumlocution, and the avoidance of clear responsibility. This system creates the risk of confusion and rashness in the very areas where clarity and sober judgment are most necessary. Hence, before reviewing the evidence relating to the cases, we briefly deal with the general subject of covert action.

Findings Concerning the Plots

1. Officials of the United States government initiated plots to assassinate Fidel Castro and Patrice Lumumba.
2. No foreign leaders were killed as a result of assassination plots initiated by officials of the United States.
3. American officials encouraged or were privy to coup plots which resulted in the deaths of Trujillo, Diem, and Schneider.
4. The plots occurred in a cold war atmosphere perceived to be of crisis proportions.
5. American officials had exaggerated notions about their ability to control the actions of coup leaders.
6. CIA officials made use of known underworld figures in assassination efforts.

Conclusions Concerning the Plots Themselves

1. The United States Should Not Engage in Assassination

We condemn the use of assassination as a tool of foreign policy. Aside from pragmatic arguments against the use of assassination supplied to the committee by witnesses with extensive experience in covert operations, we find that assassination violates moral precepts fundamental to our way of life.

In addition to moral considerations, there were several practical reasons advanced for not assassinating foreign leaders. These reasons are discussed in the section of this report recommending a statute making assassination a crime.

(a) Distinction Between Targeted Assassinations Instigated by the United States and Support for Dissidents Seeking to Overthrow Local Governments

Two of the five principal cases investigated by the committee involved plots to kill foreign leaders (Lumumba and Castro) that were instigated by American officials. Three of the cases (Trujillo, Diem, and Schneider) involved killings in the course of coup attempts by local dissidents. These latter cases differed in the degree to which assassination was contemplated by the leaders of the coups and in the degree the coups were motivated by United States officials.

The committee concludes that targeted assassinations instigated by the United States must be prohibited.

Coups involve varying degrees of risk of assassination. The possibility of assassination in coup attempts is one of the issues to be considered in determining the propriety of United States involvement in coups, particularly in those where the assassination of a foreign leader is a likely prospect.

(b) The Setting in Which the Assassination Plots Occurred Explains, But Does Not Justify Them

The Cold War setting in which the assassination plots took place does not change our view that assassination is unacceptable in our society. In addition to the moral and practical problems discussed elsewhere, we find three principal defects in any contention that the tenor of the period justified the assassination plots:

First, the assassination plots were not necessitated by imminent danger to the United States. Among the cases studied, Castro alone posed a physical threat to the United States, but then only during the period of the Cuban missile crisis, and assassination was not advanced by policymakers as a possible course of action during the crisis.

Second, we reject absolutely any notion that the United States should justify its actions by the standards of totalitarians. Our standards must be higher, and this difference is what the struggle is all about. Of course, we must defend our democracy. But in defending it, we must resist undermining the very virtues we are defending.

Third, such activities almost inevitably become known. The damage to American foreign policy, to the good name and reputation of the United States abroad, to the American people's faith and support of our government and its foreign policy is incalculable. This last point—the undermining of the American public's confidence in its government—is the most damaging consequence of all.

Two documents which have been supplied to the committee graphically demonstrate attitudes which can lead to tactics that erode and could ultimately destroy the very ideals we must defend.

The first document was written in 1954 by a special committee formed to advise the President on covert activities. The United States may, it said, have to adopt tactics "more ruthless than (those) employed by the enemy" in order to meet the threat from hostile nations. The report concluded that "long standing American concept of American fair play must be reconsidered."

Although those proposals did not involve assassinations, the attitudes underlying them were, as Director Colby testified, indicative of the setting within which the assassination plots were conceived.

We do not think that traditional American notions of fair play need be abandoned when dealing with our adversaries. It may well be ourselves that we injure most if we adopt tactics "more ruthless than the enemy."

A second document which represents an attitude which we find improper was sent to the Congo in the fall of 1960 when the assassination of Patrice Lumumba was being considered. The chief of CIA's Africa Division recommended a particular agent—WI/ROGUE—because:

> He is indeed aware of the precepts of right and wrong, but if he is given an assignment which may be morally wrong in the eyes of the world, but necessary because his case officer ordered him to carry it out, then it is right, and he will dutifully undertake appropriate action for its execution without pangs of conscience. In a word, he can rationalize all actions.

The committee finds this rationalization is not in keeping with the ideals of our nation.

2. The United States Should Not Make Use of Underworld Figures for Their Criminal Talents

We conclude that agencies of the United States must not use underworld figures for their criminal talents in carrying out agency operations. In addition to the corrosive effect upon our government, the use of underworld figures involves the following dangers:

a. The use of underworld figures for "dirty business" gives them the power to blackmail the government and to avoid prosecution, for past or future crimes.

b. The use of persons experienced in criminal techniques and prone to criminal behavior increases the likelihood that criminal acts will occur. Sometimes agents in the field are necessarily given broad discretion. But the risk of improper activities is increased when persons of criminal background are used, particularly when they are selected precisely to take advantage of their criminal skills or contacts.

c. There is the danger that the United States government will become an unwitting accomplice to criminal acts and that criminal figures will take advantage of their association with the government to advance their own projects and interests.

d. There is a fundamental impropriety in selecting persons because they are skilled at performing deeds which the laws of our society forbid.

e. The spectacle of the government consorting with criminal elements destroys respect for government and law and undermines the viability of democratic institutions.

Findings and Conclusions Relating to Authorization and Control

1. The Apparent Lack of Accountability in the Command and Control System Was Such That the Assassination Plots Could Have Been Undertaken Without Express Authorization

Based on the record of our investigation, the committee finds that the system of executive command and control was so inherently ambiguous that it is difficult to be certain at what level assassination activity was known and authorized. This creates the disturbing prospect that assassination activity might have been undertaken by officials of the United States government without its having been incontrovertibly clear that there was explicit authorization from the President of the United States. At the same time, this ambiguity and imprecision leaves open the possibility that there was a successful "plausible denial" and that a Presidential authorization was used but is now obscured.

2. Findings Relating to the Level at Which the Plots Were Authorized

(a) Diem

We find that neither the President nor any other official in the United States Government authorized the assassination of Diem and his brother Nhu. Both the DCI [director of central intelligence] and top State Department officials did know, however, that the death of Nhu, at least at one point, had been contemplated by the coup leaders. But when the possibility that the coup leaders were considering assassination was brought to the attention of the DCI, he directed that the United States would have no part in such activity, and there is some evidence that this information was relayed to the coup leaders.

(b) Schneider

We find that neither the President nor any other official in the United States Government authorized the assassination of General Rene Schneider. The CIA, and perhaps the White House did know that coup leaders contemplated a kidnapping, which, as it turned out, resulted in Schneider's death.

(c) Trujillo

The Presidents and other senior officials in the Eisenhower and Kennedy Administrations sought the overthrow of Trujillo and approved or condoned actions to obtain that end.

(d) Lumumba

The chain of events revealed by the documents and testimony is strong enough to permit a reasonable inference that the plot to assassinate Lumumba was authorized by President Eisenhower. Nevertheless, there is enough countervailing testimony by Eisenhower Administration officials and enough ambiguity and lack of clarity in the records of high-level policy meetings to preclude the committee from making a finding that the President intended an assassination effort against Lumumba.

It is clear that the Director of Central Intelligence, Allen Dulles, authorized an assassination plot. There is, however, no evidence of United States involvement in bringing about the death of Lumumba at the hands of Congolese authorities.

Strong expressions of hostility toward Lumumba from the President and his national security assistant, followed immediately by CIA steps in furtherance of an assassination operation against Lumumba, are part of a sequence of events that, at the lease, make it appear that Dulles believed assassination was a permissible means of complying with pressure from the President to remove Lumumba from the political scene.

(e) Castro

There was insufficient evidence from which the committee could conclude that Presidents Eisenhower, Kennedy, or Johnson, their close advisors, or the Special Group authorized the assassination of Castro.

The only suggestion of express Presidential authorization for the plots against Castro was Richard Bissell's opinion that Dulles would have informed Presidents Eisenhower and Kennedy by circumlocution only after the assassination had been planned and was underway. The assumptions underlying this opinion are too attenuated for the committee to adopt it as a finding. First, this assumes that Dulles himself knew of the plot, a matter which is not entirely certain. Second, it assumes that Dulles went privately to the two Presidents—a course of action which Helms, who had far more covert action experience than Bissell, testified was precisely what the doctrine of plausible denial forbade CIA officials from doing. Third, it necessarily assumes that the Presidents would understand from a "circumlocutious" description that assassination was being discussed.

In view of the strained chain of assumptions and the contrary testimony of all the Presidential advisors, the men closest to both Eisenhower and Kennedy, the committee makes no finding implicating Presidents who are not able to speak for themselves.

Helms and McCone testified that the Presidents under which they served never asked them to consider assassination.

There was no evidence whatsoever that President Johnson knew about or authorized any assassination activity during his presidency.

3. CIA Officials Involved in the Assassination Operations Perceived Assassination to Have Been a Permissible Course of Action

The CIA officials involved in the targeted assassination attempts testified that they had believed that their activities had been fully authorized.

In the case of the Lumumba assassination operation, Richard Bissell testified that he had no direct recollection of authorization, but after having reviewed the cables and Special Group minutes, testified that authority must have flowed from Dulles through him to the subordinate levels in the Agency.

The evidence points to a disturbing situation. Agency officials testified that they believed the effort to assassinate Castro to have been within the parameters of permissible action. But Administration officials responsible for formulating policy, including McCone, testified that they were not aware of the effort and did not authorize it. The explanation may lie in the fact that orders concerning overthrowing the Castro regime were stated in broad terms that were subject to differing interpretations by those responsible for carrying out those orders.

The various Presidents and their senior advisors strongly opposed the regimes of Castro and Trujillo, the accession to power of Allende, and the potential influence of Patrice Lumumba. Orders concerning action against those foreign leaders were given in vigorous language. For example, President Nixon's orders to prevent Allende from assuming power left Helms feeling that "if I ever carried a marshal's baton in my knapsack out of the Oval Office, it was that day." Similarly, General Lansdale described the Mongoose effort against Cuba as "a combat situation," and Attorney General Kennedy emphasized that "a solution to the Cuba problem today carries top priority." Helms testified that the pressure to "get rid of Castro and the Castro regime" was intense, and Bissell testified that he had been ordered to "get off your ass about Cuba."

The 1967 Inspector General's Report on assassinations appropriately observed:

> The point is that of frequent resort to synecdoche—the mention of a part when the whole is to be understood, or vice versa. Thus, we encounter repeated references to phrases such as "disposing of Castro," which may be read in the narrow, literal sense of assassinating him, when it is intended that it be read in the broader figural sense of dislodging the Castro regime. Reversing the coin, we find people speaking vaguely of "doing someting about Castro" when it is clear that what they have specifically in mind is killing him. In a situation wherein those speaking may not have actually meant what they seemed to say or may not have said what they actually meant, they should not be surprised if their oral shorthand is interpreted differently than was intended.

The perception of certain Agency officials that assassination was within the range of permissible activity was reinforced by the continuing approval of violent covert actions against Cuba that were sanctioned at the Presidential level, and by the failure of the successive administrations to make clear that assassination was not permissible. This point is one of the subjects considered in the next section.

4. The Failure in Communication Between Agency Officials in Charge of the Assassination Operation and Their Superiors in the Agency and in the Administration Was Due to:

(A) The failure of subordinates to disclose their plans and operations to their superiors; and (B) the failure of superiors in the climate of violence and aggressive covert actions sanctioned by the administrations to rule out assassination as a tool of foreign policy; to make clear to their subordinates that assassination was impermissible; or to inquire further after receiving indications that it was being considered.

(a) Agency Officials Failed on Several Occasions to Reveal the Plots to Their Superiors, or to Do so With Sufficient Detail and Clarity

Several of the cases considered in this report raise questions concerning whether officials of the CIA sufficiently informed their superiors in the agency or officials outside the agency about their activities.

(i) Castro

The failure of agency officials to inform their superiors of the assassination efforts against Castro is particularly troubling.

On the basis of the testimony and documentary evidence before the committee, it is not entirely certain that Dulles was ever made aware of the true nature of the underworld operation. The plot continued into McCone's term, apparently without McCone's or the Administration's knowledge or approval.

On some occasions when Richard Bissell had the opportunity to inform his superiors about the assassination effort against Castro, he either failed to inform them, failed to do so clearly, or misled them.

Bissell further testified that he never raised the issue of assassination with non-CIA officials of either the Eisenhower or Kennedy Administration. His reason was that since he was under Dulles in the chain of command, he would normally have had no duty to discuss the matter with these Presidents or other Administration officials, and that he assumed that Dulles would have "circumlocutiously" spoken with Presidents Eisenhower and Kennedy about the operation. These reasons are insufficient. It was inexcusable to withhold such information from those responsible for formulating policy on the unverified assumption that they might have been "circumlocutiously" informed by Dulles.

The committee finds the reasons advanced for not having informed those responsible for formulating policy about the assassination operation inadequate, misleading and inconsistent. Some officials viewed assassination as too important and sensitive to discuss with superiors, while others considered it not sufficiently important. Harvey testified that it was premature to tell McCone about the underworld operation in April 1962, because it was not sufficiently advanced; but too late to tell him about it in August 1962, since by that time Harvey had decided to terminate it. On other occasions, officials thought disclosure was someone else's responsibility; Bissell said he thought it was up to Dulles, and Harvey believed it was up to Helms.

The committee concludes that the failure to clearly inform policymakers of the assassination effort against Castro was grossly improper. The committee believes that it should be incumbent on the DDP [deputy director of plans] to report such a sensitive operation to his superior, the DCI, no matter how grave his doubts might be about the possible outcome of the operation. It follows that the DCI has the same duty to accurately inform his superiors.

(ii) Trujillo

In the Trujillo case there were several instances in which it appears that policymakers were not given sufficient information, or were not informed in a timely fashion.

(iii) Schneider

The issue here is not whether the objectives of the CIA were contrary to those of the Administration. It is clear that President Nixon desired to prevent Allende from assuming office, even if that required fomenting and supporting a coup in Chile. Nor did White House officials suggest that tactics employed (including as a first step kidnapping General Schneider) would have been unacceptable as a matter of principle. Rather, the issue posed is whether White House officials were consulted, and thus given an opportunity to weigh such matters as risk and likelihood of success, and to apply policy-making judgments to particular tactics. The record indicates that up to October 15 they were; after October 15 there is some doubt:

The standards applied within the CIA itself suggest a view that action which the committee believes called for top-level policy discussion and decision was thought of as permissible, without any further consultation, on the basis of the initial instruction to prevent Allende from assuming power. Machine guns were sent to Chile and delivered to military figures there on the authority of middle level CIA officers without consultation even with the CIA officer in charge of the program. We find no suggestion of bad faith in the action of the middle level officers, but their failure to consult necessarily establishes that there was no advance permission from outside the CIA for the passage of machine guns. And it also suggests an unduly lax attitude within the CIA toward consultation with superiors. Further, this case demonstrates the problems inherent in giving an agency a "blank check" to engage in covert operations without specifying which actions are permissible and which are not, and without adequately supervising and monitoring these activities.

(b) Administration Officials Failed to Rule Out Assassination as a Tool of Foreign Policy, to Make Clear to Their Subordinates That Assassination Was Impermissible or to Inquire Further After Receiving Indications That Assassination Was Being Considered

While we do not find that high Administration officials expressly approved of the assassination attempts, we have noted that certain agency officials nevertheless perceived assassination to have been authorized. Although those officials were remiss in not seeking express authorization for their activities, their superiors were also at fault for giving vague instructions and for not explicitly ruling out assassination. No written order prohibiting assassination was issued until 1972, and that order was an internal CIA directive issued by Director Helms.

5. Practices Current at the Time in Which the Assassination Plots Occurred Were Revealed by the Record to Create the Risk of Confusion, Rashness and Irresponsibility in the Very Areas Where Clarity and Sober Judgment Were Most Necessary

Various witnesses described elements of the system within which the assassination plots were conceived. The committee is disturbed by the custom that permitted the most sensitive matters to be presented to the highest levels of government with the least clarity. We view the following points as particularly dangerous.

(1) The expansion of the doctrine of "plausible denial" beyond its intended purpose of hiding the involvement of the United States from other countries into an effort to shield higher officials from knowledge, and hence responsibility, for certain operations.

(2) The use of circumlocution or euphemism to describe serious matters—such as assassination—when precise meanings ought to be made clear.

(3) The theory that general approval of broad covert action programs is sufficient to justify specific actions such as assassination or the passage of weapons.

(4) The theory that authority granted, or assumed to be granted, by one DCI or one Administration could be presumed to continue without the necessity for reaffirming the authority with successor officials.

(5) The creation of covert capabilities without careful review and authorization by policymakers, and the further risk that such capabilities, once created, might be used without specific authorization.

RECOMMENDATIONS

Commendable and welcome as they are, these CIA directives [prohibiting assassination] are not sufficient. Administrations change, CIA directors change, and someday in the future what was tried in the past may once again become a temptation. Assassination plots did happen. It would be irresponsible not to do all that can be done to prevent their happening again. A law is needed. Laws express our nation's values; they deter those who might be tempted to ignore those values and stiffen the will of those who want to resist the temptation.

The committee recommends a statute which would make it a criminal offense for persons subject to the jurisdiction of the United States (1) to conspire, within or outside the United States, to assassinate a foreign official; (2) to attempt to assassinate a foreign official, or (3) to assassinate a foreign official.

Democrats reportedly blocked vote. The Senate Democratic leadership, reportedly fearing too narrow a margin of approval, prevented a floor vote on adoption of the report on assassinations of foreign political leaders issued by the Select Committee on Intelligence, it was widely reported Nov. 21.

The Democratic leadership moved to block a vote on the report's release, the reports indicated, when it became convinced that Ford Administration supporters, who opposed publication, would press for a vote in the hope that a narrow margin of victory would lesson the report's impact.

As a result, the matter was returned to the committee. In turn, the committee, in an action that angered many Republicans, voted to make the report public.

Following the committee's vote, Sen. John G. Tower (R, Tex.), the committee's ranking Republican, announced he had dissociated himself from the report because of the Senate's failure to vote to adopt the report. Sen. Barry Goldwater (R, Ariz.), a committee member, also dissented with regard to publication. His objections centered, however, on "the diplomatic damage" he felt the report might cause to the U.S.

The committee's other nine members supported publication. (Sen. Philip A. Hart (D, Mich.) declined to sign the report, explaining that illness had caused him to be absent during much of the panel's investigation.)

Sen. Frank Church (D, Ida.), chairman, defended publication even though it might cause "temporary injury." "Our nation is admired in proportion to the openness of our society. Withholding this report from the public would more closely resemble the practice of totalitarian regimes."

President Ford had strenuously opposed publication and had so stated in personal letters to key senators in the days before the full Senate had been scheduled to consider the report's release. Making the report public, Ford asserted, might endanger U.S. intelligence operations.

In a subsequent statement Nov. 21, the President said through a spokesman that he "absolutely abhors government official's being involved" in coups d'etat and assassination plots abroad and had "forbidden officials in his administration from being involved."

Intelligence apparatus reforms urged. Four intelligence experts told the Senate Select Committee on Intelligence Dec. 5 that the U.S. intelligence apparatus was in need of reform. The four men said that covert intelligence actions against foreign governments had damaged the reputation of the U.S. and should be severely curtailed.

Clark M. Clifford, chairman of the Presidential Foreign Intelligence Advisory Board during the Kennedy and Johnson Administrations, testified that it was clear that covert operations had "gotten out of hand." He proposed that a House-Senate committee be formed to oversee intelligence operations. In addition, he suggested the establishment of a director general of intelligence who would preside over the entire U.S. intelligence community and report to the President.

Cyrus R. Vance, former deputy secretary of defense, said he believed the U.S. should engage in covert intelligence activities only when they were "absolutely essential" to the national security.

Clifford and Vance proposed an overhauling of the 1947 National Security Act to insure that future covert intelligence activities were conceived and approved only at the top level of the executive branch, as well as reviewed in advance by a Congressional committee.

Morton H. Halperin, former deputy assistant secretary for international security affairs, called for the outlawing of all covert actions, arguing that the possible benefits to be derived were far outweighed "by the costs to our society of maintaining a capability for covert operations."

However, David Phillips, a former Central Intelligence Agency official involved in covert operations, warned against abolition of covert operations. He likened such a move to disbanding the Army in peacetime or abolishing the office of the Presidency because it had once been abused.

JFK 'friend' reported. Sen. Frank Church (D, Idaho) denied Dec. 15 that his Senate Select Committee on Intelligence Operations had attempted to cover up a close relationship between the late President John F. Kennedy and a woman known then as Judith Katherine Campbell. The cover-up charge was made Dec. 15 by William Safire, a columnist for the *New York Times.* An account of Kennedy's friendship with the woman was first published by the *Washington Post* on Nov. 16.

The Senate panel had come across Kennedy's friendship with the woman during its inquiry into Mafia involvement in Central Intelligence Agency plots to kill Prime Minister Fidel Castro of Cuba. The committee's report referred to the woman only as a "close friend" of Kennedy and of two Mafia figures, Sam Giancana and John Roselli.

This information—her friendship with the President and with two Mafia figures as well—was said to have been relayed to the attorney general and the White House on Feb. 27, 1962 by J. Edgar Hoover, then FBI director. On March 22, 1962, according to the panel's report, Kennedy and Hoover lunched together. Subsequently, "the last telephone contact between the White House and the President's friend occurred a few hours after the luncheon," the report said.

Up to then, in the period from March 29, 1961 to March 22, 1962, she was said to have made some 70 telephone calls to the White House.

The committee's concern was that Kennedy might have learned of the Castro plot from the woman because of her association with the Mafia figures involved. The panel investigated this "very carefully," Church said Dec. 15, and "the evidence showed that she had no knowledge of assassination activities on the part of the Mafia leaders."

Church said the committee considered the details of the matter irrelevant to the report's subject and, since it felt it would not be "appropriate to wade into the personal life of the President," it made a unanimous decision to withhold them from the report.

Church said there also was no evidence to indicate that the woman's relationship with Kennedy had been encouraged by the Mafia.

The woman, Judith Campbell Exner, held a news conference in San Diego Dec. 17 to stop what she called "wild-eyed speculation." Accompanied by her husband of eight months, Daniel Exner, she denounced the implication that she "was a go-between for the Mafia" in her relationship with Kennedy.

She described that relationship as close and personal. She said she had met him in a number of private White House lunches in the President's office and occasionally when he was traveling outside Washington. Their discussions, she said, were entirely "of a personal nature" and she had never acted as an intermediary between the Mafia and the White House, nor was she aware at the time that Giancana and Roselli were helping the CIA plot against Castro.

"To me," she said, "he was Jack Kennedy and not the President." She said she last talked to Kennedy in "late 1962."

Cuba-Oswald link questioned. Associated Press (AP) reports on March 20 and 21, 1976 described recently released Central Intelligence Agency documents concerned with the assassination of President Kennedy. One memo, from the CIA to the Warren Commission, charged with investigating the assassination of President Kennedy, said that a defector had told the CIA that Lee Harvey Oswald may have been in contact with Cuban intelligence officers seven weeks before killing Kennedy.

This information, together with the defector's assertion that the Cuban intelligence service tightened its security immediately after Kennedy's assassination, was given to the Warren Commission in May 1964. A CIA June 1964 memo remarked that the commission "saw no need to pursue this angle any further."

A CIA memo prepared in May 1975 for the Rockefeller Commission asserted, however, AP said, that it "was the opinion at the working level, particularly in the counter-intelligence component in the CIA, in 1964" that the Warren Commission report "should have left a wider 'window' for this contingency [the involvement of a foreign conspiracy in Kennedy's assassination]."

The 1975 memo specified two leads that it held the Warren Commission had not adequately followed up, AP said. One was testimony to the commission by a friend of Oswald, Nelson Delgado, that Oswald had told him in 1959 that he (Oswald) had contacts with Cuban diplomatic officials. The other lead was a statement allegedly made by Cuban leader Fidel Castro to a news correspondent on Sept. 7, 1963, that "U.S. leaders would be in danger if they helped in any attempt to do away with leaders of Cuba."

An AP report March 1 said that sources on the Senate Intelligence Committee had said that day that the committee had evidence that Earl Warren, head of the Warren Commission, had been informed of CIA attempts on Castro's life, but not until three years after the commission finished its investigation.

Senate CIA Report Published

The Senate Select Committee on Intelligence April 26 issued a lengthy, but heavily censored, report that described the U.S. intelligence community as routinely engaged in covert operations that the committee said were often without merit and frequently were initiated without adequate authorization.

The committee called on Congress to pass omnibus legislation spelling out the "basic purposes" of the various intelligence agencies, their charters and structure, and the general procedures and limitations under which they would act. The report also proposed consolidating Senate oversight responsibility—divided among several committees—in a new, permanent intelligence committee. The new committee would have authority over the intelligence agencies' budgets, and would receive prior notification of planned covert operations.

The report (a section of which was held back for later publication) contained little that had not been previously disclosed. However, its detailed list of recommendations refocused attention on the faltering drive for congressional reform of the intelligence agencies.

Underlying the proposals was the committee's finding that the intelligence agencies had, at the request of presidents, and also on their own initiative, made "excessive, and at times, self-defeating, use of covert action." Programs of covert action had attained a "bureaucratic momentum" of their own, the report said, with Congress failing to provide the "necessary statutory guidelines" or to exercise effective oversight.

The report said that the Central Intelligence Agency had conducted about 900 "major or sensitive" covert operations since 1961, plus several thousand lesser operations. A great proportion of the operations, the report said, were never subject to review outside of the CIA. The 40 Committee, a branch of the National Security Council with authority over covert operations, "served generally [until 1974] to insulate the president" from the approval process, the report found.

While it stopped short of advocating a total ban on covert operations, the committee recommended tighter procedures for authorizing such projects. Officials at each level where a project came under consideration should record approval or disapproval, the committee said.

The report, while questioning the excessive use of covert activities in any form, expressed particularly strong doubts about the value of paramilitary operations. Such actions, the committee found, were often exposed, resulting both in probable failure and in embarrassment for the U.S. While admitting that U.S. paramilitary operations had recently—with the exception of Angola—been at "a very low level," the committee urged Congress to pass legislation requiring that the CIA budget proposal list each covert operation. The legislation should also make congressional approval mandatory for paramilitary operations lasting more than 60 days, the committee said.

The committee also recommended that Congress prohibit political assassinations, efforts to subvert democratic governments, and support for police forces of foreign countries which "engage in systematic violation of human rights."

Among the specific subjects considered by the committee in its report were:

Journalist contacts and publications. The report maintained that despite new CIA guidelines on employing media personnel, the agency was continuing to employ more than 25 journalists and persons otherwise associated with American news organizations.

The CIA guidelines, promulgated in February, had ended the employment of full- or part-time persons accredited by U.S. news organizations. The report said that the guidelines resulted in the termination of less than half of the approximately 50 newsmen working for the CIA at the time. The apparent reason was that the guidelines were interpreted to apply only to "accredited correspondents," but not to other employes—possibly including executives—of the news organizations.

Reporting on publications funded by the CIA for propaganda purposes, the committee said that in one year—1967—"well over 200 books" had been so subsidized. Since 1969, the report said, the CIA had produced abroad about 250 books, mostly in foreign languages.

One CIA official, the report noted, had described such publications as capable of being "the most important weapon of strategic (long-range) propaganda."

In a section entitled "Domestic 'Fallout,'" the report pointed out that CIA officials had acknowledged that there was no way to shield the American public from being occasionally misled or manipulated by covert media operations primarily directed abroad. As examples of such fallout, the report listed:

■ CIA-planted press releases picked up by international wire services.

■ A book about China, written by one CIA operative and reviewed favorably in the *New York Times* by another CIA agent.

■ *The Penkovsky Papers* was a book written by CIA agents, which purported to be the account of an executed Soviet spy. It was widely read in the U.S. in 1964. A

■ A magazine, published by a CIA-funded institution in Vietnam, which was quoted from by members of Congress in debating U.S. involvement in that country.

The committee recommended that the CIA be barred by law from the "operational use" of any person contributing material to, or otherwise influencing, the "activities of U.S. media organizations." The committee further proposed that the CIA be prohibited from undertaking any B media efforts for distribution within the U.S. or its territories, even when such distribution would be accomplished "indirectly."

Academic contacts. The report expressed concern that the covert, operational use of academics, often through their institutions, threatened "the integrity of American academic institutions." It said that several hundred American academics provided leads for C the CIA, sometimes made introductions "for intelligence purposes," and wrote "books and other material" for foreign propaganda. An additional "few score" academics were used unwittingly for "minor activities," the report said.

The report maintained that the CIA had circumvented a 1967 presidential panel suggestion that the CIA end its covert connection with academic institutions by shifting such contacts from an in- D stitutional to an individual level.

The committee recommended that the CIA be required, in any future operational use of an American academic, to notify both the academic and the head of the institution by which the academic was employed. The committee proposed that the CIA be barred from any operational use of persons receiving grants from U.S.-sponsored educational or cultural funds, and urged that the Senate consider E whether additional measures might be required to preserve academic integrity.

Proprietaries. The report faulted the CIA for allowing its proprietaries—companies owned by the CIA—to grow so large as to create unfair competition with private businesses, and to risk exposure of their function as a cover for clandestine operations. The CIA also resisted "management-oriented audits" of pro- F prietaries, the report noted.

Among the proprietaries described in the report were Air America, at one time employing 8,000 persons, and a complex of insurance companies with assets of about $30 million. The report said that the insurance companies were used primarily to handle payments for agents who could not, for security reasons, receive money directly from the U.S. government. The companies also gave "operational sup- G port" for various covert projects, the report noted.

The committee backed continuing CIA use of proprietaries, but called for closer congressional oversight of their activities.

Drugs. The report charged that the intelligence agencies had exhibited a "disregard for human life and liberty" in subjecting "unwitting" persons to tests of biological and chemical agents. The report said that CIA employes had, for 9 years beginning in 1954, slipped LSD into the drinks and food of patrons at some bars.

The report noted that the drug-testing began as a defensive reaction to suspected use of drugs by the Communist powers. However, the "defensive orientation soon became secondary," the report maintained.

The report observed that there had been an unwillingness to exchange test results between the CIA and military personnel engaged in similar testing.

The committee also found that, in addition to some test participants still suffering residual effects of the drugs, two deaths were attributable to the testing programs.

The committee recommended that the CIA and other intelligence agencies, be required to obtain the "informed consent in writing, witnessed by a disinterested third party" of any subject of a test that might be dangerous to a person's "physical or mental health." It was also recommended that an attempt be made, by the CIA and the Defense Department, to locate and provide medical care, if needed, to participants in testing programs.

Budget. The report did not put a dollar total on U.S. intelligence costs. The committee at first had decided to publish the figure. Then on April 26, the committee voted, 6–5, to let the full Senate decide whether the figure should be released. Thus the group acceded—at least temporarily—to the wishes of the CIA and President Ford that the figure be deleted for reasons of national security.

However, the April 27 *New York Times* estimated, from various indications in the report, that the U.S. annually spent a total of $10 billion to $11 billion on intelligence. The *Washington Post* estimated the annual outlay at $9.4 billion.

The *Times* projected the combined budgets of the CIA, the Defense Intelligence Agency, the National Security Agency and the national reconnaissance program at $4.5 billion. The *Post* said that direct expenses for all agencies were $4.7 billion.

The actual purchasing power of the CIA budget, the report said, had declined in recent years, so that financing for fiscal 1976 was about equivalent "to the budgets of the late 1950s." The budget decrease corresponded to a reduction in CIA covert operations, which, the report maintained, had diminished in "every functional and geographic category" over the period from "1968 to the present."

The committee called for public disclosure of the annual U.S. intelligence budget, more intensive congressional oversight of the intelligence agencies' spending and full audits of the intelligence agencies by the General Accounting Office. The committee observed that the nondisclosure of appropriations for intelligence was perhaps unconstitutional.

Performance. The committee found that the intelligence agencies had made "important contributions to the nation's security." However, the committee reported that it had also found "duplication and waste, inertia and ineffectiveness in the intelligence community."

As an example of waste, the report cited a 1970 Office of Management and Budget recommendation that 9 mergers or transfers of intelligence programs be instituted. The proposal, apparently never acted upon, would have saved an estimated $1 billion annually. The report also noted that during the Korean War, the CIA had procured $152 million worth of foreign weapons for guerrilla forces that never came into existence.

The report criticized the CIA's preoccupation with collecting raw data, in preference to analyzing information to prepare finished studies. The misplaced emphasis, the report contended, resulted in intelligence which might be adequate, but was open to "major improvement."

The report noted that in 1970 a CIA official had termed the agency's use of cover to be "lax, arbitrary, uneven, confused, and loose." More recent CIA assessments had not been so critical of CIA cover practice, the report admitted, but it maintained that "improvements and changes" were still needed.

The case of Richard Welch, the assassinated CIA station chief in Athens, illustrated the problem of maintaining cover while functioning efficiently, the report observed.

Considering counterintelligence efforts (those aimed at thwarting hostile intelligence services), the committee reported that liaison between the FBI and the CIA had a "turbulent" history. The report said that counterintelligence was necessary to the security of the U.S., noting that over 40% of the Soviet officials serving in the U.S. (1,079 in February 1975 according to the FBI) had been linked to Soviet intelligence units. The figure, the report said, was raised to 60% by taking into account conservative estimates of unidentified Soviet intelligence officials.

The committee called for a presidential study of counterintelligence, leading to a classified statement on counterintelligence "policy and objectives." The study should pay attention, the committee said, to compartmentation, operations, deception, liaison and coordination, among other matters. The committee noted that there had been reports of counterintelligence efforts that had violated the constitutional rights of U.S. citizens. It urged that the attorney general be required by law to report on any such violations to the president.

The committee also made various recommendations upgrading the role of analysts (as against collectors) in the intelligence formation process, and called for a reform to insure that analysts were "better and more promptly informed" of U.S. actions and policies affecting their area of study. (The report noted that analysts—whose function was to correlate raw data—had been deprived of relevant information about U.S. projects concerning Cambodia and Chile in the 1970s.)

Structure. The committee, assessing the responsibilities and power of the various offices and institutions in the intelligence community, came to conclusions that generally matched those contained in President Ford's revision of the intelligence agencies.

The committee found that the Director of Central Intelligence (DCI) had lacked the authority necessary to fulfill his responsibility of coordinating the intelligence acquired by the different government agencies. The DCI, the committee found, could set priorities, but could not enforce them through control of the allocation of intelligence resources.

The committee also expressed concern over the ability of the DCI to resist pressure from the White House and the Defense Department to alter intelligence estimates. The report noted that the DCI, in 1969, had modified his judgment of Soviet ability to achieve nuclear first-strike capacity, to conform with the public position of then Defense Secretary Laird.

The committee recommended statutory reforms strengthening the office of the DCI, giving him the power to set national intelligence requirements and to allocate resources, and insulating the office from outside pressures. The committee also suggested that consideration be given to removing the DCI from direct control of the CIA. Controlling the CIA was seen as a possible conflict with the DCI's role as coordinator of the different intelligence services.

The committee found that within the CIA, the general counsel and the inspector general had often been kept ignorant of activities that it was their duty to investigate. The committee recommended legislation to afford them "unrestricted access to all agency information." The committee also urged that CIA employes be required to report any agency activities in violation of either CIA regulations or its legislative charter.

Finally, the committee urged that the Department of State and, in individual countries, ambassadors engage in more active supervision of intelligence activities. The report noted that ambassadors were generally "uninformed about specific espionage activities in their country of assignment." The committee also recommended that more funds and greater attention be given to the overt collection of information by the Foreign Service.

Sens. John Tower (R, Tex.) and Barry Goldwater (R, Ariz.) did not sign the report. Tower disagreed with a number of the recommendations and Goldwater professed belief that the report would cause "severe embarrassment, if not grave harm" to U.S. foreign policy.

All the other senators signed the report, although Democratic Sens. Walter F. Mondale (Minn.), Philip A. Hart (Mich.) and Gary Hart (Colo.) complained that the deletions and rewriting demanded by the CIA had diluted and obscured the report.

They noted that three chapters originally in the report—on "Cover," "Espionage," and "Budgetary Oversight"—had been deleted, along with sections from the chapter on covert action of the CIA.

Excerpts From Senate Committee Report on Foreign and Military Intelligence

Letter of Transmittal

(By Senator Frank Church, chairman of the Senate Select Committee to Study Governmental Operations With Respect to Intelligence Activities)

On January 27, 1975, the Senate established a select committee to conduct an investigation and study of the intelligence activities of the United States. After 15 months of intensive work, I am pleased to submit to the Senate this volume of the final report of the committee relating to foreign and military intelligence. The inquiry arises out of allegations of abuse and improper activities by the intelligence agencies of the United States, and great public concern that the Congress take action to bring the intelligence agencies under the constitutional framework. . . .

The Report on the Foreign and Military Intelligence Activities of the United States, is intended to provide to the Senate the basic information about the intelligence agencies of the U.S. required to make the necessary judgments concerning the role such agencies should play in the future. Despite security considerations which have limited what can responsibly be printed for public release the information which is presented in this report is a reasonably complete picture of the intelligence activities undertaken by the U.S. and the problems that such activities pose for constitutional government.

The findings and recommendations contained at the end of this volume constitute an agenda for action which, if adopted, would go a long way toward preventing the abuses that have occurred in the past from occurring again, and would assure that the intelligence activities of the U.S. will be conducted in accordance with constitutional processes.

FRANK CHURCH.

General Findings

The committee finds that there is a continuing need for an effective system of foreign and military intelligence [but, it also finds] . . . that covert-action operations have not been an exceptional instrument; . . . that the Constitution at least requires public disclosure and public authorization of an annual aggregate figure for U.S. national intelligence activities; . . . that the operation of an extensive and necessarily secret intelligence system places severe strains on the nation's constitutional government; . . . that intelligence activities should not be regarded as ends in themselves; . . . [and] that Congress has failed to provide the necessary statutory guidelines to insure that intelligence agencies carry out their necessary missions in accord with constitutional processes.

Recommendations

1. The National Security Act should be recast by omnibus legislation which would set forth the basic purposes of national intelligence activities, and define the relationship between the Congress and the intelligence agencies of the executive branch. This revision should be given the highest priority by the intelligence oversight committee(s) of Congress, acting in consultation with the executive branch.

2. The new legislation should define the charter of the organizations and entities in the U.S. intelligence community. It should establish charters for the National Security Council, the director of central intelligence, the Central Intelligence Agency, the national intelligence components of the Department of Defense, including the National Security Agency and the Defense Intelligence Agency, and all other elements of the intelligence community, including joint organizations of two or more agencies.

3. This legislation should set forth the general structure and procedures of the intelligence community, and the roles and responsibilities of the agencies which comprise it.

4. The legislation should contain specific and clearly defined prohibitions or limitations on various activities carried out by the respective components of the intelligence community.

The National Security Council and the Office of the President

The National Security Council (NSC) is an instrument of the president and not a corporate entity with authority of its own. The committee found that . . . the president has had, through the NSC, effective means for exerting broad policy control over at least two major clandestine activities—covert action and sensitive technical collection. . . . The committee found, however, that there were significant limits to this control; . . . [that] there is no NSC-level mechanism for coordinating, reviewing or approving counterintelligence activities in the U.S.; . . . [that] until the recent establishment of the Committee on Foreign Intelligence, there was no effective NSC-level mechanism for . . . coordinating the activities of the intelligence community, ensuring its responsiveness to the requirements for national intelligence, and for assembling a consolidated national intelligence budget; . . . [and that] presidents have not established specific instruments of oversight to prevent abuses by the intelligence community.

Recommendations

5. By statute, the NSC should be explicitly empowered to direct and provide policy guidance for the intelligence activities of the U.S., including intelligence collection, counterintelligence, and the conduct of covert action.

6. By statute, the attorney general should be made an adviser to the NSC in order to facilitate discharging his responsibility to ensure that actions taken to protect American national security in the field of intelligence are also consistent with the Constitution and the laws of the U.S.

7. By statute, the existing power of the director of central intelligence [DCI] to coordinate the activities of the intelligence community should be reaffirmed. At the same time, the NSC should establish an appropriate committee—such as the new Committee on Foreign Intelligence—with responsibility for allocating intelligence resources to ensure efficient and effective operation of the national intelligence community. This committee should be chaired by the DCI and should include representatives of the secretary of state, the secretary of defense, and the assistant to the president for national security affairs. [See p. 127D1, E2]

8. By statute, an NSC committee (like the operations advisory group) should be established to advise the president on covert action. It would also be empowered, at the president's discretion, to approve *all* types of sensitive intelligence collection activities. If [a group] member dissented from an approval, the particular collection activity would be referred to the president for decision. The group should consist of the secretary of state, the secretary of defense, the assistant to the president for national security affairs, the director of central intelligence, the attorney general, the chairman of the joint chiefs of staff, and the director of OMB [the Office of Management and Budget] as an observer. The president would designate a chairman from among the group's members.

9. The chairman of the group would be confirmed by the Senate for that position if he were an official not already subject to confirmation. In the execution of covert action and sensitive intelligence collection activities specifically approved by the president, the chairman would enter the chain of command below the president.

10. The group should be provided with adequate staff to assist in conducting thorough reviews of covert action and sensitive collection projects. That staff should not be drawn exclusively from the clandestine service of the CIA.

11. Each covert action project should be reviewed and passed on by the group. In addition, the group should review all on-going projects at least once a year.

12. By statute, the secretary of state should be designated as the principal Administration spokesman to the Congress on the policy and purpose underlying covert action projects.

13. By statute, the director of central intelligence should be required to fully inform the intelligence oversight committee(s) of Congress of each covert action prior to its initiation. No funds should be expended on any covert action unless and until the president certifies and provides to the congressional intelligence oversight committee(s) the reasons that a covert action is required by extraordinary circumstances to deal with grave threats to the national security of the U.S. The congressional intelligence oversight committee(s) should be kept fully and currently informed on all covert action projects, and the DCI should submit a semi-annual report on all such projects to the committee(s).

14. The committee recommends that when the Senate establishes an intelligence oversight committee with authority to authorize the national intelligence budget, the Hughes-Ryan Amendment (22 USC, 2422) should be amended so that the foregoing notifications and presidential certifications to the Senate are provided only to that committee. A

15. By statute, a new NSC counterintelligence committee should be established, consisting of the attorney general as chairman, the deputy secretary of defense, the director of central intelligence, the director of the FBI, and the assistant to the president for national security affairs. Its purpose would be to coordinate and review foreign counterintelligence activities conducted within the U.S. and the clandestine collection of foreign intelligence within the U.S., by both the FBI and the CIA. The goal would be to ensure strict conformity with statutory and constitutional requirements and to enhance coordination between the CIA B and FBI. This committee should review the standards and guidelines for all recruitments of agents within the U.S. for counterintelligence or positive foreign intelligence purposes, as well as for the recruitment of U.S. citizens abroad. This committee would consider differences between the agencies concerning the recruitment of agents, the handling of foreign assets who come to the U.S., and the establishment of the bona fides of defectors. It should also treat any other foreign intelligence or counterintelligence activity of the FBI and CIA which either agency brings to that forum for presidential level consideration.

The Director of Central Intelligence C

The committee found that . . . while the director of central intelligence (DCI) was given responsibility under the 1947 [National Security] act for intelligence community activities, he was not authorized to centrally coordinate or manage the overall operations of the community; . . . that the DCI, in his role as intelligence adviser, has faced obstacles in ensuring that his national intelligence judgments are objective and independent of department and agency biases; . . . that the function of the DCI in his role as intelligence D community leader and principal intelligence adviser to the president is inconsistent with his responsibility to manage . . . the CIA; . . . [and] that the DCI's new span of control—both the entire intelligence community and the entire CIA—may be too great for him to exercise effective detailed supervision of clandestine activities. . . .

The committee believes that the Congress . . . should have access to the full range of intelligence produced by the U.S. intelligence community.

Recommendations

16. By statute, the DCI should be established as the E president's principal foreign intelligence adviser, with exclusive responsibility for producing national intelligence for the president and the Congress. For this purpose, the DCI should be empowered to establish a staff directly responsible to him to help prepare his national intelligence judgments and to coordinate the views of the other members of the intelligence community. The committee recommends that the director establish a board to include senior outside advisers to review intelligence products as necessary, thus helping to insulate the DCI from pressures to alter or modify his national intelligence judgments. To advise and assist the DCI in producing national intelligence, the DCI would also be empowered to draw on other elements of the intelligence community. F

17. By statute, the DCI should be given responsibility and authority for establishing national intelligence requirements, preparing the national intelligence budget, and providing guidance for U.S. national intelligence program operations. In this capacity he should be designated as chairman of the appropriate NSC committee, such as the CFI [Committee on Foreign Intelligence], and should have the following powers and responsibilities:

a. The DCI should establish national intelligence requirements for the entire intelligence community. He should be empowered to draw on intelligence community representatives and others whom he may designate to assist him in establishing national in- G telligence requirements and [in] determining the success of the various agencies in fulfilling them. The DCI should provide general guidance to the various intelligence agency directors for the management of intelligence operations.

b. The DCI should have responsibility for preparing the national intelligence program budget for presentation to the president and the Congress. The definition of what is to be included within that national intelligence program should be established by Congress in consultation with the executive. In this capacity, the DCI should be involved early in the budget cycle in preparing the budgets of the respective intelligence community agencies. The director should have specific responsibility for choosing among the programs of the different collection and production agencies and departments and to insure against waste and unnecessary duplication. The DCI should also have responsibility for issuing fiscal guidance for the allocation of all national intelligence resources. The authority of the DCI to reprogram funds within the intelligence budget should be defined by statute.

c. In order to carry out his national intelligence responsibilities the DCI should have the authority to review all foreign and military intelligence activities and intelligence resource allocations, including tactical military intelligence which is the responsibility of the armed forces.

d. The DCI should be authorized to establish an intelligence community staff to support him in carrying out his managerial responsibilities. This staff should be drawn from the best available talent within and outside the intelligence community.

e. In addition to these provisions concerning DCI control over national intelligence operations in peacetime, the statute should require establishment of a procedure to insure that in time of war the relevant national intelligence operations come under the control of the secretary of defense.

18. By statute, the position of deputy director of central intelligence for the intelligence community should be established as recommended in Executive Order 11905. This deputy director should be subject to Senate confirmation and would assume the DCI's intelligence community functions in the DCI's absence. Current provisions regarding the status of the DCI and his single deputy should be extended to cover the DCI and both deputies. Civilian control of the nation's intelligence is important; only one of the three could be a career military officer, active or retired.

19. The committee recommends that the intelligence oversight committee(s) of Congress consider whether the Congress should appropriate the funds for the national intelligence budget to the DCI, rather than to the directors of the various intelligence agencies and departments.

20. By statute, the director of central intelligence should serve at the pleasure of the president but for no more than ten years.

21. The committee also recommends consideration of separating the DCI from direct responsibility over the CIA.

The Central Intelligence Agency

The committee finds that the CIA's present charter . . . is inadequate in a number of respects. . . . A clear statutory basis is needed for the agency's conduct abroad of covert action, espionage, counterintelligence and foreign intelligence collection and for such counterespionage operations within the U.S. as the agency may have to undertake as a result of the activities abroad.

The committee believes that the U.S. cannot forego clandestine human collection [but also notes that] . . . there are certain inherent limitations to the value of clandestine sources; . . . [that] there are significant benefits to both the government and the universities . . . [in the overt] collection of foreign intelligence information from American citizens, primarily of an economic and technological nature; . . . [and that] counterintelligence requires the direct attention of Congress and the executive for three reasons: (1) two distinct and partly incompatible approaches to counterintelligence have emerged and demand reconciliation; (2) recent evidence suggests that FBI counterespionage results have been less than satisfactory; and (3) counterintelligence has infringed on the rights and liberties of Americans.

Recommendations

22. By statute, a charter should be established for the CIA which makes clear that its activities must be related to foreign intelligence. The agency should be given the following missions:

—The collection of denied or protected foreign intelligence information.
—The conduct of foreign counterintelligence.
—The conduct of foreign covert action operations.
—The production of finished national intelligence.

23. The CIA, in carrying out foreign intelligence missions, would be permitted to engage in relevant activities within the U.S. so long as these activities do not violate the Constitution nor any federal, state, or local laws within the U.S. The committee has set forth in its domestic recommendations proposed restrictions on such activities to supplement restrictions already contained in the 1947 National Security Act. In addition, the committee recommends that by statute the intelligence oversight committee(s) of Congress and the proposed counterintelligence committee of the NSC be required to review, at least annually, CIA foreign intelligence activities conducted within the U.S.

24. By statute, the attorney general should be required to report to the president and to the intelligence oversight committee(s) of Congress any intelligence activities which, in his opinion, violate the constitutional rights of American citizens or any other provision of law and the actions he has taken in response. Pursuant to the committee's domestic recommendations [contained in part II of the report], the attorney general should be made responsible for ensuring that intelligence activities do not violate the Constitution or any other provision of law.

25. The committee recommends the establishment of a special committee of the Committee on Foreign Intelligence [CFI] to review all foreign human intelligence collection activities. It would make recommendations to the CFI with regard to the scope, policies and priorities of U.S. clandestine human collection operations and choices between overt and clandestine human collection. This committee would be composed of a representative of the secretary of state as chairman, and other statutory members of the CFI, and others whom the president may designate.

26. The intelligence oversight committee(s) of Congress should carefully examine intelligence collection activities of the clandestine service to assure that clandestine means are used only when the information is sufficiently important and when such means are necessary to obtain the information.

27. The intelligence oversight committee(s) should consider whether:

—the domestic collection division (overt collection operations) should be removed from the directorate of operations (the clandestine service), and returned to the directorate of intelligence;
—the CIA's regulations should require that the DCD's overt contacts be informed when they are to be used for operational support of clandestine activities;
—the CIA's regulations should prohibit recruiting as agents immigrants who have applied for American citizenship.

28. The president . . . , in consultation with the intelligence oversight committee(s) of Congress, should undertake a classified review of current issues regarding counterintelligence. This review should form the basis for a classified presidential statement on national counterintelligence policy and objectives, and should closely examine the following issues: compartmentation, operations, security, research, accountability, training, internal review, deception, liaison and coordination, and manpower.

CIA Production of Finished Intelligence

Intelligence production refers to the process . . . by which "raw" intelligence is transformed into "finished" intelligence for senior policymakers.

The committee found that the quality, timeliness and utility of our finished intelligence is generally considered adequate, but that major improvement is both desirable and possible . . . [in the area of] resources allocated to the production of finished intelligence, the personnel system and the organizational structure of intelligence production.

Recommendations

29. By statute, the director of the directorate of intelligence (DDI) should be authorized to continue to report directly to the director of central intelligence.

30. The committee recommends that a system be devised to ensure that intelligence analysts are better and more promptly informed about U.S. policies and programs affecting their respective areas of responsibility.

31. The CIA and the intelligence oversight committee(s) of Congress should reexamine the personnel system of the directorate of intelligence with a view to providing a more flexible, less hierarchical personnel system. Super-grade positions should be available on the basis of an individual's analytical capabilities.

32. The directorate of intelligence should seek to bring more established analysts into the CIA at middle and upper grade levels for both career positions and temporary assignments.

33. Greater emphasis should be placed on stimulating development of new tools and methods of analysis.

34. Agency policy should continue to encourage intelligence analysts to assume substantive tours of duty on an open basis in other agencies (State, Defense, NSC staff) or in academic institutions to broaden both their analytical outlook and their appreciation for the relevance of their analysis to policymakers and operators within the government.

Covert Actions and Paramilitary Operations

The need to maintain secrecy shields covert action projects from the rigorous public scrutiny and debate necessary to determine their compatibility with established American foreign policy goals. The committee has concluded . . . that the U.S. should maintain the capability to react through covert actions when no other means will suffice to meet extraordinary circumstances involving grave threats to U.S. national security. Nevertheless, covert action should be considered as an exception to the normal process of government action abroad, rather than a parallel but invisible system in which covert operations are routine. . . .

While the committee believes that the executive should continue to have the initiative in formulating covert action, it also strongly believes that the appropriate oversight bodies of Congress should be fully informed prior to the initiation of such actions, [and that] congressional power over the purse can serve as the most effective congressional oversight tool.

Recommendations

35. The legislation establishing the charter for the CIA should specify that the CIA is the only U.S. government agency authorized to conduct covert actions. The purpose of covert actions should be to deal with grave threats to American security. Covert actions should be consistent with publicly-defined U.S. foreign policy goals, and should be reserved for extraordinary circumstances when no other means will suffice. The legislation governing covert action should require executive branch procedures which will ensure careful and thorough consideration of both the general policies governing covert action and particular covert action projects; such procedures should require the participation and accountability of highest level policymakers.

36. The committee has already recommended, following its investigation of alleged assassination attempts directed at foreign leaders, a statute to forbid such activities. The committee reaffirms its support for such a statute and further recommends prohibiting the following covert activities by statute:

—All political assassinations.
—Efforts to subvert democratic governments.
—Support for police or other internal security forces which engage in the systematic violation of human rights.

37. By statute, the appropriate NSC committee (e.g., the operations advisory group) should review every covert action proposal.

The committee recommends that the operations advisory group review include:

—A careful and systematic analysis of the political premises underlying the recommended actions, as well as the nature, extent, purpose, risks, likelihood of success, and costs of the operation. Reasons explaining why the objection cannot be achieved by overt means should also be considered.
—Each covert action project should be formally considered at a meeting of the OAG, and if approved, forwarded to the president for final decision. The views and positions of the participants would be fully recorded. For the purpose of OAG, presidential, and congressional considerations, all so-called non-sensitive projects should be aggregated according to the extraordinary circumstances or contingency against which the project is directed.

38. By statute, the intelligence oversight committee(s) of Congress should require that the annual budget submission for covert action programs be specified and detailed as to the activity recommended. Unforeseen covert action projects should be funded from the contingency reserve fund which could be replenished only after the concurrence of the oversight and any other appropriate congressional committees. The congressional intelligence oversight committees should be notified prior to any withdrawal from the contingency reserve fund.

39. By statute, any covert use by the U.S. government of American citizens as combatants should be preceded by the notification required for all covert ac-

tions. The statute should provide that within 60 days of such notification such use shall be terminated unless the Congress has specifically authorized such use. The Congress should be empowered to terminate such use at any time.

40. By statute, the executive branch should be prevented from conducting any covert military assistance program (including the indirect or direct provision of military material, military or logistics advice and training, and funds for mercenaries) without the explicit prior consent of the intelligence oversight committee(s) of Congress.

Reorganization of the Intelligence Community

The committee recommendation regarding the director of central intelligence [DCI] would, if implemented, increase his authority over the entire intelligence community. . . . Serious consideration also [must] be given to [making]major structural change in the CIA, in particular, separating national intelligence production and analysis from the clandestine service and other collection functions. Intelligence production would be placed directly under the DCI, while clandestine collection of foreign intelligence from human and technical sources and covert operations would remain in the CIA.

Recommendation

41. The intelligence oversight committee(s) of Congress in the course of developing a new charter for the intelligence community should give consideration to separating the functions of the DCI and the director of the CIA and to dividing the intelligence analysis and production functions from the clandestine collection and covert action functions of the present CIA.

Relations with U.S. Institutions and Private Citizens

In its consideration of the recommendations that follow, the committee noted the CIA's concern that further restriction on the use of Americans for operational purposes will constrain current operating programs. The committee recognizes that there may be at least some short-term operational losses if the committee recommendations are effected. At the same time, the committee believes that there are certain American institutions whose integrity is critical to the maintenance of a free society and which should therefore be free of any unwitting role in the clandestine service of the U.S. government.

Recommendations

42. The committee is concerned about the integrity of American academic institutions and the use of individuals affiliated with such institutions for clandestine purposes. Accordingly, the committee recommends that the CIA amend its internal directives to require that individual academics used for operational purposes by the CIA, together with the president or equivalent official of the relevant academic institutions, be informed of the clandestine CIA relationship.

43. The committee further recommends that, as soon as possible, the permanent intelligence oversight committee(s) of Congress examine whether further steps are needed to insure the integrity of American academic institutions.

44. By statute, the CIA should be prohibited from the operational use of grantees who are receiving funds through educational and/or cultural programs which are sponsored by the U.S. government.

45. By statute, the CIA should be prohibited from subsidizing the writing, or production for distribution within the U.S. or its territories, of any book, magazine, article, publication, film, or video or audio tape unless publicly attributed to the CIA. Nor should the CIA be permitted to undertake any activity to accomplish indirectly such distribution within the U.S. or its territories.

46. The committee supports the recently adopted CIA prohibitions against any paid or contractual relationship between the agency and U.S. and foreign journalists accredited to U.S. media organizations. The CIA prohibitions should, however, be established in law.

47. The committee recommends that the CIA prohibitions be extended by law to include the operational use of any person who regularly contributes material to, or is regularly involved directly or indirectly in the editing of material, or regularly acts to set policy or provide direction to the activities of U.S. media organizations.

48. The committee recommends that the agency's recent prohibition on covert paid or contractual relationship between the agency and any American clergyman or missionary should be established by law.

Proprietaries and Cover

CIA proprietaries are business entities wholly owned by the agency which do business, or only appear to do business, under commercial guise. The committee finds that too often large proprietaries have created unwarranted risks of unfair competition with private business and of compromising their cover as clandestine operations. . . .

The committee found a need for even greater accountability, both internally and externally, . . . [than] internal CIA financial controls [provided]. . . .

The committee finds that there is a basic tension between maintaining adequate cover and effectively engaging in overseas intelligence activities, [but notes,] . . . some improvements and changes are needed . . . to strengthen cover.

Recommendations

49. By statute, the CIA should be permitted to use proprietaries subject to external and internal controls.

50. The committee recommends that the intelligence oversight committee(s) of Congress require at least an annual report on all proprietaries. The report should include a statement of each proprietary's nature and function, the results of internal annual CIA audits, a list of all CIA intercessions on behalf of its proprietaries with any other U.S. government departments, agencies or bureaus, and such other information as the oversight committee deems appropriate.

51. The intelligence oversight committee(s) of Congress should require that the fiscal impact of proprietaries on the CIA's budget be made clear in the DCI's annual report to the oversight committee. The committee should also establish guidelines for creating large proprietaries, should these become necessary.

52. By statute, all returns of funds from proprietaries not needed for its operational purposes or because of liquidation or termination of a proprietary, should be remitted to the U.S. Treasury as miscellaneous receipts.

The Department of Justice should be consulted during the process of the sale or disposition of any CIA proprietary.

53. By statute, former senior government officials should be prohibited from negotiating with the CIA or any other agency regarding the disposal of proprietaries. The intelligence oversight committee(s) of Congress should consider whether other activities among agencies of the intelligence community, the CIA, and former officials and employees, such as selling to or negotiating contracts with the CIA, should also be prohibited as is the case regarding military officials under 18 U.S.C. 207.

Intelligence Liaison

Because of the importance of intelligence liaison agreements to national security, the committee is concerned that such agreements have not been systematically reviewed by the Congress in any fashion. . . . The committee notes that all treaties require the advice and consent of the Senate, and executive agreements must be reported to the Foreign Relations Committee of the Senate.

Recommendations

54. By statute, the CIA should be prohibited from causing, funding, or encouraging actions by liaison services which are forbidden to the CIA. Furthermore, the fact that a particular project, action, or activity of the CIA is carried out through or by a foreign liaison service should not relieve the agency of its responsibilities for clearance within the agency, within the executive branch, or with the Congress.

55. The intelligence oversight committee(s) of Congress should be kept fully informed of agreements negotiated with other governments through intelligence channels.

The General Counsel and Inspector General

The committee found that . . . the participation of the general counsel in determining the legality or propriety of CIA activities was limited; . . . moreover, the general counsel never had general investigatory authority.

The committee believes that . . . Congress should examine the internal review mechanisms of foreign and military intelligence agencies and consider the feasibility of applying recommendations such as those suggested for the CIA.

Recommendations

56. Any CIA employee having information about activities which appear illegal, improper, outside the agency's legislative charter, or in violation of agency regulations, should be required to inform the director, the general counsel, or the inspector general of the agency. If the general counsel is not informed, he should be notified by the other officials of such reports. The general counsel and the inspector general shall, except where they deem it inappropriate, be required to provide such information to the head of the agency.

57. The DCI should be required to report any information regarding employee violations of law related to their duties and the results of any internal agency investigation to the attorney general.

58. By statute, the director of the CIA should be required to notify the appropriate committees of the Congress of any referrals made to the attorney general pursuant to the previous recommendation.

59. The director of the CIA should periodically require employees having any information on past, current, or proposed agency activities which appear illegal, improper, outside the agency's legislative charter, or in violation of the agency's regulations, to report such information.

60. By statute, the general counsel and the inspector general should have unrestricted access to all agency information and should have the authority to review all of the agency activities.

61. All significant proposed CIA activities should be reviewed by the general counsel for legality and constitutionality.

62. The program of component inspections conducted by the inspector general should be increased, as should the program of surveys of sensitive programs and issues which cut across component lines in the agency.

63. The director shall, at least annually, report to the appropriate committees of the Congress on the activities of the office of the general counsel and the office of the inspector general.

64. By statute, the general counsel should be nominated by the president and confirmed by the Senate.

65. The agency's efforts to expand and strengthen the staffs of the general counsel and inspector general should be continued.

66. The general counsel should be promoted to, and the inspector general should continue to hold executive rank equal to that of the deputy directors of the CIA.

The Department of Defense

The committee finds that . . . most of the important collection activities conducted by the Defense Department . . . are managed relatively efficiently and are generally responsive to the needs of the military services as well as to the policymakers on the national level. . . .

The committee notes that despite the fact that the NSA [National Security Agency] has been in existence for several decades, NSA still lacks a legislative charter. . . . The committee finds there is a compelling need for an NSA charter to spell out limitations which will protect individual constitutional rights without impairing NSA's necessary foreign intelligence mission.

Recommendations

67. In order to implement the committee's and the president's recommendations for expanding the DCI's resource-allocation responsibility appropriate adjustments should be made in the secretary of defense's general authority regarding defense intelligence activities and in the department's internal budgeting procedures. At the same time, there should be provision for the transfer to the secretary of defense of responsibilities, particularly tasking intelligence agencies, in the event of war.

68. By statute, the intelligence oversight committee(s) of Congress, in consultation with the executive, should establish a charter for the Defense Intelligence Agency [DIA] which would clearly define its mission and relationship to other intelligence agencies. The committee recommends that the charter include the following provisions:

a. In order to encourage close coordination between consumers and producers of national intelligence, DIA should be a part of the office of the secretary of defense, and should report directly to the deputy secretary of defense for intelligence. A small J-2 staff should be reconstituted to provide intelligence support, primarily of an operational nature, to the Joint Chiefs of Staff. The secretary of defense should ensure full coordination and free access to information between the two groups.

b. The director of the DIA should be appointed by the president and subject to Senate confirmation. Either the director or deputy director of the agency should be a civilian.

c. The Congress must relieve DIA from certain civil service regulations in order to enable the quality of DIA personnel to be upgraded. In addition, more supergrade positions must be provided for civilians in DIA.

69. By statute, a character for the National Security Agency should be established which, in addition to setting limitations on the agency's operations would provide that the director of NSA would be nominated by the president and subject to confirmation by the Senate. The director should serve at the pleasure of the president but not for more than ten years. Either the director or the deputy director should be a civilian.

70. The Department of Defense should centralize the service counterintelligence and investigative activities within the U.S. in the Defense Investigative Service (DIS) in order to reduce wasteful duplication.

The Department of State and Ambassadors

The committee found that the role [sic] of the Department of State and the ambassadors constitute a central element in the control and improvement in America's intelligence operations overseas; . . . that neither the State Department nor U.S. ambassadors are substantially informed about espionage or counterintelligence activities directed at foreign governments; . . . that there is no systematic assessment outside the CIA of the risks of foreign espionage and counterespionage operations and the extent to which those operations conform with overall foreign policy; . . . that the Foreign Service is the foremost producer in the U.S. government of intelligence on foreign political and economic matters; . . . [and] that the State Department does not adequately train Foreign Service personnel . . . nor fund their collection operations.

Recommendations

71. The National Security Council, the Department of State, and the Central Intelligence Agency should promptly issue instructions implementing Public Law 93–475 (22 U.S.C. 2680a). These instructions should make clear that ambassadors are authorized recipients of sources and methods information concerning all intelligence activities, including espionage and counterintelligence operations. Parallel instructions from other components of the intelligence community should be issued to their respective field organizations and operatives. Copies of all these instructions should be made available to the intelligence oversight committee(s) of Congress.

72. In the exercise of their statutory responsibilities, ambassadors should have the personal right, which may not be delegated, of access to the operational communications of the CIA's clandestine service in the country to which they are assigned. Any exceptions should have presidential approval and should be brought to the attention of the intelligence oversight committee(s) of Congress.

73. By statute, the Department of State should be authorized to take the necessary steps to assure its ability to provide effective guidance and support to ambassadors in the execution of their responsibilities under Public Law 93–475 (22 U.S.C. Sect. 2680a).

74. Consideration should be given to increasing and earmarking funds for Foreign Service overt collection of foreign political and economic information. These funds might be administered jointly by the State Department's bureau of intelligence and research and the bureau of economic affairs.

75. The NSC should review the question of which U.S. government agency should control and operate communications with overseas diplomatic and consular posts, including the CIA, and other civilian agencies operating abroad.

76. The Department of State should establish specific training programs for political reporting within the Foreign Service Institute, and place greater emphasis on economic reporting.

Oversight and Intelligence Budget

The committee finds that a full understanding of the budget of the intelligence community is required for effective oversight, . . . [and] believes there is serious question as to whether the present system of complete secrecy violates the constitutional provision that: "No money shall be drawn from the Treasury but in consequence of appropriations made by law; and a regular statement and account of the receipts and expenditures of all public money shall be published from time to time." [Article I, section 9 of the Constitution]

Recommendations

77. The intelligence oversight committee(s) of Congress should authorize on an annual basis a "national intelligence budget," the total amount of which would be made public. The committee recommends that the oversight committee consider whether it is necessary, given the constitutional requirement and the national security demands, to publish more detailed budgets.

78. The intelligence oversight committee(s) of Congress should monitor the tactical and indirect support accounts as well as the national activities of intelligence agencies in order to assure that they are kept in proper perspective and balance.

79. At the request of the intelligence oversight committee(s) of Congress and as its agent, staff members of the General Accounting Office should conduct full audits, both for compliance and for management of all components of the intelligence community. The GAO should establish such procedures, compartmentation and clearances as are necessary in order to conduct these audits on a secure basis. In conducting such audits, the GAO should be authorized to have full access to all necessary intelligence community files and records.

Chemical and Biological Agents and the Intelligence Community

The committee found that U.S. intelligence agencies engaged in research and development programs to discover materials which could be used to alter human behavior. . . . These programs were kept from the American public because, as the inspector general of the CIA wrote, "The knowledge that the agency is engaging in unethical and illicit activities would have serious repercussions in political and diplomatic circles and would be detrimental to the accomplishment of its [CIA's] mission."

While some controlled testing for defensive purposes might be defended, the nature of the tests, their scale and the fact they they were continued for years after it was known that the surreptitious administration of LSD to unwitting subjects was dangerous, indicate a disregard for human life and liberty. . . .

The committee also found that within the intelligence community, there were destructive jurisdictional conflicts over drug testing.

Recommendations

80. The CIA and other foreign and foreign military intelligence agencies should not engage in experimentation on human subjects utilizing any drug, device or procedure which is designed, intended, or is reasonably likely to harm the physical or mental health of the human subject, except with the informed consent in writing, witnessed by a disinterested third party, of each human subject, and in accordance with the guidelines issued by the National Commission for the Protection of Human Subjects for Biomedical and Behavioral Research. Further, the jurisdiction of the commission should be amended to include the CIA and the other intelligence agencies of the U.S. Government.

81. The director of the CIA and the secretary of defense should continue to make determined efforts to locate those individuals involved in human testing of chemical and biological agents and to provide follow-up examinations and treatment, if necessary.

General Recommendations

82. **Internal Regulations**—Internal CIA directives or regulations regarding significant agency policies and procedures should be waived only with the explicit written approval of the director of central intelligence. Waiver of any such regulation or directive should in no way violate any law or infringe on the constitutional right and freedom of any citizen. If the DCI approves the waiver or amendment of any significant regulation or directive, the NSC and the appropriate congressional oversight committee(s) should be notified immediately. Such notification should be accompanied by a statement explaining the reasons for the waiver or amendment.

83. **Security Clearances**—In the course of its investigation, the committee found that because of the many intelligence agencies participating in security clearance investigations, current security clearance procedures involve duplication of effort, waste of money, and inconsistent patterns of investigation and standards. The intelligence oversight committee(s) of Congress, in consultation with the intelligence community, should consider framing standard security clearance procedures for all civilian intelligence agencies and background checks for congressional committees when security clearances are required.

84. **Personnel Practices**—The committee found that intelligence agency training programs fail to instruct personnel adequately on the legal limitations and prohibitions applicable to intelligence activities. The committee recommends that these training programs should be expanded to include review of constitutional, statutory, and regulatory provisions in an effort to heighten awareness among all intelligence personnel concerning the potential effects intelligence activities may have on citizens' legal rights.

85. **Security Functions of the Intelligence Agencies**—The committee found that the security components of intelligence agencies sometimes engaged in law enforcement activities. Some of these activities may have been unlawful. Intelligence agencies' security functions should be limited to protecting the agencies' personnel and facilities and lawful activities and to assuring that intelligence personnel follow proper security practices.

86. **Secrecy and Authorized Disclosure**—The committee has received various administration proposals that would require persons having access to classified and sensitive information to maintain the secrecy of that information. The committee recommends that the issues raised by these proposals be considered by the new legislative intelligence oversight committee(s) of Congress and that, in recasting the 1947 National Security Act and in consultation with the executive branch, the oversight committee(s) consider the wisdom of new secrecy and disclosure legislation. In the view of the committee any such consideration should include carefully defining the following terms:

—national secret;
—sources and methods;
—lawful and unlawful classification;
—lawful and unlawful disclosure.

The new legislation should provide civil and/or criminal penalties for unlawful classification and unlawful disclosure. The statute should also provide for internal departmental and agency procedures for employees who believe that classification and/or disclosure procedures are being improperly or illegally used to report such belief. There should also be a statutory procedure whereby an employee who has used the agency channel to no avail can report such belief without impunity to an "authorized" institutional group outside the agency. The new Intelligence Oversight Board is one such group. The intelligence oversight committee(s) of Congress would be another. The statute should specify that revealing classified information in the course of reporting information to an authorized group would not constitute unlawful disclosure of classified information.

87. **Federal Register for Classified Executive Orders**—In the course of its investigation, the committee often had difficulty locating classified orders, directives, instructions, and regulations issued by various elements of the executive branch. Access to these orders by the intelligence oversight committee(s) of Congress is essential to informed oversight of the intelligence community.

The committee recommends that a Federal Register for classified executive orders be established, by statute. The state should require the registry, under appropriate security procedures, of all executive orders—however they are labeled—concerning the intelligence activities of the U.S. Among the documents for which registry in the Classified Federal Register should be required are all national security council intelligence directives (NSCIDs), and all director of central intelligence directives (DCIDs). Provision should be made for access to classified executive orders by the intelligence oversight committee(s) of Congress. Classified executive orders would not be lawful until filed with the registry, although there should be provision for immediate implementation in emergency situations with prompt subsequent registry required.

Senate creates permanent intelligence panel. The Senate May 19 voted 72–22 to create a permanent Select Committee on Intelligence. Panel members were named the next day. The action had been recommended by an earlier Senate unit that had investigated U.S. intelligence agencies. Since creation of the committee was an internal Senate affair, neither House nor presidential action was required.

The creation of a permanent committee had appeared doubtful after the Senate Rules Committee April 29 voted out a resolution that would have established a temporary panel to investigate intelligence abuses. The Rules Committee resolution drew fire from many Senators. They argued that such a temporary panel would merely duplicate work already done by the earlier committee chaired by Sen. Frank Church (D, Idaho).

Opposition to a permanent committee also came from members of other committees—particularly Armed Services—that already had oversight over the intelligence agencies. The resolution that finally created the permanent intelligence committee partially nullified this opposition by offering a compromise; the new committee would have exclusive jurisdiction over the Central Intelligence Agency, but jurisdiction over other U.S. intelligence services would be shared with the committees that originally had the oversight authority.

The resolution also provided that eight of the 15 members of the new committee would be drawn from the four committees that previously had monitored intelligence activities—two each from the Appropriations, Armed Services, Judiciary and Foreign Relations panels. The resolution also set rules for disclosing classified material. If the committee voted to disclose such material, it would notify the president. If the president objected to disclosure, the matter would be brought before the full Senate for a vote on disclosure.

The resolution stated that it was the sense of the Senate that the intelligence agencies should keep the committee fully informed of their activities. However, the committee was not given veto power over those activities.

Just before passage of the resolution, Sen. John C. Stennis (D, Miss.), chairman of the Armed Services Committee, and John G. Tower (R, Tex.), another member of that panel, offered an amendment that would have stripped the new committee of budgetary and legislative authority over the military intelligence services. They argued that the new panel would hold a "dangerous potential" for disclosure of classified information. Opponents of the Stennis-Tower proposal said that it would render the new intelligence panel virtually impotent. The proposal, they said, would place 80%–90% of the funds going to intelligence outside of the intelligence committee's jurisdiction.

The Stennis-Tower amendment was defeated 63–31.

Church hailed the creation of the committee. He said it had been a key item in his committee's reform proposals.

Senators Mike Mansfield (D, Mont.), the majority leader, and Hugh Scott (R, Pa.), the minority leader, appointed the members of the new panel. The Democrats were: Daniel K. Inouye (Hawaii), Birch Bayh (Ind.), Adlai E. Stevenson (Ill.), William D. Hathaway (Maine), Walter Huddleston (Ky.), Joseph Biden Jr. (Del.), Robert B. Morgan (N.C.) and Gary W. Hart (Colo.). The Republicans were: Clifford P. Case (N.J.), Mark O. Hatfield (Ore.), Barry Goldwater (Ariz.), Howard H. Baker Jr. (Tenn.), Robert T. Stafford (Vt.), Strom Thurmond (S.C.) and Jake Garn (Utah).

Report on the Military

Civilians' rights violated. American civilians' rights were violated in many of the investigations conducted by military intelligence agents, according to a report made public May 16 by the staff of the Senate Select Committee on Intelligence Activities. According to excerpts reprinted in the *New York Times* May 17, the study charged that during the middle and late 1960s, agents from the Defense Department penetrated numerous civil rights and anti-Vietnam war groups to monitor the actions of private citizens.

According to the report, until 1968 the Army commanders in West Germany opened mail and wiretapped U.S. citizens they considered "threats" to the Army. Although the West German government forbade the practice after 1968, the restriction does not apply to the American sector of West Berlin. Army Secretary Martin R. Hoffman recently filed two affidavits attesting to military mail openings until 1972, and, the *Times* says, "the affidavits carried the strong implication that such practices were continuing there." [See Vol. I, p. 139]

The staff report termed the experience of the late 1960's "the most intrusion that military intelligence has ever made into the civilian community." In 1971 new Defense Department directives prohibited the collection of data on individuals "unaffiliated" with the military. Excepted, however, were individuals or groups the Pentagon considered "threats" to military security.

The committee staff estimated 100,000 individuals and a "similarly large" number of domestic organizations were subject to surveillance. Army agents posed as newsmen, recruited civilian informers, and were chosen to be young people who "could easily mix with dissident young groups of all races."

Report on Operation Chaos

Johnson, Nixon pressure the CIA. The role of Presidents Johnson and Nixon in applying pressure to the CIA for surveillance of Americans was outlined in a Senate intelligence committee report released May 18 and summarized in the *New York Times* May 19. Operation Chaos, the 1967–1974 domestic surveillance campaign ordered by the two presidents, eventually listed 300,000 A
citizens in a data bank and maintained separate files on 7,500 others. The National Security Agency was instructed by the CIA during that period to collect material from international telephone calls and telegrams "regardless of how innocuous the information may appear." [See Vol. I, pp. 11–13, 17–20, 44–51, 53–56, 140]

"Operation Chaos was not an intelligence mission sought by the CIA," the B
staff report found, but was encouraged by Johnson and Nixon. Richard Helms, then the agency's director, wrote Henry Kissinger in February 1969 to inform Nixon that "this is an area not within the charter of this agency, so I need not emphasize how extremely sensitive this makes the [report on student unrest]. Should anyone learn of its existence, it would prove most embarrassing for all concerned."

C

Karalekas Report

First CIA history released. The Senate Committee released June 6 an authoritative history written by Anne Karalekas which found that the CIA had failed to fulfill several of its goals, according to the *New York Times* June 7. The 95-page report was read and declassified by CIA officials. It is the first complete history of the CIA ever published for the public, al- D
though the agency's history was published for its own use.

Karalekas' conclusion finds that the CIA "responded to rather than anticipated the force of change" over the last 30 years, and "accumulated functions rather than redefining them." The report charges that the CIA did not consistently provide intelligence analysis of a superior quality to government leaders. It cites the agency's surprise by the North Korean at- E
tack on South Korea in 1950. Rather than being the "central" intelligence agency, the CIA never succeeded in coordinating and subordinating the intelligence services of the four armed services. Factors determining the CIA's evolution were the cold war, the inter-service jealousies, and the temptation to seek spectacular "successes" by CIA leadership. The combination led to a concentration on the covert activities to the detriment of intelligence F
analyses.

In 1952, for example, Karalekas reports that clandestine operations accounted for 74 percent of the agency's budget. Clandestine activities took a major share of funds until the late 1950's, when the perceiving of a lessening cold war tensions and budgetary pressures diminished their importance.

Karalekas spent two months studying the agency's own histories, numbering 75 G
volumes, and eight months interviewing 60 CIA officials. Her conclusions, as reported by the *New York Times* June 7, follow:

Text of the Karalekas Report on the CIA

A *Following are excerpts from the Karalekas Report on the Central Intelligence Agency written for the Senate Intelligence Committee. In the text, D.C.I. is the Director of Central Intelligence, D.D.I. is the Directorate for Intelligence, D.D.O. is the Directorate for Operations, and N.S.C. is the National Security Council.*

The C.I.A. was conceived and established to provide high-quality intelligence to senior policymakers. Since 1947 the agency—its structure, its place within the
B Government and its function—has undergone dramatic change and expansion. Sharing characteristics common to most large, complex organizations, the C.I.A. has responded to rather than anticipated the forces of change; it has accumulated functions rather than redefining them; its internal patterns were established early and have solidified; success has come to those who have made visible contributions in high-priority areas. These general characteristics have affected the specifics of the agency's development.

The notion that the C.I.A. could serve as a coordinating body for departmental intelligence activities and that the D.C.I. could orchestrate the process did not take into account the inherent institutional
C obstacles posed by the departments. From the outset no department was willing to concede a centralized intelligence function to the C.I.A. Each insisted on the maintenance of its independent capabilities to support its policy role. With budgetary and management authority vested in the departments, the agency was left powerless in the execution of interdepartmental coordination. Even in the area of coordinated national intelligence estimates the departments did not readily provide the agency with the data required.

It was not until John McCone's term as D.C.I. that the agency aggressively sought to assert its position as a coordinating body. That effort demonstrated the complex factors that determined the relative success of community management. One of the principal
D influences was the support accorded the D.C.I. by the President and the cooperation of the Secretary of Defense. In a situation where the D.C.I. commanded no resources or outright authority, the position of these two individuals was crucial. While Kennedy and McNamara provided McCone with consistent backing in a variety of areas, Nixon and Laird failed to provide Helms with enough support to give him the necessary bureaucratic leverage.

Lack of Coordination

It is clear that the D.C.I.'s own priorities, derived from their backgrounds and interests, influenced the relative success of the agency's role in interdepartmental coordination. Given the limitations on the
E D.C.I.'s authority, only by making community activities a first order concern and by pursuing the problems assertively could a D.C.I. begin to make a difference in effecting better management. During Allen Dulles' term interagency coordination went neglected, and the results were expansion of competing capabilities among the departments. For McCone, community intelligence activities were clearly a priority, and his definition of the D.C.I.'s role contributed to whatever advances were made. Helms' fundamental interests and inclinations lay within the agency, and he did not push his mandate to its possible limits.

The D.C.I.'s basic problems have been competing
F claims on his time and attention and the lack of real authority for the execution of the central intelligence function. As presently defined, the D.C.I.'s job is burdensome in the extreme. He is to serve the roles of chief intelligence adviser to the President, manager of community intelligence activities, and senior executive in the C.I.A. History has demonstrated that the job of the D.C.I. as community manager and as head of the C.I.A. are competing, not complementary roles. In terms of both the demands imposed by each function and the expertise required to fulfill the responsibilities, the two roles differ considerably. In the future separating the functions with precise definitions of authority and responsibilities may prove a plausible alternative.

G Although the agency was established primarily for the purpose of providing intelligence analysis to senior policymakers, within three years clandestine operations became and continued to be the agency's preeminent activity. The single most important factor in the transformation was policymakers' perception of the Soviet Union as a worldwide threat to United States security. The agency's large-scale clandestine activities have mirrored American foreign policy priorities. With political operations in Europe in the 1950's, paramilitary operations in Korea, Third World activities, Cuba, Southeast Asia, and currently narcotics control, the C.I.A.'s major programs paralleled the international concerns of the United States. For nearly two decades American policymakers considered covert action vital in the struggle against international Communism. The generality of the definition or "threat perception" motivated the continual development and justification of covert activities from the senior policymaking level to the field stations. Apart from the overall anti-Communist motivation, successive Presidential administrations regarded covert action as a quick and convenient means of advancing their particular objectives.

Incentive System Criticized

Internal incentives contributed to the expansion in covert action. Within the agency D.D.O. careerists have traditionally been rewarded more quickly for the visible accomplishments of covert action than for the long term development of agents required for clandestine collection. Clandestine activities will remain an element of United States foreign policy, and policymakers will directly affect the level of operations. The prominence of the Clandestine Service within the agency may moderate as money for and high-level executive interest in covert actions diminish. However, D.D.O. incentives which emphasize operations over collection and which create an internal demand for projects will continue to foster covert action unless an internal conversion process forces a change.

In the past the orientation of D.C.I.s such as Dulles and Helms also contributed to the agency's emphasis on clandestine activities. It is no coincidence that of those D.C.I.s who have been Agency careerists, all have come from the Clandestine Service. Except for James Schlesinger's brief appointment, the agency has never been directed by a trained analyst. The qualities demanded of individuals in the D.D.O.—essentially management of people—serve as the basis for bureaucratic skills in the organization. As a result, the agency's leadership has been dominated by D.D.O. careerists.

Clandestine collection and covert action have had their successes, i.e., individual activities have attained their stated objectives. What the relative contribution of clandestine activities has been—the extent to which they have contributed to or detracted from the implementation of United States foreign policy and whether the results have been worth the risk—cannot be evaluated without wide access to records on covert operations, access the committee did not have.

Organizational arrangements within the agency and the decision-making structure outside the agency have permitted the extremes in C.I.A. activity. The ethos of secrecy which pervaded the D.D.O. had the effect of setting the directorate apart within the agency and allowed the Clandestine Service a measure of autonomy not accorded other directorate. More importantly, the compartmentation principle allowed units of the D.D.O. freedom in defining operations. In many cases the burden of responsibility fell on individual judgments—a situation in which lapses and deviations are inevitable. Previous excesses of drug testing, assassination planning and domestic activities were supported by an internal structure that permitted individuals to conduct operations without the consistent necessity or expectation of justifying or revealing their activities.

'Blurred Accountability'

Ultimately, much of the responsibility for the scale of covert action and for whatever abuses occurred must fall to senior policymakers. The decision-making arrangements at the N.S.C. level created an environment of blurred accountability which allowed consideration of actions without the constraints of individual responsibility. Historically the ambiguity and imprecision derived from the initial expectation that covert operations would be limited and therefore could be managed by a small, informal group. Such was the intention in 1948. By 1951 with the impetus of the Korean war, covert action had become a fixed element in the U.S. foreign policy repertoire. The frequency of covert action forced the development of more formalized decision-making arrangements. Yet structural changes did not alter ambiguous procedures. In the late 1950's the relationship between Secretary of State John Foster Dulles and Allen Dulles allowed informal agreements and personal understandings to prevail over explicit and precise decisions. In addition, as the scale of covert action expanded, policymakers found it useful to maintain the ambiguity of the decision-making process to insure secrecy and to allow "plausible deniability" of covert operations.

No one in the executive—least of all the President—was required to formally sign off on a decision to implement a covert action program. The D.C.I. was responsible for the execution of a project but not for taking the decision to implement it. Within the N.S.C. a group of individuals held joint responsibility for defining policy objectives, but they did not attempt to establish criteria placing moral and constitutional limits on activities undertaken to achieve the objectives. Congress has functioned under similar conditions. Within the Congress a handful of committee members passed on the agency's budget. Some members were informed of most of the C.I.A.'s major activities; others preferred not to be informed. The result was twenty-nine years of acquiescence.

At each level of scrutiny in the National Security Council and in the Congress a small group of individuals controlled the approval processes. The restricted number of individuals involved as well as the assumption that their actions would not be subject to outside scrutiny contributed to the scale of covert action and to the development of questionable practices.

Independent Development

The D.D.O. have functioned as separate organizations. They maintain totally independent career tracks and once recruited into one, individuals are rarely posted to the other.

In theory the D.D.O.'s clandestine collection function should have contributed to the D.D.I.'s analytic capacity. However, D.D.O. concerns about maintaining the security of its operations and protecting the identity of its agents, and D.D.I. concerns about measuring the reliability of its sources restricted interchange between the two directorates. Fundamentally, this has deprived the D.D.I. of a major source of information. Although D.D.I.-D.D.O. contact has increased during the last five years, it remains limited.

The D.D.I. has traditionally not been informed of sensitive covert operations undertaken by the D.D.O. This has affected the respective missions of both directorates. The Clandestine Service has not had the benefit of intelligence support during consideration and implementation of its operations. The Bay of Pigs invasion was an instance in which D.D.I. analysts, even the Deputy Director for Intelligence, were uninformed, and represents a situation in which timely analysis of political trends and basic geography might have made a difference—either in the decision to embark on the operation or in the plans for the operation. In the D.D.I., lack of knowledge about operations has complicated and undermined the analytic effort. Information on a C.I.A.-sponsored political action program would affect judgments about the results of a forthcoming election; information provided by a foreign government official would be invaluable in assessing the motives, policies, and dynamics of that government; information on a C.I.A.-sponsored propaganda campaign might alter analyses of the press or public opinion in that country. Essentially, the potential quality of the finished intelligence product suffers.

Duplication a Problem

The agency was created in part to rectify the problem of duplication among the departmental intelligence services. Rather than minimizing the problem the agency has contributed to it by becoming yet another source of intelligence production. Growth in the range of American foreign policy interests and the D.D.I.'s response to additional requirements have resulted in an increased scale of collection and analysis. Today, the C.I.A.'s intelligence products include: current intelligence in such disparate areas as science, economics, politics, strategic affairs and technology; quick response to specific requests from government agencies and officials: basic or long-term research, and national intelligence estimates. With the exception of national intelligence estimates other intelligence organizations engage in overlapping intelligence analysis.

Rather than fulfilling the limited mission in intelligence analysis and coordination for which it was created, the agency became a producer of finished intelligence and consistently expanded its areas of responsibility. In political and strategic intelligence the inadequacy of analysis by the State Department and by the military services allowed the agency to lay claim to the two areas. As the need for specialized research in other subjects developed, the D.D.I. responded—as the only potential source for objective national intelligence. Over time the D.D.I. has addressed itself to a full range of consumers in the broadest number of subject areas. Yet the extent to which the analysis satisfied policymakers' needs and was an integral part of the policy process has been limited.

The size of the D.D.I. and the administrative process involved in the production of finished intelligence—a process which involves numerous stages of drafting and review by large numbers of individuals—precluded close association between policymakers and analysts, between the intelligence product and policy informed by intelligence analysis. Even the national intelligence estimates were relegated to briefing papers for second and third level officials rather than the principal intelligence source for senior policymakers that they were intended to be. Recent efforts to improve the interaction include creating the N.I.O. system and assigning two fulltime analysts on location at the Treasury Department. Yet these changes cannot compensate for the nature of the intelligence production system itself, which employs hundreds of analysts, most of whom have little sustained contact with their consumers.

Reciprocal Relationship

At the Presidential level the D.C.I.'s position is essential to the utilization of intelligence. The D.C.I. must be constantly informed, must press for access, must vigorously sell his product and must anticipate future demands. Those D.C.I.'s who have been most successful in this dimension have been those whose primary identification was not with the D.D.O.

Yet the relationship between intelligence analysis and policymaking is a reciprocal one. Senior policymakers must actively utilize the intelligence capabilities at their disposal. Presidents have looked to the agency more for covert operations than for intelligence analysis. While only the agency could perform covert operations, decision-making methods determined Presidential reliance on the C.I.A.'s intelligence capabilities. Preference for small staffs, individual advisers, the need for specialized information quickly—all of these factors circumscribe a President's channel of information, of which intelligence analysis may be a part. It was John F. Kennedy who largely determined John McCone's relative influence by defining the D.C.I.'s role and by including McCone in the policy process; it was Lyndon Johnson and Richard Nixon who limited the roles of Richard Helms and William Colby. Although in the abstract objectivity may be the most desirable quality in intelligence analysis, objective judgments are frequently not what senior officials want to hear about their policies. In most cases, Presidents are inclined to look to the judgments of individuals they know and trust. Whether or not a D.C.I. is included among them is the President's choice.

Over the past 30 years the United States has developed an institution and a corps of individuals who constitute the U.S. intelligence-profession. The question remains as to how the institution and the individual will best be utilized.

A

B

Report on Kennedy Assassination

CIA, FBI investigation scored. The Senate intelligence committee in its final report published June 23 scored the investigation conducted by the CIA and FBI into President Kennedy's assassination. The 106-page document failed to find new evidence "sufficient to justify a conclusion that there was a conspiracy to assassinate President Kennedy," but criticized the failure of the CIA to probe for a connection between its own assassination attempts against Cuban Premier Fidel Castro and Kennedy's murder in 1963. [See Vol. I, pp. 14, 22–24, 32]

According to excerpts reprinted in the *New York Times* June 24, the report stated, "Senior CIA officials should have realized that their agency was not utilizing its full capability to investigate Oswald's pro-Castro and anti-Castro connections. They should have realized that CIA operations against Cuba, particularly operations involving the assassination of Castro, needed to be considered in the investigation. Yet they directed their subordinates to conduct an investigation without telling them of these vital facts."

The FBI's investigation was characterized: "The FBI conducted its investigation in an atmosphere of concern among senior bureau officials that it would be criticized and its reputation tarnished. Rather than addressing its investigation to all significant circumstances, including all possibilities of conspiracy, the FBI investigation focused narrowly on Lee Harvey Oswald."

The Warren Commission's task to investigate the assassination was severely affected by the shortcomings of the CIA and FBI, the report charged. The Senate committee found the two agencies' motives "still unclear," but suggested several: "concern with public reputation, problems of coordination between agencies, possible bureaucratic failure and embarrassment, and extreme compartmentation of knowledge of sensitive operations."

C

D

REPORT IMPLICATES CIA IN PLOTS TO ASSASSINATE FOREIGN LEADERS

The Senate Select Committee on Intelligence Nov. 20 made public a report that said U.S. government officials had ordered the assassination of two foreign leaders and had been involved in assassination plots against three other foreign officials. Although four of the five leaders were assassinated, none of them died as the direct result of the assassination plans initiated by U.S. officials, the report concluded.

According to the committee's 347-page report, which was released over the opposition of the Ford Administration, Fidel Castro of Cuba and Patrice Lumumba of the Congo (now Zaire) were the targets of death plots originated in Washington. The others—Rafael Leonidas Trujillo of the Dominican Republic, Ngo Dinh Diem of South Vietnam and Gen. Rene Schneider of Chile—died as the result of coups. U.S. officials had encouraged or were at least privy to the plots.

The committee said it was unable to determine if any president had explicitly ordered the death of a foreign leader, but it indicated that available evidence strongly suggested that President Eisenhower had "authorized" the assassination of Lumumba. The report concluded with the recommendation that Congress adopt legislation making it illegal to kill or conspire to kill a foreign leader or politician.

Between 1960 and 1965, the CIA instigated at least eight separate plots against Castro, but none was successful. A box of the Cuban leader's favorite cigars contaminated with botulism toxin was delivered by the CIA to an unidentified person in Cuba in February 1961, but there was apparently no attempt to pass them on to Castro.

CIA action against Congolese leader Patrice Lumumba began in the late spring of 1960 with the discussion of killing an unnamed African leader. In September 1960, Sidney Gottlieb, a CIA scientist, acting on orders from Deputy Director for Plans Richard Bissell, obtained poison and hypodermic needles from Army stockpiles. He flew to Leopoldville (Kinshasha) with instructions for the CIA station officer to kill Lumumba. Members of a rival Congolese faction captured Lumumba Jan. 17, 1961 and subsequently executed him. CIA authorities in Africa later disclaimed any involvement. According to the report, cable traffic showed no CIA link to Lumumba's death.

President Eisenhower in April 1960 approved a contingency plan for the Dominican dictator's removal. The following June, Joseph Farland, U.S. ambassador to the Dominican Republic, agreed to be a link between Dominican dissidents and the CIA. A CIA memorandum dated Oct. 3, 1960 indicated that arms and explosives would be delivered to the dissidents. In March 1961, three .38 caliber pistols were delivered to the U.S. embassy in Santo Domingo in a diplomatic pouch and then passed to the dissidents through an American intermediary. Trujillo was gunned down May 30, 1961.

The Senate Select Committee on Intelligence ended its report, "The committee does not believe that the acts which it has examined represent the real American character.... We regard the assassination plots as aberrations. The United States must not adopt the tactics of the enemy. Means are as important as ends."

THE SPRINGFIELD UNION

Springfield, Mass., November 23, 1975

It shouldn't be necessary for this country to legislate against U. S. complicity in foreign assassinations, but it is. Underscoring that need is the main contribution of the U. S. Senate Committee report that was issued Thursday.

Much of the report was ambiguous, containing indications that former Presidents may or may not have been involved in initiating plots to kill two foreign leaders (unsuccessful in both cases). Nor was it clear whether U. S. participation in actions which were fatal to three other leaders had sanction, or even awareness, at the "top."

But it was quite clear that the CIA was directly involved in the unsuccessful death plots, even though 10,000 pages of testimony to the committee did not firmly establish where the authorization came from. Also, there were various degrees of CIA support in the three killings.

CIA plots against Fidel Castro centered on such devices as "poisonous cigars, exploding seashells and a contaminated diving suit," according to the report. Such tactics are demeaning to the agency and to the country, but exposing them was necessary if they are to be outlawed by legislation.

As the FBI has done within this country, the CIA has ventured far beyond its intelligence mission abroad. The agency has attempted to influence the destiny of other nations—supposedly for the security or the convenience of the United States. In this, the CIA lowered itself to the gangster level—and in fact conspired with the Mafia in plots against Castro.

For a civilized nation—and the United States still has claim to that status—"rubbing out" an unfriendly dictator with poisonous cigars is back-alley stuff, a shoddy substitute for other channels available to a powerful and prestigious nation. Even gunboat diplomacy almost looks good by comparison.

While there is talk of indictment of individuals involved in the assassination plotting, the Justice Department is not certain that existing laws provide a sound basis for prosecution. It is possible no charges will be brought.

As the committee report noted, ". . .there is presently no statue making it a crime to assassinate a foreign official outside the United States." Thus, it was recommended that a law be passed making it a crime for any U.S. official or citizen to conspire, attempt or engage in the assassination of a foreign leader.

Already pending in the Senate is a revision of the federal criminal code that make such activity a felony punishable by seven years in prison. Whatever measure is adopted, it should have enough teeth to deter such transgressions as were exposed by the Senate committee.

Rocky Mountain News

A Scripps-Howard Newspaper Reg. U.S. Pat. Off. Colorado's First Newspaper—Founded in 1859

Denver, Colo., November 24, 1975

ALTHOUGH MUCH of its content has been known for years, the Senate Intelligence Committee's report that U.S. officials had plotted to assassinate foreign leaders still is shocking and disturbing.

For the first time, the committee report formally and publicly acknowledges that the CIA planned to murder Premier Fidel Castro of Cuba and the late Prime Minister Patrice Lumumba of the Congo.

The report also shows the United States supported coups in the Dominican Republic, South Vietnam and Chile that led to the deaths, respectively, of President Rafael Trujillo, President Ngo Dinh Diem and Gen. Rene Schneider.

Fortunately for this nation's conscience, the plots against Castro and Lumumba did not succeed, and there is no evidence that the killings of Trujillo, Diem and Schneider had been planned by U.S. agents.

Two former Presidents, Eisenhower and Kennedy, emerge from the investigation with somewhat tarnished reputations.

While the committee found no absolute proof, it turned up circumstantial evidence that Eisenhower either ordered or knew about the CIA plot to poison Lumumba.

The committee did not directly tie Kennedy to the attempts against Castro's life, and it is doubtful that it tried very hard to do so. Its chairman, Sen. Frank Church, D-Idaho, has presidential ambitions and naturally hopes for the support of Kennedyites in his party.

In any case, the committee was told Kennedy chewed out a CIA official for not "doing anything about getting rid of Castro." Then the CIA repeatedly tried to kill the Cuban leader. Robert Kennedy learned of a CIA-Mafia plot against Castro, and it is inconceivable that he did not inform his brother.

The CIA comes off as a bunch of bunglers, hatching harebrained schemes to get Castro with poisoned cigars and exploding seashells. What is more scary, its bureaucratic momentum was such that it continued to try to kill him after Kennedy changed his mind and began efforts to improve relations with Cuba.

In fairness to the Kennedys and the CIA, their actions should not be judged only in today's context but also in that of the Cold War in the early 1960s. Then Castro was seen as communizing Cuba and turning it into a Soviet missile base that threatened this country.

That may explain Kennedy's desire to liquidate Castro, but it does not justify it nor make it moral nor smart. If the CIA had in fact assassinated Castro, it would not have ended communism in Cuba. He probably would have been succeeded by an orthodox Communist, one more subservient to Moscow.

THE SORDID assassination tale should not be taken as a sign of U.S. depravity, as this country's enemies will try to paint it. Many countries commit similar acts, but this is the only one that honestly investigates its wrongdoings, makes them public and tries to correct them.

President Ford has stated that assassination plotting will not be tolerated in his administration. Good. Even better is the Church committee's call for a law making such conspiring a federal crime, and in the end it is correct in declaring:

"The committee believes that, short of war, assassination is incompatible with American principles, international order and morality."

St. Petersburg Times

St. Petersburg, Fla., November 22, 1975

The report of the Senate Select Committee on Intelligence, containing the gruesome details of CIA plots to assassinate Fidel Castro and other foreign leaders, is now available to readers in the United States and throughout the world.

The accuracy of the report is attested by the fact that it was signed by all 11 members of the committee — six Democrats and five Republicans — and by the meticulous care that was shown in attributing possible, but unproved, knowledge of the assassination attempts to four presidents.

THE QUESTION that many Americans are asking is why it was necessary to spread this horror story on the public record. Or as Secretary of State Henry Kissinger said in another context: why must we continue to torment ourselves daily before the whole world?

President Ford made a last-minute appeal against publication, which was opposed also by three of the five Republican committee members. The full Senate discussed the issue in a four-hour secret session, but made no recommendation.

The reason public release of the report was necessary, we believe, lies in the kind of people we are and the kind of country we have.

The Soviet Union can suppress for a time Alexander Solzhenitsyn's expose of conditions in its political prisons, and exile the author when his book surfaces abroad.

But in an open society such as ours, which depends on the consent of the governed, the people have not only a right but a need to know what their government is doing.

COMMITTEE chairman Frank Church, D-Idaho, expressed this point of view succinctly in saying that the report "reaffirms our belief in the ability of our system of government to purge and correct itself."

The Senate report itself concludes with these words:

"The committee does not believe that the acts which it has examined represent the real American character. They do not reflect the ideals which have given the people of this country and of the world hope for a better, fuller, fairer life. We regard the assassination plots as aberrations.

"The United States must not adopt the tactics of the enemy. Means are as important as ends. Crisis makes it tempting to ignore the wise restraints that make men free. But each time we do so, each time the means we use are wrong, our inner strength, the strength which makes us free, is lessened."

THE QUESTION remains of what action should follow the committee's disclosures. The evidence that was gathered points to the direct complicity of certain top officials and area directors of the CIA and some underworld figures they recruited. The Department of Justice is examining whether these individuals should or can be prosecuted. The Cold War stresses of the period, and the implied approval of the government itself must figure in that decision.

The committee is proposing legislation that would make it unlawful for anyone "subject to the jurisdiction of the United States," and specifically including government officials acting under orders, to conspire, attempt, or actually to kill a foreign leader. Passage of such legislation is clearly indicated.

Beyond that, public disclosure and condemnation by the American people of the actions documented in the Senate committee's report will serve as a strong deterrent to their repetition.

The Sun Reporter

San Francisco, Calif., November 29, 1975

With the recent publication of the official report from the congressional committee charged with investigating the Central Intelligence Agency, Americans can no longer doubt that the CIA engaged in practices of subversion against other sovereign powers, including the ultimate subversive activity, plotting the assassination of political leaders.

Many Americans will not be shocked by these revelations. Now we have evidence about the way our government has conducted our business. While this should be a shameful and anxious period for us, we hope that our government will take the necessary actions to insure that such methods will not be tolerated and that no nation need fear such secret, shady activities of the world's most powerful nation.

Our congressmen must understand that the wrist-slapping and singling out of scapegoats for token punishment is not enough to remedy this threat. Technically speaking, we are dealing with relatively minor abuses, such as failing to report accurately on various activities and, at the worst, attempted murder. Yet, the Watergate crimes of the Nixon Administration were minor legal matters as well. What counts is the abusive, totalitarian spirit in which these heinous schemes were conceived and carried out. Clearly, the CIA was engaged in activities which are the very antithesis of a democracy, a society of free people.

The Central Intelligence Agency evolved from an information gathering source established after World War II to respond to America's new world leadership role, but the CIA evolved into a monster whose very existence mandates that its activities go unseen and consequently uncontrolled. Thus merely ordering the CIA to stop plotting to assassinate political leaders is not enough. The problem has to be attacked at its roots, the CIA must be immediately and permanently disbanded, and we must resist the urge to establish a new bureau in its place, for no matter what high principles it is founded on, or what tight controls are enforced on it, sooner or later, a new agency is bound to get out of hand.

A world without the CIA will be a world in which the average American will be able to hold his or her head just a little bit higher, knowing that the government is no longer preparing to strike in the night against some unsuspecting leader or state. But it will also be a world which harbors greater security for Americans and the freedoms which we cherish.

If our government could countenance such foreign operations by the CIA, could the CIA not just as easily unleash these same subversive forces in our country? The congress must make rapid and decisive use of the knowledge gained by its committees to destroy this possibility forever.

THE DALLAS TIMES HERALD

Dallas, Tex., November 23, 1975

THE ISSUE: Senate publication of the recent history of the CIA's involvement in assassination plots against foreign officials.

THE CONGRESS of the United States has laid bare the record of the Central Intelligence Agency and it must be found incompatible with American morality and national security needs.

We agree with Texas Sen. John Tower, co-chairman of the Senate Select Committee on Intelligence, when he condemns the past practice of the CIA in plotting assassinations with or without the knowledge of the President.

The unprecedented 347-page report, made public after a rare secret session of the entire Senate, became a controversy in the Senate over whether the findings should be made public.

Sen. Tower, while endorsing the report, did oppose making it public. President Ford's administration sought to suppress the document.

There is room for argument that the Senate should have deleted more names of intelligence agents in order to protect them. Many names were deleted but it was insisted that those whose names remained were well-known and central figures in the development of a questionable policy.

The extent of the CIA's activities have been known for years in some foreign countries, activities consistently denied by our government in playing the international spying game.

But when those activities include assassination attempts or plots to overthrow a foreign government, American citizens have a right to know the extent of the CIA's mission.

The issues that the Senate CIA report raise not only include the immorality of trying to murder foreign officials but whether such a policy by the world's leading democracy sanctions international assassination by any government.

As the late President Kennedy once said, engaging in assassinations abroad also makes American government officials targets of revenge-minded governments.

We can not kill outside of war and then condemn others for doing the same thing. Congress should accept the report's recommendation that laws be passed to make foreign assassination outside of war a crime for American citizens.

The CIA report also raises the issue of whether the CIA has been so enthralled in cloak and dagger plotting, badly bungled and futile in known cases, that it has neglected its primary mission of providing accurate and timely intelligence for American security.

THE ROANOKE TIMES

Roanoke, Va., November 25, 1975

There is no use pretending that a lot of dirty things don't go on under the cloak of intelligence-gathering abroad. Agents of many nations—certainly of all the superpowers—are spending money and fostering activities on-scene to try to influence events and policy in other countries where their interests are at stake.

Sometimes, especially when opposing agents work at cross purposes, there are attempts to kill or maim one another; conflicts like this may be unavoidable. Even before the CIA's guts began to spill over congressional conference tables, it would have been insufferably prissy to claim that U.S. agents are never involved in such as this.

But no matter what other nations do, it should simply be out of the question for the United States to plot peacetime assassinations of heads of state or other key political figures in foreign countries. To strike at a chief of state is to aim at the underbelly of an entire people, to try to upset their country's political stability, to set off a chain of events that could produce civil war or even war with a neighbor.

The consequences of such actions cannot be predicted or controlled. It is callous and arrogant for a great power—especially one that makes much of its own morality—to consider throwing a smaller, weaker country into turmoil on the chance that this would somehow advance our own interests.

More than that, such tactics can boomerang. A nation that is willing to slash at another's political jugular had better protect its own throat. A pattern of events can create a climate of international violence and intrigue, similar to the climate Americans seem to be experiencing at home as a presidential campaign nears, but a lot more dangerous.

Amid the shame that U.S. citizens should feel about the Central Intelligence Agency's immoral and reckless tactics, there is one gratification. No other nation, surely, would openly own up to such misdeeds. Some will consider that our weakness. Not so; it is our strength, this ability to conduct a more open society and government than any other country ever has. It is a tradition that allows us to drag error into the open, the better to correct it—as these CIA tactics must now be corrected.

Wisconsin State Journal

Madison, Wisc., November 25, 1975

Murder has been accepted as a foreign policy tool by the Central Intelligence Agency and, possibly four United States presidents.

That is the shocking conclusion of the Senate Intelligence Committee after an extensive investigation of the activities of the nation's huge spy apparatus.

The committee reported that the CIA tried unsuccessfully to kill Cuban Premier Fidel Castro and Congo Premier Patrice Lumumba.

It also reported that the CIA supplied arms to insurgents who—acting on their own—killed South Vietnamese President Ngo Dinh Diem, Dominican Republic dictator Rafael Trujillo and Chilean Gen. Rene Schneider.

In addition, the committee said it found evidence of CIA involvement in plans to assassinate President Sukarno of Indonesia and dictator Francois (Papa Doc) Duvalier of Haiti.

This deplorable activity was undertaken during the administrations of Presidents Eisenhower, Kennedy, Johnson and Nixon.

Although the committee found no hard evidence that these presidents authorized or knew of the plots, its report said they "should have known of them if they did not" and that they held "ultimate responsibility" for them as commanders in chief.

As distasteful as these revelations are, one can take heart in the demonstration that the American system, although far too belatedly, found out about them and presumably put an end to such activity.

The committee is to be commended for its investigation and for making its findings public over objections of the Ford Administration.

Only if the excesses of our government agencies are exposed can the public be assured that they will not be tolerated in the future.

The committee has suggested a law making it a criminal offense to conspire or attempt to carry out the assassination of a foreign official.

"'The committee believes that short of war, assassination is incompatible with American principles, international order and morality. It should be rejected as a tool of foreign policy."

That such a law and declaration should be necessary in a presumably civilized country is a depressing indictment of our society. The fact that they are needed, however, is apparent.

The Des Moines Register

Des Moines, Iowa, November 22, 1975

The report on assassination plots issued by the Senate Committee on Intelligence indicates that the Central Intelligence Agency (CIA) did not kill any foreign leaders — but not because the agency didn't try.

The CIA — and perhaps Presidents Dwight Eisenhower and John Kennedy — plotted to assassinate Congolese Premier Patrice Lumumba and Cuban Premier Fidel Castro. The CIA sent poisons to the Congo to be administered to Lumumba, but there is no evidence of direct U.S. involvement in Lumumba's eventual death at the hands of his Congolese enemies.

The CIA came up with bizarre plot after bizarre plot to eliminate Castro. It even recruited underworld figures, who were thought needed for their criminal skills and contacts.

The CIA operatives, with their double-knit cloaks and their miniaturized-transistorized daggers, presented quite a picture to the Mafia types. The outlandish and ludicrous ideas pursued by the CIA — including the use of poison cigars, exploding seashells, contaminated diving suits, not to mention the poison pills, that, alas, would not dissolve in water, and the irritating though not fatal substance to be sprayed on Castro's shoes that would make the hair in his beard fall out — must have astonished these men experienced in simpler and more direct methods of murder.

The CIA offered encouragement or was privy to plots which led to the assassinations of Rafael Trujillo in the Dominican Republic, Ngo Dinh Diem in South Vietnam and Gen. Rene Schneider in Chile. The agency's guilt in these cases is of omission rather than commission. It could have informed these officials of the plots against their lives. U.S. officials, for example, did inform Archbishop Makarios of Cyprus of plans for an assassination attempt which took place in 1970.

The Senate committee report recommends making assassinations or attempted assassinations of foreign officials by U.S. nationals a criminal offense. This would serve to punish the guilty in future assassination plotting.

Unfortunately, there may be no way to hold accountable those involved in past plots. The use of euphemism and circumlocution in oral and written contacts between officials, and the much-practiced principle of "plausible denial," have prevented the committee from pointing, with reasonable assurance, the finger of guilt at any particular president or CIA official.

This reprehensible activity by the CIA should move Congress and the public to demand an effective reform and restructuring of the agency. A first move ought to be to purge the agency leadership of representatives of its covert action sector (who always have dominated the CIA's high offices), and to replace them with representatives of its more functional and more valuable intelligence-gathering sector.

Assassination is the ultimate dirty trick. The CIA was able to become a sort of Murder, Inc., because it operated in secret and Congress abdicated its responsibility to check on the agency. Only now, nearly 30 years after the CIA was established, is Congress subjecting it to scrutiny.

The Senate is to be commended for resisting Ford administration demands for secrecy and making the assassination report public. The report is a chilling reminder to Americans of what can happen when they too readily accept "national security" justifications for secrecy and exempt a government agency from the controls a democratic government requires.

THE DAILY HERALD

Biloxi, Miss., November 24, 1975

Americans can be thankful that the best laid schemes of mice and men do sometimes go astray.

The Senate Intelligence Committee report on Central Intelligence Agency activities released last week was chilling.

The committee "found concrete evidence of at least eight plots involving the CIA to assassinate Fidel Castro from 1960 to 1965" using a variety of devices which "ran the gamut from highly-powered rifles to poison pills, poison pens, deadly bacterial powders and other devices which strain the imagination."

The eleven member panel headed by Sen. Frank Church, D-Idaho, also said it came across evidence of CIA involvement in plans to assassinate President Sukarno of Indonesia, Patrice Lumumba of the Belgian Congo and "Papa Doc" Duvalier of Haiti.

The U.S. government was also "implicated" in the 1961 assassination of Dominican strongman Rafael Trujillo and was reportedly aware of plots against South Vietnamese president Ngo Dinh Diem and Chilean army chief Rene Schneider in which the "risk of death" existed, the committee said.

All of these men are dead with the exception of Castro, although the Senate panel concluded that "no foreign leaders were killed as a result of assassination plots initiated by officials of the United States.

The committee's 346-page report, still incomplete after six months of investigation, was made public over objections from the President who wrote Senate leaders that publication would not be in the national interest.

Neither were the assassination plots.

In November of 1963 when an emissary of then-President Kennedy was meeting with Fidel Castro to explore the possibility of improved relations, a CIA official offered a poison pen to a Cuban to use against Castro.

The plots are a direct contradiction of the stated American policy of non-interference in the internal affairs of another nation.

And although the CIA's charter expressly forbids the agency from carrying out most domestic forms of police action, the Senate Select Committee on Intelligence is investigating the possibility that the CIA arranged for a hit-and-run murder in New Orleans during the late 1950's or early 1960.

The transgressions documented thus far of both the CIA and the FBI may well be "aberrations" of the American way of life, although we suspect not of government.

It's obvious that the principles this Republic prides itself on have been weakened.

THE MILWAUKEE JOURNAL

Milwaukee, Wisc., November 24, 1975

For the second time in a week, congressional revelations have confirmed grievous misdeeds reported earlier in broad outline and have fleshed out the sordid details. First it was facts about FBI domestic activities; now it is data on CIA complicity in planning and attempting the assassinations of foreign leaders. It is not a proud day for those Americans who hold the rule of law dear and see it as the foundation of our freedoms.

The CIA revelations were particularly revolting. It was not a case of an isolated instance where the CIA faltered or erred in judgment. Instead it was a case of systematic planning, involving the proposed killing of at least two foreign leaders, and complicity in or awareness of plans that led to the deaths of three more.

These plans were not the result of the work of one misguided individual. They were efforts that involved a succession of administrations, from Presidents Eisenhower through Nixon, and high officials in them. There is evidence to suggest that at least one president — Eisenhower — may have actually approved the plan to kill Congolese leader Patrice Lumumba.

Top CIA officials during these years not only initiated these plans, but at times indulged in evasion or possibly outright falsehood in failing to keep their superiors, including presidents, informed. The intelligence agency even worked with organized crime in order to try and assassinate Cuba's Fidel Castro.

It is little solace knowing that none of these specific plans was actually carried out — though four of the foreign leaders targeted eventually died violent deaths. What is shocking is the fact that such acts in peacetime were actually contemplated, for such activities show the US no better than the most common, lowly dictatorship, which coldly and callously holds that the end justifies the means.

If the US has anything to offer the world, it is that it is a moral, democratic society that believes in law. The CIA's assassination activities are a profound corruption of these very fundamental principles. As the Senate committee making the report noted, in reference to the CIA's dealing with the Mafia: "The spectacle of the government consorting with criminal elements destroys respect for government and law and undermines the viability of democratic institutions."

President Ford has stated that he has ordered an end to such activities. But, as the Senate committee making the CIA investigation said, that is not enough. Specific legislation ought to be passed prohibiting, once and for all, assassination as a tool of policy. The revelations also underscore again the lack of adequate oversight of CIA operations both by the executive and legislative branches. This must be remedied. And if penalties don't exist now, they should be instituted, so that government officials, both in and out of the CIA, cannot knowingly withhold information of this kind from those who should be informed.

The Philadelphia Inquirer

Philadelphia, Pa., November 23, 1975

Last week was one of agonizing exposure of the depths of immorality and illegality into which high and powerful American government officials have wallowed in the last 15 years and more both at home and abroad, all in the ostensible service of some greater good.

Considering those revelations and their dismaying impact, it is first of all important to judge the wisdom of their public disclosure.

To that, we believe the only answer —and the right answer—is of two elements:

• If misdeeds are hidden, it is inevitable that their repetition will be encouraged. The only effective future deterrence is through public disclosure and action.

• If the national self-confidence, the American system of laws and government and ultimately the Constitutional process were fatally vulnerable to such disclosure, then the entire American system of government would have to be found a deceitful farce.

Profoundly, we do not believe it is. On with the debate.

The Senate Intelligence Committee's 347-page report on involvement in assassination plots by the CIA and other U. S. officials was the first time a formal government body has established that murder—or contemplation of murder—had become an element of U. S. foreign policy. It found that the American government had instigated assassination plots against Patrice Lumumba of The Congo and Fidel Castro and had become involved in death plots against Ngo Dinh Diem, Rafael Trujillo of the Dominican Republic and Gen. Rene Schneider of Chile.

No firm evidence was found that the plots succeeded, although all of the five except Premier Castro died—violently. There is substantial truth in the bitterly ironic observation of Sen. Walter Mondale, Minnesota Democrat and committee member: "It shows above all that Americans are no good at all at killing, lying and covering up, and I'm glad that's the case."

The effectiveness of Americans in carrying out perfidy, however, is not the test of the issue.

The central issue, rather, is whether America will permit, at any level of its government, official planning or perpetration of murderous or otherwise fundamentally immoral acts against the leaders or citizens of other nations.

The answer must be no.

Who was responsible? The committee report could not lay a murder weapon on the desk of any president, although it came closest with President Eisenhower in ascribing to him somewhat ambiguous approval of the Lumumba plot. But in actuality, not only Mr. Eisenhower but also Presidents Kennedy, Johnson and Nixon were found guilty by circumstantial evidence at least of sins of omission in failing to prevent the plots.

Great numbers of subordinate officials in each of those administrations were, of course, involved—by act or by omission. "The committee finds," the report said, "that the system of executive command and control was so inherently ambiguous that it is difficult to be certain at what level assassination activity was known and authorized."

That ambiguity, the committee report found, had two effects: The plots may have gone on beyond the control of the President; the lines of responsibility may have been kept intentionally foggy to save Presidents or others from being held accountable.

Whichever, or both, may be true, the conclusions are clear.

The committee has a responsibility to draft, and the administration and the full Congress have a responsibility to support and to implement a system of inescapable, accountable responsibility.

Under it, no American president and no American official involved with secret intelligence operations ever again should be able to evade, or believe he may be able to evade, responsibility for the clandestine acts of government.

DESERET NEWS

Salt Lake City, Utah,

November 22, 1975

The Central Intelligence Agency cannot be condemned too strongly for having allowed itself to become involved in assassination plots against various foreign leaders over the years.

By seeking to resort to murder as an instrument of foreign policy, the CIA has in effect put the U.S. at war against other nations without even so much as the knowledge of our elected representatives, let alone the formal declaration of hostilities that is constitutionally required.

By employing the methods of ordinary gangsters, the CIA has eroded this nation's claim to moral superiority over its enemies and made it considerably harder for the U.S. to win friends among the uncommitted countries.

Likewise, by reducing power politics to its most base level, the CIA has in effect invited others to respond in kind in their dealings with us.

Granted that many of America's enemies made violence a tool of foreign policy long before the CIA became embroiled in the assassination plots that were disclosed this week by the Senate Intelligence Committee.

But a country with America's traditions and heritage simply cannot employ the same tactics without a supreme act of hypocrisy and without impairing some of the very democratic institutions the CIA is supposed to help defend.

In this whole sorry affair there are but few saving elements and they offer little comfort to Americans who want to remain proud of their country.

Even those who dug hardest to uncover the CIA's wrong-doing concede that these episodes are an aberration, not a reflection of America's true national character.

That no foreign leaders were killed as a direct result of assassination plots by U.S. officials may be no more than a testimony to CIA ineptitude. But also consider the possibility that these plots didn't succeed because the U.S. has not become as callous and closed as the hard and cynical nations which do well at foreign intrigue.

Indeed, the very fact the U.S. is washing its dirty laundry in public testifies to Washington's sincerity in wanting to avoid any repetition of such plots as those in Cuba, the Congo, Vietnam, and the Dominican Republic.

But sorrow and repentance, by themselves, are not enough. Neither is the new law that is being proposed to fill a gap in existing statutes by making it a crime to assassinate a foreign official outside the United States. Good intentions must be backed up by specific procedures for assuring that a nation at peace never lets assassination become a permissible tool of foreign policy. Such procedures must inevitably involve increased scrutiny by Congress of U.S. intelligence operations.

Human nature being what it is, the greater the power one has, the greater is the risk of that power eventually being abused.

Few agencies have greater power and authority than the CIA. Few need to be watched more closely.

CHICAGO Sun-Times

Chicago, Ill., November 22, 1975

Some of the contents of the Senate intelligence committee's report on political assassination plots had been anticipated. Yet nothing could really soften the shame or the pain that the report produced when it was officially released Thursday. In sober, measured detail, the report portrays a dimension of U.S. government policy that flies in the face of the democratic principles this country has publicly championed for nearly 200 years.

The 347-page report disclosed that U.S. officials instigated at least eight schemes to murder Cuban Prime Minister Fidel Castro. There was one plan to murder Congo Prime Minister Patrice Lumumba. The U.S. government also was "implicated" in the 1961 assassination of Dominican Republic leader Rafael Trujillo and was aware of coup plots against South Vietnamese President Ngo Dinh Diem and Chilean army Gen. Rene Schneider, the report said.

Particularly chilling was a Central Intelligence Agency official's description of an agent who had been considered for the job of killing Lumumba. The agent, code-named WI/ROGUE, "is indeed aware of the precepts of right and wrong, but if he is given an assignment which may be morally wrong in the eyes of the world, but necessary because his case officer ordered him to carry it out, then it is right, and he will dutifully undertake appropriate action for its execution without pangs of conscience. In a word, he can rationalize all actions."

That is the kind of agent the Nazi SS used to recruit. What does it say about the United States if its leaders have considered such persons as agents of official policy?

The committee found it difficult to determine whether any U.S. President had specifically ordered an assassination, partly because the process of executive command was so ambiguous. Assessing presidential involvement in murders is an important item of unfinished business.

The possibility of perjury before congressional committees also requires exploration. The Senate committee report said former President Richard M. Nixon ordered a political espionage campaign in Chile in 1970, even though U.S. officials later told Congress this country had a hands-off policy there.

Some of these investigations will take time. One action that can be taken promptly is a law banning assassinations except in wartime. That is the very least this country can do to rehabilitate its credibility and its soul.

The Washington Star

Washington, D.C., November 22, 1975

The interim report of Senator Church's select committee on intelligence, "Alleged Assassination Plots Involving Foreign Leaders," probably will do us harm abroad, as President Ford has said. It will be "exploited...to do maximum damage to the reputation and foreign policy of the United States."

A number of senators must agree with Mr. Ford, yet they chose not to suppress this sordid report. Why?

Perhaps some of them feel that it would be inappropriate for the United States to doctor or embroider its official record. Amerians have no "official" history, in the totalitarian sense. You can't imagine a report so injurious issuing from the Kremlin or the Winter Palace, but the contrast is not altogether unfavorable to American custom.

Even when a free society tries hard to hide discreditable truths about the past, the effort often fails. Someone tells. So maybe it is better to have the full story, carefully told and evaluated, than to have the bits and pieces of old skele tons falling out of the closet one by one.

These, however, are mainly tactical considerations. What we need to digest are the long-term lessons, which are often dull.

Nothing is duller, for instance, than perspective. Assassination as an instrument of policy did not originate in the U. S. nor with the CIA. The exceptional thing about the plots against Lumumba, Allende, Castro and Trujillo — none of which panned out — is that they were aimed at foreign leaders in "peacetime." We view it as unsporting perhaps, but not morally repugnant in quite the same way, that this country successfully plotted to intercept and shoot down a plane carrying the Japanese general, Yamamoto, who had commanded the attack on Pearl Harbor. That was in "wartime." In our age, the distinction is not always easy to make. In the years covered by the report, many of the accustomed differences between war and peace had collapsed.

What we have here, accordingly, is a manifestation of that doctrine called "globalism" — a doctrine having at its base the notion that vital American interests were imperiled by a crumbling colonial order in the Congo, or a Caribbean dictatorship, or the alignment of an offshore island with the communist bloc. American interest in the world was a seamless whole. Globalism involved, further, an illusion that with the right plans and tricks we would seize history by the throat and exert control over distant events, however petty.

The Senate report must be seen not only as a comment on the perils and follies of globalism, but as a scalding self-indictment by Congress, which makes the laws and handles the money.

One can't expect Congress to rise above the prevailing standard of judgment and ethics at large, and Congress in the Fifties and Sixties was as much under the spell of globalism as the rest of us. What we *can* expect is that Congress rise *to* the prevailing level of judgment and morality, which probably would have condemned the assassination of foreign heads of state. Certainly Congress ought to exceed its constituency in vigilance. One can expect Congress to know more and do more, when it's timely, about the secret projects of creature agencies than Congress knew or did in this period about the CIA. Executive secrecy was involved; but Congress has ways of penetrating that veil when it wishes. And in the present case, exposure came too long after the fact.

In a recent *Columbia Journalism Review* article, reprinted in *The Star* last Sunday, former Sen. J. William Fulbright had some wise observations about the present national mood of revelation and self-flagellation. Of these, perhaps the wisest was that as we open the old closets full of dusty skeletons we tend to dwell on the sensational facts and give "short shrift to the policy questions."

The policy questions raised by the Church committee report may be too obvious to need dwelling on. Some are questions of proper administrative procedure — for instance the unchecked capacity of a President to overbear the cautions of the professionals, as Mr. Nixon did in his design against Allende. Others are broader: Can a democracy be much good at cloak and dagger stuff? Do these operations, even when they succeed, sufficiently affect events or American interests to justify the risks and opprobrium? Can Congress give the CIA the discretion it needs and also protect the country and the country's good name against its blunders and abuses? These questions may be dull, but they beat poisoned cigars in ultimate importance.

CHICAGO DAILY NEWS

Chicago, Ill.,
November 22, 1975

Congress should, of course, give serious thought to the Senate Intelligence Committee's recommendation for a law making it a crime to conspire to assassinate a foreign official. But unfortunately, no law can be passed to spare the nation from the embarrassment wrought by the Central Intelligence Agency in its series of grim but luckily hamhanded forays into the assassination business.

What can be said of an agency that sets out to eliminate Cuba's Fidel Castro in a sequence of eight separate plans involving poison pills (twice), poison cigars, an explosive seashell, a skindiver's suit laced with tuberculosis germs, and a depilatory to make his beard fall out? Only that it's a good thing they all petered out, or the nation would have been in even worse repute than it now is.

But we would hope that a great deal more will be revealed as to who really set in motion these plots to kill Castro, Patrice Lumumba of the Congo, Rafael Trujillo of the Dominican Republic, President Sukarno of Indonesia, "Papa Doc" Duvalier of Haiti, Gen. Rene Schneider of Chile, and for all we know, others.

What the committee actually brought to light is astonishing enough. Such as the strong chain of evidence suggesting that the plot to kill Lumumba was authorized by President Eisenhower. As a matter of fact, the report holds Eisenhower, John F. Kennedy and Lyndon B. Johnson all derelict in their duties for failing to prevent "such undesired acts from taking place." In short, the conduct of foreign affairs by assassination has been an accepted practice over the past 20 years.

Even acknowledging that assassination was not invented in the United States, and that similar plotting may go on in other world capitals, the practice is totally inconsistent with everything the United States seeks to stand for in the world, and so monstrously self-defeating that it should long since have been ruled out utterly as a potential instrument of policy.

But again — as the committee perceived — no mere law will be sufficient to ensure that the practice will not be revived.

The committee said it "does not believe that the acts which it has examined represent the real American character;" that the assassination plots were "aberrations." Perhaps so. But a pattern extending across two decades and three administrations is something more than transitory. The American people had best make plain to their leaders what they consider the limits of decent global behavior. Otherwise the last shreds of our credibility may disappear.

The Morning Star

Rockford, Ill., November 24, 1975

In a frenzy of war patriotism in 1941, we in the U.S. called it "infamous" when Japanese emissaries were in U.S. State Department offices talking peace at the very moment the military forces of Japan were launching their attack on Pearl Harbor.

Yet, on Nov. 22, 1963, a U.S. Central Intelligence Agency (CIA) operative offered a poison pen to a Cuban for use against Fidel Castro at the very moment emissaries of President John F. Kennedy were with Castro exploring the possibilities of improved relationships between the U.S. and Cuba.

This is only one of many shocking revelations in the 346-page report just issued by the U.S. Senate Intelligence Committee.

The report of the committee headed by Sen. Frank Church, D-Idaho, uncloaked almost-fantastic CIA plans for assassinations and murders all over the globe.

Sen. Church's report was made public despite efforts of the Ford Administration to keep it under wraps.

And it's a good thing for the nation that the secrecy attempts were frustrated by the Senate committee.

It is secrecy over a long period of years—death plots detailed by the committee date back to 1960—that made the unholy mess possible in the first place.

Conscientious Americans would not stand still for death plots fostered by the government in peacetime if they knew about them. And they will not stand for them now.

So it is in the revealing of these plots and other CIA and spy intrigues that the remedy lies. Sunshine is good medicine for floundering official morality.

The Senate committee deserves the nation's thanks for revealing the sordid details. Knowing how our true principles were compromised before will fire our determination to not let it happen again.

THE PLAIN DEALER

Cleveland, Ohio, November 22, 1975

President Ford has promised, through his press secretary, to produce a plan that will prevent U.S. involvement in plots to kill foreign leaders.

It had better be a good one.

For reasons both moral and pragmatic, involvement in assassination schemes over more than two decades has disgraced the U.S. government in general and the CIA in particular.

As reported by the Senate Intelligence Committee, these plots have been entered with scant regard for moral principle or practical consequence. They have betrayed the declared goals of U.S. foreign policy. They have sheltered American criminals and imitated the police-state terrorism of the nation's adversaries.

They have rested on assumptions of a degree of control over other nations and their internal factions which the United States did not have and should not have.

On top of everything else, the Senate investigators concluded that none of the plots worked, though three foreign leaders did die as the result of coups initiated by this country.

In the words of former CIA Director Richard Helms, testifying before the committee. "When you go into the record, you find a lot of nutty schemes. . ."

The committee proposed that it be made a criminal act for an American to try to kill a foreign official in peacetime outside the United States. This would have the merit of clearly stating U.S. policy, which apparently was not at all clear to the numerous actors who flit through the committee's report.

But it will do little good if the lines of responsibility and accountability remain as foggy as they have been in the past. The Senate committee report shows inadequate control of the CIA by the White House and "an apparent lack of accountability in the command and control system."

Further, says the report, "Practices current at the time in which the assassination plots occurred were revealed by the record to create the risk of confusion, rashness and irresponsibility in the very areas where clarity and sober judgment were most necessary."

The White House stands in the committee report as a dismal failure in overseeing the CIA. The Rockefeller Commission's report on the CIA can be seen now as woefully incomplete.

Our belief has always been that a great deal more could be expected from the Senate, and this belief has been partly confirmed. The true test will be how much the Senate and House demand from Mr. Ford in specific plans for the future governance of the CIA and other U.S. intelligence forces.

HOUSTON CHRONICLE

Houston, Tex., November 24, 1975

Assassination should not be an instrument of U.S. foreign policy in peacetime.

President Ford has forbidden assassinations and CIA Director William Colby has issued the same orders.

If any previous president issued such an order, it certainly is unpublicized. The incredible thing is that such an order is necessary now.

How did this nation slip into a framework which has made it necessary for the President to forbid peacetime assassinations? That is one of the key questions posed by a report released by the Senate Intelligence Committee.

The report states that the use of assassination except in wartime is "incompatible with the American principles, international order and morality." It declared: "We regard the assassination plots as aberrations."

Those statements are true enough, except that when a deviation from moral standards extends through the terms of three presidents, it indicates that perhaps the standards themselves were under heavy assault.

The origins of the Central Intelligence Agency have much to do with the fact the plots were conceived. The CIA was an outgrowth of World War II, its members trained in wartime and its leaders conditioned to wartime thinking. The war ended, but not in every sense at the CIA, which was still dealing with cold war conflict on a global scale.

In addition, public attitudes then were not the same as they are today, and it is possible that popular expressions of fear and hatred could have been misread by CIA officials as encouragement for their adventuring. The climate was an unhealthy one.

The Senate report is a shocker, confirming as it does officially reports that have been circulating for months. President Ford opposed release of the document on grounds that the disclosures would not be in the national interest, and it obviously does do damage to the American image. But the controversy over release of the information should not be allowed to distract from the basic flaws, the plots themselves and the conditions that allowed them to originate. We doubt seriously if the reputation of the CIA overseas could be lower than it already is.

Attention must now be turned to ways to prevent such "aberrations" in the future.

If government agencies are not to go off on adventures of their own, our elected representatives are going to have to hold a tighter set of reins. And if our cherished American principles are to prevail, they must receive constant reinforcement against assault.

Congress can pass a law to cure the first problem; the second is up to everyone.

THE KNICKERBOCKER NEWS

*** UNION-STAR ***

Albany, N.Y., November 24, 1975

A Senate committee has revealed that the United States, through the Central Intelligence Agency, has either plotted or attempted to murder:

Fidel Castro, the Cuban dictator

Raphael Trujillo, dictator of the Dominican Republic

Patrice Lumumba, prime minister of the Congo, now known as Zaire

Ngo Dinh Diem, once president of South Vietnam

Gen. Rene Schneider Chereu, non-political military leader of Chile.

Of these five, all but Castro died at the hands of assassins, although there is no evidence that the deaths resulted from any assassination plots of the United States.

Another man who died of by violence was President Salvador Allende Gossens of Chile. While there is no evidence that the United States had marked him as an assassination victim, the evidence is abundant that it financed his political opponents.

There is a black comedy element in the attempts to assassinate Castro. Some of the plots were directly out of the old-time pulp magazines or the slick operations of James Bond, better known at 007. Nor did CIA hesitate to add to the soil on it hands by seeking to enlist the aid of mobsters. The mobsters proved as inefficient as the agency.

There were many effort made to block the report of the Senate committee, particularly on the ground that it would make our foreign relations more difficult. It is doubtful if the there is much in the report that was secret from foreign intelligence agencies.

Quite plainly, the report reveals that several governments of the United States acted with gross immorality. There is no other word for it.

But note well what the Senate committee says in an epilogue to its report:

" The committtee does not believe that the acts which it has examined represent the real American character. They do not reflect the ideals which have given the people of the country and of the world hope for a better, fuller, fairer life. We regard the assassination plots as aberrations."

Pray, God, no more such aberrations.

DAYTON DAILY NEWS

Dayton, Ohio, November 23, 1975

Americans should not pretend to be shocked by the details the Senate committee has released about official plots to assassinate foreign leaders. We have never before known the details — and they are sordid and ludicrous in the extreme — but we have known that American policy has at times meant interfering in the internal affairs of other countries and trying to bring down their governments.

A sudden change of government in most of those countries meant that the deposed leaders would die. The U.S. government knew that. The American people knew that. We just didn't like to talk about it.

It is little short of incredible that we can talk about it now — what other country's government would even consider it? — and there is reason to feel a little consolation in that.

But what must be faced is the whole question of whether the United States ought to fool around in other countries, bribing politicians, financing dissident groups, encouraging the military to revolt, or sending in Mafia hitmen or CIA agents with the minds of 10-year-olds to kill people. The question is both moral and practical.

It is easy — a bit too easy — to piously say that nations should never undertake nasty, even immoral, acts. International affairs has never been a pretty business and likely never will be. A government's prime responsibility is not to be nice but to protect its own people. But assassinations and plots likely to lead to assassinations are clearly out of bounds, particularly for a country that has always prided itself on its supposed moral superiority.

The less important argument, but the one more pertinent to national leaders, alas, is that dirty tricks and murder are extremely risky tactically and politically and that even if they succeed, the success is likely to be short-lived in countries which change their governments the way some people change clothes.

Legitimate fears of Soviet expansionism and macho posturing by American leaders seem to have led to the attitude that advancing American interests justifies any means, and that Americans are tough enough not to flinch in the face of that.

That is an attitude that allowed Richard Nixon's associates to break the law to assure his re-election. An attitude that allowed the FBI to start using some of the same dirty tricks — extortion, perhaps even violence, against domestic political figures and groups. It is an attitude appropriate to insecure adolescents, not a great power, which we are.

Not only should Congress make political assassinations of foreign leaders illegal, as several senators have proposed. It should ban all "dirty tricks" (that is, illegal covert activities other than intelligence-gathering) by the American intelligence community abroad except when specifically authorized by the President on a judgment that such a project is necessary to counter a direct threat to fundamental U.S. security.

It is time to grow up. Now that we have confessed, it is time to take the pledge. Not only are such activities ordinarily impractical and self-defeating, they are, short of considerations of national survival, wrong.

The Saginaw News

Saginaw, Mich., November 28, 1975

The interim report of the Senate Intelligence Committee establishes beyond doubt that assassination of foreign leaders has been an instrument of American foreign policy carried out through the Central Intelligence Agency.

Although many attempts were bungled and others considered in consortium with criminals were abandoned, the fact is no less incredible.

It is incredible because any such policy is not merely counterproductive and potentially dangerous to world stability. It defies belief because it runs counter to this country's profesesed aversion to violence, its spirit of fair play — and its laws safeguarding the rights of persons.

The question is how does our government deal with what it has and what it knows?

For starters let it be said that the bipartisan Senate Intelligence Committee has performed a public service by bringing these facts to light. Toward that end it has been resolute.

Once the public questions had been raised about the CIA, the facts had to be established — and illuminated. Anything short of that would have further corroded public trust of its own government. The public had to know, as desperately as CIA and some government officials tried to prevent it from knowing.

We depart with the Senate committee on only one point. It overstepped itself in making public the names of certain past CIA agents who played direct roles in assassination plots. We see nothing to be gained at this time by releasing that information.

Otherwise the case rests where it is. And it is another shameful example of what can happen when government information-gathering agencies are left to minimum or no accountability. In this report we even see the sad suggestion that past presidents chose to play God in exerting power over smaller nations — or chose to look the other way while intelligent but grossly misguided subservients ran amok.

Added to the FBI, the IRS and the Watergate chapters it makes a doleful litany.

Yet it is not merely a painful exercise in self-examination if the people's government learns from it and institutes the needed reforms to prevent future repeat occurrences.

On that score several things should happen and several things should be avoided.

Congress should properly set some new groundrules for intelligence agency accountability. As a matter of principle and checks and balances, that responsibility rests with Congress. There is enough recent history to argue against leaving the matter of institutional reform to these institutions themselves — or presidents.

The Senate committee has recommended the former, not the latter, and we subscribe to it.

What should not occur is an orgy of self-indulgence by the Congress as a purely punitive exercise.

What should not occur is any attempt to play up these findings for political gain.

Given the assumption that this country needs an effective intelligence community as a matter of national security, no laws should be written that tie that community's hands. That would be foolish and possibly disastrous. Rules that are written should define levels of responsibility, points of accountability and review and establish legitimate areas for international intelligence work. They should clearly prohibit assassination and direct involvement in the internal political affairs of other nations.

Any attempt to make political hay over these findings is totally unacceptable. Up to now, the Senate committee under the chairmanship of Sen. Frank Church, D-Idaho, has set a high standard while looking into dark and sleazy corners. Others in Congress and the administration should follow suit.

Dr. Henry Kissinger says it is now time that Congress draw the line on recrimination over past errors of judgment before we tear ourselves apart and ruin the country's ability to conduct foreign policy and gather necessary intelligence.

We think that now a reasonable request — but one which should in no way preclude possibilities of reopening probes into assassinations of domestic political figures or, for that matter, probing possible discrepancies in Mr. Kissinger's own sworn testimony on the planned Chilean coup in 1970.

Sen. Church has said, "we must remain a people who confront our mistakes and resolve not to repeat them. If we do not, we will decline, but if we do, our future will be worthy of the best of the past."

We think that is now a reasonable observation also.

Arkansas Democrat

Little Rock, Ark., November 25, 1975

The Senate report on the CIA is out, and it seems wisest to shrug off our intelligence losses and get as much credit as possible for making a clean breast of CIA misdeeds. But let's not overdo the remedies.

All the world now knows — even the Voice of America helped spread the word — that the Central Intelligence Agency tried eight times to kill Cuba's Fidel Castro and once to kill the Congo's Patrice Lumumba. The agency was also involved in plots to overthrow the governments of South Vietnam, the Dominican Republic and Chile.

The world, some Americans included, has long accused the CIA of this kind of thing — though crediting the agency with more deadliness than the Senate select Committee on Intelligence does. But there can be no doubt of the findings. All members of the committee agree on them, though some opposed making the report final and even opposed the original investigation.

We opposed it for reasons now plain — certain revelation of the findings. It was inevitable that whatever was found would be told in one way or another. The committee has taken the direct route and we think it is the best one. Congressmen can't keep silent. Anyway, silence would have ended in slow leakage of the facts and more controversy. New rumors and charges would have cropped up, and the official silence would have looked like a whitewash.

Some may call the report a whitewash anyway. The score against the CIA comes to this: No direct bloodletting (though not from lack of trying) and no direct connivance or involvement on the part of presidents in the assassination attempts, though some supported coups.

That amounts to a finding that the CIA is not DIRECTLY responsible for any of the four deaths resulting from overthrows, and that Presidents Eisenhower, Kennedy, Johnson and Nixon are probably guilty at most of lending support to internal movements to overthrow South Vietnam President Ngo Dinh Diem and Dominican Republic President Rafael Trujillo. In short, there's no proof they gave orders to kill and none that they didn't

The fact is, however, that foreign leaders died and that presidential weight was behind the coups that killed them. What that comes to in the committee report is this: "The death of a foreign leader is a risk foreseeable in any coup attempt." The committee concludes that Presidents are responsible for such deaths when they back coups, regardless of whether they know about what happens or not.

Fair enough, but the lack of proved knowledge leaves a big question mark on successive White Houses — and stimulates the House intelligence committee to find out anything further that it can.

The world, however, will probably chalk up the whole thing to past presidents. Russia is making what she can of the report and though allied countries seem to be shrugging it off, the damage is considerable.

Let's hope for what credit we can get for making a clean breast of things, but let's not go so far in assuring the world of our regret and our reformed character that we destroy the CIA to show our sincerity.

It's all right, as the committee suggests, to outlaw assassinations and perhaps — but only perhaps — support of coups, too. But if we do everything the committee suggests we do to let in the congressional sunshine on the CIA, we'll not only finish wrecking the agency — we'll frighten our friends and delight our enemies while damaging our own security.

The Times-Picayune

New Orleans, La., November 22, 1975

The Senate Intelligence Committee has climaxed its long-running melodrama with publication of a report on Central Intelligence Agency assassination plots of the '60s, despite President Ford's pleas that it would not be in the public interest. It clearly is not.

The committee would have us believe that it is protecting the public interest, that such knowledge is properly given the citizens of an open democratic society for their judgment and action. But what it does is damage the national interest beyond our borders, where our intelligence services and our foreign policy operate. We know of no other major country where such intimate, sensitive — and largely inconclusive — information would be forced out of the administration and spread before the global public in the guise of applaudable normal governmental operations.

This is not to say that congressmen should not look into such matters or that plots to assassinate foreign leaders are licit (they are, in any event, futile even if successful). But it would have been far better had the committee, composed of Republicans and Democrats of a representative spectrum of philosophies, done so behind closed doors.

There it could get information readily and make its concern and views felt. It could then release a carefully drawn report to show, without compromising detail, that the national interest was being guarded by serious men of strength and probity, not by frenetic headline hunters. To avoid scandal, disaster and stupidly wasted effort in intelligence operations it should be sufficient to have alert, interested and circumspect congressional committees to stand in the public's stead.

A similar melodrama is being staged on the House side, where Secretary of State Kissinger has been cited for contempt of Congress for refusing to give the House Intelligence Committee, for certain broadcasting to the world, staff recommendations on policy during the Cyprus crisis. Secretary Kissinger, the President and a broad group of knowledgeable supporters rightly insist that vigorous policy discussions cannot be held if each participant must weigh his comments by the prospect that they will later be publicized as breaking news.

Congress has a responsible part to play in these matters, but it is not, as here, as stage manager of breathless domestic political drama.

The State

Columbia, S.C., November 28, 1975

THE CHURCH Committee report on the Central Intelligence Agency's covert activities contained morsels that were lapped up by the CIA's liberal critics, but most Americans should find it discomforting.

On the one hand, it is unsettling to think that the United States may have employed assassination as an instrument of national policy. We agree with witnesses who believe it is immoral and impractical and that America, with its open society, "is particularly vulnerable to the risk that its own leaders may be assassinated."

On the other hand, that bulky report contained little hard evidence. The links to high American officials are tenuous at best, although the report casts suspicion by raising questions that are not fully answered.

At the end, the report concluded that no foreign official met his maker as a result of American-hatched plots. So why spread out 346 pages of half-baked tid-bits to alarm our friends and elate our enemies?

Frank Church's Senate committee and Rep. Otis Pike's House committee have dug around so much looking for old bones that the intelligence community is as pockmarked as God's Little Acre. Those juicy little items in the report might make conversation items at Georgetown cocktail parties, but they don't add much to our understanding of the real and serious nature of our intelligence efforts. Even the Church report called the assassination plots "aberrations," or deviations from the norm.

They are headline-grabbers, to be sure, and there are dark suspicions that that is what Senator Church sought as a boost to his Presidential ambitions. But no man should be awarded the Presidency for doing serious damage to our key intelligence agency and alienating our friends abroad.

That is what has happened. Allied intelligence officials can't believe that all of these ancient skeletons have been spread out for public view. Said one: "You don't have a country, you have a church — no pun intended." Our foreign informants, no longer considering us trustworthy, are said to be switching their allegiance to other countries. Our credibility in the world intelligence community is shot. Those guys know the name of the game is hard ball.

Instead of hand-wringing over decade-old plots, the Church and Pike committees should concern themselves with the present and the future. There is a need right now for CIA activities to counter Communist moves in Portugal, Spain, Italy, Lebanon and elsewhere. The democratic forces in those countries need our assistance, but the CIA has been reduced to a paper tiger.

Before the Church report was released, former Sen. William Fulbright, long-time chairman of the Senate Foreign Relations Committee, wrote that no further revelations were required to meet the real need: an effective congressional CIA oversight committee.

As President Ford has said, our intelligence capability is an essential element of any real arms limitation and is vital to our national security. He has promised to take administrative action and to recommend legislation to prevent future abuses.

Congress, working with the President, should now establish responsible safeguards and drop the subject so that our wounded intelligence operatives can pick up the pieces and get back to work.

THE KANSAS CITY STAR

Kansas City, Mo., November 25, 1975

If the disclosures by the Senate intelligence committee of alleged Central Intelligence Agency involvement in assassination plots can contain such practices, then the publicity generated in recent days will have served some purpose.

Officially or unofficially, agents of the United States have no business pursuing international politics to the point of murder except under the most extreme circumstances. Henry Kissinger, secretary of state, says such practices can be controlled. President Ford, through his press secretary, says he has a plan to foil assassination plots.

But there is a real question as to what kind of service, if any, the Senate is performing in a recital of inconclusive hints and allegations in these matters. The Federal Bureau of Investigation, in confessing error in dabbling in domestic politics (very likely at the insistence of elected presidents) is doing a bold and courageous thing in setting the record straight.

Foreign policy, however, is something else, and surely there is a limit beyond which Congress ought not to go in its soul-searching and consciousclearing hearings and pronouncements. As the committee says, there is no evidence that any President authorized assassination. Nor is there evidence that any of the alleged plots resulted in the death of a leader or foreign politician. It is possible to speculate whether the CIA really plotted to have Castro's beard fall out by dusting his shoes with a mystery powder.

But anyone knows that this no longer is a world where emperors and parliamentary bodies mobilize the army over a period of months and then with deliberation and majesty declare war on a foreign power. Wars are not declared at all these days. But subversion and espionage exist as surely as all those nuclear missiles, and states which would like to see the United States in decline or obliterated are skilled and experienced in espionage and intelligence. It is not a gentleman's game.

Such niceties as control over intelligence operations and law enforcement are of no great concern in totalitarian states. There the police power and the political leadership are the same, and the spy apparatus merely an adjunct. In a democracy the problem is to protect the nation and at the same time limit the authority of the police and contain the zeal of agencies designed to guard the national security.

In the process, is it really necessary to disclose allegations which, in the committee's own words, were based on "reasonable inferences" and "evidence of involvement"? There are some things that maybe even a member of Congress doesn't need to know. Or tell the world.

DAILY NEWS

New York, N.Y., November 22, 1975

The Senate Intelligence Committee has managed to garner a lot of headlines with its titillating disclosures of Central Intelligence Agency "assassination plots."

Sen. Church

And that, we are convinced, is all that Sen. Frank Church (D-Idaho) and his associates have done—or hoped to do.

To give the impression that it was engaged in some useful, constructive effort, the committee did tack on to its document a statement that hatching murder schemes is very nasty, naughty business for a government agency, and should be outlawed forthwith.

That point could have been put across just as effectively and forcefully by reading the riot act to the CIA privately.

But Sen. Church and some of his colleagues couldn't be content with that. They wanted a huge public blast and great fanfare to accompany their grand display of dirty laundry. And that was accomplished.

Our enemies no doubt will giggle and guffaw over our naivete. Friendly nations will wonder what kind of knuckleheads are running the U.S., and whether any delicate or sensitive information can safely be communicated to a bunch of blatherskites and blabbermouths who play show-and-tell with secret data.

Also disturbing is the manner in which the Democrats, in their eagerness to capitalize politically on the report, maneuvered to block a vote by the full chamber on whether to disclose its contents.

It was a cheap, shabby and irresponsible performance all around, and an inglorious chapter in Senate history.

Richmond Times-Dispatch

Richmond, Va., November 25, 1975

"On great occasions," Thomas Jefferson wrote, "every good officer must be ready to risk himself in going beyond the strict line of the law, when the public preservation requires it; his motives will be a justification...To lose our country by a scrupulous adherence to written law, would be to lose the law itself, with life, liberty, property and all those who are enjoying them with us; thus absurdly sacrificing the end to the means."

These are extremely important words for the American people to recall as they evaluate the Senate intelligence committee's report on Central Intelligence Agency assassination "plots" against several foreign officials. While those plots may not have been illegal, they most assuredly went beyond "the strict line" of the moral code to which this nation generally adheres. Were our leaders justified in even contemplating such abhorrent acts? Does Jefferson's rule apply in this case?

The officials who participated in discussions of the plots covered by the report, it is safe to assume, believed the proposals were essential to the security of the United States. The Cold War was on, and communism was a threat not only in Europe and Asia but in the Caribbean as well. Fidel Castro, it should be remembered, had moved into the Communist camp and had invited the Russians to install atomic missiles capable of destroying the United States on launching pads in Cuba. In a very real sense, Castro was a dangerous enemy of the United States, and the American people expect their government to guard the nation against its enemies.

That defensive security measures might include assassination attempts is indeed a revolting thought. But is it a wholly unrealistic thought? During international confrontations, morality can become a relative matter. President Truman considered it more moral to drop atomic bombs on Japan and end the war immediately than to stick to conventional weapons and allow the war to continue indefinitely. The bombs killed a total of more than 100,000 persons in the cities of Hiroshima and Nagasaki, but prolongation of the war would have resulted in the deaths of far more. During World War II, the Allied nations encouraged efforts to assassinate Adolf Hitler, and most people outside Nazi Germany would have considered his murder a highly moral and justified act.

It is true that the United States was at war with Japan and Germany but not with any of the countries whose leaders were considered possible assassination targets in the plots just revealed. But in this nuclear age, when the first strike of the war might well be the last, should the United States irrevocably eliminate assassination as a possible measure to prevent a holocaust?

In raising these points, we certainly do not mean to offer a blanket endorsement or defense of the "plots" included in the Senate report nor to advocate assassination as a normal instrument of foreign policy. We do mean to suggest, however, that it would be wrong for this nation to lacerate itself with shame, to consider itself to be the most wicked nation on earth. As abhorrent as it may be to accept, the law of the jungle remains a strong force in international relations.

Release of details of the CIA "plots," we fear, will prove, in the long run, to be more damaging than helpful to the country. Openness in government is generally to be applauded, but national interests should not be subordinated to the desire for candor. In this case, candor may make our government become overly cautious — and much less effective — in its intelligence activities and in its efforts to influence the course of foreign events that could vitally affect the security of the United States. The Kremlin, whose masters' hands are drenched in blood, must be rocking with laughter.

It seems to be a shameful fact that the Senate Democrats who insisted on releasing the report without the official approval of the full Senate were motivated primarily by political considerations. Otherwise why did they refuse to permit the Senate as a whole to vote on the matter? Democratic Sen. Frank Church of Idaho, chairman of the intelligence committee, in effect has admitted that sensationalism was his primary objective. And if there had been a Senate vote on the issue, according to news stories, those favoring its release would have prevailed by only a narrow margin, which, Church reportedly said, would have weakened the report's "impact."

"Impact" Church and his Democratic colleagues might achieve, but the result could be a dangerous diplomatic and security setback for their country.

SENATE INTELLIGENCE PANEL URGES TIGHTENING AGENCIES' SUPERVISION

The Senate Select Committee on Intelligence April 26 issued a lengthy, but heavily censored, report that described the U.S. intelligence community as routinely engaged in covert operations that the committee said were often without merit and frequently were initiated without adequate authorization. The committee called on Congress to pass omnibus legislation spelling out the "basic purposes" of the various intelligence agencies, their charters and structure, and the general procedures and limitations under which they would act. The report also proposed consolidating Senate oversight responsibility—divided among several committees—in a new, permanent intelligence committee. The new committee would have authority over the intelligence agencies' budgets, and would receive prior notification of planned covert operations.

The report (a section of which was held back for later publication) contained little that had not been previously disclosed. However, its detailed list of recommendations refocused attention on the faltering drive for congressional reform of the intelligence agencies. Underlying the proposals was the committee's finding that the intelligence agencies had, at the request of presidents, and also on their own initiative, made "excessive, and at times, self-defeating, use of covert action." Programs of covert action had attained a "bureaucratic momentum" of their own, the report said, with Congress failing to provide the "necessary statutory guidelines" or to exercise effective oversight.

The report said that the Central Intelligence Agency had conducted about 900 "major or sensitive" covert operations since 1961, plus several thousand lesser operations. A great proportion of the operations, the report said, were never subject to review outside of the CIA. The 40 Committee, a branch of the National Security Council with authority over covert operations, "served generally [until 1974] to insulate the president" from the approval process, the report found.

The report, while questioning the excessive use of covert activities in any form, expressed particularly strong doubts about the value of paramilitary operations. Such actions, the committee found, were often exposed, resulting both in probable failure and in embarrassment for the U.S. While admitting that U.S. paramilitary operations had recently—with the exception of Angola—been at "a very low level," the committee urged Congress to pass legislation requiring that the CIA budget proposal list each covert operation. The legislation should also make congressional approval mandatory for paramilitary operations lasting more than 60 days, the committee said. It also recommended that Congress prohibit political assassinations, efforts to subvert democratic governments, and support for police forces of foreign countries which "engage in systematic violation of human rights."

The report maintained that despite new CIA guidelines on employing media personnel, the agency was continuing to employ more than 25 journalists and persons otherwise associated with American news organizations. The CIA guidelines, promulgated in February, had ended the employment of full- or part-time persons accredited by U.S. news organizations. The report said that the guidelines resulted in the termination of less than half of the approximately 50 newsmen working for the CIA at the time.

THE SACRAMENTO BEE

Sacramento, Calif., May 2, 1976

The report of the Senate Select Intelligence Committee confirms in every respect the need for carefully defined guidelines for U.S. agencies involved in foreign, military and domestic intelligence operations.

Sen. Frank Church's committee set out 15 months ago to determine what secret governmental activities are necessary and how best they can be conducted under the rule of law in an open society such as ours.

Its findings should erase any doubts about the necessity for establishing charters that will impose prudent restraints on covert actions.

The abuses catalogued in two separate reports provide ample support for controls, if after the many jarring disclosures in the past Americans still require persuading.

In the foreign-military sector, the investigators could cite unethical or illegal drug tests on human guinea pigs, the paramilitary adventures with little or with tragic results, the political assassination plots and the intrusions into the political processes of countries like Chile, Korea and Greece.

Evidence accumulated by the Senate committee staff on domestic spying documents the use of government agencies for political dirty tricks for many years. The law has been disregarded in snooping into the private lives of citizens because of their political beliefs, in surreptitious mail openings and break-ins and harassment of individuals through "unsavory and vicious tactics."

There is no question about the vital role of intelligence and the importance of maintaining an effective system to beam in on hostile acts, at home or abroad, which affect U.S. security. This country — no country — can expect to preserve its interests and perhaps even its existence if it blindfolds itself against the outside world or internal enemies.

Assuredly, secrecy is essential for the success of many consequential intelligence undertakings. But just as critical is making certain secrecy is not used as a means to hide the violations of law or ethics, or brush aside operations of dubious value.

This can be avoided to a great extent by legislation which benefits from past mistakes and ensures that intelligence agencies carry out their missions in accord with constitutional processes. Congress' failure to insist on effectual controls and oversight contributed to the negative aspect of the U.S. spying apparatus. There is nothing secret about the task that challenges the lawmakers on Capitol Hill to restore confidence in the intelligence community.

HERALD-JOURNAL

Syracuse, N.Y., April 28, 1976

The ultimate effect of the restrictions recommended by the Senate Select Committee on Intelligence should be less to shackle the intelligence community than to establish orderly controls.

And it should come as no surprise that the committee is calling for curbs on covert activities to the extent that CIA agents would no longer be able to undertake projects that include assassination or other warlike covert activities.

But despite the controversy that probably will continue to swirl around the individual recommendations in the committee's report, the most beneficial result of the study may be the awakening of the American people and their leaders to the inherent danger in giving the intelligence community a free hand.

The report reveals serious inadequacies at all levels — executive congressional and within the agencies — in controlling and directing covert activities and making best use of intelligence resources, although, in most cases, there was allowance for such controls.

Now, if the committee's suggestions are heeded, there will be a joint House-Senate Oversight Committee that will function virtually in partnership with the President in guaranteeing the CIA and other intelligence agencies don't disregard their legal mandates.

Other than a limitation of certain covert activities that never were legal anyway, the CIA is in little danger of having its intelligence-gathering capabilities curtailed.

The CIA performs a necessary function in helping protect the security of the country.

But responsible, high-level controls are just as necessary.

ST. LOUIS POST-DISPATCH

St. Louis, Mo., April 28, 1976

While the report of the Senate Select Committee on Intelligence contains few new disclosures, its findings taken together ought to shock Congress into adopting its recommendations. That is, if Congress is capable of either shock or effective action in the intelligence field.

The report shows, for example, that the Central Intelligence Agency has gone far to corrupt the intelligence reaching the American people. It has planted stories abroad that were later disseminated at home. It has used and misused American journalists and still refuses to abandon such work completely. It has used and misused thousands of American scholars from several hundred American academies. It has been responsible for the publication of more than 1000 books.

Remember the famous "Penkovsky Papers," supposedly reporting the startling work of an executed Soviet spy? That work was written by CIA agents. Another book about China was not only written by a CIA agent but was reviewed by another in a New York newspaper.

This is the sort of thing the intelligence agency did to its own people. And what did it do abroad? Under the heading of covert activities, the Senate committee discusses the unsuccessful assassination plots, the secret intervention in Chile and later in Angola, the fomenting of war in Laos. There have been some 900 covert operations in the last 15 years alone, but the committee could find only one that had succeeded. Others were self-defeating or led to questionable foreign involvements.

Despite all this, the committee led by Senator Church of Idaho found that the CIA was not "out of control." Rather, it was under the control of the executive branch and the president, though executive officials were not always told what it was doing.

The CIA was, however, out of control in one important sense. It was out of the control of Congress, whose several oversight committees either defended the intelligence work or acted as if they did not want to know about it. Certainly they did not know the intelligence budget or act upon it as such. Even now the White House has managed to have the committee hold up releasing the intelligence budget, estimated at 4 billion dollars or more, and the committee has asked the Senate to consider the matter.

At this point, intelligence work has simply defied the constitutional principles of a balance of powers and of checks and balances. The Constitution requires a "regular statement" of the uses of public money. It also gives Congress the sole power to declare war. Congress has ignored both requirements in giving a free hand to the executive as to intelligence spending and covert activities.

Though the Church committee backed down on publishing the intelligence budget, and simply ignored the possibility of perjury concerning intelligence work, it has proposed legislation to overcome some of the major defects in congressional oversight, creating a single Senate committee to conduct that work.

Perhaps the most important recommendation is congressional power to authorize the intelligence budget — power it now has constitutionally but refuses to acknowledge. As for covert activities, congressional committees would have to be notified in advance and would have to approve paramilitary assistance programs. Congress itself would have to approve use of U.S. combatants in such activities. The proposed legislation also would prohibit political assassinations and efforts to subvert democratic governments.

Probably it is not surprising that such cold warriors as Senators Goldwater of Arizona and Tower of Texas thought the committee report went too far and refused to sign it. Between the Ford Administration and congressional conservatives, there is bound to be powerful opposition to carrying out any intelligence reforms. It is almost as though the Senate and House hearings had never been held and the startling disclosures of abuses never published, and secret government was to be applauded on America's bicentennial.

Yet, as the Senate committee said, "Reliance on covert action has been excessive because it offers a secret shortcut around the democratic process." What a way to defend, as the intelligence establishment insists it is doing, the democratic process. The committee recommendations should be enacted because America needs to protect its democracy from the exercise of arbitrary power assumed by its own intelligence system.

The Oregonian

Portland, Ore., April 28, 1976

The U. S. Senate will soon come to grips with the issues involved in the reform of the nation's foreign and military intelligence operations, including the more than 80 recommendations of the Senate Intelligence Committee.

Senate Resolution 400, pending in the Rules Committee, is scheduled for report to the floor by Friday with debate and a possible vote next week. The resolution would establish a single Senate committee to oversee intelligence operations, including their budgets.

Among the recommendations of the Intelligence Committee, chairmaned by Sen. Frank Church, is that to organize "a congressional intelligence oversight committee acting in consultation with the executive branch." It would have authority to approve an annual intelligence budget that would be made public. By a narrow 6-to-5 vote, the Church committee decided to delete intelligence budget figures from its report and leave the matter of their release to the full Senate.

The report deals at length with covert operations of the Central Intelligence Agency. It cites many abuses disclosed almost a year ago by the Rockefeller Commission. There will be some congressional and public concern with the CIA's subsidization of books and enlistment of scholars and journalists in the processes of gathering information and circulating propaganda.

President Ford has already imposed precautions against repetition of abuses, but there remains need for a better organization of Congress' role in keeping intelligence operations in line.

The Church committee wisely falls short of banning covert operations by the CIA. It acknowledges the need for foreign and military intelligence.

But it would ban covert operations involving "political assassinations, efforts to subvert democratic governments or support for police or other internal security forces which engage in the systematic violation of human rights." The CIA would be the only agency authorized to conduct foreign covert operations, and the president would have to approve each such project after review by a subcommittee of the National Security Council. The congressional oversight committee would have budget control.

These are among the recommendations that should have high priority in Senate debate. All the needed reforms in U. S. intelligence reorganization will not come swiftly. The Senate decision on a single oversight committee may not even clear its first hurdles next week. Powerful senators now heading committees engaging in some phases of intelligence oversight are critical of it.

But events, including the report and investigation by the Church committee, reveal the necessity, in the nation's best interest, to revise U. S. intelligence practices and controls in such a way as to prevent self-defeating operations and to keep intelligence operations under the control of officials elected by the people.

The Providence Journal

Providence, R.I., April 28, 1976

The most important thing that Congress and the President have to do about the nation's intelligence system is to restore the people's trust in it. In the light of all the excesses, violations of law and mistakes that have been committed by the various intelligence agencies, the people must be convinced that the CIA and other units are under control and that Congress is exercising real oversight of both their activities and their budgets.

The report of the Senate Select Committee on Intelligence becomes, therefore, a blueprint for assuring control by the people's elected officials. It is unlikely that all 87 of its recommendations will be adopted. But certain major proposals must be implemented.

It is true that President Ford allayed some fears about a runaway intelligence community, spending $10 billion a year on a vast array of activities and projects, from debriefing travelers to launching spy-in-the-sky satellites. But the committee is basically sound in insisting that guidelines should be spelled out in duly enacted statutes—so that intelligence, above all activities, does not become a rule of men and not of law.

Moreover, that committee and its counterpart in the House, whose report has been published, although never officially released, have both insisted that Congress must put an end to the loose budget accountability under which the CIA and others have operated for years. And they have equally insisted on budget scrutiny that might reduce substantially the estimated $4.5 billion spent by non-military intelligence units.

The Church Committee, in the report issued Monday, has urged a sharp curtailment in activities that are illegal or unethical or that amount to a kind of unauthorized war, aimed at subverting governments or helping the security forces of countries that violate human rights. None of the committee, except Senator Church himself, has suggested banning all covert actions. Undoubtedly, there will be times when the peril to national security will be such that covert projects will be necessary But when they are, they must be carried out under stricter controls, from authorization by open-eyed congressional watchdogs to post-mortem evaluation of results.

Just how serious the lapses have been in the past is not fully indicated by the new report, because of deletions and heavy censorship. The Pike Committee, whose findings were cloaked in secrecy by the House, was sharply critical of the quality of intelligence work in five interiational crises, ranging from the Tet offensive in Vietnam to the Arab attack on Israel in 1973.

There will continue to be controversy over publication of all the failures and offenses of the intelligence community. But the public exposure has been necessary to impress on the people and on Congress the urgency of reform. Duplication by different agencies must be eliminated, especially where it is expensive. The director of central intelligence should have overall authority, including the military, dificult as that may be.

Intelligence agencies must take their agents where they can find them. But there must be an end to subverting the press and the clergy to intelligence uses. The same applies to academics, especially when the latter are used without their own knowledge. But most of all, congressional and executive officials must work together to make sure that intelligence agencies, which do a necessary job, do not roll on with a "bureaucratic momentum of their own" beyond the control or knowledge of the officials who are responsible and accountable to the people.

AKRON BEACON JOURNAL

Akron, Ohio, April 28, 1976

WHILE THE problem of uncontrolled activity by United States spy agencies ought not to be overdramatized, the remedy ought not to be undersold, either.

The problem is, essentially, exaggerated human error. The penchant for people to inflate their own spheres of influence — to build their own empires — can be seen in the Senate Intelligence Committee report on U. S. spy activity released Monday. Basically, it is a report of a handful of spy agencies, insufficiently controlled by a 30-year-old law, with relatively unlimited spending power, that were left to interpret U. S. policy to their own advantage and to employ tactics worldwide that exploited that advantage.

Lost with the lack of control is the testimony to human rights and democratic principle that all American affairs — even covert ones — should exemplify.

The report, 15 months and $3 million in the making, says that the Central Intelligence Agency and the Defense Department spy network, among other things:

Engage in a great deal of busywork, wasteful of time and money, simply to justify their continued size and expenditures.

Keep several hundred American college teachers and graduate students on their payrolls as spies and propaganda writers.

Pay a network of 50 American journalists to gather intelligence overseas, despite guidelines issued in February against the practice.

Have an arrangement with 14 American clergymen and missionaries overseas actively engaged in spying for the United States.

Have conducted some 900 covert actions in foreign lands during the last 15 years without legal authority. The report says many of the actions were uncontrolled and some damaged U. S. foreign policy.

Performed experiments with LSD on hundreds of Americans during a 10-year period. Some of the test subjects were unsuspecting. Two died. The Senate report said the experiments showed "a fundamental disregard for the value of human life."

With such sweeping evidence of basic problems in the U. S. intelligence community, it stands to reason that some basic changes will be required. President Ford has said he will veto legislation that would establish perhaps the most basic change: making Congress a partner of the President in controlling spy activity.

Yet that kind of partnership would be reasonable and helpful. If enacted, the Congress would establish a permanent committee with power to authorize, and hence control, the spy agencies' now-secret budgets, estimated at more than $10 billion a year.

Covert espionage is often paramilitary in nature. Indeed, it frequently results in open, armed conflict. Because one of the American principles of international relations is that the Congress must approve military intervention, it would be logical to extend that approval to clandestine activities that can lead to such intervention.

The argument against congressional oversight is that national security might be jeopardized. Yet that is a risk — not necessarily a large risk — worth taking to uphold the democratic principle that the people have the right to decide the nature and extent of their government's involvement in world affairs.

THE TENNESSEAN

Nashville, Tenn., May 5, 1976

SO MUCH HAS already been disclosed about the U.S. intelligence community that the Senate committee's rather bland report on its investigation was anti-climactic.

In its report, the Senate Intelligence Committee said it found "duplication, waste, inertia and ineffectiveness in the intelligence community," but at the same time found "much that was good and proper." That would seem to indicate some reluctance on the part of the Congress to force any major overhaul of the intelligence units.

The report did reveal the CIA has conducted some 900 major covert action projects around the world since 1961; that it has been responsibile for publishing books, planting stories and using journalists and others for its own purposes; and that it operates a network of business enterprises to provide cover and support for agents abroad.

A major thread running through the report is that the process of intelligence gathering is marked by waste and inefficiency in that there is inadequate analysis of the material gathered. The committee said reports on evaluated intelligence available to the nation are "generally considered adequate" but that a major improvement is needed and is possible.

"In the past, the national leadership has used the CIA more for operational purposes than for its analytic capabilities," said the report. And that may be a key to the many excesses of the intelligence community, including spying on American citizens.

It may be that some improvement will occur in the process of evaluating and analyzing raw intelligence data, since the new deputy director of the CIA is a former agency analyst and presumably knows that aspect of the job far better than any of his predecessors

The Senate committee offered a list of 86 recommendations that would legally outline the purposes of the nation's spy agencies and firmly establish the role of Congress in overseeing their operations. Some of the proposed changes are already planned or carried out by the spy agencies or the administration, but the committee's recommendation is to give them the force of law.

That is needed. President Ford has made some moves in the direction of reshaping the intelligence system, but they are inadequate and presidential orders are not sufficient since future presidents could countermand or change them. There ought to be a continuity to changes.

The Senate report said that covert operations involving "political assassinations, efforts to subvert democratic governments (or) support for police or other internal security forces which engage in the systematic violation of human rights" be banned. The Congress should make that clear by law.

There is no reason why the task of reorganizing and reforming the intelligence system should be a matter of competition between the White House and the Congress, but the legislative branch ought not to buy Mr. Ford's proposal that would make it a criminal act to disclose criminal acts by government agencies. One has only to remember that it was because of leaks in the first place that the nation finally learned of the incredible abuses and the need of reform.

The process of gathering information and the subsequent evaluation of it are things that seldom get the nation in trouble and the value of these is fully obvious.

It is the covert operations — many of which go badly and are sometimes exposed — that cause problems for the country and other nations. If such abuses are to be wrapped in secrecy of the kind that Mr. Ford wants, the CIA obviously could go back to its old ways without fear that the American people might someday find out it was doing terrible and frightening things.

The Congress has a major responsibility for the sins of the intelligence community. It had an oversight responsibility which it neglected. It should make sure that it has that role and that it carries out its duty from this point on.

The best safeguard is to stake out the legal parameters of intelligence gathering and to make sure that such agencies are regularly subjected to the checks and balances of the legislative and executive branches.

It will not be enough to make cosmetic changes or to back away from the bullet that needs some biting. To do so is to invite history to repeat itself.

The Hartford Courant

Hartford, Conn., May 3, 1976

"The nation's intelligence functions should be organized and directed to assure that they serve the needs of those in the executive and legislative branches who have responsibility for formulating or carrying out foreign and national security policy." The means to do this should be provided "by statute."

This is the important essence of the Senate Intelligence Committee's report on management of the nation's intelligence operations. The report proposes that the CIA and other intelligence agencies clearly be cast as servants of the nation's policy-makers rather than as policy instruments themselves. Further, the committee proposes a solid framework of law with which to establish that a proper perspective is maintained.

The committee found that neither the President, Congress nor anyone else has in the past had the combined means and will to curb adequately such intelligence abuses as assassination plots and civil rights abuses.

President Ford recognized the same problem in February when he issued his own orders to tighten management and control of the intelligence community. The committee has proposed similar steps to those Mr. Ford has taken —their main area of difference is that the committee also favors strong congressional oversight.

But Congress can do one thing the President cannot: It can enact legislation. Thus the phrase "by statute" which introduces many of the report's 87 specific recommendations. If intelligence is to be placed firmly into its proper role of servant, this must be done on the basis of law.

In fact, many of the past abuses appear to be results of the vague purposes and unclear lines of authority and responsibility which characterize the present intelligence network. This same fuzziness promotes competition and duplication of effort among individual intelligence agencies.

The committee did not seek, as some had feared, to kill or maim the CIA. The intent instead is to strengthen this country's policies by giving our policy-makers the best possible information.

To reach this goal will still require a delicate sense of balance. The need for secrecy must be reconciled with the need for control and supervision. Congressional oversight is still a subject for controversy, even within Congress itself.

There is room to question others of committee's specific recommendations, particularly those which relate to covert operations and the spread of knowledge about intelligence operations and their costs.

But the basic goal—intelligence as servant —and the means to that end—the rule of law— are certainly valid and should be pursued.

The Wichita Eagle

Wichita, Kans., April 29, 1976

After spending 15 months investigating alleged abuses by the Central Intelligence Agency and other members of the vast intelligence community, the Senate Intelligence Committee seems to have the evidence necessary to justify recommending stricter controls by the President and Congress.

The committee's final report, for instance, included accusations that the CIA "deeply penetrated" the domestic academic life, mass communications and even the religious community.

Many Americans are convinced that the most serious aspect of the Watergate scandal — apart from the disgrace which forced an American president from office — was the obvious misuse of the nation's various intelligence agencies for partisan political purposes.

To many others, the most ominous aspect of the Watergate affair was the extent of domestic surveillance — spying, bugging, wiretapping, breaking and entering, data gathering — on individual private citizens.

The committee's key recommendations are much-needed. They call for Congress to set up a permanent intelligence oversight committee, which would have the power to authorize, and hence control, the intelligence community's budget.

Also, a special committee would be established in the National Security Council to approve all covert operations. In addition, the oversight committee would get advance notice of major operations and have the power to block them by withholding funds.

Vital as the CIA is to national security, it should be hoped that what is meant by the committee's recommendations is that there will be improvement and much closer scrutiny by the administrative and legislative branches in the future.

BUFFALO EVENING NEWS

Buffalo, N.Y., April 28, 1976

If Congress really digs into the findings of the Senate Select Committee on Intelligence Activities, as well as those of the other panels which have probed the same murky depths, the nation can benefit handsomely from past mistakes in the many ongoing moves to correct them.

We do not agree with all the recommendations of the Senate committee chaired by Sen. Frank Church. But the Church Committee, like the Rockefeller Commission and the House (Pike) investigating committee, rightly identified a dangerous past failure and the major challenge it posed as being one of wisely balancing two vital needs: The "competing demands" of secrecy in intelligence operations with "the requirements of the democratic process" in an open society.

The three investigations have usefully spotlighted illegal acts, abuses and mistakes that should alert a free nation about intelligence agencies and activities that had become all too routine, too undisciplined, too unmonitored over too many past years.

Assassination attempts on heads of foreign states in peacetime are indefensible. So are drug experiments on unsuspecting subjects. No less tolerable are paid CIA use of clergymen and journalists — members of professions especially protected under the First Amendment and thus especially out-of-bounds to covert manipulations of a sort that are bound to damage the credibility of their claims to strict independence. If any such excesses still continue, they should be stopped forthwith.

Leaders in the Congress and the executive branch also agree that intelligence agencies and activities should be monitored far more closely in the future. President Ford has set up a comprehensive apparatus for accomplishing this at the executive level. While Congress has not yet tightened its oversight mechanisms, the Church Committee joins others in recognizing the need to do so.

We believe the committee is correct in principle in proposing that individual charters, or sets of written guidelines, for the numerous U. S. intelligence agencies, should be legislated by Congress. Many an excess can result from, or be concealed by, vagueness and duplication related to an agency's misconstruing of its mission. Limits on those missions should be clear.

On another committee recommendation, however, we see no need for total budgets of intelligence agencies to be made public, so long as a responsible congressional oversight committee has them in such detail as it requires. Nor do we think future Presidents should be required to notify Congress in advance of covert operations.

In the one area most directly affecting Congress itself, we think both House and Senate committees have come up with the wrong answer. They recommend separate rather than a single joint Senate-House oversight committee on intelligence activities. Separate committees here will surely breed rivalries and magnify trivial differences, as they have in the CIA investigations themselves. What the nation needs is a single institutional check to balance the judgment of the President and the agencies under his command. A joint oversight committee could speak for a strong, co-equal branch of government. And to prevent lethargy and inbreeding in the oversight role, membership should be rotated so that no individuals stay on too long.

Finally, the prospect that Congress will really dig in and act on the findings of its committees is, unfortunately, no foregone conclusion. This is already obvious in yesterday's Senate Rules Committee rejection of a move to take intelligence prerogatives away from four seniority-encrusted standing committees in order to consolidate them in a new oversight committee.

Newsday

Garden City, N.Y., April 28, 1976

The CIA may seem like yesterday's news to many Americans, but there is one aspect of the Church Committee's report eminently worth attention. The facts concerning alleged wrongdoing and misjudgment in the U.S. intelligence community have now been submitted to two separate investigations and two independent juries, so to speak (three if you count the Rockefeller Commission). And the verdict of the Senate Select Committee is virtually identical to that rendered by Representative Otis Pike's much-criticized House Intelligence Committee last February.

This should count for something even with those people who believe the original revelations of scandal within the CIA were overblown, if not actually un-American. The dismay that greeted the Pike Committee's conclusions—and resulted in suppression of its report by vote of the House —may have led the Senate investigators to preserve the secret label on a good bit of information, but the main facts stand unchallenged.

The senators and congressmen who heard all the secret testimony and read all the secret documents agree convincingly on three points. One, the specific function for which the CIA was created in 1947—joint collection and assessment of foreign intelligence—has been seriously mishandled much of the time since. Two, the agency's attention and resources were squandered instead on an endless cycle of covert operations—dirty tricks—that might have made great sense in wartime but accomplished precious little for the country in peace. And three, significant changes in the way intelligence operations are managed and supervised should be carried out as soon as possible.

Getting on with those changes is not simply a matter of morality or economy or politics, although each is involved to a degree. At bottom it's a question of protecting the country's future. Americans with a genuine concern for national security will recall that once before in modern history U.S. intelligence operations were consigned to complacency and neglect, and the result was Pearl Harbor.

Detroit Free Press

Detroit, Mich., April 28, 1976

"The committee has found that the CIA has conducted some 900 major or sensitive covert action projects plus several thousand smaller projects since 1961. . .

"The committee finds that presidents have not established specific instruments of oversight to prevent abuses by the intelligence community. In essence, presidents have not exercised effective oversight."

THESE TWO paragraphs can be considered the heart of the report by the Senate Select Committee on Intelligence Activities, headed by Sen. Frank Church of Idaho.

And it is this point, the lack of effective oversight, that Congress must now address and correct as it attempts to prevent the kind of intelligence abuses that have been disclosed in the last 16 months.

The 474-page report of the Church committee, released Monday in Washington, added little to the known list of abuses. In some cases, the report fleshed out previous revelations—it is dismaying, for example, to learn of the extent to which American journalists and those in the academic world have allowed themselves to become handmaidens of the Central Intelligence Agency, either for pay or merely out of conviction.

But most of the more gory details of the CIA abuses had been revealed earlier, including the plots to assassinate foreign leaders.

What the Church report now does, and does with considerable restraint and reason, is to lay down a blueprint for corrective action.

The committee's recommendations go beyond those put forward earlier by President Ford. And, as the report clearly shows, with good reason.

Mr. Ford's proposed reforms were generally limited to tightening up control of the intelligence agencies within the executive branch.

However, as the Church report documents time and again, there is no guarantee that such proposals will be sufficient to prevent further abuse of the CIA's charter or its essential mission.

One distinction must be made: The foremost mission of the CIA and other intelligence agencies is to gather information from a variety of sources and methods on what America's potential enemies are up to. There has been no quarrel with this basic function, and, with few exceptions in some highly volatile situations abroad, the intelligence community has performed this task over the years quite well.

The problems have largely occurred when the intelligence agencies became involved, without sufficient executive control, in actual operations overseas, and in illegal domestic activities here at home.

As the Church committee said, covert activities became so routine that the CIA developed a "bureaucratic momentum of its own." This momentum was fueled by the 1949 law that allowed the CIA to spend public money without any accounting; over the years, among other things, the CIA secretly owned major airlines, capitalized an insurance company at $30 million, and financed major and minor wars.

From the report, it can be learned that intelligence operations have been costing $10 billion a year. Much of the cost may have been fully justified, but the total secrecy of such spending clearly spurred the "bureaucratic momentum" that led to widespread abuses.

The Church committee's recommendations would make Congress, through special House and Senate committees, a partner with the president in the authorization of covert activities. The recommendations would establish clear-cut lines of authority and accountability for intelligence activites, something that has not existed in the past. And, the committee proposed laws and regulations to prohibit certain activities, including assassinations and the use of newsmen or clergy as agents.

As the committee said: "The fundamental issue. . . was how the requirements of American democracy can be properly balanced in intelligence matters against the need for secrecy."

The recommendations are reasonable means of assuring that goal is achieved and that the damaging abuses of the past are prohibited. The proposals should be approved by Congress and the president so that there can be "effective oversight" to prevent acts alien to the American framework of law and ethics.

THE ROANOKE TIMES

Roanoke, Va., May 2, 1976

In this small and not very friendly world, the United States needs a covert intelligence capability. Without it, not only would our leaders often have to operate in ignorance of conditions and capabilities in other countries: the nation would also be deprived of certain options abroad. Put another way, instead of hitting someone quietly behind the ear with a spitball we might have to hit him in full view of the world with both our fists—provoking reaction on a scale that we don't want.

So the Central Intelligence Agency, or something like it, should be preserved. But as the recent report of the Senate Intelligence Committee reminds us, it is essential that such an agency be kept under much tighter rein than in the past. The spy's cloak conceals all manner of activity, some of it inimical to our interests overseas and to our freedoms at home.

Evidence is that the CIA has frequently operated without sufficient control, either from the White House or Congress. It has gone off recklessly on self-defined missions, making foreign policy on its own. Under every administration since Franklin D. Roosevelt's, it has dabbled in domestic politics. Because secrecy is so important to its central role, and because its backers could always wave the flag to shush its critics, it has usually gone unquestioned.

With publication last week of the Senate committee's 396-page report, we can hardly say that the CIA's record and lifestyle have become an open book. Much was excised from the final version of the report—including the figures on what the United States spends for intelligence. Surely it would not imperil any single CIA operation to have such data; but it might be very useful to compare the outlay with the kind of things it has bought. Our notion is that the dollar figures would be staggering.

The Senate committee would go farther than the President—who outlined his CIA reform proposal in February—in controlling the agency and in sharing responsibility for it with the White House. Certainly there are risks in cutting more people into knowledge of what goes on with the CIA.

But there are risks, too, in making the circle of controllers too small and too confined to the executive branch. If there is a greater chance that the whistle will be blown on some illegal or dangerous project, the more carefully must the CIA tread. An agency that can so readily short-circuit liberty and law is like a bomb that can blow up in democracy's house.

The Pittsburgh Press

Pittsburgh, Pa., May 4, 1976

There is little in the final report by the U. S. Senate Intelligence Committee on domestic spying that the public hasn't known or suspected for some time.

The facts are nonetheless deeply disturbing and warrant repetition for purposes of re-emphasis.

Needless to say, the decades-long campaign of illegal surveillance of Americans in which top governmental officials were involved since the days of President Franklin D. Roosevelt must cease.

According to the committee report, the FBI, the CIA, the Internal Revenue Service (IRS), Army Intelligence and other agencies created files on more than half a million U.S. citizens — many of which could not possibly be justified — opened nearly 250,000 pieces of first-class mail, monitored millions of telegrams and overseas phone calls, and subjected many private citizens to secret harassment designed to disrupt their lives or destroy their reputations.

The committee's work on domestic espionage activities, like that on international spying operations, was thorough and its recommendations are to the point.

It urges sharply restricting investigative activities of the IRS and Army Intelligence, together with bans on wiretaps, mail openings and other unauthorized entries by the CIA. All domestic intelligence work would be vested in the FBI.

One of its most important proposals is for a powerful, permanent congressional committee to oversee intelligence activities and to have legislative and budgetary power over the CIA and all other intelligence agenices.

Almost before the ink was dry on the report, however, the Senate Rules Committee brushed aside this recommendation. The net result would be to leave control over the various intelligence agencies in the hands of those congressional committees which now hold it so jealously — and which manifestly have been lax in exercising any control.

It remains to be seen what will happen when the subject comes up for debate in the Senate within a week or two.

In view of the evils of untrammeled surveillance in the past, the intelligence committee's recommendations for a single permanent group should be approved.

Wisconsin State Journal

Madison, Wisc., April 29, 1976

Among the more disturbing excesses of the Central Intelligence Agency is its infiltration of vital national institutions.

A few months ago it was reported that the CIA employed about 50 journalists and other employes of U.S. news organizations in its intelligence operations.

The practice of using journalists affiliated — secretly we presume — with established news agencies has been discontinued but the CIA concedes there are still about 25 free-lance journalists on the CIA payroll. The names of the past and current journalist-spies is being kept secret.

At the time the connection was revealed we editorialized that their names should be made public to clear the reputations of the vast majority of newsmen who would not think of compromising their integrity in such a manner and in so doing damage the credibility of the entire press. We renew that position.

More recently, Sen. Frank Church's Senate Intelligence Committee revealed that the CIA is currently using several hundred American university administrators, professors and graduate students for intelligence and propaganda purposes.

There is nothing wrong for the CIA or any other government agency to contact college figures for advice. But to have professors, cloaked in the prestige and protection of academic freedom, on the payroll of an intelligence agency is damaging to the entire academic community.

From a practical standpoint, it is wrong for members of the faculties and staffs of publicly supported institutions secretly moonlighting in any capacity. Most academic positions are considered full-time.

In the case of private institutions, the lines are less clearly drawn but just about all educational institutions are financed to some extent by public funds. And even for those which are not, the clandestine participation of faculty members in international espionage taints the educational process.

The CIA, probably with good intentions, has gone far afield from its purpose of gathering and evaluating foreign intelligence for use in the formation of intelligent foreign policy.

It and the other intelligence agencies in operation in this country have almost become governments unto themselves with their excesses and mistakes shrouded in secrecy which always accompanies such operations.

Extensive intelligence operations — as distasteful as they are in some cases — are necessary in an imperfect world.

But they cannot be allowed to threaten the fabric of the society they exist to protect. There is solid evidence that they have done just that and a tightening of popular control is in order.

There must be an independent congressional committee charged with constant supervision. It must have financial responsibility and control over the various agencies.

Congress has been considering legislation to establish such an oversight structure for several months.

Action, however, has been stalled by behind-the-scenes bickering among committees which now oversee the various agencies on a piecemeal basis.

The Church committee in the Senate and the House committee headed by Rep. Otis Pike, have done a good job in pointing out the dangers and the problems. It is now up to Congress to get to work on alleviating and solving them.

St. Louis Review

St. Louis, Mo., May 7, 1976

William E. Colby, former chief of the CIA, was overly disingenuous in defending the use of missionaries for intelligence purposes in foreign lands. According to Colby, "It's perfectly possible to be a good loyal American and a good loyal missionary." Of course it is, but we don't know what that has to do with using missionaries as intelligence agents.

The missionary, be he Irish or German or African or American, goes into a foreign land, but not as a representative of his homeland. He goes as a representative of the church, a representative of Christ. His principal function is to further the work of Christ, not the work of his nation. In a world explosive with political manipulation, the work of the missionary would be even more impeded than it is now were the missionary to be identified as an agent of a foreign nation. Because the work of the missions would be compromised by such identification, the use of missionaries as agents is completely unacceptable to the religious communities they represent. It is unfortunate that a man of Colby's stature can not see this.

Many nations manipulate religion for the purposes of the rulers of those nations. It is ironic that there have been numerous instances where Christian missionaries were expelled from mission territories on the allegation that they were foreign agents, when in truth the current ruler simply wanted to impose a tyranny that would be challenged by the preaching of the Gospel. Colby plays right into their hands, showing what has come to be typical CIA disregard for any other facet of American life, by insisting that intelligence-gathering by missionaries is "completely proper."

We can see the propriety of missionaries being "debriefed" on their foreign service so that the nation has the advantage of their observations. But such debriefing should not be on military or even political matters. Let the missionaries tell of the needs of the local people, of their deep-held feelings, of their exercise of or lack of freedom

Intelligence gathering is a proper function even within a democratic nation. The use of missionaries sent out in the name of God and in the name of religion for such purposes is an affront to religion.

—Father Edward J. O'Donnell

The Chattanooga Times

Chattanooga, Tenn., April 30, 1976

The report by the Senate Select Committee on Intelligence contains recommendations aimed at strengthening not only the role of the President and the director of the CIA in monitoring intelligence operations but also improving the quality of congressional oversight. With some good-faith bargaining, it could be possible to preserve the intelligence community's obvious value to this country and prevent some of the illegal abuses that abounded in recent years in the name of "national security."

In a remarkable sentence, the report summed up the key issue that must be kept in mind as its recommendations are considered: "how the requirement of American democracy can be properly balanced in intelligence against the need for secrecy."

It is obvious the committee's recommendations and actions taken by President Ford some months ago are not going to agree. The President and Congress are jockeying for power in the intelligence dispute and it is clear some compromises must be made.

One value of the report could be a move to tighten up the intelligence community's operations, thus eliminating some of the rivalry which often resulted in duplication or even triplication of intelligence efforts.

The committee was properly concerned about the covert operations and questionable activities. But it stopped short of recommending that such actions be banned, reasoning that they could be necessary in a time of true national emergency. Even so, we question the wisdom of recommending that congressional approval be obtained before such operations are undertaken. Congress' reputation for secrecy, a vital element in intelligence, argues eloquently against such a move.

More reasonable is its recommendation that political assassinations be prohibited by law. It is curious that such a law should have to be suggested. The President has argued for policy flexibility. We think he has a good case for executive flexibility in most areas — but not for political assassinations.

The report demonstrates that Congress has been lax in its oversight responsibilities, a failure made worse by its finding that Congress does have the constitutional authority to regulate intelligence programs.

In addition to its recommendation that this oversight be made more efficient, the committee's suggestion that the CIA director's authority be increased could, if implemented, do much to improve executive administration of intelligence agencies.

Finally, though it did not find that the CIA had been "out of control," as alleged earlier, it's clear the committee is on the right track in demanding more "accountability." It would be naive to expect the CIA and other intelligence agencies to function as openly as some have suggested. But it is equally naive to assume that vital intelligence cannot be gathered except through covert or illegal means, with little or no supervision.

The Charleston Gazette

Charleston, W.Va., May 12, 1976

When it was revealed that the CIA had employed missionaries as overseas agents, it was our opinion that there should be no law prohibiting the CIA from employing agents under any particular "cover," and that no clergyman should be prohibited by law from taking what he perceived as a patriotic action.

But we added our reservations about the effectiveness of a clergyman conditioned by his second role as espionage agent. We wondered what his sponsoring church would think about it. We concluded that from the point of view of the missionary movement, it isn't a very good idea for missionaries to be spies.

We have similar feelings about the employment by the CIA of journalists working abroad for employers in the print and electronic media.

If we cannot fully agree with Daniel Schorr that all the blame should fall on the media employers we can go part way with his assessment. Certainly the editors, publishers, and TV and radio executives who knew their correspondents were working for the CIA should be asked to provide explanations.

But the reflection on the integrity of the profession isn't removed by reason of the fact that correspondents worked for the CIA with the acauiescense or approval of their media bosses.

We are sure no journalist was forced to function as a CIA agent. As in the case of men and women who couldn't be objective missionaries and spies at the same time, a journalist cannot be a detached observer if he represents a particularized point of view.

Both media employers and foreign correspondents should be lectured briefly on the matter of professional ethics. Perhaps missionaries should be invited to listen, too.

The Globe and Mail

Toronto, Ont., May 1, 1976

In February George Bush, Director of the United States Central Intelligence Agency, announced that "Effective immediately, the CIA will not enter into any paid or contractual relationship with any full-time or part-time news correspondent accredited by any U.S. news service, newspaper, periodical, radio or television network or station."

But the U.S. Senate Select Committee on Intelligence Activities, in its report on CIA links with the press, has added a startling footnote to that promise. The CIA, says the committee, plans to continue to employ about 25 American journalists. They will not be accredited correspondents—Mr. Bush's statement will be technically observed—but freelancers, or executives of news organizations.

The committee also reported some startling evidence of the extent to which CIA activity has penetrated into areas Americans have believed to be the province of a free and uncommitted press.

Two news services operated by the CIA in Europe counted major American newspapers among their subscribers, even though senior executives at the newspapers had been notified that the services were the creations of the CIA.

When a supposedly objective book on China, in fact written covertly by a CIA agent, was reviewed in The New York Times, the review was written by another CIA agent—an academic, not a journalist.

The Penkovsky Papers, a successful book published in 1964, purportedly based on the diaries of an executed Soviet spy, was in fact written by CIA agents, although the publisher, Doubleday and Company, believed it to be genuine.

The Senate committee was properly concerned "that the use of American journalists . . . (was) a threat to the integrity of the press" in the United States.

But at no point did it indicate any concern about the number of journalists the CIA might have on its payroll in other countries. In fact, it recognized dissemination of propaganda abroad as a useful service, grounds for concern only if the propaganda filtered back to the United States in the guise of news.

That attitude may be satisfactory to Americans. But it is hardly reassuring to their neighbors.

THE SUN

Baltimore, Md., April 28, 1976

There was a wry little anecdote buried in the Church committee's massive report on intelligence activities. A Central Intelligence Agency agent wrote a book about China, and it was reviewed in the New York *Times* by another C.I.A. agent. The more you think about it, the less funny that is. American public opinion on a critical foreign policy question was illegally influenced by a couple of spies. The President of the United States, who must be responsive to public opinion, probably did not know of this activity. In a similar way secret subsidies to South Vietnamese journalists affected American public knowledge and opinion about the progress of the war there. Might the war have followed a different course if American attitudes had not been affected by such propaganda?

On the whole, the Church committee found, most U.S. intelligence activities over the past 30 years have been professional and honorable, but some were clearly illegal, some clearly unconstitutional, some silly, some wasteful—and some dangerous. Many of those excesses might not have occurred if there had been a reliable congressional watchdog looking on. But there wasn't. Presidents have also been less in control than they should have been. That is why the Church committee has produced 87 recommendations for legislative and executive refor.n. It had a lot of catching up and making up to do.

Some critics of the committee are already saying that too much is being asked, that, for example, it would be a mistake to tell the American people annually what they are spending for intelligence activity. Yet only with that information can the people and their elected representatives decide whether a decent sense of proportion is at work in our government. One disturbing thing about the report is that it seems to face a hostile reception on the Hill and in the White House. The decision about publicizing past as well as future budget totals has already been bucked to the full Senate. Another recommendation requiring advance notice to a congressional group before covert operations are initiated has also been watered down in the in-fighting on the Hill over which committee, if any, will oversee the intelligence operation. The President prefers that executive orders (which can be changed—and changed *back*—in a matter of minutes), rather than laws (which cannot be), be used as the avenue to "reform." Many congressmen agree.

Undoubtedly all the committee's legislative reforms cannot be enacted in an election year or in any single year. Thirty years' work can't be done in one or two. But a start can be made. And the best place to start is with the establishment of a permanent oversight committee that has the resources, determination and sense of responsibility that the Church committee has displayed over the past year.

THE LOUISVILLE TIMES

Louisville, Ky., April 29, 1976

Americans are rightly suspicious of information that originates in a Soviet publication. After all, both the press and the book publishers in Russia are arms of the government. News and history are written to reflect the official line.

This, of course, is contrary to our tradition of independence in our news media and educational institutions.

Public confidence in these citadels of objective reporting and research is bound to be somewhat shaken, however, by reports that they have on occasion served as propaganda outlets for the Central Intelligence Agency.

Nor is it especially reassuring that newsmen have served as sources for the FBI and were even asked to take part in a Nixon administration effort to find out who leaked information to *The New York Times*.

According to the report issued by the Senate Select Committee on Intelligence Activities, the CIA at one time maintained "relationships" with 50 American journalists or employes of news organizations.

In addition, the CIA operated its own news services overseas and sponsored a magazine in Vietnam. It also published numerous books.

At least some of the material turned out by the CIA, which was intended for use as propaganda in other countries, found its way into news columns and book stores in the United States.

Teachers and researchers at American colleges and other institutions, meanwhile, have violated their commitment to pursue the truth by writing books, again for propaganda purposes, for the CIA.

American journalists and scholars have traditionally scorned the role of propagandist. As the committee's report points out, the involvement of some of them with the intelligence community is a threat to the integrity of the press and academia.

These findings say something about the mentality of intelligence bureaucrats who are willing to corrupt American institutions in order to promote democracy elsewhere.

The committee suggests a law forbidding the CIA to make "operational use" of anyone employed by a news organization. Restrictions also need to be placed on the employment of academics except for legitimate research approved by their institutions.

But the press and the universities need to take steps as well to reduce the chances that they, even in a small way, will become organs for disseminating the CIA's view of the world.

St. Louis Globe-Democrat

St. Louis, Mo., April 28, 1976

Virtually the worst thing that could happen to the U.S. Central Intelligence Agency would be to accept the recommendations of the Senate Intelligence Committee that would put the CIA's budget and its operations under the supervision of a new Senate committee.

This would be the equivalent of putting Dr. Strangelove in charge of the Defense Department. Since congressional committees hold CIA secrets like a fishnet holds water, adoption of this plan would give the Russian KGB what amounts to a "hot line" to all CIA activities.

In releasing its 650-page report, the committee has given a perfect example of how it couldn't keep a secret if the life of every member of the committee depended upon it.

It thought it was concealing the amount that the U.S. is spending on intelligence operations. But careless editing of the committee's report allows any sixth-grader to figure out how much is being spent—about $4 billion to $5 billion for the CIA, Defense Intelligence Agency, the National Security Agency and the spy-satellite programs.

If the costs of tactical intelligence by the Army, Navy and Air Force, plus indirect costs are added, the overall figure comes to between $8 billion and $11 billion. But less than 10 per cent of that sum is spent by the CIA, which means its yearly budget is only about $1 billion or less.

These Senate "Boobs in Spyland" recommended legislation that would:

—Bar the CIA from using American journalists and clergymen for intelligence purposes.

—Give Congress power to authorize the intelligence budget.

—Require the CIA to give Congress prior notice of significant covert actions and obtain approval for paramilitary assistance programs from intelligence supervisory committees.

—Require congressional approval for use of U.S. combatants in such covert operations.

—Establish a permanent Senate supervisory committee that would have access to all CIA secrets and the power to make public information it judges the Congress and American people should have, even over presidential objections.

The proposal to ban the use of journalists and clergymen is probably unconstitutional, as well as dictatorial. A person who wants to offer his services to his country has the right to do this as a free individual, and Congress should not intimidate him into not doing so.

If the CIA should be required to give a committee of Congress advance notice of every covert activity, it might as well send an engraved invitation to the country in question.

The idea of making the activities of the nation's most super secret agency subject to public scrutiny would be laughable if it were not being seriously proposed by the Inspector Clouseaus on the Senate committee.

Sen. John G. Tower of Texas and Sen. Barry M. Goldwater of Arizona have commendably disassociated themselves from this odious report by refusing to sign it.

Congress already has proposed CIA reforms, most of which President Ford has adopted or is putting into effect. It should keep further hands off this vital agency that has been seriously hampered in its work by the investigatory "overkill" of congressional committees.

The very survival of the country could depend upon the effectiveness of the CIA. Any attempt to put the CIA agents in a fishbowl and require its agents to operate under the Marquis of Queensberry rules while the Russian spies operate like Svengali would be suicidal. Only half-baked isolationists would propose it.

HOUSTON CHRONICLE

Houston, Tex., May 5, 1976

The final report of the Senate Intelligence Committee points out again previously disclosed abuses by U.S. intelligence operations but the report also points up a difficulty the committee found itself in.

Despite the committee's emphasis on how intelligence operations violated the rights of Americans, there seeps through the report the conclusion that our intelligence operations are, after all, vital to the existence of this country and that where possible need to be made more efficient. This is in contrast to those who only a few short months ago were calling for the abolition of the intelligence operations.

There is no question but that the intelligence groups did exceed their authority. As the report says, "We have seen segments of our government, in their attitudes and action, adopt tactics unworthy of a democracy and occasionally reminiscent of the tactics of totalitarian regimes."

The committee concluded that there has been a "clear and sustained failure by those responsible to control the intelligence community and to ensure its accountability." And it is to correcting that fault, rather than dwelling on past abuses, that attention must now be directed.

The committee produced 96 recommendations, some of them broad generalities and others dealing with minor details. Many recommendations called for "regulations to be formulated by the attorney general" and there is a call for judicial warrants in cases of electronic surveillance and unauthorized entry. We agree that it was a lack of specific guidelines that fostered abuses in the past and that the judicial process should be involved when rights of individuals are at stake.

President Ford as a result of earlier studies has already ordered steps taken that will carry out many of the recommendations.

The final recommendation was an endorsement of the concept of Senate oversight through a new permanent committee.

The Chronicle takes the position that while better oversight is clearly needed, the proper congressional authority already exists, such as the Senate Armed Services Committee, to control the intelligence community. The idea of a new supercommittee which would have to give prior approval to covert paramilitary operations is unworkable. No new special spy panel is required.

The investigations of the intelligence community were marred from the beginning by leaks and by a tendency to go off down strange trails. On final assessment, one of the best things about the committee's report is that it is the final report.

The News American

Baltimore, Md., April 29, 1976

PROBABLY the most praiseworthy thing that can be said of the long-delayed report of the Senate Select Committee on Intelligence Activities is that it has been issued, finally, all 474 pages of it. After leaks, hints and dark mutterings during the 15 months of the committee's hearings, the other shoe has been dropped. If the humpty-dumpty of this nation's intelligence operation can possibly be pieced together again, we may go back to the task of learning what our enemies are plotting against us.

How much lasting damage has been done to the United States' intelligence arm by the super-headlined probe conducted and orchestrated by presidential aspirant Sen. Frank Church is not now known and may never be assessed fully. Despite the lofty tone of the written report there lingers the question of whether the sieve-like hearings run by Sen. Church and the nearly goldfish-bowl performance of the counterpart Pike Committee in the House did not wreak so much devastation on intelligence activities as to far outweigh any benefits that may accrue. Assuredly Messrs. Church and Pike must have evoked amusement and incredulity in other capitals.

Responsibility now rests with the Democratic-controlled Congress to weigh the merits of the recommendations in the massive report and to enact new laws, if deemed necessary.

The basic thrust of the Church report is to impose external control on the intelligence community, taking it out of the purview of the president and the existing sub-cabinet level "40 committee" and place it in the hands of Congress.

In the wake of the irresponsibility displayed by Congress toward intelligence matters (one need only recall the gift of classified information to CBS newsman Daniel Schorr) many Americans might well question whether the political pressures on members of Congress make them trustworthy custodians of sensitive information regarding the country's intelligence activities. Their performance record shows that they are not.

Another major recommendation of the Church report is that there be complete disclosure of the budget allocations for intelligence work. Most Americans do feel that we all have the right to know where and how every dime of our tax money is spent. There may be validity, however, to the contention of CIA director George Bush that disclosure of the total figure would inform enemies of our intelligence plans. A decision of this magnitude will require much study by Congress.

In many other respects the report was redolent of naivete. It pointed with alarm to the fact that the CIA, among other intelligence agencies, employed freelance "stringer" journalists to garner information, and that it enlisted people in the academic world to write books and articles favorable to the American cause. Tsk, tsk! This is certainly naughty, and somethng no other country would do — right?

All of this started in December, 1974, when it became known that the CIA had operated in violation of its charter under the Nixon administration by conducting illegal domestic operations aimed at the anti-war movement and other dissident groups. This disclosure motivated the liberals in Congress and the investigations of intelligence operations followed.

It must not be overlooked that on February 17, President Ford drastically revised the chain of command in the intelligence community in recognition of the fact that there needed to be more accountability. At the same time he structured it so that we would safeguard "critical intelligence secrets."

"We must have a comprehensive intelligence capability," President Ford emphasized at that time. No true American can disagree with that premise. If parts of the intelligence operation must function in secret, in a non-democratic way, most of us are willing to accept and live with that fact.

THE ARIZONA REPUBLIC

Phoenix, Ariz., April 29, 1976

Sen. Barry Goldwater of Arizona and Sen. John Tower of Texas, both Republicans, refused to sign the Senate committee report on American intelligence - gathering agencies.

Their action was responsible and indicates that at least some of our lawmakers aren't determined to destroy the intelligence community which all nations must, at one time or another, depend on for the conduct of foreign affairs.

It is true that spies seldom attain the glamour of a Mata Hari. On the whole, their work is grubby and painstaking. Much of their effort is wasted. If they are discovered by a foreign country, the United States denies any association with them.

But let there be no question about the effectiveness of the intelligence community in certain cases. Thousands of American lives were saved because the United States had the capability of breaking the Japanese code in World War II.

The Central Intelligence Agency muffed its chance at the Bay of Pigs, but that was largely because amateurs in the White House decided to withhold air cover without which the invasion of Cuba could not possibly have succeeded.

On the other hand, the CIA has "meddled" (if that is the word) in other Latin American countries with considerable success.

The Senate committee report made much of the fact that the CIA used some newspaper correspondents, some church workers, and some college professors to gather intelligence. That is something less than a heinous crime.

If you wanted to know about the tides at Inchon, or the best beaches for a Normandy landing, you would go to the people who should know, including the top scholars in the academic world.

If you wanted to learn the latest gossip in the United Nations press bar, you would ask the American correspondents who do their drinking there.

This is not to diminish the obvious fact that the United States is an open society. The United States doesn't want to build organizations that rival the OGPU and the Gestapo and other agencies of totalitarian countries.

But the United States does need to know what is happening in the closed societies if it does not want to be overrun by its potential enemies.

No one knows just how far Congress will go, on the basis of the committee report, to destroy the efficiency of our intelligence gatherer agencies. But it is encouraging to know that Goldwater and Tower and others will not let the CIA and the FBI be put out of business.

THE DAILY OKLAHOMAN

Oklahoma City, Okla., April 28, 1976

FOR the same reason that Humpty Dumpty—being an egg—could not be put back together after his fall, the Central Intelligence Agency will not be able soon to reconstruct its shattered worldwide intelligence operations, which were effectively destroyed by the publication of details of some of its "tools" by a publicity-seeking committee of Congress.

Any discussion of such revelations must make one clear distinction which the Senate Intelligence Committee and its staff appear to be incapable of making: some of the work of the CIA is not directly related to its primary mission of gathering and evaluating information for the highest officials of our government. That mission is so important that it should never have been jeopardized by the inclusion of information about the methods and vehicles used in its accomplishment in a congressional report.

Without accurate, timely, and correctly evaluated information, the President, the State Department, and our defense leadership cannot protect this nation from any kind of damaging attacks, whether military, economic, or political in nature.

As an example of the kind of information which the committee chose to publicize, there is the report that the CIA has "operated" a network of business enterprises with total assets valued at $37 million, to provide cover and logistic support for its agents abroad.

There are probably American business enterprises worth at least 1,000 times that total operating in foreign countries. Their activities are essential to the continued prosperity and independence of this country. They bring in between 40 and 50 per cent of the oil and gas we now consume monthly. They supply all or most of some 16 vital minerals, any one of which is required to support at least one major American industry here at home. They enable us, through exports, to afford the imports which we need or prefer to buy.

Every one of those enterprises has now been thrown wide open to attack by foreign demagogues and mobs, as a suspected CIA cover operation. The relatively tiny CIA commercial covers may be the last to be suspected, in fact.

Use of such covers is a legitimate method used by most national intelligence operations of any size. Much of the data supplied through them is acquired in open relations with foreign businessmen, but would not be as readily supplied to a foreign (American) intelligence office or government agency.

Does it serve a legitimate purpose to destroy these cover businesses, and thus deny our government the information they furnished? Is there another way to check the accuracy of intelligence gathered through military or other government channels, once they are gone?

The answer is self-evident. Yet the committee members and the staffs who have provided the report will almost certainly paint themselves, on the Washington cocktail circuit, as heroes for having cut through the CIA's defenses.

President Truman, who established the CIA and pushed through Congress the 1947 act which made it permanent, got into trouble with his famous "red herring" remark because he did not and could not believe that any Americans would be so traitorous to their country as to reveal vital intelligence data to foreign agents.

What would he think today of elected members of Congress who release such information to press conferences attended by foreign intelligence agents working in this country as reporters? That is a fact all Washington press conferences live with.

Stripping the CIA of its cover is more than taking its clothes. The revelations are stripping it to the bare bones. A massive rebuilding job now faces Director George Bush.

The Birmingham News

Birmingham, Ala., April 29, 1976

When the Rockefeller Commission reported on its investigation into activities of the Central Intelligence Agency, this newspaper expressed surprise that the agency had engaged in *so little* illegal or off-color activity in the absence of any real oversight by Congress.

The News suggested that the agency — considering its power and lack of congressional interest — should be commended for its restraint both domestically and overseas, rather than castigated and vilified.

Now that the long-awaited report by the Senate select committee on intelligence activities is out, there is more reason than ever to suspect that much of the attack against the CIA and other intelligence agencies was spawned by those who oppose and wish to discredit any kind of intelligence gathering by the United States.

To put it in Columnist Charles Bartlett's words, "Sen. Frank Church's rogue elephant turned out to be a harness horse."

In other words, accusations of all kinds of foul deeds against the CIA proved to be overblown and illusory. Rumor came to be accepted as fact, and it appeared at one time that half of the CIA and two of its directors would be convicted and jailed for heinous crimes.

Most of the hue and cry after the hide of the CIA came from the liberal establishment in Washington, New York and other eastern strongholds. Connect these attacks with the maudlin support for North Vietnam — giving tacit approval for riots, bombings, draft-card burnings and military desertions — with tearful support for the Chilean dictator, Salvador Allende Gossens, and attempts to destroy U.S. military supremacy and the evidence is sufficient to discredit the so-called liberal establishment forever in American politics.

The damage done to the CIA in reducing its effectiveness can not be calculated. Partial information leaked to the press during the circus-like hearings has given America's enemies throughout the world propaganda weapons inconceivable by supposedly responsible congressional figures.

And the damage done in this country in creating doubts about the reliability of the executive department as well as of the intelligence of Congress cannot now be measured.

And much of the blame can be laid at the feet of Democratic liberal Frank Church, a senator so blinded by his own light that he thinks his betrayal of American interests makes him a viable candidate for President of the United States.

Years will be required to re-build the CIA into an effective intelligence-gathering agency. Its operatives in foreign countries have dispersed or been indirectly exposed. Obviously operatives and officials of friendly governments will hesitate for a long time before cooperating with a government which may expose them on a whim or for political opportunity.

The obvious conclusion, looking at the entire affair is that the same results could have been obtained by closed hearings which would have been circumspect and which would have revealed nothing to the nation's enemies.

But this option was ignored for the opportunity of achieving political advantage and personal notoriety.

It is shameful, for the nation deserves much better than that.

San Jose Mercury

San Jose, Calif., April 28, 1976

It is difficult to know whether to laugh or cry over the voluminous proposals of the Senate Select Committee on Intelligence to "reform" the Central Intelligence Agency.

The Senate committee says the CIA is not out of control, which is a relief to be sure; but the Senators go on from there to propose a number of reforms that would all but put the CIA out of business as an effective spy agency.

It is ridiculous, for example, to suppose that the CIA would have a single secret left unshared with the world should Congress actually establish the proposed permanent Senate committee on oversight. This body would have access to all, repeat all, CIA secrets and would, in addition, have the power to decide which of these should be made public in the face of presidential opposition.

The problem here is not so much with the normal Executive-Congress conflict of interests as with the fact that there is no leakier sieve anywhere than a congressional committee. If a Senate committee, which is to say the sum total of its members, aides and staff assistants, has the power to rummage through the American intelligence community at will, picking up juicy tidbits here and there for public titillation and private leverage, rest assured that power will be exercised to the fullest.

If past administrations sought to misuse the intelligence community for political advantage, what is to prevent Congress from playing the same game? The temptations are equally great at both ends of Pennsylvania avenue.

Congress would be on much sounder ground in "reforming" the CIA and the other similar agencies if it worried less about which secrets—including the overall CIA budget—to publicize and concentrated instead on defining and restricting the legitimate role of the CIA and other members of the intelligence community.

It is far easier, and far more sensible, to forbid all covert activities except in time of war or congressionally-declared national emergency, than to set up an almost infinite variety of committees and review boards to pass on proposed clandestine operations.

The CIA should be given full and unhindered power to gather foreign intelligence. That information could properly be shared by the Executive and the Congress. If the CIA were ever involved in internal subversions abroad, there could be no question concerning which Americans are entitled to know about it.

In the final analysis, the United States needs an effective intelligence agency because the nation shares the globe with a large number of suspicious neighbors, some of whom are openly hostile. Often the national interest truly requires foreknowledge of their intentions and their capabilities. Beyond this, there is no need for the United States to go. Subversion and paramilitary operations are legitimate tools of war, but when the United States is not at war—which supposedly it is not now—these tools have no proper place on the spy's workbench.

It is a pity, really, that the Senate Select Committee on Intelligence failed to address itself to the root problem of past intelligence excesses.

The San Diego Union

San Diego, Calif., April 28, 1976

Sen. Frank Church was convinced that the secret intelligence apparatus of the United States was a "rogue elephant run rampant" when his Senate committee began investigating it 15 months ago. What the committee turned up was something quite different.

Abuses, yes, and some of the disclosures about activities of the Central Intelligence Agency were painful for the American people to hear. The CIA has gone down the wrong track on occasion, at times even with the tacit assent of American presidents.

But as the final report of the Church committee concludes, the CIA cannot be regarded as an agency running out of control and thus demanding a drastic curtailment of its activities. In fact, the committee report reaffirms the importance of a strong and efficient secret intelligence operation to the national security.

Having made this broad assessment of the basic value of the CIA, the committee then unreels no less than 87 major recommendations to overhaul the system for oversight of the agency by the President and Congress. Some of them seem more tailored to harness a rogue elephant than to prevent the kind of abuses which the committee turned up.

There is evident opportunity for a meeting of minds between President Ford's proposals for intelligence reforms and those the committee recommends for the chain of accountability within the Executive branch. Strengthening the role of the National Security Council in monitoring and approving covert foreign operations has obvious merit in keeping the CIA from going too far on its own. It is in the area of congressional oversight that the Church committee has not been able to resist a tendency for over-kill.

Empowering a group of senators, for instance, to overrule the President and his security advisers on whether a covert operation should remain secret or not is a formula to make such operations self-defeating. To set up a secure and leak-proof system for keeping a congressional committee informed of secret intelligence activities is challenging enough. To give it powers to disclose what it wants to could place intelligence agencies under intolerable political pressures.

Congressional probing into past activities of our intelligence agencies has done some good. It also has done some damage which may take years to repair. Congress now must make sure that over-reaction to those past abuses does not make cripples out of such agencies as the CIA.

THE DALLAS TIMES HERALD

Dallas, Tex., April 28, 1976

THE ISSUE: The Senate intelligence committee's recommendation for reforming intelligence agencies.

THE DEMOCRATIC majority of the Select Senate Committee on Intelligence is ready to endanger the security of the United States to prove a point — that intelligence gathering agencies, and especially the CIA, have gone to extremes and committed abuses which go far beyond the intent of their creation.

This majority would prove the point by passing detailed restrictive legislation for monitoring and controlling the operations of the agencies, again especially the CIA.

The intent of the committee regarding hamstringing of U. S. intelligence is apparent from recommendations in its report covering investigation of the spy agencies' foreign activities.

Certainly, the committee performed a service in revealing excesses, abuses and waste in the the operations of the nation's intelligence apparatus. These lapses should be corrected.

But in its welter of recommendations — 86 of them — the committee would not merely impose needed reforms, it would so straitjacket the agencies as to strip them of their effectiveness.

The core recommendation, in particular, is untenable on this ground. It proposes the creation of a single congressional committee with virutally unlimited powers in the monitoring and control of the intelligence agencies.

This oversight super committee would be kept informed in detail on the activities and operation of the CIA and other spy agencies and would be authorized to release this information to the public if it elects to do so.

The experience with congressional committees foretells clearly what would happen if that recommendation becomes law. What information the committee did not formally release — and that no doubt would be considerable — it would leak.

The result would be to keep the whole world informed on U. S. intelligence activites and the knowledge this nation possesses about adversaries' plans and intents.

Also, the committee would be informed in advance of foreign covert operations which would just about nullify the possibility of such operations.

Efficient, effective foreign intelligence is vital to the security of this country. The Senate committee's proposals, if enacted into law, would effectively guarantee the absence of anything more than a token U. S. intelligence program.

The Detroit News

Detroit, Mich., April 28, 1976

The Senate Intelligence Committee's report on American spy operations — a report timed, incidentally, to promote the presidential candidacy of the committee's chairman, Sen. Frank Church — seems peculiarly out of touch with reality.

A schizoid document, it concedes that the nation needs a CIA; yet the authors deplore what such an agency must do if it is to perform effectively.

"Reliance on covert action has been excessive," the committee writes, "because it offers a secret shortcut around the democratic process."

A ridiculous criticism. Nobody ever said covert action has anything to do with democratic procedures. You can't hold an election on whether to conduct a secret operation.

On the other hand, secret operations and covert actions may be vital to the preservation of a democratic government.

The committee reports with a sense of shock that by the early 1950's the CIA was spending $200 million annually on "a worldwide effort to anticipate and meet Communist aggression, often with techniques equal to those of the Soviet clandestine services."

We hope the techniques of the American intelligence network at least equal those of the Soviet Union. If they don't, the entire free world may find itself in very serious trouble. Why does the Soviet Union maintain sophisticated "clandestine services" except to place other nations at a disadvantage in her constant quest of power?

The committee notes sadly that covert support of foreign political leaders makes them vulnerable to repudiation if exposed. Certainly that risk exists. However, if covert operations must always be assured of success and never end unhappily for anyone, they would never be undertaken. The decisive factor in the planning of any operation should be, of course, whether the prize is worth the game.

Again, the committee reports with great concern that the CIA uses a false-front airline, Air America, to provide aircraft for CIA operations in Southeast Asia. Still, if you're going to move operatives from one place to another, you need some means of transportation.

Better to operate a CIA airline than to parachute into hostile territory from a Pan Am jetliner. If the committee can't see that point, at least it can take solace from the fact that the 16 largest cover businesses operated by the CIA have earned $50 million in profits.

As a means of making American intelligence operations more responsible and effective, the committee wants Congress to create a permanent intelligence panel to oversee those operations. Congress, the committee urges, should be informed in advance of all future covert operations.

To give Congress this authority over intelligence would obviously rob the intelligence community of the one factor absolutely essential to its success: secrecy. Congressional committees have proven over and over again — most recently in the case of confidential Watergate data and the widely leaked House Intelligence Committee report — that Congress can't be trusted with secrets. The surest way of blowing the cover on any future covert operation would be to tell a committee of Congress about it.

Perhaps the Senate Intelligence Committee report will compel the CIA to end some of its more unsavory and questionable practices. On balance, however, the committee's investigation and report have probably harmed the nation's intelligence services. How much confidence will foreign sources feel in an intelligence agency whose secrets and methods can be ransacked and exposed to the world by headline-hunting politicians?

This country may in time pay a very heavy price for the political ambitions of Sen. Church, who — not too coincidentally — happens to be running in his first primary of the year on May 11 in Nebraska.

Richmond Times-Dispatch

Richmond, Va., May 2, 1976

During the congressional investigations of American intelligence organizations and activities, some critics of the Central Intelligence Agency accused it of rampaging against the sovereign rights of foreign countries and against the constitutional rights of American citizens. But the report of the Senate Select Committee on Intelligence Activities, released last week, shows that the charges were greatly exaggerated. Abuses there have been, at home and abroad, but the CIA, the Senate committee concluded, is not wildly out of control.

As a matter of fact, the committee found that national intelligence agencies "have made important contributions to the nation's security, and generally have performed their missions with dedication and distinction." Moreover, the committee, some of whose members had previously indicated skepticism about the value of intelligence operations, emphatically endorsed the need for an "effective system of foreign and military intelligence." The text of the summary of the committee's report is published on this page today.

These conclusions are heartening. But the abuses and questionable practices the committee discovered in both foreign and domestic intelligence activities remain to be considered. Intelligence agencies have used some unsuspecting citizens as guinea pigs in drug experiments; unjustifiably invaded the privacy of some citizens; used clergymen, journalists and professors as paid agents; and engaged in some poorly planned and possibly unjustified efforts to influence the internal affairs of some foreign countries. The committee report showed that the sterling characteristics of the intelligence agencies far outweigh their defects, but improvements obviously are necessary. And the central need is for more effective supervision and control of the agencies.

The crucial questions are: How rigidly should intelligence operations be controlled and to what degree should the President and Congress share the responsibility for controlling the agencies?

Our fear is that the Senate committee's recommendations go too far. It would establish one congressional oversight committee that would be empowered not only to review intelligence operations but also to veto certain proposed programs. The select committee favors the enactment of laws that would prohibit the assassination of foreign leaders, prohibit efforts to overthrow democratic governments and prohibit aid for foreign security forces in countries that violate the "human rights" of their own citizens. And it recommends a legal ban against the use, ever, of clergymen or journalists as intelligence agents.

In the abstract, all of these recommendations seem to be unassailable. Yet they are in potential conflict with certain realities that the committee itself recognized. One is the reality that intelligence activities should be coordinated with the nation's foreign policy. Another is the reality that there must be some flexibility in intelligence operations. And a third reality is the need for secrecy in intelligence activities. These essential features of an effective intelligence system would be threatened by excessive congressional involvement and by severely restrictive legislation.

Should Congress assume the strong supervisory role that the select committee advocates, secrecy probably would suffer. Throughout its existence, Congress has displayed marked inability to keep secrets; and the chances are high that leaks eventually would develop in any congressional oversight committee.

Legislation prohibiting certain kinds of intelligence activities or covert operations would deprive the agencies of the flexibility they need to cope with the fluidity of international affairs. Who can truthfully say that the assassination of a foreign leader would *never* be justified by the vital national security interests of the United States? How realistic is it to argue that American intelligence agencies should never support countries that violate human rights? During World War II, our interests demanded that we align ourselves with the Soviet Union, one of the worst violators of human rights that ever existed. And, finally, who is to determine, whenever doubts arise, that a particular country has a "democratic government" that makes it immune from American interference? Many nations that call themselves democracies are dictatorships quite capable of causing the United States great harm.

As for the coordination of intelligence operations with foreign policy, too much congressional interference might make this difficult to achieve. While Congress, and especially the Senate, does indeed have an important role in foreign affairs, the primary responsibility for foreign policy rests with the White House. Conditions can and do change quickly, emergencies can arise abruptly. Prompt consultation between the President and Congress is not always feasible. The President, therefore, must have considerable freedom to react to the exigencies of the moment, and this should include the freedom to use intelligence agencies effectively.

Primary responsibility for operational control of intelligence agencies, then, should rest with the chief executive, who should develop effective policies and procedures for supervising intelligence activities. The administration should be especially vigilant in guarding the constitutional rights of American citizens. Congress should establish broad guidelines and monitor intelligence operations in a general way more diligently than it has in the past, and it should not hesitate to challenge any program that it considers ineffective or undesirable. But it should legislate with extreme caution. The object, after all, is to control the agencies, not to paralyze them.

SENATE VOTES PERMANENT COMMITTEE TO SUPERVISE INTELLIGENCE AGENCIES

The Senate May 19 voted 72–22 to create a permanent Select Committee on Intelligence. Panel members were named the next day. The action had been recommended by an earlier Senate unit that had investigated U.S. intelligence agencies. Since creation of the committee was an internal Senate affair, neither House nor presidential action was required.

The creation of a permanent committee had appeared doubtful after the Senate Rules Committee April 29 voted out a resolution that would have established a temporary panel to investigate intelligence abuses. The Rules Committee resolution drew fire from many Senators. They argued that such a temporary panel would merely duplicate work already done by the earlier committee chaired by Sen. Frank Church (D, Idaho).

Opposition to a permanent committee also came from members of other committees—particularly Armed Services—that already had oversight over the intelligence agencies. The resolution that finally created the permanent intelligence committee partially nullified this opposition by offering a compromise; the new committee would have exclusive jurisdiction over the Central Intelligence Agency, but jurisdiction over other U.S. intelligence services would be shared with the committees that originally had the oversight authority.

The resolution also provided that eight of the 15 members of the new committee would be drawn from the four committees that previously had monitored intelligence activities—two each from the Appropriations, Armed Services, Judiciary and Foreign Relations panels. The resolution set rules for disclosing classified material. If the committee voted to disclose such material, it would notify the president. If the president objected to disclosure, the matter would be brought before the full Senate for a vote on disclosure. The resolution stated that it was the sense of the Senate that the intelligence agencies should keep the committee fully informed of their activities. However, the committee was not given veto power over those activities.

Just before passage of the resolution, Sen. John C. Stennis (D, Miss.), chairman of the Armed Services Committee, and John G. Tower (R, Tex.), another member of that panel, offered an amendment that would have stripped the new committee of budgetary and legislative authority over the military intelligence services. They argued that the new panel would hold a "dangerous potential" for disclosure of classified information. The Stennis-Tower amendment was defeated 63–31.

DAILY NEWS

New York, N.Y., May 21, 1976

The painful revelations of abuses by our intelligence agencies have led the Senate to create a permanent committee which will ride shotgun on the Central Intelligence Agency. The panel also will share jurisdiction with the powerful existing committees that oversee other intelligence units, like the Federal Bureau of Investigation.

This is a long step in the right direction—toward a Joint Senate-House Committee on Intelligence. We urge that such a body be modeled on the Joint Atomic Energy Commission, which has served so admirably down the years in an equally sensitive assignment.

THE SPRINGFIELD UNION

Springfield, Mass., May 21, 1976

In creating its own Select Committee on Intelligence Activities to monitor the C.I.A. and other federal spying and intelligence - gathering agencies, the U.S. Senate responded to a need made clear by recent disclosures of abuses in such operations.

The gravity of the abuses was reflected in the Senate's 63 to 31 vote against an amendment to the resolution which would have denied the committee legislative jurisdiction over military intelligence units as such. At the core of that issue was the control given the committee over budget ceilings of those units — which include the National Security Agency and the Defense Intelligence Agency.

As noted by Sen. Frank Church, who has been chairman of the Senate's temporary intelligence committee, the budget role will give the permanent committee "the leverage it needs" to obtain information from the various agencies.

At the same time, in making itself an integral part of these intelligence operations, the committee must assume the responsibility for security in its own ranks. The legislation provides that any information the President wants kept secret on national security grounds shall be unless the committee receives permission of the full Senate, in closed session, to declassify and publish the materials.

In such instances, the responsibility would extend to the full Senate, and that is reason to hope the need for that process will not come frequently. The more people involved with classified information, the greater the chance of leakage when the national security is, or could be, at stake.

A glaring example was the leak, early this year, of a House intelligence committee report the House itself had voted to keep under wraps. If that kind of defection occurs in the new Senate committee — or in the Senate as a whole, the survival of the committee, and the purpose it serves, would be jeopardized.

No blanket pledges of secrecy can be ironclad, and the record of Congress in recent years shows an alarming trend to leakage of confidential information. That will have to be a continuing concern of the new Senate committee.

Post-Tribune

Guarding Your Interests Daily

Gary, Ind., May 24, 1976

The U.S. Senate, seeking to keep reins on further witch hunts by the federal intelligence agencies, appears to be moving carefully to avoid any charge that it is conducting a witch hunt of its own.

If that's a right conclusion it's commendable.

Here's how we arrive at the conclusion that that is the senatorial intent in setting up its new intelligence oversight committee:

–Eight members of the new committee must come from the membership of the four committees which have exercised what overview has been possible in the past — Appropriations, Armed Services, Foreign Relations and Judiciary. That tends to give both some continuity and also some guarantee against a new platoon of self-proclaimed white plumed knights.

—The 15 new committee members will be appointed by the present majority and minority leaders of the Senate. Democrat Mike Mansfield will name eight, Republican Hugh Scott will name seven. Both have reputations as reasonable men, not extremists. Both have announced their intent to retire from the Senate after this year so neither has an interest in ongoing control.

—The new panel will exercise its control over the various intelligence agencies primarily through budgetary reins.

—The Senate panel is not given veto power over operations of the spy agencies, and where it is decided that in the public interest such operations should be publicly exposed as a means of discouraging them then the President has the right to appeal that disclosure to the full Senate before it is made.

Certainly enough has been turned up in investigations by both the Senate and the House to show that the CIA, the FBI and some other agencies went to unwise extremes in seeking to protect the national security as their non-elective officials saw fit.

That being the case, it would seem wise to provide controls by elective officials beyond those granted to the President whose multiplicity of duties may be too complex to permit the watch needed.

At the same time, there have been fears expressed here and elsewhere that congressmen might go so far in their overzealousness in the other direction as to hamper intelligence operations.

That could be highly dangerous in the troubled world in which we live.

Somehow, however, there should be found a means of balancing the protection of individual rights at home with the important business of increasing awareness of what is going on abroad.

That is the compromise position the Senate apparently wants to reach.

On the surface, its action in creating the new committee seems in line with that search for balance.

The New York Times

New York, N.Y., May 23, 1976

The Senate acted as the nation's conscience when it approved creation of a permanent committee with powers to watch over the activities of the country's foreign and domestic intelligence agencies. Together with a new toughness shown by Attorney General Edward H. Levi in supervision of the Federal Bureau of Investigation, these moves represent important steps toward return to national sanity.

Though essential, such institutional reforms will nevertheless remain frail safeguards against future abuses of secret police powers and covert foreign activism. F.B.I. Director Clarence M. Kelley pointed to the deeper problem when he suggested recently that past abuses were made possible in large part by an image of the bureau's infallibility. While Mr. Kelley is right in speaking out against the popular myth created so skillfully and ruthlessly by his predecessor J. Edgar Hoover, the public affinity for glamorized and all-powerful foreign and domestic sleuths transcends the problems created by any one personality.

* * *

As a brief, dramatic interlude, the Watergate scandals reminded Americans how easily the power of government can be turned against the people. The illegal forays of the White House plumbers, and the complicity of the Federal Bureau of Investigation and the Central Intelligence Agency in disregard of citizens' rights, aroused a sense of outrage and even a momentary determination that illegal secret spying and surveillance would never again be tolerated.

The anger and the determination have long since evaporated, however. Once the rallying point for preventive action, Watergate now is more often viewed as a temporary aberration. The threat posed by unchecked secret police activities to a free society no longer appears very real. Richard M. Nixon's arrogant palace guard has departed and repented. The formidable J. Edgar Hoover is dead. Political dissent is at low ebb. The radical movements which once so alarmed the protectors of the realm and its orthodoxies have all but disappeared. The civil rights forces are on the defensive, trying desperately to halt the erosion of their tenuous gains.

THE CHRISTIAN SCIENCE MONITOR

Boston, Mass., May 24, 1976

The Senate's prolonged investigation of the intelligence agencies will have lasting results if the new permanent intelligence committee lives up to its promise.

The promise derives from the legislative strength it retained in a compromise resolution after the Rules Committee had gone so far as to try to make the proposed committee a study group without budgetary or oversight authority. But the committee's powers present it with a stiff twofold challenge: to keep the intelligence agencies from slipping once more into the abuses and illegalities of the past, and to support the effectiveness of these agencies' authorized activities, including the preservation of the nation's legitimate secrets.

Preservation of secrecy is complicated by the compromise, which involves sharing with previously existing committees the legislative jurisdiction over agencies other than the CIA. But Congress's Joint Committee on Atomic Energy has shown that secrets can be kept, and the new Senate setup gets under way with a determination not to damage domestic or national security in the effort to watch over it.

The large vote in favor of the new committee recognizes the shortcomings of previous Senate intelligence oversight. The resolution provides for jurisdiction over such matters as intelligence budget ceilings – along with means to keep them secret. If the committee should disagree with the president's judgment on secrecy it would have to get permission from the Senate for declassification.

As for covert operations, the resolution calls on the intelligence agencies to supply the committee with full and up-to-date information on what they are doing, including "significant" anticipated activities. The committee would not have veto power to prevent such activities, but it could express opposition to the president and, failing agreement, seek full Senate authorization to undercut a plan by disclosing it. Also the committee has been given subpoena power for information not voluntarily supplied.

But no one supposes that the Senate will often if ever be placed in the position of voting to disclose material over the president's objections. The hope is that the very existence of such options will help to forestall the kinds of activities that might call them into play.

Meanwhile, the committee – whose 15 members include both critics and defenders of the intelligence establishment – will have much to do in considering how to proceed legislatively along the lines of the many recommendations made by the Senate intelligence investigating committee. The zeal for institutional safeguards tends to flag when the new people in charge are trusted. But the need for such safeguards is indicated by the extent to which past abuses were found to have cut across party lines and to have occurred in many administrations.

The Virginian-Pilot

Norfolk, Va., May 21, 1976

The establishment of a Select Committee on Intelligence by the U.S. Senate is the end product of the 15-month investigation into abuses in the Government's intelligence operations.

The Senate voted Wednesday, 72 to 22, to establish a 15-member panel with exclusive authority to oversee the activities of the Central Intelligence Agency and to authorize funds for its operation.

The new committee is to share jurisdiction over other intelligence agencies, such as the Federal Bureau of Investigation, the Defense Intelligence Agency, and the National Security Agency, with the appropriate Congressional committees.

An amendment exempting the Defense Department's intelligence operations from the committee's scrutiny was rejected by the Senate, 63 to 31.

The legislation seems to be a compromise that the interested parties are willing to live with. President Ford's executive order defining the CIA's functions, which became effective on March 1, was more of a cosmetic measure than a genuine reform. But the Senate Select Committee on Intelligence will have the power of budgetary review to compel respect.

The abuses in the Government's intelligence operations occurred in the climate of the Cold War, and without effective political supervision by Capitol Hill (which didn't want to know what was going on) or the White House (which seems to have sanctioned most of the dirty work). The best guarantee that the abuses will not be repeated is the changing temper of the times.

The abuses by the FBI were encouraged by the one-man rule of the late J. Edgar Hoover. The abuses by the CIA were encouraged by its freedom from restrictions. "To a large extent," notes the Virginia Law Review in its March issue, "the only restraint upon the agency's activities has been its leaders' almost instinctive understanding of what it should not do, buttressed by the efforts of other agencies jealous of their domain."

But now the agencies are answerable to the Senate Select Committee on Intelligence, and they are also sensitive to the headlines and to the mood of the nation, post-Vietnam and post-Watergate.

The Government's intelligence operations might be divided into the political and the technological. There has been a revolution in the spy's technology. Nowadays space satellites are able to keep the planet under surveillance; cameras in the sky are so sensitive that they can spot a golf ball on a green; electronic equipment monitors the merest whispers in the airwaves.

Analyzing the space snapshots and decoding the electronic eavesdropping — these are the functions of intelligence technology. They are the work of clerks of a high order and of the computers that marry man and machine into a new sort of spy. Basically, these are the Defense Department's responsibility. For instance, it is no secret that we routinely track the movements of Russian submarines.

Although the intelligence technology accounts for most of what we learn and most of what we spend, it is not an embarrassment to the nation or a hazard to the citizen's civil liberties.

The abuses have occurred in the political sphere. The break-ins, the domestic snooping, and the heavy-handed tactics of the intelligence agencies in dealing with the antiwar movement are all political responses undertaken by the Federal Government to actual or imagined internal threats. Similarly, the CIA conducted some 900 covert operations, or more than one per week, over a period of 15 years in attempts to counter foreign threats, and to control events — often unsuccessfully. This covert foreign policy of manipulation did not parallel our open, official policy at all times.

It is here that oversight is most needed, and it is here that the Senate Select Committee on Intelligence ought to guard against the dangers we know not of. By creating an insider's industry immune from review and from political second-guessing, we encouraged the illusion that we could manage the rest of the world. We outsmarted ourselves from time to time.

Events have tempered the hubris of the insiders and encouraged a skepticism that is breeding caution generally in Washington. The creation of the Select Committee on Intelligence fits into the larger pattern.

Long Island Press

Jamaica, N.Y., May 22, 1976

Although the House has failed to act, the Senate has created a permanent oversight committee with broad powers to investigate and monitor the activities of the nation's intelligence agencies—the CIA, the FBI, plus military intelligence units.

It's too bad that a joint House-Senate committee hasn't been formed to avoid the kind of intelligence abuses unveiled by congressional committees in more than a year of investigation, but the Senate action represents a big step in that direction.

Moreover, the fact that the permanent oversight panel won by a 72 to 22 vote represents a vindication of the work of the investigative committee headed by Senator Frank Church of Idaho.

The Church committee, like the House unit headed by Rep. Otis G. Pike of Suffolk County, exposed shockingly illegal acts by the CIA and the other agencies both abroad and at home.

But whereas the Church panel's good work bore fruit in the Senate, the Pike committee's good work was scuttled in the House and its report shamefully censored.

The House can still make amends by creating its own permanent intelligence panel; better yet, by agreeing to a joint oversight committee. Meanwhile, the new Senate panel should be selected at once and put to work to assure that henceforth our intelligence agencies will carry out their necessary work within the framework of the law.

The Salt Lake Tribune

Salt Lake City, Utah, May 21, 1976

What eventually emerged, after all the backbiting, sidestepping, backsliding and compromising, was a Senate intelligence oversight committee far stronger than anything the public had a logical right to expect earlier in the game.

The Senate, with overwhelmingly encouraging lopsideness, vested its new Select Committee on Intelligence with broad exclusive powers to monitor the activites, along with authority to dole out funds, of the Central Intelligence Agency.

And continuing the no-nonsense mood the Senate also voted to give the select committee concurrent authority with other committees' jurisdiction over the intelligence operations of agencies like the Federal Bureau of Investigation and the Defense Department.

At last, after nearly 30 years of trusting neglect, Congress (or at least half of it) has started to forge the machinery for adequately policing agencies the Church Committee in 15 months of intensive investigation found had frequently and consistently abused — over a long term — the rights of American citizens, often in direct violation of laws Congress enacted prohibiting such infringements.

The finely honed instrument, one that will safeguard absolutely necessary national secrets while protecting individual Americans from abuses, won't be complete until the House of Representatives follows the example of the upper house.

Sen. Frank E. Church, D-Idaho, says, "One good committee can do the job." A single committee can, of course, "blow the whistle" when it finds inefficiency or illegality. It can block appropriations. But without a similar House committee, for instance, it will be difficult to work out the compromises needed to reconcile differences between House and Senate versions of intelligence legislation because Congressmen knowledgable of intelligence matters will be scattered throughout three or four House committees currently handling, in total secrecy, intelligence matters.

"One good committee" can do the job. But it would be much easier and more efficient if there were two — one in each house of Congress.

THE COMMERCIAL APPEAL

Memphis, Tenn., May 21, 1976

AFTER 15 MONTHS of investigating domestic and foreign spying, the Senate has, perhaps inevitably, created a watchdog committee with broad powers.

The irrefutable conclusion to be drawn from the investigation which led to the action is that for decades, through presidents dating back to Roosevelt, there has been a constant escalation of questionable and illegal activities.

The now-departed Nixon was probably ruder in the application than most, but Johnson got his kicks hearing about others' bedroom habits and the Kennedy administration thought killing castro was a good idea.

WHILE THE intelligence community must bear much of the responsibility for the abuses, the misuse of presidential power and the passiveness of Congress also contributed.

Technological advances such as computers and wiretapping and other monitoring devices made it possible to gather and process almost unbelievable amounts of information. All that information, which could be called up with the punch of a button, added to the temptation.

The 15-member panel established in the Senate will oversee the Central Intelligence Agency, the Federal Bureau of Investigation and military intelligence services. Sen. John Stennis (D-Miss.), chairman of the Armed Services Committee, made a sincere and impassioned plea to exclude the military from budgetary scrutiny. His argument died on the observation made by Sen. Walter Huddleston (D-Ky.) who said, "Oversight without legislative responsibility is toothless oversight as we all know."

But, in making his objection, Stennis points up the risk of an oversight committee. That is that in its zeal and with its political makeup it will hamper or destroy the effectiveness of the agencies.

All of the members of the new committee would be limited to eight years of service. Two members each from the Appropriations, Armed Services, Foreign Relations and Judiciary committees would be among the 15.

If conducted properly, the committee could provide a needed check against intelligence abuse and overzealousness. It also could provide the agencies with a sort of appeal board to take illegal requests from a head-strong president.

By taking on the new responsibility the senators have put their own integrity on the line, something they have been unwilling to do in the 20 years since congressional oversight was first conceived as being needed.

IF THEY FAIL, they will have done a greater disservice to the country than that done by those whose actions resulted in the establishment of the committee.

ST. LOUIS POST-DISPATCH

St. Louis, Mo., May 30, 1976

As the Senate's Select Committee on Intelligence goes out of business, the nation owes it a debt for revealing the secret abuses in government and for preparing for a restoration of constitutional checks and balances. After 15 months, the committee under Senator Church of Idaho has earned a historic place among congressional investigations.

Its reports on covert activities abroad and massive spying on Americans at home are now a matter of record: CIA efforts against elected governments and assassination plots, electronic espionage and mail openings by the FBI and a host of agencies, military spying on political dissenters, and so on.

What is important now is the result, and in this respect the Senate, after considerable controversy, has largely adopted the Select Committee's principal recommendation — that for a single permanent watchdog committee with adequate power to oversee intelligence operations. And oversight, or the inadequacy of it, by Congress has been as much to blame as executive mischief for the record of intelligence abuses.

The new committee, to be called the Select Committee on Intelligence Activities, was originally proposed 20 years ago. Still Congress left the task of intelligence oversight to nine different committees which, in the end, became more protective than critical of the agencies they were supposed to oversee. While the new committee is limited to the Senate, and will share with existing committees certain aspects of oversight, it should still have adequate authority to give the whole Congress a reasonable review of intelligence.

Its 15 members — eight Democrats and seven Republicans — will have exclusive jurisdiction over the CIA, share jurisdiction with other committees as to the FBI and defense agencies, and itself include two members each from four other committees — Appropriations, Armed Services, Judiciary and Foreign Relations. The Senate accepted this arrangement as a compromise after roundly defeating conservative efforts to deny the Select Committee any authority at all over defense intelligence agencies.

Nevertheless, the new committee will review and must approve the budgets of all the agencies, even those not entirely under its jurisdiction. If it wishes, it can inspire Senate debate on the budgets, and while the debate could be secret at least the Senate would know how it was using its power of the purse — and it has not known that highly important fact.

The Select Committee under specified procedures could both protect and release classified information, if the Senate agreed, thus giving the public a glimpse under the secrecy stamps that have hidden so many arbitrary actions. But individual senators would be prohibited from unauthorized releases.

Indirectly, at least, the committee also may regulate covert intelligence programs by obtaining prior review of proposals with the threat of exposing them through a Senate vote to do so. That might be a drastic action, but the Senate assumed this authority after learning from the investigating committee that since 1961 some 900 covert actions had not gone through formal policy review — and some of these were disastrous and self-defeating.

These are formidable powers. They also represent what the Constitution intended in demanding that the legislative branch be a check on the executive. But the final test of such powers lies in their exercise by a determined Select Committee and a determined Senate.

As Senator Schweiker of Pennsylvania noted, the weaknesses of U.S. intelligence were founded on two popular beliefs: that a claim of national security could supersede the law, and that if enemies could engage in discreditable activities, "We could, and should." It is time that Congress helped shed this democracy of the idea that the end justifies the means.

The Miami Herald

Miami, Fla., May 21, 1976

IN ITS REPORT never officially released by Congress, the House Select Committee on Intelligence chaired by Rep. Otis Pike of New York said that if its own experience were any test, intelligence agencies that are to be controlled by congressional lawmaking are beyond the lawmaker's scrutiny.

That report also said, "The key to exercising oversight is knowledge. In the case of intelligence agencies, this translates into a need for access to information often held by the agencies themselves, about events in distant places."

There is some sentiment in this country for refusing to give such oversight and knowledge to Congress. We should not endanger the secrecy of our intelligence efforts against real and potential enemies, goes the argument.

In effect, this view holds that the people's elected representatives in Washington cannot be trusted.

But what is the point of democracy and representative government if there is not that trust and confidence? Think back on the darker days of Vietnam when American officers explained that a certain village had to be destroyed to keep it from falling into the hands of the Viet Cong guerrillas. Do we destroy the American people's right to a free and open society to prevent any review of activities of the Central Intelligence Agency?

The U.S. Senate said no emphatically in the 72-22 vote to establish a 15-member Select Committee on Intelligence, the committee having exclusive authorization over funding and operations of the CIA.

Southern conservatives tried to prevent the establishment of the watchdog committee. Sen. John Tower, the Texas Republican, said sarcastically he doesn't see any evidence that the American people are quivering with fear over what the CIA might be up to.

Yet there is a growing number of people uncomfortable about what they have learned of CIA activities both abroad and here at home where intelligence agents violated the congressional prohibition against domestic activity. Even as the Senate prepared to vote on the issue of CIA oversight, there were reports in Washington that a new investigation into the assassination of John F. Kennedy will be launched by Congress because of significant information developed by Sen. Richard Schweiker's staff.

That probe will spotlight the Miami activities of the CIA and its thousands of Cuban agents paid tens of millions of tax dollars during the 1960s for futile and often slapstick efforts to get rid of Fidel Castro in Havana.

Did the United States lose a President to a sniper in Dallas because of plotting by the CIA?

A Senate oversight committee can help answer such questions and help prevent them from ever being asked.

Minneapolis Tribune

Minneapolis, Minn., May 23, 1976

To its great credit, the Senate Wednesday decided that it can no longer shrug off responsibility for overseeing intelligence activities. The strength of that belief was apparent in the 72-to-22 vote by which the Senate created an oversight committee with exclusive legislative and budgetary authority over the CIA. Existing committees and the new committee will share authority over the FBI and military intelligence.

The need for congressional supervision became a central theme in the 15-month investigation by the Select Committee on Intelligence. Its findings were largely based on the record of abuses uncovered and on the lack of accountability that led to those abuses. But the select committee also acknowledged that intelligence agencies would not have developed such seamy records if Congress had been fulfilling its own responsibilities.

This forthrightness put the question of a new committee in doubt until Wednesday, since the congressional self-criticism applied mainly to influential senior senators in whose jurisdictions what passed for oversight took place. They objected to increased possibilities of leaking classified information, despite elaborate precautions in the resolution to meet such objections. They objected to the power granted the new committee on grounds that it would weaken foreign confidence in American intelligence capabilities (a confidence already undermined, they said, by the select committee's investigation). But the idea that security is enhanced by a system that ignores lawbreaking by intelligence agencies is, we think, an obvious contradiction.

The Senate majority evidently felt the same way. Resounding support for the resolution means that the 15 senators eventually appointed to the new oversight committee can go about their work confident of bipartisan support. If their judiciousness matches that shown by their colleagues on the investigating committee, the country will be well served.

THE SAGINAW NEWS

Saginaw, Mich., May 21, 1976

The U.S. Senate has stepped forward boldly and we trust not carelessly to pass a resolution creating a special committee vested with virtually complete authority of oversight of the nation's intelligence-gathering agencies.

It remains to be seen how the House of Representatives will respond to the Senate's lead-taking and what interest, if any, it really has in grabbing a piece of the same action and assuming the responsibility that goes with it.

Up to now the House has been more disjointed than joined in determination to press on as the Senate has. Possibly the Senate's overwhelming passage of a measure dealing with spy oversight will prompt the House to act with more dispatch.

Without some House input, we're not sure where the Senate action falls. But at least in the upper chamber of Congress, there is a willingness to get on with it. It has now said that it fully intends to make agencies such as the CIA and FBI and all other intelligence offices responsible and answerable to one committee of the elected representatives of the people.

At the minimum, the Senate has passed an oversight resolution that leaves little question as to its toughness.

It also raises a few. We think it time some toughness was put into this by Congress so long as toughness is balanced against care and common sense — and raises no Constitutional questions relative to absorption or transfer of previous authority.

In terms of what the White House might think of what the Senate has completed, there could be some challenge.

Basically, though, the Senate is on the right track and has finally demonstrated its intention of taking a direct hand in ending many of the previous abuses inflicted upon the domestic public by the surveillance people.

They have been rampant enough to underscore the need for some responsible congressional oversight. Congress has always had some oversight — but it has been fragmented. And authority to check up on anything has proved farcical. A lot of congressmen knew bad things were going on and let them go on anyway — not wishing to make a fuss. Fear often overrode them. And a few, we are sure, never knew the difference between lawful and unlawful.

The Senate's new vehicle would end fragmentation for sure. And it would clearly fix the point of responsibility. Both would be taken care of by a single 15-member Senate Committee on Intelligence Oversight.

The committee would have exclusive legislative and budgetary control over the CIA. It would share with other appropriate Senate cmmmittees the same authority on all federal intelligence agencies. It would authorize and finalize all of their annual budgets. And most crucially — while it would not have the power to veto any intelligence project — it would take unto itself great responsibility for prior revue of any new ones.

This is delicate stuff. But the resolution sets up a procedure for checks and balances in this area.

If the committee did not like one, it could vote to make public any operation it disapproved. The President in that case would have the right to take an appeal to the full Senate. The Senate could ride with or override the oversight committee — or send the issue back to the committee for re-review and final decision.

That's saying a lot, to be sure. It does raise the old question of making public executive branch secrets through declassification. That could raise sticky questions, as it has in the not too distant past. But then, too, the public knows what the nation has been through as the result of this business of excessive secrecy and executive privilege under the heading of "national security." And Congress in general has come to terms with the realization that something has got to be done to put a cap on that.

One other thing bothers us just a bit about the makeup of the oversight committee. I will automatically include two members of eqch of the four committees that have had previous oversight — Appropriations, Armed Services, Foreign Relations and International Relations.

That could give some old hands who never did a very thorough job of oversighting a majority of one on the committee.

So there are some reservations about the Senate resolution. But given the assumption that no congressional oversight can ever be so perfect as to let the public in on everything without greatly damaging national security, the Senate has put down something for a starter.

This has been needed for a long time. Without somebody watching the watchdogs, we are always in potential danger of great abuses. That has been adequately documented.

THE CINCINNATI ENQUIRER

Cincinnati, Ohio, May 25, 1976

MOST AMERICANS, we suspect, were gritting their teeth and hoping for the best when they read about the Senate's decision, 72-22, to create a 15-member Select Committee on Intelligence with broad powers to oversee the activities of the nation's intelligence apparatus.

The committee will have exclusive authority in overseeing the activities of the Central Intelligence Agency (CIA); it will share with the Judiciary Committee authority over the Federal Bureau of Investigation, and with the Armed Services Committee authority over the Defense Intelligence Agency.

The Senate decision was the principal product of a 15-month inquiry into the affairs of the CIA, the FBI and other arms of the nation's intelligence establishment.

The nation would perhaps have a more optimistic feeling about the new committee and its work if the entire congressional investigation of intelligence had not been, in the main, the handiwork of outspoken opponents of covert operations abroad.

The nation has heard a great deal of late from those who feel, for example, that the CIA should confine itself to collecting and assessing information from overseas, and that it should not undertake operations that might constitute interference in the internal affairs of other nations.

The CIA got into the broad area of covert operations out of an official determination that the Soviet Union and its intelligence operation should not control the field from default.

The Soviet intelligence establishment, unhampered by ambitious politicians or crafty dissenters, has achieved remarkable sophistication in making things happen in the international sphere, of helping their friends and of punishing those who resist Communist advances.

It is useful for the United States to know what is happening abroad, to understand the scope of Soviet designs. But it is more useful, in our view, to be able to take surreptitious steps to frustrate them.

Many brave men have risked their reputations and their lives in the last three decades and stood up for a free world in the conviction that the United States, through its intelligence establishment, would not allow them to fail.

It remains to be seen whether there will be such men in crucial areas of the globe in the future. Much of the answer will stem from the manner in which the Select Committee on Intelligence deports itself, the kind of senators who shape its traditions and the quality of the staff members engaged to assist it.

The resolution creating the committee invests in the full Senate authority to make public classified information the committee assembles, and prohibits the unauthorized release of classified information by committee and staff members.

Here again, the test will be in the committee's performance.

The American people have seen too much reliance on the illicit leak as a means of frustrating official policy.

It has become an easy matter for the disgruntled congressman, staff member, or bureaucrat to attempt to discredit a policy to which he does not subscribe simply by the unauthorized and premature release of information.

Thus far, Congress has shown a shocking reluctance to come honestly to grips with the leak problem.

Certainly the most celebrated of congressional failures in this extraordinarily sensitive area was the House's refusal to deal with Rep. Michael Harrington (D-Mass.), who freely acknowledged gaining access to secret testimony before a Senate committee, promising to maintain its secrecy and then delivering the classified material to the press.

Representative Harrington's reason was that the secrets dealt with U.S. policy toward Chile—a policy of which he disapproved. Violating his own word became, in his eyes, an acceptable means of challenging U.S. policy on Chile and focusing public attention on what he perceived as its shortcomings.

By choosing to ignore the Harrington infraction, the House has raised serious public doubts about the suitabilty of congressional committees as repositories of detailed information intimately related to the nation's—and the free world's—security.

The new Senate committee needs to go on record clearly and quickly in opposition to Harrington-type pranks. It needs also to acknowledge that it is, in fact, an oversight committee and not a coadministrator with the President of the nation's intelligence apparatus. It needs, in short, to earn the trust of the intelligence community, the administration and the public.

ARKANSAS DEMOCRAT

Little Rock, Ark., April 24, 1976

Whatever happened to the great congressional crusade to tie the Central Intelligence Agency's hands abroad and get it out of spying at home? Where are the laws that will make congressional oversight of the agency more effective and perhaps even limit the CIA to intelligence gathering?

The short answer is that Congress hasn't passed any such laws and, judging by its mood and the public's, it isn't likely to do more than keep the CIA overseas, where it belongs. Like Watergate, the year-and-a-half probe of the intelligence establishment has generated far more rhetoric than lawmaking.

That won't please Sen. Frank Church, who hoped to run for president on the sensations shaken out by his committee's long pursuit of the CIA. Church very delicately waited till his committee closed shop before announcing for the White House, but there were more yawns than anything else when he bounded out of the chute at last. His colleagues appear as unimpressed by his reform recommendations as the public has been by his revelations, some of which were less than total.

Well, what's wrong? Our own view is that congressional curiosity about the super-secret CIA was built up over the years by sporadic reports of its spying on this side of the water as well as the other. Curiosity finally burst bounds when New York Times reporter Seymour Hersch accused the CIA of "massive domestic spying." The resulting Senate investigation got the headlines; the belated House probe was a botch from start to finish.

It developed that the CIA had indeed done domestic surveillance and had indeed plotted assassinations of foreign leaders, but it appeared very much as though past presidents had blessed or connived at some of the abortive plots. There appeared to be an unspoken feeling, too, among Americans in and out of Congress that though spying is a dirty business, it has a lot to do with national security. Lifting the flap of the spy tent a little is all right, but spotlighting the interior comforts only our enemies.

It also became very clear that a minority of Americans hate the intelligence establishment on grounds that have nothing to do with its misdoings. Their attitude goes beyond mere demands for an "open society" to a rage to destroy. When some rag in Washington printed the names of CIA agents abroad and when one of them, Richard S. Welch, was murdered in Athens, public revulsion at the whole probe peaked.

However concerned people may be about keeping spy agencies from surveilling Americans, they don't like seeing defenders of national security killed. Welch's burial at Arlington put the stopper on Church's probe. It may have been a piece of salesmanship on Mr. Ford's part, having a public burial, but it did avert any chance of Congress' ripping the agency apart, which was the danger all along.

Sometime next month, Congress will probably get around to adopting a minimum of Church's recommendations. The oversight structure may be tightened up, but the CIA is not going to be hauled out in the sunlight and its covert actions abroad are not going to be seriously curtailed.

Common sense said all along that they shouldn't be, and now that everybody has had a peek down the tunnel, the intelligence apparatus will go back underground, where it belongs. Hersch got the national "Headliner" award for starting the witch hunt, but Church will have to settle for less.

SAN JOSE NEWS

San Jose, Calif., May 21, 1976

Abuses by this nation's intelligence agencies can be curbed without destroying their effectiveness. Senate action to establish a Select Committee on Intelligence promises increased congressional oversight at the expense of a vastly weakened and exposed American intelligence system.

The quarrel is not with increased congressional oversight. It is with the unwieldy manner in which the Senate has chosen to provide such oversight.

An observation by Sen. Barry Goldwater (R-Ariz.) is relevant: "I don't care if you have a committee of one, it's almost impossible to stop leaks."

The Senate committee will have 15 members — eight Democrats and seven Republicans, with at least two members each from the Appropriations, Armed Services, Foreign Relations and Judiciary Committees. In addition, budget authority over U.S. intelligence agencies will continue to be shared with the Judiciary Committee and the Armed Services Committee.

Such a diffusion of oversight and funding authority increases the potential for leaks of sensitive intelligence information.

The seriousness of this problem becomes more apparent when one recognizes that this is only half of the congressional oversight picture. There's also the House of Representatives to consider.

One of the major recommendations of the temporary House Select Intelligence Committee, which completed its work in February, was for creation of a permanent House Intelligence Committee as well as full audits of intelligence agencies by the General Accounting Office. House committees will be no less reluctant than Senate committees to surrender the intelligence oversight responsibilities they presently have. The result: another crowd of congressmen picking over sensitive intelligence reports and activities.

What national secret would be secure? How could congressional accountability for protecting critical intelligence information be assured?

No quarrel is made with the need for congressional oversight. But what the intelligence agencies require is oversight not overkill.

President Ford has urged creation of a Joint Congressional Committee on Intelligence Oversight. A small, bipartisan committee of respected and well-known national legislators — as Ford proposes — could do an effective job of oversight without jeopardizing the effectiveness of U.S. intelligence operations.

U.S. intelligence agencies currently must brief no fewer than six different congressional committees. Under the Senate-approved approach this questionbable diffusion of responsibility — and sensitive information — would be perpetuated.

Congress should get on with the formation of a Joint Congressional Committee on Intelligence Oversight and recognize that responsibility for the day-to-day administration of U.S. intelligence properly belongs with the President.

The State

Columbia, S.C., May 24, 1976

THE decision of the U.S. Senate to create a special oversight committee for American intelligence agencies, with authority to approve their budgets, and to expose any covert operations it disapproves of, is a grim mistake.

It is tantamount to congressional day-to-day management of the intelligence operations of the nation, a task for which U. S. Sen. John Tower of Texas warned the Congress is "ill-suited."

The permanent committee will have exclusive legislative and budgetary control over the Central Intelligence Agency (CIA) and will share jurisdiction over other intelligence or law enforcement agencies with Senate committees which already have that responsibility. Two members of those committees will be members of the new oversight committee of 15.

It is an axiom of intelligence operations that those involved are told only what they need to know. The "need to know" practice provides greater security — all the parts of the puzzle are not kept in one place — and makes it more difficult for foreign espionage to discover secret operations and plans.

What the Senate has done is to duplicate the work of four committees, and in doing so it increases the possibility of leaks. Few Americans are unaware of the difficulty congressional committees have in keeping secrets.

Furthermore, the new oversight committee is intent on revealing the total U.S. expenditure for intelligence work, a step which U.S Sen. Barry Goldwater says will lead to pressures for more detailed accounting that would provide valuable information to our nation's enemies.

The ramifications are enormous when one considers that such a revelation will be considered by our allies as another piece of evidence that the United States cannot keep its own secrets. No other country in the world throws out that kind of information about its intelligence systems — an no other country in the world will readily cooperate with American intelligence if they think their own security will be compromised by a talkative congressman or senator, or an aide.

The Senate has overreacted to the disclosures of the abuses by intelligence agencies of their charters. Had the Senate committees already in existence done their jobs, the national ordeal might have been averted. Adding one more super-committee to the list, with such extraordinary powers, won't solve any future problems and may well turn out to be harmful to the exercise of our foreign policies.

THE BLADE

Toledo, Ohio, May 10, 1976

IF there was one clear point that emerged from the welter of investigation and testimony surrounding abuses by the nation's intelligence agencies, it was that there should be effective congressional oversight of their activities.

That central objective now appears to be threatened in the Senate by resistance from standing-committee chairmen and members who are fearful of losing some of their jealously guarded powers to a proposed separate Committee on Intelligence Activities. Armed Services Chairman John Stennis, for example, protests his committee's prospective loss of jurisdiction over the CIA. Incredibly, he admits to being "ashamed of what the CIA had done . . . but, of course, I knew nothing of it." That is hardly an endorsement of how things were handled.

Such petty considerations should not be allowed to undermine the establishment of a new oversight committee as the logical climax of the exhaustive investigations conducted by the Select Intelligence Committee. Those chairmen of committees previously charged with overseeing such agencies as the CIA and the FBI had their opportunity to do the job properly and they obviously did not do it. They have no cause for complaint now if the responsibility is taken from them and given to a separate committee charged with legislative and budgetary control over all federal intelligence activities.

As Sen. Walter Huddleston, a member of the select committee, commented, the proposed committee would not be one "to do an ordinary job. Intelligence is a whole different type of animal." And, as Sen. Frank Church, chairman of the investigating panel properly charged, the existing arrangement of congressional oversight has "conspicuously failed."

It is understandable, under the Senate's tight little system of prerogatives and perquisites, that the Rules Committee has its work cut out trying to extract intelligence jurisdiction from the several committees that have had that power. But the Senate as a whole, and the House too for that matter, cannot be unaware that the American people are in no mood to put up with any more agency dirty tricks or with "business as usual" as it has been conducted in the past simply to avoid bruising the feelings of some petty chairmen.

New York Post

New York, N.Y., April 29, 1976

The committee has found that the Central Intelligence Agency attaches a particular importance to book publishing activities as a form of covert propaganda . . . —*the Senate Select Committee on Intelligence Activities.*

* * *

Officials of the CIA were not the publishers of the Church committee's final report. But they were among its most aggressive and influential editors.

They fought publication of anything they thought might discredit the agency —even material already in the public record. They used the "national security" excuse for concealment repeatedly and indiscriminately. They began protesting early, they resorted to calculated obstruction and harassment. And, with the unremitting support of the Ford Administration, the benign approval of prominent Congressional leaders, the endorsement of some citizens and the indifference of others, they have won.

It is true that the Church committee's leadership often acquiesced in the CIA's insistent appeals to delete material or rephrase it. As a result, its findings and recommendations substantially lack the power, the credibility and the tone of independence and vitality essential to compel reform of the nation's corrupted intelligence services.

But the committee is not to blame for the snarling reception given to its plausible proposal for a new Congressional committee on intelligence "oversight." The reaction came from powerful committee chiefs who refuse to surrender their shares of the puny control authority that now exists.

The committee's final accounting lacks certain detail and determination. But its catalogue yesterday of CIA and FBI abuses of authority, while familiar, amounted to a thorough listing of the dreadfully neglected official business before Congress in the sphere of intelligence control. What, as a practical matter, has been done to interdict the murderous covert operations abroad and the poisonous spying at home, the black-bag jobs, the perversion of the intelligence function?

In the final analysis, not much. The Ford Administration has skillfully exploited the funeral of a slain CIA station chief in order to forestall reforms, instituting certain "executive order" changes which permit little, if any, Congressional or public review. Nor is official Washington alone to blame. Corrupt abuse of the CIA's authority has been actively assisted by college professors, clergymen, reporters, police, labor, industry and others.

There were, of course, those who assisted the CIA unwittingly: the tragic drug experiment victims, for example. And there are doubtless millions of Americans who feel a sickening sense of betrayal in the cynical spectacle produced by the Senate Rules Committee yesterday: an intelligence "study committee" with no power of any real dimensions. But, like the Church committee, they have not rallied the force of outrage against the corrupters to achieve any perceptible reform.

THE PLAIN DEALER

Cleveland, Ohio, April 20, 1976

A senator warned in January that "haste and simplicity may be the enemy of a solution" to the problem of congressional supervision of U.S. intelligence activities. So far, Congress has avoided all three: haste, simplicity and a solution.

The real enemy of a solution, it appears, is congressional inability to exploit CIA irregularities and power abuses as an election issue.

As a result, the nation faces an absurd situation: The only significant outcome of the disturbing CIA investigations by Senate and House committees may be an executive order broadening the government's authority to require secrecy pledges — thus handicapping any future such investigation.

The investigations made it abundantly clear that Congress should restructure the way information is gathered and processed by intelligence agencies and that it should more closely supervise U.S. operations overseas and the FBI's domestic intelligence and counterintelligence procedures.

To say this is not to attack the agencies but merely to note that they have indulged in excesses which are dangerous to foreign policy, civil rights and their own morale.

But the word from Washington now is that reform of the "intelligence community" has been lost as a political issue and that Congress is ready to settle for something far less than close supervision.

If this is true, Mr. Ford has won a battle to retain executive power. But the nation has lost, and so has the theory of representative democracy.

The Washington Post

Washington, D.C., May 2, 1976

A SLENDER Senate Rules Committee majority threatens to make a farce out of the Senate intelligence inquiry by (1) launching a tame—and utterly redundant—inquiry of its own and (2) blocking establishment of an effective permanent intelligence oversight committee. Offhand, we can think of no greater triumph of pettiness over public interest in recent times. The Rules majority, led by Chairman Howard Cannon (D-Nev.), speaks for the standing committees (especially Armed Services and Appropriations). The first thing to remember about these committees is that they did a lackadaisical and inept job of oversight in the past. The next thing to know is that they remain pretty much the captives of the agencies they are supposed to oversee, and that they do not wish to yield any of their responsibilities and perogatives to a new oversight panel. To recite these failings and frail ties is to demonstrate the magnitude of what has—or, more accurately, has not—been done.

The temporary Senate intelligence committee, which went out of business with its reports on foreign and domestic intelligence last week, is under some criticism for failing to time its biggest investigatory explosions for the period in which the oversight issue would be the first order of business in Congress. But come, now. Who can forget the earlier stark and stunning committee reports on official U.S. efforts to solve diplomatic problems with other nations by murdering their leaders or toppling their governments? Even the foreign-intelligence report issued last Tuesday, whose contents the committee negotiated out with the executive branch in order to avoid stalemate and gain consensus, had a full complement of abuses crying to be corrected by meaningful oversight. The CIA, for instance, was revealed to have bent to White House and Pentagon pressure and doctored a crucial intelligence report bearing on Soviet strategic intentions. The extent of loose and in some cases nonexistent policy control over covert actions was detailed as never before.

One could go on. The point is that the need for effective oversight has been proven beyond any serious question. To restore oversight to the very panels whose inadequacy has been so thoroughly demonstrated is an exercise in the unthinkable. Intelligence oversight is not the primary business of any of these committees, anyway. They all have plenty to do without keeping an exclusive lock on a responsibility they have discharged so poorly in the past. The whole effort to put intelligence under the rule of law is in the balance. This effort requires not just establishment of a new oversight committee but passage of comprehensive new legislation to define and delimit the tasks of intelligence. The committee issue, however, is rightly seen as a crucial test case.

Wittingly or not, the Senate barons balking committee change are handmaidens of executive abuse and patsies for executive power. Is this really the role that men like James Stennis and James Eastland, for instance, believe that a U.S. senator should play? The full Senate should reject the Rules Committee caprice when the matter comes to the floor in May, and construct oversight machinery that offers some hope of preventing recurrence of the abuses that the Church committee has so carefully and persuasively catalogued.

OREGON Journal

AN INDEPENDENT NEWSPAPER

Portland, Ore., May 3, 1976

The question of strong congressional checks and balances on the nation's intelligence community is very much in doubt with rejection by the Senate Rules Committee of a report by the Senate's Select Committee on Intelligence.

In place of the Select Committee's report, the Rules Committee substituted a proposal for a new Senate committee to oversee the intelligence agencies, but opponents of the change call the new proposal "basically weak."

In brief, the difference of opinion appears to stem from differences in point of view. On the one hand, there are those who somewhat grudgingly admit the need for covert operations but have a deep suspicion of all intelligence agencies.

On the other hand, there are those who believe deeply in the need for covert operations and have a deep suspicion that no congressional committee can keep anything secret very long.

There is good ground for both of these suspicions.

The "leaking" capacity of Congress is notorious and hardly needs documentation. The antics of both the FBI and the CIA, particularly in domestic matters such as the intrusion into the private lives of citizens, suggest the need for a tight check rein.

The Senate Rules Committee proposal emerged by a 5 to 4 vote. By contrast, only the vice chairman and one other member of the 11-man Senate Intelligence Committee refused to sign that body's report.

Recommendations of the Senate Intelligence Committee are contained in a 396-page report. In all, there are 296 recommendations, and reports out of Washington so far are sketchy. There is even less information on the recommendations of the Senate Rules Committee.

There is a basic need for good intelligence gathering, both domestic and international.

But some of the reported activities of the CIA, such as assassination attempts on the international scene and the hounding of individuals just because they once attended anti-Vietnam War meetings, border on the preposterous.

It is to be hoped that the senators do their homework before the issue goes to the Senate floor so that the debate will give the public the basis for an informed opinion.

St. Petersburg Times

St. Petersburg, Fla., April 28, 1976

Now just about the whole ugly story is out on past abuses of the CIA and other intelligence agencies. And the question today is whether anybody still cares a whole lot.

Certainly some members of Congress feel keenly that Congress and the President, between them, must act vigorously to bring CIA's secret activities under some kind of civilian control.

THAT IS EVIDENT in the report this week of the Senate's special committee on intelligence, which spent 15 months and $2.5-million exploring U.S. intelligence work, good and bad, clean and dirty, for the past quarter-century.

The committee agreed on at least 87 recommendations calculated to preserve the intelligence function but avert future excesses, from attempted assassinations to secret wars to the subversion of scholars and writers.

But committee members are not optimistic that much will come of their study. They say a slim majority of the Senate still seems interested, at least to the extent of creating a permanent CIA oversight committee to ride herd on intelligence work which, by its nature, will always have to be conducted mostly in secret.

But it is still up in the air whether such a permanent watchdog committee will get anything like the powers it needs, or the discretion to use those powers. For instance, will the committee have a whistle to blow, publicly or otherwise, on a CIA covert action which it believes illegal or contrary to the national interest?

SENATORS concerned about this are acutely aware of what happened to a similar report and a similar recommendation in the House, also prepared by a special investigating committee which now is out of business.

By the time that committee had finished its study and drafted its 338-page report, the House had lost its enthusiasm for investigating past intelligence faults. It voted not to publish the report or even, officially, to read it.

Instead, on Feb. 19, it launched an investigation, now under way and expected to cost $200,000 or more, of who leaked the report to the press.

It's not just that Congress is busy. Members say the climate has changed. They say the public has heard all it wants to hear about the CIA's goofs and outrages abroad and its violation of individual rights at home. They say they no longer detect a public demand for reform.

Many of the lawmakers trace this change, bitterly, to a slick propaganda counter-attack mounted by the intelligence community. The murder of a CIA station chief in Athens last Dec. 23, after his name was published, is said to have marked a turning point in public opinion.

CERTAINLY THE CIA and its backers seized on this unhappy event, and on the stream of disclosures from House and Senate investigating committees, to bolster their claim that vital intelligence work was being damaged or crippled.

In any event, House members have jumped at the chance to drop the whole intelligence matter. They haven't made a move even to create the oversight committee which, as in the case of the Senate report, was a key feature of the special committee's recommendations.

So it appears that after another few months the CIA and other intelligence agencies could be back to business as usual, operating secretly and comfortably under a modest reorganization plan which President Ford has imposed on his own.

WHAT THE PUBLIC wants from Congress it usually gets. But not unless it raises its voice. We hope the lawmakers this time have misread public opinion. But nothing short of a flood of protests seems likely to establish that as a fact.

Los Angeles Times

Los Angeles, Calif., May 12, 1976

Creation of a single Senate intelligence oversight committee would offer some hope that our vast intelligence agencies will be brought under more rational control.

The plan, a compromise reached by Senate leaders, would establish one permanent Senate committee of 17 members who would have exclusive oversight of the Central Intelligence Agency and partial oversight of the Federal Bureau of Investigation and military intelligence.

Specifically, the new committee would have primary jurisdiction over FBI and military intelligence, but would share this authority respectively with the Judiciary Committee and the Armed Services Committee.

Legislation affecting intelligence activities would first be considered by the new committee and then be referred to the older standing committees.

An important element of the plan is the proposed nine-year limit on committee membership. The obvious purpose of this provision is to prevent the accretion of too much power that longer periods of service would bring to committee members.

Sen. Lowell P. Weicker Jr. (R-Conn.), who began a filibuster last week to force the Senate to act, said after the compromise was reached that he considered the proposal workable. It is a distinct improvement over the present division of authority, but the plan contains one serious weakness.

Yet to be decided is whether the new committee will be given authority over the budgets of the CIA and other intelligence agencies. Budget control is where decisive power is exercised. Without that authority, the new committee's oversight function would be critically impaired. Effective control of intelligence operations means effective control of their budgets. It must not be forgotten that Congress appropriated millions of dollars for a war in Laos—a war that Congress did not know existed.

A joint congressional committee would be the most effective form of intelligence oversight, but such a committee evidently has no chance of approval. The new committee, if it has budgetary control, appears to be the next best substitute.

House CIA Investigation and Reports

Kissinger

House Committee compromises with Kissinger. The House Select Committee on Intelligence Nov. 4, 1975 voted 8–5 to compromise with Secretary of State Henry A. Kissinger over a Kissinger subordinate's memorandum criticizing the State Department's handling of the Turkish invasion of Cyprus in 1974. [See Vol. I, p. 34E2]

In so acting, the committee agreed to accept a proposal by Kissinger under which the State Department would supply the contents of the Cyprus memorandum and others like it without disclosing the names of junior- and middle-level department officers who had written them.

Kissinger had maintained that disclosure of the names of subordinate officers, who had made recommendations to department policy makers, would force these persons to answer for themselves after the fact and lead to "timidity" in future internal criticism of superiors.

The secretary's position was endorsed in a letter to the committee signed by more than 200 middle-level officers of the Foreign Service, it was reported Oct. 14. The letter, addressed to the committee's chairman, Rep. Otis G. Pike (D, N.Y.), warned that his demand for testimony by lower-level officers would damage the Foreign Service and could encourage its officers to draft "unexceptional" memoranda of internal dissent, "bland to the point of uselessness." "Many of us," the letter said, "believe that the Foreign Service is just now—after 20 years—overcoming the legacy of that bitter question: 'Who lost China?' Some of us recall the fate of those of our colleagues who were swept up—and away—in the debate."

Because of his refusal to comply with a committee subpoena for the Cyprus memorandum, Kissinger was summoned before the panel Oct. 31. He then proposed the compromise.

Contempt action sought for Kissinger. The House Select Committee on Intelligence voted Nov. 14 to cite Secretary of State Henry Kissinger for contempt of Congress for failing to produce, under subpoena, classified documents for use in the committee's investigation of the effectiveness of U.S. intelligence operations.

The committee, accusing Kissinger of "contumacious [deliberately defiant] conduct," approved, in three separate 10–3 votes, three contempt citations against the secretary of state for each of three subpoenas he had not complied with. (The committee's action had to be approved by a majority of the House before the matter could be referred to the Justice Department for investigation and possible prosecution.)

Kissinger's immediate reaction to the action was that he feared it would raise "serious questions" all over the world about "what this country is doing to itself."

President Ford, also expressing regret over the move, termed it "shocking" and predicted it would have "very broad and serious ramifications." He added that material demanded under one of the subpoenas—State Department recommendations for covert intelligence activities made to the White House during 1962–1972—was protected from Congressional scrutiny by executive privilege.

The second committee subpoena asked Kissinger to produce minutes of the meetings of the National Security Council's secret 40 Committee, which approved all covert intelligence actions undertaken by the U.S. The third asked for intelligence reports concerning the Soviet Union's compliance with the terms of the 1972 strategic arms limitation treaty. These subpoenas were addressed to Kissinger in his capacity as director of the NSC.

Action against Kissinger dropped. The House Select Committee on Intelligence Dec. 10 dropped efforts to obtain a contempt of Congress citation against Secretary of State Henry A. Kissinger for refusing to provide the committee with subpoenaed documents.

Rep. Otis G. Pike (D, N.Y.), the panel's chairman, told the House that his committee now considered the Ford Administration in "substantial compliance" with the subpoena because an accommodation had been reached over access to details of 20 State Department requests for covert intelligence operations abroad since 1961.

A. Searle Field, counsel to the committee, said the committee members had received "very good assurance" at the White House Dec. 9 that the desired information would be forthcoming. He said William Hyland, director of the State Department's Bureau of Intelligence and Research, had briefed a committee delegation directly from the 20 State Department proposals and from the minutes of the National Security Council's 40 Committee. C The committee members did not see the documents themselves, however.

Pike had announced at the beginning of a committee hearing Dec. 2 that "substantial compliance" had been obtained with two other subpoenas issued to Kissinger in his capacity as NSC director.

Navy's ex-chief accuses Kissinger. Adm. Elmo R. Zumwalt Jr., chief of naval D operations until his retirement in June 1974, charged Dec. 2 that Secretary of State Henry A. Kissinger had withheld information from President Ford about what Zumwalt characterized as "gross violations" by the Soviet Union of its 1972 agreement with the U.S. to limit strategic weapons.

Appearing before the House Select Committee on Intelligence, Zumwalt accused Kissinger of withholding negotiating information from the President, the secretary of defense and the Joint Chiefs of E Staff. Moreover, he suggested that Kissinger's lack of candor was the result of a personal and political commitment to U.S.-Soviet detente that made him "reluctant to report the actual facts."

Kissinger, in a Washington press conference Dec. 9, angrily denied Zumwalt's allegations, labeling as a "total falsehood" the suggestion that he had withheld information from President Ford. Moreover, Kissinger said that the F admiral, who had indicated interest in running for the U.S. Senate, "got carried away by his political ambitions."

After describing in detail U.S. procedures for assessing Soviet violations, Kissinger said it was difficult for the U.S. to decide whether the violations were deliberate or unintentional or, for that matter, whether U.S. intelligence had picked evidence indicating a breach of the accords where there was none.

He insisted that all suspected Soviet G violations had been immediately reported to the President. Neither the Central Intelligence Agency nor the Defense Department had ever challenged interpretations of these violations worked out by special National Security Council panels charged with assessing them, he added.

Harrington

A **Complaint against Harrington dismissed.** The House Committee on Official Standards of Conduct Nov. 6 dismissed a complaint that Rep. Michael Harrington (D, Mass.) had illegally disclosed classified information on the Central Intelligence Agency's covert operations in Chile. [See Vol. I, pp. 9, 16, 110]

Rep. Robin L. Beard (R, Tenn.) had filed a formal complaint against Harrington, charging that Harrington had
B made public secret testimony by Central Intelligence Agency Director William E. Colby before the House Armed Services intelligence subcommittee without the full committee's approval and in violation of House rules.

The panel, informally known as the ethics committee, voted, 7–3, to dismiss the complaint on the ground that no rules of Congress had been broken. The committee's chairman, Rep. John J. Flynt Jr.,
C said that because Colby's testimony had been given under conditions that were in themselves in violation of House rules, Beard's complaint was invalid. The subcommittee's meeting had been irregular Flynt said, because no public notice was issued, no quorum was present, no vote to go into executive session was taken and only one member, Chairman Lucien Nedzi (D, Mich.), was present.

In attempting to defend his actions, Harrington had not referred to the ille-
D gality of the subcommittee's meeting.

Unreleased Report Published

House intelligence committee findings reported; official publication blocked. The *New York Times* and the *Washington Post,* starting Jan. 20, 1976, published accounts of the still-unreleased report of the House
E Intelligence Committee. Described in the stories were Central Intelligence Agency operations with the news media, CIA purchasing procedures, secret aid to foreign leaders, allegations that the aid to Angolan factions had been misrepresented, and other matters. The committee report also, according to newspaper accounts, described advice given by Senator Henry M. Jackson to CIA officials on how the agency should cope with Senate investigations.

F The White House and the CIA charged that the leaking of the report violated the agreement upon the basis of which the committee had been furnished with secret information, and questioned the ability of Congressional committees to preserve the confidentiality of executive disclosures. William Colby, the outgoing director of the CIA, besides deploring the leaks, Jan. 26 characterized the report as "totally biased and a disservice to our nation."

G A. Searle Field, staff director for the House Intelligence Committee, disagreed with charges of committee responsibility for the leak. "As far as I can see, it didn't come from the committee. There's literally dozens of copies [of the report] at the State Department, at the executive offices, the Pentagon. It is a very severe blow," he said Jan. 26.

The full House voted Jan. 29, 246–124, to give the executive branch the right to review and censor the report before publication. The vote, a victory for President Ford and the intelligence agencies, was deplored by Rep. Otis G. Pike (D., N.Y.), the chairman of the intelligence committee, who said it made "a complete travesty of the whole doctrine of separation of powers." Ford said that the vote "indicates that a large majority of House members share my concern that our legitimate classified national security information be denied to our enemies and potential enemies."

The House vote came after conflicting votes by the House Intelligence Committee Jan. 23 (against executive censorship) and the House Rules Committee Jan. 28 (favoring executive censorship.)

Because the report had already been leaked, and extensively reported in newspapers, the House vote was seen as primarily a test of conflicting theories of Congress' right to disclose, on its own authority, information deemed confidential by the executive branch.

According to the newspaper accounts, the House Intelligence Committee report described the following activities:

Reporting of Angolan aid—According to the *New York Times* Jan. 20, the report disclosed that the CIA undervalued certain items in aid sent to Angola so that the total was considerably lower than the true figures. The Ford Administration had told Congress that it spent $31 million in Angola since January 1975. The case of .30-caliber semi-automatic carbines was cited: their inventory value was given as $15 apiece, but in the accounting given to Congress, they were priced at $7.55.

CIA funding of political, military groups—According to the Jan. 26 *Times* account of the report, the CIA secretly extended funds to numerous political parties and individuals, mainly in developing countries. Political parties in Italy also received substantial aid, amounting to $75 million since 1947, when the CIA was founded. One political leader in the "third world" received $960,000 over 14 years, and other heads of state received funds for over a decade, according to the report.

The report gave a breakdown by percentages of the kinds of covert operations approved by the Forty Committee. The Forty Committee was the arm of the National Security Council which the intelligence agencies went to for authorization of covert projects. According to the report, 32% of the actions approved by the Forty Committee involved political funding, about the same percentage were media projects, and 27% were proposed transfers of arms and military equipment to "secret armies" and other groups "engaged in hostilities." In most cases, the report said, the clandestine military aid projects were imposed on the CIA against its wishes, sometimes by the Defense Department or by the Administration.

The committee report said that 88% of the proposals made to the Forty Committee originated with the CIA, but other government agencies and government officials, and in one case, "foreign head of state," had also been responsible for proposals. Informed sources said that the "foreign head of state" was the Shah of Iran, who reportedly asked former President Nixon to have the CIA furnish arms to Kurdish rebels in Iraq.

Finances—The report, according to the *Times* Jan. 26 and 27, cited a number of financial practices it found questionable. It said that 85% of the CIA's contracts—amounting to "hundreds of millions" of dollars—were let without competitive bidding. However, the report did not argue with the CIA's assertion that only 2.5% of its contracts had cost overruns exceeding 15%.

The report found that the CIA "sterility codes," which were used to make untraceable purchases, had "become an over-used, expensive and often uncontrollable technique for questionable purchasing." Procurement by local stations was criticized for "overspending and underauditing." Expenditures by local stations of $41,000 in one year for liquor, and of $100,000 for furnishings for "safe houses" over five years were reported. "Safe houses" were places where CIA operatives could stay and be debriefed without fear of discovery.

The report also stated that the CIA had not complied with a 1967 order of President Johnson, to stop awarding "covert" research contracts to "any of the nation's educational or private voluntary organizations." A few universities, the report said, were still doing work for the CIA, without being aware that the work was commissioned by the CIA. The *Times* reported Jan. 26 that Colby, through a spokesman, had said he believed that the CIA had complied with the presidential order.

Finally, the report took issue with the intelligence agencies over the total amount spent by the agencies in gathering information at home and abroad. It said that these agencies had reported to Congress budgets which were "three or four times" lower than the amounts actually spent. It gave this amount as "more than $10 billion" annually.

Jackson, Symington contacts with the CIA—The report quoted a memorandum, dated Feb. 23, 1973, purportedly written by a CIA official describing a Feb. 3, 1973 meeting between the official and Sen. Henry M. Jackson (D, Wash.). At the time of the meeting, the CIA feared that some of its covert activities in Chile would be exposed in the course of an investigation, by a subcommittee of the Senate Foreign Relations Committee, into activities of the International Telephone and Telegraph Corp. in Chile, including allegations of collaboration with the CIA. Sen. Jackson, according to the memorandum, advised the agency to seek protection by having the inquiries transferred to the committee that reviewed CIA activities.

Sen. Jackson, quoted in the Jan. 26 *Times* story, denied that there had been any "coverup." He did, however, say he remembered giving officials advice on "procedural matters" in connection with the subcommittee investigation.

An article in the *Times* Jan. 28 cited "Congressional sources" as indicating another questionable link between Jackson and the CIA. According to those sources, Jackson had, early in 1973, given Richard Helms, a former director of the CIA, advice on dealing with Congressional questions concerning his, and the CIA's, involvement in Watergate matters.

Sen. Jackson said that Sen. Stuart Symington (D, Mo.) had asked him to talk to Helms about the CIA and Watergate. Jackson said that Helms feared that people in the Nixon Administration were trying to implicate him and the CIA in Watergate. Jackson said that he had had Helms and Symington to dinner one night, and that he had "just listened to" Helms' account of meetings with top Nixon aides. Jackson said that he had told Helms to "lay out all the facts" for the Senate inquiry.

Jackson also said that, as he remembered it, Symington and Helms discussed CIA activities in Chile at his home. Jackson said that he and Helms had never discussed those activities.

Sen. Symington admitted Jan. 23 that he had discussed with Helms CIA operations in Chile, and other "problems" which Helms might face in testifying before the Senate in the confirmation hearings for his appointment as ambassador to Iran. Symington strongly rejected, however, charges that he had "colluded" with Helms to prepare false testimony.

(Helms' testimony was currently being studied for possible perjury prosecution. It appeared to conflict with recent disclosures indicating extensive covert CIA aid to the opponents of the Marxist Chilean president, Salvador Allende.)

Cyprus affairs—The report, according to the Jan. 20 *Times,* made two charges concerning U.S. intelligence in Cyprus:

No firm action was taken to block the coup which overthrew the government of Archbishop Makarios, even though it was known about before it occurred: "United States officials, knowing a coup was imminent, may have simply allowed it to happen," the report said. U.S. officials in Cyprus had been told to oppose a coup against Archbishop Makarios, the report acknowledged.

Evidence concerning the killing (in August 1974) of the U.S. ambassador to Cyprus, Rodger P. Davies, had not been sufficiently followed up. The report said that information, gathered within a few hours of the killing, identifying the killers as Cypriot police officers had not resulted in the prosecution of the killers, or even their removal from the police force. The state department Jan. 20 denied that it knew the identities of Davies' murderers, or that it had been slack in investigating the murder. It said, however, that it was dissatisfied with the investigation made by the Cyprus government.

Foreign intelligence—The report said that the Navy had sent submarines inside the territorial waters of other countries to gather information, and, on at least nine occasions, the submarines had collided with other vessels, according to the Jan. 20 *Times.* The document faulted the CIA for failing, in a number of important cases, to accomplish its main task, the prediction of foreign events. As examples of such unforeseen events, the report, according to the *Times,* cited the failure to anticipate the TET offensive in 1968, the Soviet invasion of Czechoslovakia that year, the 1973 Egyptian attack on Israel, and the nuclear bomb explosion by India in 1974.

CIA-news media links—The Jan. 23 *Washington Post* quoted the report as saying, in a section entitled "Manipulation of the Media," that "the free flow of information, vital to a responsible and credible press, has been threatened as a result of CIA's use of the world media for cover and for clandestine information-gathering." According to the report, in 1975 there were 11 full-time CIA agents stationed abroad who posed as journalists. The CIA had arrangements with 15 television, radio, newspaper and magazine companies (none of them major American concerns, apparently) to provide the agents with "covers." The agency, the report said, also employed an undisclosed number of "stringers," or part-time journalists, whose connection with the CIA was not known to the newspaper or network employing them. These journalists, the report said, "are often directed to insert agency-composed 'news' articles into foreign publications and wire services."

The CIA, according to the report, distinguished between news primarily intended for American consumption, and that directed to foreign countries. News for domestic consumption was supposed to be free from CIA influence. However, as late as 1973, there were five CIA agents working in the U.S. under journalistic cover. Colby, the director of the CIA, ordered an end to those arrangements following publicity of the CIA's connection with the news media.

According to the report, the CIA did not sufficiently take into account "the possibility of its adulterating news digested by Americans." The CIA, the report said, engaged in "frequent manipulation of Reuter wire service dispatches—which regularly appear in U.S. media." (A Reuters spokesman said "I await proof that any Reuters service has been manipulated. Until I see it, I tend to think the agents have manipulated their employers.") Colby, at a Jan. 26 news conference, denied that the CIA had "manipulated" Reuters dispatches. He conjectured that the committee had fastened upon Reuters, after someone (not a CIA official) had offered it as a hypothetical example of a foreign news media.

The *Washington Post* had stories Jan. 16 and Jan. 17—not based on the House committee report—describing CIA news operations. The Jan. 16 story, based on the Senate intelligence committee report, described a propaganda effort by the CIA to block the election of Salvador Allende to the presidency of Chile in 1970. The *Post* quoted the Senate report as saying that the CIA claimed responsibility, either directly or indirectly, for "726 articles, broadcasts, editorials and similar items" in Latin American or European media. CIA funding was provided to news organizations opposing Allende. [See Vol. I, pp. 9–11, 107–110]

The *Post* Jan. 17 claimed that the CIA had set up a coordinating committee with the State Department and the U.S. Information Agency to keep those agencies advised of CIA media efforts, so that they would not be deceived by stories invented or altered by the CIA. Among the covert media operations described in the article were radio programs attacking Soviet leaders, which were broadcast so as to appear to come from mainland China, and the insertion of CIA-written stories into Chinese newspapers—done by reprinting the entire issue of the newspaper.

CIA-Media Links

Bush limits CIA-media contacts. In a directive issued Feb. 11, Director of Central Intelligence George Bush said that the Central Intelligence Agency would, "effective immediately," no longer enter into any "paid or contractual" relationships with full or part-time employes of U.S. news organizations.

The directive stated that existing relationships with such employes would be terminated "as soon as possible." An intelligence official said that "less than 20 persons will be affected by the order."

The Bush order appeared to reverse the position of the former CIA head, William Colby, who had maintained that part-time employes of American news organizations could legitimately be hired by the agency.

The directive also stated that the CIA did not presently secretly employ any American clergy, and "this practice will be continued as a matter of policy."

Bush did not acknowledge any "impropriety" in the agency's use of newsmen or clergy, but said that the order had been issued in order to avoid "any appearance of improper use."

The order did not prohibit CIA hiring of employes of foreign news organizations. It was not clear whether the CIA would be barred from using obscure American publications to provide career CIA agents with a cover identity abroad.

Senators drop request for CIA-journalist names. Sen. Walter Huddleston (D, Ky.) said Feb. 17 that the Senate Intelligence Committee had decided not to press the CIA to reveal the names of journalists who had cooperated with the agency.

Huddleston and Sen. Charles McC. Mathias Jr. (R, Md.) had met earlier that day with George Bush, the director of central intelligence, and reached an agreement whereby the CIA would give the committee information on the sorts of individuals involved, with their positions and relationship with the CIA, in CIA-media contacts. Huddleston noted that the data would probably be sufficient for the committee to infer the names of the individuals and organizations involved, but he thought this would not be necessary unless evidence of "illegal practices or absolute wrongdoing" emerged.

Huddleston said that "the name itself is not important" for the committee's task of determining the effect of the CIA-media operations on "the free press in this country."

In a television interview Feb. 15 Bush had expressed the CIA position against disclosure of the names of individuals cooperating with the agency, saying that "people can come up dead," as a result of such disclosures.

Suggested Reforms

Pike panel offers reforms. In its final act before disbanding Feb. 11, the House Select Intelligence Committee Feb. 10 voted 9–4 to submit a list of 20 proposals, including the creation of a permanent House Intelligence Committee.

The committee, chaired by Rep. Otis G. Pike (D, N.Y.), recommended, in addition to a permanent oversight committee, the following proposals:

- That the General Accounting Office be authorized to make full audits of the intelligence agencies, without exemptions for classified matters.
- That a foreign operations subcommittee be created within the National Security Council, the members of which would be required to make individual written reports to the President on the possible consequences of proposed covert operations.
- That within 48 hours of presidential approval of any covert operation, a permanent House intelligence committee be given a detailed description of it by the director of central intelligence, as well as a written statement by the President that it was necessary to national security. The House committee, under the plan, would also receive the assessments of the covert operation made by Foreign Operations Subcommittee members.
- That assassinations and paramilitary operations be prohibited except in wartime.
- That the 1947 National Security Act be amended to allow disclosure to Congressional committees of intelligence-related information, and that the intelligence committee or the House by vote could make public classified information.
- That an inspector general for intelligence be created.
- That the Defense Intelligence Agency be abolished, because it had failed in its task of coordinating military intelligence and often merely duplicated CIA efforts in an inferior way.
- That the intelligence agencies be barred from employing U.S. citizens who worked for educational, religious or news organizations.

Pike said that any action on the proposals would be "up to the leadership" of the House.

The committee report, still unreleased but extensively reported, was highly controversial. Apart from attacks by members of the administration, several committee members questioned its findings. Rep. Dale Milford (D, Tex.) said Feb. 3 that "over 50% of the charges and conclusions are not based on the committee record." Rep. Robert McClory (R, Ill.) the same day termed it "a diatribe against the CIA."

The committee staff director, A. Searle Field, however, said Feb. 3 that "almost every line is documented and footnoted."

Pike had charged on Feb. 2 that the administration was endeavoring to block release of the report because it made various officials, including Secretary of State Henry Kissinger, "look bad."

Schorr and Leaked Documents

Schorr suspended for leaking report. CBS News relieved its correspondent Daniel Schorr of all reporting duties Feb. 23 for an "indefinite period." The action was taken "in view of the adversary situation" in which Schorr was placed "in pending government investigations" as a result of his leaking the secret House Intelligence Committee report to the New York weekly, the *Village Voice.*

Schorr acknowledged Feb. 12 that he was the source of the copy of the report which the *Voice* used when it published substantial excerpts Feb. 11 and Feb. 18. Schorr said he had decided to arrange for the report's publication after he came to believe that he was "possibly the sole possessor of the document outside the government" and that he "could not be the one responsible for suppressing" its full publication. [See text, pp. 82–90]

Although CBS News and the *New York Times* had made public most of the findings of the report, the two *Voice* issues contained the first extensive excerpts from the report, publication of which had been blocked pending censorship by the intelligence agencies, by a vote of the full House on Jan. 29.

Schorr said Feb. 12 that he had obtained the "confidential cooperation" of the Reporter's Committee of the Freedom of the Press—a group that aided journalists facing legal problems in connection with their work—in finding a publisher for the report. Schorr said that an unnamed intermediary had told him that Clay Felker, publisher of the *Village Voice* and *New York* magazine, had offered to make a "substantial contribution" to the committee in return for the report.

Schorr, who had originally denied any role in the *Voice's* publishing the report, said that it had become "pointless" to conceal his part in the leak because of the committee's failure to maintain confidentiality.

The committee issued a statement Feb. 12 saying that it had agreed to accept any proceeds that might emerge from publication of the report "to be used in defense of the First Amendment" and that it had put Schorr in touch with a lawyer acquainted with publishing. It denied that it had breached the confidentiality of the arrangement with Schorr.

Robert Maynard, a trustee of the committee, denied Feb. 13 that there had been a promise of a substantial contribution. He accused Schorr of "trying to make us a partner in his calumny."

The committee announced Feb. 24 that it would not accept any proceeds from the publication "to avoid any suggestion the committee was involved in commercialization or check-book journalism."

One of *New York Magazine's* editors, associated with Felker in the transaction, said Feb. 26 that he believed that while the question of money had been raised at first, it had been in connection with the publication of the report as an independent "one-shot" book project. When it was decided to publish excerpts from the report in the newspaper, the report was made available "with no [financial] strings attached."

The House Feb. 19 voted 269–115 to have the ethics committee investigate "the circumstances surrounding the publication of the text." Schorr was cited specifically, for "alleged actions . . . [which] may be in contempt of or a breach of the privileges of this house."

Opponents of the resolution voiced concern that it would have a "chilling effect" on the freedom of the press. Supporters argued that it was necessary in order to "protect the integrity and the process of the House."

President Ford Feb. 12 had offered House speaker Carl Albert (D, Okla.) the "full resources" of the executive branch in investigating the leak. Albert Feb. 13 declined the offer.

Secretary of State Henry Kissinger Feb. 12 castigated the leak as "a new version of McCarthyism." The report had attacked Kissinger for making "comments . . . at variance with the facts" (in reference to the reporting of alleged Soviet violations of the SALT accords) and having a "passion for secrecy." Kissinger's part in an attempted revolt by the Kurds in Iraq had also been criticized.

George Bush, director of the Central Intelligence Agency, said Feb. 22 on "Meet the Press" that the *Voice* publication had done harm to national security, but he refused to identify the particular injurious passages because "that would highlight those and make things worse." He went on to say that "the fundamental thing is that Congress voted by almost 2-to-1 that the report not be made public, and it was made public . . . That's just plain wrong."

CBS said Feb. 23 that it would continue to pay Schorr's salary, and would provide him with legal aid insofar as he might need it in connection with his past reporting for CBS, or to protect the confidentiality of his sources. CBS stated, however, that Schorr had acted independently in giving the *Voice* a copy of the secret report.

Leak probe underway; Pike, CIA dispute missing documents. The House Committee on Standards of Official Conduct (known as the ethics committee), mandated by the House to investigate the publication of the classified House Intelligence Committee report, on March 3 received authority to subpoena individuals and documents. Before the House vote, 321–85, granting the powers, the ethics committee could subpoena only members and employes of the House.

The chairman of the committee, John J. Flynt (D, Ga.), announced March 4 that the committee would not use Federal Bureau of Investigation (FBI) agents in its inquiry. On March 2 Flynt had said that the committee would employ David Bowers, who had retired the previous week from the FBI, to head its investigation staff.

The House Administration Committee March 25 voted unanimously to allow the ethics committee $150,000 for the investigation. This was a major cut from the ethics committee request of $350,000.

Flynt, responding to expressions of fear that the investigation might become a witch-hunt directed particularly at Daniel Schorr, the newsman who had admitted to supplying the *Village Voice* with the copy of the report that was published, said March 2 that the committee was "not per se investigating any particular person." His committee's task, he said, was "to find out how the committee report was leaked and who leaked it."

The *New York Times* reported March 11 that the affiliates' executive committee of CBS Radio sent a telegram Feb. 17 to the top officials of CBS News urging that they consider dismissing Schorr for his role in the publication of the report. CBS officials, quoted in the *Times* story, said the telegram had no part in their decision to suspend Schorr.

In related news, Rep. Otis G. Pike, chairman of the expired House Intelligence Committee, March 9 accused the Central Intelligence Agency of "running a media event" aimed at discrediting him and his former committee. Pike's remarks referred to CIA statements that the Pike committee had failed to return 232 classified documents loaned to the committee. As described by a CIA spokesman, the documents included reports dealing with CIA purchasing and budget audits, the coup in Portugal, disarmament talks with the Soviet Union and other matters.

Pike said that 105 of the documents had been found by committee staff in the files where they were stored at CIA headquarters, and that for another 95 the CIA could produce no receipts from the committee.

A CIA spokesman March 9 said that the recovery of the 105 documents had not been "verified;" he also insisted that the 95 documents questioned by Pike had been supplied to the committee.

George Bush, director of the CIA, March 16 rejected the idea that the CIA had tried to use reports of missing documents as a media weapon against Pike or the House Intelligence Committee.

Pike March 9 also said that the committee staff director, A. Searle Field, had told him that CIA special counsel Mitchell Rogovin had, in a Jan. 23 telephone call to Field, threatened political retaliation against Pike for leading his committee to vote for the publication of its report, which was highly critical of the CIA. Pike said that Searle told him that Rogovin said: "Pike will pay for this, you wait and see—we'll destroy him for this."

Rogovin March 9 denied ever having made any such threats against Pike.

Schorr probe dropped. CBS correspondent Daniel Schorr was released from a House committee subpoena Sept. 22 after he had refused nine times in testimony on Sept. 15 to tell the committee how he had obtained a classified House report on the U.S. intelligence agencies.

Schorr, who had admitted to furnishing the copy of the report that was heavily excerpted in two February issues of the Village Voice, said that his silence was based on "professional conscience as well as [the First Amendment freedom of the press] constitutional right. . . ." To reveal his source for the report, he contended, would "dry up many future sources for many future reporters," and ultimately sap the vitality of a free press.

Schorr Sept. 22 characterized the committee's decision to release him from the subpoena as a "great victory for freedom of the press."

The House Committee on Standards of Official Conduct had voted Aug. 25 to subpoena Schorr after a five-month investigation, in which more than 385 people were interviewed, had failed to identify the person who leaked the report to Schorr. In the course of the investigation, the House panel—known as the ethics committee—had held public hearings at which members and staff of the disbanded House Intelligence Committee testified. The Intelligence Committee had produced the report that was leaked to Schorr.

David W. Bowers, a retired FBI agent who served as chief investigator for the ethics committee, told the committee at the first hearing July 19 that security had been lax in the Intelligence Committee at the time of the leak. Bowers said that Schorr had probably obtained a copy of the report on or about Jan. 25. At that time, Bowers said, the Intelligence Committee had possessed 19 copies and the original of the report, and there had been 40 copies in the executive branch.

Bowers said that the investigation had made progress but had not succeeded in identifying the individual who had leaked the report to Schorr.

Rep. Otis G. Pike (D, N.Y.), chairman of the Intelligence Committee, testified July 19 that he did not know who had leaked the report. Rep. Les Aspin (D, Wis.), a member of the Pike committee, testified July 20 that he had shown a few pages of the report to a reporter from Reuters, and lent the report to the Central Intelligence Agency. Aspin said, however, that he did not know who had given Schorr a copy of the report. Aspin added that Mitchell Rogovin, chief counsel for the CIA, had told him that the *Village Voice* excerpts contained two pages that had been missing from the copy lent by Aspin to the CIA. This meant, Aspin said, that neither he nor the CIA could have been the source of Schorr's copy.

A

At its Aug. 25 meeting the ethics committee subpoenaed three other journalists besides Schorr: Clay S. Felker, editor-in-chief of *New York* magazine, Sheldon Zelasnick, a former editor of *New York* magazine, and Aaron Latham, another *New York* magazine editor. *New York* magazine owned the *Village Voice*, and the three journalists had handled the publication of the secret report.

B

When they appeared before the ethics committee Sept. 15, Felker, Zelaznick and Latham all testified that they did not know who had been Schorr's source. Despite warnings that he was risking prosecution and citation for contempt of Congress, Latham twice refused to respond when asked if he had "any knowledge or opinion of who the source might be." The same warning was given to Schorr nine times.

C

The committee released Felker, Zelaznick and Latham from their subpoenas Sept. 22. Two votes at that session had shown that a majority of the committee did not favor punishing Schorr. A proposal to initiate proceedings against Schorr for his failure to produce subpoenaed copies of the report was rejected by a 6–5 vote; a second move to deprive Schorr of his House press credentials for the remainder of the session failed by a 7–4 vote. The committee then voted 9–1 to release Schorr and the other journalists from their subpoenas. In effect, the vote ended the ethics committee investigation of the intelligence report leak.

D

E

Schorr's attorney, Joseph A. Califano, had argued Sept. 13 in a memorandum to the ethics committee that its probe was misguided. Califano contended that the extensive disclosures of the substance of the intelligence report in the *New York Times* before the report was published in the *Village Voice* had rendered it impossible for Schorr to betray the report's confidentiality. Califano also argued that the material published in the *Village Voice* was not harmful to national security.

F

The ethics committee's final report Oct. 6 concluded that Schorr's source had been someone "on or very near" the intelligence panel. A majority of the ethics panel called Schorr's conduct "reprehensible" and urged that the House hire professionals to guard secret materials.

Schorr resigned from CBS Sept. 28. He said "the polarizing effects within CBS News of the controversy involving me" made him doubt that he could "function effectively if reinstated."

G

Excerpts from the Pike Committee's Report on the CIA

Below are excerpts from the Pike Committee's Report on the Central Intelligence Agency which was "leaked" to the Village Voice by Daniel Schorr. The excerpts were printed in the February 16, 1976 Voice.

Costs

No money shall be drawn from the Treasury, but in Consequence of Appropriations made by law; and a regular Statement and Account of the Receipts and Expenditures of all public Money shall be published from time to time. Art. 1, Sec. 9, cl. vii, U.S. Const.

Money and spending were the first topics of Committee hearings. This choice of a beginning was founded on Constitutional responsibilities, and it implemented a straightforward investigative technique—by following the dollars, the Committee would locate activities and priorities of our intelligence services.

The inquiry was fruitful and interesting. By the time it was over, GAO [General Accounting Office] accountants on loan to the Committee had concluded that the foreign intelligence budget is three to four times more costly than Congress has been told. An OMB [Office of Management and Budget] review of the domestic intelligence budget, conducted at the Committee's request, concluded that it may be five times the estimate given to Congress by federal officials.

Totals do not tell the whole story. Congressional and Executive scrutiny of these budgets was found to range somewhere between cursory and nonexistent. Spending controls by the agencies themselves were, likewise, often inadequate, as a few preliminary examples indicate.

- A CIA Station in a small country spent $41,000 on liquor, in one year.
- Taxpayer monies were spent to provide heads of state with female companions, and to pay people with questionable reputations to make pornographic movies for blackmail.
- The "accommodation procurement" mechanism was used to buy limousines for foreign dignitaries, with cash payments that were difficult to verify.
- A huge arsenal of weapons and access to ammunition have been developed by CIA, giving it a capability that exceeds most armies of the world.
- A middleman who is a close friend of top FBI officials tacked thousands, if not millions, of dollars of unwarranted markups on to covert purchases.

These examples reflect the wide range of problems with secret financing of secret activities. A more detailed review of these and other examples, along with the basic processes or mechanisms that accompany them, is a good base for suggested reforms.

1. Deceptive Budgets

Much attention is paid to numbers when the foreign and domestic intelligence budgets are prepared. Not much attention is paid to substance.

The OMB, the Director of Central Intelligence (DCI), and other officials go through an elaborate process in arriving at budget numbers. As described to Congress, it is an impressive procedure.

What is not described is the close, almost inbred relationship between OMB officials and intelligence budgetmakers. OMB also does not point out that it completely lacks the expertise to evaluate huge technological expenditures by the National Security Agency.

Executive officials do not stress the lack of a centralized budget authority in the intelligence services, which causes enormous waste, duplication and hidden costs in military intelligence. There is little consideration given to the extraordinary spending latitude granted to CIA, or to the CIA's heavy use of "unvouchered" funds. There is no explanation from FBI of the reasons for millions of dollars of "confidential" purchases.

When appearing before Congress, executive officials do not review the inadequacies of internal Agency auditors. No mention is made of items transferred elsewhere in the federal budget to keep the intelligence budget small.

These officials do not remind Congress that our government's auditors, the General Accounting Office, have been denied access to secret intelligence budgets for more than a decade. They do not explain abuses of covert purchasing mechanisms, domestic as well as foreign.

These same officials do, however, stress that anything they can or will say must be kept a secret.

All this adds up to more than $10 billion being spent by a handful of people, with little independent supervision, with inadequate controls, even less auditing, and an overabundance of secrecy.

It begins with OMB officials and their counterparts in the various agencies. Testimony before this Committee revealed that only six OMB employees work full-time on the foreign intelligence budget. Of those six, three are former CIA employees. In turn, the CIA official in charge of the Agency's budget has recently arrived from OMB, where he had primary responsibility for CIA's budget.

This, in itself, does not bode well for a vigorous review of the merits of intelligence programs. It is set back further by the fact that OMB is not told of sensitive projects as they are being planned. Even after it is told, OMB's officials are not free to evaluate all details of sensitive projects.

The absence of real involvement by outsiders in intelligence spending continues.

For example, CIA's budget appears as only a single line item in the published Federal budget. This is done in the name of secrecy, but it gives CIA an unusual advantage. Congress requires any agency wishing to transfer funds from one line item to another to come back to Congress for approval.

This is called reprogramming. Most agencies have many line items, giving Congress some check on their spending. CIA has had no reprogramming problems in the past. It could tell Congress it was spending a certain amount on covert action, then proceed to transfer large amounts to covert programs without Congress' approval.

This is not however, the most significant lack of knowledge about intelligence spending. Billions of dollars spent every year for intelligence are not included in the "official" intelligence budgets.

One way this has been accomplished has been by shifting items that have traditionally appeared in the intelligence budget into other budget categories. For example, the Department of Defense has switched the following items, by reclassifying them as "communications": Counterintelligence and Investigative Activities; Mapping, Charting, and Geodesy; and the Advance Location Strike Program. A sizeable secret reconnaissance activity at Defense was switched to "research and development." All of these activities and many more were, until recently, in Defense's intelligence budget. Defense is not alone in using this tactic.

The costs given Congress for military intelligence do not include expenditures for tactical military intelligence, which would approximately double intelligence budgets for the three armed services. Roughly 20 percent of the National Security Agency's budget is not added into the intelligence budget. It should be noted that NSA does nothing else except gather and analyze technical intelligence, and it has one of the largest budgets in the intelligence community.

Sometimes entire agencies, such as the Defense Advanced Research Projects Agency, are completely omitted from estimates of intelligence-related costs as well as the intelligence budget.

The budget for the National Security Council is omitted completely, although a sizeable portion of their staff and subcommittees work exclusively on intelligence matters.

Still another technique is undervaluation of the real cost of certain operations. The Committee analyzed one covert operation and found that the dollar amounts given by CIA for weapons supplied were about half of the Defense Department's contract prices.

At the Committee's request, OMB did add up the total cost for all federal domestic intelligence, for the first time ever. The total they came up with was more than five times the amount that had been given to the Committee in testimony by domestic intelligence officials. The FBI, for example, had neglected to include such clear intelligence functions as the National Bomb Data Center, or Counterintelligence. More significantly, there had never been an attempt to add up all the divergent intelligence operations in the federal government.

By using the new OMB figures for domestic intelligence, and by adding such items as transferred expenditures, the full NSA budget, and revalued cost figures, the Committee estimated that the cost of intelligence today is at least three to four times the amount reported to Congress.

An obvious question is how can there be such a difference in total cost estimates? One answer is the lack of coordination in approaching the budget. Another is that there are no adequate standards for what is, and is not, intelligence spending. A final answer may be that there is a conscious desire to keep the totals small, by dividing and confusing the estimates.

It should be obvious that if nobody has ever added up the costs of the many domestic intelligence units, then certainly nobody is coordinating their budgets, as intelligence per se. In foreign intelligence, the problem is, to a large degree, a lack of centralized authority. For example, the DCI presents the entire foreign intelligence budget to Congress and the President, but he only has authority for CIA's budget. Defense officials testified that a substantial part of their intelligence budget is considered the responsibility of the Secretary of Defense. The DCI, they say, merely reviews their work.

Fragmented authority leads to overall coordination problems. A good illustration is the existence of separate counterintelligence budgets in FBI, CIA, NSA, DIA, Army, Navy, and Air Force. Some are included in the intelligence budget; some are not. Some coordinate with other counterintelligence programs; some do not. The FBI testified, for example, that it does not know if CIA has a counterintelligence group, that it does not know how much CIA's operations cost, and that it does not know if CIA duplicates FBI's work.

Fragmented authority and coordination leave the budget wide open to distortions. Each agency applies its own budget standards. . . .

There is, for example, no standard for allocating the cost of a military base whose primary purpose is to support intelligence operations. The repair of a submarine damaged on intelligence duty may or may not be included in spy costs. The Committee asked OMB, GAO, and all the intelligence agencies for their standards for allocating support costs. No agency had any to offer. No agency had even a basic definition of intelligence.

In a statement prepared for the Committee, the DCI made it clear that there are no good definitions in use today. As he said, ". . . [I]n essence, it boils down to a judgment call."

The Committee has compiled its own set of suggested guidelines. In addition, a good first step would be to include the same items in the intelligence budget from one year to the next. This alone would have prevented the official intelligence budgets from remaining at constant levels over the past few years, which is fundamentally deceptive.

2. An Absence of Accountability

The General Accounting Office is the auditing arm of Congress. When it comes to intelligence agencies, that arm is no arm at all.

In the early years, GAO was generally limited to an auditing function. With the passage of time, Congress has turned to GAO for more than balancing books. Today, under authority of law, GAO is empowered to analyze the economy and efficiency with which government funds are spent.

The Comptroller General, who heads GAO, testified that he cannot even balance CIA's books, let alone analyze its efficiency. Specifically, he said that from 1962, GAO has made no attempt to audit the CIA, because it was allowed scant access to classified spending.

Last year GAO was directed to compile basic budgetary information on federal investigative and intelligence functions. It was refused information by CIA, NSA, and intelligence agencies of the Defense Department. In another recent instance, the FBI refused to permit GAO to examine case files. The Bureau offered special summaries, but refused to allow any verification of those summaries.

The Executive agencies' treatment of GAO is curious. In January 1966, the CIA enter into a sole-source contract with the management consulting firm of Peat, Marwick, Livingston & Co., for a total contract price of $55,725.00. CIA could have saved taxpayers some money, if it had given GAO access.

CIA officials conceded that these independent consultants were given complete and free access to all classified procurement documents, as well as all personnel concerned with Agency procurement activities. In June 1966, the firm completed its work and issued a full report of findings and recommendations. A cover memorandum addressed to the Inspector General expressed appreciation for the Agency's full cooperation.

By contrast, this Committee's staff encountered lengthy delays in gaining limited access to similar documents and personnel, including the report of Peat, Marwick, Livingston & Co.

The issue is not really whether Congress—with

Constitutional responsibility for federal spending—should have equal access with a private company. The issue is whether an objective look at secret expenditures over takes place.

It does not take place at OMB. GAO cannot look. Even this Congressional investigating committee has now tested access and come up wanting.

Do intelligence agencies themselves adequately audit their own operations? No.

The CIA is a good example. Their audit staff is undermanned for a comprehensive review of complex and extensive agency spending that takes place worldwide. They are allowed to balance books, but they are not always allowed to know the exact purpose of expenditures. Only five percent of all vouchered transactions are checked, even though these add up to 20 percent of CIA's entire budget. Substantive corroborating records are not kept. Their audits deviate from the standards of professional Certified Public Accountants, and CIA has not compiled a list of these exceptions to control the deviances.

These and other shortcomings in audit and control, for both foreign and domestic intelligence agencies, lead to an inevitable result—spending abuses.

3. Spending Abuses

The easiest way to illustrate problems encountered in secret spending is to examine a number of mechanisms currently in use, and a number of situations that have grown out of those mechanisms.

a. Covert Procurement

Many CIA covert actions and clandestine operations must be supported in a "non-attributable" manner, which led CIA to establish a covert procurement branch. Unfortunately, covert procurement has become an overused, expensive, and often uncontrollable technique for questionable purchasing.

The branch's activities include support of overseas stations and the procurement of weapons and paramilitary materials. To facilitate these requirements, covert procurement has under its control a number of operational proprietaries and "notional" companies. Notional companies are merely paper firms, with appropriate stationery and checking accounts. These companies make requests to the proprietaries so the proprietary can bill an apparently legitimate company for covert requirements. Needless to say, it is an expensive way to buy a refrigerator, and should not be used unnecessarily.

When an overseas station requires an item that cannot be traced to the United States government, it sends a requisition with a special code. One code is for items that should not be traceable to CIA. Another code means it should not be traceable to the U.S. government.

Theoretically, once these codes, called "sterility codes," are attached, there is no more traceable involvement with the government. However, the Committee reviewed documents which showed that items purchased in a non-traceable manner are sometimes transported by U.S. military air-pouch, rather than sent by private carrier as a truly non-government purchase would be.

Another procedure which the Committee staff questioned was the routing of requests for small quantity, low-cost, and even non-traceable items through the expensive covert process. The logical alternative would be to have the item purchased either overseas or here with petty cash, avoiding the expense of covert procurement. These included such items as quantities of ball point pens, ping-pong paddles, or hams.

The staff was also unable to determine the reason for certain high-cost items being purchased through this mechanism. Hundreds of refrigerators, televisions, cameras, and watches are purchased each year, along with a variety of home furnishings.

The question is why an American television would be purchased here and sent to Europe if someone was trying to conceal his involvement with the United States. This is especially true because the power requirements abroad are different, and a transformer has to be installed on an appliance bought in the U.S. before it will work. In fact, a large percentage of electrical appliances did not have transformers added, which raises the possibility that these items are being covertly purchased for use in the United States.

The same question arises with the purchases of home furnishings. A review of overseas station purchases showed, for example, that one station bought more than one hundred thousand dollars of furnishings in the past few years. In that context, additional covert purchases here at home seem excessive. Finally, why not buy a Smithfield ham through normal purchasing channels? There is no way that ham could be traced to the CIA or the U.S. government, no matter how it was bought.

As in every other component of the Agency, the effort to maintain secrecy, even within the branch itself, is highly emphasized.

The Committee was told that because proprietary employees do not have a "need to know," they are not put in a position to question any request the Agency might make. Three high procurement officials have conceded that the sterility code is not questioned by the covert procurement staff. The 1966 study by Peat, Marwick, Livingston & Co., stated that there was excessive use of these codes, without justification. The Committee's investigation indicates that this situation has not been remedied.

b. Local Procurement

The Committee's investigation of the covert procurement mechanism led to a review of records from local, or in-field, procurement. The staff reviewed records for the past five fiscal years from three typical overseas stations varying in size and number of employees. Over-spending and under-auditing seemed to be prevalent.

An example is a medium-sized station that purchased over $86,000 in liquor and cigarettes during the past five years. The majority of these purchases were designated "operational gifts"—gifts to friendly agents or officials in return for information or assistance.

It would appear that spending practices have an uncanny way of changing with new station chiefs. A station that purchased $41,000 in liquor in 1971, had a new chief in 1972. Liquor purchases dropped to $25,000, which is still a lot of liquor.

One station has purchased over $175,000 in furnishings for leased quarters and safehouses.

In an effort to determine whether this kind of spending is questioned by CIA auditors, the staff interviewed the CIA audit official who audited these stations. He recalled the liquor, and that when he inquired as to the quantity, he was told by the Station Chief that they would "try to hold it down in the future." The same auditor had audited the station that purchased over $175,000 in furnishings. When questioned, he was not even aware of the total figure.

This experience led the Committe staff to interview several members of the Internal Audit Division, as well as eight overseas case officers and chiefs of station. From these interviews, several things became apparent.

Auditors do not perform thorough reviews of case officers' "advance accounts." At all overseas stations, each case officer is allotted an advance, which is nothing more than a petty cash fund. From this fund, the officer pays operating expenses and the salaries of his agents. He is required by Agency regulations to obtain a receipt for every expenditure, but, due to manpower considerations, these are only spot-checked when audited—which is not often. Such funds run into millions of dollars each year.

Every case officer and Internal Audit officer conceded that the Agency must "rely solely on the integrity of its case officer." When a case officer's agents refuse to sign receipts, the case officer "certifies" that he expended the funds. A case officer might have as many as ten agents working for him, each of whom may receive between $50 and $3,000 per month, all in cash.

Finally, audits of all overseas stations are not performed on a regular basis. It may be two or three years, or more, before a station is audited. Even then, the Committee discovered that recommendations made by auditors are usually not disclosed in the auditor's report to headquarters.

c. Accommodation Procurements

In addition to procuring goods and services for its own use, CIA makes "accommodation procurements" for foreign governments, officials, agents, and others.

The Agency serves more or less as a purchasing agent for an undisclosed principal. Although the individual for whom the accommodation procurement was made advances the necessary funds or repays the Agency after delivery, the indirect administrative costs are borne by American taxpayers. These costs include the salary of the agency purchaser, certain transportation charges, accounting costs, and in some cases the salaries of training and technical personnel.

In investigating one series of accommodation procurements, the Committee learned that a foreign government received a 20 percent discount by having CIA buy equipment in the name of the U.S. government.

If the foreign government had contracted for the same items in its own name, this discount would not have been available. In just two of these actions CIA saved the foreign government over $200,000, at the expense of American suppliers.

The Agency will usually refuse to make such procurements only if the requested item might appear to be beyond the requester's financial means, and might therefore give rise to questions about the requester's sources of income. Agency security officers feel that such questions might lead to disclosure of the requester's relationship with the agency.

Accommodation procurements involving less than $3,000 require only the approval of a CIA chief of station. When larger sums are involved, approval must be obtained from the Deputy Director for Oper- A ations. When the amount is more than $500,000, it must also be approved by the Director of Central Intelligence.

The Committee examined a number of accommodation procurement records. The following two examples illustrate that the facilities and resources of the United States government are sometimes used to satisfy little more than the whims of foreign officials.

In one instance, a foreign official described his son's enthusiasm for model airplanes to the chief of station. The foreign official wanted three model airplane kits, and even advised the CIA officer precisely where the kits could be purchased in the United States. A cable was sent to Agency headquarters asking for the pur- B chase of three kits from the store in Baltimore suggested by the foreign official. Further, the cable instructed that the items were to be designated by a "sterility code," to indicate that the purchase of the kits could not be attributable to the United States government. Documents provided to the Committee in this case by the Agency were sanitized.

In another instance, the President of an allied nation was preparing to play golf on a hot afternoon. Anticipating his thirst after several hours in the sun, he made a "priority" request to the local chief of station for six bottles of Gatorade. An Agency employee was immediately relieved of his ordinary duties and assigned to make the accommodation C procurement.

Nor was this the chief of state's only experience with the Agency's merchandising talents. In the past, the Agency has purchased for him several automobiles, including at least two custom-built armored limousines, and, among other things, an entire electronic security system for his official residence. It is worth noting that these security devices are being supplied to a man who runs a police-state.

Accommodation procurements have also involved more expensive and politically sensitive items. For example, another head of a one-party state had long been fascinated by certain highly sophisticated electronic intelligence gathering equipment. He wished to develop his own independent collection capability. D As an accommodation, and to "share the take," the Agency procured an entire electronic intelligence network for him in two phases. Phase I involved contract costs in excess of $85,000, and Phase II cost more than $500,000.

In investigating one series of accommodation procurements for an oil exporting country, the Committee asked CIA officials about the coordination and effect of the Agency's purchasing favors on the foreign country's oil pricing policy. The country's oil policy, incidentally, has not been among the most favorable to the United States. Agency officials were uncertain as to the effect, but they indicated that the two policies are largely considered separate issues. E

In return for making accommodation procurements, the Agency is usually reimbursed by the requesting party. Although reimbursement may be in U.S. dollars, it is usually made in local foreign currency. The Committee was unable to learn whether the Agency has any firm policy on what rate of currency exchange is to be used in making reimbursement. In many countries, U.S. dollars exchanged for local currency at the official rate bring fewer units of local currency than if exchanged at an unofficial, but more commonly used, rate.

d. Research and Development

CIA has long prided itself on technological capability, and many of its projects operate at far reaches F of the "state of the art." Such accomplishments are made by the Agency with assistance and advice from the private sector.

Each year, CIA's Deputy Director for Science and Technology enters into hundreds of contracts with industry, usually in the name of other government agencies. These contracts total millions of dollars for Agency contracts alone. Not only does the Agency contract for its own research and development programs, but also for national intelligence programs. Total contracts for both programs amount to hundreds of millions of dollars, annually.

Committee Staff interviewed numerous members of the Science and Technology Staff. A major target G of this investigation was "contractor selection" practices. Although Mr. Colby testified before the Committee that CIA has established management controls to insure that contracting is carried out according to the intent of Congress, the investigation revealed that

84 percent of these contracts are "sole source contracts."

Staff also examined "cost overrun" aspects of research and development contracting. CIA claimed two and one-half percent of all research and development contracts involved cost overruns of 15 percent or
A more. There is no reason to doubt the figures; however, certain caveats must be considered. Contractors' cost estimates in sole-source contracts can easily be inflated to cover anticipated cost increases. Overruns can also be labeled "changes in scope."

In several interviews with contracting officers, "by the book" answers were given to questions regarding which officer is authorized, and does, accept contract changes. However, one former Agency contracting officer indicated that, to a considerable degree, the technical representative actually makes the contractual decisions, and the contracting officer then has to "catch up" by preparing contract amendments to legitimize changes already made.

Another target of the investigation was the disposal
B of Government Furnished Equipment (GFE). Regulations regarding GFE appear to be precise in determining when to "abandon" this equipment. However, the Office of Communications, for example, contracted in 1965 with an electronics company to do research work. The contract required the purchase of a large piece of industrial equipment, as well as related testing equipment. CIA provided funds for the equipment as well as the research. The testing equipment cost $74,000 and the industrial equipment over $243,000. At the termination of the contract in 1975, the testing equipment was sold to the contractor for $18,500, the large piece of industrial [equipment] was abandoned, in place.

C Calls to the manufacturer of this piece of machinery, as well as two "experts" in the field of this particular type of testing, revealed that the machinery which was abandoned, while perhaps "useless" to the Agency, was not a "worthless" piece of equipment which should have been "abandoned." According to documents provided to the Committee, CIA made no attempt to contact other government agencies, to see if the chamber could have been used by another agency.

e. Colleges and Universities

In 1967 *Ramparts Magazine* disclosed CIA support
D to the National Students Association. As a result, President Johnson issued a flat prohibition against covert assistance to educational institutions; but the Agency unilaterally reserved the right to, and does, depart from the Presidential order when it has the need to do so.

There is no evidence that a President authorized this departure from the Johnson directive.

As background, President Johnson had appointed a committee to investigate the matter and make policy recommendations.

Under Secretary of State, Nicholas deB. Katzenbach, and CIA Director, Richard H. Helms, served on the Committee. It recommended that "no federal agency shall provide any covert financial assistance
E or support, direct or indirect, to any of the nation's educational or private voluntary organizations."

On March 29, 1967, President Johnson issued a statement accepting the recommendation and directing "all agencies of the government to implement it fully."

The Agency then issued internal policy statements to implement the President's orders, stating that, whenever possible, the Agency's identity and sponsorship are to be made known. But the Agency was to clearly retain the option of entering into a covert contract with colleges and universities, after obtaining approval from the Deputy Director for Administration.

Mr. Carl Duckett, Deputy Director for Science and
F Technology, testified before the Committee on November 4, 1975, that the Agency still has on-going contracts with "a small number of universities." Mr. Duckett also revealed that some of the contracts involved "classified work," and some are covert.

4. Budget Secrecy

During Senate hearings in 1973, to confirm James Schlesinger as Secretary of Defense, Mr. Schlesinger indicated it might be possible to make public the total budget cost of foreign intelligence. When William Colby was confirmed as head of CIA in 1973, he, likewise, testified that publication of budget totals might not be harmful.

G In a television interview some years later, Dr. Schlesinger inadvertently revealed the size of the foreign intelligence budget. No great harm apparently came from that disclosure.

In 1973, a recommendation to publish the annual costs of intelligence was made by a Senate Special Committee to Study Questions Related to Secret and Confidential Documents.

On June 4, 1974, Senator J. William Proxmire of Wisconsin offered a floor amendment to a defense procurement authorization bill. His amendment would have required the Director of Central Intelligence to provide Congress with an annual, unclassified report describing the total amount requested for the "national intelligence program" in the budget submitted by the President.

In June 1975, the report of the Rockefeller Commission recommended that Congress carefully consider whether all or part of the CIA budget should be made public.

On October 1, 1975, Representative Robert N. Giaimo of Connecticut offered a floor amendment to a defense appropriations bill, prohibiting any of the funds provided for "Other Procurement, Air Force" from being expended by the CIA. Had the amendment been adopted, a subsequent amendment would have been offered to restore funds for the CIA, and a specific total for the agency would have been disclosed.

Today, however, taxpayers and most Congressmen do not know, and cannot find out, how much they spend on spy activities.

This is in direct conflict with the Constitution, which requires a regular and public accounting for all funds spent by the federal government.

Those who argue for secrecy do not mention the Constitution. They do not mention taxpayers. Instead, they talk of rather obscure understandings the Russians might derive about some specific operation, even if all the Russians knew was a single total which would be in the billions of dollars and would cover dozens of diverse agencies.

How the Russians would do this is not clear. The Committee asked, but there was no real answer. What is clear is that the Russians probably already have a detailed account of our intelligence spending, far more than just the budget total. In all likelihood, the only people who care to know and do not know these costs today are American taxpayers.

Performance

It is one thing to conclude that tens of billions of intelligence dollars have been rather independently spent, and sometimes misspent, over the past few years.

The important issues are whether this spending sufficiently meets our needs, whether Americans have received their money's worth, and whether non-monetary costs sometimes outweigh the benefits.

The latter question is a matter of risks. . . . To test the first two questions, the Committee investigated a representative spectrum of recent events. Some involved war; some involved law enforcement. Some involved American lives overseas; some involved personal freedoms at home. All involved important interests.

How did intelligence perform? Let the events speak for themselves.

1. Tet: Failure to Adapt to a New Kind of War

War in Vietnam meant that intelligence had to adapt to an unconventional war, and true perceptions could spell life or death for Americans. In Tet, perceptions were shattered.

Taking advantage of the Vietnamese lunar holiday, the North Vietnamese and Viet Cong forces launched an all-out offensive of January 30, 1968, against virtually every urban center and base in South Vietnam. The scale of attacks was unprecedented in the history of American involvement in the Vietnam War and flatly challenged the reassuring picture intelligence officials in Saigon and Washington had helped present to the American people.

With nearly all provincial capitals under siege, the American embassy compound was penetrated by the Viet Cong, and the pacification program set back in all areas; predictions of successes, announced scant months before, had turned into one of the greatest misjudgments of the war.

The Committee's investigation of Tet focused on the questions of warning in a combat situation and communicating the realities of a guerrilla war to executive branch policy-makers. Both are interrelated. Mr. William Colby and the post-mortems certify, "warning of the Tet offensive had not fully anticipated the intensity, coordination and timing of the enemy attack." A chief cause was our degraded image of the enemy.

There were at least two primary causes for such degradation. First, the dispute between CIA and MACV (Military Assistance Command, Vietnam) over enemy strength—called Order of Battle figures—created false perceptions of the enemy U.S. forces faced, and prevented measurement of changes in enemy strength over time. Second, pressure from policy-making officials to produce positive intelligence indicators reinforced erroneous assessments of allied progress and enemy capabilities.

a. The Order of Battle Controversy

According to Mr. Colby, the CIA had been suspicious of MACV's numerical estimate of the Vietnamese enemy since at least mid-1966. At an Order of Battle conference held in Saigon in September, 1967, the differences between Washington and the field, and between CIA and MACV, were thrashed out; but according to Mr. Colby, to neither's satisfaction.

A resulting compromise represented the best resolution of MACV's preoccupation with viewing the order of battle in the classic military sense and CIA's assessment of enemy capabilities as a much broader people's war. The Special National Intelligence estimate that emerged from this conference quantified the order of battle in MACV terms, and merely described other potential enemy forces. Categories now proposed from previous estimates of order of battle detailed as much as 200,000 irregular personnel, self-[one word illegible] and secret self-defense forces, and assault [one word illegible] and political cadre.

As foot soldiers realized at the time, and as different studies by the Army Surgeon General confirm, the destructiveness of mines and booby traps, which irregular forces set out, was increasingly responsible for American losses. This was primarily because American forces were engaging the enemy with increased frequency in his defensive positions. Documents indicate that, even during the Order of Battle Conference, there was a large increase in sabotage for which irregulars and civilians were responsible. It appears clear in retrospect that, given the nature of protracted guerrilla war, irregular forces were basic determinants of the nature and scope of combat.

The numbers game not only diverted a direct confrontation with the realities of war in Vietnam, but also prevented the intelligence community, perhaps the President, and certainly Members of Congress, from judging the real changes in Vietnam over time.

The Saigon Order of Battle Conference dropped numbers that had been used since 1962, and used those that were left in what appears to have been an arbitrary attempt to maintain some ceiling. It prompted Secretary of State Dean Rusk to cable the American Embassy in Saigon, on October 21, 1967: "Need your recommendation how to resolve problem of unknown percentage of enemy KIA (Killed in Action) and WIA (Wounded in Action) which comes from ranks of self-defense, assault youth and VC civilian supporters. Since these others not carried as part of VC strength, indicators of attrition could be misleading."

When the Systems Analysis office in the Department of Defense examined the results of the conference and reinterpreted them in terms consistent with prior quantification, it remarked that the new estimate should have been 395,000–480,000 if computed on the same basis as before. "The computations do not show that enemy strength has increased, but that previous estimates of enemy strength were too low."

In the context of the late 1960's, numbers were not at all an academic exercise. Mr. Colby has testified that "(T)he effort to develop a number with respect to the enemy strength was a part of the advising of our government as to the amount of effort we would have to spend to counter that kind of (guerrilla) effort by the Viet Cong. They were also used to inform Members of Congress and the American public on the progress in Vietnam.

The validity of most of the numbers was significantly dubious. Unfortunately, they were relied on for optimistic presentations. For example, while mentioning in parenthetical and classified comments that the numbers supporting its indicators of progress in Vietnam were suspect, the Bureau of Intelligence and Research provided Assistant Secretary of State William Bundy with quantified measures of success. General Westmoreland used such figures to support his contentions in the fall of 1967, that the enemy's "guerrilla force is declining at a steady rate."

In testimony before this Committee, Mr. Colby has stated that the "infatuation with numbers" was "one of the more trying experiences the Intelligence Community has had to endure." In the context of the period it appears that considerable pressure was placed on the Intelligence Community to generate numbers, less out of tactical necessity than for political purposes.

The Administration's need was for confirmation of the contention that there was light at the end of the tunnel, that the pacification program was working and generally that American involvement in Vietnam was not only correct, but effective. In this sense, the Intelligence Community could not help but find its powers to effect objective analysis substantially undermined. Whether this was by conspiracy or not is somewhat irrelevant.

b. The Consequences

Four months after the Saigon Order of Battle Conference, the Tet offensive began. On February 1, hours after the initial mass assaults, General Westmoreland explained to a press conference, "I'm frank to admit I didn't know he (the enemy) would do it on the occasion of Tet itself. I thought he would do it before or after." The U.S. naval officer in command of the river forces in the Mekong Delta and his army counterpart were similarly caught off guard. Appalled at how poorly positioned they were to provide quick and efficient response, the naval officer, now a retired Vice Admiral, has told the Committee that he "well remember(s) the words of the Army General who brought us the orders to extricate ourselves from the mudflats as fast as possible. They were, 'It's Pearl Harbor all over again.' "

The April, 1968, post-mortem done by a collection of intelligence officers discussed the general question of warning. It concluded that while units in one corps area were on alert, allied forces throughout the country generally were caught unprepared for what was unfolding. Certain forces even while "on a higher than normal state of alert" were postured to meet "inevitable cease-fire violations rather than attacks on the cities." In other areas "the nature and extent of the enemy's attacks were almost totally unexpected." One-half of the South Vietnamese army was on leave at the time of the attacks, observing a 36-hour standdown.

In testimony before this Committee, both General Graham and William Colby confirmed the fact of some amount of surprise. General Graham preferred to label it surprise at the enemy's "rashness." Mr. Colby spoke of a misjudgment of their potential "intensity, coordination and timing."

Even though quick corrective action was taken to salvage American equipment and protect U.S. personnel, the ultimate ramifications on political and military fronts were considerable. General Westmoreland requested a dramatic increase of 206,000 in U.S. troop strength, and additional equipment supplies. Secretary of Defense Clark Clifford began rethinking the substance of intelligence. A collection of intelligence officers finally briefed the President of the United States on the realities of the Vietnam War in mid-March, and a few days later he announced he would not seek re-election.

c. The Aftermath

The Committee received testimony that problems with intelligence in Vietnam were not confined to Tet. Up to the last days of South Vietnam's existence, certain blinders prevented objective reporting from the field and an accurate assessment of the field situation by Washington. Tet raised the issue of whether American intelligence could effectively account for enemy strength. Later events, among them the collapse of the Saigon government, pointed to a failure to properly acknowledge weaknesses of allies.

A real attempt to address the shortcomings of friendly forces in Vietnam was hampered by many factors. During the time of massive American presence, there was a failure to attribute at least partial South Vietnamese "success" to American air power and logistics support. Consequently, projected ARVN performance in 1975, after the U.S. pullout, was measured against the yardstick of the Easter Offensive of 1972, when American support was crucial.

Mission restrictions curtailed necessary collection activity by professional intelligence officers, and forced reliance on officials charged with military aid responsibilities. This promoted biased interpretations.

The sum total of restrictions, manipulations, and censorship no doubt led to the conclusion Secretary of Defense, James R. Schlesinger reached at an April, 1975, news conference. He pointed out that "the strength, resiliency and steadfastness of those forces (South Vietnamese) were more highly valued than they should have been, so that the misestimate, I think, applied largely to Saigon's capabilities rather than Hanoi's intentions."

Ultimately, the Vietnam intelligence experience is a sobering reminder of the limitations and pitfalls the United States can expect to encounter if it chooses to align itself in unconventional battle with unconventional allies. It illustrates how very different guerrilla war is from World War II, and how much more problematic an alliance with emerging and unstable Third World governments will be.

Reviewing the American experience in Indochina, an Assistant Secretary of Defense for Intelligence wrote a note of caution to the Secretary of Defense emphasizing the following view:

"The problems that occurred in Vietnam or Cambodia can now be occurring in our efforts to assess [an allied and an adversary Third World country's] forces, forces in the Persian Gulf or forces in the Middle East. These problems must be addressed before the U.S. becomes involved in any future crisis in the Third World that requires objective and timely intelligence analysis."

Given the substantial American involvement in these areas, strong remedies and honest restrospect appear necessary, to overcome and prevent intelligence output that fails, for whatever reason, to present comprehensive and undisguised perceptions of war.

2. Czechoslovakia: Failure Of Tactical Warning

The Czechoslovakia crisis challenged our ability to monitor an attack by the Soviet Union—our prime military adversary. We "lost" the Russian army, for two weeks.

Forces of the Warsaw Pact invaded Czechoslovakia on August 20, 1968, to overthrow the Dubcek regime which, since spring, had been moving toward liberal, independent policies the Soviets could not tolerate. U.S. intelligence had understood and reported the basic issues in the developing Soviet-Czech confrontation, and concluded that the Soviets were capable of launching an invasion at any time.

Intelligence failed, however, to provide a warning that the Soviets had "decided to intervene with force." Consequently, President Johnson first learned of the invasion when Soviet Ambassador Dobrynin visited the White House and told him.

A review of U.S. intelligence performance during the Czech crisis indicates the agencies were not up to the difficult task of divining Soviet intentions. We knew Soviet capabilities, and that the tactical decision to invade might leave only hours of advance warning. The CIA, DIA, and NSA should have been prepared for lightning-quick reaction to Soviet military moves.

Czech radio broadcasted news of the invasion at 8:50 p.m., Washington time. CIA translated and transmitted its reports of invasion to Washington at 9:15 p.m. By that time, President Johnson had already met his appointment with the Soviet Ambassador.

U.S. technical intelligence learned of the Soviet invasion several hours before—but the information did not reach Washington until after the Czech radio message. The CIA later concluded that the information "might have made a difference" in our ability to provide the tactical warning.

One alarming failure of intelligence prior to the invasion occurred during the first two weeks in August, when U.S. intelligence could not locate a Soviet combat formation, which had moved into northern Poland. Director Helms later admitted he was not "happy about those two weeks" when he could not locate the Soviet troops.

Information from technical intelligence, which would have been helpful, was not available until days later. Clandestine reporting in the previous weeks had been so slow to arrive it proved of little value to current intelligence publications.

Director of Central Intelligence Richard Helms reported to the President's Foreign Intelligence Advisory Board in October, 1968, that the intelligence record of failing to detect the actual attack "distresses me." The Director provided reassurances that the record would have been better "if West Germany had been the target rather than Czechoslovakia."

In 1971, a Presidential Commission reported to President Nixon that its review of U.S. ability to respond to sudden attack had found serious weaknesses. The Pentagon was directed to improve its warning system. Improvement to the very best possible degree is, of course, the minimum acceptable standard. There will be no more important area for Congressional oversight committees to explore thoroughly.

3. The Mid-East War: The System Breaks Down

The Mid-East war gave the intelligence community a real test of how it can perform when all its best technology and human skills are focused on a known world "hot spot." It failed.

On October 6, 1973, Egypt and Syria launched a major assault across the Suez Canal and Golan Heights against a stunned Israel. Although Israel eventually repelled the attack, at a cost of thousands of lives, the war's consequences cannot be measured in purely military terms.

For Americans, the subsequent U.S.-Soviet confrontation of October 24–25, 1973, when the Soviets threatened to unilaterally intervene in the conflict, and the Arab oil embargo are reminders that war in the Middle East has a direct impact on our own national interests.

A

The Committee's analysis of the U.S. intelligence performance in this crisis confirms the judgment of an intelligence community post-mortem that "the principal conclusions concerning the imminence of hostilities . . . were—quite simply, obviously, and starkly—wrong." Even after the conflict had begun, we did not accurately monitor the course of events.

The important question is what went wrong?

The last relevant National Intelligence Estimate before the October War was published five months earlier, in May, 1973, during a particularly bad period in Arab-Israeli relations. That estimate addressed the likelihood of war "in the next few weeks." No long-range view was presented, and the crisis soon passed.

B

The only intelligence report concerned with future political-military issues was a May 31, 1973, Bureau of Intelligence and Research (INR) memorandum to Secretary of State Rogers. The authors reasoned correctly that Egypt's President Sadat, for political reasons, would be strongly tempted to resort to arms if diplomacy proved fruitless. Accordingly, the report concluded, the "resumption of hostilities by autumn will become a better than even bet" should the diplomatic impasse continue.

By September 30, 1973—less than a week before the attack—INR had lost "the wisdom of the Spring." By then, all U.S. intelligence agencies argued that the political climate in the Arab nations was not conducive to a major war. Intelligence consumers were reassured that hostilities were not likely.

The next question is why this happened.

C

Analytical bias was part of the problem. In the summer of 1973, the Defense Intelligence Agency (DIA), CIA, and INR all flatly asserted that Egypt was not capable of a major assault across the Suez Canal. Syria, they said, was not much of a threat either, despite recent acquisitions of sophisticated Soviet . . . missile systems and other material.

One reason for the analysts' optimism can be found in a 1971 CIA handbook, in a passage reiterated and reinforced in discussions in early October, 1973. The Arab fighting man, it reported, "lacks the necessary physical and cultural qualities for performing effective military services." The Arabs were thought to be so clearly inferior that another attack would be irrational and, thus, out of the question.

D

No doubt this attitude was not far in the background when CIA advised Dr. Kissinger on September 30, 1973, that "the whole thrust of President Sadat's activities since last spring has been in the direction of bringing moral, political, and economic force to bear on Israel in tacit acknowledgment of Arab unreadiness to make war."

That analysis is quite surprising, in light of information acquired during that period, which indicated that imminent war was a distinct possibility. By late September, for example, CIA had acquired vital evidence of the timing and warlike intentions of the Arabs. The source was disbelieved, for reasons still unclear.

E

There were other positive indications. In late September, the National Security Agency began picking up clear signs that Egypt and Syria were preparing for a major offensive. NSA information indicated that [a major foreign nation] had become extremely sensitive to the prospect of war and concerned about their citizens and dependents in Egypt. NSA's warning escaped the serious attention of most intelligence analysts responsible for the Middle East.

F

The fault may well lie in the system itself. NSA intercepts of Egyptian-Syrian war preparations in this period were so voluminous—an average of hundreds of reports each week—that few analysts had time to digest more than a small portion of them. Even fewer analysts were qualified by technical training to read raw NSA traffic. Costly intercepts had scant impact on estimates.

These reports lacked visibility and prestige to such a degree that when, two days before the war, an NSA briefer insisted to General Daniel Graham of CIA that unusual Arab movements suggested imminent hostilities, Graham retorted that his staff had reported a "ho-hum" day in the Middle East. Later, a key military analyst claimed that if he had only seen certain NSA reports, which were so "sensitive" they had not been disseminated until after the war began, he would have forecast hostilities.

G

There was testimony that Dr. Kissinger's secrecy may also have thwarted effective intelligence analysis. Kissinger had been in close contact with both the Soviets and the Arabs throughout the pre-war period. He, presumably, was in a unique position to pick up indications of Arab dissatisfaction with diplomatic talks, and signs of an ever-increasing Soviet belief that war would soon break out. When the Committee was denied its request for high-level reports, it was unable to learn whether Kissinger elicited this information in any usable form. It is clear, however, that the Secretary passed no such warning to the intelligence community.

The Committee was told by high U.S. intelligence officials and policy-makers that information from high-level diplomatic contacts is of great intelligence value as an often-reliable indicator of both capabilities and intentions. Despite the obvious usefulness of this information, Dr. Kissinger has continued to deny intelligence officials access to notes of his talks with foreign leaders.

The morning of the Arab attack, the Watch Committee—which is responsible for crisis alerts—met to assess the likelihood of major hostilities. It concluded that no major, coordinated offensive was in the offing. Perhaps one of the reasons for this was that some participants were not "cleared" for all intelligence data, so the subject and its implications could not be fully discussed.

The entire system had malfunctioned. Massive amounts of data had proven indigestible by analysts. Analysts, reluctant to raise false alarms and lulled by anti-Arab biases, ignored clear warnings. Top-level policy-makers declined to share perceptions gained from talks with key Arab and Soviet diplomats during the critical period. The fact that Israeli intelligence, to which the U.S. often deferred in this period, had been wrong was small consolation.

Performance did not measurably improve after the war's outbreak, when the full resources of the U.S. intelligence community were focused [there].

The Defense Intelligence Agency, having no military contingency plan for the area, proved unable to deal with a deluge of reports from the war zone, and quickly found itself in chaos. CIA and INR also engulfed Washington and each other with situation reports, notable for their redundancy.

Technical intelligence-gathering was untimely, as well as indiscriminate. U.S. national technical means of overhead coverage of the Middle East, according to the post-mortem, was "of no practical value" because of time problems. Two overflight reconnaissance missions, on October 13 and 25, "straddled the most critical phase of the war and were, therefore, of little use."

The U.S. failure to accurately track war developments may have contributed to a U.S.-Soviet confrontation and troop alert called by President Nixon on October 24, 1973.

A second intelligence community post-mortem, the existence of which was not disclosed to the Committee until after its hearing, reported that CIA and DIA almost unquestionably relied on overly-optimistic Israeli battle reports. Thus misled, the U.S. clashed with the better-informed Soviets on the latter's strong reaction to Israeli cease-fire violations. Soviet threats to intervene militarily were met with a worldwide U.S. troop alert. Poor intelligence had brought America to the brink of war.

Administration witnesses assured the Committee that analysts who had performed poorly during the crisis had been replaced. The broader record suggests, however, that the intelligence system faults have survived largely intact. New analysts will continue to find themselves harassed and deluged with largely equivocal, unreadable, or unusable data from CIA, DIA, INR, and the collection-conscious NSA. At the same time, they can expect to be cut off, by top-level policy-makers, from some of the best indicators of hostile intentions.

4. Portugal: The U.S. Caught Napping

Do our intelligence services know what is going on beneath the surface in allied nations that are not making headlines? Quiet Portugal exploded in 1974, leaving serious questions in its aftermath.

When a group of left-leaning Portuguese junior military officers ousted the Caetano regime on April 25, 1974, State Department officials represented to the New York Times that Washington knew those who were behind the coup well. State indicated that we were not surprised by the coup, and that no significant changes in Portugal's NATO membership were expected. Nothing could have been further from the truth.

The Committee has reviewed documents which show that the U.S. intelligence community had not even been asked to probe deeply into Portugal in the waning months of the Caetano dictatorship. As a result, policy makers were given no real warning of the timing and probable ideological consequences of the coup, despite clear and public indications that a political upheaval was at hand.

The State Department's Bureau of Intelligence and Research had not analyzed events in Portugal in the month before the April coup. In retrospect, four warning signals, beginning in late February and continuing through mid-March, 1974, should have sparked "speculation at that time that a crisis of major proportions was brewing," according to the Director of Intelligence and Research, William Hyland. All four events were reported in the American press:

1. The publication in February 1974, of General Antonio de Spinola's controversial book criticizing Portugal's African colonial wars, which unleashed an unprecedented public storm.

2. The refusal of General Spinola and the Armed Forces Chief of Staff, Francisco Costa Gomes, to participate in a demonstration of military unity and support for the Caetano dictatorship.

3. An abortive coup, in mid-March, when an infantry regiment attempted to march upon Lisbon. This was followed by the subsequent dismissal of Spinola and Costa Gomes from their commands.

4. A period of rising tensions, the arrests of leftists, and a purge of military officers following the first three developments.

The intelligence community, however, was too preoccupied to closely examine the Portuguese situation. Those responsible for writing current intelligence publications had deadlines to meet, meetings to attend, and relatively little time to speculate on developments in the previously sleepy Caetano dictatorship.

The Committee's investigation indicates there were other, earlier warning signs which might have sparked some intelligence interest. Again, these indications of deeper unrest were not subjected to close analysis.

On October 26, 1973, the Defense Attache in Lisbon reported to DIA headquarters in the Pentagon rumors of a "coup plot," and serious discontent among Portuguese military officers.

On November 8, 1973, the attache reported that 860 Portuguese Army Captains had signed a petition protesting conditions. The attache quickly concluded these dissidents had no intentions of revolution. Nevertheless, the fact that over 800 military officers felt deeply enough to risk retribution was a good indication of the profound social revolution which Portugal faced.

The record does not suggest that the attache attempted to get to know these junior officers, understand their views, or even record their names. Nor had anyone in Washington assigned him the task of searching for signs of social and political unrest in the Portuguese military. One reason for this was that the Director of Attache Affairs was not allowed to assign duties to attaches. Assignments were done elsewhere, in an unbelievable demonstration of confusing and inefficient administration.

Also in November 1973, the attache attended a social gathering at the home of a retired American officer where he heard discussion of right-wing Spanish and Portuguese countercoup plans, should "extremists" overthrow the Caetano government. Neither the identities of the counter-plotters nor of the "extremists" were reported by the attache. No further reference to this report was found in a review of subsequent attache activities prior to the April coup.

In February 1974, the attache forwarded information from December 1973, on the Portuguese government response to a petition of complaints signed by over 1,500 junior military officers. There was no effort to identify the leaders of the petition campaign or to contact any of the signers. After the coup, high CIA officials would complain of the lack of in-depth biographic reporting from the attache office.

A review of all Defense Attache reports in the months prior to the coup indicated substantial delays in forwarding reports to Washington. It even took a month for the attache to send Washington the Spinola book which unleashed the public storm when it was published in February.

Twice, Defense Intelligence Agency headquarters in Washington wrote the attache office in Lisbon urging the six officers there to be more aggressive, to travel more, and frequent the diplomatic party circuit less. Only the most junior attache, A Navy lieutenant, made an attempt to probe beyond the obvious.

The Committee was also told that a serious problem in DIA is a tendency to reward senior officers, nearing the ends of their careers, by assigning them to attache posts. Not only were these officers often untrained and unmotivated for intelligence duties, but the Director of Attache Affairs testified that he was powerless to assign substantive duties to the attaches in the case.

The Committee did not have the opportunity to review raw CIA reports during the six months prior to the coup. CIA officials who relied on these reports told this Committee that the CIA Station in Lisbon was so small, and so dependent upon the official Portuguese security service for information, that very little was picked up. In fact, attaches were in a better position than CIA to get to know the Portuguese military. There is no indication that attaches and the Chief of Station attempted to pool their resources and combine CIA's knowledge of the Portuguese Community movement with attaches' supposed military contacts.

The National Intelligence Officer (NIO) for Western Europe did attempt an analysis. A draft memorandum on trends in Portugal, titled, "Cracks in the Facade," had been in preparation for nearly a month, and was almost complete when the April coup erupted. It had to be re-titled. The document itself, despite its titles, was not attuned to the real causes of intense discontent which produced a leftist-military revolt.

That same National Intelligence Officer testified that he had some twenty-five European countries to monitor, with the help of only one staff assistant. NIO's do not have command authority over CIA's intelligence or operations directorates. They cannot order that papers be written, that staffers be detached from the current intelligence office to work on an in-depth estimate. They cannot instruct clandestine operations to collect certain types of information. Nor will the NIO always be informed of covert actions that may be underway in one of his countries.

The most disturbing testimony before this Committee was official satisfaction with intelligence prior to the Portuguese coup. The Director of Attache Affairs told the Committee that intelligence performance had been "generally satisfactory and responsive to requirements." The National Intelligence Officer for Western Europe said intelligence reports had described "a situation clearly in process of change, an old order coming apart at the seams."

However, both officials quickly admitted under questioning that the attaches had not, in fact, been very aggressive. Nor had any intelligence document warned when and how the old order was "coming apart at the seams." Without access to intelligence reports, this Committee might have believed official claims that the system was functioning well.

5. India: Priorities Lost

How well does U.S. intelligence keep track of non-military events that affect our foreign policy interests? Not very well, if the first nuclear test in the Third World is any indication.

The intelligence community estimated, in 1965, that India was capable of conducting a nuclear test, and probably would produce a nuclear device within the next few years. In 1972, a special estimate said the "chances are roughly even that India will conduct a [nuclear] test at some time in the next several years and label it a peaceful explosion."

DIA, in reports distributed only within the Joint Chiefs of Staff, had stated since 1971 that India might already have a nuclear device. However, when India did explode a nuclear device on May 18, 1974, U.S. intelligence was caught off-guard. As the CIA's post-mortem says of the community's surprise: "This failure denied the U.S. Government the option of considering diplomatic or other initiatives to try to prevent this significant step in nuclear proliferation."

Only one current intelligence article was published in the six months before the May explosion. That article, by DIA, stated for the first time that India might already possess such a device. Perhaps one reason the article did not provoke more debate and initiative was the title: "India: A nuclear weapons program will not likely be pursued in the near term."

In 1972, U.S. intelligence had picked up 26 reports that India would soon test a device, or that she was capable of doing so if the government made the decision to proceed. There were only two reports on the subject from August 1972, to May 1974, when the device was exploded. Neither was pursued with what the CIA can claim was a "real follow-up."

An April 17, 1974 report indicated that India might have already conducted an unsuccessful nuclear test in the Rajasthan Desert. The CIA did not disseminate this report to other agencies, nor did CIA officials pursue the subject.

The Director of Central Intelligence had established the bureaucratic device of "Key Intelligence Questions" in 1974. Although nuclear proliferation was on the list, few officials outside the upper reaches of the bureaucracy expressed much interest. The CIA's general nuclear developments priority list did not address India, and the military attaches received no clear instructions on nuclear matters. Nevertheless, previous estimates on India had identified "gaps" in our information.

After India exploded the nuclear device in May 1974, Director Colby wrote Dr. Kissinger to say he intended to mount a more aggressive effort on the nuclear proliferation problem.

One of several justifications for national technical means of overhead coverage over India in the two years prior to May 1974, was the nuclear test issue. However, the Intelligence Community technical analysts were never asked to interpret the data. The CIA's post-mortem stated, in effect, the system had been tasked to obtain data, but the analysts had not been asked to examine such data. After the explosion, the analysts were able to identify the test location, from pre-test data.

Following the failure to anticipate India's test, the United States Intelligence Board agreed to hold one committee meeting a year on nuclear proliferation. Interagency "coordinating" mechanisms were established. Teams of experts traveled to various countries to impress on American embassy personnel the importance of the proliferation threat. Analysts once again were encouraged to talk to each other more.

The missing element, as the bureaucracy reshuffled its priorities after the Indian failure, is quite simple: the system itself must be reformed to promote anticipation of, rather than reaction to, important world events.

6. Cyprus: Failure of Intelligence Policy

Cyprus presented a complex mix of politics, personalities, and NATO allies. Unfortunately, a crisis turned to war, while intelligence tried to unravel events —and America offended all participants.

On the morning of July 15, 1974, Greek strongman General Dimitrios Ioannides and his military forces on Cyprus overthrew the elected government of Archbishop Makarios. Five days later, Turkey invaded the island, ostensibly to protect the Turkish minority there and to prevent the Greek annexation long promoted by the new Cyprus leadership. Unsatisfied with its initial military success, Turkey renewed its offensive on August 14, 1974.

The failure of U.S. intelligence to forecast the coup, despite strong strategic and tactical signs, may be attributed to several factors: poor reporting from the U.S. Embassy in Athens, in part due to CIA's exclusive access to Ioannides; the general analytical assumption of rational behavior; and analysts' reluctance to raise false claims of an impending crisis.

The failure to predict the coup is puzzling in view of the abundance of strategic warnings. When Ioannides wrested power from George Papadopoulos in November, 1974, analysts concluded that relations between Greece and Makarios were destined to worsen. Ioannides' hatred of Makarios, whom he considered pro-Communist or worse, has been described as having "bordered on the pathological." Moreover, Makarios was seen as a stumbling block to Ioannides' hopes for *onosis*. Observers agreed that a serious confrontation was only a matter of time.

By spring of 1974, that confrontation would at times appear imminent, with intervening lulls. Each trip to the brink elicited dire warnings to policy officials from Near East desks in the State Department. However, the nuances of these events, indicating a gathering of storm clouds, were largely lost on analysis as their attention remained focused on the Greek-Turkish clash over mineral rights in the Aegean. Cyprus remained a side issue despite growing evidence that the Ioannides-Makarios relationship was reaching a critical stage.

There would soon be several tactical indications that a coup was in the works. On June 7, 1974, the National Intelligence Daily warned that Ioannides was actively considering the ouster of Makarios if the Archbishop made an "extremely provocative move." On June 29, intelligence officials reported that Ioannides had again told his CIA contact nine days before, that if Makarios continued his provocation, the Greek would have only two options: to write-off Cyprus, with its sizeable Greek majority, or eliminate the Archbishop as a factor.

On July 3, 1974, Makarios made that "extremely provocative move," by demanding the immediate withdrawal of a Greek National Guard contingent on Cyprus. The ultimatum was delivered in an extraordinary open-letter to the Greek government, accusing Ioannides' associates of attempting his physical as well as political liquidation.

On June 29, 1974, Secretary Kissinger, responding to alarms sounded by State Department desk officers, approved a cable to U.S. Ambassador Henry J. Tasca in Athens, instructing that he personally tell Ioannides of U.S. opposition to any adventure on Cyprus. The instruction was only partially heeded.

Tasca, assured by the CIA station chief that Ioannides would continue to deal only with CIA, and not sharing the State Department desk officer's alarm, was content to pass a message to the Greek leader indirectly.

Tasca's colleagues subsequently persuaded secretary Kissinger's top aide, Joseph Sisco, that a general message passed through regular government channels would have sufficient impact. The Ambassador told Committee staff that Sisco agreed it was unnecessary for Tasco himself to approach Ioannides, who had no official government position. That interpretation has been vigorously disputed. It is clear, however, that the Embassy took no steps to underscore for Ioannides the dept of U.S. concern over a possible Cyprus coup attempt.

This episode, the exclusive CIA access to Ioannides, Tasca's indications that he may not have seen all important messages to and from the CIA Station, Ioannides' suggestions of U.S. acquiescence, and Washington's well-known coolness to Makarios, have led to public speculation that either U.S. officials were inattentive to the reports of the developing crisis or simply allowed it to happen, by not strongly, directly, and unequivocally warning Ioannides against it.

Due to State Department access policies, the Committee was unsuccessful in obtaining closely-held cables to and from the Secretary of State during this period including a message the Secretary sent to Ioannides through the CIA the day after the coup. Accordingly, it is impossible to reach a definitive conclusion.

On July 3, 1974, a CIA report stated that an individual, later described as "an untested source," had passed the word that despite new aggressiveness on Makarios' part, Ioannides had changed his mind: there would be no coup after all. For reasons still unclear, this CIA report was embraced and heeded until July 15, the day of the coup. The Intelligence Community post-mortem, appears to have concluded that the "tip" was probably a ruse.

Ioannides' dubious change of heart went virtually unquestioned despite Makarios' open-letter, despite further ultimatums from the Archbishop to remove the Greek officers, and despite the en masse resignations of three high-level Greek Foreign Ministry officials known to be soft-liners on Cyprus. In this setting, the grotesquely erroneous National Intelligence Bulletin of July 15, 1974, is not surprising, nor are Ambassador Tasca's protestations that he saw no coup on the horizon.

Almost at the moment Ioannides unleashed his forces, a National Intelligence Bulletin was reassuring intelligence consumers with the headline: "Ioannides is taking a moderate line while he plays for time in his dispute with Archbishop Makarios."

Results of the events triggered by the coup included: thousands of Cypriot casualties and refugees, a narrowly-averted war between NATO allies Greece and Turkey, a tragic worsening of U.S. relations with all three nations, and the death of an American Ambassador. U.S. intelligence must be accorded a share of the responsibility.

The intelligence community somewhat generously termed its performance during the Cyprus crisis as "a mixture of strengths and weaknesses." The Committee's conclusion, after an analysis of the record, is less sanguine. Intelligence clearly failed to provide adequate warning of the coup, and it performed indifferently once the crisis had begun.

The analytical failure in the Cyprus crisis brings to mind several parallels with the 1973 Middle East debacle. In both cases, analysts and policymakers were afflicted both with a past history of false alarms, and with the rigid notion, unsupported in fact, that foreign leaders invariably act "rationally." In the Cyprus crisis, as in the Mid-East, analysts were deluged with unreadable and redundant data subsequent to the initial intelligence failure. Still, given the ample indications that Makarios had sufficiently aroused Ioannides' ire, these analytical quirks should not have prevented a correct interpretation of events.

There appear to have been collection failures in this period, although additional evidence could probably not have overcome the analytical deficiencies that caused erroneous conclusions. For example, CIA personnel had been instructed by the U.S. Ambassador not to establish contacts within the Turkish minority, and to obviate any allegations of collusion with the anti-Makarios EOKA-B movement. They were told to seek intelligence on EOKA-B by indirect means, rather than through direct contact with members of that organization. Finally, signals intelligence in the area was focused elsewhere and even after the coup was not a significant factor.

Since the coup inevitably led to the two Turkish invasions and the Greek-Turkish confrontation, the performance of intelligence in predicting military hostilities after the coup is both less important and unremarkable in its successes.

Along with most newspaper articles of the time, U.S. intelligence concluded that Ioannides' installation of Nicos Sampson, notoriously anti-Turk, as Cypriot President insured a Turkish invasion of the island. Despite prominent stories in Turkish newspapers and undisguised troop movements at the coast, DIA did not predict the invasion until literally hours before Turkish forces hit the beaches on July 20, 1974. A National Intelligence Officer's report had picked July 20 as a likely invasion date, but was never disseminated to the intelligence community.

Perhaps flushed by its "success" in calling the first Turkish invasion just after the Turkish press did, U.S. intelligence appeared to lose interest, in the belief that the crisis was over. Thus, there was no real forewarning that the Turkish forces would launch an even more ambitious invasion on August 14, resulting in the capture of fully one-third of the island.

In terms of both its immediate and long-range consequences, the sum total of U.S. intelligence failure during the Cyprus crisis may have been the most A damaging intelligence performance in recent years.

Risks

The American taxpayer clearly does not receive full value for his intelligence dollar. The costs of intelligence should not, however, be measured in dollars alone. Many day-to-day activities inevitably pose real risks.

The Committee has found that when results are measured against hazards alone, certain intelligence programs may be wholly unacceptable; other projects may too easily stray from wise and worthwhile courses, without detection. B

It is disturbing that the consequences of intelligence activities are sometimes apparently given scant consideration by policy makers. Even more troubling are indications that this insensitivity continues when dangers reveal themselves.

1. Covert Action

The Committee has examined CIA covert action operations and has considerable evidence that they are irregularly approved, sloppily implemented, and at times have been forced on a reluctant CIA by the President and his National Security Advisor.

"Covert action" may be defined as clandestine activity other than purely information-gathering, which C is directed at producing a particular political, economic, or military result.

Successive administrations have cited Section 102 of the National Security Act of 1947 as the legal justification for covert action. During the course of this investigation, the Special Counsel to the Director of Central Intelligence has argued that the President, in his conduct of foreign relations, has an inherent Constitutional mandate to authorize these activities.

On the other hand, in recent years, commentators have maintained that in establishing the CIA, Congress had no specific intention that covert operations apart from intelligence-gathering missions be conducted. Witnesses before the Committee likewise disputed any inherent Constitutional power to conduct D covert actions. In any event, Congress has implicitly acquiesced in covert action through the oversight process.

It may be argued that there has been explicit approval as well. Just as the War Powers Act acknowledges the authority of the President to conduct overt military hostilities, albeit for a limited period, without a Congressional declaration of war, the Ryan-Hughes Amendment to the Foreign Assistance Act of 1974 formally acknowledges the existence and legality of covert action.

The Committee has surveyed all Forty Committee approvals since 1965, and has delved deeply into three recent covert action projects. It is believed that E the Committee's review of ten years of covert action is without precedent in the Congress or the executive branch.

a. Ten Year Survey

Our primary purpose was to determine whether the Forty Committee and its predecessors had been exercising their oversight and control responsibilities from 1965 to date. To do this, it was necessary to trace the process from proposal to final approval.

Like other aspects of covert action, fixing responsibility for the initiation of various covert action projects was a difficult task. As recorded in Forty F Committee records, the vast majority of projects was submitted by the CIA, 88 percent of the total projects since 1965. The high number of covert action proposals represents a general activism within the foreign affairs bureaucracy, especially within CIA.

The overall picture, however, does not support the contention that covert action has been used in furtherance of any particular principled form of government, or identifiable national interest. Instead, the record indicates a general lack of a long-term direction in U.S. foreign policy. Covert actions, as the means for implementing a policy, reflected this band-aid approach, substituting short-term remedies for problems which required long-term cures.

Covert action proposals came from a variety of G interest areas: a foreign head of state, the Department of Defense, the Department of State, an Ambassador, CIA, the Assistant to the President for National Security Affairs, a cabinet member, or the President himself.

Proposals involving a large expenditure of funds or classified as "politically sensitive," required review and approval of the Forty Committee. Unfortunately, the executive branch does not have a clear definition of what constitutes a large or politically
A sensitive operation. Projects of less sensitivity are approved within the CIA, usually at the level of the Deputy Director for Operations, with the determination of "political sensitivity" being left to the Director of Central Intelligence.

The Forty Committee is chaired by the Assistant to the President for National Security Affairs and includes the Deputy Secretary of Defense, the Undersecretary of State for Political Affairs, the Chairman of the Joint Chiefs of Staff, and the Director of Central Intelligence. Theoretically, a detailed proposal is presented to this group. The members are then afforded an opportunity for a full discussion of the merits and a reporting of their views to the President.
B In practice, the Forty Committee has often been little more than a rubber stamp.

The procedures for approval of covert action have changed with administrations, political conditions and personalities. At various times, the approval process has been relatively informal, extraordinarily secretive, and pro-forma.

While on occasion some projects have been considered in depth, at Committee meetings which included the approval or disapproval by formal votes, several informal procedures have frequently been used. These informal procedures, such as telephonic votes, do not allow each member to benefit from the views of his colleagues. At times, members have been
C given only the barest of details, and instead of formal votes have simply been allowed the opportunity to acknowledge the project's existence.

The Forty Committee has only one full-time professional staff member. Because of the high degree of compartmentation attending these projects, committee members—who are among the busiest officials in government—are frequently in the position of evaluating a complex proposal without adequate staff support. The Assistant to the President for National Security Affairs and the Director of Central Intelligence, having the incentive and the resources to cope with Forty Committee business, clearly dominate the process.

The origin of many covert action projects is murky
D at best.

The CIA, as the prospective implementation arm, is often directed to produce proposals for covert action and is, therefore, incorrectly seen as a plan's original proponent. It is clear that on several occasions involving highly sensitive projects, CIA was summarily ordered by the President or his National Security advisor to carry out a covert action program. It is further clear that CIA has been ordered to engage in covert action over the Agency's strong prior objections.

All evidence in hand suggests that the CIA, far from being out of control, has been utterly responsive to the instructions of the President and the As-
E sistant to the President for National Security Affairs. It must be remembered, however, that the CIA Director determines which CIA-initiated covert action projects are sufficiently "politically sensitive" to require Presidential attention.

From 1965 to 1972, a majority of approvals occurred subsequent to a formal committee meeting; although many telephonic approvals also took place during this period. In 1972, the process became quite informal, often involving mere notification to members that an operation had already been set in motion by the President. The Forty Committee, as the review and approval mechanism for covert action, fell into virtual disuse, with telephonic approvals being the rule and formal meetings the exception. One formal
F meeting was held in 1972, none in 1973 and 1974. This process did not begin to reverse itself until 1975.

b. Election Support

From 1965 to date, 32 percent of Forty Committee approved covert action projects were for providing some form of financial election support to foreign parties and individuals. Such support could be negative as well as positive. This is the largest covert action category, and its funding has occurred in large part in the developing countries. With few exceptions, financial support has been given to incumbent moder-
G ate party leaders and heads of State.

Certain projects have had a long life. One Third World leader received some $960,000 over a 14-year period. Others were financially supported for over a decade.

c. Media and Propaganda

Some 29 percent of Forty Committee-approved covert actions were for media and propaganda projects. This number is probably not representative. Staff has determined the existence of a large number of CIA internally-approved operations of this type, apparently deemed not politically sensitive. It is believed that if the correct number of all media and propaganda projects could be determined, it would exceed Election Support as the largest single category of covert action projects undertaken by the CIA.

Actitivies have included support of friendly media, major propaganda efforts, insertion of articles into the local press, and distribution of books and leaflets. By far the largest single recipient has been a European publishing house funded since 1951. There are a number of similar operations in the region. About 25 percent of the program has been directed at the Soviet Bloc, in the publication and clandestine import and export of Western and Soviet dissident literature.

d. Paramilitary/Arms Transfers

The 23 percent approvals in this category from 1965 to 1975 have taken one of especially four forms: secret armies, financial support to groups engaged in hostilities; paramilitary training and advisers; and shipment of arms, ammunition and other military equipment. Military ordnance is typically supplied by CIA out of its large inventory of U.S. weaponry and captured foreign weapons.

The Committee scrutinized these projects carefully, since this category is the most expensive and represents the greatest potential for escalating hostilities and deepening American involvement. By far the most interesting, and important, fact to emerge was the recognition that the great majority of these covert action projects were proposed by parties outside CIA. Many of these programs were summarily ordered, over CIA objections. CIA misgivings, however, were at times weakly expressed, as CIA is afflicted with a "can do" attitude.

At times, CIA has been used as a conduit for arms transfers in order to bypass Congressional scrutiny. A State Department-proposed project which could have been accomplished under the Military Assistance Program was tasked on CIA because the Department of Defense did not desire to return to Congress for additional funds and approval.

e. Organizational Support

A plethora of foreign, civic, religious, professional, and labor organizations have received CIA funding. There has been no real geographical concentration, although the Third World was again well represented. For example, one labor confederation in a developing country received an annual subsidy of $30,000 in three successive years.

f. Trends

Since 1965, there has been a general decline in the number of covert action projects approved by the Forty Committee. There are indications that the low figure represents the Director of Central Intelligence's determination that not as many projects should be considered "politically sensitive" and taken to the Forty Committee for approval. This, in turn, may reflect his recognition that the Forty Committee had fallen into disuse and their approvals pro-forma.

There is no indication that the passage of the Ryan-Hughes Amendment to the Foreign Assistance Act of 1974, requiring Presidential certification and briefings of Congressional oversight committees, has had a significant impact on the national covert action program. As the events of 1975 have shown, those who had warned that the Amendment and the Congressional probes into the U.S. intelligence community would make covert action impossible, have not seen their fears realized.

g. Three Projects

The three projects examined in depth were selected from major recent operations, apart from the American experience in Indochina, and involved different types of covert activity. One was election funding of pro-U.S. elements in an allied country. The second was Presidentially-directed arms support of an insurgency movement at the behest of the foreign head of a third country. The last involved a mix of political action, military training, and assistance to pro-Western forces in Angola. The last project was also initiated in part at the request of a third party.

The Committee became aware of each of these operations through other parts of its investigation and through information provided to staff by sources outside the intelligence community. For example, a study of CIA arms inventories and shipments led to the major Agency para-military support operations.

The case studies are not representative of all covert action since 1965. The Committee does believe that they are not atypical of most major programs of this type. CIA has indicated its agreement with the completeness and factual accuracy of the staff's analysis, though not necessarily with the conclusions.

Case 1: Election Support

The U.S., perhaps needlessly, expended some $10-million in contributions to political parties, affiliated organizations, and 21 individual candidates in a recent parlimentary election [1972—*editor's note*] held in an allied country [Italy—*editor's note*].

The program was initiated by our Ambassador [Graham Martin—*editor's note*], who later persuaded the Assistant to the President for National Security Affairs [Henry Kissinger—*editor's note*] to authorize him, rather than CIA, to select funding recipients and otherwise control the program's implementation. The results of the aid were mixed, and short-lived.

With national assembly elections less than two years away, the U.S. country team concluded from a CIA-contracted survey that the pro-U.S. elements, which had governed the country since the post-war period, were being seriously challenged by the Communists. The opposition, apparently heavily financed by Moscow, had scored gains in regional elections and trailed the incumbents by only a few points in the opinion polls.

Pro-West parties and affiliates had received substantial funding in the past. CIA reports total U.S. election financing over a previous 20-year period at some $65 million. Despite this massive aid, the beneficiaries had suffered repeated electoral setbacks. American observers apparently concluded that another "quick fix" was necessary to see our clients through the next vote.

Anxious to gain control of the covert program, and fearing that inter-agency consideration would be inhibiting, the Ambassador has originally sought the President's personal approval of this proposed political action.

This course would avoid the Forty Committee and, with it, the inevitable role of CIA in implementing the program. The Ambassador was rebuffed. Ironically, the Assistant to the President then requested that CIA draft a proposal without the knowledge of the Ambassador or the Department of State.

It is known that during this period the President was indirectly approached by prominent international businessmen, who were former nationals of the allied country. Their communications to the President were not available to the Committee.

The Forty Committee subsequently approved the CIA proposal, but with unusual implementation. Despite the usual near-automatic control of covert action by CIA, the Ambassador, by all accounts a man of unusual force, successfully extracted from the Assistant to the President the commitment that he would have total control of the "mix and implementation" of the project. Thus, the Ambassador, who had been in the country less than two years and did not speak the language, would determine which individuals and organizations would receive U.S. funds. The CIA station would be reduced to couriers. The Agency expressed concern that a high profile by the Ambassador would needlessly compromise the program; their complaints fell on deaf ears, despite the agreement of all that exposure would bring down the pro-West government.

A major political party received $3.4 million; a political organization created and supported by CIA, $3.4 million; other organizations and parties, a total of $1.3 million. Substantial funds were provided to several incumbents whose seats did not appear in jeopardy. Of a total of $11.8 million approved by the Forty Committee, only $9.9 million was actually spent. The reserve was held to be spent in the following year.

CIA concurred in most of the recipients chosen by the Ambassador, although differences were expressed on precise amounts. There were serious disagreements over some recipients. One of these was a high local intelligence official to whom the Ambassador wanted to give over $800,000, to conduct a propaganda effort. The Ambassador was unmoved by CIA warnings that the man was clearly linked to antidemocratic elements of the right, and went ahead with the funding.

Embassy control of the funds was poor. Participants in the program testified before the Committee that little effort was made to earmark grants or, failing that, at least seek assurances that the money was spent as intended by the Forty Committee. The Ambassador resisted most CIA control suggestions, insisting that such monitoring would insult the recipients. Thus, there was almost no accounting or control of the expenditures. There is no indication that the Ambassador began to encounter interference from Washington at this point.

The fruits of this U.S. investment are difficult to assess. The pro-U.S. elements retained control of the government by a small plurality, and most of the incumbents supported were returned to office. On the other hand, the ruling coalition quickly lost public support and suffered severe reverses in subsequent local elections.

Case 2: Arms Support

[At this point in the committee report one manuscript page was missing. It is clear from the context that the missing material opened a discussion of a U.S. scheme, involving the Shah of Iran, to channel secret aid to the Kurds in their rebellion against the government of Iraq.]

The program, ultimately to involve some $16-million, was apparently endorsed by the President after a private meeting with the foreign head of state and Dr. Kissinger.

There was no Forty Committee meeting at which a formal proposal paper containing both pros and cons could be discussed and voted on. Instead, members were simply directed to acknowledge receipt of a sparse, one-paragraph description of the operation. In a setting of almost unprecedented secrecy within the U.S. government, John B. Connally, the former Treasury Secretary, about to assume a major role in the President's re-election campaign, personally advised the head of state that the U.S. would cooperate.

The recipients of U.S. arms and cash were an insurgent ethnic group fighting for autonomy in a country bordering our ally. The bordering country and our ally had long been bitter enemies. They differed substantially in ideological orientation and in their relations with the U.S.

Evidence collected by the Committee suggests that the project was initiated primarily as a favor to our ally, who had cooperated with U.S. intelligence agencies, and who had come to feel menaced by his neighbor.

As our ally's aid dwarfed the U.S. aid package, our assistance can be seen as largely symbolic. Documents made available to the Committee indicate that the U.S. acted in effect as a guarantor that the insurgent group would not be summarily dropped by the foreign head of state. Notwithstanding these implicit assurances, the insurgents were abruptly cut off by our ally, three years, thousands of deaths, and 16 million U.S. dollars later.

It appears that, had the U.S. not reinforced our ally's prodding, the insurgents may have reached an accommodation with the central government, thus gaining at least a measure of autonomy while avoiding further bloodshed. Instead, our clients fought on, sustaining thousands of casualties and 200,000 refugees.

There is little doubt that the highly unusual security precautions and the circumvention of the Forty Committee were the product of fears by the President and Dr. Kissinger that details of the project would otherwise leak—a result which by all accounts would have mightily displeased our ally. It is also clear that the secrecy was motivated by a desire that the Department of State, which had consistently opposed such ventures in the region, be kept in the dark.

Perhaps more than the President's disregard of the Forty Committee, the apparent "no win" policy of the U.S. and its ally deeply disturbed this Committee. Documents in the Committee's possession clearly show that the President, Dr. Kissinger and the foreign head of state hoped that our clients would not prevail. They preferred instead that the insurgents simply continue a level of hostilities sufficient to sap the resources of our ally's neighboring country. This policy was not imparted to our clients, who were encouraged to continue fighting. Even in the context of covert action, ours was a cynical enterprise.

It is particularly ironic that, despite President Nixon's and Dr. Kissinger's encouragement of hostilities to keep the target country off-balance, the United States personally restrained the insurgents from an all-out offensive on one occasion when such an attack might have been successful because other events were occupying the neighboring country.

All U.S. aid was channeled through our collaborator, without whose logistical help direct assistance would have been impossible. Our national interest had thus become effectively meshed with his. Accordingly, when our ally reached an agreement with the target country and abruptly ended his own aid to the insurgents, the U.S. had no choice but to acquiesce. The extent of our ally's leverage over U.S. policy was such that the apparently made no effort to notify his junior American partners that the program's end was near.

The insurgents were clearly taken by surprise as well. Their adversaries, knowing of the impending aid cut-off, launched an all-out search-and-destroy campaign the day after the agreement was signed. The autonomy movement was over and our former clients scattered before the central government's superior forces.

The cynicism of the U.S. and its ally had not yet completely run its course, however. Despite direct pleas from the insurgent leader and the CIA station chief in the area to the President and Dr. Kissinger, the U.S. refused to extend humanitarian assistance to the thousands of refugees created by the abrupt termination of military aid. As the Committee staff was reminded by a high U.S. official, "covert action should not be confused with missionary work."

Case 3: Angola

For reasons not altogether clear, and despite the opposition of senior government officials, the U.S. has been heavily involved in the current civil war in Angola.

The CIA has informed the Committee that since January 1975, it had expended over $31 million in military hardware, transportation costs, and cash payments by the end of 1975. The Committee has reason to believe that the actual U.S. investment is much higher. Information supplied to the Committee also suggests that the military intervention of the Soviet Union and Cuba is in large part a reaction to U.S. efforts to break a political stalemate, in favor of its clients.

The beneficiaries of U.S. aid are two of the three contesting factions: the National Front for the Independence of Angola (FNLA) and the National Union for the Total Independence of Angola (UNITA). The third faction contesting for control of the government, following independence on November 11, 1975, is the Soviet-backed Popular Movement for the Liberation of Angola (MPLA). CIA estimates that the fighting had claimed several thousand casualties by the end of 1975.

The main U.S. client is the National Front, headed by Holden Roberto, a longtime associate and relative of President Mobutu Sese Seko of neighboring Zaire. Subsequent to President Mobutu's request last winter to Dr. Kissinger, as independence for Angola became a certainty and liberation groups began to jockey for position, the Forty Committee approved furnishing Roberto $300,000 for various political action activities, restricted to non-military objectives.

Later events have suggested that this infusion of U.S. aid, unprecedented and massive in the underdeveloped colony, may have panicked the Soviets into arming their MPLA clients, whom they had backed for over a decade and who were now in danger of being eclipsed by the National Front. Events in Angola took a bellicose turn as the U.S. was requested by President Mobutu to make a serious military investment.

In early June, 1975, CIA prepared a proposal paper for military aid to pro-U.S. elements in Angola, the cost of which was set at $6 million. A revised program, costing $14 million, was approved by the Forty Committee and by President Ford in July. This was increased to $25 million in August, and to about $32 million in November. By mid-summer, it was decided that U.S. aid should not be given solely to Roberto, but instead, divided between him and UNITA's Jonas Savimbi.

The Committee has learned that a task force composed of high U.S. experts on Africa strongly opposed military intervention; instead, last April they called for diplomatic efforts to encourage a political settlement among the three factions to avert bloodshed. Apparently at the direction of National Security Council aides, the task force recommendation was removed from the report and presented to NSC members as merely one policy option. The other two alternatives were a hands-off policy or substantial A military intervention.

Of CIA's $31 million figure, said to represent expenditures to the end of 1975, about half is attributed to supply of light arms, mortars, ammunition, vehicles, boats, and communication equipment. The balance includes shipping expenses and cash payments. The Committee has reason to question the accuracy of CIA's valuation of military equipment sent to Angola.

A staff accountant on loan from the General Accounting Office has determined that CIA "costing" procedures and the use of surplus equipment have resulted in a substantial understatement of the value of U.S. aid. Examples include .45 caliber automatic weapons "valued" by CIA at $5.00 each and .30 B caliber semi-automatic carbines at $7.55. Based on a sampling of ordnance cost figures and a comparison with Department of Defense procedures, staff advises that the CIA's ordnance figure should at least be doubled.

Dr. Kissinger has indicated that U.S. military intervention in Angola is based on three factors: Soviet support of the MPLA and the USSR's increased presence in Africa, U.S. policy to encourage moderate independence groups in southern Africa, and the U.S. interest in promoting the stability of Mobutu and other leadership figures in the area. Past support to Mobutu, along with his responsiveness to some of the United States recent diplomatic needs for Third World support, make it equally likely that the para- C mount factor in the U.S. involvement is Dr. Kissinger's desire to reward and protect African leaders in the area. The U.S.'s expressed opposition to the MPLA is puzzling in view of Director's Colby's statement to the Committee that there are scant ideological differences among the three factions, all of whom are nationalists above all else.

Control of resources may be a factor. Angola has significant oil deposits and two American multinationals, Gulf and Texaco, operate in the off-shore area. Gulf had deposited some $100 million in concession fees in a national bank now under MPLA control. At the suggestion of the U.S. government, the company suspended further payments. D

Until recently, the U.S.-backed National Front was supported by the People's Republic of China, which had provided about 100 military advisors. Mobutu has provided a staging area for U.S. arms shipments and has periodically sent Zairois troops, trained by the Republic of North Korea, into Angola to support Roberto's operations. Small numbers of South African forces have been in the country and are known to have been in contact with Savimbi's UNITA troops.

Pursuant to Section 662 of the Foreign Assistance Act of 1974, the President has found that the Angola action program is "important to the national security." As directed by the Act, CIA has briefed the Congressional oversight committees as to the Forty E Committee approvals of increased amounts of military aid.

CIA officials have testified to the Committee that there appears to be little hope of an outright MPLA military defeat. Instead, U.S. efforts are now aimed at promoting a stalemate, and in turn, the ceasefire and the coalition government urged by the long-forgotten NSC task force.

2. Intelligence Collection

Human and diplomatic risks are not confined to covert action. Certain methods of intelligence-gathering invite the same danger of war and infringement of F the Constitutional rights of Americans.

The Committee has examined both technical and non-technical intelligence-gathering programs and has concluded that the risks accompanying them are often unacceptably great; that information obtained often does not justify the risk; the policy-makers have been insensitive to dangers, especially of the violation of U.S. citizens' rights; and, that there are inadequate policy-level mechanisms for the regular review of risk assessment.

a. Submarines

A highly technical U.S. Navy submarine reconnaissance program, often operating within unfriendly waters, has experienced at least 9 collisions with hostile vessels in the last ten years, over 110 possible detections, and at least three press exposures. Most of the submarines carry nuclear weapons.

The program clearly produces useful information on our adversaries' training exercises, weapons testing, and general naval capabilities. It is also clear, however, that the program is inherently risky. Committee staff's review of the program suggests if both Congress and the Department of the Navy were sufficiently motivated to provide the funds, technical capabilities could be developed which would make possible the acquisition of the same data through less hazardous means.

The Navy's own justification of the program as a "low risk" venture is inaccurate, and has, therefore, not met or resolved the Committee's misgivings. Documents provided the Committee by the Defense Department indicate that, while risk assessments are made prior to operations, they are ritualistic and pro forma. In fact, their mission risk assessments do not vary despite constant changes in political conditions, information sought, distance from enemy shores and hostile forces, and our adversaries' ability to detect the presence of U.S. submarines. During the hundreds of missions these submarines have conducted, the Navy has never assessed military risk as anything but "low." The Committee is, therefore, troubled by the completely pro forma nature of the mission risk assessment as it is presently accomplished.

Just as the Navy's assurances that the program is secure are inconsistent with the collisions, apparent detections, and press stories, their claims that the sensitive missions are closely monitored are belied by the scant tactical guidance given commanders and regular communications gaps. Once a U.S. submarine enters the 12-mile limit of another nation, communications security and the lack of certain technical capabilities make it impossible to independently verify the location of a submarine at any given moment. Many of these difficulties result from factors which are inherent in the nature of this covert operation.

Naval inquiries into collisions and other "untoward incidents," if held at all, are almost always conducted at a low level, effectively keeping policy-makers in the dark on changing operational conditions. Thus, it took a field-initiated, low-level investigation, conducted after three collisions in 1970, to determine that pre-mission training and operational guidelines for U.S. submarines on this type of sensitive mission needed revision and up-grading. If Washington-based review had been adequate, it would not have taken this field investigation to determine that U.S. submarines were following other submarines too closely. In addition, staff found no evidence which would indicate that commanders of submarines colliding with hostile vessels have ever received disciplinary action of any kind. At times, commanders have escaped censure despite recommendations to that effect by a review panel.

Despite these faults, the Committee noted the procedures implemented by the Navy to insure the safety of the mission and the crew in situations which are inherently risky. Washington-based control, review, and coordination of this program has been an evolutionary matter over the years. At present it appears to be extremely well managed, with the exception of the risk assessment area and the failure to forward the results of low-level investigations for Washington-based review.

In reviewing past investigations and formal reviews, the Committee noted the Navy's implementation of previous suggestions for change. There is, however, one unfortunate exception. A previous review of this program suggested that the Department of the Navy make a firm commitment to the necessity of maintaining an intelligence capability with U.S. submarines by allocating funds to research and development efforts designed to increase both the capabilities and the security of their missions. The Navy has paid only lip service to this commitment.

Given these factors, the Committee urges a thorough review of the program's product and hazards, to avert another *Pueblo*, or worse, and to insure that important intelligence collection continues with significantly less risk than presently exists.

b. Interpretation of International Communications

The National Security Agency (NSA) systematically intercepts international communications, both voice and cable. NSA officials and the Director of Central Intelligence concede that messages to and from American citizens and businesses have been picked up in the course of gathering foreign communications intelligence. They maintain, however, that these messages are small in number and usually discarded in any case.

Earlier NSA programs of questionable legality focused on international narcotics traffic and radicalism, and even targeted Americans. The Committee's preliminary investigation reveals at least one new area of non-political and non-military emphasis in international intercept—economic intelligence. Communications interception in this area has rapidly developed since 1972, partly in reaction to the Arab oil embargo and the failure to obtain good information on Russian grain production and negotiations for the purchase with American corporations.

The Committee is not convinced that the current commercial intercept program has yielded sufficiently valuable data to justify its high cost and intrusion, however inadvertent, into the privacy of international communications of U.S. citizens and organizations. Inasmuch as the technical complexity of the program defies easy or quick evaluation, the Committee is hopeful that a permanent oversight mechanism will closely and comprehensively scrutinize the operation to determine whether the risks are necessary and acceptable.

c. Manipulation of the Media

The free flow of information, vital to a responsible and credible press, has been threatened as a result of CIA's use of the world media for cover and for clandestine information-gathering.

There are disturbing indications that the accuracy of many news stories has been undermined as well. Information supplied to the Committee suggests that some planted, falsified articles have reached readers in the U.S.

Intelligence agencies have long prized journalists as informants and identity-covers. Newsmen generally enjoy great mobility, and are often admitted to areas denied to ordinary businessmen or to suspected intelligence types. Not expected to work in one fixed location, both bona fide journalists and masquerading intelligence officers can move about without arousing suspicions. They also have extraordinary access to important foreign leaders and diplomats.

CIA, as no doubt every other major intelligence agency in the world, has manipulated the media. Full-time foreign correspondents for major U.S. publications have worked concurrently for CIA, passing along information received in the normal course of their regular jobs and even, on occasion, traveling to otherwise non-newsworthy areas to acquire data. Far more prevalent is the Agency's practice of retaining free-lancers and "stringers" as informants. A stringer working in a less-newsworthy country could supply stories to a newspaper, radio, and a weekly magazine, none of whom can justify a full-time correspondent. This may make the use of stringers even more insidious than exploitation of full-time journalists.

The Committee has learned that the employment of newsmen by CIA is usually without the knowledge or agreement of the employers back in the U.S. Publishers have been unable, despite strenuous effort, to learn from the Agency which, if any, of their employees have had a clandestine intelligence function. Newsmen-informants apparently do not often disclose this relationship to their editors. The Committee has learned of cases in which informants moved from one bona fide press position to another, without ever making employers aware of their past or present CIA status.

CIA acknowledges that "stringers" and others with whom the Agency has a relationship are often directed to insert Agency-composed "news" articles into foreign publications and wire services. U.S. intelligence officials do not rule out the possibility that these planted stories may find their way into American newspapers from time to time, but insist that CIA does not intentionally propagandize in this country. CIA insensitivity to the possibility of its adultering news digested by Americans is indicated by its frequent manipulation of Reuters wire service dispatches—which regularly appear in U.S. media. Because Reuters is British, it is considered fair game.

A number of CIA officers employed by U.S. and foreign publications write nothing at all. Their journalistic affiliation is a "cover"—a sham arrangement making possible full-time clandestine work for the Agency. With these arrangements, the employer's cooperation has been obtained.

After the Washington *Star-News* discovered a CIA-media relationship in 1973, Director Colby ordered a review of these practices. Subsequently, the Agency terminated the informant relationships of five full-time employees of American periodicals. Stringers and free-lancers are still on the payroll, despite their periodic reporting for a U.S. media usually unaware of the writer's CIA connection.

The use of American press enterprises as a cover has been tightened somewhat. No longer, for example, can a CIA officer in the field arrange for cover without headquarters approval.

d. CIA Presence in the Executive Branch

CIA personnel may be found in a host of U.S. departments and agencies, in the National Security Council, and in the White House itself.

Typically, their Agency affiliations are unknown to colleagues and to all others, except one or two leadership figures. They sit on interagency panels whose members are unwitting. In some cases these panels already include another, official CIA representative, giving CIA undue representation. Some of them work in positions involving evaluation of CIA's work product and proposals.

These individuals are "detailees"—CIA employees on loan to the Executive, usually at the latter's request. They include all types, from gardeners and typists, to intelligence analysts and practitioners of covert action.

Detailees are requested for a variety of reasons—because the White House wants to circumvent Congressional budget ceilings, because there are no other available secretaries with security clearances, because CIA professional expertise is highly regarded, or because the position had always been staffed by an Agency officer.

The Committee has found no indications that CIA detailees are instructed to make clandestine reports to headquarters on the inner workings of the host-employer. Nor is there credible evidence that they are asked by CIA to perform in any manner which is inconsistent with the best interests of the host. Nonetheless, the Committee believes that detailing as presently practiced reflects an unwise policy.

At best, intelligence personnel such as electrical help are diverted from CIA duties thus frustrating the budget allocating intent of Congress. A far worse spectre is that of CIA officers assigned to such posts as the National Security Council where they are susceptible, despite all good intentions, to substantial conflicts of interest on the most sensitive issues. The latter problem is compounded by the fact that the detailee's background often is unknown to NSC colleagues who are also charged with CIA-related responsibilities.

The Committee discovered detailees, whose Agency ties were closely held secrets, making recommendations on CIA covert action proposals to unwitting senior NSC officials. Such individuals also help conduct the NSC's evaluation of the intelligence product, and in that capacity regularly compare CIA's performance with that of rival agencies.

These individuals have impressed staff as highly motivated professionals, acutely aware of the problems resulting from divided loyalties. Their integrity is not at issue. But neither the White House nor the CIA is well served by an unnecessary policy which invites cynicism and compromises the quality of Executive Branch oversight of the intelligence community.

HOUSE INTELLIGENCE PANEL VOTES TO CITE KISSINGER FOR CONTEMPT

The House Select Committee on Intelligence voted Nov. 14 to cite Secretary of State Henry Kissinger for contempt of Congress for failing to produce, under subpoena, classified documents for use in the committee's investigation of the effectiveness of U.S. intelligence operations. The committee, accusing Kissinger of "contumacious [deliberately defiant] conduct," approved, in three separate 10–3 votes, three contempt citations against the secretary of state for each of three subpoenas he had not complied with. The committee's action had to be approved by a majority of the House before the matter could be referred to the Justice Department for investigation and possible prosecution.

Kissinger's immediate reaction to the action was that he feared it would raise "serious questions" all over the world about "what this country is doing to itself." President Ford, also expressing regret over the move, termed it "shocking" and predicted it would have "very broad and serious ramifications." He added that material demanded under one of the subpoenas —State Department recommendations for covert intelligence activities made to the White House during 1962–1972—was protected from Congressional scrutiny by executive privilege.

The second committee subpoena asked Kissinger to produce minutes of the meetings of the National Security Council's secret 40 Committee, which approved all covert intelligence actions undertaken by the U.S. The third asked for intelligence reports concerning the Soviet Union's compliance with the terms of the 1972 strategic arms limitation treaty. These subpoenas were addressed to Kissinger in his capacity as director of the NSC.

The State Department Nov. 15 offered a more definitive response to the committee's assertion that Kissinger was responsible for the material covered by the subpoenas. William G. Hyland, head of the department's bureau of intelligence and research, insisted that Kissinger had no responsibility for compliance with the two subpoenas concerning NSC documents. Since Kissinger had relinquished the post of director of the NSC Nov. 3 and since the subpoenas had been served after that date, Hyland argued, Lt. Gen. Brent Scowcroft, named to succeed Kissinger as NSC director, was the individual to whom the subpoenas should have been directed. [See pp. 1334–1343] Regarding the subpoena addressed to Kissinger as secretary of state, Hyland said Kissinger's failure to respond was the result of an order by President Ford, who had been advised by the attorney general that the documents need not be produced on the ground they were privileged presidential communications.

Rep. Otis Pike (D, N.Y.), chairman of the committee, said Nov. 17 his committee would seek House approval of the contempt citations despite State Department arguments that the committee had erred. Such a contention was faulty, Pike said. He said his committee had produced research that the post of NSC director would technically have to be occupied until Scowcroft was sworn in. "Technically that person is Kissinger," Pike said. He also questioned the contention that Kissinger's responsibility for the subpoena addressed to the secretary of state had been preempted by a claim of executive privilege.

The Miami Herald

Miami, Fla., November 23, 1975

A House committee has voted 10-2 to hold Secretary of State Kissinger in contempt because he refused to submit certain foreign policy documents to it.

Kissinger

Naturally, Dr. Kissinger is angry. No Cabinet officer has ever been held in contempt of Congress, although contempt has been expressed for more than one on occasion. The Secretary holds further that the attitude of the House committee weakens his administration of foreign policy.

Naturally, too, Dr. Kissinger threatens to resign if the House supports the Intelligence Subcommittee. It's natural because he has made the same threat before. After spending some years in his corner as the brilliant architect of detente and the absence of war in the Middle East, at last he has put us under compulsion to depart.

When a House committee votes three subpenas by such a margin it is not, as a White House source told newsmen, a "helter-skelter" operation.

Rather, we think, it is a reaction to the ego round-trips which Dr. Kissinger takes with regularity. According to Aldo Beckman of The Chicago Tribune, "Kissinger was in a fit of temper at the time" of the committee action.

Temperamental Cabinet officers are nothing new. Lincoln had a hard time putting a halter on Secretary of State William Henry Seward, who wanted his own way on government policy, but he succeeded through artful persuasion.

We are aware that Secretary Kissinger has his unfriends in and about the White House, and we understand that even Gerald Ford is becoming weary of the Kissinger arrogance and frequent publicized threats to quit.

The bottom line of the matter is that no man is indispensible under our form of government. The House committee has enjoyed the cooperation of every other agency in pursuing information about foreign policy decisions which have been made in the dark — such as, for example, suppression of dissenting views on the Cyprus crisis and unreported Soviet violations of SALT agreements.

If Dr. Kissinger must have his way without question or challenge we suggest that he have it outside the State Department.

Newsday

Garden City, N.Y., November 16, 1975

Americans mustn't be misled by the rhetoric surrounding the contempt citation voted against Henry Kissinger Friday by Representative Otis Pike's House Intelligence Committee.

The confrontation is *not* simply another outbreak of political infighting between the Democratic Congress and the Republican President.

Nor is it just a personal feud between an ambitious committee chairman and the secretary of state over documents that Pike would like to see in the headlines and Kissinger wants to protect. Anyone personally acquainted with Pike, as many Long Islanders are, knows better than that.

It isn't even an argument about the public's right to know. The Pike committee hasn't sought to release the subpoenaed documents, which deal with Soviet adherence to the SALT agreements, State Department recommendations for covert operations and White House decisions thereon. It merely demands the right to read them under its mandate to investigate the conduct of U.S. intelligence.

No, what's really at stake is far more significant. The Pike-Kissinger confrontation is the inevitable test of everything the country should have learned from the Bay of Pigs, Vietnam and Watergate about Congress' responsibility to oversee the policies carried out by the executive branch in the name of the American people. Either Congress has the absolute right to examine the operations of the executive branch, or the executive is effectively free to exempt itself from oversight whenever it sees fit. There is no middle way.

Even the CIA seems to have learned that lesson. Director William Colby has cooperated fully with the Pike committee and its Senate counterpart. There have been no pleas of executive privilege from CIA headquarters, because the intelligence community now recognizes the need for the public support that can only come with oversight on behalf of the public.

It's hard to believe that Gerald Ford hasn't learned. Can he really have forgotten in 15 months that it was confrontation over a cov[er-] up that drove Nixon from office? More like[ly,] in our opinion, Ford has come to anoth[er] grossly unwise decision by the same route th[at] has led him astray so often in the past (on [aid] to New York, for instance): his almost pa[ra]noid desire to appease the right and someh[ow] head off Ronald Reagan's challenge, his v[ul]nerability to self-serving advice from one [or] two favored advisors and a vacuum in th[e] corner of the White House where every Pre[si]dent should be able to turn for disinterest[ed] counsel.

Kissinger's motives are less clouded. [Re]gardless of his protestations that the subp[oe]naed documents concern previous administ[ra]tions, the fact remains that he stands to [be] personally embarrassed by his own role [in] some of the grievous policy mistakes now co[m]ing under congressional scrutiny. If that's [a] false assumption, Kissinger need only ha[nd] over the subpoenaed documents to prove [it.] He certainly won't accomplish that by rev[iv]ing the Nixonian rhetoric of a year or two a[go.]

Arkansas Gazette.

Little Rock, Ark., November 18, 1975

Secretary of State Henry A. Kissinger we are sure will never actually do any time, as Senator Lowell F. Weicker, one of the first on the Republican side of the aisle to have had enough of all this business, has said that Kissinger so richly deserves to do.

We are just about as sure that the full Congress will not follow through on the contempt action that Representative Otis G. Pike's House Committee on Intelligence has recommended, though the Congress sometimes is loath to reject out of hand actions by a responsible committee of either House initiated with such a show of near unanimity (10-to-1 on two of the three counts of contempt recommended by the Pike Committee, 10-to-2 on the remaining one.)

None of this is to say that Kissinger ought not to be cited for contempt by the full Congress, or that he should not pay one of the legally prescribed penalties for such, though we ourselves would be reluctant to play the role of turnkey for Senator Weicker. If there had been no such expression as "contempt of Congress" written into the law, one would have had to be invented, and what more likely inventor—or, rather, cause—than Henry Kissinger, who positively *reeks* of contempt for these legally elected representatives of the American people, whom he, deep down under, regards as beneath contempt or even of meaningful notice. As Lowell Weicker puts it, Kissinger throughout his public life has operated on the assumption that "there is one set of rules for Kissinger and another for the democracy called the United States of America."

Chairman Pike didn't do badly either in drafting the language of the contempt resolution with the advice and consent of the overwhelming majority of the other Committee members: Kissinger as he (and they) said had been guilty of "contumacious conduct" in his dealings—more properly, non-dealings—with the Congress, most immediately, with those members of the Congress who have tried so valiantly to get at the truth of what has been done to the country in recent years under the catch-all, excuse-all cloak of national "security."

KISSINGER for his part, was regretful that the Pike Committee had done what it had no honorable choice but to do, dragged out his threadbare security blanket again and started wringing his hands publicly about possible outside reaction, that the Pike Committee's contempt recommendations might "raise serious questions all over the world at what this country is doing to itself and what the necessity is to torment ourselves like this *for month after month.*"

This is vintage Kissingerese. Does "month after month" cover only the period in which the Pike Committee and its counterpart in the Senate, the Church Committee, have been at work? Or is it a more sweeping description, going back to the whole of the Watergate story, including the still untold full story of Kissinger's role in the unauthorized wiretaps laid on by or for the National Security Agency, the wiretaps that resulted in a civil action for damages by Kissinger's onetime trusted assistant, Morton Halperin. On the whole central issue that Kissinger tries to raise, the answer is of course that the country is and has done nothing to "itself." What it has had is things done to it by identifiable individuals, as we have tried to point out many times. That is what both the Pike and the Church investigations have been about, and the earlier ones before them. The analogy is more that of someone bringing the hockey puck to the rim of the net by the sharpest sort of sharp practice and the goalie (Congress, the courts, the press) lunging desperately to block the shot if it can.

Kissinger was regretful, then, and President Ford, who is easily shocked, was of course shocked by Congress's contempt action. In the case of one of the subpoenas, he "reluctantly" invoked executive privilege, thus taking Kissinger out of it, he said, and making the showdown one between him, the President, and the Congress. Here is, again, the dreary familiarity of everyone (or, at least, almost everyone) rushing to batten "the Secretary" in cottonwool, as if this tough old global political operator were some kind of innocent foundling.

This is a sentiment not unknown in the Congress itself, as we are fully aware. In the end it is only the Congress that can determine whether it—meaning the Congress as a whole—wants seriously to restore its full-partnership in the governance of the country.

THE SACRAMENTO BEE

Sacramento, Calif., November 18, 1975

The contempt citation against Secretary of State Henry Kissinger by the House Intelligence Committee, for failure to turn over subpoenaed documents, is one more necessary step in Congress' assertion of its prerogatives in relation to the executive branch.

It comes on the heels of the contempt citation against Commerce Secretary Rogers C. B. Morton, spearheaded by Rep. John Moss, D-Sacramento, chairman of the House investigation subcommittee.

In the latter case, the citation resulted from Morton's refusal to hand over lists of American firms pressured to join the Arab economic boycott against Israel.

Both actions dramatically signal congressional determination to hold the executive branch to account in vital actions and policies affecting the nation's interests.

In the Kissinger case, the secretary of state has refused to give the committee documents on eight covert intelligence operations. The Congress clearly has a right to know about covert actions by our intelligence apparatus pertaining to foreign and domestic policies, so long as such disclosure doesn't compromise security.

Both contempt actions bring to a head a long-needed showdown over the respective powers of legislative and executive branches. While it's obvious Congress should not go overboard to the extent of violating legitimate executive privilege, the matters involved in the contempt citations do not constitute any such intrusion.

The documents sought are vitally necessary if the respective congressional committees, and ultimately the full Congress, are to have an appropriate voice in a wide range of covert intelligence operations which Congress has the right and duty to oversee.

Long Island Press

Jamaica, N.Y., November 17, 1975

The House Intelligence Committee has voted, by 10-to-2, to cite Secretary of State Henry A. Kissinger for contempt for refusing to comply with subpenas that sought documents on covert activities by the Central Intelligence Agency.

That's strong stuff. But, as explained by Rep. Otis G. Pike, the Suffolk Democrat who heads the committee, the panel exhausted all other ways to get the documents, and time is running out on the committee's investigative mandate.

"I, for one, am weary of this whole business of waiting and delaying," Mr. Pike commented. So are we.

The full House may not go along with a contempt citation against Mr. Kissinger. The fog in Foggy Bottom is being made still thicker by White House claims of executive privilege.

But surely Congress is entitled to full information about illicit CIA activities. The Pike committee deserves praise for opening the door to a confrontation between the executive and legislative branches of government over this important issue.

New York Post

New York, N.Y., November 15, 1975

In its protracted attempts to obtain critical information on certain secret intelligence operations from the Department of State, the House Intelligence Committee has employed patient negotiation without success. It has now been obliged to issue what amounts to an ultimatum. It should not be required to declare unlimited legal war.

The Pike committee, with three decisive votes, has decided to recommend to the full House that Secretary of State Kissinger be cited for contempt of Congress. He has, assertedly on White House instructions, ignored a committee subpena for the information; President Ford evidently plans to invoke "executive privilege."

The committee's decision is fully warranted and demands backing on the floor. Unless it is sustained, neither Congress nor the American people may ever regain control of an intelligence apparatus that has repeatedly abused its high authority.

But that is far from the only serious issue at hand. How often, for example, have the nation's intelligence services been shamefully misused by the White House—before Watergate? How many times have carefully drafted intelligence estimates been ignored? What have been the resultant effects on U. S. policy and posture? These are some of the questions embodied in the Pike committee's quest for information on the secret operations. We cannot envisage any "executive privilege" that justifies refusal to answer.

Unless the Administration modifies its stand, only a full-scale legal test can clear the air.

ST. LOUIS POST-DISPATCH

St. Louis, Mo., November 25, 1975

Shortly after Congress returns from its Thanksgiving recess, the House of Representatives is expected to consider the three contempt citations voted by its Select Committee on Intelligence against Secretary of State Kissinger, who had declined to comply with three subpenas issued by the panel. What follows then — in debate and subsequent action by the chamber and possibly the courts — again will focus public attention on the question of how the nation is best to be served when the interests of the executive and legislative branches collide on basic constitutional issues.

In the case of one of the subpenas, that concerning State Department recommendations of covert intelligence activities, the Administration has asserted the claim of executive privilege. So what may emerge here is a further clarification of what the executive argues is its inherent constitutional right to withhold certain material from Congress. All three subpenas, the other two of which deal with covert operations authorized by the National Security Council's "Forty Committee" and with documents relating to strategic arms negotiations, are pertinent to a somewhat broader issue. And that is the extent, as a practical matter, that it is desirable for the legislative branch to be able to peer into the workings of the executive.

As to executive privilege, it is a claimed right because it is nowhere mentioned in the Constitution and it has never been definitively upheld by the courts. Here, however, it is important to note that in the Nixon tapes case, Chief Justice Burger declared in passing that executive privilege "is inextricably rooted in the separation of powers under the Constitution." To what degree remains to be tested.

Yet, as Richard Dudman pointed out Sunday in a thoughtful analysis from Washington, there is a long tradition of parliamentary thought — dating back at least to the eighteenth century — on both sides of the Atlantic that the executive must yield to the legislative on matters of how the laws are being carried out. Quoting from Woodrow Wilson, Mr. Dudman wrote that "unless Congress both scrutinize . . . (acts of the executive) and sift them by every form of discussion, the country must remain in embarrassing, crippling ignorance of the very affairs which it is most important that it should understand and direct."

It would seem to us that in the instant case Congress is acting with utmost responsibility in scrutinizing and sifting material relating to covert intelligence activities. Those activities, Americans need scarcely be reminded after recent revelations, have been a repugnant affront to both personal and public morality and, in encompassing assassination plots and schemes for the overthrow of governments, gross violations of international law.

But does it necessarily follow that Congress may properly regard the executive as a goldfish bowl, the activities therein to be constantly on exhibit? The answer, we think, must be based on a case-by-case assessment. If, for example, there is reason to think that there are crimes being committed or that the executive is failing in its constitutional mandate to "take care that the laws be faithfully executed," then Congress surely is entitled to use the strongest investigative tool at its disposal — the subpena — to get at whatever information is needed.

If, however, that investigative power is used frivolously or for the purpose of malicious harassment, as with the case of the McCarthy hearings of the early 1950s, the executive has every right to resist it and a responsible congressional leadership will restrain it — as indeed happened with the censure of Senator McCarthy. The threat of congressional action ought not to be allowed to chill the process of legitimate policy-making.

Even so, we would argue that in a democratic society in the last analysis the claims of secrecy must yield to those of openness and public accountability. As Prof. Raoul Berger of Harvard has written, "there is the proven fact that . . . (confidential) interchanges have time and again served as a vehicle for corruption and malversation . . ." The solution, of course, lies in responsible co-operation: candor on the part of the executive, sensitivity on that of Congress. Without it, as the contempt citations demonstrate, confrontation is inevitable.

THE DENVER POST

Denver, Colo., November 20, 1975

Secretary of State Kissinger is peeved once again with the U.S. Congress. It's Kissinger's contention that a House committee, in citing him for contempt, has destroyed his credibility abroad and will make it all but impossible for him to conduct effective foreign policy.

If Kissinger feels that way, he should quit immediately.

It's too bad that the latest Congress-Kissinger imbroglio should erupt over peripheral issue of doubtful urgency. However, it serves to spotlight once again Kissinger's belief that Congress has no business in the State Department.

It's high time that the secretary understand that U.S. diplomacy is a cooperative venture between the executive and legislative branches of government and that the old days when Congress shrugged off foreign policy involvement are gone forever. For too long, going back to at least the early months of World War II, the formulation of our foreign policy was left largely in the hands of only one branch of government—the executive. The will of the people was effectively circumvented.

Of late, however—and especially since the nightmare in Southeast Asia, the people of these United States have demanded that they be heard and listened to before vital commitments are made in their name. The message has been passed on to their elected congressmen in the House and Senate. And now Secretary Kissinger chafes at what he considers congressional interference in his pursuit of "creative," i.e. highly personal, diplomacy.

But is public opinion a poor guide to foreign policy creation, as the secretary would appear to suggest? It seems not. Ample evidence can be provided to show that the public has often been ahead of its leaders and its diplomats when decisions were being made about military involvement. For example, the people seemed to sense far ahead of our military leaders that it would be difficult to win the kind of war that was fought in Vietnam. Only a few months after the Bay of Tonkin incident in 1964, many citizens were predicting "another Korea."

Instead of clandestine wheeling and dealing on foreign policy matters by their diplomatic, political and military leaders, U.S. citizens are demanding candor and openness.

Kissinger timed his latest petulant outburst very poorly indeed. He ignores the fact that the Johnson and Nixon administrations suffered giant-sized credibility gaps on the conduct of the Vietnam war. And that the Ford administration of which he is a member is dealing with an increased level of skepticism on the part of the public regarding the conduct of foreign policy.

Moreover, this skepticism and criticism is apt to increase, rather than lessen, as the nation enters the election year of 1976. Already, Ronald Reagan is sniping at Kissinger's framework of detente with Russia; the Democrats can be expected to get him in their sights soon.

But that's the way the American political system operates—or should operate, even though it's been overlooked during much of the past quarter-century. Every issue up for debate and discussion. A full revelation of American feeling on every matter. This, to be sure, goes against the grain with Henry Kissinger. He fears that he'll lose respect abroad and that foreign leaders will hesitate to do business with the United States.

This is nonsense—or will be as soon as it's generally known that the conduct of U.S. foreign policy no longer is a cozy business worked by cronies. What harm could there be in reemphasizing that, in the American political system, Congress and the presidency represent coequal branches of government, that both have important roles to play in framing and implementing foreign policy, and that no agreement in which both partners haven't fully participated can be considered valid or binding? None whatsoever.

As mentioned earlier, the secretary might happen to be the aggrieved party in the contempt citation that provoked his latest outburst. He was named in three separate counts by the House Select Committee on Intelligence for failing to make documents available. In two of these, the citations were issued in his former capacity as head of the National Security Council, a post he no longer holds. He apparently withheld the data mentioned in the third on direct orders from President Ford. But these are complex issues which face long legal and congressional journeys before the secretary is finally found guilty or innocent of contempt.

It's likely that history will deal kindly with Mr. Kissinger, will find that, on balance, he played his role capably and with style. If—and it's a big if—he can now accept the fact that he has a new partner in his act, a partner demanding equal billing.

For some 20 years now, Kissinger has been saying that broad public support is essential to successful foreign policy. Somehow, he still finds it distasteful to take the simple steps necessary to ensure that support. Put simply, he dislikes taking the American people into his confidence. This is a fundamental, possibly limiting, error on his part.

For, above all, American foreign policy is obliged to be public policy, subject to public scrutiny and appraisal.

The Salt Lake Tribune

Salt Lake City, Utah, November 17, 1975

Contempt of Congress recommendations pending in the House of Representatives against Secretary of State Henry A. Kissinger raise anew the delicate question of how much Congress—and the public—need to know about secret affairs of government.

Similar action is pending against outgoing Commerce Secretary Rogers C. B. Morton. Both men refused, on grounds of executive privilege, to provide information sought by House committees. They acted on orders of President Ford.

With presidential election preliminaries in full swing the actions of both Democrat-controlled committees have clear political links. But the issue the contempt recommendations pose is basic and a source of longstanding conflict between executive and legislative branches.

President Ford and his secretaries of State and Commerce contend that release of the information requested would violate confidences of previous secretaries and Presidents. Mr. Kissinger said the committee action was hurting the United States' image and could interfere with his handling of foreign policy.

The House Intelligence Committee subpoenaed documents on covert U.S. intelligence operations and intelligence estimates on Soviet compliance with arms agreements.

No doubt there are valid reasons for refusing to comply. But in the case of the request for data on arms agreements compliance, Congress has a legitimate claim on such information.

Mr. Kissinger has been accused, by ousted Defense Secretary James R. Schlesinger among others, of playing down alleged evidence of Soviet violations of Strategic Arms Limitation Talks (SALT) agreements. With the United States and the Soviet Union hoping to begin SALT II negotiations before many months the question of Soviet violations of past agreements becomes paramount.

Since Congress will eventually have to act on agreements reached at SALT II it has a legitimate, yea compelling, need to learn what U.S. intelligence agencies know about the charges of Soviet cheating.

Because of accusations that the Secretary of State has been too easy on alleged Soviet violations, the attempt to withhold what could be convincing evidence of his innocence or guilt appears more a move to protect Mr. Kissinger than the United States.

Still, there may be other, less sinister reasons for Mr. Kissinger's refusal and he should hasten to get them on the record. As for the greater question of a President's right to invoke executive privilege, no explicit answer is likely. Each confrontation must be decided on its particular merits. By the time a final court ruling is obtained (if indeed one can be had) the original conflict is often history.

Good sense, good faith and a willingness to compromise for the good of the country can resolve most such impasses quicker and better. At this stage, however, none of these ingredients is apparent.

OKLAHOMA CITY TIMES

Oklahoma City, Okla., November 15, 1975

FOR all of this nation's devotion to open conduct of public affairs, it must be candidly confessed that there are some things which must remain secret, at least for some time after they take place, in order to assure the very survival of the country.

Friday, the House Intelligence Committee, headed by Rep. Otis Pike, D-N.Y., voted three contempt citations, two of them by 10-2 margins and the third by a 10-1 vote, naming Secretary of State Henry Kissinger for his refusal to supply certain information on covert (undercover) intelligence requests made by the State Department over the past 15 years. President Ford was reported ready to claim executive privilege as the basis for Kissinger's refusals.

Elsewhere on this page today, columnists Evans and Novak praise the Pike Committee, in contrast to its Senate counterpart under Sen. Frank Church, D-Idaho, which has been called "irresponsible" by some members of Congress. But the matter is relative. Neither committee has demonstrated an understanding of the nature of intelligence gathering. The very fact that our government does or does not know certain things can affect history. The fact that a certain type of inquiry is made by high officials indicates to foreign powers how much we already know and don't know. That can be an important secret in the conduct of our foreign affairs. It can also affect our national security—and not in abstract terms.

One of the State Department requests covered by the subpoenas from the Pike Committee is said to refer to a period in 1961 when the Kennedy administration was assessing Cuban intent. And another is reported to refer to a similar request in 1962, when Russian missile bases were being built in Cuba.

From about February, 1962, Soviet vessels were arriving at Cuban ports at the rate of one per day, delivering arms, heavy equipment for construction of bases, and massive supplies of ammunition, electronics gear, and other war materiel. By July, this country was flooded with Cuban exile reports that Soviet long range missiles were being installed. Photo reconnaissance by the U.S. Navy and the U.S. Air Force proved the sites were being developed, but did not prove the arrival of missiles. By August, Sen. Kenneth Keating, R.-N.Y., began a series of ten major Senate reports on the situation and calling on the President to take action. Finally, reconnaissance confirmed the arrival of the big Soviet missiles, and in some cases their delivery to the launch sites.

But the vital ingredient that was to decide the case was missing. Some reliable and vital intelligence devices, located on friendly allied soil, had not reported the passage of nuclear warheads enroute from Russian ports. When—and only when—those menacing weapons did sound the sophisticated alarms, Kennedy acted.

On Oct. 22, 1962, in the strongest and most belligerent speech by any American President in peacetime, Kennedy warned that Cuba had been quarantined and that the missiles would have to be removed. By then, the warheads were enroute across the Atlantic. The two ships carrying them were being trailed by our navy. Faced with the alternatives of withdrawal or war, Khrushchev ordered them home.

That is an abbreviated bit of history, but it illustrates the importance of such intelligence. Our intelligence community had watched the Soviet weapons buildup in Cuba for ten months. Reports from clandestine sources were confirmed by reconnaissance and other means. But when it came time for the vital decisions that might mean the survival of the nation, the President and his advisers did not have to rely on spies or photographs, both of which can be misled. There were other, secret but reliable, ways to supply the final pieces of the jigsaw.

The Soviet leaders may, or may not, know by now how it was done. The details are still secret, and should remain so as long as the threat exists and any foreign power is determined to dominate the world—and we have the capacity to deny them the element of surprise.

Congressional committees should know the use to which tax money they vote for intelligence is put, in general terms. But the need to know does not go as far as some committee members profess to think. Sensational publicity is fatal to good intelligence work, a fact responsible members of Congress recognize.

And there are occasions when the true facts can be obtained only by secret means, but are vital to our survival.

TULSA DAILY WORLD

Tulsa, Okla., November 17, 1975

AFTER Watergate, it was natural that Congress should attempt to put some restraints on the EXECUTIVE BRANCH. Since the New Deal Era, the power balance had been increasingly weighted toward the White House and away from Capitol Hill.

Today, the urgent question is whether the pendulum hasn't swung out of bounds in the other direction.

Last week, the House Intelligence Committee performed what can be described as a childish tantrum. Members voted to cite SECRETARY OF STATE HENRY KISSINGER for contempt because he refused to turn over a number of top secret documents on intelligence operations and estimates.

PRESIDENT FORD called the citation shocking. SECRETARY KISSINGER said it raised serious questions all over the world of what this country is doing to itself and what the necessity is to torment ourselves like this month after month.

All of this is obvious, of course. Certainly, the country cannot conduct normal foreign relations, much less effective intelligence operations, if every secret report is in danger of exposure by headline hunting Congressional committee chairmen.

In this case, the headline hunter is OTIS G. PIKE, chairman of the House Intelligence Committee, a New York Democrat who often behaves like a spoiled child who has been told he can't have any more candy.

British and Canadian spy agencies have recently demanded—and obtained—a written guarantee that no secrets they provide to the CIA under an exchange agreement will be revealed to U.S. Congressional investigating committees.

In other words, if Americans want to let small-minded egotists like OTIS G. PIKE wreck their own intelligence operations, fine. But the British and Canadians want no part of it.

The Watergate impeachment process, RICHARD NIXON's forced resignation and related court decisions and Congressional action have all combined to curb the power of the Presidency. The time has come now to demand some restraints on a power-happy and irresponsible Legislative Branch.

LEDGER-STAR

Norfolk, Va., November 15, 1975

The danger all along in Congress' probe of the various government intelligence operations has been that in its zeal to uncover improprieties Capitol Hill would take steps that could greatly weaken the nation's security.

The contempt-of-Congress citations issued yesterday against Secretary of State Henry Kissinger show how great that danger really is. This was a reckless action by Rep. Otis Pike's House Intelligence Committee. It amounts to an unjust and unfair attack on Dr. Kissinger and actually complicates the issue with respect to the administration and Capitol Hill coming together in some measure of understanding on the sensitive questions involved.

Dr. Kissinger reacted angrily but also offered some sobering observations on the potential harm in the citations.

'I profoundly regret," he said, "the committee saw fit to cite in contempt a secretary of state, raising serious questions all over the world what this country is doing to itself and what the necessity is to torment ourselves like this month after month."

The Pike committee's action of course represents only the start of contempt proceedings. Approval by the full House would be required, and then the matter would be turned over to a U.S. attorney for prosecution. So Dr. Kissinger has not actually been held in contempt or confronted with the penalties, the maximum being a year in jail and a $1,000 fine on each citation.

But the mere resort of the committee to the use of what amounts to a criminal charge in pursuing its efforts to obtain from the administration sensitive documents relating to foreign intelligence operations and estimates on Soviet compliance with arms agreements is irresponsible.

According to the State Department, Dr. Kissinger refused to give the committee the documents at the specific direction of President Ford, and a spokesman described the issue as "between the committee and the White House."

By coincidence, The Pike committee's citation was the second by a congressional body this week against a Cabinet member, a procedure that, according to records, had never been invoked before. Secretary of Commerce Morton was cited on Tuesday by a House Commerce subcommittee for his refusal to release the names of American firms asked by the Arabs to participate in a boycott against Israel.

The battle between members of the Congress and the administration over the release of intelligence documents has created, as Secretary Kissinger suggested in his statement, a kind of self-punishment that not only impedes progress toward a resolution of legitimate problems concerning intelligence operations but threatens the country's basic foreign relations.

Unless the members of the Congress curb their own excesses, politically inspired and otherwise, then the dangers for the United States will grow ever larger; this country's participation in international affairs will become riskier, and it will be the Congress which, deservedly, will be held in the nation's contempt.

The Washington Post

Washington, D.C., November 19, 1975

IF ANYONE NEEDED a clinching argument for better intelligence oversight by the standing committees of Congress, it lies in the current performance of the House special committee led by Rep. Otis Pike (D-N.Y.). By no fault of its own, the committee began its work months late. It is now playing catch-up ball with an abandon inconsistent with the sensitivity and seriousness that the object of its inquiry warrants. We refer specifically to its decision to hold the Secretary of State in contempt for refusing to produce certain documents. By this act the committee has forced an unnecessary and unwise confrontation with the executive branch. For the American system of government is simply not built to sustain such direct institutional clashes. It is built to have these clashes blurred and deterred by political compromise and a shared respect for the system's own vulnerabilities. That the Pike committee's single-minded quest for information has come to the issuance of subpoenas and the threat of a contempt citation by the full House, is evidence enough that the system has broken down.

Consider the sorts of information the Pike committee seeks. There are some 10 pre-Kissinger State Department recommendations, to pre-Ford Presidents, for covert operations. Mr. Ford was regrettably slow to assert a claim of executive privilege in the correct (direct) manner to protect these documents but that does not diminish the validity of the claim. If executive privilege does not mean that such pre-decision secretarial recommendations are protected, then it really means nothing at all. Second, the Pike majority asked for National Security Council documents on Soviet and American adherence to strategic arms agreements. These documents, besides containing technical material not readily mastered by an untutored committee in a hurry, presumably bear not only on sensitive intelligence-gathering methods but on the prospects of current negotiations. Their transmission to Congress could directly invade the President's prerogative to conduct foreign policy. Third, the committee asks for the NSC "Forty Committee's" records on covert operations approved since 1965. But these records too are bound to include pre-decision discussions, and to touch on some matters still current, and, of course, to intrude on the President's conduct of foreign affairs.

It is perfectly true that past Presidents abused the specific claim of executive privilege and the general claim of national security as rationales for secrecy. But that does not mean those claims are without substance. Excesses of the executive branch are not remedied by excesses of Congress. In its zeal, the Pike committee—unlike its Senate counterpart—has brushed by the time-tested "political" ways in which responsible standing committees can and do gain access discreetly to material which would not be forthcoming in the context of a hostile political confrontation. Indeed, the House panel has seemed to be unwilling to grant that there are any legitimate barriers to its inquiry—either in constitutional principle or in practical effect. But there are such barriers. The intelligence inquiry is not being pursued in a vacuum. The legitimate powers of the office of the Presidency need to be kept intact. These include the confidentiality of the presidential decision-making process and the conduct of the nation's foreign policy. Mr. Kissinger is not always his own best advocate. In this instance, he has been gratingly quick to identify his own discomfort with national misfortune. Yesterday, for instance, he belittled his citation for contempt as "frivolous"—hardly a response calculated to mollify his attackers. Yet in a congressional investigation the burden of responsibility does fall on the Congress. We do not yet see the Pike committee measuring up.

The Standard-Times

New Bedford, Mass., November 20, 1975

A committee of the U.S. House moved emphatically and, as the Associated Press told its worldwide readership, "dramatically" last week in the area of foreign policy.

The development could have been helpful. The U.S. policy establishment could do with Legislative Branch backing. In the United Nations, America had been steamrollered on the Zionism-racism issue. The Soviet Union is stirring the Angola cauldron while blaming Washington. Upcoming are crucial talks with Moscow on nuclear weapon controls. The President was heading for Europe for economic parleys and soon is to leave for a first visit to China.

But the committee had other things in mind. Muckraking. Scavenging in long-closed U.S. intelligence cupboards, looking for possible garbage to strew on the record. Needed for this exercise in defamation: National Security Council secret records going back 14 years on covert operations.

"We're weary of waiting, you know," said its headline-hunting committee chairman Otis Pike, D-N.Y., after President Ford declined to submit the records — because previous presidents had personally approved them — and ordered Secretary of State Kissinger to stand firm. The Pike brigade made an historic decision. It rose above its principles, as they say, and indicted Kissinger.

What a message of confidence in the American way to put before the world! What statesmanship! While terrorists heave bombs in a strife-ridden globe an arm of the U.S. Congress takes the violent course against the secretary of state (penalty if convicted, three years in jail, $3,000 fine).

We lament with Secretary Kissinger, that this detestable adventure in publicity raises questions everywhere about "what this country is doing to itself and what the necessity is to torment ourselves like this month after month."

It is the Pike committee that has first claim on contempt.

Los Angeles Times

Los Angeles, Calif., November 19, 1975

Oversight of government is one of Congress' most important jobs. The legislators must inquire, review, ensure that each federal agency and bureau serves the public interest effectively.

But that is no charter for a kind of heavy-handed oversight that, by itself, maims the workings of government.

The House Select Committee on Intelligence and its chairman, Rep. Otis G. Pike (D-N.Y.), have gone too far. They have mocked their responsibility by recommending that the House find Secretary of State Kissinger in contempt of Congress—all because of a bitter and confused dispute over sensitive intelligence reports. The committee's action is politically motivated; it is unnecessary; it is plainly damaging to the country.

The vote for contempt proceedings grew out of three committee subpoenas for documents showing the intimate details of how intelligence-gathering decisions are made and how the results are interpreted. The Pike committee's stated goal is to see whether policies affect assessments—whether intelligence officials distort the information they collect to make it support the policies and projects they favor.

This is obviously a valid and important question. It is also one that demands the greatest care and sensitivity.

We now know that intelligence estimates of Communist strength during the Vietnam war were heavily influenced by officials' desire to believe that the war could be won quickly. That abuse should not be repeated.

But neither should the abuses of the McCarthy era be repeated. Experts on China were silenced, then purged from government, for holding opinions that a prying—but intolerant—Congress did not want to hear.

The Pike committee has ignored the risk that its quest for too much detail could silence dissent and debate within the executive branch. It has issued subpoenas demanding records of the State Department's recommendations to the White House for covert operations during the Kennedy, Johnson and Nixon administrations; minutes of the highly secret covert-operations committee of the National Security Council, and intelligence reports on alleged Soviet violations of the strategic arms limitation agreements.

Reasonable people recognize that the committee should know about covert operations, that it should be kept aware of how well the Russians are behaving under disarmament agreements.

But this kind of information should not be acquired in a way that either inhibits debate and dissent in the executive branch or puts middle-level officials on the spot for the decisions of their superiors.

These things can be worked out if both sides are serious. Only two weeks ago Kissinger and Pike reached a sensible compromise: The committee got the data it sought on an Administration debate over what to do about Cyprus. But the names of the debaters were removed.

If Congress seems excessively suspicious of the intentions of the executive branch, there is a lot of recent history to thank for that. And Kissinger's lament that the country is "tormenting" itself will be discounted by many who have heard him talk that way before. But he has a point—a serious point.

A citation of contempt by a House committee against a secretary of state should be undertaken only for the gravest reasons. It was undertaken here in haste, without solid grounds. It is not too strong to call it at best frivolous, at worst cynical.

FORT WORTH STAR-TELEGRAM

Fort Worth, Tex., November 19, 1975

The House Intelligence Committee did the country an enormous disservice last week when it voted to begin contempt of Congress proceedings against Secretary of State Henry Kissinger.

The committee may be justified in its frustration over not being able to obtain, by subpoena, the documents it wants concerning covert U.S. intelligence operations and intelligence estimates on Soviet compliance with arms agreements. It may actually need information in these documents to guide it in the shaping of future legislation.

But the contempt vote goes much too far. Since a majority of the House would be required to force a Justice Department investigation of the charges, the move would have little hope of success, even if the legal grounds were good. And they're not.

At least two of the three counts may have been misdirected. They cited Dr. Kissinger in his role as the President's national security affairs adviser, a post he no longer holds.

More important, though, Dr. Kissinger is said to have refused to turn over the documents on orders from President Ford.

That brings the whole question of executive privilege into the picture.

Executive privilege is a tough nut to crack. Even in the Watergate case, when there was reason to suspect high crimes, it came close to prevailing.

Further weakening the current contempt case is the apparent political motivations behind the charges. Its timing marks it as part of a continuing political power play which finds some members of Congress trying to encroach on the executive domain of foreign policy.

The perpetrators of the move, Rep. Otis Pike of New York and Sen. Lowell Weicker of Connecticut, to name two of the most outspoken, wrap their scheme in talk about the people's right to know.

People with any discernment, however, will note two things. First, the Constitution assigns responsibility for conducting foreign policy to the President, with the advice and consent of the Senate. Second, the members of Congress responsible for the contempt move couldn't possibly have the interests of the American people uppermost in their minds.

Coming, as it did, on the eve of the economic summit conference in Rambouillet, the President's trip to China and an important NATO meeting, and while the Mideast situation still sputters on the brink of explosion, this undermining of the nation's foreign policy leadership could only be harmful—possibly seriously so.

With its record of the past several months, Congress would do well to avoid use of the term contempt in any context. It might merely serve to remind the people of what a contemptible Congress we have.

San Francisco Chronicle

San Francisco, Calif., November 18, 1975

A LOT OF PEOPLE are kicking Kissinger around and seeming to enjoy it at the moment, unfairly, in our opinion, and to the detriment of the proper and effective conduct of U.S. foreign policy.

The Otis Pike Select Committee on Intelligence cited the Secretary of State November 14 for failing to comply with three subpoenas issued November 6. One was a demand for recommendations for covert intelligence acts made by the State Department in previous administrations and sent to Presidents Johnson and Nixon. Two other subpoenas were issued to Kissinger as the President's adviser on national security (which he no longer is.)

THE FIRST THING to be noted is that the House committee allowed the Secretary and the President precious little time to weigh, consider and argue the propriety of these subpoenas, which may involve serious constitutional questions.

President Ford, who specifically ordered the secretary to reject the first subpoena, is probably the real target of the committee's move. He has said he is "shocked," and he is entitled to be. He and Kissinger should at least have been given a chance to make their case for resistance.

SECOND, if highly confidential deliberations are going to be open to the summons of any groups of congressmen taking a partisan interest in them, how are the security interests of the United States going to be protected by any Secretary of State or President? The uproar and dismay at the revelation that Nixon taped diplomatic conversations in his office should have taught the lesson that confidentiality in sensitive areas of government must be unbreachable.

If Congress, encouraged by the anti-Soviet, anti-detente lobby, is becoming slap-happy at issuing subpoenas for intelligence materials, Kissinger's comment is apt: he feared it would "raise serious questions all over the world about what this country is doing to itself." The point is particularly well made that it is "unbelievable" that a congressional committee would plaster the secretary with contempt citations on the eve of a Chinese summit.

WORCESTER TELEGRAM

Worcester, Mass., November 21, 1975

The House Select Committee on Intelligence has voted to begin contempt of Congress proceedings against Secretary of State Kissinger, thus triggering another confrontation with the executive branch. Another House subcommittee plans to seek contempt charges against Interior Secretary Rogers Morton.

The case against Kissinger stems from a wide-ranging congressional investigation of various U.S. intelligence gathering methods. He is being held in contempt by a panel, chaired by Rep. Otis G. Pike, for alleged refusal to produce documents demanded in three subpoenas.

Two subpoenas call for the production of minutes of the National Security Council's "Forty Committee," which approves covert intelligence actions, and for various intelligence reports on the Soviet Union's compliance with the 1972 arms limitation treaty. They were addressed to the "President's adviser for national security affairs" — after Kissinger stepped down from that job on Nov. 3. Thus the State Department's claim that the secretary had no responsibility for complying with the requests.

The third subpoena has to do with recommendations for covert intelligence actions sent by the State Department to the White House over the last 15 years. That request was addressed to Kissinger, who said President Ford ordered him not to produce the documents on the grounds that they represented privileged presidential communications.

Openness is essential in a democratic government, and the various investigating committees had been formed to combat undue secrecy and possible transgressions within the intelligence community. It seems, however, that the Pike committee stretches its mandate pretty far.

Is there a real need for looking into 15 years of intelligence-gathering decisions by a number of administrations? And if yes, why not 25 or 100 years? Is national interest served by airing our secret knowledge of Soviet compliance — or the lack of compliance — with a nuclear treaty? Should the concept of presidential privilege be entirely discarded just because it was abused during the Watergate crisis? Should the country be exposed to the trauma of contempt procedures involving high government officials who follow legitimate presidential orders? Should there be no limit to unveiling this country's intricate intelligence system?

Previous clashes between the State Department and the Pike committee have been resolved through compromise. Perhaps the Kissinger contempt charge, too, should be settled without a fight.

KISSINGER'S CANDOR QUESTIONED; PIKE DROPS CONTEMPT CHARGES

Adm. Elmo R. Zumwalt Jr., chief of naval operations until his retirement in June 1974, charged Dec. 2 that Secretary of State Henry A. Kissinger had withheld information from President Ford about what Zumwalt characterized as "gross violations" by the Soviet Union of its 1972 agreement with the U.S. to limit strategic weapons. Appearing before the House Select Committee on Intelligence, Zumwalt accused Kissinger of withholding negotiating information from the President, the secretary of defense and the Joint Chiefs of Staff. Moreover, he suggested that Kissinger's lack of candor was the result of a personal and political commitment to U.S.-Soviet detente that made him "reluctant to report the actual facts."

Kissinger, in a Washington press conference Dec. 9, angrily denied Zumwalt's allegations, labeling as a "total falsehood" the suggestion that he had withheld information from President Ford. Moreover, Kissinger said that the admiral, who had indicated interest in running for the U.S. Senate, "got carried away by his political ambitions." After describing in detail U.S. procedures for assessing Soviet violations, Kissinger said it was difficult for the U.S. to decide whether the violations were deliberate or unintentional or, for that matter, whether U.S. intelligence had picked evidence indicating a breach of the accords where there was none. He insisted that all suspected Soviet violations had been immediately reported to the President.

The House Select Committee on Intelligence Dec. 10 dropped efforts to obtain a contempt of Congress citation against Secretary of State Henry A. Kissinger for refusing to provide the committee with subpoenaed documents.

Rep. Otis G. Pike (D, N.Y.), the panel's chairman, told the House that his committee now considered the Ford Administration in "substantial compliance" with the subpoena because an accommodation had been reached over access to details of 20 State Department requests for covert intelligence operations abroad since 1961. The committee's ranking Republican, Rep. Robert McClory (Ill.), said separately that the compromise had been personally ordered by President Ford, who had previously declined to relinquish the material on the ground that to do so would violate the confidentiality necessary to Presidential decision-making.

The Virginian-Pilot

Norfolk, Va., December 12, 1975

Admiral Elmo Zumwalt fired a shot across the bow of Secretary of State Henry Kissinger when testifying before a Congressional committee last week.

He got a broadside in return this week.

Admiral Zumwalt accused Mr. Kissinger of withholding information about alleged Russian violations of the arms control pact signed in 1972.

That is a "total falsehood," Mr. Kissinger responded at his press conference Tuesday.

"The charge that information has been deliberately withheld is false," he said. "The charge that the President has not been briefed is false. The charge that either I, as Secretary of State or as Assistant to the President, have refused to deal with compliance issues is false. The charge that there were secret agreements is essentially false."

The last denial was qualified only on technicalities, explained the Secretary of State.

As to the charges made by Admiral Zumwalt, Mr. Kissinger suggested that "the admiral got carried away by his political ambitions." Mr. Zumwalt is expected to run for the Senate against Harry F Byrd Jr. in Virginia. Whether he helped himself by attacking Mr. Kissinger is unclear. Certainly the Secretary of State seems to have gotten the better of the exchange; he has answered the retired admiral's charges unequivocally.

But that is hardly the end of the matter. There is no question that Admiral Zumwalt feels strongly that detente is permitting the Russians to take advantage of American trustfulness to achieve a decisive military superiority in the world. Nor is he the only person who holds that view.

If he was mistaken to accuse Mr. Kissinger of bamboozling the President, it does not discredit entirely the questions that he has raised in his Congressional testimony and in his recent speeches and writing.

Mr. Kissinger is not unable to defend himself and his policies, to be sure. And there is no alternative to coexistence and detente as goals of our policy, which may be described fairly in the famous advice of Teddy Roosevelt to speak softly and carry a big stick. The question is really how big a stick, and do we have enough sticks stockpiled?

The Providence Journal

Providence, R.I., December 4, 1975

Charges of Soviet cheating on the 1972 strategic weapons agreement have taken on grave new import with the assertion by Retired Adm. Elmo R. Zumwalt Jr. that information about the alleged violations is being deliberately withheld from President Ford.

Admiral Zumwalt, the former Chief of Naval Operations, charged on Tuesday that Secretary of State Henry A. Kissinger "has not been candid" with Mr. Ford about what he said have been "gross violations" of the pact by the Soviet Union. Moreover, said the admiral, the President himself has not studied the issue enough to be aware of what material is being kept from him. He even went so far as to say that there has been collusion between the administration and the Soviet Union to cover up the alleged cheating.

These are serious charges that demand a prompt and thorough response from the administration. The charges of Soviet violations, calling into question the Soviets' good faith and reliability, are going to foster new skepticism about the Kissinger detente strategy. So be it. Detente is valuable only insofar as both superpowers deal with each other fairly and honestly. If the Soviets indeed are cheating on the 1972 arms agreement, the Congress and the American public deserve to know about it, and the sooner the better.

Admiral Zumwalt and some other critics of the 1972 agreement, known as SALT I, say that the Soviet Union has been making unauthorized conversions of "light" missiles to "heavy" missiles; interfering with U.S. satellite efforts (permitted under the 1972 pact) to check on Soviet compliance; upgrading air defenses; and secretly increasing the number of its missile launchers.

The administration's response has been that the agreement contains "ambiguities" that are subject to differing interpretations. Mr. Kissinger himself, while not denying that alleged violations have been kept quiet, says that they all have been "energetically pursued" with Soviet officials. And former Defense Secretary James R. Schlesinger, while saying that the Russians have violated U.S. expectations, says that specific violations of the agreement itself cannot be proven.

The dispute is reminiscent of the non-existent "missile gap" that became a central issue in the 1960 presidential campaign. John F. Kennedy asserted then that the Soviets were overtaking the United States in long-range missiles, but after his election the alleged "gap" somehow disappeared. Some of the same sort of confusion and exaggeration may be developing now, with the Ford administration trying to head off attacks on its detente policy.

The overriding need now, as we see it, is for Congress to obtain the facts. A start on this has been made with Secretary Kissinger's delivery to the House Intelligence Committee of subpoenaed material about the arms negotiations. This data should help the committee, and eventually the country, assess the charges of Soviet violations for what they are worth.

Few Americans, except for the most self-deluding converts to the idea of Soviet beneficence in world affairs, would be astonished to learn that the Russians indeed had been cheating on the arms limitation agreement.

What simply cannot be concerned, however, is any official deception by high American officials about what Soviet strategists are up to. Congress is obliged to pursue Admiral Zumwalt's testimony and to try to learn whether such deception has been going on.

There has to be room for some latitude, of course, in any set of negotiations as complex as those on strategic weapons. And the prime goal of detente — to head off the risk of nuclear war — probably requires that both superpowers bend a bit in evaluating what each other is doing. But it is critical that the United States proceed in these negotiations with eyes open and feet firmly on the ground. The Soviets continue to prove themselves as tough adversaries, and any deception in this high-risk contest could prove fatal.

The Saginaw News

Saginaw, Mich., December 11, 1975

For a long time presidents, people and the Congress have considered Henry Kissinger the indispensable man in the conduct of the country's foreign policy and national security operations.

Yet of late it becomes increasingly evident that Dr. Kissinger's indispensability is under considerable strain. Even Kissinger now perceives his role as secretary of state in terms of limited duration.

Lately, however, it is not so much a question of his usefulness or his consumate diplomatic skill that doggedly shadows his career in high government service. It is the questions that arise over the secretary's powers and the way he perceives himself in relation to his obligations both as confidant of presidents and subservient of Congress. And, frankly, questions that seem to be centering on his candor.

Difficulties are mounting from both directions. For the moment, at least, it appears that Mr. Kissinger has become trapped in dual loyalties that are his.

Only delicately handled 11th hour accommodation by the White House has rescued Secretary Kissinger from a possible contempt citation from the U.S. House.

Dr. Kissinger's refusal to supply the House Intelligence Committee with all of the information it wanted on covert operations abroad, considered or carried out by the State Department in recent years, certainly flew in the face of Constitutional checks and balances — and won him no new friends.

The committee is an official arm of the House which had a mandate from the House to get the information that Kissinger had and could supply. That has not all been submitted, but enough of it has that the committee headed by Rep. Otis Pike, D-New York will spare Kissinger from a contempt action.

Considering the depth and seriousness of congressional investigations spanning activities of the nation's intelligence and security agencies, Kissinger's refusal to the people's representatives suggests at least hautiness — if not some fuzziness on his part about his role in government.

There is a glimpse here, perhaps, of a mentality that still has difficulty coming to terms with answerability to Congress. That seems particularly true in cases of those dealing in foreign affairs.

We do not believe Mr. Kissinger is in business to protect Mr. Ford or other presidents — or that Mr. Ford is in business to protect Mr. Kissinger. Yet there is a trace of that evident in the showdown over covert operations materials.

It is now possible that the material finally obtained from the White House under subpoena may indicate the accuracy of or further illuminate the discrepancies in the secretary's own sworn testimony earlier as to what he knew about the planned Chilean coup in 1970.

The worst of it may not yet be over for Dr. Kissinger.

Charges by retired Adm. Elmo Zumwalt, former chief of naval operations, that Kissinger withheld information from Mr. Ford about alleged Soviet Union violations of 1972 arms agreements, doesn't shorten any shadows.

These are serious charges made by Zumwalt. And they have drawn Kissinger denials in language far stronger than he customarily uses.

Allowances on this are necessary. Automatic assumptions are out of the question. Zumwalt has political aspirations for the U.S. Senate. He is highly critical of detente in its present course. Kissinger naturally makes a handy target if, indeed, gross errors have been committed or deceptions practiced. But then, detente is raising a good many suspicions lately.

So either Elmo Zumwalt is totally and irresponsibly off course himself, or he has what's called classic proof in his bag that Dr. Kissinger has strayed from the narrow. The latter could prove disastrous to the secretary's career.

Either way, there is an indication of anti-Kissinger sentiment building. It isn't clearly defined. Yet it seems centered around deep concerns that Dr. Kissinger has assumed too much power and may have succumbed to its lures with resulting bad judgment. Or shading of the truth.

Not a scintilla of this is proven. But it is doing nothing for the former image of indispensability. Ultimately it could shorten Dr. Kissinger's secretariat considerably.

Chicago Tribune

Chicago, Ill., December 12, 1975

It is reassuring to read Secretary of State Kissinger's denial that he withheld information from President Ford about possible Soviet violations of the strategic arms limitation agreements. The charge had been made by Adm. Elmo Zumwalt, retired chief of naval operations.

Dr. Kissinger went further and denied that the Soviets had been guilty of violations. This, too, is somewhat reassuring. It is less than fully reassuring because:

● The secretary may have some secret and highly restricted definition of "violations." He is adroit in the handling of words. Aviation Week magazine said last month that "as the chief architect of SALT politics" he has become "a skilled practitioner of the art of not telling the truth without actually lying."

● The secretary said that two of the suspected violations investigated by the United States proved to be "borderline" cases. A borderline case strikes us as being so close to an actual violation as to offer no assurance about the Soviets' honorable intentions. In one of these cases, antiaircraft radars were employed in such a way as to make them usable as antiballistic-missile radars, an activity forbidden by a Soviet-American treaty. When the U.S. protested, Dr. Kissinger said, the Soviets stopped some of this activity. An honest man who is doing what is right does not normally desist simply because someone questions him about it.

● Though Adm. Zumwalt is planning to run for the Senate [which makes his comments less reliable, in Dr. Kissinger's opinion], he is not the only presumably authoritative source of such charges. Others include former Secretary of Defense Melvin Laird, Sen. Henry Jackson, Sen. James Buckley, Sen. James McClure, Aviation Week magazine, and Colin Gray, associate director of the International Institute for Strategic Studies in London.

Mr. Gray wrote last fall in Air Force Magazine that "Soviet avoidance or evasion of the terms" of the first SALT agreement make it questionable whether the U.S. should enter into a second one. This is precisely why the charges are so important just now. Dr. Kissinger is soon to go to Moscow to do some carpentering on another SALT agreement. With so many knowledgeable people saying there are violations and with Dr. Kissinger seeming to say there are not, the public has a right to be made fully reassured. The facts should be laid out more frankly before we plunge ahead into new agreeemnts that may prove booby-trapped.

St. Louis Globe-Democrat

St. Louis, Mo., December 6, 1975

The former chief of naval operations, Adm. Elmo Zumwalt, has made the serious charge that Secretary of State Henry A. Kissinger is withholding information of Soviet violations of the nuclear arms agreement made with the Russians.

Zumwalt said he had gained this impression by the public statements that President Ford has made on the arms agreements.

The former naval chief charged that the Russians were interfering with methods of detecting violations; exceeding missile size limits and numerical limits on missile silos; upgrading air defenses in violation of the ABM provisions and deploying mobile intercontinental ballistic missiles.

A State Department spokesman (acting in behalf of Kissinger who is with President Ford on his Asian trip) called Zumwalt's charge "preposterous." Former Secretary of Defense James R. Schlesinger said he believed the Russians might have violated the strategic arms agreement but would be inclined to disagree that Kissinger had concealed information concerning alleged violations.

Schlesinger pointed out that there are two primary allegations of violations. One is that the Soviets are extensively deploying their SS-19 land-based missile. The other is that they are using air defense radar as part of an antiballistic missile system.

Deployment of the SS-19s "may have been a violation of the unilateral statement of the United States. It was not a violation of the treaty," said Schlesinger.

What Schlesinger referred to was the controversial "unilateral statement" that Kissinger inserted into the SALT I agreement when the Russians refused to agree on a definition of a heavy missile.

This statement said the U.S. would consider an ICBM "having a volume significantly greater than that of either the largest ICBM now operational on either side to be a heavy ICBM. The U.S. proceeds on the premise that the Soviet side will give due account to this consideration."

If Zumwalt's information is correct, the Russians simply have ignored this unilateral statement in the treaty and have broken a number of provisions in the treaty as well.

In any event, Kissinger should give a complete answer to the Zumwalt charges upon his return. They are far too serious to be brushed off by an aide. As long as they are allowed to remain unanswered by Kissinger, the public will be inclined to believe the charges by Zumwalt are true.

The Boston Globe

Boston, Mass., December 4, 1975

Charges that the Soviet Union is violating terms of arms limitation agreements, made by retired Chief of Naval Operations Elmo Zumwalt, deserve public attention. At the same time, they must be understood in the context of Adm. Zumwalt's broader views on the subject of disarmament. The admiral is in favor of more, not less reduction of arms expenditures by both sides.

The whole history of disarmament talks between the United States and the Soviet Union has been marked by fears on each side that the other was secretly going to take advantage of the other and build up a force clandestinely that could not be defeated.

At first glance that appears the purport of the Zumwalt views, expressed most recently in testimony Tuesday before the House Intelligence Committee.

But as recently as Nov. 22 Adm. Zumwalt told the National Democratic Issues Convention in Louisville, that "the Soviet Union must be persuaded to reduce armaments," and to use the resources for the good of her own people.

The admiral probably had no way of knowing that just as he was delivering his testimony Tuesday, Soviet leaders were revealing that serious problems with crops this year would mean a sharp slowdown in the improvement of the Soviet standard of living in 1976. Now the Soviet Union will have to spend more money buying food rather than other kinds of foreign goods that would have made Soviet life more agreeable. No point illustrates more clearly the need for general reductions in the use of resources for arms.

It is impossible to make any quick judgment about the specific charges of violations made by Adm. Zumwalt. They involve size, number and deployment of various weapons systems in the Soviet Union itself. Much of the question turns on interpretation of photographs and other data, and on the wording of international agreements.

More serious is the Zumwalt charge that Secretary of State Henry Kissinger has been keeping these thorny questions away from the full attention of President Ford. Merely asking the question in a sense answers it. The President is now alerted to the issue and may satisfy himself on the matter.

Former Secretary of Defense James Schlesinger yesterday denied both of Zumwalt's charges — that the Soviets are violating terms of the agreement and that the truth is being kept from the President.

There are other serious issues associated with but not specifically part of the Zumwalt charges. He and others contend, for example, that agreements reached by President Ford and Soviet leader Leonid Brezhnev at Vladivostok are destructive because they set such high "limits" on arms — and the Soviets will squander their resources reaching them while we lose relative strength by failing to match their outlays.

There is also the much more difficult problem of the Helsinki accords, ratifying the status quo in Europe for the first time since the end of World War II. That agreement also included provisions that nominally guaranteed at least some human rights of all individuals, East and West. The Soviet Union has trodden on the spirit if not the letter of the accords on a number of occasions — making the Zumwalt charges on armaments more credible in the process.

Adm. Zumwalt has, it is to be hoped, performed a service with his testimony. If the Soviet Union has been nibbling at the edges of the permissible within the limits of the arms agreements, it now has overt if unofficial warning that there are responsible Americans who want them to stop.

But the larger truth of the Zumwalt position is still very much intact. Enormous buildups of strategic weapons systems are an unforgiveable waste of assets. Meaningful agreements can halt that waste. And that is really what Adm. Zumwalt is talking about.

THE COMMERCIAL APPEAL

Memphis, Tenn., December 4, 1975

THE HOUSE investigation into possible Soviet violations of nuclear arms agreements has brought forth charges that could indicate the nation's security is being threatened. If the Soviet Union is, indeed, playing the United States for the fool with regard to the agreements, the whole policy of detente needs to be carefully reviewed.

Another and equally serious cause for concern was the testimony of Adm. Elmo R. Zumwalt, former chief of naval operations, that Secretary of State Henry Kissinger has withheld information about Soviet violations from President Ford. Zumwalt told the House Select Committee on Intelligence that "the President has not gone into the material in sufficient depth" to understand all phases of the arms issue. He also said, "The secretary of state has not been candid with him in the gross nature of the cheating."

IF THIS is true, Kissinger has done a disservice to his country. Congress and the public deserve to hear the secretary's answers to the charges at once. And the House committee should provide the public with any added information it can about breakdowns in arms agreements.

The Defense Department has charged the Soviet Union with concealment of submarine and missile-silo construction. There also are reports that three U.S. satellites have been bombarded with Soviet infrared laser beams, which could indicate an attempt to blind this country's system for detecting Soviet missile launches.

It's hard to imagine the President wouldn't have been fully informed of these possibilities because he is the person ultimately responsible for national security. He must have available to him any facts that could affect his decisions about foreign policy. Efforts to withhold information from him would lead to the inference that someone feared he would change his mind and, in this case, the direction of detente.

ZUMWALT'S CHARGES, of course, have not been proven. Former Defense Secretary James R. Schlesinger, testifying yesterday before the Senate Foreign Relations Committee, said only that the Soviet Union may have violated the Strategic Arms Limitation Agreement. He said, however, he did not think Ford had been kept in the dark.

But this is no time to leave such charges without thorough and immediate investigation. Ford is being criticized by the Chinese and by many leaders at home for Kissinger's approach to detente. The critics claim that the Soviet Union will violate the agreements and that, by doing so, it will develop a dangerous military superiority over the United States. The new charges can't help but arouse public concern and damage the credibility of both the President and the secretary of state. Kissinger has a solemn responsibility to cooperate with the House investigation and any other that might be started. The true situation concerning detente and how well the President is being kept informed must be made known.

THE SACRAMENTO BEE

Sacramento, Calif., December 9, 1975

For some time, former chief of naval operations Adm. Elmo R. Zumwalt has been circulating disturbing reports about "massive" Soviet violations of the strategic arms limitation agreements and an administration cover-up of the fact.

Such reports are obviously disturbing because they call into question both the adequacy of America's nuclear defenses and the veracity of our highest public officials. Equally unsettling, however, is the fact such charges come at a time when the administration appears determined to rush through another and more elaborate nuclear arms deal with the Russians.

In his recent remarks before the House Intelligence Committee, however, Zumwalt's accusations reached a new pitch of intensity and seriousness which can no longer be dismissed out of hand as old-fashioned defense doomsaying.

Zumwalt is convinced the Soviets have been cheating on their part of the SALT bargain by interfering with the U.S. means of detecting violations. Under this intelligence blackout, according to Zumwalt, the Soviets have exceeded limits on the size of their missiles and on the number of their missile silos. In addition, they have illegally upgraded their air defenses and secretly deployed a battery of intercontinental ballistic missiles.

Unfortunately for both sides in the SALT debate — those who support continued U.S. arms limitation efforts as well as those who oppose them — Zumwalt has remained closemouthed as to the source of his provocative information. He insists "only Kissinger knows the full details."

But Secretary of State Kissinger has called such charges "preposterous" and considers the work of the committee which handles disputes over arms violations between the two superpowers as "quite successful." Even former Defense Secretary James Schlesinger — fired for pushing too hard for more defense spending — disagrees with Zumwalt's charges although he believes there have been instances where the Soviet Union has violated the spirit, if not the letter, of the nuclear arms accords.

If nothing else, these conflicting statements throw the SALT political ball back into Adm. Zumwalt's court where it belongs. The burden of proof is now his. If tangible information about massive Soviet arms control violations exists, he should place it squarely in evidence. And with a new SALT accord nearing completion, it is in the highest national interest that he do so quickly.

HOUSTON CHRONICLE

Houston, Tex., December 11, 1975

If a person is planning to make a political race and wants to attract attention, it can be expected that he will take a stand on an issue and present his position in as persuasive a manner as he can, even up to and including stretching a point. This is standard political practice.

But there are times when one wishes that when the candidate, avowed or potential, has a highly specialized background in the field from which he takes his issue that he would be more thoughtful in the way he handles his treatment of it.

Specifically, we wish that former Chief of Naval Operations Elmo Zumwalt, believed to be on the way to running for the Senate, would choose the low-key route instead of telling a House intelligence committee that the Russians have turned the SALT talks into a "grotesque mockery" and that Secretary of State Henry Kissinger had purposely withheld information on Soviet arms agreement cheating from the public, the Congress and the President.

Zumwalt's contentions of Russian cheating fell somewhat short of being convincing. Some of the committee members picked his allegations down to the point where he had to begin to qualify them so sharply that much of their original sensationalism was extracted.

Then former Secretary of Defense James Schlesinger, no great champion of Kissinger's, told a Senate committee that Kissinger did not withhold any Russian-cheating information from the President. And Kissinger heatedly denied as a "total falsehood" he concealed any arms violations from President Ford.

We have always had a certain admiration for Zumwalt, and we respect his views on national security because he is an expert in the field. But if he is going to try to blend this expertise with his political ambitions, we would like him to do so in a way that enhances his credibility instead of tarnishing it. The national defense is too important a subject to play fast and loose with.

The Salt Lake Tribune

Salt Lake City, Utah, December 20, 1975

For months there have been vague accusations leveled against Secretary of State Henry A. Kissinger that he has been "soft" on alleged Soviet violations of the 1972 Strategic Arms Limitation Talks (SALT) accords.

The other day Mr. Kissinger denied the charges in non-diplomatic language that seemed to leave no grounds for further doubting his performance.

Mr. Kissinger summed up his defense thusly:

"The charge that information was withheld is false.

"The charge that the President was not briefed (on the alleged violations) is false."

"The charge that I, either as Secretary of State, or as assistant to the President, have refused to deal with the compliance issue is false."

In view of the secretary's categorical denial, his critics, including former Secretary of Defense James R. Schlesinger and retired Adm. Elmo R. Zumwalt, should produce evidence to back their claims or keep quiet.

Rocky Mountain News

A Scripps-Howard Newspaper · Reg. U.S. Pat. Off. · Colorado's First Newspaper—Founded in 1859

Denver, Colo., December 16, 1975

A POTENTIALLY explosive confrontation has happily been avoided in Washington with the decision of the House Select Committee on Intelligence to withdraw its recommendation that Secretary of State Henry A. Kissinger be held in contempt of Congress.

Kissinger had refused to provide the committee with 20 documents relating to State Department requests to presidents since 1961 for covert operations abroad.

Time and again the committee chairman, Otis G. Pike, D-N.Y., had argued that the committee needed the actual documents to determine whether presidents had exercised proper control over intelligence agencies.

President Ford had refused to relinquish the material on the ground that to do so would violate the confidentiality needed for presidential decision-making.

The conflict was resolved by traditional means.

That is, both sides — the executive branch and Congress — stated their claims vigorously but didn't press them to an unalterable conclusion. Instead, they compromised and again left unanswered the constitutional question of whether Congress has an absolute right to information collected by the executive.

Under the compromise, a State Department official briefed Pike's committee extensively on the contents of the documents and the committee agreed not to press its claim to see the documents.

Pike kept his ego intact by saying that although the committee didn't get everything it wanted it did get more than the State Department had been willing to give.

The final word came from a congressional official who said the documents were "certainly not spectacular or dramatic" and "the information was not worth the battle."

Would that all such potential tempests could be so neatly confined to their teapots.

The New York Times

New York, N.Y., December 13, 1975

The confrontations in which House subcommittees were threatening the Secretaries of Commerce and State with contempt of Congress citations were aborted this week after eleventh-hour agreements with the executive branch. First, Commerce Secretary Morton yielded on the request to furnish subpoenaed information concerning Arab pressure on American firms to boycott Israel. The next day, the Administration agreed to what the House Intelligence Committee accepted as "substantial" compliance with its subpoena seeking a record of all State Department recommendations to the White House for covert action between 1961 and 1974.

Both conflicts involved efforts by Congressional committees to improve upon past oversight performance; they also involved resistance by the executive branch to requests for information which the committees thought they needed. The Morton issue turned on the relatively simple problem of interpreting a section of the Export Administration Act of 1969. Though the Department of Justice interpreted the act to support Secretary Morton's position, the Secretary decided to reach an accommodation with the committee just as a group of 37 distinguished law scholars released a letter asserting that his legal position was baseless.

In the other averted clash, the Administration justified the withholding of information sought from Secretary of State Kissinger on the assertion that it was contained in confidential executive branch communications and thus protected by executive privilege. The interest usually protected by such an assertion is to permit the Chief Executive to have the freest and most candid exchanges between himself and his closest associates as he explores facts, opinions and options in the process of formulating policy.

Sheer logic would probably have dictated a resolution in favor of the committee on the ground that the information sought involved the formal policy recommendations of a department of Government rather than informal and candid exchanges between the President and his closest advisers. Whatever interest the Administration might have in withholding such information would appear to be subordinate to the committee's need for the information if the oversight function is to have any meaning. In any event, while the documents were not made available, their content was; and the committee presumably was satisfied.

In both these cases, the executive branch presented less than compelling reasons for resisting requests for information. Ultimately, in each case, it wisely changed its position and provided more information, thus paving the way for resolution by accommodation—the traditional and substantially more satisfactory way of concluding such disputes.

Prior to reaching these compromises, regrettably, the Administration displayed a reflexive instinct for secrecy. If the last three-and-a-half years have demonstrated anything, they have demonstrated the twin dangers of a breakdown in the Congressional oversight system and of governmental power exercised in secret. While it would be foolish to assert that the executive never has legitimate interests to protect in such contests with Congress, an instinctive policy of withholding requested information reflects insufficient sensitivity to the need for true accountability in the exercise of governmental power.

New York Post

New York, N.Y., December 11, 1975

No colorful signing ceremonies, briefings from the "senior U. S. official" who insists on anonymity or Delphic communiques accompanied the conclusion of the agreement between the Ford Administration and the Congress of the U.S. The accord was nevertheless noteworthy and may make relations a little more diplomatic.

The events were simple: the director of the Department of State's Bureau of Intelligence briefed members of the House Select Committee on Intelligence on documents previously withheld from the panel. The committee chairman, Rep. Pike (D-N.Y.), then moved to quash a contempt of Congress citation against Secretary of State Kissinger for defying a subpena ordering him to produce the records.

In other words, the Congressional investigators, who had withstood an extraordinary Administration onslaught representing them as irresponsible snoopers at best and dangerous triflers with the nation's security at worst, finally prevailed. The outcome should hearten Americans committed to federal freedom-of-information.

The dispute can hardly be regarded as the last of its kind, but the next one may be easier for Congress to win. The committee did not secure everything it sought. But it clearly obtained vastly more than what the Administration was originally willing to grant: nothing.

Detroit Free Press

Detroit, Mich., December 10, 1975

ON THE domestic front, it's good to see that Secretary Kissinger has been spared a possible contempt of Congress citation after the administration "substantially complied" with a House Intelligence Committee subpena.

Committee Chairman Otis Pike said he would drop the contempt action in light of a White House briefing on State Department requests for covert activities abroad. Subpenaed documents covering such activities dating back to 1961 also apparently will be produced.

The Pike Committee can't be expected to do its job of exposing the full extent of "intelligence" abuses if it doesn't get cooperation from the executive branch.

The initial resistance of the administration to extending that cooperation threatened a needless confrontation, and dragged out what should have been an expeditious undertaking.

Now that the conflict has been resolved, perhaps the committee can get on with its more important work of determining where the origins of governmental abuses lay.

The Hartford Courant

Hartford, Conn., December 12, 1975

The attempt to cite Secretary of State Kissinger for contempt of Congress may have fallen flat for no better reason than that its sponsor, Representative Otis G. Pike, couldn't muster enough votes.

But that reason is good enough. The citation threatened to increase the degree of legislative-executive confrontation in a matter in which neither side is entirely wrong, nor entirely right. In such cases it is better to seek accommodation and compromise, as Mr. Pike's Intelligence Committee finally did.

The specific question was whether the committee should be given full details of covert intelligence operations initiated, or even thought of, by the State Department. It is part of the much larger issue of the degree to which Congress should oversee this nation's foreign policy.

The committee's motives may have been good: To determine whether there is sufficient Presidential accountability for these operations; or bad: To stir up a little more scandal.

On the State Department side, it could have been interested in avoiding embarrassment to this country in the eyes of foreign leaders, or embarrassment to the department in the eyes of this country.

There are equally mixed motives with regard to the larger issue of Congressional oversight. Mr. Kissinger resents attempts by Congress to second-guess his activities which, he points out, must necessarily be conducted in some degree of privacy. One can certainly hope that diplomats —Mr. Kissinger included—are more direct and communicative in their private conversations than they are in their obtuse public statements.

But Congress feels, with equal justification, that foreign policy should not be a one-man show in which Mr. Kissinger gives away a fighter squadron here, a grain shipment there, and in general gives more than he receives. This is done with too little oversight and accountability, particularly when deals are made through executive agreements rather than formal treaties—only the latter require Congressional ratification.

The public has a direct interest in both points of view. Foreign policy must be subject to the usual checks and balances. The public, through Congress, is entitled to know, and to reject when it sees fit, those commitments the government has made on the public's behalf. Secret agreements—or plots—do not serve that end.

But at the same time, privacy is an important element of the established system through which nations conduct business with each other. The public will not be served if a desire for open government locks this nation out of that system.

An all-out constitutional confrontation would mean that one element, or the other, of the public's interests must eventually lose. Whether it responded to that reality, or merely to political winds, the Pike committee did reach an accommodation with the administration on its access to the plot data. The same approach must be applied to the larger question as well.

The Morning Star

Rockford, Ill., December 11, 1975

Secretary of State Henry Kissinger is off the hook—and off to Europe on a trip to assess NATO's defense capability.

The secretary left as the House of Representatives dismissed proceedings that were leading to a contempt of Congress citation against Kissinger.

The issue between Kissinger and House members was more than just a test of wills.

What the House Intelligence Committee was demanding of the secretary were documents identifying the State Department's role in covert operations abroad, dating back to 1961.

As Otis Pike, committee chairman, explained it, there is rampant doubt extant in the land about the trustworthiness of our government.

Watergate, he went on, occurred because Congress had not carried its weight in demanding to know how government was functioning, how it was working.

Based on these and other lessons, Pike argued—correctly, we think—that the White House and Kissinger could not tell congressmen to "get lost," when it was the constitutional duty of Congress to know about secret operations in support of national policy.

Finally, it was the White House that saved Kissinger by promising a Pike committee delegation to provide the documents demanded, meantime giving the delegates a detailed briefing on the operations under scrutiny.

Unless a further hitch develops in the transfer of documents, the right of Congress to know has been upheld.

Thus is restored one more of the checks and balances that keeps our democracy going.

The Pike committee battle spilled no blood. But it did something that enhances peace of mind—and when was the last time that happened?

The Washington Post

Washington, D.C., December 10, 1975

COMMERCE SECRETARY Rogers C. B. Morton, under threat of a contempt citation, has wisely agreed to comply with a House investigations subcommittee's subpoena for reports from American companies that came under pressure to support the Arab boycott of Israel. Mr. Morton had no good grounds for refusing to furnish the information when Rep. John Moss' panel first requested it last July. By pushing the Commerce Committee to the brink of a contempt vote, the Secretary managed only to stir up unnecessary controversy and delay a potentially important congressional inquiry into the government's implementation of its stated anti-boycott policy.

Mr. Morton's reasons for withholding the subpoenaed reports were much flimsier than the case advanced by Secretary of State Henry Kissinger in his dispute with the Pike committee. The Morton-Moss conflict did not involve executive privilege, the secrecy of decision-making processes, or the confidentiality of advice to the President. Mr. Morton had relied only on a self-serving reading of section 7 (c) of the Export Administration Act, which holds that the companies' reports may be deemed confidential unless the Secretary "determines that the withholding thereof is contrary to the national interest." In Mr. Morton's view, that gave him the latitude to resist the congressional subpoena. Yet the statute gives no indication that Congress intended to foreclose its own access to the facts needed to oversee the administration of national policy. Indeed, as a number of legal scholars emphasized, Congress' power to obtain information is so fundamental that it need not be reasserted in every law.

Mr. Morton also argued against release of the reports on the Catch-22 ground that disclosure of various companies' responses to secret Arab pressures might generate new pressures on the firms involved. That concern may not be entirely baseless, but the Moss panel is entitled to the presumption that it is capable of handling the material responsibly. Under the agreement reached Monday between Mr. Morton and Mr. Moss, the reports will be turned over in executive session and released publicly only by subcommittee vote. That is a sensible arrangement which recognizes Congress' prerogatives and enables the subcommittee to find out what has really been going on, and how the anti-boycott laws need to be bolstered. Now that Mr. Morton has finally ended his stubborn resistance, perhaps the administration will cooperate with Congress in pursuing this important inquiry.

The Tennessean

Nashville, Tenn., December 13, 1975

THE WHITE HOUSE has backed down from its position against releasing secret information on foreign policy and thereby stopped House contempt action against Secretary of State Henry Kissinger.

Chairman Otis Pike of the House Intelligence Committee, told the House that President Ford's aids have "substantially complied" with a subpoena against Mr. Kissinger for details on State Department requests for covert political operations abroad since 1961.

The President apparently ordered the 11th-hour compromise and subsequently a committee delegation was briefed on the documents in question.

It was the second time in days that the administration had backed down on requests for secret information. The first was when Secretary of Commerce Rogers C.B. Morton agreed to turn over subpoenaed information about U.S. corporate compliance with the Arab boycott of Israel. A House subcommittee withdrew its contempt action against Mr. Morton and pledged to treat the information "in consonance with their asserted confidentiality."

The efforts to open up executive files and reveal decisions have not been timid, and they are evidently a harbinger of new laws and procedures to insure legislative control over some U.S. operations overseas.

Chairman Pike has already suggested new laws giving Congress full access to information about covert acts while insuring that the Central Intelligence Agency and other spy groups are working from set laws outlining their powers.

"How can Congress ratify covert acts that it cannot be told about?" asked Mr. Pike. It is a good question.

The Des Moines Register

Des Moines, Iowa, December 16, 1975

House Intelligence Committee Chairman Otis Pike (Dem., N.Y.) announced last week that his committee no longer will seek a contempt of Congress citation against Secretary of State Henry Kissinger. Pike gave as the reason for this shift the White House's "substantial compliance" with a committee subpoena for State Department documents concerning covert foreign operations since 1961.

The documents have been and continue to be withheld from the committee on the ground of executive privilege.

In what is being described as a "compromise" by the Ford administration, the committee was briefed on the contents of the documents by the director of the State Department's intelligence bureau.

The "compromise" allowed the White House to maintain strict control over access to information necessary to a congressional investigation. The White House denied the committee the opportunity to study the documents and forced the committee to take its word that the information was complete and had not been deceptively edited. The Nixon White House acted similarly in its release of transcripts of the Watergate tapes.

The Pike committee, pressured by time to wind up its investigations, has backed down from a confrontation which, if taken to the courts, might have helped resolve the issue of executive privilege. It also has backed away from at least rebuking Kissinger for inexcusable conduct toward congressional committees.

Kissinger delayed the Pike committee's work for months haggling over State Department documents on the 1974 Cyprus invasion and on covert operations abroad. He refused to testify before the Senate Intelligence Committee when it held hearings on Chile. He was one of the forces behind keeping information on the Arab boycott from another House committee.

Kissinger and others in the Ford administration hold firm to the belief that congressmen cannot be trusted with keeping classified information secret. Executive officials, however, are free to reveal intelligence data when they serve policy or personal interests.

An illustration of this came the other day, when Pike and Central Intelligence Agency Director William Colby appeared together before a Washington, D.C., audience. Colby spoke freely of the Soviet Union's activity in Angola and gave intelligence estimates of Soviet and Cuban military forces there. Pike, who had read files on U.S. involvement in that African civil war, was under White House restrictions not to give factual evidence on a potentially dangerous U.S. policy.

HOUSE CIA REPORT TO BE CENSORED; UNAUTHORIZED SECTIONS PUBLISHED

The full House of Representatives voted 246–124 Jan. 29 to give the executive branch the pre-publication right to review and censor the House Intelligence Committee's report on the Central Intelligence Agency. The vote, a victory for President Ford and the intelligence agencies, was deplored by Rep. Otis G. Pike (D., N.Y.), the chairman of the intelligence committee, who said it made "a complete travesty of the whole doctrine of separation of powers." Ford said that the vote "indicates that a large majority of House members share my concern that our legitimate classified national security information be denied to our enemies and potential enemies." The House vote came after conflicting votes by the House Intelligence Committee Jan. 23 (against executive censorship) and the House Rules Committee Jan. 28 (favoring executive censorship.)

The New York Times and the *Washington Post* Jan. 20 began to publish accounts of the still-unreleased report. Described in the articles were CIA operations with the news media, CIA purchasing procedures, secret aid to foreign leaders, allegations that the aid to Angolan factions had been misrepresented, and other matters.

The White House and the CIA charged that the leaking of the report violated the agreement upon the basis of which the committee had been furnished with secret information, and questioned the ability of Congressional committees to preserve the confidentiality of executive disclosures.

According to the newspaper accounts, the House Intelligence Committee report described the following activities:

CIA-news media links—The Jan. 23 *Washington Post* quoted the report as saying, in a section entitled "Manipulation of the Media," that" the free flow of information, vital to a responsible and credible press, has been threatened as a result of CIA's use of the world media for cover and for clandestine information-gathering." According to the report, in 1975 there were 11 full-time CIA agents stationed abroad who posed as journalists.

Reporting of Angolan aid—The report, according to the *New York Times* Jan. 20, said that, by undervaluing certain items, the CIA had arrived at a total for aid given to factions in Angola which was considerably lower than the true figure. (The Ford Administration has told Congress that it has spent $31 million in Angola since January 1975.) The case of .30-caliber semi-automatic carbines was cited: their inventory value was given as $15 apiece, but in the accounting given to Congress, they were priced at $7.55.

Finances—The report, according to the *Times* Jan. 26 and 27, cited a number of financial practices it found questionable. It said that 85% of the CIA's contracts—amounting to "hundreds of millions" of dollars—were let without competitive bidding.

THE CHRISTIAN SCIENCE MONITOR

Boston, Mass., February 2, 1976

America's saga of governmental secrecy last week took another turn that a spy novelist might have thought too incredible for fiction. After months of investigating secret intelligence activities, the House of Representatives decided to keep its own final report secret.

The decision may have seemed purely symbolic, since the report had been leaked by sources unknown. But it was in fact a valuable assertion by the House of a sense of responsibility that has sometimes seemed lacking in both the House and Senate investigations.

The vote served notice that the House did not intend to be a channel for the official publication of the kind of classified information said to be in the report. Nor did it intend to except the final report from the agreement reached between the White House and the leaders of the intelligence committee — that in return for receiving classified material the committee would not disclose it without Mr. Ford's approval or a decision by the courts.

Some have argued that this approach threatens the equality of Congress among the three branches. By this reasoning, Congress would have as much right as the executive to maintain secrets or disclose them in what it regarded to be the national interest. And the legislation now being fashioned for control of the intelligence agencies will have to take account of some knotty questions as to the role of secrecy in strengthened congressional and administrative oversight. How can Congress ensure against unauthorized disclosure of the secrets it must have to exercise effective oversight? Under what circumstances can it authorize disclosure of such secrets?

The development of answers requires the kind of trust of Congress that the House sought to encourage by its vote to keep its report secret. It promises to withhold release unless the President approves a version that meets his specifications of secrecy.

It is to be hoped that this display of cooperation and responsibility will have a long-term benefit in helping Congress and the executive work together for the kind of strong intelligence capacity the United States needs — and whose "activities must be conducted in a constitutional and lawful manner and never be aimed at our own citizens" — as Mr. Ford said at the swearing-in of the new CIA chief, George Bush, on the weekend.

In the short term, the public is left with the press's selective version of a leaked report rather than the full version of an authorized one. Is it likely that Mr. Ford will now designate passages for removal that can be compared with the uncensored version? Will the whole report remain officially secret? Will the Senate committee be able to publish its final report without White House censorship?

Perhaps not everyone will agree with Mr. Ford that "the abuses of the past have more than adequately been described." But the present situation suggests that the thrust should and will have to be to go on from them to preventing abuses of secrecy in the future.

The Standard-Times

New Bedford, Mass., February 4, 1976

"WASHINGTON — The House yesterday voted to block publication of a 338-page Intelligence Committee report until the White House clears it of material regarded as still secret and harmful to U.S. agencies." — News report.

The House acted wisely in voting s it did and possibly this action will igger an end to the mistakes and ccesses that have marked much of e investigation of the American telligence apparatus.

There have been mistakes, with- it a doubt.

Probably the first was when the ongress and the White House en- ered into a "gentlemen's agree- ent" under which President Ford as at least left with the im- ression he would have some voice ver what classified information as made public.

Such an arrangement tends to lur the separation between the ex- cutive and legislative branches of overnment and could set a most fortunate governmental prece- ent.

There also have been excesses on ne part of members or staff employes of the Intelligence Committee, some of whom have seemed bent on releasing classified information to the news media almost as soon as it was in their hands.

Although some disclosures of this sort can be justified, it is also equally true that some information, by its very nature, should not be made public in the interest of national security.

Bluntly, this distinction appeared — and appears — lost on some committee members and functionaries.

A prime example of this sort of myopic thinking is the chairman of the House Intelligence Committee, Rep. Otis Pike, D-N.Y., who childishly pouted that the House vote had made "a complete travesty of the whole doctrine of separation of powers." That is nonsense.

There isn't the slightest question that individuals connected with the committee who think as does Pike gave away the nation's secrets without thought of or concern for the inevitably adverse results.

The 246-to-124 majority decision to block disclosure of intelligence secrets without the President's approval is a sensible one.

Anchorage Daily Times

Anchorage, Alaska, February 1, 1976

COMMON SENSE prevailed in the House of Representatives at Washington yesterday when members halted attempts to disclose publicly the nation's intelligence secrets.

No nation can be secure in today's world without covert operations to keep advised of the powers and plans of other nations. It is well known that all the great powers have far-reaching networks of intelligence operations.

In the United States, much of the information that ought to be kept secret from enemies is published for all to see. The foreign spy assigned to the U.S. must have the lushest of all assignments. All he has to do is use scissors and paste and the daily newspapers to make up reports for his home office.

IT IS INCREDIBLE that there are members of Congress who would penalize their own nation by requiring intelligence secrets to be published. That would make it illegal for security information to be withheld from publication.

It is also incredible that senators could propose a requirement that secret operations be approved by a committee of senators before they are undertaken. It is well known that a senator and his staff cannot keep a secret and the security of the nation would be lost if such a course was followed.

Let's hope the Senate will kill its silly idea the way the House killed the proposal to require publication.

THE DALLAS TIMES HERALD

Dallas, Tex., February 2, 1976

THE U. S. HOUSE of Representa- ves displayed a genuine sense of esponsibility in stopping its intelli- ence committee from releasing the anel's report containing informa- on on highly secret government telligence operations.

The report deals with the lengthy vestigation by the House Select ommittee on Intelligence of such telligence agencies as the CIA. ontained in the report was exten- ve description of secret U. S. spy nd other CIA operations abroad hich could have done considerable amage to this country's security ow and in the future.

The entire House, disagreeing ith its intelligence committee on e advisability of making all these ecrets public, voted 246 to 124 gainst releasing the report without e approval of President Ford.

Considerably piqued by the House ction, Committee Chairman Otis ike declared that as far as he is oncerned the report is dead. pparently his fellow Democrats, in e majority on the committee, agree with the New York congressman.

That attitude is wrong. Certainly the information on the wrongdoings of the CIA—and apparently they were many—should be revealed and could be, we feel sure, without the release of security damaging secrets.

The Times Herald Washington Bureau reported that the House vote was a victory for two Texans, Rep. John Young of Corpus Christi, a member of the rules committee, and Rep. Dale Milford of Grand Prairie, a member of the intelligence committee.

"Our sole concern," said Rep. Milford in arguing against release of the report in its present form, "deals with the fact that the committee report contains classified information that will be very damaging to this nation's ongoing intelligence effort and damaging to our foreign relations with certain nations."

The House rightly agreed with Rep. Milford.

THE RICHMOND NEWS LEADER

Richmond, Va., January 30, 1976

Well, blow us down: There remains in the House of Representatives about a 2-1 majority in support of standing by its word. For a while, many Americans had begun to doubt that such a majority could be mustered. But yesterday the House voted 246-124 *against* allowing its intelligence committee to disclose certain secret information without presidential approval; the committee had received the information from the CIA and from the White House on condition that the committee would not make the information public. Nevertheless, the committee had voted 8-4 on January 21 to release secret information in its final, 300-plus page report — despite the committee's prior pledge *not* to release secret information.

Yet despite yesterday's vote by the full House, in effect forcing the committee to abide by its word, the contents of the committee's report has been given to *The New York Times*. And *The Times* has published the essence of it. And the consequent damage has been done.

What is happening to America's intelligence operations is, simply, a crying shame. The CIA is an instrument of American policy. As outgoing CIA Director William Colby has commented, "the government needs an ability to conduct large, unattributed, unadmitted operations. Otherwise we're in a position of either having to complain with a diplomatic protest and be ignored, or having to threaten to use military force, which nobody wants to do." But of late, opponents of the CIA have exploited the natural American antipathy towards secrecy. Ask Mr. Average American on the street, and he's likely to tell you that secrecy in American government — secrecy in American policy — is a sin.

Indeed, so "up" is the CIA as a topic for discussion, that it is the subject of ponderous debate and lugubrious prose — all of it seemingly endless. And the increasingly accepted attitude is essentially this: Secrecy has no place in an "open" society, hence an institution such as the CIA — which depends on secrecy — is an unacceptable instrument of policy.

In dreamland, where only good guys dwelled, such a dreamy theory would be just fine. But this is the real world, in which real enemies dwell. America's current enemies, the most proficient and brutal that ever have arrayed against her, are the Communists. At present, the principal Communist thrust in the West is political. A sound philosophic and patriotic argument can be made that goes something like this: In certain circumstances, particularly when your enemy is using a political thrust against you, one's most effective weapon against that thrust ought to be secret. Such a circumstance pertains now. To the degree that we are diluting the strength of the CIA, we are removing from our arsenal our most effective weapon against the Communists.

Yet the relentless assault goes on — not an assault on the Communists, but on the CIA. So we read of the CIA's non-assassinations, and of CIA money to non-Communists in Italy, and of CIA efforts to aid the anti-Communists in Angola. Frustration and cynicism about the CIA increase: The dark insinuation is that somehow all this is wrong. No. One need only look at a map, and reflect upon the advance of Communism across continent after continent. Operation Hobble proceeds. But the damage we are doing to our intelligence community — the damage we are doing to the CIA — is damage we are doing to ourselves.

THE BLADE

Toledo, Ohio, February 5, 1976

THE vote by the House decisively overruling its own Intelligence Committee in the conflict with President Ford over publication of classified CIA information was, obviously, of considerable significance. That makes it particularly important that the specific point at issue be clearly understood. Unfortunately, key statements on both sides invited misinterpretation.

Chairman Otis Pike, arguing against the floor vote, defended on two grounds the committee majority's desire to include in its final report data that Mr. Ford had asked be withheld. To accede, the chairman said, would amount to sweeping serious things under the rug and to giving the President a veto over anything he did not want in the legislative report. But neither contention was really valid. The CIA's misdeeds, both in general and in great detail, have been subjected to glaring exposure in several investigations. And the presidential request for protection of certain information was not only specific but in accord with an agreement with the committee governing its access to the data. It was the honoring of this agreement — and only that — which was the question before the House.

But the President, after having been strongly supported on that score, regrettably responded with a misleading comment of his own. The vote, he said, showed that "House members recognized that the American people want a strong and effective foreign intelligence capability." That could easily be taken to mean that a sound intelligence operation depends upon a blanket of executive secrecy. This is precisely the kind of attitude which allowed the CIA to go astray in the first place, and it seems highly unlikely the American people want to return to it.

The full House, commendably, kept its eye on the main issue and properly insisted that the committee abide by an understanding with the executive branch that was made in good faith. Nothing more nor less should be made of the vote.

The Evening Gazette

Worcester, Mass., January 31, 1976

Just as the various committees investigating our national intelligence community seemed about to get out of hand, the House, in a move of commendable responsibility, put an end to the indiscriminate airing of sensitive information.

House members overwhelmingly voted to prevent their own intelligence committee from disclosing its secret findings without presidential approval. The vote seems both a repudiation of some methods used by the Pike committee and an effort to keep American intelligence gathering effective.

The committee, under the chairmanship of Rep. Otis G. Pike, obtained its data on the Central Intelligence Agency and other spy organizations through the full cooperation of the federal agencies—after Pike and his colleagues promised discretion. They also agreed not to publish the final report if President Ford objected. But the ink was still wet on the 338-page document when many of its details were leaked.

Those who would like to see the C.I.A. and other intelligence bodies crippled are up in arms, claiming that the rug was pulled out from under the investigations. They are wrong. The probes have served their purpose, and as a result the intelligence community is likely to be very careful not to commit future transgressions. But a seemingly unending disclosure of sensitive material by over-zealous investigators would be counterproductive.

Commenting on the House vote, President Ford says the "House members recognize that the American people want a strong and effective foreign intelligence capability." That recognition came none too soon.

The Oregonian

Portland, Ore., January 31, 1976

The House of Representatives acted with more maturity than its intelligence investigating committee in instructing that committee to honor its agreement with President Ford not to make public portions of its report the President believed would endanger national security or intelligence personnel. The vote of 246 to 124 overturned the committee's recommendation which rejected any "censorship" by the President or the Central Intelligence Agency. The committee report is to be submitted to the House as a secret document or released only with President Ford's approval.

Dispatches from Washington called this a "precedent-setting victory" for the President. Maybe. But a copy of the report was delivered to the New York Times days ago and its contents have been published. The "leak" provided more evidence that Congress rarely can keep a secret and is not constituted to manage intelligence agencies. The CIA director has had to testify recently before eight congressional committees. A small, joint committee should be given exclusive authority to oversee spy operations.

President Ford, speaking at the swearing in ceremony for the new CIA director, George Bush, said "we cannot improve this agency by destroying it" and that the director's first duty will be "to restore public confidence" in the CIA. But the President has yet to make known the plans he has been studying for strengthening and reorganizing all federal intelligence agencies.

Congressional committees have served the public by exposing some abuses of power by the CIA and other agencies in years past. Congress now has the obligation to cooperate with the executive branch in establishing review procedures directed to preventing misdeeds while protecting secrecy justified by the national interest.

BUFFALO EVENING NEWS

Buffalo, N.Y., January 31, 1976

Chairman Otis Pike (D., N. Y.) and his House CIA investigating committee stand properly rebuked, in our judgment, by the decisive 246-124 vote of their House colleagues to prevent the publishing of their final committee report until the President has had a chance to remove any secret material he considers damaging to the security of U. S. intelligence operations abroad.

The issue, to be sure, is in one sense largely academic, since the substance of the Pike report had already been leaked to a New York City newspaper which, to the dismay of the CIA and the White House, has been printing excerpts all week. But the basic question concerns the proper exercise of Congress' oversight powers, and on this the House as a whole has shown a much higher sense of responsibility and restraint than the Pike committee has.

For, despite Chairman Pike's anguished cry that the House has made a "travesty of the whole doctrine of separation of powers," it has actually, in our judgment, done the reverse. For it was Mr. Pike and his committee who, after receiving classified information from the CIA and the White House on a pledge of confidentiality, then decided to do their own declassifying by publishing whatever secrets they thought the public should have.

Instead of themselves respecting "the doctrine of separation of powers," in short, they sought to flout it by arrogating unto themselves the power to declassify secret material, a power until now clearly reposed in the President.

But even though this showdown closes the Pike investigation on a sour note, it should not wipe out any of the positive values of this searching look at CIA transgressions. Nor can it justify a congressional or public brushoff of any proposed reforms or other committee recommendations that have validity. The next step, obviously, is to obtain a quick clearance from the White House for the speedy publication of everything in the report that does not actually and seriously jeopardize any intelligence operation abroad. On that, the President's policy at this stage, bearing in mind that there is no point in trying to recapture anything that has already been leaked, should be one of maximum disclosure so that the country can move on as quickly as possible to the more constructive mop-up phase.

Certainly in the aftermath of this year-long orgy of publicly washing our dirty intelligence linen, we must, as the President said in his State of the Union message, "take action to reform and strengthen our intelligence community."

The Evening Bulletin

Philadelphia, Pa., February 2, 1976

The necessary plan to increase Congress' control over U.S. intelligence operations has raised one particularly troubling objection. Critics have rightly pointed out that only one informed but irresponsible member of Congress could destroy any intelligence operation simply by leaking its existence.

Fears of this danger have focused more on the larger and more diverse House of Representatives than on the Senate. Yet the House's participation remains essential to the creation of a joint committee to oversee intelligence. And the executive has far less likelihood of "co-opting" a committee of both houses rather that of just a single house.

The House took a major step in establishing its responsibility last week by voting, 246 to 124, not to release the report of its own Committee on Intelligence.

Admittedly the leaking of the report must have influenced many members. The prior publication of much of its contents allowed them to vote on the right side after the fact — always a luxury.

Nevertheless, the House's refusal to release the report until the President censored it was important. The report contained classified information which the committee had obtained only after agreeing not to disclose it. As some members argued, the House's reputation was in fact at stake.

Leaks do have a useful function as in the U.S. involvement in Angola. But they serve when government is concealing an abuse from the public, not when it has agreed to cooperate with a major investigation.

Preventing abuses from reoccuring will certainly require far tighter oversight by Congress. And that certainly necessitates confidence by the executive in Congress so that the overseer has adequate information.

Now is the time not for leaks but to build that confidence. The House has taken a step in that direction. It will have to take more by building safeguards against leaks into legislation creating a new joint committee.

Just as this country's security needs an effective intelligence agency so does that agency need security.

HOUSTON CHRONICLE

Houston, Tex., February 3, 1976

In the wake of criticism and sensational disclosures concerning real and imagined activities of the Central Intelligence Agency, the U.S. Senate on Jan. 27, 1975, created a Select Committee to Study Government Operations With Respect to Intelligence Activities. The U.S. House of Representatives followed suit by establishing a Select Committee on Intelligence on Feb. 19.

The two committees stayed as busy as politicians the week before the first primary—except for frequent congressional holidays. Whether the result of all this scurrying about, nail biting and finger pointing will be legislation in the public interest or a political exercise that could disillusion the public and perhaps emasculate the U.S. intelligence operations remains in doubt.

Practically everything of any importance, sensitive or not, has been leaked by members of the two panels. The speed with which the testimony went public was astounding, indicating competition of sorts among eager congressmen.

The American public couldn't help but be confused. The CIA obviously overstepped its authority, yet the average citizen is aware that world realities demand that the United States have an effective intelligence system.

The exposure has been sufficient. The Chronicle agrees with President Ford that the House acted properly in voting overwhelmingly to prohibit public release of the committee report that contains classified material apparently much more sensitive than that included in the recently released Senate report.

Even though most of the House information has been leaked already, there is no need to supply the full details to the KGB and other interested parties.

Enemies and potential enemies of the United States must be pleased with the way things have been going. The CIA has been caught in a withering cross fire that to some extent will undermine its effectiveness, even if restrictive legislation does not follow.

The State

Columbia, S.C., February 5, 1976

THE U.S. House of Representatives used common sense in stopping U.S. Rep. Otis Pike's intelligence study committee from publishing national security secrets and intelligence activities in its final report.

No one should believe, however, that the House's action means the secrets will be kept. Sections of the drafted report have already been printed in *The New York Times* and other newspapers. The information was leaked by sources on Capitol Hill.

Of course, if American journalists can get that kind of information, then foreign agents have also been able to get it. The presence of the Soviets' agents on Capitol Hill is well-known — remember the Russian-made "bug" that was found in a congressional committee room?

So, it is fair to conclude that most of the damage probably had already been done by committee leaks before the House voted to let President Ford cut top secret information from the final report.

In doing so, the House lived up to its agreement it made with the President to obtain the information.

The action of the House was important, however, in another respect; it prevented the United States from committing an act of unsurpassed official stupidity. The activities of Mr. Pike's and Sen. Frank Church's committees have appalled our friends — no nation in history has so deliberately bared its intelligence secrets and operations as this country has done.

The self-destructive nature of those disclosures is not lost upon our allies or our enemies, who surely must marvel at our naivety. But blind to it are those with the compulsion to purge publicly this nation of all wrong-doing, to send it walking naked and innocent into the future, sure that purity is sufficient defense against evil in this world.

What the Congress voted, in substance, was not to place an official stamp on the previously leaked stories. The intelligence systems of the United States could have been totally overhauled, reformed, and reconstituted without disclosing so much sensitive information.

But the emphasis in Washington has been on exposure, not on reform. And we thank Congress for saving us the embarrassment of watching another committee feast on the final tidbits of publicity on which they thrive.

The Detroit News

Detroit, Mich., February 13, 1976

Rep. Otis Pike's Select Committee on Intelligence has finally gone out of business. Good riddance. The committee's investigation of the federal intelligence system was a cheap shot all the way.

On the day the committee closed its books, the Village Voice, a liberal weekly in New York, underlined the character of that investigation by publishing 21 pages of excerpts from the committee's "secret" report.

There is a touch of Wonderland in the history of this report. And in Pike's complaint, as he finished his inquisition, that the White House had blocked the report so that unnamed administration officials wouldn't be embarrassed.

First, it is true that the White House vigorously objected when the committee threatened to release secret intelligence data without first checking with the President, as previously agreed. However, it was the full House of Representatives, made up of Pike's own colleagues and dominated by his own party, that actually blocked the report — by a vote of 246-124.

Second, the House resolution admitted that Mr. Ford might have substantial reasons, beyond protecting administration officials from embarrassment, for objecting to the release of secret data.

The resolution said the document would remain frozen until "certified by the President as not containing information which would adversely affect the intelligence activities of the CIA" or other federal agencies abroad. In short, the House recognized that national security and the integrity of the intelligence system might be at stake.

Third, however, the report was leaked to the New York Times, CBS and other news organizations and has now been reproduced in part by the Village Voice. Media consistently unfriendly to the administration and the intelligence system have published selective and critical accounts of a report which the public cannot check.

As a commentary on the Village Voice's objectivity, that newspaper published its excerpts from the report under the headline "The CIA Report the President Doesn't Want You to Read," ignoring the House's vote to withhold the report.

The quality of the criticism contained in the report may be judged from the statement that U.S. intelligence "failed" in the 1973 Middle East war. Here was a case in which Israel, the country directly affected by the Arab attack, failed to detect what her enemies were up to. Perhaps U.S. intelligence could be forgiven for also being surprised.

No country's intelligence system can be totally effective. Operatives are not as omniscient as congressmen with 20-20 hindsight; they do what they can within their limitations. And as a result of congressional meddling, their limitations are growing more stringent all the time.

By the way, doesn't it seem a bit contradictory that a committee which sought to expose the CIA's inner workings to the world now deplores the agency's "failure" to obtain good intelligence?

The Pittsburgh Press

Pittsburgh, Pa., February 2, 1976

The House has shown a welcome sense of responsibility in voting overwhelmingly to prohibit public release of the full 338-page report by its intelligence committee describing secret CIA activities.

The action was a victory for President Ford and former CIA director William E. Colby, who had argued strongly against release of the report in its present form — even though much of it has already been divulged without authority.

★ ★ ★

But more important than the issue of who won this particular confrontation between the legislative and executive branches of the federal government is the fact that the House action may be a foretoken of more workable understandings between Capitol Hill and the White House on future Congressional policing of the nation's intelligence operations.

Had the House agreed to allow its committee to publish its report as is, it would have violated an agreement reached months ago that certain secret information about the CIA made available to the committee would not be made public. Faith in any House pledge would then have been wrecked.

Committee chairman Otis G. Pike, a New York Democrat, is disgruntled. However, he will let his panel vote either to kill the report or let the President make deletions and then publish it even though he himself opposes any outside editing.

★ ★ ★

Be that as it may, a secret intelligence agency such as the CIA is a necessity to our national security.

In a democracy such as ours, it cannot be permitted to function independently. But it cannot function with assurance nor can its activities be monitored effectively if there is a lack of mutual faith and understanding between the agency and its overseers.

Now, after months of back-biting between the executive and legislative branches over the issue of covert intelligence activities, the House vote gives citizens some hope that such faith and understanding are at least a step nearer.

Chicago Tribune

Chicago, Ill., February 2, 1976

Rep. Otis Pike's colleagues in the House of Representatives have given him a well deserved lesson in honor. By a thumping majority, they followed the advice of the Rules Committee and prohibited Mr. Pike's Intelligence Committee from publishing a report on its investigations into "illegal and improper" actions by the intelligence agencies until the report had been approved by the White House.

Last September, after White House complaints that Mr. Pike's committee was leaking secrets like Niagara Falls, Mr. Pike reached an agreement with the White House under which the committee would be allowed to have its secret material, provided that the White House be given a day's notice before any of it was released to the public. This would give the White House a chance to express its views.

Now that the committee is closing shop, it voted 9 to 4 to publish its report without reference to the White House.

Questioned about this, Mr. Pike said that the material was simply "too atrocious" to "sweep under the rug"; that to carry out his promise would amount to "censorship by the CIA"; that this would be "a complete travesty of the whole doctrine of separation of powers"; and that most of the material in the report had already been leaked to the press anyway.

If we may borrow Mr. Pike's words, his logic is atrocious. It is not at all clear, in the first place, that the September compromise called for censorship; it merely gave the White House time to object. And now that he has acknowledged all the leaking, why didn't he do anything to stop it—especially since it is fairly well agreed that most of it came from the offices of his own committee?

As for separation of powers, it is designed precisely to prevent the unilateral sort of action that Mr. Pike advocated. In effect, he is arguing that since the committee or its agents have already leaked so much of the material, it may as well be permitted to break its promise and publish the material officially. Some separation.

Up to a point, Mr. Pike's committee did a job that needed to be done. It let the intelligence agencies know that they do not operate in a total vacuum, free from any rules or control at all. Because of the committee's work, future administrations will no doubt watch the agencies more closely than they have in the past.

But since last fall, it has begun to look as if Mr. Pike was using secret government documents to build a launching pad for his own political propulsion in directions unspecified.

We're not going to try to judge how much damage has been done by the leaks [the New York Times discreetly acknowledges that a copy of the whole report—tho still officially unpublished—has been "made available" to it]. What we are saying is simply, first, that a Congress that makes promises and breaks them will lose the respect of the rest of government and the public; and, second, that separation of powers doesn't mean—and never was intended to mean—the unilateral right of Congress to grab executive branch secrets and spread them about the country, by leakage or otherwise. Mr. Pike and those who supported him have some dented halos to repair.

The Des Moines Register

Des Moines, Iowa, February 3, 1976

The 246-to-124 vote by the House of Representatives blocking its Intelligence Committee from publishing a report on the CIA should be taken as showing a lack of confidence in the committee rather than as an endorsement of the views on secrecy of President Ford and William Colby, former Central Intelligence Agency director.

The House action forbids the committee to make its report public without President Ford's approval because of alleged secrets in it. Ford, Colby, and some members of the committee felt that secret information had been given in confidence and that the committee would be breaking an agreement with the President if it made the report public without "sanitizing." Committee Chairman Otis Pike (Dem., N.Y.) denied any such agreement.

Most of the secrets in the report already have been leaked to the press, so whatever damage could be done has been done.

The right to keep certain public business secret exists, but that right is limited and must be subject to checks and balances from Congress and from the courts.

Congressional oversight in practice must be exercised primarily through a committee. Congress has been poorly served in the past by oversight committees too anxious to keep secrets or not to inquire into them. Perhaps the Pike committee has swung too far in the other direction. But the number of foolish and dangerous projects the committee found emphasizes the need for vigilant congressional oversight.

Living in the sunshine — even in a fishbowl — is more suitable to a democratic, constitutional government, and is not as dangerous as the secret-keepers assume. The House vote should not become a precedent for presidential control over the output of congressional watchdog committees.

DAILY NEWS

New York, N.Y., January 31, 1976

Much to the chagrin and embarrassment of Rep. Otis Pike (D-N.Y.), the House has voted overwhelmingly to hold up publication of the final report prepared by his intelligence-investigating committee.

Not a very good loser, the Suffolk Democrat spluttered after the vote, "I'm not quite as proud of being a member of the House of Representatives today as I was yesterday. I'm still proud, but not as proud." Pike really ought to get a grip on himself.

We regard the chamber's action as a wholesome, healthy display of responsibility and concern for the national interest—and we believe most Americans so see it.

The panel's leaks of classified information on Central Intelligence Agency operations—and its attempt to publish secret data on its own hook—raised serious questions about whether tighter congressional supervision of the CIA would destroy the agency.

By its vote, the House has taken a long step toward quieting those fears.

FORT WORTH STAR-TELEGRAM

Fort Worth, Tex., February 4, 1976

It's going to take some doing. The competition is tough. But Rep. Otis Pike, D-N.Y., holds the inside track in the race for a new individual indoor record for being wrong.

As chairman of the House Select Intelligence Committee, Pike has headed up an investigation into activities of the Central Intelligence Agency, better known as the CIA. The investigation has turned up all sorts of information about the CIA.

Some of that information the American people ought to have. The people need it to form the new opinions that, hopefully, will shape the new policies needed to govern the operations of this secret agency.

But some of the information would be of little or no use to the people. Its only value would be to America's enemies. It would help them to neutralize U.S. intelligence activities and thwart U.S. policies in various parts of the world.

Congressman Pike, whose responsibility it is to control releases of information from his committee, already has allowed some damaging "leaks" of this information.

In so doing, Pike was wrong.

Pike announced his intention to release a report including all the information, except the names of intelligence agents who had not testified at public hearings.

Wrong again.

President Ford asked if Congress couldn't do something to bring Pike and his committee under control before they did some irreparable harm.

Texas Democrats Dale Milford of Grand Prairie and John Young of Corpus Christi came through, sponsoring a measure allowing the President to censor the report prior to its release.

The House approved the measure by a whopping 2-to-1 margin.

Pike responded to this like a spoiled brat. All right, then, he said, he just wouldn't file the report at all. "As far as I'm concerned," he said, "it's dead and buried."

Wrong again.

As we said, that report contains some information the people should have. With his juvenile insistence on having his way or refusing to play, Pike could deny the public access to this important information. That would be wrong.

Apparently, to be chairman of the House Select Intelligence Committee, there's one qualification that isn't needed: Intelligence.

Long Island Press

Jamaica, N.Y., January 31, 1976

We share Rep. Otis G. Pike's deep disappointment over the House's decision to withhold release of his committee's final report on intelligence activities. Allowing President Ford to censor what can be told the American people is, as the Suffolk congressman said, "a complete travesty of the whole doctrine of separation of powers."

The Select Committee on Intelligence, like its counterpart in the Senate, was assigned not just to determine the extent of the Central Intelligence Agency's illegal activities, but also to recommend ways for Congress to exercise its constitutional right to act as an overseer. Sadly, Mr. Pike may be right in suggesting that the House may now never have a strong oversight committee.

The House action in hiding the report of the Pike committee is a shameful surrender to the White House, which for years has been the sole arbiter of secret foreign policy decisions. That these high level decisions led to the CIA abuses — such as participation in assassination plots against foreign leaders and coups to overthrow foreign governments — became known before Congress began its own investigations.

Mr. Pike's committee, however, was especially useful in not just confirming the scary revelations by the news media, but also in uncovering new abuses that must not be kept secret from the public. Indeed, the panel went beyond illicit spying activities into the shadow area of secret diplomacy, as well as exposing highly questionable budgetary practices.

Mr. Pike feels that his committee's work had been "entirely an exercise in futility." Not so.

To the contrary, the House's surrender to White House censors may well have shocked the public far more than would release of the panel's full report. After the traumatic Watergate scandal that drove former President Nixon from office in disgrace, we would be very surprised if there were any public feeling in favor of still another coverup.

Indeed, the retreat in the lower chamber should stiffen enough backs in the Senate to make sure that its intelligence committee, headed by Sen. Frank Church of Idaho, succeeds where the House failed.

THE SAGINAW NEWS

Saginaw, Mich., February 3, 1976

Accepting the thesis that the government must have the latitude to carry out intelligence work, two things are of paramount importance, more important at this juncture, we believe, than telling the world everything we know.

One is that those operations are conducted with strict regard to Constitutional provisions. The other is that congressional reform be undertaken to see that they are.

Thus it would behoove Rep. Otis Pike, D.-N.Y., to subdue his anger over the House vote last week long enough to give President Ford the full report of the finding on the CIA and FBI compiled by the House Select Committee on Intelligence.

The House has directed the committee chaired by Rep. Pike to do that — before making any of it public.

To an extent we can understand Rep. Pike's resentment. He is hickory-hard, high principled and a stubborn defender of the separation of powers. In a very real way he is not wrong when he considers such a directive as so inimical to those powers as to make a farce of his committee's work.

Rep. Pike obviously feels that the White House will blue pencil much of the report and reduce it to something meaningless via administrative censorship. That could happen, to be sure. The risk of whitewash is there.

Yet Rep. Pike conveniently forgets a couple of things.

One is that the committee has not exactly set a record for keeping a lid on its findings up to now. There have been a number of leaks which have already divulged some of the more serious CIA and FBI transgressions.

Another is that the committee agreed last year to report to the President and thereafter fight him on anything it considered unwarranted censorship or unwarranted use of executive privilege on materials it sought. To argue now that those promises did not apply to the finished report is, at best, dubious.

Lastly, it seems somewhat foolish now that Rep. Pike threatens to issue no report — ever — because of the House mandate to his committee. Better he send the report forward and fight afterward.

Both Congress and the White House are walking a thin line in the entire intelligence issue. The questions of what should be made public and what should not in the best interests of the U.S. abroad are heavy indeed — regardless of urges for full disclosure.

Making everything public is not necessarily any better than unbridled censorship. But when all is done, what is needed is the kind of congressional oversight reform that will keep these agencies in line. Rep. Pike will not help that by folding up everything and abandoning the essential task.

His leadership is needed.

CHICAGO DAILY NEWS

Chicago, Ill., February 1, 1976

The House of Representatives branded its own Select Committee on Intelligence as untrustworthy when it voted to suppress the committee's report — at least until the executive branch has had a chance to censor it. If the faults of the intelligence apparatus are to be corrected — and the need for correction is clear — the findings of the committee need to be laid on the table for public scrutiny.

The committee chaired by Rep. Otis G. Pike (D-N.Y.) has made its own mistakes, to be sure. The leakage of information by committee members or staff, some of it sensitive in nature, has kindled the suspicion that politics and publicity were being put ahead of a genuine concern for reforming the Central Intelligence Agency and other information-gathering bodies.

But there is another side. Censorship by the executive branch of a report already screened for national security purposes leads to the suspicion that deletions may be made merely to avoid embarrassment where no real question of security is involved. The only way to resolve this dilemma is to publish the report and let the chips fall where they may.

Enough is already known about the committee's work to clinch the case for better control of the CIA and related intelligence operations. The problem becomes one of restoring public trust in agencies that have clearly overrun their bounds, but are still vitally needed. This will be no easy task, for it requires guidelines that insure secrecy, but not too much secrecy, and who is to decide?

The legislative and executive branches must collaborate in setting these guidelines. Congressional oversight of the CIA failed to prevent abuses in the past. One of the shocks that has come from the House and Senate investigations is the revelation that some congressmen charged with the responsibility of oversight simply ducked their duty — they "didn't want to know" what was really going on.

This must change. Certainly in the House and Senate there are tough-minded, honest, responsible men and women who can be trusted to put the national interest above all other considerations. A joint, bipartisan committee, identified and accountable, working with the President to separate the real problems of national security from the chaff of petty politics, could go far toward restoring the trust that is lacking.

If the House committee report can help bring that about, it will be of great service to the nation. But it cannot help while it lies hidden, generating new suspicions.

THE DENVER POST

Denver, Colo., February 2, 1976

Rep. Jim Johnson, R-Colo., put it forthrightly and well to his colleagues in the House of Representatives: "The issue before you today is to decide if despicable, detestable acts should be reported. Your choice today is whether to continue hiding shameful conduct."

Unwisely, a majority of the House members did not heed Johnson's admonition and voted 246 to 124 to prevent release of the final report of the House Select Committee on Intelligence on the Central Intelligence Agency until the report had been censored by the White House.

Through this action, the House abdicated responsibility for overseeing the activities of the intelligence community and reverted to the subservient role it has taken on the CIA over the years.

If this action is permitted to stand, then with support from the White House, the CIA could again be in the familiar position of engaging in widespread covert activities without accountability.

That must not be allowed to happen. For far too many years Congress has literally given the CIA a blank check and asked few questions on what the agency did with the taxpayers' money.

The year-long investigations by the intelligence committees in the House and the Senate have raised serious questions about the "dirty tricks" undertaken by the CIA in the guise of serving the national interest. Gathering essential intelligence information for foreign policy decisions by the White House is one thing, but what mandate did the CIA have to engage in plotting assassinations of foreign leaders or in attempting to subvert foreign governments?

The leaks of information from the committee hearings that produced these shocking disclosures were strongly criticized by the administration. And indeed a number of these leaks were unfortunate. But it is also true that without this disclosure, the American public would have no knowledge of, and therefore no opportunity of acting on, the CIA's abuse of power.

As they were in the Watergate scandal, leaks to a free press can turn out to be the last resort in our democratic society of dealing with such abuse of power.

The way to deal with leaks is not to damn them — as the White House has done — but to produce reforms in the intelligence apparatus that will make leaks unnecessary.

Congress must not go so far as to incapacitate the CIA by irresponsible disclosure of all of its activities, and thereby endangering the lives of its operatives. But Congress must establish a tough, yet fair, system of overseeing the agency.

An outline for such reforms has begun to emerge from the Senate Intelligence Committee, headed by Sen. Frank Church, D-Idaho. Among the proposals is one calling for establishment of a joint House-Senate oversight committee with control over the CIA's budget, which now is hidden in the budgets of various federal departments.

A debate is also under way on whether such an oversight committee should be told before a covert operation takes place — to prevent such CIA activities as the secret funneling of arms to one side in the civil war in Angola. Both houses of Congress have voted to ban covert aid to Angola.

Another item for discussion is whether a congressional oversight committee should have the right —by majority vote — to make public information on the CIA as a measure of last resort.

But whatever reform finally take shape, Congress must keep in mind the continuing need for the nation to maintain an effective intelligence service.

The effort, therefore, must be directed at ending past abuses of the CIA—without wrecking it.

Newsday

Garden City, N.Y., February 8, 1976

The CIA may have wound up with the worst of all possible results from its investigation by Congress.

Instead of being presented fully and openly, the Pike Committee's findings have dribbled out in a series of leaks. And no doubt the leaks will continue as it suits the various interests of Democrats or Republicans, in Congress or in the White House, to put a particular tidbit before the public. The agency's travail will be needlessly prolonged.

And instead of grappling with the substance of the problem, which is how to prevent future misuse of the CIA, Congress and the White House have been diverted into a debate on the public's right to know what went wrong in the past. Since the detour includes a presidential election campaign, it may be a year or more before the critical problems of American intelligence get the serious attention they deserve.

If that serves the national security, as President Ford's spokesmen claim in defense of their demand to withhold parts of the report, then we'd like to know how.

More likely the administration's prime concern with the Pike report is not national security but national politics. There are two pieces of evidence on that score. One is that Republicans on the committee showed no reluctance to declassify those sections of the Pike report that deal with Democratic Presidents; apparently the national security problem occurs only with Republicans. The other is that, according to a responsible source who has read the report (but would not leak it), some of the more damning sections that the White House would censor do not embarrass the CIA so much as Henry Kissinger, who ordered the operations concerned.

Under questions, Kissinger told a Senate committee at an acrimonious hearing last week that some of the CIA operations revealed in recent weeks could properly be construed as national secrets. Senator Lowell Weicker (R-Conn.) retorted, "I would characterize them as a national shame rather than a national secret."

The U.S. intelligence community will no doubt survive, just as the Defense Department survived public knowledge of the Pentagon Papers after a strikingly similar attempt to cover up the lies told the American people about Vietnam. But delaying the final disposition of the House and Senate investigations can only postpone the restoration of credibility and efficiency at the CIA and further embroil its future in partisan politics. And the fault for this lies with the White House. By using the pretext of national security in an attempt to protect Kissinger and his patrons, the administration is itself playing loose with the country's safety.

The Charleston Gazette

Charleston, W. Va., February 4, 1976

By its 246-124 vote to prohibit public release of the report of the House Intelligence Committee, the House of Representatives has subscribed to the bankrupt political philosophy that the people are better off kept in the dark about the workings of their government.

This philosophy prevailed during the dark days of Vietnam when the elected representatives of the people quailed before executives who psychopathically mistrusted the people.

It is being revived by the current House apparently because the elected representatives of the people have been convinced that revelation of illegal acts by espionage agencies will somehow damage the effectiveness of those agencies.

We think such a contention rests not merely on fatuous thought but also on an inability to understand the American tradition of the "consent of the governed."

Espionage agencies aren't going to be asked to publish a record of their daily activities in the future. We hope they will be asked to provide a record to the proper oversight committees in Congress, however, and that they will be forbidden to engage in activity specifically forbidden by law.

Disclosure of past sins won't hurt espionage agencies. It will, on the contrary, make them more sensitive to the civil rights they ostensibly protect. When democracy must rely on totalitarian techniques for protection, it ceases to be a democracy.

New York Post

New York, N.Y., January 31, 1976

A series of forthright, courageous efforts to challenge and override the Ford Administration's flawed domestic and foreign policies has been recently mounted by Congress. The insurgence has doubtless heartened the nation. It is a discouraging anticlimax to see the House not only uphold the President but vote him new veto power to which he has no constitutional claim.

What the House has done, by a crushing vote of 246 to 124, is confer upon the White House authority to review, revise and otherwise censor the final report of the House Intelligence Committee. It is true that classified copies of the unaltered document will be distributed to members and details which have not already been leaked may shortly be published. This "compromise" makes the decision an even more uninspiring, unwarranted capitulation.

Perhaps the majority felt some concessions were necessary to an Administration that has been overruled on Angola aid, overridden on social welfare funding and defied by a large vote in favor of the public employment bill. Whatever the explanation, the issue demands immediate review, leading to public release of the intelligence committee's report.

Giving the Administration the opportunity—indeed, the authority—to suppress independent findings on the abuse of the intelligence system is virtually to guarantee that there will be more of the same abuses already exposed. What possible point is there to an investigation of this urgency and depth if the results are subject to ultimate control by its targets?

* * *

It is hardly conceivable that any fateful disclosures contained in the report are inaccessible to foreign intelligence operatives—or even constitute very hot news to them. The real victims of the exercise in suppression are the American people, who were told so often in the aftermath of Watergate that a new era of "open government" was at hand. Now coverup has been given new sanction and respectability by the House vote.

The outcome has been called a big "victory" for Ford. Over whom?

ST. LOUIS POST-DISPATCH

St. Louis, Mo., February 1, 1976

By its 246-to-124 vote to bar public release of the report of the House Intelligence Committee, the House of Representatives has delivered a slap in the face to one of its own committees and has surrendered to the Executive on a matter in which the Ford Administration has provided little reason for trust in its judgment. The House action stipulates that release of the 338-page report on intelligence activities must depend on certification from President Ford that disclosure would not harm the national interest. Chairman Otis Pike of the committee has rightly said that, in putting the issue to a committee vote, he will vote to kill the report rather than allow the President to make further deletions.

Under White House pressure, the Intelligence Committee had already deleted some material from its final report and then voted 9 to 4 to release it. That decision was overridden Thursday by the full House, whose members had not even had a chance to read the document but were merely reacting to importunities from the White House and from outgoing CIA Director William Colby, who castigated the committee for irresponsibility and harped on the need for stopping leaks. But in its efforts to prevent disclosure of CIA covert aid to Angola, covert aid to Italian political parties and involvement in assassination plots against foreign leaders, the Administration has clearly demonstrated that it is more interested in avoiding embarrassing revelations than in stopping questionable and illegal intelligence operations—which is the real purpose of the House report.

Far too few members of Congress have shown any recognition of the need for that body to have a role in the declassification of secret material and of the fact that, as long as the Executive is the sole judge of what may be properly disclosed, the potential will remain for covering up crimes and other despicable acts which threaten the fabric of a democratic society. The House should reconsider its censorship action and vote to release the report, which Mr. Pike has emphasized has nothing in it to endanger the national security.

The Salt Lake Tribune

Salt Lake City Utah, February 2, 1976

"The issue before you today is to decide if despicable, detestable acts should be reported. Your choice today is whether to continue hiding shameful conduct," said Rep. James P. Johnson, D-Colo.

And the U.S. House of Representatives voted on the side of darkness. It succeeded in turning what had the potential of being a roaring, frightening lion for good into an almost certain emasculated tabby.

The decision of the whole House to permit the White House to censor its own Select Committee on Intelligence's report is just about as despicable and detestable as the acts Rep. Johnson alluded to. The action virtually assures that Americans will never know just how bad the intelligence agencies they are paying for are. Conversely, American may never know how good the same agencies might be.

And the very Congressmen who voted to permit White House censorship of the Intelligence Committee's report are denying themselves the very information they need in order to make rational judgments on legislation governing the operation of the nation's intelligence apparatus.

It was with great enthusiasm that the House created the Intelligence Committee about a year ago. Great things were expected. Now those same Congressmen aren't particularly anxious to hear, and to let the public learn, what the committee discovered.

Why the sudden change of attitude?

Perhaps the "leaked" revelations from the Senate side concerning the unusual relationship between Judith Campbell Exner and the late John F. Kennedy engendered some substantial re-thinking

It is conceivable that many a Congressman began to worry about just what the unexpurgated version of the Pike Committee's report would contain

In that context, better a meowing kitty than a roaring lion. And what better way to assure a cuddlesome feline than to have a threatening lion stilled under the wraps of "national security."

BUSH CURTAILS CIA'S EMPLOYING NEWSMEN FROM U.S. PUBLICATIONS

In a directive issued Feb. 11, Director of Central Intelligence George Bush said that the Central Intelligence Agency would, "effective immediately," no longer enter into any "paid or contractual" relationships with full or part-time employes of U.S. news organizations. The directive stated that existing relationships with such employes would be terminated "as soon as possible." An intelligence official said that "less than 20 persons will be affected by the order."

The Bush order appeared to reverse the position of the former CIA head, William Colby, who had maintained that part-time employes of American news organizations could legitimately be hired by the agency. The directive also stated that the CIA did not presently secretly employ any American clergy, and "this practice will be continued as a matter of policy." Bush did not acknowledge any "impropriety" in the agency's use of newsmen or clergy, but said that the order had been issued in order to avoid "any appearance of improper use."

The order did not prohibit CIA hiring of employes of foreign news organizations. It was not clear whether the CIA would be barred from using obscure American publications to provide career CIA agents with a cover identity abroad.

The Evening Gazette

Worcester, Mass., February 23, 1976

George Bush's first public decision as the new director of the Central Intelligence Agency was a good one: He decided to cancel all CIA recruiting of American newsmen as agents.

The news that the CIA had been using some newsmen, both full-time reporters for major news gathering organizations and part-timers or free-lancers, first came out several years ago. Not until recently, however, was it acknowledged that the practice of recruiting reporters was relatively widespread.

It's easy to understand why the CIA looked to journalists. Reporters, by reason of their profession, often have access to foreign leaders and information that is not available to the average man on the street, spy or not.

But reporters are in a unique position. There is a certain public trust inherent in the job that cannot be maintained when a man or woman serves two masters. The freedom of the press protection offered by the U. S. Constitution should not be tainted by conflict of interest and the opportunities for conflict are many when there are two employers.

It can be argued that a patriotic duty is involved in this type of situation, but the credibility of the news media and the credibility of government depends on reporters impartially relating events. When a reporter is paid by the CIA as well as the news gathering agency, that credibility is damaged.

The arrangement raises disturbing questions. Did reporters employed by the CIA send factual reports back to their newspapers, magazines, television or radio stations or did they send back something that the CIA wanted the American public to receive? Did they withhold information and deliberately alter events? Was their role limited simply to intelligence gathering?

These questions, and the many others that arise, are clear indication of the unhealthy nature of the situation. It's best for the nation and best for the news media for Bush to put an end to use of journalists as paid agents.

The Washington Post

Washington, D.C., February 22, 1976

NO MORE BUT NO LESS than a lot of their fellow Americans, we surmise, journalists were drawn into the sticky web of "national security" during the cold war years. Their access to people and places as news gatherers, and their access to the public as news disseminators, gave them an obvious attractiveness to intelligence operators oriented more towards specific political missions than towards a journalistic quest for truth. Some journalists and news organizations responded to the agencies, which seemed then at least to be devoted to goals shared by other anxious and concerned citizens contemplating the world scene.

In today's political climate, operational cooperation with the CIA is widely perceived to be corrupting and unacceptable. But this is a relatively recent perception. As we see it, the question is how to combine the arm's length detachment of intelligence and news now so plainly required, with the commitments that intelligence and news people made to each other in the past when they sometimes saw their relationship to each other in another light.

One broad answer, we note, has already emerged out of the internal deliberations of the CIA and its discussions with news organizations, legislators and others. That answer, stated as a policy by the new CIA director, George Bush, is to end the employment of all full-time and part-time reporters accredited to "any" United States news organization, but to keep confidential the names of those journalists or organizations cooperating in the past. We find this a reasonable policy as far as it goes. The mixing of the intelligence and news functions, whatever its residual value (small and declining, we suspect) to the CIA, offers only the possibility of perversion to the press. But naming those who formerly worked with the CIA would require the CIA to break the bargain of confidentiality it struck with them, and might conceivably put some of them in personal jeopardy. True, not to name the cooperators risks leaving a taint on some non-cooperators. However, some part of this burden should be eased by the CIA's pledge to remove from its payroll those journalists remaining on it. The Senate Intelligence Committee has, properly, endorsed this arrangement, agreeing not to press for names but getting in return a CIA promise to share "certain files," which will let the panel determine the impact on the American press of the CIA's past ties with American and foreign journalists.

The CIA's policy declaration (which also applies to churchmen and missionary organizations) leaves open the possibility that the agency will employ journalists, including some Americans, accredited to *foreign* news organizations. This is at face an offensive formulation: The United States government would be exercising abroad an option—exploiting newsmen, polluting news —which it denies itself at home. But this is part of the larger question of what kind of covert operations should be conducted in the first place. Careful congressional oversight, rather than CIA policy declarations alone, would seem to offer the best mechanism for finding an answer.

For American news organizations and journalists themselves, the matter is really much simpler. The Constitution and the practice of American democracy confer special privileges upon the press. In return, the public has a right to expect that the press will be exactly what it professes to be: the eyes and ears and voice of a free people. Perfect detachment from the state may be impossible. The performance of voluntary services for the state, for instance, would be devilishly hard to control. But for practicing newsmen to be on a government payroll—on a secret payroll at that—is an intolerable violation of a solemn trust. If the perception of that responsibility was previously clouded, there is no excuse whatsoever for misreading it now.

Post-Tribune

Guarding Your Interests Daily

Gary, Ind., February 13, 1976

Newsmen can be patriots, too — and quite properly so.

In view of that, we see nothing wrong with a reporter, particularly an overseas correspondent, passing along to his country's intelligence apparatus information which might serve his nation's security.

But, we nevertheless are pleased that George Bush, new chief of the Central Intelligence Agency (CIA), has announced that he is doing away with hiring of news correspondents as CIA agents. We further regret that such hiring was a practice for however long it may have been.

That's because (1) a newsman should devote his efforts to digging out and writing facts for the sake of telling people what is going on and not for any other motive — even one conceived as patriotic, and (2) because no newsman should be under control of any government insofar as carrying out his reporting duties are concerned.

Actually, using newsmen to serve national security is hardly new. As a young man, Winston Churchill mixed active military service with profitable war correspondence. We happen to know a man of brief military and long and respected newspaper experience, who, when breaking into journalism in Hawaii in the 30s, had a side assignment (from the government) of telling what he observed when greeting Japanese ships. (We don't know if he ever passed on anything of value, but obviously it wasn't enough to forestall Pearl Harbor.) Investigative reporters, when no violation of confidence is involved, often and properly pass on tips to the police.

But in the interest of effectively giving the public the sort of information on which individuals can make up their own minds, it is much to be preferred that a reporter work at his own trade, and not with a sideline of espionage.

Damning as have been some of the revelations about it, we still believe that the CIA serves a vital need. But so does the press, and while in the general sense of serving the public good, those needs may be parallel, from an operations standpoint they should be kept separate.

Tulsa Daily World

Tulsa, Okla., February 13, 1976

AT LEAST one good thing has come out of the Congressional investigation of American intelligence activities. The CIA has announced U.S. journalists no longer will be used as paid agents.

The hiring of newsmen as intelligence agents — and the practice of agents posing as journalists — have long been sore points with the news profession. It goes to a question of credibility. Those of us in the news business have enough trouble trying to insure that we are believable; when intelligence agencies are known to be using journalists in their operations, they merely confirm the suspicions already in the minds of our critics.

GEORGE BUSH, the new CIA Director, says his force also will not use any American clergymen or missionaries as intelligence agents. That will take the same kind of onus off religious people as journalists suffer in foreign countries.

The CIA still doesn't admit any impropriety in using these people in its work. The feeling among intelligence people seems to be that they must have *some* kind of covers and they have merely taken advantage of the best ones available.

That is probably true, but it doesn't take into account the damage that can be caused to the professions affected. The press in this country needs to be *believable* in order to play its special role in our society. Ministers also must be free of any possible taint of hidden motives. Sources of information must feel free to talk to journalists and men of the cloth without fearing loss of their confidential relationship.

To some extent, even the new policy by BUSH cannot immediately undo the damage already caused. Some skeptical people aren't going to believe the change no matter how many times the CIA announces it. Nor can we find out how many journalists and ministers-missionaries have been involved in CIA work. The intelligence agency isn't telling; in fact, it says that will be a permanent secret.

This again indicates part of the problem. U.S. news media — the newspapers, wire services, broadcast companies and magazines — don't know how many of their employes, if any, have been on the CIA payroll. They would like to find out who the double-identity persons are; otherwise they may suspect innocent workers.

But the most important thing is to stop the practice, no matter how infrequent or extensive it has been in the past. We hope BUSH sticks tightly to his new policy.

NEW ORLEANS STATES-ITEM

New Orleans, La., February 13, 1976

The decision of the new director of the Central Intelligence Agency, George Bush, to halt the agency's long practice of employing American news people as overseas spies is a healthy development for the news media.

Public confidence in the news media is not as high today as it has been. Disclosures that some reporters have compromised their professional integrity by doubling as government espionage agents will increase public doubts as to the objectivity and impartiality of the news media.

The proper relationship of the press, including newspapers, television and radio news agencies, to government frequently is misunderstood by both public and politicians. In a free society, the proper role of the press is to keep an eye on government to see that it responds to the will of the people, adheres to the law and does not overstep its authority.

Credibility is essential to the press. Like Caesar's wife, news reporters should avoid even the suspicion of compromise. When news people become extensions of the government, they damage their credibility as government watchdogs.

Much has been made in the press of government spying on news reporters in connection with Watergate and government news leaks. News people are particularly sensitive to government spying on their lives. Like other citizens, they resent it as an invasion of privacy and an intrusion on their civil liberties. But in addition, they see it as a transgression by government on the function of a free press. And it is.

Disclosures that news people have been on the other end of the spying game is an embarrassment to those who recognize the dangers in such practices.

THE COMMERCIAL APPEAL

Memphis, Tenn., February 17, 1976

THE CENTRAL Intelligence Agency says it has quit hiring reporters who work for American news organizations to act as its agents.

It never should have begun such a policy.

It is not hard to understand how a few — a senior intelligence agency official says "less than 20 persons" — got involved in such a business.

During World War II, the Office of Strategic Services, which was a sort of predecessor of the CIA, sought out and hired newsmen, especially those who had been foreign correspondents and had special knowledge of foreign countries. It was an open policy, and the newsmen left their reporting jobs to be OSS employes.

Then, during the cold war period everyone was concerned about communism and when asked to cooperate with the CIA did so. Again, newsmen with special access abroad and with some special knowledge of situations were often questioned about what they knew. And most cooperated because it was the patriotic thing to do.

From those beginnings it was easy for some reporters to take in stride offers from the CIA to do a sort of double duty, drawing regular pay from their news organizations and some supplemental pay from the CIA. Since the names of those agents are being withheld, it is not possible to know how widespread the practice was or who and what organizations were involved.

But it was wrong for those newsmen to serve two masters. Newsmen must know that their job is to report the news, not to make it. Failure to realize that can destroy the credibility of the news organizations they represent and their own credibility as news reporters.

CONFLICTS OF interest within the news organization have been a matter of increasing concern, whether it involves reporters accepting junkets provided by private firms, or expensive gifts or sideline jobs. Professional journalism organization have adopted codes of ethics, and many news organization managements have adopted such codes as strict policy for their employes. The Commercial Appeal is one of the organizations which has such a policy in effect.

It was good to see that CIA Director George Bush also said in his statement of policy about hiring newsmen that the CIA was ending the practice of sending CIA employes abroad disguised as accredited representatives of U.S. news organizations. That was a corruption of the constitutional provision of free press just as bad as the hiring out by regular journalists, and without an end to that practice the task of honest newsmen overseas would be made difficult if not sometimes impossible.

The Des Moines Register

Des Moines, Iowa, March 12, 1976

The Inter American Press Association, an organization concerned about press freedom in the Americas, has condemned infiltration of the press by government intelligence agencies. The head of the association's Committee on Freedom of the Press called on journalists to demand "that those governments that are still democratic order immediate cessation of the insidious and Machiavellian infiltration of the media by their espionage services."

The Central Intelligence Agency (CIA) has admitted that it has had newsmen in its employ as part of a long-standing policy. The agency last month announced revision of the policy. It said:

"Effective immediately, CIA will not enter into paid or contractual relationship with any full-time or part-time news correspondent accredited by any U.S. news service, newspaper, periodical, radio or television network or station."

The Inter American Press Association has no reason to be satisfied with the change of policy. The new policy prohibits infiltration only of the U.S. news media. The CIA is free to keep on its payroll journalists working for Latin American and other foreign publications.

U.S. newsmen working for the CIA apparently were used for the most part to pass along information to the agency. According to Stuart Loory in the Columbia Journalism Review, foreign newsmen "were used to float false or misleading stories. Some reporters were directed by CIA agents in the same way any clandestine field man is run by his 'control.'" Loory said the CIA bought the services of newsmen working for Reuters, Agence France-Presse, Tass "and dozens of newspapers around the world."

A number of U.S. newspapers and Editor & Publisher, the newspaper trade publication have applauded the new CIA policy. We believe they are being shortsighted. The U.S. news media cannot be isolated from the media of the rest of the world. Misleading stories planted by government agents abroad inevitably find their way back to this country and pollute the U.S. news media. Many newspapers, including this one, make extensive use of foreign news sources.

Even if the U.S. news media did live in isolation, there would be no justification for shielding American readers from CIA manipulation of the press while subjecting foreign readers to such manipulation. The deliberate distortion of news by secret government agents is anathema to the concept of a free press.

All of the press needs to be made off-limits to infiltration by intelligence services, as the Inter American Press Association has urged. U.S. news organizations need to protest the partial and unsatisfactory CIA ban on infiltration.

The Evening Telegram

St. John's, Nfld., February 24, 1976

In the aftermath of the congressional investigation into the overt and covert activities of the U.S. Central Intelligence Agency, including revelations of attempts on the life of the leaders of foregin countries, President Ford recently imposed a new set of rules on CIA operations, coinciding with the appointment of its new director George Bush.

The agency will not be permitted to infiltrate domestic organizations except those of non-Americans "reasonably believed" to be acting on behalf of foreign governments; domestic break-ins will be outlawed; also physical surveillance in the U.S. of everyone, except employees or contractors of intelligence agencies. These rules don't apply to the FBI who'll get their own directive from the justice department.

It's a moot point as to how far these rules will go to prevent the sort of thing that happened in the past. However, since new legislation requires the CIA to report to a number of congressional committees, that is tantamount, says one British source, to "having it printed in the papers". What that will do for national security in this dog-eat-dog world is something to think about.

FORT WORTH STAR-TELEGRAM

Fort Worth, Tex., March 3, 1976

New CIA Director George Bush deserves high commendation for one of his first official acts as head of the nation's huge and troubled intelligence unit.

Bush has agreed to one of the recommendations of the House Intelligence Committee by removing any full-time or part-time U.S. journalists from the CIA's payroll.

As part of the same action, he clarified the agency's policy with respect to use of clergymen or missionaries as sources of intelligence. This has been a matter of concern to many church leaders, including Dr. James Harris, president of the Southern Baptist Foreign Mission Board and pastor of University Baptist Church here.

The policy, according to Bush's statement, is for the agency to have "no secret paid or contractual relationship with any American clergyman or missionary."

The action does not bar either journalists or missionaries from offering information voluntarily to the CIA. But it goes about as far as Bush or the agency can go in freeing the two groups from suspicion by foreign governments as agents of the spy organization.

It will be up to individual journalists and missionaries and the organizations they represent to decide whether missionaries and journalists volunteer information to the CIA as acts of patriotism.

The Detroit News

Detroit, Mich., February 15, 1976

This newspaper had and still has reservations about the appointment of George Bush as director of the Central Intelligence Agency. In our view, his experience as a professional politician and chairman of the Republican National Committee should have disqualified him for such a sensitive job.

To his credit, however, in his first public action he has publicly barred the CIA from recruiting agents from among full-time or part-time reporters for American news organizations.

The CIA practice never has been widespread and currently the ban will affect fewer than 20 persons. Yet a few bad apples tend to spoil the whole barrel. The integrity of all U.S. reporters both at home and abroad has been brought under question by the CIA practice, limited though it was.

The agency pointed out that over the years it has had relationships with Americans in many walks of life, reflecting both the individuals' desire to help their country and the CIA's intent to further its foreign intelligence mission.

But the CIA said it had ordered the ban on churchmen and newsmen in view of the concern expressed about the agency's relationships with both, to avoid any appearance of impropriety and in recognition of the two groups' "special status" under the Constitution.

The public should welcome the order, which in effect protects the constitutional guarantees of a free press and freedom of religion. It also points up the difference between the U.S. press and the Communist press, which is simply an arm of the Communist states.

That doesn't stop the Soviet Union, of course, from pretending to protect the free press. It has just forced the International Olympic Committee to cancel the accreditation of Radio Free Europe's reporters to cover the winter Olympics at Innsbruck.

True, Radio Free Europe (RFE) is financed in part by the U.S. government as well as by private U.S. contributions. But its purpose is to provide a fair presentation of news to the people behind the Iron Curtain. For the USSR to call a halt to RFE reporting is not only ironical. It also is an unacceptable example of Soviet censorship — and proof of RFE's effectiveness.

Buffalo Evening News

Buffalo, N.Y., February 16, 1976

The CIA's decision to end any paid or contractual relationships with American journalists or clergymen signifies a measure of healthy reform, a step back from rank cynicism. Without doubt this first public action by the new CIA director, George Bush, reflects an improved sensitivity to significant U. S. values.

For the same reasons, the CIA should adhere to its pledge not to send any of its agents abroad under the false cover of journalists for accedited American news organizations.

The CIA announcement that it saw no impropriety on its part in "the limited use made" of people connected with news, church or missionary groups in the past leaves a doubt, unfortunately, that the right lesson has been learned even yet. For it shows a continuing insensitivity to the fact that the now-admitted use of only a few has the effect of tarnishing the credibility and independent standing abroad of all members of these two professions.

But if this mistake is now truly behind us, not to be repeated, so be it. At least the CIA announcement does now recognize "the special status afforded these institutions under our Constitution." Honoring that special status must now involve scrupulous adherence in the future to the publicly proclaimed no-paid-or-contractual-relationship standard. On this matter, the CIA must practice what it preaches.

St. Louis Post-Dispatch

St. Louis, Mo., February 16, 1976

George Bush, the new director of the Central Intelligence Agency, has properly moved to discontinue all use by the agency of news media employes, clergymen or missionaries as undercover agents. The CIA should have realized before this that it was a reprehensible intelligence practice to use people from these occupations. If the press does not maintain an arms length relationship with government, it can hardly perform its proper function of reporting on government in a disinterested and credible fashion. If members of religious organizations are to ethically serve their constituencies, with whom they often have a confidential relationship, they too must be uninvolved in any covert intelligence activity.

Since the CIA in the past has not understood the corrupting influence of what it was doing and since some journalists and clergymen have not been sensitive to the problem either, the best way to avoid the problem in the future is to bar the agency from infiltrating organizations which must maintain a position of trust with the public.

The Morning Star

Rockford, Ill., February 13, 1976

George Bush, who has now taken over direction of the Central Intelligence Agency (CIA), is canceling from the payroll any agents who are full or part-time U.S. journalists.

The move was recommended by the House Intelligence Committee which investigated the CIA. And it will be applauded as a necessary step by all who care for the independence of the American press.

Newspaper people have two things going for them, neither of them expendable. One is their talents. The other is their credibility.

It is the latter that was imperiled by the CIA practice of recruiting journalists to double as spies.

When a newsgatherer loses independence, credibility goes next.

Journalists who can't see that for themselves cast no credit on their profession. Fortunately, they are an infinitesimal minority.

With Bush's new directive, the vast numbers of journalists will be spared the suspicions and doubts created by the few.

We commend Bush's move.

He said the CIA, however, would welcome any tips it receives regarding foreign threats to domestic security. In other words, a private citizen would still be expected to do a citizen's duty.

That's something quite apart from masquerading as a journalist while conducting spy work. The distinction should not be lost or fogged over.

The Christian Science Monitor

Boston, Mass., February 13, 1976

The first publicly announced action by the new director of the CIA, George Bush, was a promising one. He prohibited the agency from entering into further paid relationships with news correspondents accredited by American organizations and said such "existing relationships" would be brought into conformity "as soon as feasible." The directive also said there are not now and would not be secret paid relationships with American clergymen or missionaries.

According to the House intelligence committee, there already had been some tightening of the use of U.S. press enterprises for CIA cover: "No longer, for example, can a CIA officer in the field arrange for cover without headquarters approval."

Now, by establishing headquarters policy against CIA use of reporters, Mr. Bush takes a step further against a situation raising the gravest questions of press freedom and conflict of interest. Only a few newsmen have been named as alleged CIA employees, but clearly no one should be in the pay of the CIA while attempting to preserve objectivity in informing the public. The House intelligence committee found "disturbing indications that the accuracy of many news stories has been undermined" as a result of CIA use of the press.

The CIA use of clergymen raises the additional question of separation of church and state. The revised CIA policy recognizes the "special status" of both press and religion under the Constitution and seeks to "avoid any appearance of improper use." It will be up to the agency's accountability procedures — and to its executive and congressional watchdog — to see that the policy is carried through.

Meanwhile, the CIA quite rightly continues to welcome information volunteered by individuals, and it notes that cooperation from those in many walks of life in the past has "reflected the desire of Americans to help their country." This is in line with the current effort at correcting the abuses of the intelligence community so it can help the country more. Mr. Bush has started well.

The State

Columbia, S.C., February 17, 1976

THE CENTRAL Intelligence Agency has announced that, effective immediately, it "will not enter into any paid or contractual relationship with any full-time or part-time news correspondent accredited by any U.S. news service, newspaper, periodical, radio or television network or station."

The CIA's use of newsmen informants was curtailed after 1973 disclosures of such employment, but apparently the practice has continued, particularly the use of stringers or free lancers.

We have deplored the hiring of U.S. foreign correspondents for intelligence-gathering activities and the use of press "covers" for CIA agents. The practice threatened the credibility of the U.S. press abroad and had the potential of impairing the press's mission to keep the American public fully and accurately informed on developments in foreign lands.

We further question the professional ethics of newsmen who took pay from the CIA and their employers, who in almost all cases had no knowledge of the CIA connection.

If a newsman comes into possession of information of importance to the U.S. government, he has a duty as a citizen to report it voluntarily to the CIA if he cannot for some reason write it as news. But acting as a paid informant is something else.

We welcome the new hands-off policy by the CIA. It is long overdue.

Rocky Mountain News

A Scripps-Howard Newspaper Reg. U.S. Pat. Off. Colorado's First Newspaper—Founded in 1859

Denver, Colo., February 19, 1976

AMERICANS HAVE a right to expect that what they read and hear from overseas is being reported by newsmen whose only allegiance is to the truth rather than to the CIA or some other government agency.

There simply is no way that a reporter can maintain his contacts or his credibility if his own government insists on using the press as a cover for intelligence activities.

Though only a handful of reporters ever have done intelligence work, CIA Director George Bush wisely has decreed that newsmen, or imposters posing as newsmen, no longer will be used as informants or undercover agents.

The country has more to gain from protecting the lives and reputations of the great majority of legitimate newsmen than from hiring a few reporters and bogus reporters to serve as part-time spies for the CIA.

Los Angeles Times

Los Angeles Calif., February 13, 1976

The Times has asked the Central Intelligence Agency to make public the names of journalists, past and present—including our own, if any—in the employ of the CIA.

We have argued previously that the names of CIA agents should not be disclosed. Recent stories have reported on American journalists in the CIA's employ, and a few have been named. The press-CIA connection is a unique and troubling situation, one that demands disclosure.

The credibility of every news organization is damaged by the allegations. So the record should be set straight.

The Times, as a matter of policy, forbids its correspondents to work for the CIA or any other governmental agency. While we know that this is our policy, and while we can state it unequivocally, we fear that our readers will not be persuaded in light of the revelations of CIA employment of reporters.

Without credibility, a newspaper is compromised. That's why the CIA must tell the American people the names of journalists whom it has employed, full time or part time, as undercover intelligence operatives.

CIA Director George Bush announced Wednesday that, effective immediately, the agency would not employ correspondents working for American news organizations. Existing arrangements will be brought into compliance with the new policy "as soon as feasible."

We applaud the directive, but it does not obviate the need for full disclosure of journalists' past and present CIA employment.

The House Intelligence Committee report, published Wednesday, said the CIA had terminated informant relationships with five correspondents for American periodicals, although the agency continued to use "stringers and free-lancers." The report also said these journalists "apparently do not often disclose this relationship to their editors."

It's possible, then, that news organizations, whose policies may forbid CIA connections, have been compromised.

Without full disclosure, the American press and individual journalists will be tainted. There are some correspondents, to be sure, who will have to account to themselves and the public. But those who have conducted themselves professionally and ethically deserve the protection of the truth.

The Houston Post

Houston, Tex., February 17, 1976

George Bush has begun his new career as director of the Central Intelligence Agency with a sound decision. Acting on a recommendation of the now-defunct House Intelligence Committee, Bush is removing all journalists, both full- and part-time, from the CIA payroll. News people had no business being in the hire of the intelligence agency in the first place. It was bad for the profession, bad for the government and bad for the public.

Such an association, if it becomes public knowledge, jeopardizes the journalist's credibility. Beyond that, it raises questions about the reporter's professional integrity. What's wrong, some may ask, with newsmen and women giving the government information they feel may be important to this country's security? Nothing at all, so long as they do it voluntarily—no strings attached.

To bring the issue closer to home, reporters covering the police beat are as opposed to crime as any other citizen. And they are as bound by the obligation to uphold the law as any other citizen. But they should not be on the police department payroll.

The journalist should not put himself in a position of divided responsibilities. The reporter who agrees to be a paid informant of the CIA or any other agency—possibly even without the knowledge or consent of his employer—may be able to avoid a conflict of interest. But it is doubtful. At the very least, such arrangements create suspicions of protective bias by the reporter toward his secondary benefactor.

These suspicions taint not only the journalists who engage in such activities, but their colleagues in the professional as well. This, in turn, damages the news media's believability and their ability to gather information. George Bush has done journalism a big favor.

Newsday

Garden City, N.Y., February 14, 1976

Representative Otis Pike says that publishing the names of reporters who worked for the CIA would serve no useful purpose. Maybe not, but we think the reporters who didn't—and the people who read their reporting—would rest easier if the stigma were removed from the many and attached solely to the few who earned it. Newspapers in a free society are most effective when people have some degree of faith in their independence. That independence doesn't come easy, and it doesn't take much to shake some readers' faith.

The media have little enough credibility as it is. If people believe that a great many journalists received part of their salaries from the CIA, that credibility would be damaged even more. The press depends as much as any government institution on the appearance of fairness. So long as a cloud hangs over part of it, everyone's hurting.

The announcement by the new CIA director, George Bush, that neither journalists nor missionaries will be enlisted to gather intelligence is welcome, but it does nothing to remove the suspicion against past or present moonlighting agents. The agency should make public the names, not only for its own sake but for the sake of a free press in this country.

PIKE ACCUSES CIA OF STAGING MISSING PAPERS 'MEDIA EVENT'

Rep. Otis G. Pike (D, N.Y.), chairman of the expired House Intelligence Committee, March 9 accused the Central Intelligence Agency of "running a media event" aimed at discrediting him and his former committee. Pike's remarks referred to CIA statements that the Pike committee had failed to return 232 classified documents loaned to the committee. As described by a CIA spokesman, the documents included reports dealing with CIA purchasing and budget audits, the coup in Portugal, disarmament talks with the Soviet Union and other matters.

Pike said that 105 of the documents had been found by committee staff in the files where they were stored at CIA headquarters, and that for another 95 the CIA could produce no receipts from the committee. A CIA spokesman March 9 said that the recovery of the 105 documents had not been "verified;" he also insisted that the 95 documents questioned by Pike had been supplied to the committee. George Bush, director of the CIA, March 16 rejected the idea that the CIA had tried to use reports of missing documents as a media weapon against Pike or the House Intelligence Committee.

Pike March 9 also said that the committee staff director, A. Searle Field, had told him that CIA special counsel Mitchell Rogovin had threatened political retaliation against Pike for leading his committee to vote for the publication of its report, which was highly critical of the CIA. Pike said that Searle told him that Rogovin threatened: "Pike will pay for this, you wait and see—we'll destroy him for this." Rogovin March 9 denied ever having made any such threats against Pike.

St. Louis Globe-Democrat

St. Louis, Mo., March 6, 1976

More than 230 "top secret" and "secret" documents which the Central Intelligence Agency turned over to the House Intelligence Committee are reported missing and the chairman of this committee doesn't have the foggiest idea what happened to them.

This is one more incredible, sordid chapter in the story of this committee headed by Rep. Otis G. Pike, New York Democrat. Only a few weeks ago it made headlines by leaking its entire voluminous report attacking U.S. intelligence operations to CBS newsman Daniel Schorr, who then turned it over to the Village Voice for publication.

The missing CIA documents cover such sensitive subjects as the CIA budget, strategic arms limitations, the 1974 coup in Portugal, the agency's use of business firms to cover their actions and the assignment of CIA personnel to other agencies.

What does Pike, a constant critic of the CIA, have to say about this?

He discounted the possibility of theft and said the documents probably had been turned over to the National Archives, destroyed or returned to another agency by mistake.

If any of the things happened to the missing CIA documents that Pike surmises, it would prove that his committee is even worse than many people suspected.

Sending top secret CIA documents to the National Archives? Is there actually someone on the committee staff that brainless? Destroy secret CIA documents? Is this what the committee does with documents?

Pike has given those who have been critical of congressional oversight of U.S. intelligence operations more valuable ammunition. He has demonstrated how carelessly sensitive materials sent to the committee are handled, which is almost as bad as the practice of leaking this secret information to the media.

Unless these documents are recovered, the Executive Branch should not permit any more secret documents to be sent to these oversight committees. This apparently is one of the fastest ways for transmitting them to the public and making secret U.S. intelligence operations an open book to foreign countries.

Perhaps the nation would be better served if the CIA investigated Chairman Pike and his committee instead of vice versa.

The Houston Post

Houston, Tex., March 11, 1976

It seems Congress just can't keep secrets. If it doesn't leak them, it loses them. The latest instance of slipshod congressional handling of sensitive national security information is the disappearance of documents the Central Intelligence Agency gave a House committee during the panel's investigattion of U.S. intelligence agencies.

Rep. Otis Pike, D-N.Y., chairman of the now-defunct House intelligence committee, now says his staff has accounted for 200 of the 232 papers, 189 of them top secret, which the CIA had reported missing. Commenting earlier on a letter from CIA Director George Bush inquiring about the missing documents, Pike said they had probably been destroyed or were in the archives. He also said it was possible some of the papers had been sent to the State Department by mistake. "I think it's nothing, frankly," he said. Some of those document contain information on the CIA budget, nuclear arms limitation, the 1974 Portugal coup and the CIA use of business firms for cover.

The New York congressman's belief that the missing documents have not been stolen is not particularly reassuring since the final report of his intelligence committee, which was secret, was leaked to CBS newsman Daniel Schorr. Another House committee is investigating the leak but has refused FBI assistance.

Pike claims that some of the documents did not have to be returned to the CIA anyway. But even if that is true, the committee had an obligation to keep closer track of them. The fact that some are still unaccounted for means they could be floating around Washington open to theft, if, indeed, they haven't already been stolen.

The case of the missing documents, disturbing in itself, also illustrates the difficulty of defining a congressional role for intelligence oversight. Yet, in the wake of House and Senate committee investigations of the intelligence agencies, efforts are afoot in Congress to exert greater control over them. The Senate Government Operations Committee, for instance, has voted to create a committee with power to release classified information over presidential objections and review covert operations in advance.

Congress should have a part in overseeing the activities of the nation's intelligence community, and not the moribund role played by congressional oversight committees in the past. Unfortunately, the leaks of secret information and the sloppy handling of classified documents by congressional committees and individual lawmakers expose a dangerous immaturity in the legislative branch's approach to this critically sensitive function of national security.

THE KNICKERBOCKER NEWS
··· UNION-STAR ···

Albany, N.Y., March 6, 1976

Secrets can be serious, but when a committee of the House of Representatives has to admit it lost or inadvertently destroyed more than 200 secret CIA documents, the situation becomes absurd.

Charged with failing to return the documents to the CIA is the House Intelligence Committee, whose own "secret" report was leaked by Daniel Schorr, the broadcaster, after the full House had voted it should not be made public.

The documents in question shouldn't have been easy to either mislay or lose. There were more than 200 of them, which would make substantial bulk, and they were stamped either "Top Secret" or "Top Secret-Codeword." The committee chairman, Representative Otis Pike, believes they probably were destroyed. As alternatives he suggests they might have been turned over to the national archives or sent to another agency.

It is obvious, however, that Mr. Pike doesn't really know what happened to them. He must be considered less than a vigilant guardian of the nation's classified information.

How many of those 200 or more documents really should be considered secret is another matter entirely. Probably some bore "Top Secret" classifications only from a bureaucrat's whim. But that is beside the point in the current instance.

The documents had been delivered to the committee by the CIA in good faith. They were classified, and that classification deserved at least sufficient respect from the House committee and its staff to insure their safe return.

Representative Pike has discounted the possibility the documents were stolen. He may be right. But then again they might be published in full some day by some off-beat newspaper or magazine or blabbed by some commentator.

Wait and see.

DAILY NEWS

New York, N.Y., March 6, 1976

The Central Intelligence Agency is more than a trifle upset because 232 documents it loaned to the House Intelligence Committee have not been returned, and nobody seems to know for sure where they are.

Rep. Pike

Included are some top-secret items—including 13 that deal with the strategic arms limitation talks, and others concerning Portugal.

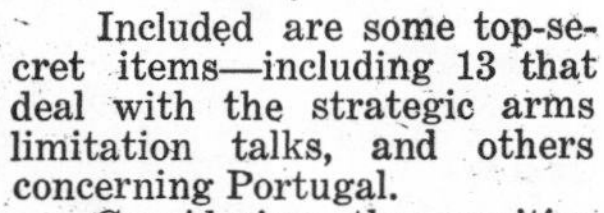

Considering the sensitive nature of the missing material, Committee Chairman Otis Pike (D-N.Y.) is taking a pretty casual attitude toward the whole affair.

Rep. Pike has pledged to cooperate in a hunt for the papers. At the same time, he suggests that perhaps the CIA's bookkeeping is shoddy, or that his staffers mistakenly bundled the reports up and sent them to the National Archives.

We trust that the House as a whole will take a more serious view of the situation. Its reputation for responsible conduct already has been grievously damaged by the wholesale leaks from Pike's panel. The chamber will sink even further in public esteem if it turns out that the committee was wantonly careless in handling classified reports.

New Orleans, La., March 6, 1976

Sad — and revealing — to say, the confusion over what happened to some 200 highly classified Central Intelligence Agency documents supplied to the House Intelligence Committee is a fitting finale to that committee's performance as scourge of the spymasters.

CIA Director George Bush wrote to committee chairman Otis Pike, D-N.Y., after the probe wrapup to say 232 "sensitive classifed CIA documents" were missing at roll call. They involved, says CIA special counsel Mitchell Rogovin, such things as the CIA budget, arms control, the 1974 coup in Portugal and CIA use of business firms as cover.

Rep. Pike and his former chief aide say the documents were probably destroyed. But "probably" doesn't quite do it when you're dealing with top secret intelligence data and making a media melodrama out of telling the nation's intelligence services how to run their businesses better.

The CIA's letter, further, provided a list of what had not been turned back, but Mr. Pike wrote for more information such as when they were given to the committee and to whom. Since they were only "probably" destroyed — or sent to the national archives or to some other agency, as also suggested — there must be no burn logs or receipts, the basic instruments of secret document control.

The chief characteristic of the House Intelligence Committee and its Senate counterpart seemed to be their leakiness — assertedly in the cause of establishing better congressional oversight of undercover activities. In the old Cold War days, when congressional oversight committees were little more than rubber stamps, security at any rate was virtually absolute.

We agree that better congressional monitoring of covert operations is desirable. But the record of the committees espousing it inclines us — and doubtless the concerned public — to wonder whether the potential ills of the old system are not much to be preferred to a new system involving such groups.

THE DALLAS TIMES HERALD

Dallas, Tex., March 8, 1976

IF THERE was doubt that Texan George Bush would move swiftly and surely into leadership of the maligned CIA, he is removing it in the first days with direct action in protecting vital, secret functions of the intelligence agency.

Bush has demanded of the leaking House Intelligence Committee headed by Rep. Otis Pike, D-N.Y.—now defunct—that it produce 232 missing CIA documents, including 13 top secret papers on the strategic arms talks.

Somewhere, the documents have been "misplaced." It is the kind of stuff that made the House committee suspect and caused the entire House to vote against full revelation of the Pike committee report.

Bush, in an exchange of letters with Rep. Pike dating back into February, pointedly has asked for an inventory of material supplied the committee for its recent investigation.

Rep. Pike is suggesting that perhaps the 232 missing documents could be in sealed files delivered to the National Archives. But Bush's efforts so far have already turned up a few of the files and he strongly urges that the whole batch be reinventoried in the search for the vital top secret papers.

It suggests that, just perhaps, there could be new and damaging revelations from the dead committee that would parallel those CBS Correspondent Dan Schorr made available to the Village Voice, a New York weekly just prior to dissolution of the Pike committee.

Critics who opposed the confirmation of Bush as CIA Director indicated that he was politically oriented and could not serve in the sensitive secrecy of an intelligence agency with full distinction.

We argued at the time that they did not know the depth of Bush's integrity and capability in any field. He has given full demonstration in the Congress, the United Nations and as special envoy to the Republic of China.

He will perform with the same intensity in the CIA. And he has started by assuring Congress that he wants no more hanky panky in dealing with his agency's secrets. He is right and the documents should be found — wherever they are — and returned to the CIA, not the New York Times or the Village Voice.

HERALD EXAMINER

Los Angeles, Calif., March 12, 1976

Of unusual significance was the overwhelming House vote last week to investigate the shortcomings of one of its own committees.

The vote called for an inquiry into the scandalous leakage of confidential information by the so-called Pike Committee during its now defunct probe of the nation's security agencies, particularly the Central Intelligence Agency. It came as the CIA made formal protest that 232 documents loaned to the committee have not been returned.

Rep. Otis G. Pike (D-N.Y.), chairman of the House Select Committee on intelligence, took his usual casual attitude toward the lack of responsibility shown from start to finish in his inept and gravely damaging probe of our security agencies. He suggested that maybe the CIA is mistaken, despite the fact that 13 of the missing documents are stamped Top Secret. On the other hand, he admitted, the missing material might have been sent to the National Archives, or simply burned by error.

His attitude reflects the conduct of his special committee right up to its final report. Although veiled with secrecy by vote of the full House, parts of the final report were leaked to some newspapers and printed in full by one. This was too much for the full House, which thereupon voted an inquiry into the Pike Committee leaks by its Ethics Committee. The latter has requested $350,000 to do the job.

The situation deserves the widest possible emphasis for two reasons. It is extraordinary, in the first place, for congressmen to vote an investigation of each other — and this is really encouraging news. Far more important, however, is that the forthcoming probe of bungling probers may instill a more serious sense of responsibility among our lawmakers with regard to national security matters.

Our national security operations have been damaged severely by the publication of secrets leaked through both the Pike Committee and its Senate twin headed by Sen. Frank Church (D-Idaho). It is not too much to say that both committees, in seeking the political limelight, have committed a huge and threatening act of sabotage against the welfare and even the safety of all American citizens.

HERALD-JOURNAL

Syracuse, N.Y., March 9, 1976

The seemingly cavalier attitude of Rep. Otis Pike, chairman of the House Intelligence Committee, toward 232 "lost" documents that were borrowed from the CIA but never returned is nothing short of irresponsible.

With an unnerving lack of concern, Pike throws up his hands and says maybe the documents were destroyed; or maybe they went to the National Archives; or maybe . . . or maybe. . .

Daniel Schorr delivered a major blow to the prestige of the Congress when he peddled the Pike Committee report to a New York City newspaper, and Pike's casual approach to the matter has not helped to heal the wounds.

We're beginning to understand why government agencies are hesitant to open their books to Congress.

THE MILWAUKEE JOURNAL

Milwaukee, Wisc., March 13, 1976

The latest scuffle between Rep. Pike's House Intelligence Committee and the CIA over so-called lost documents has caused Pike to cry foul. He has good grounds for such complaint.

The focus of the latest incident has been a number of highly sensitive CIA classified documents supposedly given to the Intelligence Committee but not returned. CIA Director Bush wanted to know where they were. Pike initially could not find them, saying that they were either destroyed by the committee or carted off to the National Archives in sealed files. That was disputed by the CIA.

If the documents were unaccounted for, it was another example of what appeared to be sloppy management by Pike and his committee. After all, the committee had the look of a sieve because of the massive leaks of its findings following investigation of the intelligence community.

Now it appears, however, that not all the lost documents were "lost." Pike says about half the documents have been found and another large portion purported to be missing never left the CIA. They had been examined by the committee on the CIA premises; the CIA has had them all the time.

The CIA lamely says the incident has been blown out of proportion by the press. The intelligence agency only intended to ask politely about locating the classified papers, it says. But there seems to be more than a hint of political motivation behind Bush's queries — putting the heat on Pike would take the heat off the CIA.

Pike and his committee are not lily white in the handling of their investigation of the intelligence community. In this instance, however, they suffered more abuse than they deserved.

BUFFALO EVENING NEWS

Buffalo, N.Y., March 12, 1976

The CIA official involved has flatly denied threatening that his agency was out to destroy Rep. Otis Pike (D., N. Y.), as charged on the House floor by Mr. Pike, and there is probably no way to prove what was really said. But surely the last thing we need, in the wake of the CIA investigations, is any lingering shadow of a threat by members of that beleaguered agency to wreak vengeance on their congressional tormentors.

The House's undisciplined probe of the CIA wasn't well-handled. But the House had every right, even a duty, to pursue its legislative oversight functions. Rep. Pike may not have been the ideal chairman, but he is an elected legislator doing his job. Any threats by the CIA — like those reported in Mr. Pike's House speech — would be wholly indefensible.

Nor does the CIA seem very convincing with its complaint that the Pike committee failed to return 232 secret documents. Rep. Pike told the House that his committee staff found 105 of the documents in material returned to the CIA, which he said also had admitted it had no record of sending most of the rest to the committee in the first place.

The CIA has reason to feel put upon by some of the loose-lipped excesses during the Pike investigation, but vengefulness and spite won't help matters. Let the CIA stick to its own knitting, concentrating on intelligence functions abroad — which aren't beyond improvement — and forget any idea of paying back its critics here at home.

CBS SUSPENDS SCHORR; HOUSE VOTES TO INVESTIGATE LEAK OF CIA REPORT

CBS News relieved its correspondent Daniel Schorr of all reporting duties Feb. 23 for an "indefinite period." The action was taken "in view of the adversary situation" in which Schorr was placed "in pending government investigations" as a result of his leaking the secret House Intelligence Committee report to the New York weekly, *The Village Voice*. Schorr acknowledged Feb. 12 that he was the source of the copy of the report from which the *Voice* published substantial excerpts Feb. 11 and Feb. 18. Schorr said he had decided to arrange for the report's publication after he came to believe that he was "possibly the sole possessor of the document outside the government" and that he "could not be the one responsible for suppressing" its full publication. Although CBS News and *The New York Times* had made public most of the findings of the report, the *Voice* issues contained the first extensive excerpts from the report, publication of which had been blocked pending censorship by the intelligence agencies, by a vote of the full House on Jan. 29.

Schorr said Feb. 12 that he had obtained the "confidential cooperation" of the Reporter's Committee of the Freedom of the Press—a group that aided journalists facing legal problems in connection with their work—in finding a publisher for the report. Schorr said that an unnamed intermediary had told him that Clay Felker, publisher of *The Village Voice* and *New York* magazine, had offered to make a "substantial contribution" to the committee in return for the report. The committee issued a statement Feb. 12 saying that it had agreed to accept any proceeds that might emerge from publication of the report "to be used in defense of the First Amendment" and that it had put Schorr in touch with a lawyer acquainted with publishing. Schorr, who had originally denied any role in the *Voice* publication of the report, said that it had become "pointless" to conceal his part in the leak because of the committee's failure to maintain confidentiality.

The House Feb. 19 voted 269–115 to have the ethics committee investigate "the circumstances surrounding the publication of the text." Schorr was cited specifically, for "alleged actions ... [which] may be in contempt of or a breach of the privileges of this house." Opponents of the resolution voiced concern that it would have a "chilling effect" on the freedom of the press. Supporters argued that it was necessary in order to "protect the integrity and the process of the House." President Ford Feb. 12 had offered House speaker Carl Albert (D, Okla.) the "full resources" of the executive branch in investigating the leak. Albert Feb. 13 declined the offer.

Secretary of State Henry Kissinger Feb. 12 castigated the leak as "a new version of McCarthyism." The report had attacked Kissinger for making "comments ... at variance with the facts" (in reference to the reporting of alleged Soviet violations of the SALT accords) and having a "passion for secrecy."

THE ROANOKE TIMES

Roanoke, Va., February 25, 1976

The case of Daniel Schorr, suspended CBS newsman, is in the gray area—but a very dark gray area. When he released a House committee's report on intelligence, the committee itself had approved the release so there was justification for what Mr. Schorr said on television.

The full House of Representatives, however, voted to keep the report secret so Mr. Schorr released his copy not to his employer, CBS News, but to this other crowd, in the print media, the *Village Voice*, anti-establishment New York newspaper. Mr. Schorr may have gotten too big for his britches.

The Miami Herald

Miami, Fla., February 25, 1976

WHEN a newsman gets involved personally in a story, he's in trouble. Daniel Schorr did exactly that in turning over to the weekly Village Voice a copy of what has come to be called The Pike Papers, a report of the House Select Committee on Intelligence. CBS did the proper thing in suspending him of all duties as a correspondent.

Mr. Schorr played the role of a good investigative reporter in getting the report which tells of efforts by the Ford Administration, Secretary of State Kissinger and the CIA to frustrate a congressional search for truth about matters important to a free society. Mr. Schorr went on the air with as much of the report as a 30-minute network news show can handle.

When the television newsman went farther at that point, it needs to be remembered that he had been the victim of an illegal investigation and smear campaign orchestrated by the Nixon White House as part of the Watergate scandal. Mr. Schorr sought a quick paperback publication of The Pike Papers because he saw in the House committee report additional evidence of abuse by the Executive branch of government in classifying information.

Unable to get a paperback worked out, Mr. Schorr did as Daniel Ellsberg did in releasing the Pentagon Papers to The New York Times. We are confident Mr. Schorr sought no personal profit, but he stumbled badly when he suggested a contribution by The Village Voice to the Reporters' Committee for Freedom of the Press.

Here again he got involved with his own story in seeking to make the owners of the weekly newspaper "do good" at the same time they were going to do well with the exclusive publication of what the House had voted to keep secret.

We have read the findings of the Pike committee. They reveal little that had not been known before. What is new is not dangerous to the national security of this country. The report is valuable because it reveals, as the Pentagon Papers did, how close this free nation has come to the dictatorship of an imperial presidency. It reveals how the Administration whispered plans into the ears of sympathetic congressmen to sneak around any real oversight of intelligence activities.

It also reveals such heights of bureaucratic stupidity as classifying as secret a Jack Anderson column that appeared earlier in hundreds of newspapers.

Congress should never have voted to keep this report on the CIA secret. And we see no profit to anyone in the House Ethics Committee search for the person who made it available to a newsman.

But Daniel Schorr should have taken himself off the story when he found himself a part of it. That is when a reporter's objectivity is lost and when the reader has to worry about the role of the press.

THE PLAIN DEALER

Cleveland, Ohio, February 18, 1976

Daniel Schorr never was regarded as a real top-flight news journalist. Still, he had a good rating as a news correspondent for CBS, a man skilled in investigative journalism. No question that his reputation rose when former President Nixon tried to get Schorr's job because Schorr became inquisitive about Nixon's shady affairs. Schorr gained public sympathy because he was on Nixon's blacklist.

The broadcasting media now have been hurt by Schorr who admitted he leaked a House Intelligence Committee report to the Village Voice newspaper which printed classified information contained therein. So Schorr turns out to be short of moral scruples, same as the Nixon bunch. We are sorry that a semi-hero turned out to be a semi-bad guy.

OKLAHOMA CITY TIMES

Oklahoma City, Okla., February 17, 1976

RISING concern over leaks of highly classified information from the House Select Intelligence Committee has prompted a New York state congressman, Rep. Sam Stratton, to seek a contempt citation against Daniel Schorr, the CBS television network reporter.

The concern is understandable, but Stratton's proposal is an over-reaction that should be rejected by the House.

It is true that the unauthorized flow of information out of the committee during its six-month investigation of intelligence agency operations more nearly resembles a flood than a leak. And members of Congress ought to be disturbed at the damage being done to national security and U.S. foreign policy by detailed disclosure of sensitive dossiers and files.

But in seeking punitive action against Schorr, Stratton is aiming the wrong weapon at the wrong target.

Schorr is completely within his First Amendment rights in refusing to reveal who slipped him a draft of tne committee's report before it had been approved and issued. If the Congress is really concerned over leaks, it should zero in on the committee staff.

Schorr obviously could not have obtained the draft without the cooperation of somebody on the committee or staff with access to the secret material. Sen. William Brock, R-Tenn., is more nearly on the right track with a bill to impose stiff fines and jail terms on congressional staffers who violate their positions of trust.

However, Schorr did his own case and journalistic ethics no service by fatuously arguing that he had a duty as a newsman to arrange for publication of the secret draft by a New York City weekly in addition to his own broadcast commentary on it.

It is one thing for a reporter to exercise some degree of voluntary restraint and responsibility when commenting on classified material, regardless of how it came into his possession. It is quite another thing to have an unauthorized report printed in its entirely and thereby disseminating information that could be misleading or damaging to U.S. relations with other countries.

The Dallas Morning News

Dallas, Tex., February 27, 1976

"I GOT hit," says Daniel Schorr, "by a swinging pendulum." He may be right. If so, it was high time the pendulum got to swinging.

Schorr, of course, is the CBS correspondent who turned over to the Village Voice the officially suppressed report of the House Intelligence Committee, for which act he is under investigation by the House. The investigation led to his suspension by CBS.

"There have always been in our country two great urges," Schorr said in a news conference apologia Wednesday, "one toward security, one toward liberty. The pendulum constantly swings between them . . .But security always comes back. And the pendulum appears to have started its return course. . ." The veteran correspondent aches where the pendulum struck him.

One reason for the violence of the blow is the vast distance the pendulum had to travel for it to find Daniel Schorr. For months the two congressional committees investigating the U.S. intelligence establishment—aided and egged on by much of the media—have thought fit to tell national security secrets that only a few years ago would never have been let out.

Disclosure after disclosure has eroded the prestige and effectiveness of once-respected organizations like the FBI and CIA. Not only has their effectiveness been damaged here at home but also abroad. All too little thought has been given to the rather fundamental proposition that the American public's "right to know" means, by extension, the world's "right to know." We have hung our dirty laundry out in view of the whole planet, and the sight has been manifestly unappealing.

But now the pendulum has begun swinging back. The House overrode its intelligence committee chairman's objections and voted to keep secret the committee's report until it could be edited with a view to the national safety.

Enter Schorr at this point. He has a copy of the report. The House will not publish the report, will it? Very well; Daniel Schorr will see that the Truth Comes Out. The Village Voice, a somewhat seamy Greenwich Village publication, is eager to strike a blow for liberty. And so the Truth Comes Out.

One point in Schorr's analysis of the ensuing flap is regrettable.

He poses a dichotomy between freedom and security. There need be no such dichotomy—not if responsible freedom is what is aimed at and not the brand of who-cares-let-it-all-hang-out freedom espoused by Schorr.

There most assuredly exists a right to know. But as The News has observed before, that right is far from absolute. The safety and security of the nation is a consideration that matters, if only because without public safety, there can be no real freedom—something Schorr would know had he ever read Thomas Hobbes.

Ideally, the pendulum ought to dangle somewhere midway between liberty and security; between the right to know all and the right to know nothing. By no means ought security to become a secular deity. Balance is what we need; balance, sad to say, is what we have so conspicuously lacked for so many months now.

THE INDIANAPOLIS NEWS

Indianapolis, Ind., February 18, 1976

CBS news correspondent Daniel Schorr has admitted his responsibility for the publication of most of the Select House Intelligence Committee's still-classified secret report.

"I decided that with much of the contents already known I could not be the one responsible for suppressing the report," Schorr stated after his role became known.

Working through the Reporters Committee for the Freedom of the Press, Schorr arranged for publication in the Village Voice. His fee, amount as yet unrevealed, was paid to the Reporters' Committee.

Schorr said that when he realized he had a copy of the report which would probably not become public, "I felt myself confronted with an inescapable decision of journalistic conscience."

Obviously Schorr will not name the House committee member who leaked the report, but he said he received it at a time "when its general release was expected within a few days." He had reported highlights on CBS news, but he said he believed a wider publication of the contents was necessary even though the House had voted 246 to 124 to keep the report a secret.

Evidently Schorr solved his moral dilemma by reasoning he could not cooperate in supressing a report "originally meant for public distribution."

The contents of that report were classified information released to the House committee under the explicit agreement with the President that they not be made public. It was not Schorr, however, who made that agreement, but in our opinion what he did was a mistake in judgment.

Newsmen partially earn their keep through use of inside sources and news leaks, yet there are some cases in which national security interests and a higher ethic than reporting the news prevail. It is a situation not without its irony, because at this point a journalistic ethic does dictate Schorr protect the confidentiality of his sources.

Rep. Samuel Stratton, D-N.Y., has said he will move in Congress to cite Schorr for contempt. Stratton is undeniably justified in his anger, yet it is misdirected.

The issue is not one of Schorr's being willfully "good" or "bad." Schorr received no personal reward. The ethics of the Reporters Committee is more questionable than Schorr's.

Whether there is some legal means for disciplining Schorr is something lawyers may wish to debate. Whether he did, in the long run, do the right thing is something for his conscience to decide.

But the House should take care of its own. Representatives are in no position for verbal mudslinging until they deal with whomever among them willfully violated their own ruling. That individual is the one who truly deserves the contempt.

The Register-Republic

Rockford, Ill., February 17, 1976

Daniel Schorr, CBS newsman, has himself become an item in the news for having received, and "leaked" to a weekly New York City newspaper the contents of a secret House report on CIA intelligence activities.

Schorr may be cited for contempt by the House which voted 246 to 124 to withhold the report from the public until sensitive security material could be deleted.

The legal aspects are reminiscent of the troubles Daniel Ellsberg invoked upon himself when he "leaked" the so-called "Pentagon Papers" to the public. Ellsberg contended the public's need to know about Vietnam blunders exceeded any secrecy guidelines.

That case never came to trial because the government itself was found to have abused the defendant's constitutional rights by breaking into the office of Ellsberg's psychiatrist and by tapping the defendant's phone.

But legal aspects aside, the Schorr incident raises short-term as well as long-range questions, some of them of the somberest nature.

The immediate question is why Schorr saw fit to share his information with the Village Voice, a newspaper competitor, rather than broadcasting it over the facilities of CBS.

There is a heavy hint here that CBS was not prepared to reap the discontent that would obviously ensue, although the network has said it will support Schorr and the confidentiality of his sources.

So there's that quandary.

Of over-riding import, however, is the ethical question that Schorr's action raises.

Was he acting in the best interests of journalism when he siphoned the House report into print?

Schorr says that he agonized over the decision and concluded that it was not his judgment to make, that he had no choice but to release the information.

Considering the adversary nature of a free press reporting upon a free government, we are wary of all restraints that officials would place on the press aside from the obvious rules of libel.

But in this instance, we are mindful that House members who know intimately the findings of the CIA report were constrained not to publicize it for reasons of national security.

And, however misused "national security" was as a device by the Nixon administration to cloak illegal conduct, there is a bona fide area known as "national security."

It embraces those acts that foreign powers could use for our nation's peril.

At least tacitly, CBS seems to have acknowledged this same principle.

It's worth pondering. it mandates self-discipline and immense restraint.

BUFFALO EVENING NEWS

Buffalo, N.Y., February 20, 1976

However he may try to sugar-coat his own rationalizations, CBS Correspondent Daniel Schorr has covered himself, his employer and his profession with no glory or honor by his inexcusable merchandising of a leaked copy of the still-classified House Intelligence Committee report. His act of arrogant bravado in taking it wholly upon himself to declassify a document which the House had voted 2-to-1 to keep classified was a clear abuse of his credentials as a correspondent for a reputable news agency.

Far from striking a blow for the public's right to know, as he evidently intended to do, Mr. Schorr succeeded only in muddying that important issue while compromising his own role as a bona fide journalist and thereby diminishing in some degree the credibility of all his professional colleagues. For he was not here acting the aggressive reporter, bringing in a sensitive story about which his editors could then make responsible judgments on whether or how much to broadcast or publish. He was making himself rather the conduit — idealizing himself perhaps in the role of a "Daniel Ellsberg" who, having obtained a kind of bootleg access to classified secrets, was determined to use whatever means he could to break it out into the public domain.

And, what is perhaps most ironic about Mr. Schorr's ethical lapse is that he has done to his profession's reputation the very kind of damage that some CIA agents have done by posing as journalists or that some journalists have done by moonlighting for the CIA. In Mr. Schorr's case, instead of taking information he obtained on his reporter's credentials and peddling it to the CIA, he peddled it for a consideration to a publication willing to print classified secrets despite the strong feeling of both the President and the House that this would risk damaging our national security or putting the lives of U. S. agents in jeopardy.

MANCHESTER NEW HAMPSHIRE UNION LEADER

Manchester, N.H., February 22, 1976

We hope the House Committee on Standards of Official Conduct comes down with all fours on one Daniel Schorr, the insufferable CBS news correspondent who admits responsibility for publication of a classified intelligence report in a New York newspaper.

Schorr's part was just the latest act in an incredible comedy being performed by the "leaky Congress." It was the subject of an earlier editorial on this page two weeks ago.

The "secret report" was compiled by the House Select Committee on Intelligence and concerned certain CIA and State Department activities over the last two decades. Even before the report was finalized, juicy bits of it had made the newspapers. Still, the full House overruled select committee chairman Otis Pike's desire to "tell all" and voted to let the White House review the report for possible deletion of sensitive information.

As it turns out, relatively little of what has been published was shocking or detrimental to national security in itself. But the fact that a mere handful of publicity-seeking congressmen, aides and newsmen can deliberately disregard Congressional and Executive Branch pleas, regulations and warnings is most damaging. How can foreign governments be expected to deal candidly with the U.S. if their security problems and ours are going to be splashed all over the liberal newspapers for our joint enemies to see?

Getting back to Mr. Schorr, he had the gall to excuse his action by saying, "I could not be the one responsible for suppressing the report." That's true enough. It wasn't Mr. Schorr's "responsibility" or any of his damn business since an overwhelming majority of the House, whose responsibility it is, had already voted to suppress the report.

Of course, liberal defenders of CBS and Mr. Schorr will argue that punishing him (a move is underway to cite him for contempt and strip him of his House press card) would mean little since some of the report had previously been "leaked." To that, we argue that not only should Schorr be censured but so too should the Congressman or aides who gave Schorr and others the information.

THE CINCINNATI ENQUIRER

Cincinnati, Ohio, February 20, 1976

"THE IDEAL journalist, the ideal newspaperman," said J. Russell Wiggins, once the editorial page editor of the Washington Post, a former president of the American Society of Newspaper Editors and a former U.S. ambassador to the United Nations, "is a man who never forgets which side of the footlights he's on, who never forgets that he is a reporter, a recounter, a narrator and not an actor, who never forgets that he is an observer and not a mover and shaker."

That elemental rule of orthodox journalism is one that Daniel Schorr obviously has forgotten. For as the Columbia Broadcasting System's (CBS) correspondent specializing in the multifaceted investigation of the Central Intelligence Agency (CIA), Mr. Schorr has stepped over the line that separates observers from actors and become himself an actor — a starring actor, at that—in the CIA drama.

As such, Mr. Schorr was not content to let the CIA investigation unfold at the pace of the investigators' choice. He elected instead to hasten the process by causing to be delivered into the hands of the Village Voice, a New York City publication, the final report of the House Select Committee on Intelligence, despite the fact that the full House had voted, at President Ford's earnest urgings, not to make the report public. Mr. Schorr did so, judging from his own explanations, because he felt chosen by destiny to frustrate and confound those who, in his view, were seeking to perpetrate a massive cover-up of CIA misdeeds.

Mr. Schorr would be a more convincing hero if he had revealed the full scope of his report on CBS television, which is, after all, his employer. Why did he choose a competing medium—a hippie newspaper? Could it be that CBS had its chance and preferred, in the national interest, not to reveal what the President and the House felt should not be revealed? If that was the case, shouldn't CBS' refusal have been a signal to Mr. Schorr to think twice about revealing it?

Unless the President, the CIA and the House majority are wrong, Mr. Schorr has done serious damage to the security of the CIA and its operatives around the world.

Just as important in the long run, perhaps, he has strengthened the suspicions of many longtime media watchers that Washington-based television correspondents are not the detached, disinterested, objective, professional reporters they are assumed to be and that they themselves invariably claim to be, but are instead the self-anointed purveyors of a specific point of view about the nature of which their audiences can only speculate.

It may turn out that Mr. Schorr has broken no law, although the Department of Justice is certainly warranted in determining whether he has.

But he has seriously embarrassed the House of Representatives and challenged the House to utilize whatever means are available to it to determine who made the committee's secret report available to Mr. Schorr in the first place.

Some in the House undoubtedly have delved into the alleged misdeeds of the CIA out of a sense of righteous indignation, with the nation's best interests at heart. Others, we fear, have had as their goal the permanent disabling of the CIA. The net results of their efforts, whatever their purposes, has been to shake the public's faith not so much in the CIA as in the House itself.

The House has emerged, in the public's view, as a floundering institution incapable of policing itself, much less a sensitive and crucial agency like the CIA.

And if anyone needed proof that the House of Representatives is ill equipped to exercise a significant role in overseeing CIA covert activities in the future, the House itself has provided an abundance.

The State

Columbia, S.C., March 1, 1976

THE involvement of CBS newsman Daniel Schorr in the publication of the secret report of the House Intelligence Committee on intelligence reforms raises again questions about the proper function of newsmen.

Mr. Schorr, long a correspondent in Washington, procured a copy of the first draft of the committee report when its publication appeared imminent. He has not said from whom he obtained it.

In response to appeals by the White House and responsible congressmen, the House voted 246 to 124 to bar the committee's release of the report because it contained secret information which President Ford said would adversely affect American intelligence agencies.

On the same day the House committee filed the report, *Village Voice*, a publication in Greenwich Village in New York City, published excerpts of it in a 24-page supplement. Two days later Mr. Schorr confirmed that he had given the report to *Village Voice* because, "I decided that with so much of the contents already known, I could not be the one responsible for suppressing the report."

CBS responded at first by switching Mr. Schorr from his Capitol Hill reporting duties, and a week later suspended him indefinitely from its news staff. We do not know at this writing what the final disposition of Mr. Schorr's employment with the network will be.

It is our belief that newsmen have the obligation to seek out and to report the truth. But, as in all endeavors, there are boundaries. Newsmen are not obligated to receive stolen government documents.

Furthermore, Mr. Schorr's turning the secret over to another medium strongly suggests malice — an unacceptable trait for journalists. Indeed, we wonder at the purpose of the giver of the secret documents to Mr. Schorr in the first place.

We suggested long ago in connection with the Pentagon Papers theft that journalists enjoy no special status as American citizens that exempts them from ordinary responsibilities. Receiving stolen classified government documents is a serious offense, and at a minimum, Mr. Schorr should be held accountable for that.

He deserves no prize for American citizenship — or journalism.

The Evening Gazette

Worcester, Mass., February 17, 1976

Through enterprise and good contacts, presumably, Daniel Schorr of CBS obtained a copy of the secret House Intelligence Committee report. He caused a mild sensation by broadcasting parts of it. There were other leaks, in other media.

Then the Manhattan weekly, the Village Voice, printed a long excerpt. From where? From Schorr. It seems that he arranged secretly for the information to be sold. The proceeds were to go to a third party, the Reporters' Committee for Freedom of the Press.

This was a dark business. Reporters who obtain government documents ought not to sell them under the counter to other media or to anyone else. Schorr obviously got the document because he was working in Washington as a CBS representative. It would be interesting to know whether CBS authorized the sale to the Village Voice.

And the Reporters' Committee, a group that has done constructive work up to now, did not enhance its reputation by accepting payment for this transaction.

There are many questions to be answered in this matter. On what is known already, the incident reflects serious discredit on Schorr, the Village Voice and the Reporters' Committee. They, and CBS, owe the public a full explanation of the entire transaction. To the extent that they stay silent, they will feed the false notion that reporters obtain secret government information to peddle it or for some purpose other than to inform the public through the news organization for which they work.

Chicago Tribune

Chicago, Ill., February 17, 1976

Few people are more indignant over corporate bribery and other forms of official misconduct, we suspect, than CBS correspondent Daniel Schorr, New York's anti-establishment weekly Village Voice, and the Reporter's Committee for a Free Press, a group committed to the 1st Amendment rights of reporters.

Yet we now learn from Mr. Schorr that it was he who obtained a copy of the secret House Intelligence Committee report on the CIA and the FBI, and that it was he who arranged for it to be published last week in the Voice in exchange for the Voice's agreement to make a cash payment to the Reporter's Committee.

The Reporter's Committee emerges from this the worst of the three. By its willingness to turn a profit on this transaction, it has put price before principle and done more to damage its own cause than could be done by a dozen court gag orders, subpenas for the files of reporters, and threatened citations for contempt. No matter how much the committee may need cash, its participation in this payoff was a tragic blunder.

As for Mr. Schorr, his right to receive the material and to refuse to say where he got it is precisely what the Reporter's Committee is dedicated to defending. And this goes also for his right to use the material on his CBS program if he determined that it would not damage national security. Mr. Schorr has become a favorite target of the administration, indeed, for prying secrets out of government offices and airing them over CBS.

But this time neither he nor CBS handled the story. Maybe CBS had had enough of "checkbook journalism" after the criticism it received for paying H. R. Haldeman last year for an interview on Watergate. Maybe Mr. Schorr had his own doubts about airing a report which both the White House and a majority of the House of Representatives had declared should be kept secret. Or maybe he simply thought he was doing a favor for the Reporter's Committee, or for the Voice.

In any event, he chose what looks like a back door deal with a payoff attached. There is a move in the House to hold him in contempt of Congress. The House would be wiser to forget Mr. Schorr and search its own premises for the source of this and the hundreds of other leaks that have come out of the Pike committee. The crime in which Mr. Schorr and the Reporter's Committee have participated is not against Congress; it is against their own profession and their own cause. When a career reporter has information that he feels should be made public, it is his duty to do so; not to offer the material to somebody else in exchange for a payoff.

And of all people, the Reporter's Committee should be least willing to take part in such a deal.

THE MILWAUKEE JOURNAL

Milwaukee, Wisc., March 2, 1976

CBS correspondent Daniel Schorr, perennially controversial in his style of reporting, is in the middle of another mess, this time one that does not reflect well on him or the journalistic profession.

Schorr's most immediate problem is a House decision to investigate his role in the release of the House Intelligence Committee's classified report on the US intelligence community to the weekly newspaper Village Voice. The Voice published a 24 page verbatim transcript of parts of the report. The House may also seek to learn who leaked the report to Schorr. In the end, the House could find him in contempt, or it could refuse him credentials to cover the body.

If the House were to carry through to either of these conclusions, its act would represent retaliation in a fit of pique. The fact is that security around the report had been a sieve. Much of what Schorr turned over to the Voice had been revealed before. What differentiated Schorr from other newspeople who had had the report leaked to them was that Schorr obtained a full copy of the report. If the House wants to punish, it can't stop with Schorr. And if the House were to look at its own members and staff, it could prove very embarrassing.

Schorr has been suspended by CBS until the legal problems surrounding the incident are resolved. His credibility has been damaged. But CBS rightly will help to defend Schorr in protecting the source of the committee report.

What Schorr deserves is a reprimand from his own profession for the way he handled the release of the document. When it became clear that he had been involved in the Voice caper, he initially denied that he had a copy of the report and that he had given it to the Voice. It was stonewalling reminiscent of Watergate participants, not exactly the kind of behavior expected of a reporter supposedly dedicated to opening the affairs of government to sunshine.

Just as shabby was the entry of money in the deal. Schorr declared, "I don't sell government documents." But it seems that, if Schorr personally did not receive money, some kind of arrangement was worked out between Schorr, the Voice, and a journalistic legal defense group, the Reporters Committee for Freedom of the Press, so that the Voice would pay the committee for the document Schorr gave the newspaper. This denigrates Schorr's supposedly altruistic motives and also casts a cloud over the committee and the Voice. The Voice appears quite willing to buy the news. The reporters' committee was willing, with Schorr's help, to trade in government documents.

If the press is to be a public watchdog and point moral fingers at other segments of society, it must play the role of Caesar's wife. In this instance, those high minded ethics are severely in question.

Portland Press Herald

Portland, Me., February 25, 1976

The publication of the House Intelligence Committee's report of the CIA is bad news for the press.

In our viewpoint, CBS newsman Daniel Schorr goofed. So did the Village Voice and so did the Reporters Committee for Freedom of the Press.

Schorr, who has been covering the intelligence beat for CBS, got a copy of the secret report. He did a series of radio and television accounts based on that report. Then the entire House voted not to release the committee report on grounds of national security.

Schorr then sold the report, not for personal gain but for what he deemed a worthy cause, the Reporters Committee for Freedom of the Press. On Feb. 11, the Village Voice, a New York weekly, printed much of the report.

Schorr goofed more than once. There is the initial propriety of scoring a scoop by broadcasting material still a committee secret.

Then after the House vote Schorr said he could not, as a matter of "journalistic conscience," maintain the secrecy the House had imposed on its members. He could not make a unilateral decision to suppress the information but he could make the unilateral decision to release it.

He erred again, although acting in behalf of charity, when he sold the report. He should have known full well the peril that attends the selling of news.

Schorr now has himself and his network under threat of a contempt of Congress citation. He is in danger of having his congressional credentials revoked. CBS has pledged to support him but it's also removed him from the intelligence beat.

As we said, we think Schorr erred—and more than once. But the House in its indignation should not confine its investigation or disciplinary action to him. There is no indication that Schorr stole the report. So someone connected with the committee, perhaps even a member of the House, was a party to the initial leak. As President Ford said, Congress should act to clean up its own House. It should pursue that angle vigorously and be no less severe in its discipline if the guilty party is found than it is with Schorr and CBS for their roles in the disclosure.

The Oregonian

Portland, Ore., March 10, 1976

It has been widely reported in the news media that CBS reporter Daniel Schorr gave The Village Voice the House Intelligence Committee report so that it would be placed on the public record, despite the almost two-to-one House vote against the same proposition advanced by the committee. Accuracy In Media, a nonprofit organization that publicizes what it regards as foibles of the press, cogently points out that Schorr's act had a price.

Schorr stipulated that the secret report could be published by The Voice, if the publisher would make a "voluntary" contribution to an organization (The Reporters Committee) favored by the newsman. Thus, Schorr obviously recognized that the information had monetary value, and Accuracy in Media argues that the right to designate to whom payments will be made is a valuable consideration.

In effect, a case has been made, albeit a thin one, that Schorr was trafficking in secret documents.

Whether the House was correct or not in trying to suppress the report is irrelevant. It was not an arbitrary decision; it was democratically arrived at, with bipartisan support.

Whoever leaked the report to Schorr was anxious to frustrate congressional intent, and though the newsman may believe his motives and actions conform to press rights and responsibilities, he undermined his position first by treating the First Amendment as a blank check and then by writing a price on it.

AKRON BEACON JOURNAL

Akron, Ohio, February 26, 1976

THE SWIRL of controversy over the publication of a secret House report on the CIA is kicked up largely by peripheral circumstances surrounding the case.

The biggest cloud hangs over the head of the principal figure, veteran CBS newsman Daniel Schorr, a long-time foe of government secrecy. Schorr has the distinction of being thrown out of Russia and later, as a Washington correspondent, being clumsily investigated by the Nixon administration, presumably in hopes of finding some "dirt" on him to get him ousted from Washington, too.

Schorr has been suspended by CBS because he has become a part of the story, rather than an outsider reporting it. Both Schorr and his superiors at CBS recognize the awkwardness of that position and have agreed that "he will be relieved of all reporting duties for an indefinite period."

The story concerns a report on the CIA and other intelligence agencies by the House Intelligence Committee. Schorr got hold of a copy of the report before it was released and he and other newsmen reported chunks of the findings which, while certainly not a threat to U. S. security, proved embarrassing to the cloak and dagger community. It also suggested that Secretary of State Henry Kissinger lied to the committee and tried to block the investigation.

The House blocked publication oi the 338-page report on Jan. 29 after the Ford administration said its disclosure would damage national security.

Schorr, accepting this as a challenge of the public's right to know and a test of the First Amendment guarantees of press freedom, moved to have the report published in a New York weekly, the Village Voice. He arranged for money to be paid for the secret report, but it wasn't to go to him: It was to be paid to the Reporters Committee for Freedom of the Press.

Schorr then denied he had a copy of the secret report or that he was connected with the appearance of the text in the Village Voice — until the Washington Post reported differently. Schorr has since angrily acknowledged his connection, but charged that the Post betrayed him by reporting "off-the-record" conversations. In other words, the press leaked his secret to the public just as it reported the contents of the House secret report.

The way Mr. Schorr chose to handle publication of the House report leaves a bad taste in the mouth, and tends to throw the issue out of perspective. Why didn't he publish the report himself, or at least have it appear under his byline? It can be argued that the limitations of television forced him to dissect the report and give the television audience only the choice filets, but trying to sneak the publication without taking credit detracts from Mr. Schorr's apparent purpose.

But it is money that really muddies the waters. The Reporters Committee for Freedom of the Press couldn't have needed money that badly. If the issue was freedom of the press, profits shouldn't have entered into the matter.

But what's done is done, and the focal point is not Mr. Schorr's tactics, but whether publishing a "secret" report and the use of leaks is patriotism or treason. The Ford administration, the CIA and some members of the Congress would have the American people believe that the Village Voice and Mr. Schorr have somehow torpedoed American foreign policy and put our spies in danger. That's hard to swallow. No, it's impossible.

The key issue is whether the government can cover up embarrassing disclosures by marking them "secret." There is no question it would be tidier: no reports of Watergate burglaries, assassination plots, a $10 billion secret police operation with almost no controls. But it would also shut off the public's need to know the bad as well as the good about government; and therefore it would increase the danger not only to First Amendment freedoms of the press, but of constitutional guarantees to individuals.

The press, by nature, is an adversary of the government, and should be — not to the point of giving away legitimate national secrets, which it has not, but to the point that it is not afraid to tell the public what its officials are up to in Washington and around the world.

Detroit Free Press

Detroit, Mich., February 25, 1976

THE Daniel Schorr case is as troubling for the journalism profession as it is for other advocates of greater openness in government. Mr. Schorr, a Washington correspondent for CBS News, was attempting to force a measure of that openness when he delivered a copy of a House committee's intelligence report to a New York weekly newspaper for publication.

Mr. Schorr says an "inescapable decision of journalistic conscience" compelled him to do this, after it became clear to him that CBS News already had broadcast as much of the report as it wanted. It must be remembered that, explosive as the report might ordinarily have been, virtually every major disclosure had been leaked long before the official report was assembled.

What is troubling about Mr. Schorr's action is not his making the report available for publication, which is the focus of the current House Ethics Committee investigation. Since the House had voted to keep the report on U.S. intelligence abuses secret, Mr. Schorr might technically be in "contempt of Congress." But it can be convincingly argued that the public's right to know superseded any such decision.

It's what Mr. Schorr did with the report after he was given a copy by an unnamed source that sets the case apart from the earlier "Pentagon Papers" case, for example, in which Dr. Daniel Ellsberg leaked suppressed government documents on the conduct of the Vietnam war.

Mr. Schorr did not simply deliver the intelligence report to media outlets for their consideration and possible publication, as Dr. Ellsberg had done. He apparently attached a condition: that the Village Voice, the weekly publication he chose to *publish the report, make a contribution to the Reporters' Committee for Freedom of the Press.*

This doesn't quite constitute the "selling" of the report that some of Mr. Schorr's critics have charged. But it comes close. Mr. Schorr offers the weak argument that he didn't want to see the Voice "profit" from the report's publication.

"I suggested it would be appropriate for (the publisher) to make some gesture to the free press idea which has animated me," he explains, "by a voluntary contribution to the Reporters' Committee."

Mr. Schorr's intent may have been innocent enough. But no matter how it's sliced, putting any condition whatever on presenting the news is reprehensible. It's an unwarranted phase of "checkbook journalism" that the profession must renounce if it's to retain public credibility.

CBS News has acted responsibly in removing Mr. Schorr from his active reporting duties, while providing legal counsel for defending his actions as they related to his CBS duties. Presumably that would include his obtaining the report from an unidentified source, and his refusal to name that source.

Beyond that, Mr. Schorr apparently will have to answer for his own actions. The distinction should not be lost on the House investigators. The freedom of the press and the peddling of the news are completely separate issues, and they must be treated in that light.

St. Louis Globe-Democrat

St. Louis, Mo., February 25, 1976

The co-culprit along with Daniel Schorr in the leak of the secret House Intelligence Committee report clearly is the person who provided the suspended CBS newsman with the document he was not entitled to have.

In pursuing its investigation, the House Ethics Committee should concentrate on finding the worm within its own woodwork, whether Schorr chooses to cooperate or not. Little good may come from citing Schorr for contempt. He has admitted his misdeed of making the report available to the Village Voice, a New York weekly publication that printed the classified information.

CBS News may have acted in its own interest by relieving Schorr of his role as a Washington correspondent pending the outcome of the case. He remains on the payroll and the network says it will provide him with legal counsel.

Schorr cannot be defended for accepting and passing onto others material whose publication is deemed damaging to the national interest. Nor can his appeal to his own "journalistic conscience" justify his decision "not to suppress" the report.

By no legitimate standard of newsgathering was Schorr entitled to the report. It was not enterprise on his part. Rather, he was the recipient of stolen goods. The person who gave him the report betrayed a trust.

The House Ethics Committee, which does a poor job of policing misdeeds by its own congressional members, will be whistling in the wind if it cites Schorr for contempt because he refuses to divulge his source. This will only make him a martyr in some misguided eyes.

The House should have the ability to close its own sieve of security leaks. CBS must decide whether a person of Schorr's character deserves continued employment. And the Justice Department should be looking into the Village Voice.

If the transmittal and publication of classified reports is to become accepted practice, perhaps Benedict Arnold should be disinterred and turned into a national hero for the Bicentennial Year.

San Jose Mercury

San Jose, Calif., February 26, 1976

There is something positively gamy in the House of Representatives contemplating a contempt citation against newsman Daniel Schorr in the matter of the leaked CIA report.

The concept is bad, and the way the House is going about this particular bit of business is worse. It adds up to an arrogant assault on the people's right to know; it is patently an attempt to abridge the First Amendment guarantee of a free press.

It is worth recalling, briefly, how the House and the Columbia Broadcasting Co. newsman arrived at the present unhappy situation. The special House committee investigating past misdeeds of the Central Intelligence Agency had completed its work and voted to publish its report. Somebody, presumably an employe or staff member of the committee, slipped Schorr an advance copy, large portions of which had already been leaked to the press piecemeal.

At this point, the White House requested that publication be held up until President Ford could censor the document. The House agreed. Schorr, after ascertaining that the broadcast and book publishing potential of the report was small, turned it over to a New York weekly newspaper with the suggestion that any profits derived from it be passed along to the Reporters' Committee for Freedom, a group devoted to defending the First Amendment.

The report, which was hardly news by this time and which contained about as much "sensitive" national security data as a Sears Roebuck catalog, was duly published, and the House, in a fine display of moral indignation, turned the matter over to its ethics committee.

The ethics committee, with admirable feeling for its work, went into secret session and proceeded to debate whether it could get the Federal Bureau of Investigation to do a job on Daniel Schorr, who by now had been suspended by CBS from reporting for the duration of the investigation.

Interestingly, neither the ethics committee nor the House itself seems the least bit interested in pursuing the matter of who handed the CIA report to Schorr and what, if anything, should be done to him, her or them. That, of course, will come later when, it is anticipated, Schorr will be summoned before the committee and threatened with further contempt action if he refuses to reveal his source.

The hypocrisy in all this is as monumental as it is revolting. For better or for worse, official Washington lives by the leak. Congressmen and women do it; members of the Executive do it. Newsmen do it—but with one big difference. It's their job to see that the public is as fully informed as possible.

And that is what makes the House vendetta against Daniel Schorr as serious as it is reprehensible. In the words of Rep. Don Edwards (D-San Jose), one of the few House members to oppose the contempt proceedings:

"It has been said that this is not a matter of freedom of the press at all, but I believe the issue of freedom of the press is very much involved. . .I think by bringing it up in this particular way and by naming Mr. Schorr, there is a very large and dangerous chilling effect on the right of the reporters to receive information."

The point is well taken. The House is going after the wrong man for the wrong reasons. If it persists in this miscarriage of justice it will serve the American people badly, indeed.

ALBUQUERQUE JOURNAL

Albuquerque, N.M., February 28, 1976

Once more the inevitable conflict and confusion between national security and the public's right to know is making the waters hopelessly muddy.

It is a virtual replay of the infamous "Pentagon Papers" debate, except that now the administration has injected a demand for something dangerously akin to an official secrets act which could severely abridge the freedoms of speech and press and the correlative right of all Americans to know what their government is about.

The President's shift to the cause of secrecy is consistent with and closely follows his earlier offer of FBI assistance to Congress to identify the congressman, if any, who leaked contents of the House intelligence report to radio-television newsman Daniel Schorr. The administration moves have been followed up by congressional moves to investigate the leak, to cite Schorr for contempt and to revoke his official press credentials.

We submit that there is nothing in the material presumably leaked that should be concealed from the media or the public; that publicity of past diplomatic blunders or past blunders by an intelligence agency cannot affect national security adversely except, perhaps to shake the public's confidence in past diplomatic, intelligence and security performance, and we don't see that to be necessarily bad; that there is no reason to discipline Schorr or to put an official investigative agency on the trail of a congressman who may have caused those blunders to be publicized; that any congressman or any other citizen in possession of such knowledge should be free to shout such knowledge from the rooftops without fear of recrimination; that it is no crime, and it should not be made a crime, for a congressman or any other to leak information in which the public has a right and an interest.

We acknowledge that Schorr, the anonymous congressman and, in the case of the Pentagon Papers, Daniel Ellsberg may have violated confidences in making public certain information, but we believe their moral obligation to respect that confidence was, or could have been, counterweighted by public interest in that information — an interest that would not have been satisfied except for the leaks.

We also acknowledge that disclosures which could "blow" a sensitive and ongoing diplomatic strategy or intelligence effort could adversely affect national security, and we believe the criminal code, with reasonable safeguards, should prohibit and provide penalties for such disclosures. We also must deplore the "fingering" of persons concurrently engaged in such security-sensitive operations either by publication or by word of mouth.

But we must strongly protest the growing implication in official quarters that the public should be deprived of knowledge about official actions that tend to outrage the national sense of decency and fair play; or actions, such as **our secret involvement** in Angola, that could lead to armed hostilities — hostilities that could jeopardize the lives of the nation's young people as well as the freedom, property rights and personal options of all Americans.

HOUSE ETHICS COMMITTEE REJECTS CHARGING SCHORR IN REPORT LEAK

The House Ethics Committee Sept. 22 ended an inquiry nto the leaking of the House Intelligence Committee report on he Central Intelligence Agency. Daniel Schorr, a CBS news eporter, had admitted in February that he had given a copy of he report to the *Village Voice* after the House had voted to eep the report secret.

The House committee voted against citing Schorr for con-empt, bringing criminal charges against him in federal court, nd depriving him of his congressional press credentials. On a –1 vote, it released him from the committee's subpoena, but oted specifically that it made no judgment on his claim to rotection under the Constitution's First Amendment. Schorr ssued a statement after the voting, "The most significant thing s that the committee has decided not to press for a contempt itation against a reporter who has exercised his First Amend-nent privilege and honored his professional obligation to pro-ect his confidential source." Throughout the hearings held the veek before, Schorr had refused to name his congressional ource for the document or to produce his copies of the report.

The House had voted in February to investigate the leaking f the report. Almost 500 people were questioned by 12 re-ired agents of the Federal Bureau of Investigation, but the ource's identity was not divulged. The investigation cost nore than $150,000.

Schorr resigned from CBS Sept. 28, having been sus-ended since his February acknowledgement that he had given he report to the *Voice*. Schorr wrote in his letter of resigna-on, "Aware of the polarizing effects within CBS News of the ontroversy involving me, I would doubt my ability to function ffectively if reinstated."

CASPER STAR-TRIBUNE

Casper, Wyo., September 23, 1976

The House Ethics Committee investigation of CBS newsman Daniel Schorr leaking a secret report on abuses in U.S. intelligence gathering activities to the *Village Voice*, a New York City Green avant garde newspaper, has died.

Schorr refused to name the source from whom he received the alleged secret documents. And the Ethics Committee, while threatening Schorr with a prison sentence if he did not tell them, finally conceded defeat Wednesday and lifted its subpoena against Schorr, leaving him free to report on Congress.

The hesitation on the part of the committee in taking any punitive action arises from their own fears that such an act would invoke a constitutional question of the powers of Congress versus the freedom of the press guarantee in the First Amendment, which Schorr used as part of his defense.

The committee in its vote Wednesday simply avoided a constitutional confrontation. Defeated 6 to 5 was a motion which would have recommended to the full House that criminal charges be lodged against Schorr for refusing to return his copy of the House intelligence committee document. A 9 to 1 vote released Schorr and three other witnesses from subpoenas.

As an example of the cavalier manner in which the Congress spends tax money this case was outstanding. When it concluded it had expended $150,000 on the investigation and earlier was turned down on a request for $100,000 more.

More than 5,000 newsmen throughout the country appealed to the committee not to cite Schorr because of the principal of confidentiality of news sources.

So $150,000 and five months later, the question of the power of Congress versus the First Amendment still remains in limbo.

THE TENNESSEAN

Nashville, Tenn., September 17, 1976

THE HOUSE Ethics Committee members would do best to forget about Mr. Daniel Schorr, and hope that the voters forget about them and their ridiculous and misguided attempts to discover who leaked the Pike Committee's report on the Central Intelligence Agency.

In the final act of this seven-month, $150,000 farce, the committee questioned Mr. Schorr, a CBS correspondent, on his source for the Pike report.

Despite the threat of being found in contempt of Congress, Mr. Schorr refused to answer the committee's questions.

"In some 40 years of practicing journalism, I have never yielded to a demand for the disclosure of a source that I have promised to protect and I cannot do so," he said.

Citing the First Amendment guarantee of a free press, Mr. Schorr eloquently told the committee that if he were to violate his source's confidence "the ultimate losers would be the American people and their free institutions.

"But, beyond all that, to betray a source would be to betray myself, my career, and my life. It is not as simple as saying that I refuse to do it. I cannot do it."

The committee was not prepared to face this constitutional question straightforwardly. Committee members tried to engage in cat-and-mouse questioning based on other witnesses' statements in hope of trapping Mr. Schorr. However, he avoided these traps and maintained his simple confidence in the First Amendment.

To cite Mr. Schorr for contempt would only compound the committee's foolishness to date and would probably lead to further embarrassment if the full House refused to go along.

And the committee should have doubts about its support in the full House. The House Administration Committee has refused to appropriate any more money for the ethics panel to continue its investigation and 36 representatives petitioned the committee not to force Mr. Schorr to testify.

By dropping the matter now, the committee members may be lucky enough to be forgotten by most voters before November.

Wisconsin State Journal

Madison, Wisc., September 20, 1976

The words "national security" have become a catch-all phrase used by the federal government to justify just about anything from FBI burglaries, to illegal wiretaps, to over-classification of government documents.

As columnist Anthony Lewis notes elsewhere on the Page of Opinion, even in a country that values freedom and individuality above almost everything else the words "national security" are expected many times to prompt individuals to "bow automatically to the state."

Those two magic words were used again and again in the case of CBS reporter Daniel Schorr, the subject of hearings before the House Ethics Committee.

Schorr obtained the secret report of the House Intelligence Committee, used some of it on CBS news reports and gave the entire document to the Village Voice, which published it.

Congress immediately was up in arms over how Schorr obtained a copy of the report and the Ethics Committee began hearings in an attempt to force Schorr to reveal his source or face contempt of Congress charges.

Schorr has steadfastly refused to reveal his source and to do anything else would seriously undermine the ability of all reporters to obtain controversial and suppressed information. The principle of protecting one's sources is as old as journalism. If it is compromised, access to the free flow of information will be endangered.

It is difficult to say flatly that the publication of the report will not affect national security in any way, but so far there has been no evidence that it has.

The government's record to date in crying wolf at the least breach of government secrecy does not support its concern.

When the Pentagon Papers were published, the State Dept. warned of "irreparable harm" it would cause the United States.

They were published. Where's the irreparable harm?

If Congress would concern itself more with declassifying material that is more embarrassing to the government than vital to security, it would be easier to keep secret material that really should be kept secret.

It is entirely too easy to stamp "Top Secret" on a document. There were reports a few years ago that newspaper clippings were so classified.

There is a need for some secrecy in government, but nowhere near the current, excessive use.

Reporters such as Schorr are not trying to undermine foreign policy or damage national security when they obtain controversial material and inform the public of it.

On the contrary, they are strengthening one of the principles upon which this country is founded, that the governed shall decide who the governors are and the directions they take. Unless they know what is going on in governing circles, they cannot make intelligent decisions. That, more than an occasional security leak, is what endangers this society as the Watergate scandals helped prove.

It is now reported that the Ethics Committee will back off of its option of recommending that Schorr be cited for contempt and instead let the matter quietly die. It should.

The San Diego Union

San Diego, Calif., September 17, 1976

Correspondent Daniel Schorr's appearance before the House Ethics Committee should bring an end to any effort to make him the scapegoat for a breakdown in the machinery for control of secret documents in the hands of congressional investigators.

Mr. Schorr quite properly refuses to say who gave him a copy of a report on the House investigation of the Central Intelligence Agency. Petitions signed by 5,500 of his fellow journalists are backing up his position that the First Amendment protects the confidentiality of his notes and that to disclose the source of the CIA document he gave to a New York newspaper would violate his professional ethics.

When the document was published seven months ago it appeared that Mr. Schorr had been a party to a breach of national security. That is hardly the case. The breach was not Mr. Schorr's. At the time he received the document the House investigating committee had decided to make it public, a decision later reversed by the full House. Further, it has been learned that the committee staff was woefully lax in keeping copies of the report from circulating in Washington.

Mr. Schorr is not the first reporter to stand firm against a powerful arm of government in protecting a source, and we hope he is not the last. Unfortunately the CIA investigating committee was also not the first to be embarrassed by a leak of confidential information. It could be the last if the Ethics Committee confines its attention where it belongs — on congressmen and staff members who deliberately or carelessly are responsible for leaks in the first place.

New York Post

New York, N.Y., September 17, 1976

Television reporter Daniel Schorr was impressively back on camera at the hearings of the House Ethics Committee in Washington. Although he was not covering the session but appearing as the principal witness, he was well prepared and authoritative, and spoke with quiet dignity.

Schorr declined, for reasons he set forth with solemnity, clarity and restraint, to reveal to the committee how he was supplied with the officially secret report of the House Intelligence Committee. He explained, on behalf of all journalists who take their profession seriously, why sources must have protection and the significance of that stand in relation to the nation's free institutions.

Seemingly as a consequence of Schorr's forthright, firm presentation at the televised hearings, it now appears that the committee will not proceed with punitive action against him or further investigation of the case.

That would be good news. Too much federal money and official time have been squandered on an inquiry which had no serious constitutional justification or any real relevance to national security.

Many TV news viewers will be awaiting Schorr's early return to the screen in his professional capacity. They must also hope that the House Ethics Committee finds more useful and defensible areas of exploration than this ill-conceived inquisition.

THE STATES-ITEM

New Orleans, La., September 17, 1976

The House Ethics Committee, which has not been overly aggressive in policing its own, pulled out all the stops in its pursuit of television newsman Daniel Schorr. The committee demanded that Mr. Schorr name the person who gave him a House intelligence report, and they threatened nine times during a hearing to hold him in contempt of Congress.

Mr. Schorr, a tough newsman who made the Nixon Administration's hate list, did the only thing he could do. He refused on grounds that to reveal his sources would betray a confidence. Naming his source would have a chilling effect on every reporter's ability to report the news, he told the committee.

"To betray a confidential source would mean to dry up many future sources for many reporters," Mr. Schorr said. "The reporter and the news organization would be the immediate losers. The ultimate losers would be the American people and their free institutions."

Rep. F. Edward Hebert, a member of the Ethics Committee and a former newspaper reporter and editor, was totally unsympathetic to the pressuring of Schorr.

"I would not ask any newsman under any circumstances, under any conditions, to reveal his sources," Mr. Hebert said.

The committee apparently will not hold Mr. Schorr in contempt. Half of the members already are on record against such action.

Mr. Schorr is something of a "fall guy" for a Congress frustrated by information leaks to newsmen. He obtained the intelligence report after the House Select Committee on Intelligence had voted to publish it. Much of the material contained in the report already had been leaked to newsmen, and had been used.

Certainly, there are instances when the news media should not publish material. This is the case where publication could adversely affect national security or jeopardize lives. The House Intelligence Committee's original decision to publish indicates that this was not true with the intelligence report.

The Ethics Committee's $150,000 investigation to find out who leaked the report to Mr. Schorr is just one facet of a much broader attempt to discourage reporters determined to inform the public. Four California newsmen currently are serving contempt sentences for refusing to reveal news sources.

Mr. Schorr might have been speaking for all of them when he told members of the Ethics Committee that, "To betray a source would be to betray myself, my career and my life."

The Virginian-Pilot

Norfolk, Va., September 17, 1976

All right. So Daniel Schorr is a bit over-the-hill to be playing the role of Daniel in the lions' den. But then the House Ethics Committee is hardly a pride of lions. It's more on the order of a litter of tabbycats.

And so the confrontation was something less than cosmic when this Daniel ventured into that lions' den this week. Nine times Mr. Schorr refused to disclose the details of how he had obtained a copy of the Pike Committee's report on intelligence operations.

Aaron Latham, a journalist for New York magazine, refused twice to answer questions relating to the same subject.

Representative John J. Flynt Jr. (D-Ga.), the committee chairman, threatened the two with contempt-of-Congress citations for refusing to answer the questions. But having marched his troops to the top of the hill, he marched them back down again.

At the conclusion of the lengthy hearing Wednesday, six of the committee's twelve members said that they would refuse to support a citation for contempt of Congress. That ought to be the end of a the futile investigation into the question of who gave Mr. Schorr a copy of the report.

The Pike report was the end product of the House investigation into the government's intelligence operations. Although the committee itself voted to make public the report, its recommendation was overridden by the full House of Representatives.

A copy of the report then was furnished by Mr. Schorr to The Village Voice, which published extensive excerpts in February. Since the choicest details had already leaked into print in Washington, fuller publication was an empty sensation.

But many members of the House of Representatives thought they had been held up to ridicule, something that the Honorables prefer to do themselves. And so the House launched an investigation, questioning more than 500 persons — and spending more than $150,000 — to discover who gave the report to CBS correspondent Schorr. The effort was unsuccessful. And since Mr. Schorr isn't telling, it seems that we'll never know who the culprit was.

It hardly matters. While Mr. Schorr may have behaved with excessive self-righteousness at times, the confrontation was needless and pointless. Congress leaks like a sieve. In pursuing the vendetta with Mr. Schorr, the Ethics Committee was wasting its time and the taxpayers' money. When push came to shove Wednesday, the committee members were unwilling to force a showdown on the constitutional question. That was wise.

For if the confrontation over the Pike report was small potatoes, Mr. Schorr was standing upon large principles. They are not to be hazarded idly by miffed politicians.

DAILY NEWS

New York, N.Y., September 17, 1976

Newsman Daniel Schorr has invoked the protection afforded the press under the First Amendment in refusing to tell a House committee who supplied him with a copy of the chamber's Intelligence Committee report.

Rep. Flynt

Technically, Schorr laid himself open to a contempt citation by doing so. Ethics Committee Chairman John Flynt (D-Ga.) made a point of reminding Schorr of the peril.

At least half of the panel members, however, have indicated a commendable reluctance to push the issue to that extreme. We earnestly hope that, in the long run, those cooler and wiser heads will prevail.

Punishing Schorr would be manifestly unjust, and an admission by the lawmakers of their impotence to deal with the problem at the source—which is within the House itself.

There was not just one leak involving the intelligence report, but an almost continuous stream of them. The Congress as a whole is, in fact, a vast sieve where classified information is concerned.

Such indiscretion ought to be a matter of concern to Congress. But it should be able to regulate and discipline its members without assaulting—

A VITAL FREEDOM

—which must be protected if the press is to carry out its obligation to inform the public.

A free press needs more than merely the right to publish what happens on the surface. It needs access to information that many people—some of them very powerful—would prefer not to have known.

Very often, it is the shielded tipster who puts a newspaper on the scent of a smelly scandal, criminal connivance in high places, and shady political manipulations.

Without the guarantee of anonymity, and the protection from retaliation that it provides, the lips of informants would be sealed, and much wrongdoing would go undiscovered.

Rep. Flynt and his colleagues may believe that there are important reasons for trying to break Schorr's silence in this particular case. But they should realize that using threats and punishment to abridge freedom of the press would set a very dangerous precedent.

It takes no great imagination to see other politicians dreaming up equally plausible excuses for putting the screws on newsmen simply to cover up their own misdeeds, or to intimidate persons who might bear witness against them.

For its own good and that of the country, the committee should retreat as gracefully as possible from a confrontation which was a mistake to begin with.

THE DENVER POST

Denver, Colo., September 19, 1976

The House Ethics Committee's attempts to intimidate CBS reporter Daniel Schorr are both unjust and unnecessary.

Using the threat of a contempt citation, the committee tried to get Schorr to disclose where he obtained possession of a secret House report he had made public. Other reporters also had gained access to all or parts of the report, and had published or broadcast most of its contents.

Schorr, in his appearance before the Ethics Committee, sought the protection of the First Amendment guarantee of freedom of the press, and rightly refused to reveal where he got the report. If he did, he told the committee, "the ultimate losers would be the American people and their free institutions."

And that is indeed the case. If newsmen, such as Schorr, or the four editors and reporters (the Fresno Four) who were unjustly jailed for refusing to reveal sources of confidential information, did betray their sources, many of such sources would dry up in the future—to the detriment of a free press and a free society.

Charles B. Seib, respected critic and observer of the mass media for the Washington Post, wrote in a column published in this newspaper Friday that "what is really at stake in both these cases is the confidentiality of news sources (which is) essential to an effective free press, and a free press is vital to our system.

"So when officials, no matter in what branch of government or at what level, crack down on journalists for protecting sources, it is a matter of concern for everybody, not just for those of us in the news business."

New York Times writer Anthony Lewis, in a column on this page today, declares that Schorr "and other reporters like him . . . serve their country by doing their job, even when it annoys."

And the Los Angeles Times, in an editorial about the Fresno case, commented Wednesday that "it is an important case of rights denied, of the public interest subverted for the sake of judicial autonomy . . . An informed electorate requires information; freedom to express opinions is an empty right indeed unless people have the basis for forming opinions. And the confidentiality of sources is basic to a free press."

We emphatically agree with the observations of our colleagues.

Surely, the House Ethics Committee has more ethical things to do than try to weaken the First Amendment by threatening Schorr. Surely, the two California judges who are the villains in the Fresno case would be hard put to find a jury which would sanction their abuse of authority in jailing the four reporters and editors of the Fresno Bee.

The Bee workers were released Friday by an appeals court judge, but the stigma of an undeserved sentence is attached to them. Their record should be wiped clean of alleged wrong-doing and Schorr, under suspension by CBS as a result of the Ethics Committee's implications and charges, also should be allowed to return to work with a clean slate. The cause of freedom requires no less.

THE SAGINAW NEWS

Saginaw, Mich., September 17, 1976

Having stood up the House Ethics Committee under the glare of hot lights wasn't an easy thing for CBS newsman Daniel Schorr to do. But he met his testing moment with courage, resolve and a touch of eloquence on the deeper meanings of the First Amendment — and in so doing has served all journalism with distinction.

At the end, it was the committee that was on the verge of melting in the grand presence of what it had started by taking on Mr. Schorr. What the committee will now do is not clear.

But it is instructive that at least half of the 12-member committee wants to drop it and forget Mr. Schorr rather than promote a constitutional confrontation between government and press in this country.

That would be the sensible thing to do. Maybe it will, maybe it won't. Schorr could get fined and go to jail for refusing to tell the committee who gave him information contained in House Intelligence Committee reports on CIA activities.

The issue here is not making a triumphant hero out of Schorr. There are larger issues. Mr. Schorr recognized them and joined them nicely for the committee as he nine times refused to divulge what the committee wanted to hear.

"To betray a source would be to betray myself, my career, and my life," said Schorr. It is not as simple as saying that I refuse to do it. I cannot do it. To betray a confidential source would mean to dry up many future sources for many future reporters. The reporters and the news organizations would be the immediate losers . . . the ultimate losers would be the American people and their free institutions."

Here is the crux of the Schorr issue, as we noted earlier. While it is the right of Congress to investigate, it also the right of a free press to gather information and publish it.

When government preempts both powers under threat of punishment, the delicate line that separates these two rights under First Amendment guarantees have been breached and we are entering a terrible danger zone.

The Ethics Committee would do well to think on the essence of this as Mr. Schorr phrased it — and act accordingly.

DAYTON DAILY NEWS

Dayton, Ohio, September 16, 1976

CBS reporter Daniel Schorr has said exactly what he said he was going to say: Nothing.

Now it is up to the House Ethics Committee to decide whether it wants to try to throw Mr. Schorr in prison. The issue, at least superficially, is the committee's effort to force the reporter to reveal the source of a House committee report on U.S. intelligence activities, which Mr. Schorr obtained and made public. The real issue, however, may be the ethics committee itself, which has become infamous for letting congressmen get away with murdering ethics and might like to seem tough now by snarling and snapping at the reporter.

It ought to go without saying that the committee, having now made a monkey out of itself, ought to back off without making a martyr out of Mr. Schorr. Formal contempt charges and the likelihood of a jail term won't shake the name from Mr. Schorr and won't deter other journalists from continuing to report important information that comes into their hands.

The House's beef, if it really has one at all, is with the House member or staff person who leaked the intelligence report in the first place. Mr. Schorr is a secondary participant. In the circumstances, he did as virtually any other journalist would have done.

Of course, the committee has a perfect right to make a big to-do of this affair. Its legal powers are awesome. No one doubts that. It's the committee's intellectual powers that remain in question.

The Cleveland Press

Cleveland, Ohio, September 18, 1976

Having already wasted a great deal of time and money, the House should quietly close the books on the case of Daniel Schorr, the CBS correspondent who refused under oath the other day to reveal his confidential sources of information.

For six months the House Ethics Committee has been trying to find out how Schorr was able to obtain a secret House report (containing no secrets) on the CIA, which he then turned over to a New York newspaper, Village Voice, for publication last February.

Schorr won't talk — for the very good reason that press freedoms are protected by the Bill of Rights. His source won't talk. Yet the investigation is costing the taxpayers a cool $150,000, with an additional $100,000 now being sought to write a final report.

To spend even a nickel more on this fiasco would be an insult to common sense. The committee cannot drum up enough support within its own ranks to hold Schorr in contempt of Congress. More than 35 congressmen, in fact, have signed a petition opposing a contempt citation.

One may question whether the now-forgotten document should have been made public. But it is hard to quarrel with Schorr's contention that the American people would be "the ultimate losers" if newsmen were forced to betray confidences at congressional (or judicial) request.

Chicago Defender

Chicago, Ill., September 22, 1976

When the House Ethics Committee failed to cite Daniel Schorr for contempt of Congress, a victory of some consequence was won for the American press as a whole. Schorr, a brilliant CBS correspondent, had refused to disclose to the committee details of the way he had obtained a copy of the Pike's Committee's report on intelligence activities.

He was subpoenaed. Citing freedom of the press provisions in the First Amendment as the ground for his refusal, Schorr told the committee that to comply with its demands would cause irreparable injury to the journalistic principle of confidentiality and to his integrity.

For a journalist, he said, the most crucial kind of confidence is the identity of a source of information. "I consider it a matter of professional conscience as well as constitutional right not to assist you in discovering the source."

He went on: "To betray a confidential source would mean to dry up many future sources for many future reporters. The reporter and the news organization would be the immediate loser. I would submit to you that the ultimate losers would be the American people and their free institutions."

Courts and some Congressional committees, here of late, have attempted to coerce reporters into identifying the source of their information, without success. Just a few weeks ago, four California editors were jailed for refusing to reveal the source of their information. Newsmen have a deep commitment to journalistic ethics.

THE ATLANTA CONSTITUTION

Atlanta, Ga., September 17, 1976

Nine times Ethics Chairman John Flynt warned CBS newsman Daniel Schorr that if he refused to answer questions he could face a contempt citation. And nine times Schorr refused to tell who gave him the copy of the secret House intelligence committee report.

A big hero? Perhaps some will view him that way. In reality Schorr is just exercising his right under the First Amendment. Lately too many journalists have had to exercise or try exercising their rights under that amendment. And too many have been hauled off to courts and jails.

The Congress has gotten into the Schorr case because the material in question, the material Schorr received and subsequently made available to CBS and The Village Voice, originated from a congressional committee. Since that august group sees fit to go to such lengths to find Schorr's source—not the least of those lengths is the $150,000 spent so far by the ethics committee—it is only logical Mr. Flynt and his Seekers would do a little digging in their own backyard.

The source the probers are trying to pry from Schorr generally is believed to be from the the House staff, the intelligence committee staff or from the executive branch. And it is generally known that copies of that intelligence committee report were not exactly rare. At any rate, the places to look, it seems, certainly should include the House's own house.

The fact that the House ethics committee is spending good money in a bad—possibly futile cause—and the fact that it is spending the money in a ridiculous fashion (strangely refusing to probe its own with the zeal it directs toward Schorr) should not detract from one basic and alarming point in this case: freedom of the press—under constant attack during recent years—and the public's right to know are being tested again. If Flynt and his committee do something silly, such as citing Schorr for contempt, that freedom and that right will have been dealt a severe blow. And this country will have taken a dangerous step toward a situation which finds the press reduced to mere distributors of the crumbs the government decides to toss out.

HERALD-JOURNAL

Syracuse, N.Y., September 20, 1976

Daniel Schorr went one step too far.

Nobody seemed very disturbed when he broadcast a series of reports on the findings of the Congressional Intelligence Committee.

Although it was apparent that if he did not have a copy of the report, he at least had seen it and was familiar enough with its contents to reveal them in detail to his television audience.

On Capitol Hill, it's generally acknowledged there are very few true secrets. Sooner or later, some legislator, or staff member, or an employe with access to secret material, probably will turn it over to the press.

It's been going on as long as Congress has been meeting and it's not likely to stop soon.

Schorr, a veteran broadcaster, has been on the receiving end of probably hundreds of leaks, but he handled this differently.

After getting as much tv newscast mileage out of it as he thought was reasonable, he sold the text of the report to the Village Voice, an underground weekly newspaper in New York City.

In doing this, he was, in effect, issuing a challenge to the Congress. His action said: "Yes, I have the report and I'll do with it what I want to."

* * *

This put Congress on the spot. It had to respond. While there has been plenty of lip service down through the years about stopping leaks, there never was much in the way of action.

Now, however, to save face, Congress had to do something. It had to make an example of Schorr.

Schorr invoked the protection of the First Amendment's guarantee of a free press in refusing to reveal who slipped him a copy of the report.

Technically, he risked the threat of a contempt citation, as Rep. John Flynt, chairman of the House Ethics Committee, reminded him.

Schorr was not the only recipient of information on the Intelligence Committee's report. In truth, by the time the text of the report appeared in print, it was not really "news." The bulk of it had been reported in detail by both the print and electronic media.

If the Congress doesn't want a repeat performance of this incident, it would do better to clean up its own act than to lay the blame for its indiscretions on reporters who are doing what they feel is their job.

When a reporter tries to capitalize on doing his duty, either for profit or publicity, he is subject to censure like everyone else. That's the trouble with many First Amendment conflicts. They are not clear cut.

* * *

But attempting to shackle the press through intimidation is a repudiation of the freedoms guaranteed by the Constitution.

A nation needs a free press to remain free.

The Washington Post

Washington, D.C., September 16, 1976

IT TAKES NOTHING AWAY from the performance of Daniel Schorr before the House Ethics Committee yesterday to observe that he had a lamentably easy act to follow. Some news executives of the Village Voice, who testified before Mr. Schorr was called to the stand, and some members of the committee as well, had twisted the First Amendment so far out of shape that it was barely recognizable—even to those of us who believe in it deeply and defend it zealously. The distinctions drawn by Mr. Schorr and his attorney, Joseph A. Califano Jr., between the rights of journalists to protect their confidential sources and to publish information and the right of government to try to withhold certain information from the public were a breath of fresh air.

Under our view of the First Amendment, contrary to what our colleagues from the Voice said yesterday, there is no obligation on the part of the press to publish every bit of information or every government secret it stumbles on. The First Amendment imposes no *obligations* on the press. It creates only protections—although certain responsibilities can be inferred from those protections. Even so, the First Amendment does not confer on anybody an obligation to publish the report of the House Select Committee on Intelligence, which Mr. Schorr obtained last winter. Whether the decision to publish it was a responsible one is a different question, on which individuals can reach different judgments. But it is reckless to rely, as one witness did, on the fact that one third of the members of the House had voted to make the report public, as support for the decision to publish.

We have no doubt that the government, and the House for that matter, have a right to keep some information secret. And we have no doubt that Congress was entitled to make it a crime for government employees to release legitimately classified national security information without proper authority. Similarly, we have no doubt that certain kinds of government secrets ought not to be made public if they fall into the hands of the news media. Indeed, the First Amendment provides little protection for the press against criminal charges of violating the espionage laws. The constantly recurring questions concern which classified documents really merit secrecy—and when. Given the way classified information moves around this town—and out of government control—even documents that may have been properly classified can easily lose their standing as authentic secrets; the highest government officials traffic in secret materials with the press when it suits their political purposes. Like Mr. Schorr, we have in addition seen all too many instances in recent years when the stamp of national security has been used to withhold information that was embarrassing or even incriminating but had nothing to do with national security. And we, like Mr. Schorr, also think that while it is the government's right to create secrets, it is also the government's responsibility to keep them; once the government has lost control of its secrets, the decision about whether they should be published rests with the news media; it needs to be remembered that a wrong decision can result in a criminal conviction. That is the tension—of which Mr. Schorr spoke so eloquently—that is created by the First Amendment between the power of the government and the protections afforded a free press by the First Amendment.

The Birmingham News

Birmingham, Ala., September 18, 1976

CBS correspondent Daniel Schorr has refused to tell the House Ethics Committee who his source was for the copy of a secret House intelligence report which he obtained and had printed in a New York newspaper.

The refusal was in the face of possible contempt of Congress charges, which, upon conviction, carry a maximum of one year in prison and a $1,000 fine.

It is doubtful that Schorr is very worried about possible punishment, because spending time in jail would only enhance his status as a celebrity among much of the media and a certain portion of the public.

But a very important principle is involved.

Schorr insists that the First Amendment protects him against having to reveal his sources. If the situation were different, any journalist would agree with Schorr. But the situation is not the usual case of investigative reporting. It involves national security, which Schorr breached by making the secret report public.

Certainly the First Amendment guarantees freedom of the press, but the Ninth Amendment says, "The enumeration in the Constitution of certain rights shall not be construed to deny or disparage others retained by the people."

Among the most basic rights of the American people is to be protected by its government from malevolent acts of foreign powers. And government cannot fulfill its responsibility to protect its people if the press presumes to be the arbiter of what information shall or shall not be made public for all to see, including foreign powers.

Also, it is a legitimate function of government to make laws, and the responsibility of all citizens—including journalists—to obey those laws.

Schorr certainly did not respect the law, and neither did his unnamed accomplice, when the secret document was made public.

A nation cannot survive an atmosphere in which its most confidential secrets are splashed in the press. This is especially true when the subject is as sensitive as intelligence operations.

Thus, it is the opinion of this newspaper that Schorr is wrong in principle. He was wrong to have participated in the disclosure of the report and he is in no more tenable a situation now in refusing to reveal the name of the person who helped him breach security.

If we come to the point where the press will be stripped of some of its freedom, it may well be because certain journalists failed to exercise their freedom responsibly.

No doubt there are a good many members of the press who applaud Schorr's stand and believe that the right of a journalist to refuse to name his source is absolute. But many other journalists don't.

If Schorr's case is ever carried through the appelate process for a definitive Supreme Court ruling, it would be a bad case upon which to form a general rule about sources. For Schorr has a weak position. The issue of national security looms large. Yet, if Schorr loses, the issue of confidentiality of sources in ordinary circumstances would be clouded. And that in itself would tend to diminish the effectiveness of the press.

So Schorr may be doing his own cause, the cause of the press and the cause of the people's right to know a grave injustice by taking a stand on shaky ground.

The Providence Journal

Providence, R.I., September 18, 1976

In his tense appearance on Wednesday before the House Ethics Committee, CBS correspondent Daniel Schorr spoke of "that constitutional Great Divide which separates the roles of the Congress and the press." This divide is real: it is a fundamental and precious distinction between the role of the government and that of the press, and the distinction is far more important than the question of how Mr. Schorr obtained copies of a House report on U.S. intelligence activities.

The committee had subpoenaed Mr. Schorr in an effort to find out how he obtained a copy of the report — excerpts were later published through Mr. Schorr's assistance — that the House had voted to keep secret. Mr. Schorr on Wednesday insisted that he could not reveal his confidential source, and on this point we agree with him. The press depends heavily on such sources to obtain information, and its right to protect the condifentiality of sources must be protected.

As the Schorr case has shown, though, confidentiality of sources is only one of two issues. The second issue here is the responsibility of the press to publish classified information only when its disclosure is clearly in the national interest.

While we feel that official documents tend to be over-classified we firmly believe that some sensitive materials must remain protected. Publication of certain secrets in the past has harmed the interests of the United States, and could do so again.

The difficult task, in trying to reconcile the conflicting roles of press and government in such a sensitive area, is to conceive of some way by which the interests of both sides are protected — and we find it just about impossible to imagine any official mechanism that could do this without eroding the First Amendment.

The seriousness of the Mr. Schorr's releasing the report, it should be noted, was mitigated considerably by events beforehand and afterward. The CIA itself had gone through the report to remove possibly sensitive information. The House Intelligence Committee itself had voted to make the report public (only to be reversed by the House after a plea from the Ford administration). The Justice Department, asked to investigate the source of the leak, was unable to find that Mr. Schorr had broken any laws.

This said, however, Mr. Schorr's own handling of the report is at least open to question. He did not publish in his own medium but went outside (to the New York weekly *The Village Voice*, and this raises questions of its own. He exercised poor judgment, we think, in arrogating to himself the ultimate decision as to the degree of national security affected by the report's release. But we also believe that he is on solid ground in declining to name his source. By pursuing the matter, the committee is tampering with one of the most vital principles of journalism, and we take no exception to Mr. Schorr's refusal to yield here.

If there can be no formal means of resolving such disputes, is the prospect for more such confrontations? Probably so. Any law, committee or other official mechanism for filtering official documents would leave the decision solely in the hands of the government, and would move the United States closer to the sort of Official Secrets Act that prevails in Britain. Untidy as it is, we feel that the best solution is for the press to exercise rigorous self-scrutiny whenever such a case comes up — and be prepared to take the legal consequences that may follow.

CIA Foreign Covert Operations

Greece

CIA station chief slain near Athens. Richard S. Welch, the station chief of the Central Intelligence Agency in Greece, was shot and killed by three masked gunmen outside his home in a suburb of Athens Dec. 23, 1975. Greek President Constantine Caramanlis launched a special investigation into the assassination Dec. 24, but no arrests were reported despite numerous claims of responsibility by various extreme left- and right-wing political groups in Greece. Anti-U.S. sentiment had been rife in Greece after the demise of the military dictatorship in 1974.

Welch, 46, had been officially listed as a member of the U.S. diplomatic corps, as a special assistant to the ambassador. However, his CIA identity had been widely known—he resided in the suburban Athens home which had been used by many of his CIA predecessors—and he had earlier been named in Greek and U.S. publications as a CIA agent.

Although the CIA at first declined, in line with its policy, to confirm the link, President Gerald Ford Dec. 27 attributed the assassination to the publication of Welch's identity as a CIA operative and waived restrictions to enable Welch to be buried in Arlington National Cemetery, where burial was normally reserved for those who had served in the armed forces or who had died in the service of the country.

Welch's body arrived in Washington Dec. 30 where it was met by CIA Director William E. Colby and presidential counselor Philip Buchen, Jr.

Welch had been named as a CIA agent in a letter published in the English-language daily *Athens News* Nov. 25. The letter, signed by a group calling itself "The Committee of Greeks and Greek-Americans," said Welch's job was "to see that the Caramanlis government does not get out of control." The names, addresses and phone numbers of Welch and six other members of the U.S. embassy staff were provided in the published letter which charged all seven with being CIA agents. The others listed, as reported by the *Financial Times* of London Dec. 3 were: William Lofgren, a political officer at the embassy, James Macwilliams, a junior embassy officer, and four members of the U.S. military mission—Ronald Estes, John Palavich, Stephen Winsky and William Bright.

(A letter sent to foreign wire services and to the *Athens News* Dec. 3 from "The Committee to Keep Greece Greek" named 10 alleged agents of the U.S.S.R.'s KGB [state security police] who were active in Greece. The letter, which named Sergei Tokhine, nominally first secretary of the Soviet embassy, as the chief KGB agent in Athens, was not published by the Greek press, which turned it over to the government for further consideration. Other agents named, as reported by the *Financial Times* Dec. 3, included: Viktor Boiko, embassy press officer; Gennady Bakanov, embassy third secretary; Ruben Martikian, consul; Yuri Muraviev, Sovinflot representative; Gennadi Pivovarov, cultural attache; Boris Shegolev, Sovexportfilm representative; and Vyachislav Safronov, Tass correspondent.)

The Greek government Dec. 25 increased its security guard on U.S. and Soviet personnel and embassies in Athens and Dec. 27 imposed a ban on all domestic reporting on the assassinations. Athens offered a $175,000 reward Dec. 29 for the capture of the assassins and $30,000 for information on the murder. It was reported Dec. 27 that all border exit points had been placed under surveillance.

Although both left- and right-wing groups in Greece Dec. 28 asserted responsibility for the assassination, these claims were generally discounted by the government. Reports in the Greek press Dec. 25 had suggested that Welch's assassination had been a case of foreign agents "settling a score."

Welch's CIA links had previously been cited in a U.S. publication, *Counterspy* published by a group which called itself the Fifth Estate for Security Education. The Fifth Estate's membership comprised a number of former CIA agents and figures who had been prominent in the movement against the Vietnam War. In its January and June issues, *Counterspy* had included Welch in a list of active CIA agents. The magazine named him as operating in Peru, where Welch had served as CIA station chief in 1972–73. (Welch had previously served in Guyana, Guatemala and Cyprus.)

The Fifth Estate Dec. 24 issued a statement charging that the CIA was responsible for Welch's death in so far as the agency had sent him "to spy, perhaps even to intervene in the affairs of the Greek government." The statement was denounced that day as "shocking" by CIA chief Colby who, in an unusual declaration, assailed the group for trying to use Welch's murder "as fuel for its irresponsible paranoic attack on Americans serving their country here and abroad."

State Department stops printing rosters. The State Department said March 18, 1976 that it was discontinuing the publication of the *Foreign Service List* which had been available to the public. A second publication, *The Biographic Register* would still be printed but classified "for official use only."

A State Department spokesman explained the action: "A new dimension was added to the problem when an American official was assassinated in Athens in December 1975, whose identification was attributed in part by the news media to the manner in which his name and biographic sketch were listed in the *Biographic Register* and *Foreign Service List*."

The list gives the names and assignments of high-ranking employes in each U.S. embassy. It had been issued four times a year; the August 1975 issue was the last. The register gives names and short biographical sketches including education and previous posts. An annual publication, the list had not appeared since 1974.

Probe of CIA agent's murder ends. Chief prosecutor Spyros Kaninias presented to a Greek magistrate the findings of a five-month investigation into the assassination in Athens Dec. 23, 1975 of Richard Welch, U.S. Central Intelligence Agency station chief, it was reported May 21. The probe had concluded without determining who was responsible for the murder. Kaninias said he had begun proceedings against "persons unknown" in connection with the incident.

Angola

Covert U.S., other aid reported. Huge sums of money were reportedly being funneled into Angola by the U.S., China and the Soviet Union, according to Washington sources cited in a *New York Times* article by Leslie Gelb Sept. 24, 1975.

The covert financial operations by the U.S. Central Intelligence Agency were being conducted with the approval of President Gerald Ford and the knowledge, as prescribed by law, of several congressional committees, the Washington sources said.

CIA assistance had been responsible, the sources asserted, for the resurgence of Holden Roberto, leader of the anti-Soviet movement, the National Front for the Liberation of Angola (FNLA). Roberto had been sponsored and supported with U.S. money and arms between 1962 and 1969, but had been "deactivated" thereafter. Recent support and aid from the U.S. had enabled Roberto to challenge the Marxist group, the Popular Movement for the Liberation of Angola (MPLA), which was reportedly backed by pro-Communist elements in the Portuguese government.

The sources said the U.S. was maintaining its aid to the FNLA, despite the increasingly greater strength of the MPLA forces in Angola, in an effort to demonstrate its support for Zaire President Mobutu Sese Seko, who backed the FNLA.

China, too, was providing financial and military aid to the FNLA, according to the article. The sources indicated that both China and the U.S. might also have been assisting the National Union for the Total Independence of Angola, led by Jonas Savimbi.

Soviet aid was allegedly in excess of U.S. aid and reportedly had included several direct shipments of arms to the MPLA as well as transhipments through the Congo Republic and materiel delivered on Yugoslav and East German vessels. The arms supplied were said to have included AK-47 assault rifles, the standard weapon of Soviet bloc armies, and Degtyarev light machine guns.

Kissinger warns vs. intervention—U.S. Secretary of State Henry Kissinger Sept. 23 warned non-African nations against interfering in Angolan affairs, declaring, 'We are most alarmed at the interference of extracontinental powers, who do not wish Africa well, and whose involvement is inconsistent with the promise of true independence." He made the statement in an address to representatives of African nations in New York.

In a related development, a special commission of the Organization of African Unity, met in Kampala, Uganda Oct. 1–4 to assess the Angolan situation. The commission comprised Burundi, Morocco, Ghana, Niger, Algeria, Somalia, Kenya and Lesotho. Representatives of the three Angolan liberation movements and Portugal also participated in the meetings.

Independence brings rival regimes. Angola's rival liberation movements proclaimed two distinct governments in the war-aggrieved nation Nov. 11 as Portugal granted independence to its final African colony.

In ceremonies in Luanda Nov. 10, Vice Adm. Leonel Cardoso, the last Portuguese high commissioner in Angola, announced the transfer of sovereignty to "the Angolan people," indicating that Portugal was not yet recognizing the authority of any of the nationalist movements, still waging battle throughout Angola.

Shortly after midnight Nov. 11 the Popular Movement for the Liberation of Angola (MPLA) proclaimed its leader, Agostinho Neto, president of the People's Republic of Angola. The proclamation and subsequent celebrations were conducted in Luanda, the Angolan capital and stronghold of the MPLA which also controlled the band of territory across the middle of the nation.

Hours later in Nova Lisboa, the joint formation of the People's Democratic Republic of Angola was announced by the National Front for the Liberation of Angola (FNLA) and the National Union for the Total Independence of Angola (Unita). The two movements had agreed in Kinshasa, Zaire Nov. 10 to form a joint government headed by a 24-member National Revolutionary Council. Unita leader Jonas Savimbi presided over the ceremonies in Nova Lisboa, Angola's second largest city and Unita stronghold, which thereupon reverted to its indigenous name of Huambo, used before 1925.

FNLA leader Holden Roberto headed independence observances on behalf of the joint government in Ambriz, a Front stronghold 75 miles north of Luanda. Other ceremonies for the People's Democratic Republic of Angola were held in Carmona, another FNLA center, 170 miles northeast of the capital.

The Luanda government of the Soviet-backed MPLA was promptly recognized Nov. 11 by the former Portuguese colonies of Mozambique, Guinea-Bissau, Cape Verde and Sao Tome e Principe. Other nations recognizing the MPLA regime that day were: the U.S.S.R., the Congo Republic, Cuba, Guinea, Algeria, Brazil, Hungary, Poland, Rumania, Bulgaria, Czechoslovakia, East Germany, Mali, Mauritania and Mongolia. The support of the Soviet Union for the MPLA precipitated a diplomatic incident in Uganda resulting in the recall of the Soviet ambassador to Moscow.

The U.S. and other Western nations withheld recognition of either regime. In denying U.S. recognition, U.S. Secretary of State Henry A. Kissinger charged Nov. 11 that the MPLA was using Cuban as well as Soviet arms; he further stated that Havana's involvement in Angola was one of the reasons for Washington's delaying improvement in relations with Cuba.

The U.S. consul, Thomas Kilhoran, and his staff left Angloa Nov. 3, advising all U.S. nationals to quit the territory as well.

(In another U.S. development, Central Intelligence Agency Director William E. Colby Nov. 6 defended the supply of covert U.S. aid to Angola, asserting that the U.S. interest there was one of general need to prevent a new country from falling under Soviet domination. His remarks, made to a closed session of the Senate Foreign Relations Committee in Washington, were cited by a senator present at the hearing.

CORE recruiting for Angola. The Congress of Racial Equality (CORE) had reportedly been recruiting black American military veterans for service as mercenaries in Angola as part of the CIA's operation there to assist the anti-Soviet FNLA and Unita forces, according to U.S. intelligence sources cited in a report by the Long Island (N.Y.) newspaper *Newsday* which was published in the *Washington Post* Dec. 12.

At a press conference Dec. 11, CORE president Roy Innis acknowledged that the civil rights organization had been recruiting experienced black combat medics and would consider sending black U.S. army veterans to serve as combat advisers in Angola. He denied any CIA link, however, and asserted that the CORE recruits would act as a "neutral force" under the mandate of the Organization of African Unity, if the OAU so wished. He said he would offer CORE's services to the OAU chairman, Ugandan President Idi Amin Dada, who was reportedly a friend of Innis'.

U.S. Congress moves to bar aid. Members of Congress Dec. 14–16 began a number of legislative actions to bring a halt to the growing U.S. role in the Angolan war as Administration officials mounted campaigns to maintain American financial assistance to the two anti-Soviet movements fighting in the war-torn nation.

President Ford Dec. 16 expressed through a spokesman his "serious concern" over the involvement of the Soviet Union and Cuba in Angola and appealed for "discussion in the Congress of the geopolitical significance of that part of Africa to the United States and the West."

The Senate Foreign Relations Subcommittee on Foreign Assistance and Economic Policy voted unanimously Dec. 16 in favor of an amendment and joint resolution which would prohibit, without specific Congressional authorization, covert military assistance for any party in the Angolan conflict. Participants in the session later reported that they had been informed by Administration spokesmen that there were between five and eight Americans presently in Angola, reputedly Central Intelligence Agency officials who had reporting functions only.

The Senate Dec. 15 had postponed action on a $120.9 billion defense appropriations bill in order to consider further the issue of U.S. involvement in Angola. Meeting in closed session Dec. 16, the Senate heard state department and CIA officials urge that funds for Angola not be cut off. The Senate action was initiated by Sen. Mike Mansfield (D., Mont.), the majority leader, who asserted, "What we are doing in Angola is unknown to most Americans."

House Democratic Leader Thomas P. O'Neill (Mass.) said in a Dec. 14 television interview that the House Intelligence Committee had asked the Administration to explain the U.S. role in Angola. He noted that recent reports of millions of dollars in military aid to Angola had "really caught the House by surprise."

Ford reported to rule out combat role. President Ford had reportedly ruled out any form of combat intervention in the Angolan war, including the sending of advisers, but would maintain the acknowledged program of financial and material aid, according to high and authoritative Administration officials quoted in the *New York Times* Dec. 16.

The officials cited in the *New York Times* report sought to stress that U.S. interests in Angola were limited and did not endanger detente with the Soviet Union. The anonymous disclosures in defense of non-combat U.S. involvement were reportedly made in an attempt to defuse growing public and Congressional suspicions that "another Vietnam" might be developing in the former Portuguese colony.

In contrast to the reputed Ford position, recent statements by Secretary of State Henry Kissinger, while disallowing the Vietnam analogy, had suggested a growing U.S. stake and possible U.S. action in Angola.

Other Administration officials also hinted at strategic U.S. interests in the war-torn nation. Speaking in the United Nations Dec. 14, Ambassador Daniel Moynihan alleged that if the U.S. discontinued its opposition to Soviet activities in Angola, "the Communists will take over Angola, and thereby considerably control the oil shipping lanes from the Persian Gulf to New York."

Other Administration sources, noted in the *Times* report, cited as reasons for possible U.S. concern in the Angolan situation potential consequences for South Africa in the event of a victory by the Soviet-supported Popular Movement for the Liberation of Angola (MPLA). The interests of Zaire and Zambia were also emphasized as potent policy factors, particularly in the early phases of U.S. involvement.

The two movements which had proclaimed a rival government to the one declared by the MPLA—the National Front for the Liberation of Angola (FNLA) and the National Union for the Total Independence of Angola (Unita)—had reportedly received $25 million in arms support funds sent via Zaire by the Central Intelligence Agency during the preceding three months, a high-ranking Washington official confirmed Dec. 11. A further $28 million was scheduled for continued aid and $7 million more was already "in the pipeline," according to Administration testimony Dec. 16 before the Senate Foreign Relations Subcommittee on Foreign Assistance and Economic Policy. This would bring total reported U.S. financial support to $60 million.

The $28 million allocation, it was reported, would deplete the CIA funds for such contingencies and the Administration was prevailing upon Congress not to cut off the aid which was aimed at countering the growing Soviet and Cuban involvement in Angola. (An Administration source said Dec. 11 that the number of Cuban troops supporting the MPLA had risen to 5,000.)

The U.S. aid was described by officials Dec. 11 and 12 as intended to "create a stalemate" in light of the heavy Soviet assistance, rather than to secure a victory. The Administration apparently envisioned creation of a coalition government by the three Angolan movements which had for years battled one another. (Numerous tenuous agreements and ceasefires between the traditionally rival groups—whose allegiances were based more on tribal and ethnic grounds than on political ideologies—had collapsed since the January signing of the Alvor pact which first enunciated the plan for a coalition administration in Angola after Portugal's departure.

U.S. arms assistance to the FNLA and Unita reportedly included large numbers of antitank missile launchers and antipersonnel rocket launchers, as well as five artillery spotter planes and other weapons. The materials had been turned over to the Zaire army, which was said to have 1,000 soldiers on the northern Angola front above Luanda.

Kissinger hints role, warns Moscow. Secretary of State Henry Kissinger said Dec. 12 that, in the absence of a negotiated settlement reached by the Angolans "free of outside interference, . . . the U.S. will try to prevent one party, by means of massive introduction of outside equipment, from achieving dominance." In his strongest statement to date on possible U.S. action in Angolan developments, the secretary of state asserted that the U.S. "cannot be indifferent" to shipment of arms and equipment to the MPLA.

Kissinger asserted that Angola "cannot but affect relations between the U.S. and the Soviet Union" if the U.S.S.R. engaged "in a military operation or massively supports a military operation thousands of miles away from Soviet territory in an area where there are no Russian interests and where it is therefore a new projection of Soviet interest." He maintained that there was a difference between arming countries and arming factions, in that the latter might establish "new patterns of dominance."

He further stressed that the Angolan situation was not "analogous to Vietnam because in Vietnam the conflict had a much longer, more complicated history." "There should not be a war by proxy by the great powers" in Angola, he said.

Kissinger made his remarks in Brussels where he was attending a meeting of foreign ministers of the North Atlantic Treaty Organization. The group was said to have devoted considerable discussion to Angolan developments and growing Soviet involvement on the African continent. A

Davis resignation linked to Angola—A dispute within the state department over the Administration's Angola policy had led Nathaniel Davis to resign in August as assistant secretary of state for African affairs, according to government sources quoted in a *New York Times* report Dec. 13. At the time of his departure from the department, Davis' resignation had been attributed to African and Congressional opposition regarding his alleged role in earlier CIA activities in Chile. B

The sources stated that Davis had resigned the post after Secretary of State Henry Kissinger rejected his recommendation that the U.S. seek a diplomatic solution in Angola and play no active role in the civil war there. Davis' action came shortly after the Administration authorized the covert shipment of $10 million in arms to two Angolan factions, the FNLA and Unita, the sources said. C

In Dec. 15 remarks aboard the secretary of state's airplane, en route between European capitals where Kissinger was participating in international meetings, reporters were told that the anti-Soviet forces in Angola would have collapsed if the U.S. had not provided military aid in July.

D

Senate votes to end covert Angolan aid. The Senate Dec. 19 approved, 54–22, an amendment to the fiscal 1976 Defense Department appropriations bill cutting off covert financial aid to factions battling for control of Angola. The vote ended a three-day struggle between liberal senators opposed to the aid and the Ford administration and its backers, who argued that failure to extend the funds would be a serious blow to the national interest of the U.S. E

President Ford Dec. 19 called adoption of the amendment "a deep tragedy for all countries whose security depends on the United States."

As a result of the vote, final action on the Defense Department bill was delayed until January 1976 when Congress was scheduled to return from its Christmas-New Year recess. The House Dec. 12 had adopted, 314–57, the House-Senate conference report on the appropriations bill, and the Senate Dec. 17 had approved it, 87–6. Passage of the Angolan amendment meant, however, that the bill would have to be returned to the House for another vote. (The Defense Department, meanwhile, continued to operate under a resolution continuing spending at fiscal 1975 levels until the fiscal 1976 appropriations measure was enacted.) F

G

Following a secret session of the Senate Dec. 17, Sen. John V. Tunney (D, Calif.) introduced an amendment calling for a $33 million reduction in defense monies,

the amount he said had been recommended by the Central Intelligence Agency for continued aid to Angola. In addition, his motion prohibited use of funds "for any activities involving Angola
A directly or indirectly."

Sen. Robert P. Griffin (R, Mich.) then offered a substitute amendment barring use of fiscal 1976 defense funds to support U.S. combat operations in or near Angola. This amendment, which would have allowed additional military grants for Angola, was overwhelmingly defeated Dec. 18, by a 72–26 vote. But an amendment by Sen. Jacob K. Javits (R, N.Y.) Dec. 18 retaining the $33 million in the bill while barring use of any defense
B funds for activities involving Angola was passed on a 93–4 vote.

Failing to defeat the Tunney amendment, supporters of the Administration began a filibuster Dec. 18. The White House-backed filibuster continued until Dec. 19 when President Ford, seeking to free the defense appropriations bill for Congressional passage, agreed to a vote on the Tunney amendment.

During the three-day debate, the
C Administration sought to compromise, announcing Dec. 18 that $9 million for Angolan aid would be acceptable. By the next day, however, opposition to the aid had stiffened, and the Administration was told by Senate liberals at a closed session of the Foreign Relations Committee that the whole purpose of their efforts was to end all aid to Angola.

Following adoption, Tunney (who was facing a primary challenge in California
D from Thomas Hayden, a peace activist) and the other sponsors of the amendment were jubilant. They earlier had expressed anger that covert aid to favored factions in Angola had been given without what they considered proper consultation with Congress. They also likened the situation to the early years of U.S. involvement in Vietnam, when Congress accepted at face value Administration statements that U.S. interests were involved in Indochina. Others indicated qualms about backing
E Angolan factions that were being aided by the Republic of South Africa. U.S. alignment with South Africa, they said, would only damage U.S. relations with black nations of Africa.

U.S.S.R., Cuba criticized on Angola. President Ford spoke out strongly at his news conference Dec. 20 against Soviet
F and Cuban involvement in the Angola civil war.

It was "harmful" for any foreign power "to try to dominate that country," Ford said. Soviet activity in Angola, he asserted, "certainly does not help the continuation of detente."

"I want to get it on record as forcefully as I can," Ford continued, "to say the action of the Cuban government in an effort to get Puerto Rico free and clear of
G the United States" as well as Cuba's involvement in Angola "erodes any chance for improvement of relations" with the U.S.

The President also was critical of the Senate's vote to cut off funds for U.S. covert military support of two of Angola's warring factions.

The Senate action "unfortunately has tied our hands," he asserted, and was "a serious mistake." "I feel a great country like the United States should have flexibility," he said. "The action of Congress is crucial in that it has deprived us of our ability to help the people of Angola. It is a broader problem in that many other countries consider the United States as friendly and helpful."

"Those countries dependent on us," Ford continued, "cannot help having misgivings because the Congress prevented us from helping Angola and may feel they will have the same fate."

In a statement released Dec. 19, Ford had called the Senate action "a deep tragedy for all countries whose security depends" on the U.S. "Ultimately," he said, "it will profoundly affect the security of our country as well." Urging the Senate to reverse its action, Ford said "failure to do so will, in my judgment, seriously damage the national interest" of the U.S.

"The issue in Angola is not, never has been and never will be a question of the use of U.S. forces," the President stressed. "The sole issue is the provision of modest amounts of assistance to oppose military intervention by two extra-continental powers, namely the Soviet Union and Cuba."

How could the U.S. take the position, Ford asked, that these countries could "operate with impunity" with troops and "massive amounts of military equipment while we refuse any assistance to the majority of the local people who ask only for military equipment to defend themselves?"

Kissinger on U.S. Angola position. Secretary of State Henry A. Kissinger held a news conference Dec. 23 to emphasize that the U.S. would continue to oppose imposition of a Soviet-backed regime in Angola. Kissinger met later in the day with Soviet Ambassador Anatoly F. Dobrynin.

"Unless the Soviet Union shows restraint in its foreign policy actions," Kissinger cautioned, "the situation in our relationship is bound to become more tense, and there is no question that the United States will not accept Soviet military expansion of any kind."

While pledging that no American forces would be sent to Angola, Kissinger said the U.S. would continue to supply its available military aid to the Angolan factions fighting the Soviet-backed faction and to press for diplomatic solution, primarily through the Organization of African Unity. He spoke of $9 million still in the pipeline for covert military aid and said the U.S. would make "every effort" militarily with that aid.

If necessary, Kissinger said, the Administration would seek more such financing from Congress in the next session.

In relating the Angola situation to other areas of U.S.-Soviet relations, Kissinger asserted the Administration would do nothing to promote Congressional approval of trade concessions for the Soviet Union. But he said he would wait a while to see if his planned trip to Moscow early in 1976 for arms-limitation talks was "in jeopardy or not." As for the talks, Kissinger stressed their importance to both countries and said the problem facing the U.S. was "avoiding nuclear war without giving up any interests."

That was "the preeminent problem of our period," Kissinger said, the problem of "how to manage the emergence of Soviet power without sacrificing vital interests."

The issue at hand "is not whether the country of Angola represents a vital interest to the United States," he continued. "The issue is whether the Soviet Union, backed by a Cuban expeditionary force, can impose on two-thirds of the population its own brand of government." If the U.S. support in Angola ended, he said, "we are practically inviting outside forces to participate in every situation in which there is a possibility for foreign intervention, and we are, therefore, undermining any hope of political and international order."

The Senate action against covert aid, Kissinger said, had "severely complicated" the U.S. effort for a diplomatic solution.

Moscow rebuffs U.S., vows more MPLA aid. The Soviet Union Dec. 24 and 25 defended its support for the Popular Movement for the Liberation of Angola (MPLA) and rejected the U.S. demand that it halt its involvement in the Angolan war.

The government newspaper *Izvestia* Dec. 24 declared that "support for the national liberation struggle of the people," as realized in Moscow's support of the MPLA, "is an important principle of Soviet foreign policy, the same as the steadfast struggle for improving international relations." It added, however, that "detente [between the U.S. and the U.S.S.R.] cannot mean the freezing of the status quo around the world."

The Communist Party newspaper *Pravda* charged Dec. 25: "There is enough evidence to confirm that South African aggression is performed with the agreement and assistance of certain U.S. circles and circles in other NATO [North Atlantic Treaty Organization] countries."

In a statement in the Dec. 25 edition of *Izvestia,* Moscow expressed its further commitment to the MPLA with the assertion that "the anti-colonial revolution does not end with the achievement of independence. It is quite natural that assistance should be continued."

According to Western sources cited by United Press International Dec. 22, Soviet aid to the MPLA had totaled $100 million. U.S. aid to the other two movements, the National Front for the Liberation of Angola (FNLA) and the

National Union for the Total Independence of Angola (Unita), had previously been reported as amounting to $60 million.

(The *New York Times* reported in a Dec. 18 article by Seymour Hersh that Washington officials had confirmed that the Ford Administration's initial authorization for substantial Central Intelligence Agency financial operations in Angola had come in January 1975, more than two months before the first significant Soviet build-up.)

A high-ranking Administration official observed Dec. 24 that the U.S. had been slow to express its concern to the Soviet Union about Angolan developments. The first such statements were reportedly made in September and a formal protest was issued in late October. Secretary of State Henry Kissinger and Soviet Ambassador Anatoly Dobrynin were said to have met "four or five times" since September, most recently Dec. 23.

U.S. seeks to counter MPLA support—William E. Schaufele, Jr., newly confirmed assistant secretary for African affairs, left Washington Dec. 25 for talks in Zaire, Gabon, Cameroon, the Ivory Coast and Senegal, in a move seen as an attempt by the U.S. to rally African nations to withhold recognition of the MPLA at the emergency meeting of the Organization of African Unity set for January. The January meeting, the first extraordinary session in the organization's history, had been called to consider the Angolan crisis.

The Schaufele trip was launched as OAU Chairman Idi Amin Dada, president of Uganda, declared in a Dec. 25 statement: "We should not let ourselves be brainwashed by the Western powers that the presence of Soviet technicians in Angola is an indication that the Soviet Union wants to colonize Africa."

Amin's statement represented a reversal of his previous stance advocating OAU neutrality and formulation of a government of national conciliation in Angola. With the recognition of the MPLA Dec. 25 by Burundi and Ghana, a total of 19 OAU member nations had defied Amin's earlier appeal to withhold recognition of any of the Angolan parties. No nation had recognized the government proclaimed by Unita and the FNLA.

U. S. mercenary training charged—The U.S. Army was reportedly training 300 mercenaries, half of them Americans, to join 300 other U.S.-trained forces, most of them American, assisting pro-Western forces fighting in Angola, according to an article in the Boston daily newspaper *Christian Science Monitor* Jan. 2, 1976.

The report alleged that the training program, a refresher course at Fort Benning, Ga., was sponsored by the Central Intelligence Agency. The U.S. mercenaries, most of them on indefinite leave from the Army's Special Forces or recently discharged military men, were reportedly being paid $1,000–$1,500 a month.

The White House Jan. 2 denied that Americans were being trained for combat roles in Angola, but would not comment on whether foreigners were being trained.

(The Associated Press reported Jan. 3 that Cuban refugees were recruiting exiles in Miami, Fla. to fight against the Soviet-supported Angolan movement. The two Cubans organizing the recruitment drive claimed to have been working through a U.S. organization but declined to identify it.)

Sen. John V. Tunney (D, Calif.) charged Jan. 6 that American pilots were airlifting weapons from Zaire into Angola aboard U.S.-built C-130 cargo planes. The White House Jan. 7 denied as "totally false" the claim that Americans were flying weapons into Angola, but conceded that Zaire might be using U.S. foreign assistance funds to subsidize an airlift operation.

U.S. denies mercenary role—The White House, the State Department and the Central Intelligence Agency Feb. 2 issued separate statements denying that the U.S. had been involved in financing the recruitment in Britain or elsewhere of mercenaries to fight alongside western-backed forces in Angola. The U.S. embassy in London Feb. 2 specifically denied a British press report that Maj. James E. Leonard, an assistant Army attache, was helping to recruit the mercenaries.

In a related development, Justice Department sources said Jan. 30 that the Department had asked the Federal Bureau of Investigation to look into violations of federal neutrality statutes by mercenary soldiers reported to have signed up to fight in Angola and by those who were recruiting them.

Italy

CIA aid to centrists reported. The U.S. Central Intelligence Agency had made $6 million worth of secret cash payments to individual anti-Communist leaders in Italy in 1975, it was disclosed Jan. 7, 1976. The payments, reportedly authorized Dec. 8, 1975 by President Ford, were said to have been part of a program to counteract growing Communist influence in Italian politics.

Spokesmen for the Christian Democrats, the Socialists, the Liberals and the Republicans Jan. 7 denied that any members of their parties had received any funds from the CIA.

According to the *New York Times* Jan. 7, which cited well-informed sources, the secret fund also had the strong approval of Secretary of State Henry A. Kissinger. Kissinger was reported to have been concerned about Communist gains in the June 1975 local Italian elections. When he visited Europe in December 1975 for the NATO and Paris energy conferences he assertedly had informed Western leaders that the United States would oppose the entry of the Communists into European coalition governments.

U.S. Senate and House of Representatives intelligence review committees were briefed on the CIA covert aid program Dec. 8 and Dec. 9, 1975, respectively, by CIA Director William E. Colby. Colby reportedly disclosed that the major portion of the $6 million was intended for helping finance centrist Christian Democratic Party politicians and members of the Socialist Party. A slight percentage, A he said, would go to the minority Republican Party.

Rep. Wayne L. Hays (D, Ohio) Dec. 9 reportedly challenged Colby, in the closed-door hearings, to prove that CIA payments would not ultimately end up in the private accounts of the designated recipients of the funds.

According to other unconfirmed accounts cited in the *Times* article, John A. Volpe, the United States ambassador to B Italy, had also objected to the operation, warning that, if it were divulged, it might prove to be extremely embarrassing to the politicians who received the aid and to the Ford administration.

An American official interviewed by the *Times* said that the $6 million figure was "peanuts" when compared with the total amount of sub rosa aid to Italian political parties spent each year. This included, the *Times* said, substantial amounts funneled into the Communist Party and its allied C trade unions by the Soviet Union as well as large subsidies to centrist politicians made by large multinational corporations, such as those disclosed in 1975 by the U.S. Mobil Oil and Exxon corporations.

The Jan. 7 news accounts did not indicate the names of the Italian figures who were said to be recipients of the CIA payments.

President Ford Jan. 7 was described by his press secretary, Ron Nessen, to have D been angered by the publication of reports of the CIA covert funding operation in Italy. Nessen, in a meeting with reporters, said that there was "a strong suspicion" in the White House that the press leaks had come from the congressmen who had been briefed by Colby. The leaks, Nessen added, were believed by the President to undermine "our capability to carry out our foreign policy."

Meanwhile, other White House officials E Jan. 7 had confirmed the veracity of the newspaper stories, the *New York Times* said Jan. 8.

Communists score CIA aid charges. The Italian Communist Party Jan. 8 responded to reports of the previous day that the U.S. Central Intelligence Agency had given $6 million in secret cash payments to anti-Communist politicians beginning Dec. 8, 1975. F

An article published in the party newspaper *L'Unita* accused the CIA of "brutal interference in our domestic affairs." The money had only succeeded in funding "bad government and corruption" and exacerbating "the general crisis of the country," *L'Unita* said.

Jan. 9 news reports said that while most Italian publications were down-playing the CIA story, Christian Democratic leaders had expressed concern that their already G crisis-ridden party could be damaged by the disclosures.

In a related development, CIA Director William E. Colby Jan. 9 said that no money had been spent by his agency in Italy "in the past few months." Colby, interviewed on a U.S. television program, refused, however, to discuss what future plans the CIA might have.

A The *Washington Post* reported Jan. 9, citing an informed source, that there had been no disbursement of funds in Italy because the CIA director's contingency fund had been depleted by paramilitary expenditures in Angola. Furthermore, because the cash payments were allegedly geared toward upcoming Italian elections, no money had to be transferred immediately last year.

B **Covert foreign aid scored by parties.** The national executive body of the ruling Christian Democratic Party Jan. 26, 1976 urged that details of the alleged secret Central Intelligence Agency payments to Italian anti-Communist politicians be made public. It adopted a resolution calling on the government to seek to persuade President Ford not to impose any restrictions on "the publication of documents or information on the subject regarding
C Italy." It noted "there cannot and should not be any doubts about these matters."

The Italian Communist Party, acting to counter widespread charges levied in the aftermath of the CIA revelations that it had received comparable massive subsidies from the Soviet Union, had held a news conference Jan. 16 to make public its financial statement for 1975.

Party spokesman Guido Cappelloni emphatically denied that the Communists
D had obtained any money from Moscow. Operating funds, he declared, came "very largely from party members, workers and electors."

The financial report Cappelloni released showed that the party had sustained an over-all deficit of $356,000 for 1975. Over 27% of its $34.8 million 1975 income, it said, came from party member contributions. Less than 45% was derived from state contributions fixed by law, according to the report.

Politicians named as CIA aid recipients. According to Jan. 31 reports, several top politicians were among the recipients of the estimated $75 million in covert anti-communist aid the U.S. Central Intelligence Agency funneled into centrist parties and individual political campaigns since 1947.

Following the Jan. 20–26 "leakage" of portions of the report of the U.S. House of Representatives' Select Committee on Intelligence, an investigation conducted by the Turin daily *La Stampa,* reported Jan. 31, disclosed that U.S. Ambassador to Italy Graham Martin in 1972 had obtained approval from Secretary of State Henry A. Kissinger for the payment of $800,000 to the head of Italian military intelligence, Gen. Vito Miceli.

Miceli, who served until 1974 as chief of the Defense Intelligence Service (SID), was currently under indictment for alleged subversive activities in 1970.

The *Washington Post* Jan. 31 said that *La Stampa* had also reportedly identified the names of four politicians it claimed had received CIA payments in December 1975. These included former Christian Democratic Premier Giulio Andreotti, Industry Minister Carlo Donat-Cattin, also a Christian Democrat; labor leader Vito Scalia; and former President Giuseppe Saragat, a Social Democrat.

The *Post* article noted, in addition, that charges had been levied in a soon-to-be-published book by two Italians alleging that Cardinal Giovanni Battista Montini, now Pope Paul VI, had cooperated closely with the U.S. wartime Office of Strategic Services and the CIA between 1942 and 1950.

In a related development, the French newspaper *Le Monde* Feb. 14 carried a report originally published in the Rome weekly *L'Expresso* maintaining that the Vatican had been infiltrated by both the CIA and SID. *L'Expresso* asserted that the late vicar general of Rome, Msgr. Angelo Dell'Acqua, had communicated developments in the Holy See to both intelligence services from the accession of Pope John XXIII to Dell'Acqua's death in 1972.

In another development, Giulio Andreotti, Italy's budget minister, said Feb. 2 in Rome that he saw no reason why President Ford should think it was in Italy's best interests to ban publication of reports on CIA Italian activities. The importance of such matters could be decided in Italy, Andreotti said.

Alleged CIA agents' named. The newly-founded leftist newspaper *La Republica* Jan. 16 published a list of eight alleged CIA agents operating in Italy. The report said that more than 40 agents worked out of the U.S. embassy in Rome. It claimed that other agents maintained covers in the Rome and Milan consulates and in U.S. military organizations and multinational corporations throughout Italy.

An Italian Journalist Interviews William Colby

Oriana Fallaci, the Italian journalist, spent "one long Friday morning and a long Sunday afternoon" in February interviewing former CIA Director William Colby at his home in Washington. She regards the encounter as an "exhausting and nasty fight" between spy and victim. But it was a strange fight. While her voice "trembled with rage," Colby was unperturbed—cool, controlled, polite—as he answered her accusations. She thought she saw anger occasionally in his blue eyes, but "his lips did not stop smiling, his hands would not stop pouring coffee in my cup."

This article was condensed from a longer version which appeared in The New Republic, March 13, 1976.

Oriana Fallaci: The names, Mr. Colby. The names of those bastards who took CIA money in my country. Don't you think that Mr. Pertini, the president of the Italian Parliament, should have those names?

William Colby: No, because our House has said by vote that those reports must remain secret. CIA should protect its associates and people who work for them. Of course the decision of to give or not to give those names does not depend on CIA; it depends on the government of the United States and I am not speaking for my government; I'm speaking for CIA.

But my judgment is no; my recommendation would be no. No names. It's the only thing I can do to maintain my agreement with the people I worked with . . . because, if I break my promise, when I go to someone new he'll say that my promise is no good. Why don't you ask the Soviet government for the names of the Communists who take Moscow's money in Italy? The Soviets are doing exactly the same.

Fallaci: We'll talk later about the Russians, Mr. Colby. Now let's talk about CIA. Tell me, please, if I came here, as a foreigner, and financed an American party, and 21 of your politicians, and some of your journalists, what would you do?

Colby: You would be doing an illegal thing and, if I found it out, I would report it to the FBI and have you arrested.

Fallaci: Good. So I should report you and your agents and your ambassadors to the Italian police and have you all arrested.

Colby: I won't say that.

Fallaci: Why not? If it is illegal that I come here to corrupt your politicians, it is as illegal that you come there and corrupt my politicians.

Colby: I am not saying that you would corrupt. I am saying that it is against our law for you to come and do that.

Fallaci: It is also against mine, Mr. Colby! And I'll tell you more: There is only one human type that is more disgusting than the corrupted one. It is the corruptor.

Colby: We don't corrupt at CIA. You may have a problem with corruption in your society but it was in existence long before CIA got there. Saying that we corrupt is like saying that we give money to do things for us. That isn't why we give money.

We give money to help somebody to do what he wants and cannot do because he hasn't enough money. We are basically supporting the democratic countries and, of all the countries that should understand this, Italy should. Because the American assistance in Italy helped it from becoming an authoritarian communism for 30 years . . .

Fallaci: Your clients, as you call them in the Pike report. Tell me, Mr. Colby, what do you mean by the word "clients"?

Colby: Well . . . What is an attorney doing when he deals with a client? An attorney helps a client.

Fallaci: I see! You consider yourself the attorney of the Christian Democrats and of the Social Democrats in Italy.

Colby: Right. Well, no . . . I will not comment about any particular situation.

Fallaci: Why? Had you answered with a lie when saying "right?"

Colby: I don't lie! And I suffer when they accuse me of lying. . . . Sometimes I refuse to give information; sometimes I keep a secret; but never lie. My Congress won't let me, my press either. The head of intelligence in America cannot say that it is not true when it's true. Our intelligence is under the law, not outside the law.

Anyway, I want to put a question to you: would it have been right or not if America had helped the democratic parties against Hitler?

Fallaci: There is no Hitler in Italy. And the $800,000 that Ambassador Graham Martin wanted to give to Gen. Vito Miceli, with Kissinger's blessing, did not end up in democratic hands. It ended up in the hands of Hitler's followers, the neofascists.

Colby: I will not discuss any specific CIA operation. First, I have great respect for Ambassador Martin. We have been together in different parts of the world and I have always found him a very strong ambassador, always taking positions and responsibilities in the interest of the United States. Secondly, I believe that in this kind of activity CIA can have a view and the government can have another. It is up to the President to decide. In any of these kinds of operations, CIA follows the directions of its government. . . . Until a year ago, the President could call the head of CIA and say to him: "Do that and don't tell anybody."

Fallaci: We all know that SID (Italian Secret Service) is the pied-a-terre of CIA in Italy. Now tell me, Mr. Colby, what right do you have to spy on me at home and use the secret service of my country? What right do you have, for instance, to control my telephone there?

Colby: I get news from around the world. There is nothing wrong with trying to understand what is happening in the world, what people are doing or thinking. It isn't a matter of invading others' privacy. It's a matter of looking to see if you have a pistol to shoot me or another weapon to hurt me, and prevent it. You ask if a nation has the right to conduct clandestine intelligence activities in other nations? Well, there is a law in every country that says no, and almost every country does it. So do I have the right to try to find out what happens in order to protect my country? Yes, I morally have it. Though it is illegal.

Fallaci: Let's see if I have understood you. You're saying that it is illegal yet legitimate to spy on me in my country even through the secret service of my country. . .

Colby: It depends. Sometimes another intelligence agency will help you. It depends on a country's policy. Sometimes two countries have a mutual interest and they are very close to their allies and very concerned about penetration, so we work together.

Fallaci: Only agents or clients also?

Colby: Those too. Some have said, don't give me anything anymore because you will reveal it. People who were new and people who were old clients. They felt betrayed. We have fought very hard at CIA to keep those names, you know. Very hard. And we have won, I must say. But the publicity has hurt us all the same.

These things do not happen with KGB. You have quite a few KGB agents in Italy and there are many Italians working for KGB of course. Yet nobody asks KGB to make those names public. One finds all these wrongs about CIA, and KGB—nobody accuses them.

But suppose that the Communists are clean. And because of that you let them run the government? Are you going to run that risk, letting them run the government? Name a country that has been communist and has then changed from communism. Name one! Name one!

Fallaci: Mr. Colby, what would you do to us if the Communists win the elections in Italy?

Colby: Name a country! Name one!

Fallaci: Mr. Colby, would you punish is with a coup as in Chile?

Colby: Name a country.

Just one! Rumania? Poland? Czechoslovakia? Hungary?

Fallaci: Please answer my question, Mr. Colby Another Chile?

Colby: And suppose there is not another election? The way it happened with Hitler and Mussolini? Don't you understand that they played at the democratic game all these years because they were a minority? Do you really think that when they are on the top they will still go on being democratic? . . .

Fallaci: I insist you answer the question. What would the Americans do to us if the Communists came to power in Italy? A

Colby: I don't know. This is the policy of the United States. I don't know.

Fallaci: Sure you know. Another Chile?

Colby: Not necessarily. This is an hypothetical question I cannot answer. It depends on so many factors. It could be nothing, it could be something, it could be some mistake.

Fallaci: Some mistake like Chile? Come on, Mr. Colby. Do you think it would be legitimate for the United States to intervene in Italy with a Pinochet if the Communists came to power?

Colby: I don't think I can answer that question. Your Pinochet is not in America. He's in Italy. B

Fallaci: I know. But he needs you. Without you, he can do nothing. Mr. Colby, I am trying to make you admit that Italy is an independent state, not a banana republic, not a colony of yours. And you don't admit it. I am also trying to explain to you that you cannot be the policemen of the world.

Colby: Chiaro ma sbagliato. After World War I we said that the war had been wrong and badly fought, and we had a period of innocence. We reduced our army to something smaller than the Romanian army, 150,000, and we decided to have an open diplomacy, and the Secretary of State dissolved the intelligence service saying that gentlemen don't read others' mail. C

And we thought that we were going to live in a world of gentlemen, and that we wouldn't involve ourselves any more in foreign affairs. Then we had problems rising in Europe. But we did not intervene. And we had problems in Manchuria, it was too far away. But we did not intervene. Then Spain. And we were neutral.

But it did not work very well, no, and we had economic problems; authoritarian leaders who believe they could dominate their neighbors. And then came World War II. And after World War II we did as we had done. In 1945 we dissolved our intelligence service, the OSS, and we said: peace again. But the Cold War started and it was obvious that Stalin was . . . becoming a threat in Greece, in Turkey, in Iran. And we learned the lesson. And we applied the lesson. D We collected our security again, and we attempted to contain the expansionist Soviet Union through NATO and through the Marshall plan and through CIA.

Liberals and conservatives together, both of us convinced that we had to help. I was one of those liberals. I had been a radical when I was a boy and . . .

Fallaci: For Christ's sake! How could you change that much?

Colby: Clemenceau said that he who is not a radical when he is young has no heart; he who is not conservative when he's old has no brain. But let me go on.

NATO worked. The containment of Soviet expansionism worked. The subversive plans of the Communists were frustrated. E It wasn't the right against the left. It was a democratic solution. We decided that we would go any distance to fight for freedom. And in the course of this there were some situations in which local leaders were somewhat authoritarian or more authoritarian than people liked.

Fallaci: From Gen. Franco to Caetano, from Diem to Thieu, from Papadopoulos to Pinochet, without counting all the fascist dictators in Latin America, the Brazilian torturers for instance. And so, in the name of freedom, you became the supporters of all those who killed freedom on the other side.

Colby: Like in the World War II when we supported Stalin's Russia against a greater threat. We work now in the same way we worked with him then. F In the '50s wasn't communism the biggest threat? If you support some authoritarian leader against a communist threat, you leave the option that the authoritarian state could become democratic in the future. With the Communists, the future offers no hope. My government recognizes Pinochet's Chile as the legitimate government. True. But don't I accept that 200 million Russians live under Soviet communism? Pinochet is not going to conquer the world. Nobody is worried about Pinochet.

Fallaci: I'll tell you who's worried about Pinochet, Mr. Colby. The Chileans, first, who are imprisoned and persecuted and tortured and killed by Pinochet. Secondly, those who really care about freedom. G Thirdly, the countries that are afraid to become a second Chile. Like mine.

France

Paris paper links 44 to CIA. The radical Paris newspaper *Liberation* Jan. 13, 1976 A published a list of 32 men and women it claimed were among the top 50 U.S. Central Intelligence Agency members in the French capital. The pro-Marxist paper, which was founded by the French philosopher Jean-Paul Sartre, said that the investigatory work for the article had taken three months and had been carried out in conjunction with *Counterspy*, an American magazine published by disaffected former CIA agents.

Liberation identified Eugen F. B Burgstaller, officially listed as an attache in the U.S. embassy in Paris, as the head of the CIA Paris station. It also printed what it said were his office location, home address and telephone number. Similar revelations that had appeared in the Athens press in November 1975 had been widely regarded as having contributed to the exposure and Dec. 23, 1975 assassination of CIA station chief Richard S. Welch.

C Also linked to the CIA in Paris were Oleg Selsky, whom the paper claimed was an "expert in the struggle against the KGB," the Soviet intelligence network; John Berg, an attache; Dominic Tacconelli, allegedly the paymaster for CIA missions; and Michael Bergen.

In making the disclosures, *Liberation* said that it did "not wish the death of anyone," but that CIA agents always ran the risk of retaliation when they engaged in subversive activities. The paper also de- D fended itself against charges that it was only exposing American agents to jeopardy by expressing the view that all Soviet officials were automatically suspect whereas foreign nationals could easily be misled by an "engaging American cultural attache."

The Paris newspaper Jan. 14 added 12 more names, six men and six women, to its list of alleged CIA agents.

The London *Times* Jan. 14 reported E that only three of the 32 names listed in *Liberation* were to be found in the 1974 foreign service list of the U.S. State Department, its most recent edition. In addition, none were listed in official diplomatic reference sources as being stationed in Paris.

A U.S. State Department spokesman Jan. 13 denounced the Paris disclosures as "contemptible and inflammatory."

In a related development, it was F reported Jan. 19 that the French weekly news magazine *Nouvel Observateur* had named Soviet counsellors Ivan Kislyak and Nikolai Vevdokimov as Paris heads of the KGB security services and GRU military intelligence, respectively.

Spain, Great Britain

Alleged CIA agents named. The *London Times* Jan. 14 reported that the Madrid G weekly *Cambio-16* had named nine men it claimed were operatives of the U.S. Central Intelligence Agency working in Spain. The magazine identified Robert Gahagen, an attache at the U.S. embassy, as the station chief and said the list had been drawn up with the help of Philip P. Agee, a former CIA agent. [See Vol. I, p. 99F3]

The London *Socialist Worker*, a small left-wing publication, Jan. 22 identified the names and addresses of five individuals it said worked for the CIA in London, including the alleged chief of station.

The London weekly magazine *Time Out*, which in 1975 had disclosed the names of 60 alleged CIA agents, added three more to the list in its Jan. 15 issue. The article also said that the number of CIA agents working in London had increased from 60 to 70 people in recent months.

West Germany

Leftist journal publishes CIA list. The leftist weekly periodical *Informations-Dienst* Feb. 9 published a list allegedly containing the names of 10 U.S. Central Intelligence Agency operates in the country. The names of five men and women, their home addresses and telephone numbers were printed. All were said to be employed by the U.S. embassy in Bonn.

The periodical had published the previous week a similar list of 15 names, the London *Times* reported Feb. 10.

Denmark

Communist deputy bugged in '58. The Danish Justice and Defense Minister Orla Moeller Jan. 9 confirmed that the Copenhagen apartment of Communist deputy Alfred Jansen had been wired with listening devices in 1958 by "foreign secret agents." Moeller, questioned by a Socialist People's Party deputy who asked him about a Radio Denmark report that the U.S. Central Intelligence Agency had been involved, refused to identify the nationality of the agents. He denied, however, that the Danish intelligence service had been involved. Moeller said no action had been taken when the matter was discovered in 1964 because the statute of limitations had expired.

South Vietnam

Vietnam troop estimates defended. William E. Colby, outgoing director of the Central Intelligence Agency, Dec. 3 denied that the CIA and military intelligence had conspired to deliberately downgrade enemy troop strength figures before the 1968 Tet offensive in South Vietnam to make it appear that the U.S. and its allies were winning the Vietnam War.

In prepared testimony before the House Select Committee on Intelligence, Colby said that the CIA in 1967 had concluded that the overall strength of the Communists "was probably in the 500,000 range and maybe even higher." This estimate was in sharp contrast to the official military intelligence figure of 292,000 enemy troops, Colby said. "The CIA did not shrink from pushing the case for higher figures and made no attempt to produce 'politically acceptable' estimates," he added.

Colby said the difference between the CIA's and the military's estimates were primarily the result of "differing assessments of who presented a danger in Vietnam."

Samuel A. Adams, a former CIA analyst, had testified previously before the committee that Communist strength had been falsified to give the appearance that the allies were winning in Vietnam.

Saigon 'rebellion' crushed. Armed dissidents staged a rebellion in a Roman Catholic church in Saigon Feb. 12 but were suppressed after security forces stormed the building Feb. 13. A security officer was killed at the outset and two of the dissidents were slain the following day. Five persons, including a priest, were arrested.

According to the official accounts, the security man was shot as he and a fellow officer approached the church. The rebels continued to fire after rejecting a government ultimatum to surrender. Security forces then hurled hand grenades and broke into the building. Leaflets, letters, weapons, radio transmitter equipments, and printing machinery to forge banknotes were found in the church. "It is an armed rebellion opposing the revolutionary government and undermining the economy and life of the people," a government statement said Feb. 15. The U.S. Central Intelligence Agency, it said, "is involved in this political plot to sabotage the security" of South Vietnam, a charge denied by the U.S. State Department.

A government official told newsmen Feb. 15 of other instances of armed rebellion in the past few months, some of which involved sniping and grenade-throwing. Other incidents were marked by the secret distribution of leaflets signed by two generals of the former regime.

Japan

CIA informed of Lockheed bribes. The Central Intelligence Agency was kept informed of secret Lockheed bribe payments to Japanese officials in the late 1950s, the *New York Times* reported on April 2, 1976.

The account said that a Japanese citizen, who in 1958 had worked for Lockheed, had admitted passing on the information to a U.S. embassy official in Tokyo. The embassy official reportedly worked for the CIA.

The *Times* report, which quoted both Japanese sources and a former CIA official, said that the CIA had failed to forward the data to either the U.S. State Department or the U.S. Grumman Aircraft Corp. Grumman then was competing with Lockheed for Japanese defense contracts.

Spokesmen for both the CIA and Lockheed denied the allegations, the *Times* reported.

Chile

CIA role in Chile detailed. A staff report by the Senate Select Committee on Intelligence, made public Dec. 4, 1975, absolved the Central Intelligence Agency of direct involvement in the military coup in 1973 against the late Chilean president, Salvador Allende. However, the report said that the CIA had spent $13.4 million on covert operations in Chile between 1963 and 1974, most of it in a campaign against Allende.

Although most of the information in the 62-page report had been made public earlier, some new facts concerning U.S. involvement in Chile were disclosed:

- After President Nixon ordered a stepped-up effort against Allende in September 1970, the CIA secretly channeled $1.5 million to *El Mercurio,* Chile's largest daily newspaper, to insure continuation of anti-Allende coverage and to keep the paper solvent.
- International Telephone and Telegraph Corp. put $350,000 of its own money into the Chilean presidential election of 1970, and other, unnamed U.S. businesses provided another $350,000 to candidates opposed to Allende.
- The 40 Committee, which approved covert U.S. intelligence operations, did not authorize funds to support lengthy strikes by Chilean truck drivers during 1971–73. But some money passed by the CIA to private sector groups supporting the strikes might in turn have been passed on to the strikers.

Nixon testimony on Chile released. Former President Nixon acknowledged, in sworn Congressional testimony released March 11, 1976, authorizing secret efforts to undermine the presidency of the late Salvador Allende in Chile in 1970. He said, however, that he did not recall specifically ordering a military coup or knowing that the CIA had tried to stir up a military coup that year.

The testimony was in answer to written interrogatories from the Senate Select Committee on Intelligence.

Nixon told the panel he also did not recall discussing in a key planning session "specific means to be used by the CIA to prevent Mr. Allende from assuming the presidency." He said he did recall discussing some ways to achieve it, such as "the direct expenditure of funds to assist Mr. Allende's opponents, the termination of the United States financial aid and assistance programs as a means of adversely affecting the Chilean economy, and the effort to enlist support of various factions, including the military, behind a candidate who could defeat Mr. Allende in the congressional confirmation procedure."

Nixon defended the intervention as being motivated by "the same national security interests" that prompted Presidents Kennedy and Johnson to authorize the CIA in the early 1960s to support Allende's political opponents financially. He also said, "It is quite obvious that there are certain inherently governmental actions which, if undertaken by the sovereign in protection of the interest of the nation's security, are lawful but which undertaken by private persons, are not."

As an example of the latter, he cited the 1969 wiretapping program against 17 government officials and newsmen to stop security information leaks.

Concerning that area of activity, Nixon remembered "learning on various occasions that during administrations prior to mine, agencies or employes of the United States government, acting presumably without a warrant, conducted wiretaps, surreptitious or unauthorized entries, and intercepts of voice and non-voice communications."

Nixon was queried by the panel on his statement, on a June 23, 1972 tape transcript, that his administration had protected former CIA director Richard M. Helms "from one hell of a lot of things." The reference, according to Nixon, was to his support of efforts by Helms to defend the CIA and prevent, by legal action if he chose, disclosure of CIA secrets in a forthcoming book.

'Dangerous doctrine' deplored—The select committee's chairman, Sen. Frank
Church (D, Idaho), March 11 denounced A
Nixon's advocacy of a doctrine of "the sovereign presidency" as "pernicious and dangerous."

U.S. presidents, he said, "unlike monarchs which we replaced 200 years ago, must, as any ordinary citizen be servants of the law."

The lesson to be learned was "not that illegal actions were justified," Church said, "rather it is that once government officials start believing that they have the
power and right to act secretly outside the B
law we have started down a long, slippery slope which culminates in a Watergate."

U.S. Citizens

CIA surveillance of Americans overseas. CIA Director George Bush stated that some Americans living overseas have been targets of CIA break-ins and electronic surveillance, the *Washington Post*
reported July 17. In a sworn statement C
released July 16, Bush made virtually the first official acknowledgement of U.S. spying on Americans abroad. Bush's statement was filed in U.S. District Court in New York City in connection with a $37 million suit filed by the Socialist Workers Party against the CIA, FBI, and other agencies.

Bush's sworn statement, given in response to questions from lawyers
representing the party, said: "The files of D
the CIA do contain information indicating that certain of the individual plaintiffs . . . were overheard by means of electronic surveillance conducted abroad; and that certain other information, apart from the conversations that were overheard, was acquired as a result of several surreptitious entries that were made into premises abroad. . ."

CIA STATION CHIEF IN ATHENS SLAIN; HAD BEEN NAMED AS AGENT IN PRESS

The Station chief of the U.S. Central Intelligence Agency in Greece, Richard S. Welch, 46, was shot and killed by three masked gunmen outside his home in a suburb of Athens Dec. 23. Greek President Constantine Caramanlis launched a special investigation into the assassination Dec. 24, but no arrests were reported despite numerous claims of responsibility by various extreme left- and right-wing political groups in Greece. Anti-U.S. sentiment had been rife in Greece after the demise of the military dictatorship in 1974.

President Ford Dec. 27 attributed the assassination to the publication of Welch's identity as a CIA operative and waived restrictions to enable Welch to be buried in Arlington National Cemetery, where burial was normally reserved for those who had served in the armed forces or who had died in the service of the country. Welch had been named as a CIA agent in a letter published in the English-language daily *Athens News* Nov. 25. Welch's CIA links had previously been cited in the January and June issues of a U.S. publication, *Counterspy,* published by a group which called itself the Fifth Estate for Security Education. The Fifth Estate Dec. 24 issued a statement charging that the CIA was responsible for Welch's death in so far as the agency had sent him "to spy, perhaps even to intervene in the affairs of the Greek government."

The Standard-Times

New Bedford, Mass., December 29, 1976

Violence takes no holiday. But the Christmas-time death of Richard S. Welch of the American Embassy in Athens was a particularly horrifying reminder because exponents of nonviolence may have helped seal his doom.

Last summer, a publication founded by U.S. protesters against the Vietnam war identified Mr. Welch, described by one who saw him shortly before he was gunned down as "an amiable man with a trim white mustache and the manners of a tweedy college professor," as a clandestine operative of the Central Intelligence Agency.

Meanwhile, the CIA came under attack in the U.S. Senate and House. Current and former heads of the agency protested that some of the publicity would expose the agency's personnel and informants to danger. The Ford administration vigorously opposed a Senate probers' plan to publish names of certain CIA agents.

The spectacle in Washington produced anti-CIA waves abroad, particularly among leftist factions. One, in Greece, delivered to an English-language newspaper in Athens the names and addresses of what it contended were CIA agents in Greece. Welch's was included. The list was published (but the same newspaper refused to publish a list of alleged Soviet undercover agents submitted by another faction).

The chain of events — how else could it be described? — came to its conclusion. Richard S. Welch stepped out of his car at his home and was assassinated.

We do not know how many, if any, American lives may have been saved by this "amiable man" in intelligence duties, or what he may have contributed to the nation's security. But intuition tells us his death was a needless sacrifice, and that some of his own countrymen should feel deep remorse.

Minneapolis Tribune

Minneapolis, Minn., December 30, 1976

A Washington newsletter called Counter-Spy recently published this prophetic quotation by Philip Agee, a former CIA agent who has written a muckraking book about the agency: "The most effective efforts to combat the CIA," said Agee, "are, I think, the identification, exposure and neutralization of its people working abroad." Richard Welch, CIA chief in Greece, was "neutralized" last week by assassination.

That was probably not what Agee had in mind. A spokesman for Counter-Spy said that "we obviously don't want to see anyone shot," but that identifying key CIA employees is a necessary public service. The publication this year named 150 individuals who it said are CIA station chiefs around the world. So the outrage shown against Counter-Spy in recent days by CIA Director William Colby, by the president of the Association of Retired Intelligence Officers and by many other Americans is understandable. We share the belief that singling out individuals in such a way is deplorable. And the practice is not unique to Counter-Spy. Athens newspapers last month published names, addresses and telephone numbers of CIA agents in Greece. Their doing so may not have caused Welch's death, but certainly made the gunmen's job easier.

The Athens shooting could have other repercussions. One is the linking of irresponsible criticism —exposure for the sake of exposure — with the more thoughtful investigations of American intelligence agencies. Already one sees attempts to imply that blame for Welch's death rests partly with congressional committees, which their critics say have helped generate public opposition to the CIA (and FBI). If the disclosures of wrongdoing were unfounded, that view might be justified. But it seems to us that the discovery of past shortcomings is necessary to devise remedies for the future. Moreover, the focus of the investigations has been accountability and policy-making by senior officials, including presidents, and not agents in the field.

Another possibility is rebirth of the belief that the intelligence services ought to remain secret in the sense they were in the past — with illegal activities tolerated, with top administration officials insulated from having to approve certain operations, with congressional oversight constrained to an uncritical few. That would be as dangerous as going to the extreme of eliminating covert intelligence.

Highly classified intelligence work does pose problems for a democracy. To immunize it from the political process jeopardizes the political process itself; to emasculate it by virtually eliminating secrecy exposes a free society to unacceptable dangers from others. The shooting in Athens should emphasize the importance of striking the right balance.

Sentinel Star

Orlando, Fla., January 1, 1976

RICHARD WELCH is to be buried with honors in Arlington National Cemetery but the questions swirling about his death in Greece won't be interred with him.

Was our CIA man in Athens fingered by the American anti-CIA group who blew his cover by identifying him, along with others, in their newspaper? Do dissidents have the right, legally and morally, to put counterspies in mortal danger by revealing secret data?

AT THIS writing there is no conclusive evidence that Welch's death was related to the publication of his name. Actually, in fact, we seriously doubt that our principal adversaries, such as the old pros of the Soviet KGB, would need to rely on such data. They probably knew as much about Welch as his wife or boss did.

The hazard of such irresponsible publicity is that it can incite the suggestible crazies of the world, who need little urging to kill and terrorize.

Anyway, what possible good comes of "telling all" about America's espionage network? Assuming there is a case against the CIA, how is it advanced by printing the agency's roster? Other agents may die if this abuse of free speech continues.

The State

Columbia, S.C., January 4, 1976

NO ONE in his right mind could expect that the constant exposure of American intelligence systems, mainly the Central Intelligence Agency, would not eventually result in some impairment of that essential function.

Just how much capability has been lost to conduct the dark but necessary part of our foreign policy may never be known, but the United States is not faring well in the ideological contest around the world with the Soviet Union.

The murder of Robert S. Welch, the CIA's station chief in Athens, must sound an alarm in the minds of congressional investigators, Sen. Frank Church's Select Committee on Intelligence in particular.

It may be, as Senator Church contends, that his committee did not name the names of any intelligence agents. But there can be little doubt that the Senator's showy handling of his committee's work contributed to the atmosphere in which Mr. Welch was gunned down.

The United States in general and the CIA in particular have been extremely unpopular in Greece. The agency has been repeatedly accused of supporting the military government which ran Greece for seven years until it was overthrown in 1974. The CIA is also suspected of having promoted the coup against Archbishop Makarios in Cyprus, an event that triggered an invasion by Turkey which left the Greeks fuming at their own inability to respond.

Add to that atmosphere the long run of disclosures about the CIA's alleged misdeeds from the congressional committee hearings. Those disclosures charged the political climate in Greece with greater tension and animosity for the United States and its CIA.

The conditions were ripe, then, for political gunmen to slay an American agent on his own doorstep. As one correspondent in Athens suggested, the assassination of a CIA agent had become a "desirable objective" for extremists.

As for naming the names of intelligence agents in the field, the culprit is *Counterspy*, a magazine manned by ex-intelligence agents and embittered Vietnam veterans who apparently wish to see the CIA destroyed. They may find some defense in claiming that the names of the agents named by them, including Mr. Welch, had already been published elsewhere.

We do not excuse them. The fact is that in their zealous condemnation of the CIA for its violent covert activities and planned assassinations, the magazine embraces the very tactics they are deploring. The writers and editors know full well that listing agents by name is making marked men of them somewhere in the world. *Counterspy* may not pull the trigger, but they finger the targets.

While we resist the idea of prior censorship in our free society, there needs to be some parameters in dealing with matters of national security and the Americans who seek to maintain it. Perhaps Robert S. Welch did not die in vain if his murder provokes a greater sense of reason and patriotism in dealing with individuals and institutions which serve our national interests.

THE INDIANAPOLIS STAR

Indianapolis, Ind., January 2, 1976

"The gentleman is misinformed, since the committee has made no disclosures . . . that could possibly jeopardize the life of any CIA agent."

So said Senator Frank Church (D-Idaho) taking issue recently with comments of a retired Central Intelligence Agency officer that inquires into the CIA by Church's Senate Intelligence Committee should have been conducted without disclosing sensitive information.

The implication was that disclosures made by the committee had played a part in the assassination in Greece last week of CIA agent Richard S. Welch. A career civil servant, Welch was attached to the United States embassy at the time he was gunned down outside his home in an Athens suburb — an event strongly deplored by President Ford.

Obviously ruffled at the tagging of his often moralizing-prone committee as instrumental in the death of a respected U.S. government employe, Church was quick to explain that the committee never had announced the names of CIA agents.

Is Church on that safe ground, however, in thus hastening to absolve his committee of blame in the Welch killing?

For more than a year, obedient to New York Times publication of a story in late 1974 accusing the CIA of spying on some Americans, various congressional committees — including the Church committee — have busied themselves digging into CIA activities.

Unlike a committee of the House of Representatives disbanded due to internal strife and replaced by another which has gotten virtually nowhere, Church's Senate committee has kept its investigation going and has been ladling out at regular intervals tidbits clearly calculated to make Church look almost saintly and the CIA devilish.

The steady stream of anti-CIA propaganda thus churned out not only has raised doubts about the agency among many Americans — an end some observers believe intended — but it has had inflammatory repercussions on Left-leaning and terrorist elements in many parts of the world. From Cuba, South America, Africa, the Middle East, India and the Communist bloc nations comes a more and more insistent clamor that the world's ills mostly have been brought on by that intrusive instrument of "imperialist" America — the CIA.

Who killed CIA agent Welch? Greek authorities say they still don't know, though they consider the killing "a professional job" likely to be the work of organized terrorists. Doesn't it seem altogether possible, therefore, that inspiration for this repulsive assassination could have been a spin-off of the publicity-seeking goings-on of the Church committee — despite Church's rush to protect the committee by his claim it never actually announced names of CIA agents?

And doesn't all this suggest that Representative Samuel S. Stratton (D-N.Y.), a member of the House Armed Services Committee, knew what he was talking about when he said in backing a move to terminate the House's initial CIA probe:

"Why do we have to have a bunch of guys fiddling around and possibly jeopardizing the CIA? It seems to me clear this is not going to be a responsible inquiry."

THE RICHMOND NEWS LEADER

Richmond, Va., January 2, 1976

In February, 1973, some 500 of Norman Mailer's best friends gathered at a New York restaurant to celebrate the author's 50th birthday. They paid $50-per-couple for the honor of being present. Mailer announced that the takings would finance an organization called The Fifth Estate, which would expose American intelligence activities. Calling Fifth Estate a "democratic secret police," Mailer said: "We must see how much our paranoia is justified."

Since then, little has been heard of Fifth Estate — little, that is, until Richard Welch was gunned down in Athens, and CIA director William Colby angrily denounced the group's magazine, *Counter-Spy*, as having set Welch up for the hit. *Counter-Spy* denies Colby's charges: Its spokesmen say that most of those listed in the quarterly magazine are already known as CIA men. Indeed, according to *Newsweek*, many of the names listed in *Counter-Spy* also were included in a book called *Who's Who in the CIA* that appeared in Europe in 1967. *Who's Who* is believed to be the work of the Soviet secret police — known as the KGB.

Fifth Estate exhibits a distinct ambivalence in its denial of responsibility for Welch's death. "It's not our fault," said spokesman Tim Butz. But author Kirkpatrick Sale, a member of Fifth Estate's advisory board (a board that includes revolutionaries such as David Dellinger), told *Newsweek:* "The CIA is in the business of killing. Our job is to expose every clandestine agent until the CIA abandons its covert actions." That is hardly the rhetoric of moderation. Moreover, to seek "to expose every clandestine agent until the CIA abandons its covert actions" is to seek to put the CIA out of business. Implicitly, it is to seek to put the United States out of business as well.

The Fifth Estate evidently has decided that Norman Mailer's paranoia is justified, and Fifth Estate has taken to publishing hit lists of American agents. Regarding the murder of Richard Welch — an unsurprising consequence of Fifth Estate's decision to publish his name as an agent of the CIA — Fifth Estate is at least a moral accomplice.

The Birmingham News

Birmingham, Ala., January 4, 1976

Senate Intelligence Committee Chairman Frank Church disavows any responsibility for the murder of the Central Intelligence Agency's Richard S. Welch on grounds that his panel has in no way disclosed the names of any CIA agents.

Historians, however, will probably see things in a different light. It is doubtful that they will overlook the fact that Sen. Church has dragged the good name of the United States and the names of some of its presidents through the mud and slime of backroom politics for personal gain.

From his exalted seat in the U.S. Senate Church should know better than most how the jackals of international terrorism await opportunities to deface the American image and to call attention to our willful helplessness by assassinating U.S. officials.

With the nation nearly paralyzed by a Congress gorged on self-righteousness or suffering from timidity, it is no wonder terrorists, tools of the Soviet's KGB or simply common criminals feel they can prey on American citizens without fear of retaliation.

Whether Church revealed names or not, he has made a major contribution to the three-ring circus that has made the United States the laughing stock of the international community and the goat for political opportunists around the globe.

The Oregonian

Portland, Ore., January 7, 1976

The assassination of Richard S. Welch, 46, Harvard graduate in classical studies who became a brilliant strategist in espionage for the Central Intelligence Agency, by unknown terrorists in Athens, Greece, shocked official Washington. This was not a case of an unknown spy being cut down behind the iron or the bamboo curtain.

Welch was a cultured gentleman who did not even carry a gun and who had no dealings with the Mafia. His addresses were in embassies of the United States. He was an intimate of ambassadors. And his identity as a CIA official was exposed by an American counter-culture sheet in the midst of the congressional investigation and denunciation of alleged CIA misdeeds.

The nation should note well that President Gerald Ford issued a special ruling which made Welch the first CIA agent to be buried in the military cemetery at Arlington, Va., and that the President attended the funeral Tuesday. The presidential attention was a signal to Congress and all Americans, including those steeped in the sex-and-violence distortions of pocketbook and television spy thrillers, that American intelligence operations are manned by real men and women whose work is absolutely vital to national security and world peace.

Congress knows that, but some of its members have made the CIA, the FBI and military intelligence agencies the objects of political attack. And shoddy, so-called "activist" sheets such as "Counterspy" have endangered the lives of American agents by circulating identifications here and abroad. In an age of unchecked terrorism, every spy must live in fear and take fewer chances to do his job.

None of this is to say that violations of law and morally indefensible actions by intelligence personnel should be tolerated and hidden. It is to say that the agencies do what they must do and must not be exposed to needless dangers in the name of sensationalism. This world is real, not the creation of script writers, and men like Richard Welch are serving their country in a unique way. They deserve a maximum of protection and a minimum of harassment.

St. Louis Globe-Democrat

St. Louis, Mo., January 8, 1976

If there isn't a law that bans the publication of the names of CIA agents and others performing secret missions for the U.S., there should be. Safeguarding security agents by forbidding disclosure of their foreign assignments should be part of an official secrets act. Violation should be no more permissible than publishing troop movements during wartime.

In the wake of the murder of Richard S. Welch, the CIA's station chief in Greece, the Central Intelligence Agency has asked the Department of Justice to determine whether federal laws were violated in connection with the publication of the identity of Welch and 149 other CIA station chiefs last year by the Organization Committee for the Fifth Estate which publishes the magazine, "Counter-spy."

There is no question why the Fifth Estate group published the names of Welch and the other CIA agents. They wanted to subject them to reprisal from local people in the countries where the agents are assigned.

There is good possibility that Welch was assassinated as a direct result of being fingered by this crummy assortment of anti-Americans.

In the same issue in which the CIA agents' names were listed, Philip Agee, the former CIA case officer whose recent book, Inside the Company; CIA Diary, also carried many names of former agency colleagues, advocated "the identification, exposure, and neutralization" of CIA agents abroad. He added: "Having this information, the peoples victimized by the CIA . . . can bring pressure on their so-often compromised governments to expel the CIA people . . . And in the absence of such expulsions . . . the people themselves will have to decide what they must do to rid themselves of the CIA."

If that isn't a call to violence and an invitation to murder, then what is?

Unless the government shows some backbone and acts to protect the CIA from these traitorous "counterspies," it may find it difficult or impossible to get the caliber of men it needs.

The Evening Bulletin

Philadelphia, Pa., January 5, 1976

The Central Intelligence Agency has received frequent attention of late, and most of the attention has been critical in nature.

But the murder of Richard S. Welch, CIA operations chief in Athens, was the sad consequence of the most irresponsible kind of attack on the agency.

A career intelligence officer, Mr. Welch had endured many hardships in the service of his country. But, by most accounts, he eschewed dirty tricks in favor of scholarly analysis.

However, Mr. Welch's "cover had been blown," his identity and the nature of his assignment disclosed, by the magazine Counterspy. Published in Washington, this magazine seems to be dedicated to the destruction of the CIA. Books written by former CIA agents have similarly exposed the identities of other current employes of the vital federal intelligence agency.

The authors of these publications apparently labor under the incredibly twisted conviction that this country should have no intelligence agency. And to make their point they are willing to risk the lives of good men who serve the nation in essential and honorable posts.

No place exists in this democracy for "black operations" such as assassinations or overthrows of foreign governments. But intelligence about foreign governments, albeit clandestinely obtained, remains essential to the conducting of America's foreign policy. Insuring compliance with the Strategic Arms Limitation Treaty is only one of many uses for such intelligence.

Restructuring and overseeing the CIA remains essential. But in a democracy the method must be through Congressional action and the Joint Congressional oversight committes this newspaper has consistently supported.

Disclosing the names and the assignments of individual employes of the CIA is the wrong method. It is, in fact, no better than the political blackmail employed by terrorist kidnappers. It is an invitation to assassination, an invitation almost certain to lead to murder.

The murder of the 46-year-old father of three children gives a tragically painful lesson in restraint to all who would criticize a service with many dedicated men and women.

Los Angeles Times

Los Angeles, Calif., January 2, 1976

It is probably true that the names of CIA agents in foreign countries can be discovered one way or another by elements within those countries. Still, it is a wretched practice, akin to an invitation to murder, to publish their identities.

After an Athens newspaper identified Richard S. Welch as the CIA station chief in Greece and printed not only his name but also his address, three gunmen shot him to death outside his home. A Washington, D.C., quarterly called Counterspy previously identified Welch as a CIA agent in Lima, Peru. A quarterly spokesman announced that Counterspy next month will publish the names of CIA agents in Angola, France and Sweden.

The operation of the CIA is a matter to be determined by the government in response to public opinion as represented in Congress. The issue can be debated fully without any need to disclose the identities of CIA agents abroad. It is not an issue to be resolved by inspired assassinations under the spurious claim of devotion to democracy.

Albuquerque Journal

Albuquerque, N.M., January 7, 1976

The assassination of Richard S. Welch, scholarly intelligence agent for the Central Intelligence Agency attached to the U.S. embassy in Athens, should have invoked the grief of all Americans. The unprecedented hero's burial accorded him in Arlington National Cemetery was appropriate, for his tragic death was a proximate result of the hazardous activity in which he was engaged in the interest of national security.

But it is regrettable that Welch's extreme personal sacrifice should be overshadowed by the game of finger-pointing that the tragedy generated. President Ford, who attended the funeral to dramatize his deep personal concern, blamed Sen. Frank Church's investigating committee for going too far in its public disclosures — particularly in naming names — of past abuses of authority by the CIA. Others point to an organization calling itself the Fifth Estate and its publication, "Counterspy," as being responsible for identifying Welch to his enemies."

Now comes columnist Jerry F. terHorst, himself a former press secretary to President Ford, and points out that the U.S. State Dept. itself provided a foolproof means of identifying Welch as a CIA agent. Its snobbish means of distinguishing career State Dept. personnel from those borrowed from other federal agencies in its official directories could have been used to identify Welch as the target of his assassins.

While the American people are duly outraged by the far-ranging nature of CIA covert activities — activities which go far beyond American rules of decency and fair play — they will not be appeased by the knowledge that CIA agents, in carrying out the lawful and essential functions of their agency, are deprived of their all-important "cover" or anonymity by short-sighted governmental actions.

The Dallas Times Herald

Dallas, Tex., January 1, 1976

CIA AGENT Richard Welch, shot down in Athens, died in the service of his country, just as thousands of men and women in uniform have done throughout this nation's history. He deserves every honor a thankful country can bestow.

Welch will be buried with full military honors Friday in Arlington National Cemetery, after President Ford waived some requirements. The tribute was marred only by the protests of the head of the Veterans of Foreign Wars.

Thomas Walker, commander-in-chief of the VFW, said that although Welch's death was tragic, "interment in Arlington . . . should be for those uniformed servicemen who answered the call of their country in time of need.

Making an exception in Welch's case is "unjust and an insult to the dead servicemen who fought in battle for their country," Walker said.

Thoughtful Americans surely must disagree with the VFW leader. CIA agent Welch died in the service of his country just as much as any GI charging an enemy gun emplacement or an airman killed in a bombing run.

At a time when intelligence agents are risking their lives to enhance the security of their fellow citizens, it is appropriate for the President to waive rules on burials in Arlington National Cemetery.

The VFW's commander ought to apologize to the Welch family and to the nation for his remarks.

Long Island Press

Jamaica, N.Y., January 8, 1976

The murder of Richard S. Welch, the chief CIA agent in Athens, has slowed efforts by Congress to curb illegal intelligence activities abroad.

Congressional investigative committees have established that the CIA has been operating beyond its mandate by taking part in assassination plots against foreign leaders, trying to overthrow governments, and in other ways interfering in their internal affairs. The need to confine the agency to intelligence gathering was—and is—obvious, as demonstrated anew by the charge yesterday that the CIA is still sending money to anti-Communists in Italy with the approval of President Ford.

Clearly it was the duty of Congress to expose the wrongdoing, even at the risk that exposure might harm the CIA's legitimate operations, or endanger the lives of some agents.

* * *

Sadly, Mr. Welch's murder has served to emotionally intensify the debate and stifle those who believe that strict congressional oversight is vital. Instead of reasoned debate, the major question now is: Who blew the CIA agent's cover?

During the congressional investigation, the identities of the agency's undercover employes were correctly and successfully shielded. Unfortunately, the names of some agents—including that of Mr. Welch—were publicized abroad and—shamefully—by an underground magazine in this country.

The murdered agent's identity was exposed as long ago as 1968 by a leftist publication in West Germany, a year ago in Peru, and by an Athens newspaper only a month before he was gunned down. Mr. Welch was also named recently by Counter-Spy, a magazine published by CIA critics in this country.

Did any of these disclosures cause Mr. Welch's death? We may never know. But the story in Counter-Spy helped convince Rep. Robert H. Michel of Illinois, the House Republican whip, to propose legislation making it a crime to identify undercover American intelligence agents.

* * *

Whether such a law could be effective without violating First Amendment rights is a question Congress must resolve. We believe that no responsible American journalist would knowingly identify this country's intelligence people.

Besides, there are other ways for foreign nations to uncover our agents, just as we find out about theirs. In reality, the clandestine services are not all that secret. A CIA station chief in a foreign capital, for example, is nearly always a medium-to-high ranking State Department diplomat whose real mission becomes apparent to trained eyes.

There is no easy way to protect spies against exposure, any more than there is an easy way for Congress to keep the CIA in check. The related problems deserve priority attention from Congress and the White House, but hasty decisions may do more harm than good.

ST. LOUIS POST-DISPATCH

St. Louis, Mo., January 8, 1976

The recent slaying in Athens of Richard W. Welch, head of the Central Intelligence Agency's operations in Greece, has fathered a new rationale for proposals to limit free speech. What formerly was sought on the ground of national security is now sought on the ground of the personal security of the nation's intelligence employes.

It is understandable that an individual human life is a lot more real than "national security" to a people to whom "national security" has become a vague term to cover a multitude of political sins. But that does not make vague fears of personal danger a good reason for tampering with the Constitution. And all proposals to do so—such as that of Representative Bob Michel of Illinois to make it a federal crime to reveal the identity of an American intelligence agent—should be rejected.

That having been said, we must say also that we fail to understand the motivation of CIA critics in listing the identity of agents. Criticism of CIA operations and even the identification of particular agents involved in questionable activities certainly add to needed public discussion of the nation's conduct abroad. But nothing is accomplished by simply compiling and releasing lists of agents. The practice can be harmful to proper intelligence activities and dangerous to the agents involved.

Although Americans may be exercising a constitutionally protected right in identifying spies and in particular circumstances may be fulfilling a duty in doing so, there is no good reason for wholesale publication of such information. Therefore, we believe that if those groups who have made public such lists wish to be acknowledged as serious and responsible critics of this nation's policies they must either rethink or better defend their tactics.

The Boston Globe

Boston, Mass., January 15, 1976

Exposure of Central Intelligence Agency operatives by foreign publications is, as the State Department has said, "contemptible and inflammatory." For the sake of neutralizing the effectiveness of the CIA abroad — which the listing of agents' names certainly accomplished — the foreign journals have subjected these men and women and their innocent families to grave personal risk. Richard Welch, gunned down in Greece, may be only the first victim.

Appalling as the trend is, it is not likely to stop. Publications in Mexico, Britain, Spain, Portugal, Sweden, Greece and now France have listed our agents there, helped by the American magazine Counter-Spy — and those countries are friendly to us. Agents in Africa, Asia and South America will probably be exposed next, and they will be in greater peril.

We cannot simply wring our hands, nor does it gain anything for President Ford to denounce Counter-Spy. From the perspective of foreign governments, political movements, and journalists, it is to expose people who may be engaged in covert and illegal attempts to manipulate their elections and economies.

And if an American newspaper, television station or magazine acquired a list of Russian KGB agents operating undercover here, could we realistically say the news agency would suppress the information?

The reason the CIA is in trouble is because it has offended much of the world. Our meddling in Chile and Italy, and suspicions of even more heavy-handed intervention in other countries, have done more to harm America's international relations than anything except the Vietnam war.

Whatever solution we undertake must be more than cosmetic, must recognize that the fundamental problem is not the revelation of CIA agents' names but foreign outrage about what those agents do.

America must have an intelligence-gathering agency. But can that intelligence agency continue to be a paramilitary organization carrying out secret warfare to advance our foreign policy — and sometimes, if the CIA is as headstrong as believed, foreign policy objectives of the agency's own?

President Ford, his rivals for the White House, and the Congress will be struggling with the problem all year. In his State of the Union address, which reportedly will include a separate discussion of intelligence agencies, the President must begin the process of redefining the CIA's role and reforming its structure to keep it to that role.

Congress, which has been seeking the power to veto covert activities and to disclose them to the public, must develop a proposal that recognizes the need for secrecy, especially about vital military information.

Presidential candidates will be tempted to use the CIA debate as a spring-board springboard to accuse liberals of disloyalty and conservatives of endorsing Watergate-style secret police activities.

Reforming the CIA, in recognition of the fact that we cannot presume to run the rest of the world, is inevitably a crucial political issue for America. We hope it will be debated with dignity, leadership and concern for future national security rather than present electoral gain.

The Courier-Journal

Louisville, Ky., December 31, 1975

PRESIDENT FORD'S belief that publication of the name of CIA agent Richard Welch was at least "partly responsible" for his death is a heavy charge to lay at the feet of the press. This is especially so because publication had occurred only in *Counterspy*, an underground, anti-CIA publication issued quarterly in Washington, and in the *Athens Daily News*, an English-language publication in Greece.

But "the press" can't pick and choose; it must be answerable even for the most extreme publications that enjoy our First Amendment privileges or its parallel freedoms elsewhere. Even the most bawdy student newspaper or underground periodical is known as part of the press, and by its actions brings credit or blame to all others.

The issue becomes particularly sensitive when it involves publishing secret information, a question that continually plagues all journalists, especially in peacetime. Public sentiment usually is strongly opposed to such publication, as all of us saw during the Pentagon Papers dispute. Yet there have been cases in which decisions to cooperate in keeping mum have been opposed — at least eventually — by the very engineers of the secret. The best known case of this probably was President Kennedy's regret that *The New York Times* did not print what it knew about the planned invasion of Cuba, since publication would have forestalled the operation and thus have averted a disaster at the Bay of Pigs.

It is improbable, however, that anyone ever will celebrate the publication of Richard Welch's name, and with the benefit of hindsight it's even harder to justify. Philip Agee, who identifies many CIA agents in his new book, *Inside the Company: CIA Diary*, supplied the one possible rationale last summer in an interview in *Playboy*:

"What you've got to understand is that in revealing the names of CIA operatives, I am revealing the names of people engaged in criminal activities. These people live by breaking the law. . . . It's nonsense to say that by exposing the CIA officers and agents I knew, I have endangered their lives. I have exposed some to problems, but the Company can solve those problems. . . ."

Mr. Agee, a former CIA agent himself, elaborates on this thesis in the winter *Counterspy*, in an article written before the slaying of agent Welch: "The most effective and important systematic efforts to counter the CIA that can be undertaken right now are, I think, the identification, exposure and neutralization of its people working abroad."

The trouble with this tidy thesis, obviously, is that it doesn't take into account the kind of terrorist actions, using the CIA as a symbol of American intervention, that took the life of Mr. Welch. Nor does it provide an effective argument for alerting the man on the street, who least needs to know, to what most other governments — including the Communists — are in little doubt about. By reading public documents, as *Washington Monthly* observed last year in an article reprinted in *The Courier-Journal & Times Magazine*, a practiced eye can easily single out the CIA agents in the lists of diplomatic officials stationed overseas. That's presumably how *Counterspy* obtained the names of the 225 CIA employes and 150 station chiefs it has listed so far this year.

So publication of these names does not jeopardize national security in the normal sense of revealing to the Communists information they don't already have. But it does offer a source of embarrassment, in denying the U.S. the cover of what diplomats call "plausible deniability." Thus it subjects our agents to possible loss of effectiveness, since it becomes harder for officials of other countries to be seen with people publicly known to be U.S. spies. And it does expose these agents to greater risk of assassination, since their public identification suddenly makes them notorious, in a sense.

None of this, it seems to us, supports Mr. Agee's thesis that the way to curb the CIA is to publicize the names of individuals who carry out its policies overseas. But if the Central Intelligence Agency is ever to free itself of this type of vindictive attention, it will not be by trying to suppress what is readily obtainable anyway. It will be by concentrating on the root causes of the agency's sinister reputation.

Let's face it. What started out as an intelligence-gathering arm of our government, totally defensible as a way of protecting ourselves and our allies against those with hostile intentions, rapidly evolved into a way of "destabilizing" foreign regimes we didn't like, (sometimes because they jeopardized our business interests on the scene). It even became a license to snoop on U.S. citizens whose views on the CIA or on America's role in the world seemed disruptive to those in our own government.

In the final analysis, it sometimes would be easiest if the secret abuses of government could be cured without publicity, especially when that publicity means the kind of fate that has overtaken our CIA chief of station in Athens. But in a free country such as ours the dirty linen eventually gets washed in public.

So, despite this painful incident, the death of Richard Welch may not have been in vain. It may be a turning point in the reform of our intelligence agencies. Thirty-one other CIA agents have died in the line of duty since the agency was formed in 1947. But none of those deaths had taught us an essential lesson. It's that unbridled intervention in the domestic affairs of foreign countries may score short-run successes but, in the long run, can only persuade Americans and everybody else that we are no better than the hostile forces we say we're trying to combat.

Arkansas Gazette.

Little Rock, Ark., January 2, 1976

What we fear we are witnessing in the controlled publicity following on the slaying of the CIA's "station ...ef" at Athens is a kind of hark-back a similar use of medal awards cere...nies, the POW welcoming parties, ..., with which earlier national admin...rations used to try to re-sell the ...erican people on the Vietnam War, ...s latest example a rather more ...teless one, if anything, in its use of ...nan grief and other human emo...ns, and one with possibly an even ...s innocent motive.

...rom almost the moment that the ...ts rang out in the Athens streets, ... the agent, Richard Welch, fell ...d, CIA Director William E. Colby ... used the tragic occurrence in an ...empt to do something that he had ... quite been able to do before for all ... trying, which was simply to queer ...n the House and Senate investiga...s of the CIA's past breaches of law ... restore the agency to its former ...ition as the one tentacle of the fed... government that nobody, but no...y, dared question, even if he were so ...osed, which, up to now, was seldom.

So transparent has Colby's design been, in fact, that Senator Frank Church of Idaho, the head of the Senate Select Committee, has been obliged to deny with some heat that the blood of Mr. Welch was on the Committee's hands in any way.

If anyone is showing disrespect to the dead CIA agent and his family, it is the people who have surrounded the regrettable fact of the Mr. Welch's death with such stagy P. R. aspects as the return of the body of a middle-echelon civilian employe of the government by a military honor guard and President Ford's use of an executive order to permit burial in Arlington National Cemetery in contravention of the rules. It is not critics such as Thomas G. Walker, commander-in-chief of the Veterans of Foreign Wars, who, while expressing all sympathy for the Welch family, said that the rules governing who may or may not be buried in Arlington and the nation's other national cemeteries were there for a reason, and should not have been abridged by executive order.

If Agent Welch, like his chief, Director Colby, was a "Company" man first, last and always — as we are sure he was — he would not object to the use being made of his death now, if he could know of it, because it all might redound in the end to the benefit of the beloved agency. But the relevant question here is, will it all work for the larger benefit of the country, if this one incident can be successfully manipulated in such fashion as to allow the CIA to again run free without let of the law? We say not. (In this matter of observance of the law, there is a certain irony in Ford's setting aside the Arlington burial rules in furtherance of the CIA's effort to regain its law-free status, though Ford, we are sure, would be the last to recognize it.)

As for the slaying itself, nobody at this writing knows who the killers were. Or, rather, certain someones know, but they aren't telling.

All we know for starters is that counter-intelligence is a high-risk calling, which explains part of the mystique of the CIA and its wartime American predecessor agency, the Office of Strategic Services. It is a high-risk calling for Americans so engaged, and for their counterparts and/or adversaries in other countries.

In terms of the ultimate reminder at Athens of just *how* high risk a calling counter-intelligence can be, it must be noted that while the name of Mr. Welch and the job he held had been published both by one newspaper in Athens and by a publication in this country calling itself "Counterspy," it seems unlikely that the identity of the CIA "agency chief" in Athens or in any other foreign city would be unknown to "unfriendly" counter-intelligence people from other countries or to local people with a compulsion to do him in. Non-identity is the ideal, the hope of a CIA or any other kind of "cover", but the very definition of intelligence and counter-intelligence is the finding out of something that the other side doesn't want you to know.

This is not only so, but so much so, that two rival counter-intelligence efforts frequently turn out to be mutually self-cancelling. That is the game.

U.S. SAID TO SPEND $50 MILLION IN ANGOLA TO OPPOSE USSR, CUBA

The United States government has supplied one side in the Angolan civil war with arms and funds totaling $25 million, and plans to send another $25 million in supplies, the *New York Times* reported Dec. 12. The *Times* quoted a high-ranking official as saying that the covert operation was designed "to create a stalemate" in the war raging since independence was granted Angola Nov. 11.

The Russians and Cubans support the Popular Movement for the Liberation of Angola. The administration source said that the Soviet Union had sent 200 military advisers to Angola, as well as numerous supply missions. Cuban combat troops were estimated between 4,000 and 5,000. No American advisers were said to be in Angola. The Central Intelligence Agency was reported to distribute the American aid through Zaire, which borders on Angola.

Secretary of State Henry A. Kissinger warned Nov. 24 that the U.S. "cannot remain indifferent" to Soviet and Cuban military intervention in the civil war in Angola. Addressing the Economic Club of Detroit, Kissinger cautioned that "time is running out; continuation of an interventionist policy must inevitably threaten other relationships.... we will never permit detente to turn into a subterfuge of unilateral advantage."

Angola's rival liberation movements had proclaimed two distinct governments in the war-aggrieved nation Nov. 11 as Portugal granted independence to its final African colony. In ceremonies in Luanda Nov. 10, Vice Adm. Leonel Cardoso, the last Portuguese high commissioner in Angola, announced the transfer of sovereignty to "the Angolan people," indicating that Portugal was not yet recognizing the authority of any of the nationalist movements, still waging battle throughout Angola.

Shortly after midnight Nov. 11 the Popular Movement for the Liberation of Angola proclaimed its leader, Agostinho Neto, president of the People's Republic of Angola. The proclamation and subsequent celebrations were conducted in Luanda, the Angolan capital and stronghold of the MPLA which also controlled the band of territory across the middle of the nation.

Hours later in Nova Lisboa, the joint formation of the People's Democratic Republic of Angola was announced by the National Front for the Liberation of Angola (FNLA) and the National Union for the Total Independence of Angola (Unita).

The San Diego Union

San Diego, Calif., November 29, 1975

At the European Security Conference in Helsinki, Finland the Soviet Union signed on Aug. 1 documents which said that the Kremlin would respect the territorial boundaries of other nations.

Before long the Soviet Union was pouring millions of rubles into Portugal to foment a revolution against constituted authority.

Today the Soviet Union is pouring armaments and supplies into the African state of Angola in an overt attempt to establish a Communist government in that country although the majority of the people there do not want Russian Marxism. Cuba, a Soviet satellite state, is actively helping the Communist effort with troops and equipment.

The Soviet participation in Angola is completely contrary to the letter of the Helsinki agreements, which Moscow sought, as well as the spirit of detente generally.

Secretary of State Henry Kissinger is right when he says that the United States cannot "ignore the substantial Soviet buildup of weapons in Angola . . . nor can we ignore the thousands of Cubans sent into the African continent."

If the Soviet Union ignores the secretary's warning the first major power confrontation in Africa in the last 15 years will likely ensue and the entire spectrum of detente will be threatened.

The chips that the big powers are playing in Angola are the blue ones.

THE  SUN

Baltimore, Md., December 10, 1975

American foreign policy in the post-Vietnam era is more likely to be defined by what Washington does about Angola than by the vague premises of President Ford's "Pacific doctrine." The latter was a modest rephrasing of the so-called Nixon doctrine, with the American profile a notch lower However, U S policy in Asia really will be manifest only when actual crises arise that require specific responses.

On the other side of the world, in Angola, an actual crisis requiring specific responses has arisen, and before it subsides the world should know a lot more about America's post-Vietnam policy. Not much was learned from the Mayaguez incident, which was little more than a jingoistic spasm. Strategic arms negotiations and Middle East diplomacy have mainly followed lines established when American forces were still dug into the soil of Indochina. But Angola is something different, something new, something forcing Washington to face up to questions about the proper use of American strength in situations that might well have precipitated U.S involvement not so long ago.

The civil war sweeping Angola is the result not only of tribal rivalries but of outside meddling By far the biggest meddler has been the Soviet Union, which has poured in arms to a pro-Moscow provisional regime in Luanda Other meddlers aiding a rival government in Huambo have included South Africa, which has sent mercenaries into southern Angola; Zaire, which has helped tribally affiliated forces in northern Angola; China, which tried to offset the Russians until it evidently had second thoughts, and the United States. Washington has avoided direct involvement but has funneled arms through Zaire and has denounced Moscow for trying to impose a new colonialism.

The American response to the Angola crisis has so far been somewhat uncertain and contradictory Secretary Kissinger has warned Moscow that its Angola meddling could undermine detente, but he has not as yet cut back on the economic benefits the Soviet Union reaps from detente. Ambassador Moynihan has flailed the Soviet Union for its arms trafficking, but his flank is exposed to Russian charges that U. S. weaponry is also present in Angola. If Washington rhetoric is to have logic, the administration should consider: (1) Making the Russians suffer where it hurts for their outrageous conduct in Angola; (2) curtailing even indirect U. S. involvement to the point where the Russians will be exposed as the only major power seeking an African foothold. Once that happens African states might awaken to the Soviet threat and bring their voting strength to bear in favor of a United Nations peacekeeping force in Angola.

Foreign policy is often hammered out on hard anvils like Angola Before that conflict is over, the Soviet Union may have to ponder the wisdom of trying to dominate a large, far-away country. And the United States may for the first time have to apply a post-Vietnam policy to a major strategic problem.

THE ATLANTA CONSTITUTION

Atlanta, Ga., December 13, 1975

Because of the tragedy of Vietnam, because of the extended hostilities in the Middle East, because of several other reasons, many Americans have become almost "deadened" to "hot spots" around the world. Well, here's one where you'd better sit up and pay attention: Angola.

There is a bloody civil war going on in Angola, a mineral-rich nation in southwest Africa. And the Soviet Union and the United States are rapidly getting involved there. The potential for eruption and escalation is great.

Reports from Washington say that the U.S., through the CIA, has already sent $25 million in arms and support funds to Angola over the last three months, and plans to send another $25 million in supplies to counter the large-scale military intervention there by Russia and its Communist friend, Cuba.

The American aid is reportedly an attempt "to create a stalemate" in the Angolan civil war between pro-Communist and anti-Communist forces. Portugal, which had controlled Angola for several centuries, "freed" the African nation last month after years of fighting various native forces seeking independence.

Now, factions of the Angolan forces are fighting each other for control of the country. The intensity and bloodshed of the war have increased, with many thousands killed.

The Soviet Union has sent several dozen ship and plane loads of military supplies to pro-Communist forces among the Angolans, and Cuba has sent 4,000 to 5,000 combat soldiers and equipment. And now the U.S. is pouring in supplies to anti-Communist forces.

Top American officials have wasted no words in condemning the Soviet intervention. Daniel Moynihan, the U.S. ambassador to the United Nations, accused Russia of trying to colonize Africa. And Secretary of State Henry Kissinger told NATO foreign ministers that the U.S. would never accept the establishment of Soviet bases in Angola.

Kissinger and President Ford both have warned that Angola threatens detente between the U.S. and Russia. In fact, some officials have warned in the past that the Soviets see detente only as a time "of peace and non-nuclear war" beween the two superpowers while it attempts to spread Communism around the world with efforts such as those in Angola.

Angola is a bad situation that could get far worse. But the United States must react strongly to it to counteract growing Communist influence in Angola and Africa. And it is right to do so.

THE INDIANAPOLIS STAR

Indianapolis, Ind., December 6, 1975

It no longer seems possible for a small nation to have its own quiet little civil war.

The other day it was reported—one might almost say it was announced—that the United States Central Intelligence Agency is flying arms and other military equipment into Africa for use of the anti-Communist side in the Angola civil war.

The CIA used to be thought of as engaged in assiduously clandestine activities. The report says the arms and such for Angola are being flown into neighboring Zaire in Air Force cargo planes. That's about as clandestine as a circus parade.

Contemporary outside intervention in Angola began years ago with Soviet aid to the Communist-dominated Popular Movement for the Liberation of Angola, a guerrilla organization seeking to throw off Portuguese colonial control.

On Nov. 11 Portugal in line with the policy of its new regime formally withdrew and declared Angola independent, but did so without any pretense of orderly transition to an organized local government. The PMLA proclaimed a government, but it is disputed by two other liberation groups, both anti-Communist. The three already had been fighting among themselves as well as against the Portuguese.

For some time there have been credible reports of substantial and increasing Soviet aid, in money and supplies, to the PMLA, and lately there are said to be some Soviet technicians on the ground. Reportedly present are Cuban troops, estimated to number about 2,000.

Red China for a time was reported to be giving aid to the anti-Communist groups, presumably in the interest of foiling the Soviets. The Chinese aid is now said to have terminated. Before the current report of an airlift of arms the U.S. was reported to be supplying money to the anti-Communist groups for purchase of arms.

The whole pattern seems very familiar. The Soviet Union, unabashedly and Red China somewhat more discreetly make a practice of encouraging and aiding "liberation" movements, meaning ones aimed at supplanting existing governments with Communist governments.

Since Communist-aided movements are always anti-Western and anti-American, the U.S. is left with little practical choice but to try to counter the Communist aid where it seems feasible to do so. The case of Angola seems to offer very good prospects for such countering aid, though of course a hard decision must be made as to how much it is worth while to invest there.

It is too bad the Angolans have not been left to settle their future for themselves. But they haven't been, and there is a clear U.S. interest in trying to prevent a Communist victory.

The Birmingham News

Birmingham, Ala., December 1, 1975

While detente holds out a wispy promise of blissful coexistence between the U.S. and the Soviet Union, lulling the West with yet-unrealized hopes, a very real struggle is being waged by Russia to extend its dominance into fresh fields.

Of course, there is Portugal, where the Soviets have supported minority leftists' attempts to impose communism on an unwilling majority. Although the administration has issued warnings about Soviet provocations in Portugal, the trouble-making has been more or less tolerated.

But in contrast to the largely political and financial assistance the Soviets have given their cohorts in Portugal, in Angola, the struggle is on the battlefield. There the Russians have poured in a vast arsenal of sophisticated weapons—as well as providing pro-Communist local forces with help from Cuban mercenaries and Russian advisers.

So, despite Moscow's propaganda sweet-talk about peace, the Soviets have become involved in open warfare. At stake is a country which not only is rich in oil, diamonds and minerals but which also is strategically located along ocean trade routes plied by oil tankers from the Persian Gulf.

Granted, the U.S. is helping the two pro-Western forces vying for control of Angola. But the help, by comparison, is meager.

The Russian-aided Popular Movement for Liberation of Angola is being supplied with T-54 tanks, PT-76 armored cars, 25-mm recoilless rifles, SAM-7 missiles, 122-mm rockets and MIG-21 jets with Algerian pilots, based in the Congo.

The two pro-Western Angolan forces are the National Front for the Liberation of Angola and the National Union for the Total Independence of Angola.

A leader of the former said, "While we can only buy weapons in parts on the open market and assemble them, the Russians bring shiploads of tanks, missiles and armored cars into Luanda."

The same leader said further, of his pro-Communist opponents, "They have missiles by the thousands and we have none. They have armored cars, tanks and jeeps coming every day, and meanwhile our friends in the West and Peking hesitate."

Unfortunately, the struggle in Angola comes at a time when the U.S. has little stomach for a continued policy of checking Soviet probes for weakness. We want to wish away the fact that the aim of the Soviet government is for world dominance. We want to ignore warnings from a growing number of quarters that detente merely fits into the Soviet plan for lulling the West into disarmament while Russia races ahead militarily.

In recent days, Secretary of State Henry Kissinger, in calm diplomatic tones, expressed U.S. displeasure at Soviet expansionism in Angola. These grumblings were similar to those uttered in the past about Portugal. Yet, this country continues to tolerate such behavior on the part of Russia, hoping somehow that harsh realities will dissipate on their own.

We trusted Russia as an ally in World War II, and our trust was betrayed; the Soviets seized and imprisoned Eastern Europe. Subsequently, Russia has armed the North Koreans, the North Vietnamese and insurgent forces everywhere it could get a foothold. In 1962, the Soviets put nuclear weapons in Cuba. In 1968, Russian troops crushed Czechoslovakia. Russia tried unsuccessfully to gain the upper hand in the Congo in the early Sixties.

The post-war history of Russia has been one power-play after another. We should now be fully aware of the true nature of our opponents in the Kremlin. We have two choices: Oppose Soviet bayonet thrusts in the remote arenas of the world or capitulate to the constant extension of Russian hegemony.

Peace is a two-way street. With detente, we are getting a one-sided deal. What is happening in Angola speaks for itself.

Richmond Times-Dispatch

Richmond, Va., November 30, 1975

After 400 years under Portugal's thumb, Angola ceased being a colony on Nov. 11. But it is not yet an independent nation. Hardly. Rather, that southwest African land—so vast, so rich in oil, diamonds and gold—is more nearly a big piece of juicy raw meat for possession of which three factions, aided by outsiders, are vying voraciously.

The most blatant intervention by far has been that of the Russian and Cuban Communists on the side of the Marxist Popular Movement for the Liberation of Angola (MPLA), which holds the capital of Luanda. Fidel Castro, the dictator who supposedly had gone out of the revolution-export business, has dispatched 2,800 Cuban officers and men to the fray. Russia has sent hundreds of "advisers" and many weapons.

Communist China and neighboring Zaire (the former Belgian Congo) are supporting another "liberationist" outfit—the National Front for the Liberation of Angola (FNLA)—but apparently only with training and arms and not their own nationals—so far. The third group, considered the most Western oriented, is the National Union for the Total Independence of Angola (UNITA). It is backed by South Africa and Zambia (formerly northern Rhodesia)

Despite its domination in the capital city, MPLA is being hard-pressed in the outlying areas, where fighting is ferocious. FNLA and UNITA, despite their ideological differences, are currently cooperating to prevent Moscow from establishing a beachhead, including a naval port, in Angola. Their benefactors, Zaire and Zambia, would look equally askance on such a development because both depend upon an Angolan rail route to the sea for their copper exports.

So, too, ought the United States be alarmed about the Soviets setting up naval quarters in Angola by brute force. Such a facility would greatly aid the Soviet swimming bear in making the south Atlantic the kind of big honeypot for him that the Indian Ocean has become. American and European shipping access to the Middle East and southern Asia via the Cape of Good Hope could be threatened.

Washington ought to offer its good offices as a peacemaker in Angola, the only spot on the globe just now where a full-fledged war rages, with all the horrors of any war. But if the Russian-Cuban war of conquest continues unabated, we see no reason the U.S. ought to shrink from the responsibility of openly assisting—with arms, not men—those native forces resisting the takeover. Who knows? Maybe Angola will be Moscow's Vietnam.

St. Louis Globe-Democrat

St. Louis, Mo., December 4, 1975

Will Soviet Russia risk turning Angola into its own Vietnam?

The question, no longer abstract, is tantalizing to political and military analysts because there is a superficial similarity to the Russian intervention in the former Portuguese colony and the first stage of American involvement in South Vietnam.

Presently there are at least several hundred Russian "advisers" assisting the so-called Popular Movement for the Liberation of Angola in the fighting for control of the country. Reports that thousands of Russian troops are involved have been denied, but it is a fact that Cuban regulars numbering at least 3000 are fighting there at Moscow's bidding. And it is a fact too that Russia has poured tens of millions of dollars in arms and military supplies into Luanda, the seaport capital city.

The long native rebellion which ended 400 years of Portuguese rule succeeded only in driving out hundreds of thousands of European settlers and leaving Angola in turmoil. The Portuguese high commissioner, anticipating Angola's Independence Day last Nov. 11, but noting that there were only warring factions and no stable government, commented bitingly "We may have to mail them the flag."

The Soviet-backed MPLA immediately proclaimed itself The People's Republic of Angola. Two anti-Communist rivals, the National Front for the Liberation of Angola (FNLA) and the National Union for Total Independence of Angola (UNITA), joined forces and declared their own coalition regime.

Fighting which was stalemated at first has intensified with the unloading of 13 Soviet cargo ships in the last week. Saturation shelling of up to 1000 artillery rounds an hour has held back an advance of National Front and National Union forces on Luanda.

☆ ☆ ☆

AN INDICATION of intense Soviet interest came in a front page story in Pravda, the official Communist Party newspaper, which claimed that U.S. servicemen, along with regular troops from South Africa and Western Europe, were being sent urgently to Angola. The distorted Pravda report conveniently ignored the presence of Russians and Cubans.

The seriousness with which the U.S. views the situation is reflected in Secretary of State Henry A. Kissinger's warning that detente will not permit continued Soviet or Cuban intervention. Moscow in reply has hardened its attitude by saying that detente in no way precludes Soviet support of the "national liberation struggle."

U.S. Ambassador Daniel P. Moynihan countered in the United Nations by accusing Russia of trying to colonize all of Africa. This blunt assessment wounded the sensibilities of Russia's Third World stooges, who are too stupid or too naive to see the threat to themselves.

Evidence that Russia has committed itself to play for keeps in Angola came in an editorial in Izvestia, the official government newspaper. The editorial said in part:

"Some would like to convince us that the process of detente in the world and support of the national liberation struggle are incompatible things. Similar things have been maintained before, but in vain. The process of detente does not mean and never meant the freezing of the social-political status quo in the world and cessation of anti-imperialist struggles of the people for a better and just fate, and against foreign interference and oppression."

Such twisted commentary is to be expected from a source that regularly employs others to do its dirty work.

☆ ☆ ☆

IF RUSSIA SUCCEEDS in dominating Angola it will have won for itself a strategic country with 1000 miles of seacoast, and its first port on the South Atlantic. Soviet naval strength in Angola would permit Russia to control supertanker traffic around the Cape of Good Hope. Already Soviet bases in the Far East are being improved and new bases are being constructed in the East African nation of Somalia to control the approaches to the Indian Ocean.

It appears certain the Soviets are more concerned with the strategic value of Angola than in its oil and mineral riches.

The resemblance between American interest in South Vietnam and Soviet expansion into Angola is not genuine. The United States sought to protect a partitioned people from takeover by Communist oppressors. The Russians are seeking a stranglehold on native African blacks who are fighting a civil war.

The question confronting the United States is whether it is going to sit by and let Russia accomplish its will, or whether it will apply more than vocal pressure to make the Soviets back off and get out of Angola.

LEDGER-STAR

Norfolk, Va., December 3, 1975

Angola is beginning to look like the newest East-West poker table, if not an actual cockpit for a test of military and economic muscle.

And the question for Americans, underscored by warning signals to the Soviet Union from Secretary of State Kissinger and ambassador-to-the-U.N. Moynihan, is this: Should the U.S. commit itself to frustration of the Soviet designs? And how far should we go in carrying out such a commitment?

It seems quite obvious, as Mr. Moynihan pointed out in his speech to the Pacem in Terris convocation Tuesday, that the Soviet Union and Cuba are lending help to the Communist faction trying to seize control in the wake of Portugal's departure from its one-time colony. And that here as elsewhere the Soviet Union is still embarked on a policy of expanding its influence wherever the United States is unlikely to intercede.

It is also clear that America's ultimate interests and the interests of its free friends in the world are threatened by the still unabated expansionist appetite of communism. Those who would fight this tooth and nail in Angola or anywhere else have much right and logic on their side. But some of them can be recklessly simplistic, too.

★ ★ ★ ★

Vietnam is a miserable example of what can happen through an ill-thought-out commitment—or disastrous choice of battlefields. Moreover, Vietnam's scar and the sensitivity it has created among the nation's youth toward foreign military operations requiring draft manpower constitute a formidable, continuing impediment to almost any fresh U.S. military action abroad, perhaps even in cases where our security is much more directly at stake than Angola—as in Europe and the Mideast and South America.

But the prospect of a Soviet-assisted Communist take-over in Angola is surely something the United States cannot passively accept. And the answer to the question posed earlier—Should there be an American commitment?—almost surely has to be yes.

★ ★ ★ ★

But at this juncture the wise course is not to make this any kind of win-at-all-costs proposition. Calling Moscow to account before the court of world opinion for its violent designs, as Secretary Kissinger has done, is one intermediate measure that may produce a restraining effect. More strenuous forms of public censure may well be undertaken as a following step. Substantial aid and public encouragement to the non-Communist elements could have a measure of effectiveness, too.

But each such step would have to be taken with the greatest care, and with eyes wide open to the high probability that a stopping point might be reached and that a total pledge to prevent Communist victory would be foolhardy and perhaps unfulfillable against the weight of unforeseen realities.

Angola isn't Vietnam, but the legacy of Vietnam must be reckoned with.

Events and the assessments of Soviet purpose could, of course, drive America to a soberly reached conclusion that Angola was a crossroads, that a flat, militarily backed "no" was the only remaining answer to Communist purpose there.

But that's a leap to showdown we mustn't take now and should work by every reasonable means to avoid

The Washington Star

Washington, D.C., December 15, 1975

It is time to blow the whistle on the growing American involvement in the civil war in Angola. There is no conceivable American interest that would justify a commitment to one or another of the contending nationalist factions in the former Portuguese colony. There is every reason to limit the scope of an international intervention that threatens to reach the proportions of the Spanish Civil War of the 1930s.

The American involvement so far has been discreetly limited The well-publicized "covert" operation of the Central Intelligence Agency appears to have been confined to the shipment of some $25 million in small arms for the more pro-Western (or more anti-Russian) of the three nationalist factions, with another $25 million worth supposedly on the way. This American aid, sent indirectly through Zaire, is small potatoes compared to the massive shipments of heavy armaments and rockets supplied by the Soviet Union to its proteges in the Popular Movement for the Liberation of Angola (MPLA) and the presence in the country of some 200 Soviet advisers and more than 4,000 Cuban combat troops.

But this is only the beginning of foreign involvement in the civil conflict in Angola. In one way or another, China, Western Europe, South Africa, former Portuguese colonists and troops from Zaire are lined up in support of the anti-Russian elements, represented by the National Front for the Liberation of Angola (FNLA) and the National Union for the Total Independence of Angola (UNITA). Most recently, there have been reports that the Congress of Racial Equality is recruiting black American volunteer Vietnam veterans for service in Angola as a neutral "police force" under the direction of the Organization of African Unity, which has been trying to mediate the conflict.

Meanwhile, Secretary of State Henry Kissinger has been making ominous pronouncements about the situation. The Soviet intervention in the war in Angola, he told the NATO meeting in Brussels, represents a potential shift in the world balance of power to which the United States cannot remain indifferent. The possibility of the Soviet Union's establishing a foothold in southern Africa, he says, is "inadmissible" so far as the United States is concerned. Other officials have said that the Russians are out to "win all of Angola," suggesting that this amounts to a challenge to the United States on a global scale.

For our part, the situation in Angola strikes us as a classic can of worms that the United States would do well to steer clear of. We do not see what American interests are served by any of the factions contending for power there. We are doubtful that, even if it should "win" there, the Soviet Union would find Angola much of a long-range asset. A modest contribution of money and arms in the hope of achieving a stalemate in the civil war and a negotiated solution of the conflict may still be justified. Anything more than that, in our view, would not.

DAYTON DAILY NEWS

Dayton, Ohio, December 11, 1975

Secretary of State Henry Kissinger only conceded an open secret when he admitted that, yes, indeed, the United States roundaboutly is supporting the two Angolan liberation groups that are locked in a civil war against the Soviet-backed provisional government.

The admission hardly merits the visions of Vietnam II that some Democratic presidential candidates are too eagerly trying to invoke.

So far, U.S. aid has been washed through Zaire (the old Congo), an appropriately indirect method that keeps the United States from establishing or thinking it has established a stake that must be invested in ever more heavily. This is one involvement Washington can walk away from without actually having been there.

Not that it should. The issue is not inconsequential. Its importantce is underscored by the crazy band of nations aiding the anti-Soviet coalition — black African Zaire, white-racist South Africa, Peking China and, of course, Uncle. An unlikelier cabal would be difficult to fantasize.

For different reasons, each of those nations fears any growth in Soviet influence in Africa. That influence is not yet large, but it is solidy established in Somalia, in east Africa. An equally solid influence in the west, particularly in the potentially oil-rich Angola, would alter the international strategic board disturbingly, especially in the south Atlantic.

It is by no means certain that, even if the Soviet-backed force prevails in Angola, the Soviet presence will be as extensive or as apparently durable as it has become in Somalia.

The supply line is much longer and many more times more tenuous. Whatever the outcome now, Angola is likely to remain politically volatile for years. If Russia's favorite wins, troops from Zaire, though they should not, well might nip off the Cabinda enclave, the site of much of Anogla's off-shore oil.

The U.S. interest in the outcome in Angola is sufficient to justify the once-removed role American policy is playing there. If an armed standoff could be achieved, there would be a chance, at least, of compelling a UN-supervised plebescite, the best way, for the Angolans themselves, to resolve the struggle.

This is not Vietnam II. It is Angola I, which is quite issue enough in its own right.

WINSTON-SALEM JOURNAL

Winston–Salem, N.C., December 5, 1975

Was the lesson of Vietnam, like the "Mission: Impossible" message, destined to "self-destruct" moments after it was received? If America's 14-year ordeal in Southeast Asia should have taught us anything, it was the moral and political bankruptcy of trying to promote American ideology by military intervention in another country's civil war. Vietnam also showed this nation the tremendous danger of allowing presidents the power singlehandedly and secretly to direct American foreign policy.

In the wake of Vietnam we have begun the painful process of probing our recent history and discovering the extent to which our government's role in the world — and at home, for that matter — was shaped by faceless, unaccountable men in secret cloisters.

But what has been accomplished? The ink has scarcely dried on the Senate report of CIA assassination plots when the news arrives of a CIA airlift of $20 million worth of arms to one faction in Angola's civil war. The official explanation is bland and simple: Russia and Cuba have been supplying the other side.

The warning ought to have a familiar ring to those who read American history from 1955 to 1965. U.S. Air Force transport planes are ferrying arms to the Angolan fighters. Will one of them suddenly figure in a "Tonkin Gulf incident"? Is the CIA's secret army already engaged in Angola? Will American Special Forces troops soon begin shipping out for service as "advisers"?

The point is not so much a matter of where the policy of intervention in Angola will stop as where it began. Who decided that American force should weigh in on the side of Holden Roberto and his Front for the Liberation of Angola (FNLA)? Who authorized the expenditure 20 million American tax dollars on his behalf? The answer to the first question is, apparently, someone in the Kremlin. The answer to the second is, nobody. Neither the American people, nor their elected representatives, have ever been asked to formulate or express a policy toward Angola. The Senate has never been asked to ratify a treaty with the FNLA; the House has never authorized $20 million in military aid to that faction. The CIA has conducted its airlift in secret, not to keep it from the Russians — they undoubtedly know about it — but conveniently to spare Congress its Constitutional responsibility for foreign policy.

It is regrettable that liberation from Portugese colonialism has spawned civil war in Angola, even more so that the Soviet bloc is meddling in the country. We are told that the faction we are opposing is "Communist-dominated." Twenty years ago we were told that about the faction led by Ho Chi Minh, when the truth was that he had turned to Moscow and Peking only after being spurned in Washington. Whatever the case in Angola, there is no excuse for the U.S. once again to mimic the contemptible habits of other, non-democratic countries. That was the lesson of Vietnam. We seem to have forgotten it already.

THE MILWAUKEE JOURNAL

Milwaukee, Wisc., December 15, 1975

The US rightly ought to express its concern over Soviet intentions in Angola. Soviet and Cuban intervention with arms and men threatens to make the former Portuguese colony an African Vietnam. Soviet adventurism in Angola puts into question the very tenets of detente.

But America can't assume a "holier than thou" attitude. Its hands are not clean of the Angolan affair. The US has been funneling money and arms to its favored side in the Angolan civil war. American assistance has been nowhere near the magnitude of Soviet aid, but there have been reports that initial American help triggered a Soviet response earlier this year.

What is particularly disturbing are the reports that Washington has given its blessing to efforts of the Congress of Racial Equality (CORE) to recruit black Vietnam veterans for volunteer service in Angola, possibly as medics or as part of a pan-African police force. American blacks may find appeal in rediscovering their heritage and playing a role in black Africa. But before they decide to turn Angola into a black Spain of the '30s, they ought to know whom they are supporting. Ideological lines are blurred in the Angolan fighting, unlike the Spanish conflict. Sides have been picked as a result of superpower rivalry. Blacks could easily find themselves used. The US government should put a halt to this effort.

The Boston Globe

Boston, Mass., December 15, 1975

Instead of one-sided debates and resolutions, the UN might spend more energy the raw adventurism being carried out by Cuba and the USSR in newly-independent Angola.

Cuban troops and Soviet arms are pouring into that mineral-rich West African country in support of the Popular Movement for the Liberation of Angola (MPLA) in its struggle for power against two rival groups, the FNLA and UNITA, supported by the United States, Western Europe, neighboring Zaire and China.

The Soviet Union has made no pretense about its military intervention in the affairs of a country thousands of miles from Moscow.

It cynically defends its role as support for a "national liberation struggle" and promotes its intervention in Angola as required "against foreign interference and oppression."

The United States and other anti-communist nations have directed only modest support to the factions in Angola. Secretary Kissinger has admitted that a covert program of support is underway to the FNLA and UNITA and estimates in Washington are that the United States has spent more than $50 million in military aid to Angola since April.

Indirect support is also being given through American military aid to Zaire. The Ford Administration is asking Congress for a total of $80 million for "security support" to Zaire.

NATO countries are divided on what to do in Angola but the Dutch probably have the right idea. The Dutch are against any move that might suggest NATO involvement in Angola and favor a hands-off approach. This should go for the United States as well. In any case, covert American aid should be stopped. The nation should be informed regularly about the nature of the commitments being made in Angola

Meanwhile the UN has a responsibility to speak out against imperialism and expose the USSR and Cuba to world censure. By failing to act on such adventurism while acting with uncommon alacrity against all resolutions directed against Israel, the UN is seriously devaluing its currency as a responsible world organization for peace.

Los Angeles Times

Los Angeles, Calif., December 4, 1975

The Soviet-Cuban intervention in the civil war in Angola requires a stronger response from the United States than the public criticism and private diplomatic protest directed thus far from Washington.

But this is not to argue for an American intervention in Angola itself. On the contrary.

No matter what happens in the three-way struggle for control of Angola, it is not likely to emerge as anybody's puppet. Angola will probably embrace the commitment to nonalignment that characterizes most of the African nations. Given that prospect, it is in everyone's interest to get the war over with as quickly as possible. For all its oil and other minerals, Angola is an impoverished and undeveloped nation that can in no way afford the waste of war.

There is now little or no chance that the Organization of African Unity will be able to realize its sensible plan for a coalition of the three rival groups. The prospect for a coalition has been killed by the massive flow of arms from Moscow and the entry of at least 3,000 military technicians from Havana. They have given an overwhelming advantage to the Popular Movement for the Liberation of Angola (MPLA).

The prospect of an MPLA victory accounts for the aggressive response being advocated by South Africa, whose trust territory, Namibia (South-West Africa), borders on Angola. In Pretoria, events in Angola are perceived in much the same way that Washington once perceived events in Vietnam, dominoes and all. South Africa, which kept hands off Mozambique when it gained independence from Portugal last June, now is advocating intervention in Angola, and reportedly has troops operating across the Namibia frontier into Angola.

Only two options realistically remain open to the United States. It could mount a massive program of aid and advisers that just might bolster the failing forces of the National Front for the Liberation of Angola (FNLA) and the National Union for the Total Independence of Angola (UNITA); the best possible result of such an intervention probably would be partition of the country and continued warfare at a reduced level. Or the United States could withhold assistance on the grounds that the war in Angola is a matter that does not affect American national security or interests and that intervention in itself would only make matters worse.

To do what the United States was reported doing Wednesday—sending in $20 million in assorted arms—is hardly enough to turn the tide, but more than enough to deepen the agony for all.

We find the arguments for abstinence persuasive.

Nonintervention has a number of advantages. It would undermine any rationale for Soviet assistance; until now, a relatively modest flow of aid from China and the United States to FNLA has allowed Moscow to defend its role as a response to other intervention. More important, nonintervention would leave to the African states themselves and their organization the peacemaking role. That process already has isolated the Soviet Union and brought condemnation of Moscow's activities.

Put another way, an Angola controlled by the MPLA is not likely to be the monster some portray. Regardless, however, the price of reversing an MPLA conquest is too high for either the United States or the people of Angola to pay.

But nonintervention in Angola by the United States should not mean quiet acquiescence by the United States of what the Soviet Union and Cuba are doing.

Their intervention challenges the fundamentals of detente.

Izvestia, the official Soviet government newspaper, has affirmed that detente and national liberation are compatible. That begs the question. National liberation is not at stake in Angola. Portugal agreed to grant independence 17 months ago. The Soviet-Cuban aid program reached its record level long after that. Moscow's only purpose is to frustrate a shared democratic rule, to reinforce the imposition of a Marxist regime where the Marxist organization admits its own unpopularity by sabotaging the plebiscite proposed by Portugal.

Secretary of State Kissinger has told Moscow that "continuation of an interventionist policy must inevitably threaten other relationships." Kissinger must now make sure that Moscow learns that this was no idle threat. The events in Angola give extraordinary credibility to the cautions that he and President Ford have been hearing in Peking regarding Moscow's real intentions in the world today.

The gravity of this intervention requires reconsideration by the United States of the normalization of relations with Cuba. If Cuba will lend its troops to a war so distant from its interest, it must be held a risk to the security of its own hemisphere.

The intervention requires, furthermore, reconsideration of Ford's plans for another Moscow summit. A freeze on credit, on trade concessions and on other liberalizations of America's relationship with the Soviet Union would be appropriate.

Those are serious measures. But this is a serious matter.

THE ARIZONA REPUBLIC

Phoenix, Ariz., November 16, 1975

If there's one country in the world toward which the United States should adopt a policy of benign neglect, it's Angola.

The former Portuguese colony is a country without a government. Three factions, armed with an amazing array of modern weapons, are warring for control.

One, the Popular Movement for the Liberation of Angola (MPLA), has received arms from Soviet Russia and troops from Cuba.

Another, the National Front for the Liberation of Angola (FNLA) is getting French and Communist Chinese arms from Zaire.

The third, the National Union for the Total Independence of Angola (UNITA), which has the backing of Portuguese businessmen and mercenaries, recently formed an uneasy alliance with the FNLA and is now getting arms from Zaire, too.

In addition, Congo may or may not have invaded the country. That report comes from Zaire. It may have been concocted as a prelude to a Zairean invasion of Angola.

Also, several tribal wars are raging.

The fighting already has cost an estimated 10,000 lives and it bids fair to develop into the bloodiest civil war in Africa's bloody history, one that is expected to last for years.

The whole situation is a mess, and the farther the United States stays away from it the better. The United States shouldn't recognize any of the warring factions and it shouldn't give aid to any of them.

This, we think, is obvious. However, Secretary of State Henry A. Kissinger doesn't agree.

Kissinger has said: "We would support any move that keeps outside powers out of Angola."

If this remark means anything, it means that Kissinger wants the United States to support the FLNA and UNITA against the MPLA.

Lending support to that interpretation is the fact that the administration recently asked Congress to appropriate $20 million in military aid to Zaire. One way or another, most of those arms almost certainly would be used in Angola.

No matter which side eventually wins in Angola, outside powers will be inside the country, wielding an influence. In one case, it will be the Russians and the Cubans; in the other, it will be the Zaireans, the French and the Chinese Communists.

The civil war cannot end happily for the United States.

It's none of this nation's affair, anyway; so let's keep hands off.

The Washington Post

Washington, D.C., December 15, 1975

THE SOVIET UNION'S intervention in Angola is reprehensible and alarming and bound to erode further the crumbling ground of "detente." But is the proper American response to sponsor a counter-intervention? A counter-intervention, moreover, which—far from being a lame response to an admittedly greater Soviet effort—has already reportedly cost $50 million, with no end yet in sight? The answer is, No. The foreseeable costs in dollars and in political credit abroad are simply too large for the benefits likely to be gained. If the Russians are so perverse as to proceed, let them then harvest the scorn of much of the international community, the burden of carrying Angola if their client prevails, and the embarrassment of "losing" Angola if their client's gratitude subsequently falters, as usually happens in these situations.

Zaire, the administration's favorite black African state, is the channel for most of the American aid going to Angola. The president of Zaire is directing the aid to the Angolan faction led by his brother-in-law, himself long known for his CIA associations. But what does this have to do with the welfare of the people of Angola or of the people of Zaire? It is a tribal power struggle, which probably will end in partition. Washington could live with that. The real reason the United States is playing the game is because the Russians are backing another horse and the administration, viewing Africa as usual through its great-power lens, does not wish the contest to be lost to Moscow by default. We would have thought the United States had learned from Vietnam that it is not wise or necessary to match the Communist competition everywhere—least of all by an automatic military response. If Zaire and its implicit partner in this struggle, South Africa, feel otherwise, that is their business. They live there. Americans don't. Americans should not be panicked by talk of a Soviet "foothold" in Angola (we've been around that track with Fidel Castro) or by the specter of the Soviet navy "commanding" the sea lanes off the African coast.

It is indeed disturbing that the Soviet Union, manipulating Cuba, is taking a plunge into Angola. The enterprise bespeaks a policy fundamentally inconsistent with a stable and improving Soviet-American relationship. But there are other ways for that point to be registered. In the United Nations the other day, for instance, the Russians suffered a smart setback—one of their first of this sort in years—when the bottom fell out from under a proposed amendment that would have ignored Soviet intervention and condemned only the Angolan role of South Africa, whose intervention is at once much smaller than Moscow's and more justified. Also, as we mentioned in a recent editorial, Soviet access to extra American grain might well be conditioned on Soviet performance in Angola and other political trouble spots. In any event, secret or semi-secret sponsorship of one side's fight in a savage and prolonged civil war is wrong and should be halted now. That will be the outcome, we confidently predict, if the question is opened up to close scrutiny and thoughtful public debate.

The Globe and Mail

Toronto, Ont., December 8, 1975

Portugal's record in Angola is dismal: 90 per cent illiteracy among black Africans, a life expectancy estimated at 40 years, an almost total lack of elementary political rights or even of opportunities to prepare for participation in any political structure beyond the scale of the tribe. To Portugal the richest of its African colonies mattered as a source of oil, diamonds, copper, iron and coffee, not as a community of human beings.

Now the Portuguese are gone but Angola is still a prize fought over by powerful outsiders for its resources, for its potential value to the opposing sides in any conflict between South Africa and its black neighbors, or even between rival blocks within the Organization of African Unity, fought over most of all for its strategic importance in the struggle between East and West for control of the sea lanes around the Cape of Good Hope.

The cruel irony is that while the rival Angolan liberation movements managed to some extent to make common cause against the Portuguese imperialists the new imperialism pits them one against another, front-line soldiers in the service of causes that mean little but hardship and suffering to the Angolan people.

There is little doubt that the most massive intervention is from the Soviet Union. Hundreds of tons of Russian armaments have been shipped into Angola since last spring to supply the forces of the Popular Movement for the Liberation of Angola (MPLA) and its Cuban "volunteer" supporters, whose numbers are estimated at up to 3,000. Russian arms include mortars and anti-tank rifles, armored personnel carriers and, according to American analysts, tanks and MIG-21 aircraft, to be flown by Algerian pilots.

Meanwhile, the United States denies that it is sending support to the rival coalition of the National Front for the Liberation of Angola (FNLA) and the National Union for the Total Independence of Angola (UNITA). But American officials admit that heavy military aid being supplied to Zaire "may" be ending up in Angola. The arrangement is hardly that casual. President Mobutu Sese Seko of Zaire is a close relative of FNLA leader Holden Roberto, like him a member of the Bakongo tribe on which the FNLA is based, like him an implacable foe of the MPLA. Moreover, President Mobuto has himself given every indication of a desire to add the oil-rich Angola province of Cabinda to his own territory, either as part of Zaire or as a nominally independent satellite.

South Africa's involvement is more direct. South African soldiers, described as mercenaries, are reported fighting in support of the FNLA-UNITA coalition, mainly in southern Angola, across the border from Southwest Africa. This puts South Africa into a working alliance with the United States, Zaire and China.

It is not hard to understand South Africa's interest in Angola. A heavily armed and militant Soviet-backed regime directly across the border from Southwest Africa, the resource-rich former protectorate which South Africa is determined to keep, in defiance of the United Nations, would be a black African spearhead aimed threateningly at the very survival of South Africa itself.

But the political judgment of the United States, China and South Africa in supporting the FNLA and UNITA is open to question. Most observers, including most westerners, see the MPLA as the movement almost certain to win in the long haul. For, unlike its rivals, each of which is based largely on a single tribe, the MPLA support cuts broadly across tribal lines and includes as well most educated Angolans and most urban workers.

Mr. Roberto, the dominant figure in the opposition coalition, was dropped as a weak reed by the American Central Intelligence Agency in 1969. He had been adopted for support by the CIA in 1962 when the Kennedy administration became convinced Portugal was fighting a losing war to hold its African colonies.

The Soviet Union has been and remains the dominant outside contributor to the prolongation of the civil war that is destroying the promise that independence might have offered to Angola's people. But the United States, South Africa, China, and Zaire, by shoring up and arming the opposition to the most broadly based of the liberation movements, are themselves contributing significantly to the scale of the Russian intervention. They are also increasing the probability that before the MPLA comes out on top, as it is expected to do, it will have become, not an instrument of Angolan nationalism as it began, but a pliable tool of Soviet foreign policy.

Meanwhile, the United Nations, paralyzed by superpower rivalries, and the Organization of African Unity, split between rival camps in black Africa, stand by helplessly as civil war goes on in Angola, fed by foreign intervention far beyond that which sent UN forces into the Congo in 1960.

Newsday

Garden City, N.Y., December 11, 1975

The Popular Movement for the Liberation of Angola, equipped with Soviet weapons and reinforced by Cuban troops, seems to be winning Angola's civil war. Perhaps the most frustrating thing about this is that the United States may have only itself to blame. For all the self-righteous U.S. denunciation of the Russians' meddling in this former Portuguese colony, some intelligence sources in Washington say the U.S. itself made the first move last summer and the Soviet buildup in the fall was merely a reaction.

Recriminations aside, the question for the policymakers in Washington is what to do next: (1) Raise the stakes again, as the Russians have already done? (2) Continue shipping equipment to Zaire for the factions the U.S. has been supporting in Angola? Or (3) end the whole clandestine enterprise and concede Angola to Soviet domination? Bear in mind that the U.S. has no vital interest in Angola.

The trouble with escalation is that it might be unsuccessful and it's bound to be expensive. The trouble with the status quo is that lining up with South Africa on the Angolan conflict will destroy what little rapport the U.S. still has with the Africans and Asians in the United Nations. And the virtue of withdrawal is that it leaves the Russians to play the same quasi-colonial role that eventually turned Egypt against them. We think the U.S. should leave Angola alone and let Africans learn once again that Soviet imperialism is just as bad as all the other brands.

The Sun Reporter

San Francisco, Calif., December 13, 1975

Imperialism dies hard. It's demise is nearly always ugly and painful, accompanied by terrible suffering afflicted on the newly independent country as the departing power extricates itself and other forces clamour for whatever political and economic spoils they can grab up.

We see this happening today in the world's newest independent nation - Angola. Freed on November 11 after half a millenium of inhuman Portuguese rule, the former colony is now engaged in a brutal civil war among the three forces which so recently combined to throw off the oppressors.

The battle field is being bloodied largely by millions of dollars of American equipment which has been supplied to two of these groups by the American government. The National Front for the Liberation of Angola (FNLA) and the National Union for the Total Independence of Angola (UNITA) have been receiving American arms shipments, sent covertly through neighboring Zaire, since before independence was declared.

Reacting to this situation, the Soviet Union has recently begun to help arm the rival Popular Movement for the Liberation of Angola (MPLA) and the battle continues, with the MPLA controlling the national capital at Luanda and the US-aided groups occupying much of the countryside.

The United States is clearly the main aggressor in this tragic situation. Our intervention has already begun to ape the secret war that we waged in Laos during the Nixon presidency, and if events are allowed to continue, we could easily become more directly involved in a new Vietnam-type invasion. The spectacle of thousands of young American soldiers, with exaggerated proportions of Black Americans, sent to Africa to gun down Black freedom fighters, is too horrifying to comtemplate.

But without even thinking about the future, the present American intervention in Angola is wrong. Events in that country in no way threaten our national security and a continuation of our present activities could only serve to jeopardize our future relationship with the MPLA, should they prevail in the end. Worse yet, our arming of UNITA and FNLA has already begun to provoke an unhealthy competition with the Soviet-Union which is liable to threaten detente if allowed to go on much further. Secretary of State Kissinger's "warning" to the Soviets to stop aiding the MPLA is just a smokescreen to distract national and international public opinion from the embarrassing fact that we, not the USSR, are the aggressor.

Black Americans must also take cognizance of Angola's strategic geographical location. It lies directly north of Namibia, a colony held illegally by the Republic of South Africa, and a place where the most vicious repression of Black Africans is practiced by the white minority government. A unified, independent Angola could conceivably pose a serious threat to the racist regime in Namibia which maintains the Black popultion in conditions approaching slave labor for the sake of maximizing profits among white-owned corporations in South Africa and the United States.

In order to insure freedom for the people of Angola, we recommend support for measures introduced in Congress by Representatives Michael Harrington of Massachussetts and Don Bonker of Washington these provisions would specifically forbid any of this country's "International Security Assistance" funds from going to political groups in Angola and prohibit the sale of military equipment to Zaire until that country has ceased to function as a funnel to Angola.

The Providence Journal

Providence, R.I., December 11, 1975

If the decolonization of Africa is not to become a travesty, then all foreign governments with troops participating in the Angolan civil war should be forced to withdraw them. That includes Cuba and South Africa, if the whites helping the coalition in the south of Angola are indeed South Africans.

That there are about 3,000 Cubans fighting for the Popular Movement for the Liberation of Angola (the Soviet-backed leftist faction) seems pretty well established. And U. S. officials report that they are turning the tide in favor of the Popular Movement.

The United States reportedly is supplying arms and other materiel to the National Front and the National Union, which have only recently joined forces against the Popular Movement. It would be better if the United States were not involved at all. But if the Russians are providing a massive amount of supplies to the leftists, then it is understandable that the Americans are helping the other side.

The Soviets already have a firm foothold in Somalia on the east coast of Africa, close to the Suez Canal and the sea lanes to the Persian Gulf. If they are successful in helping the Popular Movement in Angola, they will have a base from which to control shipping along the west coast of Africa.

Secretary of State Kissinger can hardly be blamed, then, for his warning that the Soviet government is endangering the detente between the United States and Russia that has been built up slowly and with great effort over the past six or seven years.

Since alien soldiers are being used in Angola, the country is a proper subject for investigation and action by the United Nations Security Council. Angola and the continent of Africa would be better off if all foreign assistance to the warring factions were to be halted and the dispute mediated by the Organization for African Unity.

The meddling of the Soviet Union, which has in turn prompted meddling by the Americans, is dangerous. Neither of the superpowers can afford to become embroiled in a dispute stemming from a new colonialism in Africa. Africans themselves must be extremely unhappy to find this sort of meddling. The whole thrust of African policy has been to eliminate outside influence and to give the African nations a chance to develop in their own way. That is good policy, coming as it does in the aftermath of more than 100 years of bitter, often brutal, colonial exploitation.

The United States has already spoken bluntly in the U. N. General Assembly about the situation. If there is no change, an attempt ought to be made in the General Assembly or the Security Council to pinpoint the responsibility of the Soviet Union and Cuba, too, for the dangerous state of affairs in Angola. The attempt may not be successful, but at least it will put the world on notice that we are trying to observe the proper neutrality in Africa, and it will spotlight the new Russian imperialism.

The Miami Herald

Miami, Fla., December 13, 1975

IT was a close call, but for once in the Western world the Marxist left has been dealt a sharp and telling defeat. The moderate parties of Portugal have ousted and isolated the Communist minority which proved to have neither strength at the polls nor in the streets.

This is the kind of victory that makes democracy, and not just another extreme, a viable agent of freedom. Since President Francisco da Costa Gomes faced up to a Communist military putsch two weeks ago, the hardline Marxist element has been sliding into national disrepute. As evidence of its strength, the Lisbon government easily wrested the press and radio from their Communist squatters. Now the dominant Armed Forces Movement, working with civilians, can bring off the promised free elections.

This would be wholly good news if it did not stand in the shadow of bad news from Angola, which is of more direct concern to the United States at the moment.

That former colony of Portugal, which sits strategically on the South Atlantic, has become what Portugal did not — an international battlefield with contending Soviet agents and arms, Castroite Cubans, South Africans, Chinese Maoists and, as it develops, the U.S. Central Intelligence Agency.

The CIA, it has been disclosed, is spending $50 million on arms for the two groups opposing the Soviet-backed Popular Movement for the Liberation of Angola (MPLA). Put "liberation" in quotes.

The money was authorized last spring in an unannounced action by the Forty Committee, the group which oversees the CIA. It is described as a "covert activity." It would involve Congress, which alone has the constitutional right to make war, if the CIA has to go back to Congress for more money. Its present resources for this kind of activity have been exhausted.

Lest this country slip and slide into another Vietnam on another continent, covert activity in Angola should be the subject of public debate. At that time, of course, it is no longer covert. Yet this is the sort of thing that has brought the CIA criticism in that very same forum.

No one wants to see Angola fall under Soviet control, but what the United States alone can do about the matter is a highly complex technical problem. Do we match U.S. troops with the forces backing the MPLA as we endeavored to match the Viet Cong? That would be the ultimate solution if there has been a commitment to the defeat of the MPLA, again covertly through Zaire or any other agency

Angola has every appearance of another international snake pit. Congress should determine at once what is best in the national interest lest we go from a few arms to a few advisers to Green Berets and ultimately to a heavy investment of U.S. manpower once again halfway around the world.

Des Moines Tribune

Des Moines, Iowa, December 5, 1975

U.S. Ambassador to the U.N. Daniel Patrick Moynihan told a Washington, D.C., audience Tuesday that recent developments in Angola indicate an intention by the Soviet Union to colonize all of Africa. Moynihan was referring to a stepped-up Soviet supply of military equipment and technicians to the Popular Movement for the Liberation of Angola (MPLA) and to the introduction of Cuban soldiers in MPLA ranks.

The Soviet moves in Angola since the Portuguese colony became independent on Nov. 10 are a cause for alarm in the West and in the rest of Africa. But Soviet actions are not taking place in a vacuum.

What makes Angola attractive to the Russians are hoped-for port facilities on Africa's southwest coast, the country's oil and mineral wealth and the political benefits of influencing liberation forces in Namibia (South-West Africa) and of checking Chinese influence on the continent. A pursuit of these interests does not necessarily constitute an attempt to "colonize" Africa.

The United States has pursued its own military, political and economic interests in southern Africa. In 1970, the Nixon administration adopted a plan to extend the U.S. and NATO naval presence in the region. U.S. Navy ships made increasing use of ports in Angola and in the then-Portuguese colony of Mozambique. NATO surveyed ports and airports as part of a contingency plan for the defense of South Africa and Cape shipping.

The Nixon administration then stopped the minimal amounts of aid that had been shipped to liberation groups in Angola and Mozambique and started to help Portugal retain its colonies by supplying military equipment and training to fight those same liberation groups.

The support by the Nixon and Ford administrations of Portugal and now the National Front for the Liberation of Angola (FNLA) also was an effort to protect growing American financial holdings in Angolan oil production and diamond mining in the north, and to bolster European interests in the mining industry in the south.

The U.S. support of the FNLA is based less on the politics of that particular movement than on its close association with the government of Zaire, which the administration perceives as an anti-Communist bulwark.

The Soviet actions since November have been out of proportion to what went before, but an acknowledgement of "what went before" is important for an understanding of the present Angolan crisis.

Moynihan should know that when it comes to international meddling in Angola, few nations' hands are clean.

THE CHRISTIAN SCIENCE MONITOR

Boston, Mass., December 15, 1975

There seem to be conflicting strains in the national mood in the field of foreign policy. On the one hand concern grows that the Soviet Union is expanding its influence and that the United States is politically and militarily on the defensive. On the other there is a clear reluctance in Congress to get involved in foreign ventures again after the bitter experience of Vietnam.

Angola is now at the heart of that dichotomy. President Ford has been quietly trying to force the Russians to scale down their intervention in the former African colony by providing arms — reportedly as much as $50 million — through neighboring Zaire. Members of Congress, meanwhile, are challenging any covert CIA operation in Angola on grounds it will suck the U.S. into another impossible conflict. Even within the State Department disagreement has surfaced over how best to deal with this thorny, intractable problem.

The dilemma is that there are no facile solutions. Clearly the United States cannot put its troops into Angola. Nor does it even like to be seen "fighting" on the same side as the South Africans, who are trying to contain the Soviet-backed faction. Yet Washington cannot simply wash its hands of the whole affair.

It is of course far from certain what the Russians will gain even if the pro-Soviet group wins out. They presumably are counting on a naval foothold on the western coast of Africa — just as they have on the eastern coast in Somalia. They undoubtedly would like to influence the political development of Angola in a Marxist direction, although how much success they would have given the primitive, tribal animosities there is open to question.

Then, too, there are those who argue that the MPLA, the pro-Russian faction, whatever criticism of it, is the only group competent in the end to run the country.

However, there is ample evidence that the Soviet penetration of Africa is growing and that a "victory" in Angola would greatly expand Moscow's sphere of influence and threaten the West's freedom of the seas in the South Atlantic. With the Russians having poured an estimated 150,000 tons of military equipment into Angola and supporting at least 3,000 Cuban guerrilla troops there, the situation grows more and more ugly.

In the face of this threat, U.S. countervailing aid to the anti-Soviet factions is understandable. Perhaps it should now even be publicly acknowledged and legitimatized. Such aid should serve the limited purpose of inducing the Russians to cut down their own involvement and to keep the fight from spreading to the borders of other countries, where it could destabilize the entire region.

Aid, however, is but a means of pressure. Above all there must be vigorous U.S. diplomatic efforts along two fronts. One, to try to reach some understanding with the Russians that all East-West power struggle in Angola will only exacerbate the already parlous state of detente. And, second, to induce the African states themselves, through the Organization of African Unity, to assume leadership in this matter, throw their weight behind a coalition in Angola, and call for an end to all foreign intervention on the continent of Africa.

In any case, as Washington wrestles with the problem, two realities are emerging from Angola.

The first is that detente — a policy never really understood by many Americans — has not ended the active rivalry between the two superpowers. The Russians have not abandoned their great-power goals. They will continue to project their force to the extent they can do so, though detente provides the framework for avoiding all-out confrontation and exercising restraint.

The second reality is that Vietnam did not put a finish to American involvement abroad. In a world where authoritarian systems are the rule rather than the exception and where force is used to gain political ends the U.S. will go on confronting situations where it must decide how much force to use in return. The judgments for the President are not easy. But they can be made in cooperation with an informed Congress that fully understands the stakes involved.

SENATE VOTES TO CUT OFF COVERT U.S. AID IN ANGOLA

The Senate Dec. 19 approved, 54–22, an amendment to the fiscal 1976 Defense Department appropriations bill cutting off covert financial aid to factions battling for control of Angola. The vote ended a three-day struggle between liberal senators opposed to the aid and the Ford administration and its backers, who argued that failure to extend the funds would be a serious blow to the national interest of the U.S.

Following a secret session of the Senate Dec. 17, Sen. John V. Tunney (D, Calif.) introduced an amendment calling for a $33 million reduction in defense monies, the amount he said had been recommended by the Central Intelligence Agency for continued aid to Angola. In addition, his motion prohibited use of funds "for any activities involving Angola directly or indirectly." Sen. Robert P. Griffin (R, Mich.) then offered a substitute amendment barring use of fiscal 1976 defense funds to support U.S. combat operations in or near Angola. This amendment, which would have allowed additional military grants for Angola, was overwhelmingly defeated Dec. 18, by a 72–26 vote. But an amendment by Sen. Jacob K. Javits (R, N.Y.) Dec. 18 retaining the $33 million in the bill while barring use of any defense funds for activities involving Angola was passed on a 93–4 vote.

Failing to defeat the Tunney amendment, supporters of the Administration began a filibuster Dec. 18. The White House-backed filibuster continued until Dec. 19 when President Ford, seeking to free the defense appropriations bill for Congressional passage, agreed to a vote on the Tunney amendment. During the three-day debate, the Administration sought to compromise, announcing Dec. 18 that $9 million for Angolan aid would be acceptable. By the next day, however, opposition to the aid had stiffened.

Following adoption, Tunney (who was facing a primary challenge in California from Thomas Hayden, a peace activist) and the other sponsors of the amendment were jubilant. They earlier had expressed anger that covert aid to favored factions in Angola had been given without what they considered proper consultation with Congress. They also likened the situation to the early years of U.S. involvement in Vietnam, when Congress accepted at face value Administration statements that U.S. interests were involved in Indochina. Others indicated qualms about backing Angolan factions that were being aided by the Republic of South Africa. U.S. alignment with South Africa, they said, would only damage U.S. relations with black nations of Africa.

President Ford spoke out strongly at his news conference Dec. 20 against the Senate action. He said it "unfortunately has tied our hands," and was "a serious mistake." "I feel a great country like the United States should have flexibility," he said. "The action of Congress is crucial in that it has deprived us of our ability to help the people of Angola. It is a broader problem in that many other countries consider the United States as friendly and helpful." "Those countries dependent on us," Ford continued, "cannot help having misgivings because the Congress prevented us from helping Angola and may feel they will have the same fate."

ST. LOUIS POST-DISPATCH

St. Louis, Mo., December 23, 1975

The Senate, to its credit, voted overwhelmingly to cut off funds for covert military support operations in Angola. President Ford, who had lobbied strenuously against the amendment to a defense appropriations bill, deplores the vote and has called upon the Senate to reconsider. "The sole issue," Mr. Ford said, "is the provision of modest amounts of assistance to oppose military intervention by two extra-continental powers . . . " Nothing could be further from the truth.

Until earlier this month not many Americans were aware of Angola, a former Portuguese colony on the southwest coast of Africa which achieved independence on Nov. 11 and has been torn by civil war since. On Dec. 8 the U.S. Ambassador to the United Nations, Daniel Patrick Moynihan, brought the issue before the General Assembly in a major speech condemning Russian intervention in Angola. The Soviet Union was attempting to colonize Africa, he said, and for the General Assembly to pretend otherwise would be to settle for the "big lie." He made no mention of any American involvement in Angola.

On the following day, Dec. 9, Secretary of State Henry Kissinger held a press conference. In response to a question on Angola, Mr. Kissinger would only say that the "U.S. has tried to be helpful to some neighboring countries." And furthermore, "Whatever we have done has started long after massive Soviet involvement became evident . . . the Soviet Union has been active there in this manner since March." So no American involvement, of any kind whatsoever, began until "long after" the "massive Soviet involvement" which began last March.

The American people have since learned a good deal more about what has been done in their name in Africa. Government leaks, which the Ford Administration has not denied, indicate that military equipment worth $50,000,000 is being funneled into Angola through neighboring Zaire. And the *New York Times* has reported, again quoting government sources, that the U.S. commitment began last January—or well before the subsequent build-up in Soviet assistance.

Mr. Kissinger denies the *Times* report. He still maintains that the U.S. has acted only in response to Soviet intervention. There has been one significant change, however, from statements made during the Dec. 9 press conference. Mr. Kissinger now claims that the U.S. acted not only in response to Soviet military aid extended last March but to Soviet financial aid which began in October 1974. By pushing back the alleged start of the Soviet commitment, Mr. Kissinger thus protects himself if he later has to concede the accuracy of the *Times* report.

We are not now in a position to say who intervened first in Angola. At this point no one is, outside of the Ford Administration. But clearly the Administration has tried to conceal the extent of the American involvement, and its spokesmen have engaged in a campaign of half-truths and outright distortions.

President Ford claims that the national interest of the United States is at stake in Angola, and that to remain passive in the face of military intervention would be a "deep tragedy for all countries whose security depends on the United States." To the contrary, the paramount issue is whether the American people can expect their Government to tell the truth.

Arkansas Gazette.

Little Rock, Ark., December 23, 1975

We wrote many times during the Vietnam War, which itself was conspicuously not such a situation, that not the least of the consequences of our needless involvement over there would be the diminution of our will to make a similar type of response in some unforeseen and unforeseeable situation in the future where — unlike in Vietnam —our vital interests *were* engaged. We thought this was so then, and think it is so now. Such is the nature of human disillusionment after the inevitable folding up of such a star-crossed enterprise as that one.

This is by way of preface to our saying now that neither is any vital American interest involved today in Angola, and, if we were ever surprised by anything these people say or do, we would be a little surprised by the shrill insistence of President Ford, Secretary of State Kissinger and others that we do, too, have a do-or-die stake in yet another civil war, this time across the other big ocean in Black Africa. The American people may have a low attention span in a lot of ways, but we think the lesson of Vietnam is still etched rather more deeply than that in the public consciousness.

The lessons of the past certain have impressed themselves deeply on the memories of a majority of members of the United States Senate, which last week voted 54-to-22 to cut off all the surreptitious aid that was being funneled through the CIA to "our" side in the Angola fighting, thus touching off some fairly high-pitched screams from the aforementioned Mr. Ford and Mr. Kissinger, all of which boil down to the "pitiful, helpless giant" that Richard M. Nixon said the United States would be reduced to if it pursued the course of sanity in Vietnam and got out of a place where we should never have been in the first place.

In the event, withdrawal from Vietnam meant no such thing so far as America's standing in the world was concerned. What Vietnam *did* do was make it a whole lot easier for the Congress to read the road signs for booby traps before getting drawn along, step by step, into another worthless, costly, undertaking in another corner of the globe that many millions of Americans had never even heard of before being seriously told by their leaders that here was another test of American resolve at least on a par with Valley Forge.

When Henry Kissinger says that Angola is not "another Vietnam," he is right only to the extent that no sequence of events involving a shooting war replicates itself precisely.

But the more Kissinger talks of how different the Angolan and Vietnamese situations were and are, the more we, and the Congress, are reminded of the similarities.

Angola is a recently freed former colony that those pioneer colonists, the Portuguese, finally turned all the way loose of, as France finally got out of Indochina — only to have us rush in and try to salvage what the French could not save after an occupying presence there of a hundred years.

What the Ford administration had done on the quiet and all that it says it wants the Senate to let it go on doing in the future is to pour a "modest" amount of money ($50 million projected or already given, so far) into Angola.

So was only a "modest" investment at the beginning in Vietnam, until the thing began feeding on itself, growing into an immodest investment with no hope of any kind of return that almost bankrupted the country before it was over.

"The Pitiful Helpless Giant" theory now is enunciated by Richard Nixon's successor in these terms:

> "How can tne United States, the greatest power in the world, take the position that the Soviet Union can operate with impunity *many thousands of miles away* [Angola] with Cuban troops and massive amounts of military equipment, while we refuse assistance to the majority of the local people who ask only for military equipment to defend themselves?"

Here again, there is the curious notion that only we, because we are "the greatest power in the world", are entitled to throw our weight around or have our proxies throw their weight around "thousands of miles" and oceans away from our own shores.

It is distressing, we know, for Ford and Kissinger to see little Cuba being conned by the Russians into behaving in Angola as the mighty power that lies "only 90 miles away" from the Cuban mainland once behaved itself thousands of miles and an ocean away in Vietnam.

We are tempted to say that if the Cubans want to make as big fools of themselves now in faraway Angola as we did then in Vietnam, why, then, let them.

Minneapolis Tribune

Minneapolis, Minn., December 28, 1975

The Senate this month voted 54 to 22 to cut off funds for the administration's covert military activities in Angola. It wasn't just liberal Democrats who voted against the Ford-Kissinger Angola policy, either; there were Republicans who usually support the administration, too — Clifford Case of New Jersey, Robert Packwood of Oregon, Robert Taft of Ohio and Jacob Javits of New York. The administration did little to help its supporters. It concealed whatever case it had until the last moment. And when President Ford and Secretary of State Henry Kissinger did open up, their case was not convincing. There was too much of the old Vietnam rhetoric for the majority of the Senate to stomach. Ford and Kissinger weren't helped, either, when it was revealed that many of the U.S. government's own African experts had advised the administration to stay out of the Angolan civil war.

The administration has not given up. Last Tuesday, Kissinger turned his attention to the House, upon which the administration is now centering its hopes for reversal of the Senate action. "If the Soviet Union continues action such as Angola, we will without any question resist," he said. "Failure to resist can only lead other countries to conclude that their situation is becoming precarious. . . ." To many of his critics in Congress, Kissinger's words sounded like more Vietnam rhetoric.

But whatever Congress might think of Kissinger's warnings, it does not appear that many Africans are taking them seriously. There is no argument in Africa about the Soviet and Cuban involvement in Angola. But, reported the Washington Post's David Ottaway recently, "for the majority of African leaders, the presence of Soviets and Cubans in Angola is of far less concern than the 'penetration' by South Africans for the first time into a black-ruled nation and the presence of hundreds of white mercenaries there."

The United States, the Post writer continued, is "in danger of finding itself linked in the African mind with South Africa and of being condemned with it for helping to divide rather than preserve the unity of Angola." In a similar vein, the British Guardian commented; "To have South Africa as an ally is not a position which any African liberation movement covets."

With the notable exception of West Germany, which traditionally follows Washington policy lines, the administration's Angola policy has won little support from Western allies, either. The British and French, especially, view Angola with nervousness and some uncertainty. Britain has told the administration that neither it nor NATO can afford to be seen by Africans to be making common cause with South Africa. Canada, Norway and the Netherlands support the British position and Britain's call for a cease-fire and the formation of a coalition government in Angola.

"We should not feel we have to become involved in this civil war simply because the Russians have chosen to do so," Minnesota's Rep. Bill Frenzel said. "Knee-jerking in the power-politics game is a poor substitute for a careful assessment of whether or not our vital interests are at stake in this struggle. . . . In my judgment, our interests would be better served if we stayed out of the conflict. Instead, we should use whatever diplomatic leverage is available to us in support of the Organization of African Unity's call for a cessation of all foreign intervention." That is sound advice. We hope that when Congress reconvenes next month, the House will follow it. If the administration can make no better case for U.S. involvement in Angola than it has to date, the House should vote "no," as the Senate did.

FORT WORTH STAR-TELEGRAM

Fort Worth, Tex., December 24, 1975

President Ford stated to Congress and to the nation, as clearly as possible, that the issue for the United States in Angola "is not, never has been, and never will be, a question of the use of U. S. forces. The sole issue is the provision of modest amounts of assistance to oppose military intervention by two extracontinental powers, namely the Soviet Union and Cuba."

The president asked: How can the United States, the greatest power in the world, take the position that the Soviet Union can operate with impunity many thousands of miles away with Cuban troops and massive amounts of military equipment, while we refuse any assistance to the Angolan majority who ask only for military equipment to defend themselves?

He already had the answer, underscored by a 54 to 22 vote in the U. S. Senate calling for a ban of any further aid to Angola from the United States, in the congressional debate which repeatedly raised the specter of "another Vietnam" in West Africa. Congress was telling the White House that its constituents wanted no part of Angola aid..

If this move to cut off military equipment needed by the Angolan opponents of the Marxist, Soviet-backed Popular Movement results in a flat forfeiture of that country to the Communists—as it likely will—we in the United States will have learned some doleful lessons:

The Russians do not intend to let their end of the detente policy to get in the way of the inexorable march of Communist conquest that has plagued the world for almost half a century. Seen in this realistic light, detente seems but a minor adventure in diplomatic opportunism by comparison.

And the Cubans under Fidel Castro likewise cannot be relied upon to exploit the recent openings toward normalization of relations with the United States when those openings coincide with a "greater opportunity" to further the worldwide sweep of communism in Angola or elsewhere.

The Cuban aid to the Marxists in Angola, added to Havana's constant meddling in Puerto Rican politics and its refusal to compensate American companies for its takeover of $1.8 billion in American property, amounts to a hardening intransigence that rolls back U. S.-Cuban relations a decade or more.

President Ford gave the Angolan aid ban action in Congress a bleak assessment. He said it "tied our hands" and called it a serious mistake for this nation which should have flexibility in helping people of other nations decide their own fate.

It will remain for history to determine how much of a mistake it was. But one thing seems certain: the congressional opponents of Angolan aid cannot be accused of acting counter to the wishes of most of their constituents—leaving the question of wisdom aside.

Portland Press Herald

Portland, Me., December 23, 1975

Congress is right to put a brake on covert U.S. operations in Angola.

It is comforting to see the Congress reassert itself in matters of this sort. For too long the initiative for such foreign adventures has been left to executive whim.

Conversely, it is unnerving to see the President pressing so vigorously to move the United States more deeply into the Angolan situation, where three different political factions are locked in a struggle for control of the newly-independent African country.

"America's tragic intervention in the Vietnam civil war should be a clear enough warning to our policy makers," declares Senator Edmund S. Muskie. "The wisest policy for the United States is to stay out of the Angolan conflict."

Since Senator Muskie, like most Americans, staunchly supported our Vietnam policy throughout most of that wrenching chapter in our nation's history, his comments on the Angolan matter are instructive. Our guess is that he reflects the view of the vast majority of Americans today.

Secretary of State Kissinger, arguing the Administration's case, has denied that American involvement in Angola is in any way analogous to the Vietnam experience. Almost nobody else, however, has failed to perceive the striking similarities between Indochina in the late 1950s and early 1960s and Angola in West Africa today.

As George Santayana observed, "Those who cannot remember the past are condemned to repeat it." The Ford Administration presents a chilling demonstration of historical amnesia in secretly shipping arms to the so-called anti-Communist forces in Angola's civil conflict.

Americans may very well wonder whether their government learned anything from Vietnam.

The President has warned the Soviets and the Cubans that their intervention in Angola threatens future relations between those countries and the United States. But such warnings are meaningless if our response is to get involved in the conflict ourselves.

We tend to agree with Senator Muskie and other congressional leaders who say that a much more effective and less dangerous response would be for the U. S. to apply economic and diplomatic pressure.

"If the Russians are prepared to make a mockery of the detente relationship," argues Muskie, "then let them lose some of the material advantages of detente."

That makes better sense than pouring millions of dollars worth of arms into a complicated civil conflict in an area of the world where our national interests or security simply are not involved.

Amsterdam News

New York, N.Y., December 27, 1975

Secretary of State Henry Kissinger is driving an American-made-Ford through the back roads of Angola and the American people should charge him with reckless driving.

The Ford which is illegally touring the roads of Angola is named Gerald — but the driver's name is Henry.

Frankly speaking, it is difficult for us to imagine that President Ford realizes the dangers of the back roads in Angola. His entire performance thus far in the field of foreign affairs has been so immature that most students of foreign affairs are willing to shake their heads and say the President simply does not know what he is doing in the field of international relations.

But Henry Kissinger definitely knows — and the fact that he does know is what qualifies him for the charge of being a reckless driver in Angola.

The United States has about as much right poking its nose into the affairs of Angola as the Imperial Wizard of the Ku Klux Klan has trying to tell Roy Wilkins how to run the NAACP.

We simply have no business in Angola and Henry Kissinger knows this.

The Senate, by a vote of 54 to 22, tried to tell this to President Ford this week. But more and more it is becoming increasingly clear that Mr. Ford only listens to Henry.

What if Russia is cultivating Angola?

Didn't the French try the same thing in Vietnam?

And when the French failed, didn't we try the same thing — only to get our ears pinned back in a war that never should have been fought in the first place?

The Portuguese victimized, exploited and decimated the people of Angola for decades while we sat by and never raised an official murmur of protest.

And now, a few months after these poor people become independent, and start going through the struggles that go along with independence, along comes Henry Kissinger, Hell bent for elections, screaming that we must hurry over there and save them from the Russians and the Cubans, in what could end up as another war in which Angola itself would be virtually destroyed as Vietnam was.

With such friends as Kissinger was to Vietnam — Angola does not need any enemies.

Let's get out of Angola now — and stay out!

The Courier-Journal

Louisville, Ky., December 24, 1975

THE SENATE'S INSISTENCE on cutting off all U.S. assistance to Angola, despite President Ford's plea that such aid is in our "national interest," is not surprising. After 30 years of the Cold War, and especially after Vietnam, that phrase finally has lost its power to charm Congress into approving any and every request that comes from the White House.

Things conceivably could be different if someone were able to clearly define what aspect of our national security is supposed to be at stake in Angola. Most of the time, the Ford administration seems to be hinting that Soviet domination of this West African country would pose a threat to the South Atlantic shipping lanes that carry an increasing proportion of U.S. oil supplies. But it's hard to believe that such pressure would ever be exercised unless we were already at war with the Soviet Union. In any event, the existing Soviet foothold in Somalia, on the east-coast horn of Africa, would be far more effective for that purpose, since it is much closer to the Persian Gulf oil ports.

A more plausible case could be made — though it hardly would be in the interests of a Republican administration to try — for attempting to crush the Soviet-backed Popular Movement for the Liberation of Angola (MPLA) because of the American business interests in that country. The size of the investment of Gulf Oil Corporation, for instance, is indicated by reports that it has been paying $500 million a year in royalties on its petroleum production. And the futility of what the Ford administration was trying to accomplish in Angola is underscored by the fact that the Gulf payments, all of which have gone to the MPLA, amount to 10 times the U.S. government aid to the opposing factions.

More cogent still would be the reasoning that if the MPLA can establish control over the whole of Angola, its next step, with eager Soviet encouragement, would be to press southward to liberate South-West Africa. At that point, the long-expected black-white showdown in southern Africa would be under way.

Clearly, South Africa sees that possibility down the road, which is one reason its forces already have been committed on the side of MPLA's opponents in southern Angola. But if that struggle is to come to a head in a few years' time, the best course for the United States is to try to steer clear. The worst we could do would be to find ourselves dragged in on the side of the white South African government, with its apartheid policy of racial segregation, because of an association in Angola.

What seems to be forgotten by those who advocate U.S. intervention, even in its most limited form, is not only the whole lesson of Vietnam, but the entire experience of post-colonial history. Both African and Asian nations have accepted outside assistance in their liberation struggles. But the welcome mat never has stayed out for long, especially when the help came from a powerful, white government with its own purposes to serve.

The United States was kicked out of Vietnam, the Russians were sent home (admittedly in a less ignominious fashion) from Egypt, and many African leaders are disturbed at the prospect of a strong Soviet influence in Angola. If it hadn't been for South Africa's intrusion, the Russians might already be feeling African pressure to back down. As it is, the introduction of foreign troops, mainly Cuban but also from Eastern Europe, could turn out to be the Kremlin equivalent of the U.S. mistake of sending troops to Vietnam in 1965.

An Angola dominated by the Marxist MPLA would be no more threatening to U.S. national security than are the other left-wing regimes in Africa, among them Mozambique and Tanzania. This was the advice given to the Secretary of State by State Department experts in African affairs, and its rejection prompted the resignation of several officials, including Nathaniel Davis as Assistant Secretary of State for African Affairs. But what raises administration hackles is the role of the Soviet Union. To the President and to Secretary Kissinger, Angola has become a Soviet vehicle for testing U.S. determination after Vietnam.

Some evidence, to be sure, suggests that our initial maneuvering for advantage is what caused the Kremlin to respond. In any event, the best way to combat Soviet assertiveness in Africa is not to start a new arms race or try to outbid the Russians in a military way. Instead, the aim should be to give whatever diplomatic help we can, particularly to the Organization of African Unity, which has been trying to bring about a ceasefire and a negotiated settlement in Angola. Above all, South Africa should be kept at arm's length. Let the Russians be the ones to dig themselves into an impossible situation in which they are unlikely to receive much gratitude and, in the long run, few tangible benefits.

The Senate appears to understand what's at stake better than do the President and his Secretary of State. Mr. Ford's plea that only a limited amount of assistance is involved is not easily swallowed by senators who remember that that was the way Vietnam began. If the administration wants to resume its efforts when Congress resumes after the holiday recess, it will have to come up with something more palatable than these indigestible allusions to our undefined national interests.

The Philadelphia Inquirer

Philadelphia, Pa., December 29, 1975

"What is surprising," the Soviet government newspaper Izvestia declared the other day, "is that some people in the West are trying to conjure up some sort of contradiction between the relaxation of international tension and the Angolan People's Republic's efforts to repulse external forces, primarily the South African racist regime."

Is it surprising that the Soviet government believes, or professes to believe, that there is no contradiction between U. S.-Soviet detente and the Kremlin's massive intervention on the side of the Popular Movement for the Liberation of Angola, one of the three factions contending for power in the former Portuguese colony?

Perhaps not. The one consistent principle in Soviet policy has always been inconsistency. The Kremlin line is that Western intervention into the affairs of other countries is "imperialism," and therefore bad, because it is Western; Soviet intervention outside its borders is "support for national liberation struggles," and therefore good.

Unhappily, the Russians score more propaganda points with that line than they deserve. By its covert intervention to assist Angolan factions opposing the Popular Movement, the U. S. government found itself on the same side as South Africa, which has also dispatched a thousand or so men to Angola.

If any single issue unites the countries of black Africa, it is opposition to the apartheid policies of Pretoria. The Ford Administration argues that it is not allied with South Africa but only happens to be taking parallel actions. It should not be surprising, either, that the Soviet Union, attempting to expand its influence in Africa, should link "certain U. S. circles" to "South African aggression" and that this strikes a responsive chord among many Africans.

This is a major reason, although not the only one, that we agree with the Senate's vote, 54-22, to cut off new military and economic aid for clandestine support of the other two Angolan factions. It is easy to understand Secretary of State Henry Kissinger's frustration at this congressional interference (as he sees it) with his own conduct of foreign affairs. Mr. Kissinger, though, should also understand the national temper which the Senate vote reflects — a profound reluctance to wade into another quagmire where our interests are indiscernible and our ability to shape events is minimal.

Possibly the vote would have gone the other way if the administration had adequately consulted with Congress last spring before acting on its own, although we doubt that it would have. In any case, the danger does not arise from our "domestic disputes," as Mr. Kissinger asserts. Detente, as he also says, "requires conscious restraint by both sides," and we think he would have the support of Congress in making this clear to Moscow.

The Virginian-Pilot

Norfolk, Va., December 22, 1975

The Senate's refusal to play the Russians' game in the Angolan civil war was not only a stinging rebuke to the Administration but an early and welcome Christmas gift.

Before packing up for a month's vacation Friday, the Senate rallied behind liberal Democrats to deny, by a decisive 54 votes to 22, further covert aid through CIA channels to two of the three factions fighting for control of the former Portuguese African colony. The $32 million already spent or committed would be all if the House, when it returns in January, agrees to a Senate amendment to the $112.3 billion defense appropriations bill cutting off aid to Angolan belligerents.

Opponents of aid were haunted by memories of the Vietnam involvement: a trickle now (the Administration has estimated that $100 million might be committed to Angola) could become a torrent, involving not only cash but military hardware, advisers, even troops. Further, they were persuaded of the folly of matching Moscow in a contest that may have no outside winner: the emerging black African states have consistently shrugged off powers that tried to embrace them, as the Russians should have learned from their experiences in Mozambique and Zaire.

Moscow has committed arms, advisers, and 3,000 of its Cuban comrades to the Popular Movement for the Liberation of Angola (MPLA), which holds the capital of Luanda and at the moment appears to have winning chances. American aid has flowed through Zaire to two other contenders for power that have now combined, the National Front for the Liberation of Angola (FNLA) and the National Union for the Total Independence of Angola (UNITA). South Africa, jittery at the implications for that segregationist country of a black Marxist neighbor, is supporting the FNLA-UNITA coalition with perhaps 1,000 troops.

The presumed reward for the great powers would be access to Angola's Atlantic ports, whose strategic importance is belittled by Senate critics, and to her minerals and petroleum (Gulf Oil, whose royalties are Angola's largest single revenue source, is being pressured by the Administration to withhold a pending $100 million payout to the MPLA regime in Luanda). But there is no assurance that the winning side, having settled a tribal war for supremacy over a black nation newly delivered from 500 years of European colonialism, would be eager to share the benefits with a white ally. The basic issue in the fighting is which group of Angolan nationalists will run Angola.

The Administration's defeat eroded both President Ford's constitutional authority over foreign affairs and his support among Senate partisans. Party leaders were among the 16 Republicans who went against him, as were Virginia's William Scott and North Carolina's Jesse Helms. On the Democratic side, Mr. Ford won only the sympathy of a hawkish seven, among them Virginia's Independent Harry F. Byrd Jr. and North Carolina's Robert Morgan. Mr. Ford's assessment of the setback as "a deep tragedy" for countries relying on the United States for their security and a threat to American national interests overstated the case.

The vote was a measure of the gulf between Congress and the Administration in their appreciation of Angola's importance. The Administration wished to maintain a presence in Angola both to influence African affairs and to impress the Russians that it hasn't been scared away from overseas encounters by the Indochina debacle. But the stakes are low and the game in the end unwinnable for interlopers. Losing out to the Russians would be a severe blow to American prestige, and coming out on top as an implied ally of South Africa would be a poor way to win friends in black Africa. Let Moscow pay and learn.

THE COMMERCIAL APPEAL

Memphis, Tenn., December 23, 1975

A GRIM PRESIDENT Ford told the White House press corps last Friday he regards the Senate action toward ending covert U.S. aid to an Angolan faction as an "abdication of responsibility" by the lawmakers.

A great nation, he added, cannot escape its responsibilities because "responsibilities abandoned today will return as more acute crises tomorrow."

He may be right.

There have been times in this nation's history when it has sought to shy away from its responsibilities in the world's affairs. The failure of the U.S. to join in the League of Nations after World War I surely must be regarded now as one such failure.

But it is also true that in recent years presidents and their close advisers all too often have sought to involve this nation in foreign affairs which we could not really influence. Our reactions in those cases made this nation look just as foolish as it did when it bobbled on the side of inaction.

The Senate remembers, too.

After all, this is the post-Vietnam Congress which has been uncovering a lot of information about involvement of this country in dubious foreign affairs.

We don't have great confidence in the ability of this or any other Congress to make U.S. foreign policy. Its effort in that direction during the Greek-Turkish clash over Cyprus was hardly a great success. But we do understand the reluctance of the senators to be a party after the fact to another involvement that some believe could prove to be another Vietnam situation.

The President and Secretary of State Henry Kissinger don't seem to comprehend that reaction on the part of Congress. Their failure to consult adequately with the congressional leadership on the Angolan matter when the policy was being established at the White House inevitably led to this reversal in the Senate last week.

If the President wants to develop and carry out a foreign policy that he considers responsible, he is going to have to take Congress into consideration in the future.

Pittsburgh Post-Gazette

Pittsburgh, Pa., December 20, 1975

THE SENATE vote blocking aid to Angola may prove to be strategically in the best interests of the U.S. . . . or, as President Ford commented in deploring the action, it may not.

The significance lies in the fact that Congress rightly is insisting that in foreign ventures of this kind it be involved in the takeoffs and not just whistled in if there is a crash landing.

We have learned that lesson from Vietnam. It could be argued, of course, that we are overreacting to the Vietnam experience, that the failure of our investment there has made us too leery of involvement anywhere else, to the detriment of our world struggle against Communist expansion. Angola has come to the fore because of Soviet Russian backing for one of the three factions in the civil war there, reinforced by Communist Cuba's dispatch of troops to that former Portuguese colony.

But there should be no argument against the concept that for American policy to work and to have the long-term support of the American public, it is vital that it be publicly discussed and understood. That is particularly true if the involvement is on the order of the $25 million reportedly already funneled into the two Angolan groups fighting the pro-Soviet faction.

* * *

The basic question is whether our national security is sufficiently threatened by Soviet activities in Angola to warrant this degree of involvement. Beyond that, should we make commitments which could lead us into a mini-Vietnam quagmire?

The time to find out is now, before we are overcommitted. The United States Senate, once badly burned because it went along with the executive for years on the Vietnam venture, is not making that mistake again.

We still may need to make some sort of commitment in Angola. But it should be only after a proper public debate, an opportunity the Senate action makes possible.

Wisconsin State Journal

Madison, Wisc., December 31, 1975

The Ford Administration's continuation of military aid to two factions in the civil war in Angola despite a Senate vote to the contrary is another example of arrogant use of power by the executive branch.

The Senate voted 54-22 on Dec. 19 to cut off future funds for covert aid to the Angolan groups, neither of which has been recognized by any African government as a functioning authority in Angola.

The opposing faction, the Popular Movement, is backed by the Soviet Union and Cuba, but it also has been extended diplomatic recognition by 21 of the 49 African countries and is seen as the ultimate winner by a State Dept. African expert who resigned in protest of United States intervention.

The House recessed without taking action on the Senate measure, leaving the door ajar for Secretary of State Henry Kissinger to keep the arms shipments going to Angola.

So far, everything about U.S. involvement in Angola leaves a bad taste in the mouth.

The Ford Administration sneaked into the civil war before the action could be debated in Congress. It kept the involvement quiet despite the lesson of Vietnam committing $32-million of the taxpayers' money.

After the involvement was made public, debated and rejected by the Senate, the Administration ignored the rejection and continued the aid, apparently juggling the financial books to come up with the money.

"I'm not going to say how much or where it is coming from," a "high United States official," presumably Kissinger, was quoted by the New York Times as saying.

The members of the House must share blame for this sad state of affairs.

It should have stayed in session to act on the Senate measure, which was an amendment to a defense appropriations bill. It had another chance to return to Washington during the holiday recess before many of the members took off for overseas junkets — some justified, some not.

It is interesting that while the members of Congress are touring everywhere from Peking to the South Pacific to Western Europe, there are no reports of anyone going to Angola.

If senators and representatives feel compelled to leave their desks to study various foreign nations, the obvious nation to look at at this stage is the latest hot spot in Africa.

The Dallas Morning News

Dallas, Tex., December 18, 1975

THE SENATE has been debating what to do about aid to the factions in the Angolan civil war. It is a subject that deserves a full airing. The problem involves not only Angola, but all of the new and unstable nations in the Third World.

The problem is that the easy, extreme answers are obviously the wrong ones. After Vietnam, it is not likely that any government official would call for an all-out effort to support any Third World faction. Politically, Americans would not stand for a commitment in which the ante might be raised, step by step, as it was in Vietnam.

On the other hand, a decision to cut off all aid to the anti-Soviet factions would amount to an announcement that we will not oppose Soviet attempts to take over the Third World, one country at a time.

There are few governments that operate without a radical opposition. If the Soviets continue to arm and organize these movements to topple the existing governments and if we make it clear that we do not intend to do anything, then the road to Soviet domination is clear.

We can be quite sure that those governments that have not already made an accommodation with the Soviet Union will swiftly do so. In the country of the unarmed, the man with a sword is king— and the Soviets are handing out weapons that are much more deadly than swords.

A Senate subcommittee has recently voted out a resolution calling for an end to U.S. aid to Angolans and urging other "foreign" interveners — the Soviet Union and Red China — to get out. The Senate has proved in Southeast Asia that it can effectively cut off U.S. arms aid. Unfortunately, the lawmakers have not been so effective in getting the Communists to heed their cease-and-desist resolutions. The Soviet managers of the take-over offensive, we can be sure, will not give this weak, toothless protest a moment's consideration.

A better approach, we believe, is to give the diplomatic bargainers something to work with in gaining Soviet attention.

The Soviet leadership apparently wants to continue the detente policy, and with it the shipments of American food and technology upon which the Russians increasingly depend.

Some in the Senate have suggested that it is time to make the Soviet leadership decide which it wants more, detente and American trade or Angola. Our diplomats should inform the Kremlin that if it continues the drive to overthrow existing governments in the Third World, it will sacrifice detente and any hope of future cooperation or trade with the U.S.

This is no panacea. Indeed, there is no guarantee that it will work.

But at least the either-or approach would be a more promising one than passing congressional resolutions calling on the Soviets to be good world citizens. As we should have learned decades ago, all that we accomplish with such resolutions is to demonstrate our own weakness and indecision.

THE SACRAMENTO BEE

Sacramento, Calif., December 19, 1975

If the American people are confused and disturbed about the U.S. role in Angola, it can be traced directly to the fact the administration has failed to keep Congress and the public fully informed.

It's not entirely clear how deeply this country is committed to factions opposed to the Russian-backed MPLA — the Popular Movement for the Liberation of Angola. Nor has President Gerald Ford made a persuasive case for pouring substantial military materiel into the civil strife that broke out after Portugal pulled out of its African colony.

As a consequence of the blurred picture of U.S. involvement, there is an underlying fear that, despite the many protestations, another Vietnam is in the making. It is an understandable reflex, considering the hush-hush beginnings in the Indochina debacle.

The Bee does not support the move in Congress to cut off all funds for American intervention. But we feel strongly the administration erred badly in waiting until after the fact to fill in and consult with Congress on what it has done and is doing.

The situation has reached the point where it is imperative for the legislative branch to be lifted out of the shadows and given information on the basis for not-so-covert CIA operations in the African nation rich in minerals and with deep-water ports which could be useful to the Soviets. The lawmakers have the right and the obligation to share in foreign policy decisions; to do so they need to be cognizant of developments affecting their course of action, mostly the matter of approving defense spending.

In that respect, Sen. John Tunney, D-Calif., has performed an estimable service in stirring up debate over his proposal to prohibit expenditures "for any activities involving Angola other than intelligence gathering."

Tunney's amendment to a defense appropriation bill provided exposure for such questions as why the U.S. has implicated itself in Angola. Realistically, however, his attempt to erect an absolute barrier to sending aid there would handcuff the administration from taking what may be necessary steps to protect U.S. interests against Soviet encroachment.

The best thing the White House can do, and quickly, is to level with the country on where it is taking us and why.

Winnipeg Free Press

Winnipeg, Man., December 22, 1975

The vote of the United States Senate to bar further American aid to pro-Western factions in Angola is another alarming sign of the crippling legacy of Vietnam on U.S. foreign policy.

In effect, the Senate has given the Soviet Union a clear message, if any were needed, that the U.S. is retreating into an isolationist cocoon.

By the defeat of President Ford's request for funds to buy Angolan arms, Moscow has been given virtually a free hand to play out its imperialistic game in that African country and an open invitation to indulge in other power plays with little fear of American intervention.

The implications of the Senate vote, which seems likely to be backed by the House of Representatives when Congress returns from its Christmas recess, are alarming both for the United States and her NATO allies.

The renunciation of any American responsibility to counter the blatant Soviet intervention in the Angolan civil war also is likely to be seen as a poignant lesson in other Third World countries. To the governments of these nations, particularly on the African continent, it will be clear that the Soviet Union is the more reliable big-power ally. In the unstable political climate characteristic of most Third World countries, the alternative to alliance with Moscow will be the spectre of Soviet-assisted revolution uncountered by Washington.

What is at stake in Angola, however, is far more important to Western interests than merely courting friends among the developing countries of Africa.

In its unsuccessful fight for congressional authorization to continue supplying funds to pro-Western factions in the civil war, the Ford administration cited two critical strategic and diplomatic interests. One is that the Popular Movement for the Liberation of Angola (MPLA), backed by Moscow with arms and 6,000 Cuban mercenaries fighting by proxy, might grant the Soviet Union a submarine base. The other equally unsettling prospect is that another radical regime on South Africa's borders would bring black-white relations on that continent to the explosion point.

The ever-growing Soviet fleet is steadily gaining ascendency in the Indian Ocean and in the vital eastern approaches to the Cape shipping route via the Mozambique Channel. Almost all supertankers from the Middle East for Western Europe and North and South America take that route because they are too big to navigate the re-opened Suez Canal. If the Soviet Union is allowed to establish a base in Angola, on the western approach to the Cape, the route used by the West to supply its oil requirements would be subject to blockade. Indeed, air power would affect the balance of power in the whole South Atlantic.

There are two courses the Ford administration may pursue in an attempt to counteract the shortsighted vote in the Senate. It seems likely that Washington will attempt to persuade some of its European friends to take up the burden of backing the anti-Soviet forces. Secretary of State Henry Kissinger is reported to be considering approaches to both Belgium and France, both of which have been sources for arms and mercenaries in central Africa, but what success he will have is difficult to predict. Washington is also weighing the value of a major diplomatic effort to promote a black African move against all foreign intervention when the Organization of African Unity holds an emergency meeting on Angola in Addis Ababa, Ethiopia, next month. The MPLA already has been recognized by 16 African governments, but there are 49 members in the OAU and two-thirds of them have indicated they will attend the emergency session. (The MPLA, which has the support of only a minority of Angola's population, would be quickly defeated if all outside intervention were ended.)

Unfortunately for the National Front for the Liberation of Angola (NFLA) and a smaller third group that have been receiving covert U.S. aid, the Senate vote will result in an increase in the importance of aid from South Africa. That support is a major embarrassment for the NFLA and could prove to be an Achilles' heel if the OAU gets involved in trying to impose a diplomatic settlement.

The reaction of the Senate to the Angola issue is clear evidence that the traumatic American experience in Vietnam will haunt and possibly hamstring U.S. foreign policy for years to come. The debate which ended in the 54-22 vote to cut off aid centred on fears that an initial commitment of money and arms would inevitably lead — as it did in Vietnam — to the use of American troops in the struggle. The senators' refusal to accept administration assurances to the contrary is the price President Ford is paying for a decade of deception over the Asian war and Watergate by his predecessors.

The senators who voted to abandon Angola to the Soviet Union don't want history to repeat itself. However, their historical perspective, as the United States reverts to the mood of isolationism that preceded the Second World War, is rather short.

DAILY NEWS

New York, N.Y., December 23, 1975

The Senate vote to cut off military aid to anti-Soviet groups in Angola was a rash act born of panic. Unless the House shows better sense, the ability of the U.S. to carry out an orderly foreign policy will be gravely harmed.

The most immediate and serious consequence would be to give the Soviet Union the idea—rightly or wrongly—that it can press forward with its policies of subversion and aggression unchallenged.

It is not just foolish to send the Kremlin such a signal; it is downright dangerous.

The Salt Lake Tribune

Salt Lake City, Utah, December 21, 1975

There is great, good reason for a full-scale congressional airing of United States involvement in Angola. But the Senate's attempt to cut off all U.S. aid before adequate discussion has taken place is ill-advised.

The Angola aid cutoff tactic recalls Congress' bumbling attempt to dictate U.S. policy in the aftermath of Turkey's invasion of Cyprus. A congressional ban on sale of arms to Turkey prompted that nation to take over American military bases on its soil and in other ways spoiled relations between the United States and a critical ally.

As has been the case with so many Executive-Legislative branch troubles, the Angola aid controversy springs from Ford administration attempts to keep U.S. involvement in Angola a secret from the American people.

The aid cutoff strategy in the Senate is a direct outgrowth of this policy of launching huge covert military aid projects without consulting Congress. Belatedly appraised of the extent of U.S. involvement, many senators want more definite answers to questions about the wisdom of past and future U.S. moves in Africa, particularly Angola.

Cutting off military aid right now would at least force the administration to explain, for the benefit of the public, its true Angola policy. But such potentially drastic action might also jeopardize benefits, if any, that past U.S. assistance has procured.

The question of United States involvement in Angola is too critical to be decided by a handful of high officials in the executive branch alone. Likewise, the U.S. role must not be determined by members of Congress seeking to take formulation of foreign policy into their hands.

There was a time when such potentially risky ventures were approached as a joint enterprise of the President and Congress and presented to the country as bi-partisan foreign policy. That didn't prevent foreign policy mistakes but it served to let the rest of the country in on what was being done and built a consensus for whatever action emerged.

The time for covert operations in Angola is over. From here on out President Ford and Secretary of State Henry Kissinger should work closely with Congress in determining U.S. response to events in Angola. And Congress, in return, should stop attempting to preempt policy-making duties of the White House.

BUFFALO EVENING NEWS

Buffalo, N.Y., December 22, 1975

The refusal of the Senate to authorize further covert military aid for Angola is one more example of the recent excessive attempts by Congress to intrude in the making of foreign policy.

Cutting off aid to a friendly faction in Angola would be bad enough, but President Ford hinted at the larger implications when he said that the Senate's action was tragic for "all countries whose security depends on the United States." The constant intrusion by Congress hampers the President in the exercise of his constitutional prerogatives in foreign policy and necessarily creates doubts as to U. S. resolve among U. S. friends and allies everywhere.

The strong opposition in Congress stems, no doubt, not from the merits of the case but from similarities, real or imagined, between Angola and Vietnam. But the President has properly made clear his opposition to any escalation of the U. S. role to include U. S. personnel. A civil war is going on in Angola, and the outlook for that newly independent country is turbulent, no matter which side wins. Thus, it only makes sense to make a modest contribution to a friendly group — or to the group that is friendly to our friends in that part of Africa — especially when the opposing group in the civil war is being aided by Cuban troops and massive arms aid from Russia.

We agree with the arguments of some aid opponents as to the risks involved in committing U. S. prestige or of being tarnished through being on the same side as South Africa, but that is no reason for doing nothing. It was a reason, however, for keeping the operation secret, but now we have an absurd situation in which Congress is holding a public debate about a secret operation. Now that the aid has reached its present proportions, there is a case for ending the secrecy and sending the arms openly.

As Mr. Ford stressed, "the issue in Angola is not, never has been and never will be a question of the use of U. S. forces." The sole issue here is whether a great power can simply abdicate responsibilities for providing even military equipment to oppose Communist intervention.

The unfortunate Senate cutoff vote all seems part of the effort of an overzealous Congress to limit the powers of the executive branch — an effort that killed the U. S.-Soviet trade bill, impaired ties with Turkey through the arms embargo and continues to chip away at the old and new SALT negotiations through partisan criticism.

The News and Courier

Charleston, S.C., December 27, 1975

Congress has extended a clear invitation to the Soviet Union to proceed with bold and dangerous strategy in Africa. That, in a nutshell, is what recent action on Capitol Hill calling a halt to American intervention in Angola amounts to.

That there should be many in Congress under misguided impression that drawing back in the face of a Russian push is the best way to avoid trouble is understandable. Congress has been profoundly influenced by feelings in the aftermath of Vietnam which run against any form of foreign policy except the use of words.

What Congress has done is nevertheless to be condemned. To fly from before the Soviets in Africa invites trouble, instead of avoiding it.

The threat in Africa is not of a new form of colonialism, Red Russian style, but of chaos and global stress arising from the internationalization and expansion of local, African conflicts.

Pursuing its African strategy, the Soviet Union has tested and eliminated the U.S. as a possible stabilizing factor. Its next target will be to test and turn back, if possible, the increasing Chinese influence in Africa.

Until the other day, a bulwark of American power in Africa protected against confrontation between the Russians and the Chinese. With that bulwark leveled, a way is cleared for Red tides to flow toward each other unrestrained, until they collide with explosive implications for the world.

Chicago Tribune

Chicago, Ill., December 30, 1975

The most striking thing about the battle over Angola is that the battle lines are much more clearly defined in Washington than they are in Angola.

To Congress, the issues seem to be pure and simple: We don't want to get bogged down in another Viet Nam, so the Senate has arbitrarily cut off funds for aid to the anti-Soviet forces in Angola. To Secretary Kissinger, the issue is equally clearcut: The Soviet Union is helping the Popular Movement for the Liberation of Angola, one of the rival factions in that newly independent country, in the hope of winning access to its strategic bases and resources; so it is essential for the free world that we thwart this effort to subvert an African country.

The trouble is that both sides are fighting old wars over again. Many of those who once urged us into Viet Nam in order to avoid another Munich are now urging us out of Angola in order to avoid another Viet Nam. In all of this shouting, neither side has pointed out that the principal trouble in Viet Nam was ignorance and often misrepresentation of conditions in that country.

Intelligence reports, we've since learned, were systematically tilted so as to minimize the strength and public support of the Communists in South Viet Nam and to exaggerate the strength and popularity of the Saigon government. Under Presidents Eisenhower and Kennedy we allowed a commitment to develop which was based more on theory than on realities. Under President Johnson, the American people were deliberately soothed with deceptive reports purporting to show that we could win the war even without cutting off the Communist supply routes. We were told that our troops would be "home by Christmas [1965, that is]." We labored under constant illusions about the degree of support we could expect from our allies.

In short, the Viet Nam war was lost not necessarily because the theory was bad, but because in Washington and in American public opinion the battles were fought in a minefield of misinformation or, at best, wishful thinking.

Of all the possible similarities between Angola and Viet Nam, this is the one that we find most disturbing. The arguments for helping anti-Soviet forces in Angola are valid; but so is the fear of another Viet Nam. If an intelligent judgment is to be made, it requires much more in the way of facts than we now have.

How do the people of Angola feel? Do they have any feelings at all, or is it the tribal chiefs who decide, perhaps for personal reasons, which team their tribe will be on? How do the neighboring African countries line up [we know, for example, that Zaire and South Africa are backing the anti-Soviet Front for the National Liberation of Angola; and so, for a time, were the Chinese]? Is there any hope that the Organization for African Unity can negotiate effectively to bring about a peace [this would be the best solution]? At what point does military aid turn into a commitment that may keep us trapped even if the going should get bad? Can the Soviet Union realistically expect to profit even if it does manage to install a puppet regime —or is it likely to find itself mired down by continuing strife? Are our European friends irrevocably committed to noncommitment?

Granted, these aren't questions that can be answered with precise numbers and dates. But so far as we have seen, there hasn't even been a sincere effort to answer them, either by the administration or by Congress. The lessons of history are important, of course, but no strategy can be successful, in diplomacy or in war, without studying the terrain ahead as well.

Given only what we now know, we are opposed to any policy that leaves us with an ironclad commitment. But it is easy to conceive of answers which would show that the Senate was dead wrong in opposing any sort of military aid. Congress should be as interested as the State Department in seeing that we all understand the facts and the odds better than we now do.

The Detroit News

Detroit, Mich., December 24, 1975

The Senate's action in barring any more U.S. aid for Angola may well assure the victory of the Soviet-backed faction in the former Portuguese colony.

For why should the Marxist Popular Movement for the Liberation of Angola (MPLA) now wish to resume negotiations with the two anti-Soviet factions over the future government of the country?

Nobody is cutting off the Soviet aid to MPLA or the help it is receiving from an estimated 4,000 Cuban soldiers. On the other hand, the ending of U.S aid no doubt will limit the activities of the anti-Soviet factions and make it even more difficult for them to win or bring their MPLA foes back to the negotiating table.

Thus President Ford was right in assailing the Senate for halting U.S. aid unilaterally and thus tying the hands of the administration in Angola. But the effect is much wider than that, as the President pointed out:

"Those countries dependent on us cannot help having misgivings because the Congress prevented us from helping Angola and may feel they will have the same fate."

That would be especially true of any anti-Soviet nations whose governments would be subjected to subversion or other attack by the USSR in the future. In other words, the Senate's rebuff to any aid for Angola must raise new questions about this country's will to resist Soviet expansionism in Angola or anywhere else.

True, the action cutting off funds for Angola still could be reversed by the Senate itself or be rejected by the House of Representatives when Congress returns to Washington in January. But neither action appears to be likely at the moment.

Mr Ford also was right to attack the actions of the USSR and Cuba in Angola. He warned the USSR its involvement with weapons was "harmful" to detente but used tougher language to tell Cuba its intervention in the Puerto Rican independence movement and in Angola "destroys any opportunity for improvement of relations with the United States."

Obviously, this country would prefer peaceful relations with a stable Angolan government selected by the Angolan people than helping one side or the other in any civil war.

But if the Soviet-backed faction takes over, the chances are Angola will become a base for new Soviet operations in Africa and in the Atlantic. Under those circumstances, there would be little reason for the United States to have any relations with Angola.

In view of the current mood of neo-isolationism on Capitol Hill, perhaps that is what the members of Congress really want. Congress' present motto seems to be, "Hear no, see no, speak no evil" about anybody — except the President and the U.S. State Department.

HOUSE CUTS OFF AID TO ANGOLA; FORD SAYS CONGRESS 'LOST GUTS'

President Ford castigated the members of Congress Feb. 10 as having "lost their guts" when they voted to ban further aid to the forces in the Angolan civil war that were opposing the faction supported by the Soviet Union and Cuba.

The House Jan. 27, in a 323–99 vote, adopted the amendment. The defense appropriations bill provided $90.5 billion for fiscal 1976 and an additional $21.8 billion for the three-month transition period between the end of fiscal 1976 and the start of fiscal 1977. The aid-cutoff amendment, authored by Reps. Joseph Addabbo (D, N.Y.) and Robert Giaimo (D, Conn.), specified that none of the funds could be used in Angola for other than intelligence-gathering purposes.

The bill had originally been approved by the House without the amendment. The Senate had added the aid-cutoff amendment to the conference report on the bill and it was moved back to the House. In the vote, 72 Republicans joined 251 Democrats in supporting the amendment.

Democrats had criticized the Ford request for Angolan aid on grounds that U.S. security was not imperiled by events in Angola, that continued intervention would alienate the people of Angola and other African nations from the U.S., and that the amount of aid requested by Ford—$28 million—was inadequate to achieve the ends sought. Carl Albert (D., Okla.), speaker of the House, said "There's no use in doing anything if you don't do enough. This is a typical Ford operation where you wave your hand and make a gesture and then forget it." Rep. John Rhodes (R, Ariz.), GOP leader in the House, attributed the strength of the anti-Angolan vote to "a lingering fear of getting involved in another Vietnam."

President Ford had sent a letter to Albert before the vote expressing "grave concern over the international consequences of the situation in Angola." The letter said that the cutoff would "inevitably lead our friends and supporters to conclusions about our steadfastness and resolve," and that "resistance to Soviet expansion by military means must be a fundamental element of United States foreign policy."

THE  SUN

Baltimore, Md., February 2, 1976

In quick succession last week the House of Representatives voted 323 to 99 to cut off further aid to western-backed factions in Angola and 246 to 124 to permit the White House to censor the report of its Select Committee on Intelligence. Both issues touched fundamentally on the question of executive versus legislative power in the control of foreign policy. And if the House seemed contradictory, this may reflect a growing uncertainty about the prudent American role in an era of Soviet expansionism.

The 94th Congress, be it remembered, was elected at what may have been the high point of legislative resistance to foreign involvement. Watergate had just removed Richard Nixon from the scene and Vietnam had yet to fall in ignominious fashion. Lawmakers chosen in this atmosphere came to Washington with a mandate to check the executive, to bring the Super-Secretary of State to heel, to cut defense spending, to prevent further foreign entanglements. And this they did, as the Angola vote so well exemplified. Mr. Kissinger could compare modern Russia to the imperialist Germany that brought on two world wars. The President could speak of the "Soviet-Cuban expansion by brute military force into areas thousands of miles from their country." But the 94th Congress was sure of its mandate, and so voted on Angola.

But was it really so sure? Politicians traditionally pay more attention to changing popular moods than to any mandates fixed at a given point in time. It may be that the House rebuff to its own Intelligence Committee two days after the Angola vote was but a well deserved slap at the high-handed methods of its chairman, Representative Pike. But then again, it may reflect a stiffening in the public attitude toward the Soviet Union that election-minded legislators reflected by shying away from actions that could undermine the intelligence agencies.

American foreign policy in its post-Vietnam phase has been spectacularly incoherent, not least because of a legislative-executive struggle that has left Washington-based diplomats wondering if there really is a (singular) U. S. government to which they are accredited. This probably was inevitable in a nation that dares to have built-in tensions among its branches of government, even on security matters. If the ordeal finally convinces the executive that it must bring Congress more openly into the making and implementation of foreign policy, Congress may in the end be more constructive in its responses. This would be in the nation's interest. Having to deal with the Soviet Union through a complex mixture of detente and toughness, the United States can ill afford either all-out struggle between the executive and the legislative branches or the kind of congressional abdication of responsibility that Lyndon Johnson called consensus.

THE DENVER POST

Denver, Colo., January 30, 1976

Congress has dropped the other shoe on administration attempts to send more military supplies to pro-Western forces fighting for control of Angola.

The House rejected a last-minute appeal from President Ford and approved an Angolan aid cutoff by the lopsided margin of 323 to 99. Several weeks ago, the Senate took a similar stand, also by a big margin.

Secretary of State Kissinger plans still another last-ditch appeal for aid funds, but his chances for success appear slim.

Specifically, the House and Senate action prohibits some $28 million in supplies from being sent to the stricken former Portuguese colony. This amount was earmarked in the $112.3 billion over-all defense appropriation bill.

The congressional position was that the United States isn't willing to match massive Soviet aid to the African nation and therefore shouldn't waste the $28 million, a sum so small when compared to Russian commitment as to be termed a "mere gesture."

President Ford, on the other hand, argued that the U.S. goal in Angola was not victory for a faction, but rather a bid to force peace negotiations.

No matter. The message from Capitol Hill now seems clear: Congress will no longer sanction what might become an open-ended commitment to a remote conflict where no United States interest has been established except that of thwarting the Soviet Union.

And by congressional standards, it was obvious that the administration did not demonstrate how additional American aid could further a peaceful resolution of the Angolan civil war.

The days of automatic congressional majorities for overseas operations of this sort are clearly over with and behind us.

There is one vital lesson that the administration might be able to learn from this latest foreign policy defeat. It must accept a larger role for Congress in the shaping of foreign policy than has heretofore been accorded the legislative branch of government. Until this basic tenet has been learned, there will continue to be embarrassing rebuffs similar to the Angolan fiasco.

THE ATLANTA CONSTITUTION

Atlanta, Ga., January 30, 1976

At least one national poll shows that by a narrow margin Americans support President Ford and Secretary of State Henry Kissinger in their view that we should send money to Angola to aid the factions fighting the factions supported by Russia and Cuba.

Yet it is a safe bet that all but a very few Americans don't know the names of the Angolan factions we propose to support, don't know their leaders, don't know anything about their ideology, their plans, their past, present or future and, frankly, don't really care. All we *do* know is that when the Russians support one side in any country, we automatically support the other because it automatically becomes our friends.

This week Congress stopped thinking that way. The lawmakers, by a solid and fairly bipartisan majority, refused the administration request for funds to send to "our" side in Angola. Are we thus *giving* Angola to the Russians? An echo from the Vietnam years should remind us that Angola is not ours to give. Nor, if the Communist-backed faction wins, is Angola a Russian possession. It has been suggested that Angola could be a Russian Vietnam. Probably not — but it is hard to see what overwhelming advantage Russia would gain in world affairs if it does achieve influence in a future Angolan regime.

Angola—a country most of us never heard of until the Portuguese pulled out last year after centuries of imperial control—has become the catalyst for a renewed debate on American foreign policy: what it has been, what it is, what it should be. It is a complicated debate, muddied by all sorts of more or less irrelevant issues. The memory of Vietnam figures large in it—especially with Congress, which in effect shirked its constitutional responsibilities in having rubber stamped anything the executive branch wanted to do in that country for most of that long and tragic episode. Watergate, too, is a factor because Watergate reminded Congress again that it is supposed to be an equal branch of government, not an assembly of yea sayers. Plain old fashioned politics and personality clashes are also factors. Some think Henry Kissinger is too big for his britches, is too devoted to secrecy, and conducts a foreign policy based on *faits accompli* (like China). When the tally was in some congressmen could hardly conceal their glee in handing Kissinger a setback in Angola which, it is widely assumed, is *his* baby, not Ford's.

There are other complicating factors. But the essential issue is very simple and very clear. Everyone can understand it. It is this: Will the U.S. allow the Russians a free hand to interfere in the internal affairs of other nations without doing a thing to prevent it?

When the question is put that way, the almost instinctive reaction of most Americans, not to mention our allies, is a resounding No!

Yet Vietnam and other setbacks have taught us that we cannot by ourselves police the entire world. Some European statesmen are deploring our lack of action and decisiveness in Angola, but nobody has noticed a large commitment of money and troops flowing to Angola from Europe. Some critics say American foreign policy is based mostly on *reacting* to moves by the opposition, is essentially defensive. That, of course, is not fair and not true. But Angola does seem to provide an example of a Soviet move calling for an automatic U.S. response. President Ford and Dr. Kissinger clearly feel we should respond in Angola. Congress is clearly persuaded we need not. But does this action by Congress mean that America has embraced "neo-isolationism?" Those who criticize the congressional vote fear it is so. If they are right, then the vote was a shortsighted and potentially dangerous action. But it is possible that Congress has sensed that from now on in foreign policy we must be more choosy about where, when and why we spend money or, conceivably, go even farther in supporting countries exposed to communist influence. Congress is saying that we cannot automatically send millions to any point on the globe thus threatened. But that is not necessarily to say that we will not act if and when we perceive that we or our allies are truly menaced.

In brief, the President and Dr. Kissinger say we must respond to every threat to anybody made by the Communist powers. Congress is saying we ought to play a tighter hand than that because we simply don't have the power and resources we once had. Perhaps the American people, in this election year, will be able to help decide which approach is the right one.

The Washington Post

Washington, D.C., January 15, 1976

THE ADMINISTRATION'S insistence on compounding the error of its Angolan ways is downright masochistic. With the Soviet-backed Popular Movement taking town after town, scattering the organized units of its Angolan rivals and recognized now by the Organization of African Unity, you would have thought it was a good time for the United States to start cutting its losses and adjusting to the new realities. But no. Precisely the opposite tack is being pursued.

President Ford, for instance, the other day accused congressmen who differ with him on Angola of having "lost their guts"—a tasteless and tactless charge made, one is forced to suspect, to protect his right flank against Ronald Reagan's New Hampshire onslaught. Why else would Mr. Ford so heedlessly further antagonize his congressional adversaries? Why else would he broadcast his embarrassment in a way calculated to encourage Kremlin interventionists to believe they had scored in Washington a psychological victory surpassing any gain they might claim in Angola? In fact, if "guts" is the issue, one can imagine several more valid tests. It would take "guts" for the President to admit he had made a mistake in Angola. It would have taken "guts" —and would have been wise—to have gone to Congress last summer with a forthright appeal for public support of a reasoned proposal to join the struggle in Angola. Mr. Ford is rather poorly placed to taunt the Congress on "guts."

Meanwhile Mr. Kissinger continues to warn in effect that as goes Angola, so goes the world. He seems troubled most by the fear that Congress' interruption of the executive's Angolan operation will set a "precedent," or will be seen as one by Moscow. We think it correct as well as prudent, however, to treat the Angolan case on its own merits. It could become a "precedent" but it need not if the administration draws from it the conclusion that, in the current political setting, the Congress can be asked to support only those military operations which can be shown—to a broad public—to matter. The administration's mistake has been to think that it had the political resources to support an operation undertaken on its own private and quite esoteric perception of a foreign threat. In post-Vietnam post-Watergate Washington, the executive does not have such political resources. Accordingly it must be selective when it undertakes to use or sponsor force abroad.

The French and British, among others who earlier supported the "American" side in Angola, are now preparing to recognize the Popular Movement. Zaire, worried about the Popular Movement's intentions, is hesitating but the Angolan winners have offered Zaire a not unreasonable deal: Stop supporting the Angolan losers and we'll get along just fine. Zambia is so needful of Angola's good will, for economic and other considerations, that it will be hard put not to accept the new regime soon. Even from South Africa one hears murmurs of readiness to consider coexistence with Angola, on certain terms.

Why is it not then possible—it already seems to us desirable—for the United States to conform its own policy to the realities in Angola in order to open up the best possible relations with the new government? The Popular Movement's leader, saying he will countenance no foreign bases, has extended Washington a hand. By attentive diplomacy, the United States has an opportunity to help ensure that its own dire prophecy—that Angola will become a Soviet "stronghold in Africa"—will not come true. The United States could then turn to a much more important diplomatic enterprise in Africa—composing an intelligent policy toward the great racial divisions in southern Africa. The temporary implicit alliance which Washington was forced to make with South Africa in an earlier phase of its Angolan operations put the United States much too close to Pretoria, and on the "wrong" issue—narrow-gauge anti-communism. The "right" issue on which American policy in Africa ought to be shaped is how to deal with the great racial drama unfolding in the continent without becoming, in the name of anti-communism, a partner of apartheid in South Africa.

The Providence Journal

Providence, R.I., February 4, 1976

Both the Ford administration and Congress seem uneasy about the fumbling U.S. response to the civil war in Angola, and for good reason. Secrecy and mutual suspicion have derailed whatever chance there might have been for Washington to develop a coherent policy on Angola that commanded broad agreement.

What Americans are witnessing in the drawn-out debate over Angola is an unsettling confusion over this country's global means, ends, tactics, purposes and that indefinable quality called our national will. This confusion is the tragic — and perhaps inevitable — legacy of the stormy decade of Vietnam and Watergate that rocked the presidency and shocked Congress into reasserting a major foreign-policy role.

The confusion of means and ends is most acutely seen in cases such as Angola, where the U.S. response to Soviet intervention has been an ill-timed, on-and-off process that has only made an unsettling situation worse. Between Congress and the executive, the level of trust has grown thin. By insisting on secret military aid to the anti-Marxist factions in the former Portuguese colony, the administration triggered a categorical ban by Congress on such aid. Instead of an open and careful weighing of the pros and cons of any U.S. move on Angola, there has been a wave of warnings and recriminations. Overreaction is the result, and thus there is little wonder that our Angolan policy lies in ruins.

The most important foreign-policy issue for the United States, as it has been for the past generation, is how to deal with the Soviet Union in ways that show this country as neither supine nor belligerent. The sober realities of the late 1970's demand an approach to the Russians that is carefully balanced between a hesitant neo-isolationism and a reflexive reversion to the brinkmanship of the Cold War. But the chances for such a balanced policy disappear when an administration elects to move unilaterally and secretly, and when a Congress reacts by saying: Stop.

Secretary of State Kissinger responded to the House cut-off of secret U.S. aid to the two anti-Soviet factions in Angola by indicating that the administration might ask Congress to authorize open military help. However belated this shift may be, it at least represents a useful change in the direction of open policy-making. With most of Angola now under the domination of the Soviet-supported faction, any such aid almost certainly would be too little and too late. But Mr. Kissinger's suggestion of an open aid request at least might give an opportunity for a searching debate about how the United states *should* counter Soviet expansionism, and this kind of debate is badly needed.

Secretary Kissinger, for example, told senators last week: "The Soviet Union must not be given any opportunity to use military forces for aggressive purposes without running the risk of conflict with us." This is profoundly important as a strong statement of the administration's policy, but it also is a statement fraught with implications and unanswered questions. Does Mr. Kissinger mean for it to be taken literally? Does it apply to the entire world? Does "aggressive" Soviet behavior, in Mr. Kissinger's view, also mean aid to indigenous factions engaged in what Moscow likes to call "wars of national liberation"? These kinds of questions demand answers if the United States expects to draw its tangled foreign-policy threads together.

The issues raised by the Angolans' battle for supremacy run far deeper than the fate of that African country. The issues go to the essence of that overworked term, "detente," and to the process by which U.S. decisions on foreign policy are reached. American policy toward the Soviet Union must be based on consistency, on an agreed-upon array of what constitutes U.S. national interests and on the measures the United States can best employ to protect those interests. Such a policy can be crafted neither through administration secrecy nor through Congress reacting to deceptive administration moves with sudden alarm.

THE DALLAS TIMES HERALD

Dallas, Tex., January 29, 1976

YOU CHANGE a word or two, a place and a time, and the debate over U.S. aid to Angola sounds too much like we're still living in the sixties rather than the late seventies.

Where is the new leadership that would guide the President and Congress to shape a foreign policy to cope with world realities?

President Ford has not, and perhaps can not, identify the importance of Angola and whatever happens there to the strategic national interests of this country.

What we have received are old cliches attempting to justify an open-ended policy that would escalate American involvement in Angola and tie our fate with factions about whom we scarcely know a thing.

Hardly one in a thousand average, high school educated Americans can give you either the geographical location of Angola or an outline of its history, resources and politics.

Defending freedom, democracy and capitalism with our guns, money and lives is a noble cause for which sacrifices will be demanded of us in facing the world's realities.

But to do so foolishly, impetuously and without a firm national resolve and understanding of clear goals is to squander our resources in the same open-ended manner Vietnam cost us $150 billion, 55,000 lives and more than a decade of economic and political turmoil. We are still paying the price for our mistakes in Vietnam.

Angola represents a point of Cuban and Soviet aggression to unbalance the tribal and political factions in favor of their chosen friends. They could be taking an action in Africa which could do more to warn Third World nations of Communist aggression than anything we have ever said. We must be careful of polarizing the situation into another pro and anti-American confrontation. We must take care of trapping ourselves in an indefensible posture by selecting an opposing faction as our allies without regard to its strengths and weaknesses. There is a wide range of responses this country can take and each must be evaluated for its practicality.

The U.S. House of Representatives reflected a necessary caution in banning further open-ended U.S. military aid to Angola which only brings more American involvement each time our new found allies suffer setbacks.

President Ford, who devoted so little of his State of the Union address to foreign affairs, should not use another discredited cliche to condemn the Congressional action.

Instead he must set about providing leadership and gathering support for a foreign policy that carefully defines American strategic interests and provides for a range of responses to world events.

President Ford can make a valid point that it is the function of the President to evolve foreign policy, not Congress. However, he must concede that American foreign policy must be ratified by the American people.

The Sun Reporter

San Francisco, Calif., February 7, 1976

With the overwhelming 323-99 vote against military appropriations for Angola, the House of Representatives has joined the Senate in reasserting the responsibility given to Congress by the U.S. Constitution to decide whether or not our country engages in a foreign war.

In this case, wisely, Congress has told the President that we will not become involved in the Angolan struggle. They have spoken out clearly and decisively, and what's more important, they made their decision at the very beginning of the administration's attempts to involve us in the action, rather than stalling until a great deal of damage could be done. Had Congress acted with similar courage and timing in Vietnam, the country might have been spared a great deal of the tragedy which President Ford was leading us into on the African continent.

However, the administration has incidated that it doesn't intend to take the Congressional mandate as the final word on the subject. Already, President Ford and Secretary of State Kissinger have begun to issue strong statements reaffirming their neo-colonialist position that America's duty is to "save Angola from the Soviets."

That viewpoint has been amply refuted in these pages in recent weeks. The point to be made now is that Congress has seen fit to support our words with their actions. They have spoken, and theirs is the voice of authority.

Detroit Free Press

Detroit, Mich., January 30, 1976

THE FORD administration shouldn't have any doubts about the will of Congress on aid to Angola, after the House vote this week that seconded an earlier Senate position. Both houses overwhelmingly rejected the administration's tiresome argument that U.S. interests are somehow at stake, and that we should remedy the situation by dispatching $28 million in aid to the "other side" than that backed by the Soviet Union.

The aid request was made all the shakier by the way the "other side" is looking more and more like the losing side as well. House Speaker Carl Albert made the point that if we're really serious about turning the war around, it's going to take a lot more than $28 million.

It would take, in fact, something approaching full-scale intervention to repulse the Marxist MPLA forces that apparently already have secured most of the northern half of the country. This week the Western-backed factions abandoned their makeshift capital of Huambo in central Angola and shifted it 100 miles eastward, in anticipation of a Marxist drive.

These developments don't exactly inspire confidence, either among the troops that are being routed or in the American taxpayer.

Still President Ford and Secretary of State Kissinger continue to wave the standard of loyalty to "our friends and supporters," who would lose faith in the United States if it "refused help" to its friends in Africa.

Mr. Kissinger made his most impassioned pitch yet Thursday in saying the administration was thinking of asking Congress to grant "overt financial aid" to the beleaguered anti-Soviet forces.

But deciphering who is "friend" and who is otherwise in a civil war on the scale of Angola's is exceeedingly tricky business. Rather than justify U.S. involvement positively, the administration so far has been able only to argue that our help is needed to repel the Soviets.

The Congress obviously doesn't buy that reasoning, and it's fairly certain the American public doesn't either. Past examples of "token" involvement are all too clear in the public's mind.

The president should accept the will of Congress and declare outright that this country is ending its Angolan aid effort, particularly now that the Soviets have indicated some willingness to help negotiate a political settlement.

While such a settlement might well be within reach, it's important that the Russians understand that in any event, Angolan sovereignty must remain intact. It also must be made clear that any attempt by the Soviet Union to lean on Angola's neighbors, as Zambia and Zaire now fear, will be taken as a serious affront to world peace.

It should be obvious to all outside powers that the days of colonialism in Africa are over.

AKRON BEACON JOURNAL

Akron, Ohio, January 31, 1976

HENRY KISSINGER pulled out all the stops, conjuring up visions of dominos and darkly suggesting that World War III hinges on the United States' "resolve" in an African nation most Americans couldn't find on a map.

It is to the credit of the Congress, which cut off secret military aid to that nation, Angola, that such talk seems no longer enough to get this nation involved in new Vietnams. But it is dismaying that Secretary Kissinger and President Ford cling to outdated and unsophisticated theories of international relations.

The lawmakers rejected President Ford's last-minute effort to save a secret $28 million expenditure to back the Angolan factions fighting the side supported by the Soviet Union and Cuba. Two days later, Mr. Kissinger went before the Senate Foreign Relations committee and said that the administration may be forced to come out of hiding and ask for above-board money for Angola instead of sneaking the cash to Africa through the CIA. Let it ask; the Congress seems to have the right answer at hand.

When President Ford pleaded for the $28 million, he sounded like Harry Truman writing from a draft prepared by John Foster Dulles, arguing that Russia is outspending us by 10-to-one and American refusal to bridge the spending gap would make us look weak. That, as any Dulles fan can tell you, opens the door to the surge of godless, atheistic, monolithic communism.

Then comes Mr. Kissinger, and he sounds like Mr. Dulles the cold warrior himself. "Any other course will encourage more dangerous crises tomorrow," he warned. He told the senators, "I believe we must discourage the view that the Soviet Union can move anywhere it wants without serious risk."

The Congress seems equally concerned about weakness — and weakness also can be a refusal to learn from past mistakes.

As for the Soviets and their Cuban allies in Angola, they seem not to have learned the bitter lesson of the folly of intervening in another nation's civil war.

For Secretary Kissinger to insist, as he has in the past, that Russia can gain a "foothold" in West Africa by supporting one of the factions in the Angolan war suggests that he doesn't appreciate the rudiments of Bantu nationalism. Having just gotten rid of the Portuguese in Angola, the native people are hardly going to welcome another imperialistic power. Their Bantu cousins didn't do so in neighboring Zaire (formerly the Belgian Congo), after all, despite the best efforts of both Russia and the United States to gain a foothold there when the Belgians left.

We, too, are concerned about a "lack of resolve." We hope the Congress doesn't lose its resolve to avoid being trapped in another no-win situation by a question of ego rather than national interest.

THE SPRINGFIELD UNION

Springfield, Mass., January 29, 1976

"Self-determination," which was widely accepted as a South Vietnamese objective justifying U.S. aid, is now making its way into the rhetoric of aid-to-Angola proponents.

White House Press Secretary Ron Nessen used the meaning, if not the words, Tuesday in a statement following the 329-99 House vote against behind-the-scenes U.S. military aid to Angola.

Nessen said, "By its action the Congress has put the United States on record as refusing the request for help from an African people who seek nothing more than to decide for themselves their own political future free of outside intervention."

But there is even less unity in Angola than there was in South Vietnam on what the country's political future should be. Supporting one or two supposedly "pro-West" factions would be an enormous risk, and very likely a waste, of U.S. resources.

Furthermore, making different factions the fighting puppets of this country and the Soviet Union would be to stage a long-term war that could virtually destroy that small nation. It would be a costly and tragic route to "self-determination."

As for letting the Soviet Union "get away" with helping the Popular Movement (MPLA) faction — to the tune of an estimated $200 million so far—the Kremlin is betting it all on the slim prospect that the MPLA would stabilize Angola on a pro-Soviet basis.

How stable or lasting the government of any newly independent African nation will be is hard to predict. Independence means tribal influences become stronger—as they already have in Angola, where the factions are tribally-based.

If, as Nessen said, the future of Angola should be free of outside intervention, it is not for the United States to turn the civil war into a conflagration. Whatever the outcome, it would not be worth the devastation of Angola, or the cost to this country.

THE SAGINAW NEWS

Saginaw, Mich., January 29, 1976

The resounding vote in the House against further U.S. military aid to Angola virtually seals the decision against any big American involvement in a situation that is changing rapidly.

What is surprising in the House vote supporting an earlier Senate rejection of further aid, is the number of prominent Republican defections to the side of turning off the war materiels spigot.

The message to Mr. Ford seems to be clear and concise. There simply isn't any strong sentiment in Congress to invest in a civil war that may already be decided. This says that Henry Kissinger is going to have a tough time trying to resuscitate the cause before a Senate committee.

In spite of congressional anti-sentiment on more aid to support U.S.-backed forces, Angola does remain a vexing situation. At the same time there are strong suggestions of late that it is also one capable of being misread, thus luring our government to over-response. The memories of Vietnam are still vivid, no matter what.

This is what Congress is trying to get across with Mr. Ford. And the somewhat amorphous state of affairs in Angola would seem to support congressional attitude.

Within the past week South African forces have completed a full withdrawal under orders from their own government. That presence alone was enough to drive certain African nations into hard positions on the side of Soviet and Cuban supported political elements in Angola.

Through our earlier secret involvement we found ourselves siding with South Africa. That, in turn, has placed the U.S. in an uncomfortable and equally unpopular position.

More recent reports indicate that the Communist-backed MPLA may not be as hard-line as thought. Apparently it has been making "discreet" overtures in hopes Washington will soften its stand in Angola and thus give its moderate leadership greater credence.

The congressional vote may, in the long run, be just the signal that is looked for. That could help to resolve Angola's problem without the establishment of a rock-hard Communist regime. This may also be pipe-dreaming. Angola must be watched. We can hardly turn our backs on it.

Yet a less doctrinaire government willing to do business with the U.S. would be preferable to proliferating U.S. intervention, unmitigated bloodhshed and a complete loss of Angola as base for diplomatic interchange. Congress pursues the more prudent course for now.

THE MILWAUKEE JOURNAL

Milwaukee, Wisc., January 28, 1976

The House, following the Senate's lead, has cut off US aid to the Western backed factions in the Angolan civil war. The congressional decision is difficult to quarrel with.

US interests in the Angolan fighting essentially have been negative. The Ford administration primarily has been concerned with stopping Russian influence in southern Africa rather than with the merits of the Angolan groups struggling for control of the country. American involvement there was causing the Ford administration as much grief in the rest of black Africa as it was in Congress because white racist South Africa was supporting the same side the US was. It was a no-win situation.

Part of the Ford administration's problem at home was the way it initially approached the situation in Angola. The method chosen was to channel aid secretly to Angola through the CIA. When US support was revealed it came as a surprise to a majority in Congress, reawakening old fears that a "new Vietnam" was in the making. The White House probably could have avoided a great deal of congressional antagonism initially by dealing with the Angolan problem openly and asking for congressional debate. After all, the Russians and their Cuban shock troops were anything but covert about their Angolan presence.

In trying to persuade the House to continue aid, President Ford warned that Angola would be lost without US assistance. That probably is true and would be true even with aid, since the US assistance has been nowhere near the magnitude of that provided by Russia and Cuba.

How concerned should the US be over the extension of Soviet influence in Africa? There is reason to doubt from past big power experience in black Africa — the Congo, for example — whether Russia will be able to make it stick. There should be concern about Soviet aggressiveness, now that it has shown that it has Cuban fodder for its adventures. But this should be a Western, not just an American, concern. And our allies were conspicuously silent about joining the cause in Angola.

THE TENNESSEAN

Nashville, Tenn., January 29, 1976

THE MASSIVE vote in the House to ban all behind-the-scenes aid to Angola is an affirmation that the Congress learned something from Vietnam if the White House did not.

President Ford was reportedly angered by the action and felt some House members voted against him on the issue for election-year reasons. That might have been, but many seemed to share the view of Speaker Carl Albert, who said after the voting that the administration's decision to get involved in Angola "was about the most useless enterprise I have ever seen undertaken."

So the administration has failed with Congress. It has not had much luck on the diplomatic front. The Russian leaders wouldn't discuss their own and Cuban operations in Angola with Secretary of State Henry Kissinger. They classify their aid as going to a liberation movement, not interference in a foreign land.

The White House response to the vote in Congress came in a statement approved by Mr. Ford:

"The Congress has stated to the world that it will ignore a clear act of Soviet-Cuban expansion by brute military force into areas thousands of miles from either country."

But the White House statement assumes that the Soviet Union is going to be in control of Angola from here on. That is speculation, for the Russians have not done so well in other African nations where they sought to establish influence. And the tribal animosities in Angola are not likely to fade away any time soon, whichever side declares itself the winner.

The $28 million in aid requested by the administration for the anti-Communist forces was not the amount of aid they would need to wrest victory from the other side or force negotiations between the warring factions.

Mr. Ford may be angry now, but the Congress may have saved him and the nation from a foolish misstep in Africa.

NEW ORLEANS STATES-ITEM

New Orleans, La., January 29, 1976

President Ford and Secretary of State Henry Kissinger have encountered a brick wall in their efforts to gain congressional support for U.S. involvement in the Angolan war. By voting 323 to 99 to cut off some $28 million earmarked for Angola, the House underscored similar action taken earlier by the Senate.

The congressional action is reminiscent of the cutoff of aid to Vietnam which contributed significantly to ending this nation's costly involvement in that war. Fears of "another Vietnam" obviously underlay Congress' vote against more money for Angola.

The rationale in Ford Administration arguments on Angola recall arguments for continuous U.S. involvement in Vietnam. "Failure of the United States to take a stand will inevitably lead our friends and supporters to conclusions about our steadfastness and resolve," the President said, speaking of Angola. The U.S. goal in Angola is not victory but to force negotiations, the President argued.

In several respects, the conflict between Congress and the White House is an extension of the Vietnam debate, which has yet to be resolved. Again, the fundamental question of where the nation's basic interest lies is unanswered.

Congress is justified in its wariness of the Angolan situation. The U.S. interest in Angola is not sufficiently clear at this point to justify extended U.S. involvement there.

The real setback to the Ford Administration is the flaw in detente which the Soviet Union's stubborn involvement in Angola has exposed.

Portland, Ore., February 2, 1976

Angola is not the best issue on which the Ford administration can make a case against excessive interference by Congress in the conduct of foreign policy.

What the Soviet Union and Cuba are doing in Angola is an outrage. But there is no way the U.S. can effectively counter this blatant intervention without emulating the Russians and the Cubans.

Part of the reasoning in Congress in the vote to cut off funds for support of groups opposing the Soviet and Cuban-backed Popular Movement for the Liberation of Angola (MPLA) is that both money and blood would be wasted in a hopeless cause.

After Vietnam, the American people simply would not support the massive involvement that would assure successful resistance.

The battle has to be fought in other arenas. Secretary of State Henry Kissinger has let the Russians know that what they are doing in Angola will have a serious effect on detente.

There is strong resentment among black African nations against the Russian-Cuban intervention. This will grow if South Africa withdraws from Angola, which it seems to be doing. That resentment ought to be shared by the world community of nations.

The Russians have not always been successful over the long run in their attempts to influence independent nations. They may not be in Angola even with a victory of the force they are backing.

It is possible to cite chapter and verse where congressional interference in foreign policy has been detrimental to the national interest and the cause of peace. Angola is not one of those chapters.

DAYTON DAILY NEWS

Dayton, Ohio, January 29, 1976

The House's agreement with the senate's ban on further U.S. aid to the anti-Soviet factions in the Angolan civil war virtually seals that issue. President Ford may come back with a specific aid proposal to Congress — at least, he has said he may — but that is unlikely to change many minds on Capitol Hill.

Reacting more to memories of Vietnam than to the presence of Angola in its own terms, Congress hasn't bothered to give the issue detailed consideration. The votes in the Senate and in the House simply launched a "principle" and then retired from the field.

Some principle. It means that the Soviet Union is welcome to muck deeply in such situations without worry of any serious U.S. counter.

In Angola, U.S. aid was small compared to what the Soviet Union has been shoveling in. U.S. aid was indirect, mostly provided to legitimately interested black African nations. Soviet aid amounted to direct intervention. The United States sent no troops. The Soviet Union has sent several thousand Cubans, in one of the era's more classic dramatizations of the dictum "let's you and him fight."

The United States dosen't have to get involved everywhere just because the Soviet Union seems interested. But neither can it afford to shun all involvements. The U.S. project in Angola was limited, indirect and in proportion to the U.S. interests implicated there.

If Congress can't learn to live with that, it ought to begin explaining to the American people that, if only by default, it proposes to concede to the Soviet Union whatever advantages the Kremlin decides to muscle up for itself.

HOUSTON CHRONICLE

Houston, Tex., February 2, 1976

Congress is a blunt instrument when it deals with foreign policy.

Congress has demonstrated this over and over again in the last few months and seems determined to keep pounding away in the same fashion.

We believe Congress is making a mistake, not in being involved in foreign policy—for there is a role for them to play in that field—but in the manner in which they are acting.

Illustrations of the problem are easily cited. Regardless of which side of the issues is favored, the results of congressional foreign policy action in a number of instances are clearly questionable.

Congress involved itself in U.S.-Soviet relations through the Jackson amendment denying most-favored-nation status to Soviet trade unless the Soviet Union changed its restrictions on emigration of minority groups. Russia has increased its trade with other countries and emigration has not improved.

Last February, Congress cut off military aid to Turkey because of the Cyprus dispute, and the result was alienation of Turkey and no progress over Cyprus.

Now, Congress has voted to cut off funds for Angola, giving the Soviet Union a green light to pour in heavy weapons and Cuban troops so a Communist minority can seize control of that African nation.

In each of these instances, Congress created additional obstacles to the resolution of a foreign policy problem, and posed the possibility of open confrontation when finesse was in order.

The U.S. Constitution gives the president authority to represent the nation in foreign affairs. In prior years, there has been a concept of bipartisanship in foreign policy that strengthened the president's hand in dealings abroad. But lately, such a concept has disappeared under a welter of individual presidential ambitions and partisan squabbling.

We don't need self-serving political maneuvers in the conduct of our foreign affairs.

As Rep. Jim Wright of Texas aptly put it: "Congress, made up of 535 individuals, cannot conduct sensitive negotiations with foreign powers. It cannot be secretary of state."

This being a presidential election year, Congress might try to make it impossible for President Ford to conduct foreign affairs by undercutting both the President and Secretary of State Henry Kissinger. The rest of the world would look at the United States and see a weakened executive and a capricious Congress. Nothing would please our opponents abroad more.

Tulsa, Okla., January 29, 1976

THE panicky move in Congress to stop U.S. aid to pro-Western forces in Angola is disturbing in itself. But even more frightening is the illogical reasoning behind the action.

Because the United States tried and failed to stop the Communist conquest of South Vietnam, so the argument goes, we must not make any effort to halt the Soviet takeover of Angola. We might get "bogged down" and lose thousands of American lives as we did in Vietnam.

This is reasoning?

In the first place, Angola and Vietnam are two different places. They represent two entirely different situations. About the only commonality is that both are victims of Communist military aggression supported from the outside.

In the second place, it is unthinkable that, in the wake of Vietnam, an American Government would send troops to a foreign war of intervention except under the most grave conditions. It is unthinkable in Angola. No one has seriously suggested it.

Nevertheless Congress rushes to cut off aid to the popularly-supported, pro-Western forces in Angola, almost certainly assuring their defeat by a Cuban invasion force financed by Russia.

To make matters worse, many of the Congressmen are opposing aid to the friendly Angolan forces on the grounds that helping them resist Communist aggression would be "immoral" just as our intervention in Vietnam was "immoral."

It's a strange new world where helping people fight for self-determination is "immoral" while passive encouragement to foreign intervention is "moral."

WORCESTER TELEGRAM.

Worcester, Mass., January 31, 1976

The House vote to cut off all U.S. aid to the anti-Communist factions fighting in Angola apparently reflects the country's post-Vietnam reluctance to get involved in another foreign conflict half-way around the world.

While the wisdom of the decision has yet to be tested by history, Congress, in effect, made it clear that it is not willing to resist armed Soviet expansion in areas regarded strategically or politically important by Moscow.

Congress represents the public, and the public evidently wants no part of even limited U.S. involvement. Some wonder whether, in the long run, Angola may become Russia's Vietnam.

But President Ford and many others believe that the recent House action "can only result in serious harm to the interests of the United States."

Our hands-off policy plays into the Kremlin's interpretation of detente: Peaceful coexistence and economic cooperation with the West should not hinder Moscow's plans to spread Communist influence around the globe.

St. Louis Globe-Democrat

St. Louis, Mo., January 29, 1976

The U.S. House of Representatives has now joined the U.S. Senate in telling the Soviet Union that the United States, the traditional leader of the free world, will no longer help its friends oppose Russian-Cuban expansion in Africa and other parts of the world.

In voting to cut off all aid to two Western-backed factions in Angola, the House sealed the fate of these forces that are opposing more than 10,000 Cubans and other Marxist troops that have heavy military and financial backing from the USSR.

Following the vote, the White House said:

"The Congress has stated to the world that it will ignore a clear act of Soviet-Cuban expansion by brute military force into areas thousands of miles from either country."

Angola now may soon join South Vietnam in the dustbin of history, the victim of a craven Congress that no longer has the will to face up to open Communist aggression.

Historians may one day refer to these two votes, along with the aid cutoff to South Vietnam at the time of its greatest peril, as the American Munich.

And they will quote the American Chamberlains who acquiesced to the butchery of freedom in Southeast Asia and Africa, such as the whimpering House speaker, Carl Albert, who in speaking in favor of an aid cutoff, said:

"One thing about foreign aid, military aid or war itself. You either do enough or you're better off not doing anything."

The United States, said Albert, should cut off aid to Angola because it is not prepared to match the huge Soviet and Cuban support for the pro-Marxist Angolan faction.

And so a once proud nation is now led by cowardly lions who, having exhausted the nation's resources on welfare and foreign aid to countries that had no common interest with this country, choose to turn their heads while free nations are conquered and incorporated into the Russian colonial empire.

WINSTON-SALEM JOURNAL

Winston-Salem, N.C., January 31, 1976

Last year, there was Cambodia, then South Vietnam, then Laos. This year, there will be — short of a miracle — Angola. The Congress of the United States on the one hand, and the Soviet Union and Cuba on the other, do not approve of miracles and are not about to provide any. So Angola, perched atop the drain spout, looks to President Ford and Secretary of State Kissinger for salvation. The African nation might as well close its eyes and dive downward, for there is nothing to see but a charade.

To be sure, the President and Kissinger are saying the obligatory things, and the obligatory things make a great deal of sense. The President, for example, has noted that the "failure of the United States to take a stand will inevitably lead our friends and supporters to conclusions about our steadfastness and resolve." Though baroquely phrased, the President's point is unarguable: Should Angola share Southeast Asia's fate, United States' "friends and supporters" — those few remaining around the world — will necessarily decide that American "steadfastness and resolve" are at best obsolescent.

The points being harped on by Kissinger are no less valid. In Senate testimony the other day, Kissinger correctly observed that "Congress has ignored the crucial truth that a stable relationship with the Soviet Union based on mutual restraint will be achieved only if Soviet lack of restraint carries the risk of counter action" by the United States. Moreover, "a demonstration of a lack of resolve could lead the Soviets to a great miscalculation, thereby plunging [the United States and the Soviet Union] into a major confrontation neither [country] wants."

Wise words, nobly spoken: It is unfortunate that they are addressed to the deaf. A majority of this Congress remains so paralyzed by the Vietnam experience that the imminent fall of Canada might not arouse them to action, let alone the pending demise of Angola. Strategic arguments go unheard: No matter that Angola is resource-rich, no matter that Soviet access to Angolan ports will threaten international shipping routes around the Cape of Good Hope. Human arguments are not listened to either: No matter that a clear-cut majority of Angolans are trying to resist tyrannization at the hands of a minority backed by endless Soviet support and by more than 10 per cent of Cuba's entire armed forces.

But for sheer lack of concern, Congress must take second place to the Soviet Union. As long as Moscow meets mush and not bone, it will drive the knife just as deeply as it can, wherever it can. Without some display of American "steadfastness and resolve" beyond the mouthing of words, Moscow will neither hear nor heed anything except the rumbling of Soviet tanks moving toward victory in Angola. For the Soviets, deafness is a function of detente: Their ears tune in to the sweet strains of peace only after they and their friends have won.

The President and Kissinger will keep talking even so, for that is all they can do. Worse still, they know that that is all they can do; they know that they are just going through the motions, as they did during the Southeast Asian crisis last year. Soon now, the sad charade will end, for Angola will no longer be looking — it will be lost.

THE CINCINNATI ENQUIRER

Cincinnati, Ohio, February 6, 1976

THE FORD administration has sustained a highly significant foreign-policy defeat in Congress' frustration of administration efforts to prevent the Soviet-backed faction in Angola from seizing complete control of that new African nation.

What the President had sought was an appropriation to buy arms and other aid for the National Front, which has been struggling against heavy odds to defeat the Popular Movement, a faction backed by Soviet arms and several thousand Cuban soldiers.

One look at a map of Africa suffices to illustrate Angola's importance. It lies astride the sea route by which Western Europe receives its petroleum from the Middle East, and it is situated north of the rich and strategic Republic of South Africa, west of copper-rich Zambia and south of uranium-rich Zaire (formerly the Belgian Congo).

Angola, in pro-Soviet hands, would offer the Soviet Union an ideal naval base to complement the base the Soviets have already installed in the Somali Republic on Africa's East Coast.

But even if Angola were, in itself, of absolutely no strategic importance to the United States or the free world, Congress' prohibition of U.S. aid constitutes an extraordinarily risky incursion by the legislative arm into a province normally and necessarily superintended by the executive.

The President of the United States needs flexibility if he is to deal realistically on a day-to-day basis with both friends and potential enemies around the world.

The President is obviously denied that flexibility when Congress, acting without the information to which the executive branch is privy, lumbers forward and prohibits specific courses of action or, worse yet, proclaims specific parts of the world to be of no interest or concern to the United States.

Such legislative intrusions tell the Soviet Union, for one thing, that it has a free hand to do as it pleases in Angola and, very probably, beyond. Such intrusions also come as sobering signals to other African states and to states even beyond Africa that they resist Soviet incursions at their own distinct peril.

The cause of peace and world order is rarely served by such proclamations and signals.

Congress may well have been animated by some vague determination to avoid falling into "another Vietnam" —even though it is difficult to draw a parallel between what President Ford has sought to do in Angola and what Presidents Kennedy and Johnson undertook in Vietnam. For Congress to imagine that there is suggests that key members of Congress have been hypnotized by their own mythology about the origins of the U.S. commitment in Southeast Asia. That mythology teaches that Vietnam was somehow an executive action, which Congress neither authorized nor was capable of controlling.

The fact, of course, is that President Johnson asked and received a blank check from Congress to do what needed doing in Vietnam. Congress, moreover, consistently refused until the very end to back down from its original commitment.

Critics of U.S. policy in Vietnam grew to laugh at what was widely known as the domino theory—the view that a failure of American purposes in Southeast Asia would have ramifications in other parts of the world.

Who would have imagined that the next domino to fall would be Angola?

The Birmingham News

Birmingham, Ala., January 30, 1976

With a decisive 323 to 99 vote, the House has joined the Senate in banning further U.S. aid to the embattled anti-Soviet factions in Angola despite massive Soviet aid to their Angolan allies.

There were a number of arguments made against the administration's pleas for aid. One was made by Speaker Carl Albert when he said, "One thing about foreign aid, military aid or war itself: You either do enough or you're better off not doing anything."

Of course, if the majority in Congress felt that the administration was not asking enough in aid (only $28 million was requested) then it could have upped the ante

But the matter of the proper scope of aid wasn't really the issue. Vietnam was the issue. It loomed large in the minds of the majority—even though no one in the administration has suggested direct U.S. military intervention. And interwoven in the arguments against aid was a recurring thread: Congress must assert its power to determine foreign policy and say how funds will be spent in commitments abroad.

No one can question now that Congress has asserted itself. Many of its members are probably still chuckling about how they put Secretary of State Henry Kissinger in his place.

But was Congress wise?

It has been said of military leaders that they are always preparing their troops to fight the last war. Perhaps Congress, still smarting from early support of the Vietnam conflict, is equally backward-looking in making foreign policy decisions.

Angola is unique. It is not Vietnam. This nation's objectives are not the same as they were in Vietnam.

Earlier, there might have been a chance, with prompt U.S. aid, of turning the tide of battle against the pro-Soviet faction. Now a pro-West military victory is doubtful, but the chance remains that military aid still could strengthen the position of anti-Soviet forces enough to promote a settlement.

President Ford, still hopeful of securing enough aid from Congress to force negotiations, said, "Failure of the United States to take a stand will inevitably lead our friends and supporters to conclusions about our steadfastness and resolve."

If the United States refuses to spend $28 million in an effort to deny Soviet hegemony over Angola, then what prospects are there that other remote, threatened countries will be able to turn to the U.S. for help?

"Conclusions about our steadfastness and resolve" are indeed being made as a result of the Angola vote. Our apparent reluctance to lift a finger to block Soviet expansionism in Africa can only invite further acquisitions of territory by the Russians.

With the steady diminution of U.S. credibility as a power in world affairs, it will be much more difficult sometime in the future to take a hand when Soviet expansionism threatens U.S. interests in areas more vital to us than Angola. We are allowing the Soviets to build momentum in their scheme of conquest. Congress, now exultant in its own reaffirmation of its powers, may well regret it's timid position on Angola.

THE DAILY OKLAHOMAN

Oklahoma City, Okla., January 29, 1976

TUESDAY two related developments in Washington reflected the disarray in our government. At the same time, they showed the frightening ability of small groups of dedicated pacifists to dominate congressional voting, without regard to the long-term best interests of the nation.

Rejecting a last-minute plea from the President not to tie his hands by cutting off funds for aid to Angola's anti-Communist factions, the House of Representatives completed congressional action to deny all further aid to that African state.

At the same time, the Secretary of Defense, Donald Rumsfeld, was urging Congress to act promptly to reverse the dangerous shift in the military power balance in the world.

In his short tenure as defense chief, replacing the popular and able Dr. James Schlesinger, Rumsfeld has not warmed many Pentagon hearts with his approach to his new job. But he has impressed many veteran officials there with his close contacts at the White House, and his related ability to get impossible things done. For example, he was able to restore $2.7 billion of defense funds in the budget submitted to Congress by President Ford, after the Office of Management and Budget had cut them out as "unavailable." But Rumsfeld is a thorough student of whatever job he undertakes, and has briefed himself on the deterioration of our international prestige, influence, and power.

He was thus not talking in generalities when he told Congress Tuesday that restoration of modernization money to the defense appropriations bills is essential. In defense of the record (in current dollar terms) proposed budget of $100.1 billion, he was candid in his report. "Security is not available at bargain basement rates," the report stated simply.

If Congress needs proof of the price we pay for the paring of the defense budget, it need look no farther than Angola. A few years ago, the present massive Communist intervention that has been taking over larger and larger portions of the country would have been unthinkable, except in some area of the world that was already surrounded by Communist armies and air fleets.

Today, the American aid is at a token level, and even though that level might prove decisive in time, the Congress has decided it represents a risk not worth taking.

That decision is announced despite the fact that Angola occupies a vital geographic spot on the globe. It is reported officially that 80 per cent of Europe's oil must now come around the Cape of Good Hope, and thus pass Angola, enroute to European refineries and depots. A Communist naval base on the Angolan coast would dominate the waters through which the supertankers travel.

Sen. Dewey Bartlett told the Senate Wednesday that he feels Congress "has done a disservice to American national interests" by shutting off our aid to Angola's defenders. But Congress seems determined—convinced that the pacifists will dominate the voting next fall—to pare defense costs and such inexpensive but effective aid budgets. The hitch is that the entire nation will pay later for such "thrift" today, and so will the rest of the Free World.

CIA ALLEGED TO SUPPORT ITALIAN ANTI-COMMUNISTS

The U.S. Central Intelligence Agency had made $6 million worth of secret cash payments to individual anti-Communist leaders in Italy in 1975, it was disclosed Jan. 7. The payments, reportedly authorized Dec. 8, 1975 by President Ford, were said to have been part of a program to counteract growing Communist influence in Italian politics. Spokesmen for the Christian Democrats, the Socialists, the Liberals and the Republicans Jan. 7 denied that any members of their parties had received any funds from the CIA.

According to the *New York Times* Jan. 7, which cited well-informed sources, the secret fund also had the strong approval of Secretary of State Henry A. Kissinger. Kissinger was reported to have been concerned about Communist gains in the June 1975 local Italian elections. When he visited Europe in December 1975 for the NATO and Paris energy conferences, he assertedly had informed Western leaders that the United States would oppose the entry of the Communists into European coalition governments.

U.S. Senate and House of Representatives intelligence review committees were briefed on the CIA covert aid program Dec. 8 and Dec. 9, 1975, respectively, by CIA Director William E. Colby. Colby reportedly disclosed that the major portion of the $6 million was intended for helping finance centrist Christian Democratic Party politicians and members of the Socialist Party.

An American official interviewed by the *Times* termed the $6 million figure "peanuts" when compared with the total amount of sub rosa aid to Italian political parties spent each year. This included, the *Times* said, substantial amounts funneled into the Communist Party and its allied trade unions by the Soviet Union as well as large subsidies to centrist politicians made by large multinational corporations, such as those disclosed in 1975 by the U.S. Mobil Oil and Exxon corporations.

The Jan. 7 news accounts did not indicate the names of the Italian figures who were said to be recipients of the CIA payments. President Ford Jan. 7 was described by his press secretary, Ron Nessen, to have been angered by the publication of reports of the CIA covert funding operation in Italy. Nessen, in a meeting with reporters, said that there was "a strong suspicion" in the White House that the press leaks had come from the congressmen who had been briefed by Colby. The leaks, Nessen added, were believed by the President to undermine "our capability to carry out our foreign policy." Meanwhile, other White House officials Jan. 7 had confirmed the veracity of the newspaper stories, the *New York Times* said Jan. 8.

Rocky Mountain News

Denver, Colo., January 9, 1976

CONGRESSIONAL OPPONENTS of covert activities by the CIA anywhere in the world finally seem to have found a way of stopping the practice — by leaking about it.

That is the conclusion one must draw from the disclosure that the CIA passed $6 million in the last month to anti-Communist politicians in Italy to help them prevent further Communist party gains in future elections.

Now that the secret is out, the CIA efforts will have to cease, even though President Ford and Secretary of State Henry Kissinger are convinced that the U.S. national interest lies in blunting the Communist drive for power in Italy.

Under a 1974 law the CIA cannot carry out a covert operation unless the President determines it is important to national security and it is reported to the six Congressional committees overseeing the intelligence agency.

Complying with the law, CIA director William Colby briefed congressmen last Dec. 8 and 9 about the Italian operation. Less than a month later the secret was on the front pages of the nation's newspapers.

A similar technique was used to leak the CIA's provision of arms to the anti-Communist factions fighting in Angola and thus to end that program.

A separate and difficult question is whether the CIA should be putting money into Italian domestic politics. In an ideal world the answer would be a clear no. In the real world, however, with the Soviet Union heavily subsidizing the Italian Communist Party, there are no easy answers.

For one thing, contributions by foreign governments and by foreign and domestic corporations are a traditional and accepted part of Italian political life.

For another, the United States had great success with the practice in the past. American financing of the infant Christian Democratic party in 1948 helped it win a crucial election against a powerful Communist threat.

Had communism taken power in Italy at that time, the face of Europe would be entirely different today — and much less favorable to the United States and its democratic allies.

Unfortunately, the Christian Democrats have become inept, corrupt and paralyzed after a generation in power. In recent years the Communists have been gaining votes steadily, and it is not certain that U.S. campaign contributions can keep them out of the government.

Ford and Kissinger thought it worth a try because they fear that a Communist government role in Rome could have a domino effect in France and West Germany and destroy NATO as a viable alliance.

What is disturbing is that there are not enough votes in Congress to plainly ban covert CIA actions. But since by definition a covert operation must be kept secret, a small number of Congressmen can stop any such CIA move by blabbing about it.

In pleading with Congress not to outlaw CIA covert operations, Colby said the President should have an option in between sending a diplomatic note and sending in the Marines. The congressional leakers of secret information have decided otherwise. It is doubtful that the country will be safer because of it.

Pittsburgh Post-Gazette

Pittsburgh, Pa., January 9, 1976

ANY AMERICAN with more than a passing interest in international affairs long has known that, since the close of World War II, Washington has been offsetting Moscow's aid to the procommunist left in Italy by aiding the noncommunist center. It was never much of a secret, but it wasn't page-one news either. Why it is now may have something to do with the advent of the New American Age of Naivete.

Its exponents include some journalists whose idea of history is anything that they happened to write or to read about two weeks ago. The fact is that 30 years ago West Europe's economies and political structures were in shambles, especially in Italy, France and West Germany. Throughout the war, only the communists had remained well organized, and with Moscow's help were in excellent positions to take over.

* * *

The U.S., for the sake of its own people and of Europe's democrats, felt obliged to help out. The U.S. poured money into the rebuilding of West Europe's economies. It helped finance democrats' campaigns.

That help, overt and covert, worked well almost everywhere except in Italy, which had known nationhood only recently, as measured on the European scale of history. Rome's postwar noncommunist governments have been less efficient and more corrupt than those elsewhere in Europe.

Perhaps, over three decades, occasional, small-scale U.S. financial help to some anticommunist politicians contributed in a small way to the Italian political system's inadequate ability to slough off the less able politicos, just as U.S. government's providing protectionist legislation or subsidies to certain industries may reward, by keeping alive, the inefficient while punishing the efficient competitor.

Whether continuing to subsidize Italian anticommunists for so long came to be more harmful than helpful is a legitimate matter for debate. That the U.S. is somehow responsible in any major way for the weaknesses in post-war Italy is not debatable; it's absurd. Just as it's absurd to argue that the U.S. should never have lifted a finger to help noncommunist politicians.

In congressional and public debates that are about to ensue, let that fact be kept well in mind. Be it remembered also that the "CIA anticommunist funding" stories broke just when the Christian Democrats lost the support of the Socialists and will try to form a new government or have to call for new elections.

If ignorance, naivete and partisan pettiness characterize the debate in the U.S., the noncommunist politicians — the competent and honest as well as the incompetent and dishonest — in the next elections will be put at a further disadvantage against an ever-strengthening Communist party.

* * *

Let no one mistakenly believe that it will make little difference to the legitimate self-interests of the American people whether Italy goes communist. So long as the majority of Italians believe that it has been better to live under an imperfect capitalist democracy than under even the most honest and efficient of communist governments, so long should the American people remain willing and eager to help out.

OKLAHOMA CITY TIMES

Oklahoma City, Okla., January 10, 1976

ONCE the secrecy of the Central Intelligence Agency's request for money to aid the anti-Communist political parties in Italy, where the Communists are given a chance to become the first freely elected majority government in the world, was violated, it was too late to save the project, under any kind of circumstances.

It is true that the charges that the money had already been spent, or at least committed to the beleaguered anti-Communist Italian politicians, were false. It is true that the carefully worded statement of CIA Director William Colby was soon reduced to a transparent effort to cover the agency's tracks. But it is also true that some members of Congress acted in a completely irresponsible manner in shouting that they knew of a secret and then blabbed what they knew—even though they were wrong about the timing—to the world.

There is no way for such aid to those who are often fighting for the very independence of their countries to be given openly. It is more effective and far cheaper for this country to do what it can through covert financial support, if such support is justified, and it can be seen in advance that it will make the difference in an election. Those who moralize that we should not become involved in the internal political affairs of other lands ignore the fact that the Communists are lavishly financed from Moscow, and that their opponents usually are unable to tell their story to the voters because of the lack of funds.

Once such a plan becomes known, it is as completely shattered as a bubble, and as impossible to reconstitute. What is worse, the Communists will now be able to cry that they are the targets of capitalist intrigue and interference, and gain some voter support thereby.

Congress is going to have to return to its proved system of permitting only members of the "oversight" committees to learn CIA secrets. It worked for 28 years.

TULSA DAILY WORLD

Tulsa, Okla., January 8, 1976

THE CENTRAL Intelligence Agency, under mounting Congressional pressure for its role in Angola, now is "disclosed" to be working covertly in Italy.

Stories of CIA attempts to aid non-Communist parties in Italy were printed yesterday in the NEW YORK TIMES and WASHINGTON POST and quickly spread to the wire services. Now everyone who wants to know what American intelligence is up to in Italy can see it in type.

It is hardly a surprise to have such a revelation. SECRETARY of STATE HENRY KISSINGER has indicated earlier that the U.S. is determined to do what it can to keep the Communists from taking over Italy. Our presence in Italy has been felt for many years in the continuing struggle with Communism.

KISSINGER'S thinking is that if Italy falls to the Reds, France may be next, and NATO is bound to be weakened. That goes to the heart of U.S. foreign policy in Europe. Could we have any faith in a NATO honeycombed with Communists?

One wonders if the anti-CIA movement in Congress will now switch its fire to the Italian front? The Angola argument isn't settled yet, but the CIA is so weakened there that it might as well pack its bags.

Italy may be another story, but in the present hostile atmosphere for American covert activities, the presumption seems to be that the CIA has no business operating secretly anywhere. If that is so, why have an intelligence organization?

Are we ready to say we don't care whether the Russians are winning control of Third World countries? If we *do* care, must the CIA be constantly crippled by having its operations exposed in public?

Critics of the CIA do not acknowledge that they would like to kill the agency outright. They indicate they merely hope to limit its activities, confining them to a corral they consider appropriate.

This is a neat theory, but unfortunately the warfare at the intelligence level doesn't allow itself to be regulated so precisely. It isn't easy to tell where "proper" intelligence stops and "improper" begins. The Congressional detractors will discover that fact when they try to write their new rules spelling out exactly how far the CIA is allowed to go.

The Virginian-Pilot

Norfolk, Va., January 9, 1976

The apparently coincidental collapse of the government in Italy at a time when the American press reported that the Central Intelligence Agency channeled some $6 million to Italy's non-Communist political parties is sure to confuse things.

The CIA will be blamed by Italian politicians of every stripe for Italy's ills and another debate about the bungling of the CIA and American meddling overseas is likely to ensue in Washington. It is desirable to keep the issues in perspective.

The reason why the government of Premier Aldo Moro fell is that the Socialists withdrew their backing of the coalition in parliamentary voting. The Socialists seem to have acted for their own political reasons and figure to profit from the shake-up. Any outrage over the CIA's involvement will be inspired by those who don't like the United States.

The Moro government is the 32nd Italian Cabinet to fall since the end of the Second World War. The fact that it lasted for 13 months is more surprising than its collapse this week.

Although the Italian political parties are denying that they received any CIA funds, there is little reason to question the essential truth of the reports that were first published in The New York Times and The Washington Post.

It is no secret that American covert funds have helped to support the non-Communist political parties of Western Europe since the Second World War. And, indeed, in better days the CIA claimed credit for preventing the political takeover of Western Europe.

And while President Ford is reported to be outraged by the leaks, the White House is not denying the sum and substance of the stories.

Mr. Ford is right in thinking that the leaks are damaging to our national interests. The CIA story is embarrassing to Italian politicians sympathetic to us, who are forced now to deny the seemingly truthful. And the episode furthers the image of the CIA's incompetence at routine skulduggery. The net result is to embarrass Rome and Washington.

At the same time, it is easy to exaggerate the hullaballoo. The fall of the Moro government is not so serious. And American dollars cannot save the Italian politicians from themselves. The Italians live from crisis to crisis politically and seem to like it that way. The failures of the Italian political system have less to do with the Americans or the Communists than with the Italian reluctance to tax themselves and the Catholic Church's influence in paralyzing reforms. And from the Caesars to Mussolini, the Italians have seen a lot of governments come and go.

It is idle to debate whether the CIA involvement in Italy is "wrong." Just last month, Leslie H. Gelb wrote in The New York Times Magazine that "the Ford Administration has used the CIA to funnel millions of dollars into the hands of non-Communist parties in Portugal," and that "the CIA plowed money and arms through President Mobutu of Zaire to support two liberation movements in Angola." There has been little outrage over either operation. Surely we have a greater interest in Italy than in Africa.

Nor is the CIA acting independently of the White House or the State Department. If anybody is to blame for the bungling, it is Mr. Ford and Mr. Kissinger — not the available whipping-boys of the CIA. Obviously somebody in Washington wants to embarrass Mr. Ford and get Mr. Kissinger. Whoever is doing the leaking is succeeding in the first and may succeed in the second.

New York Post

New York, N.Y., January 8, 1976

Conceding that some of their past performances regularly featured lock-step drilling and abrupt about-faces, it is no longer profitable to think of the world's Communist parties as so many marching bands, forming hammer-and-sickles and other designs, all to the music of Moscow. They have been following the beat of different drummers.

The Yugoslavs left the parade long ago; others marched behind. Increasingly discordant sounds have been heard lately from the Italian, French and Spanish Communists. Moscow's chances of arranging a compliant conference of European parties this year —it was utterly unable to do so in 1975 —is not significantly brighter than its own bleak economic situation.

Against that background, it comes as incredible, incomprehensible news that official Washington, through the CIA, has been secretly pouring millions in cash into the pockets of non-Communist politicians in Italy.

Last fall, expressing his personal distress at the fact that Italian Communists had scored heavily in elections, Secretary of State Kissinger conceded that the U. S. could not "determine the domestic structure of Italy . . . the future of Italy is not an American foreign policy problem . . ."

Why, then, in the name of sanity—or, perhaps, insanity—has the U. S. government dumped at least $6 million into an enterprise that is massively counterproductive, utterly unwarranted and indicative only of a relentless, dangerous, and fundamentally stupid determination to meddle in other nations' political affairs? As with Indochina and Angola, it is again vital for Congress to assume the responsibility that the Administration has abandoned and throttle this witless waste of desperately short public money, decreed by an Administration that seems to have lost its reason.

The Dallas Morning News

Dallas, Tex., January 9, 1976

IT IS NOW customary to hiss and shudder when the name of the Nixon "plumbers" comes up. But it would be well to take another look at that name and recall how it came about.

The stated purpose of the "plumbers" group was to stop leaks of state secrets during the Nixon administration. Such leaks are more than a political problem. They were then and are now a serious national problem. They have significant effect, not only on our foreign policy and its operation but on the process of government here at home.

The latest leak, disclosure by the New York Times that the U.S. has been slipping money to anticommunist political parties in Italy, is a case in point.

Release of this information at a time when the Christian Democrat government was tottering did not, apparently, greatly influence the subsequent collapse. And the actual information itself is not that much of a bombshell. The U.S. has given aid to these parties in the past, while the Soviet Union has financed the Italian Communist party throughout its history.

Nevertheless, the leak will undoubtedly be a handicap to friends of the U.S. in coming elections. With the Communist party now within 2 percentage points of the Christian Democrats, as indicated by regional and local elections, that may help the Communists into the driver's seat.

Few thinking Americans, let us hope, would favor trying to stop these leaks with restrictions of the news agencies who print them. The real problem lies in the irresponsibility of the government officials who give secret information out.

President Ford was reportedly furious when he saw the news stories. The leak was centered on information recently given to some members of Congress in confidence. There is obviously suspicion that someone thus briefed betrayed this confidence. And based on past instances of congressional gabbiness with state secrets, the suspicion is understandable.

It is, of course, possible that the congressmen briefed on the funding are innocent. The leak might well have come from some bureaucrat settling a score or scoring a point in the Byzantine mazes of office politics. It could have come from some obscure member of the administration itself, someone playing the game of "Look how many secrets I know."

But whatever the source, the probable result of this sort of thing is that it will drive this president and future presidents to keep more and more secrets tightly locked up at the top of the executive branch. Efforts to guard security information from the headlines can also keep such information away from the legislative branch.

Congress has said it wants to be kept in the picture on all foreign policy operations of the government. We believe that it should be, indeed must be, kept informed, if the legislative is to regain its proper constitutional status as an equal partner in national leadership.

But so long as chief executives expect that every bit of sensitive or confidential information provided Congress will shortly thereafter be published around the world, that's not likely. What is likely is that presidents, Democratic or Republican, will return to the former policy of keeping Congress as much in the dark as possible.

You may not think that is a healthy policy—we do not— but considering the record, it is easy to see why it was adopted.

AKRON BEACON JOURNAL

Akron, Ohio, January 10, 1976

NOW COMES news of the "Italian connection" in which the CIA secretly slips wads of cash to non-communist political parties in Italy, a brilliant move that ranks right up there with boring a hole in the bottom of a leaky boat to let the water out.

The latest reports, coming as Italy's 32nd rubber band government since the end of World War II snapped, estimated the current handout program at $6 million. Most goes to the Christian Democratic Party.

There is certainly nothing wrong with supporting your friends, and the United States is vitally concerned with keeping Italy in the Western European non-communist community. But pumping cash into the black bag of politicians didn't work in Vietnam, and apparently isn't working in Rome. If anything, secret contributions are counter-productive, undermining hopes for exactly what they were intended to promote.

The Italian connection, it seems to us, tends to give aid to the communists. It is ammunition which they can use to blaze away at the Christian Democrats, screaming that its leaders are puppets of the CIA, etc. And because it was done in such a sneaky manner, it is yeast to make suspicions rise.

It should be hard for Secretary of State Henry Kissinger, President Ford or CIA director William Colby to defend the practice before the U. S. Senate in the wake of an overwhelming Senate vote against secret funds for Angola. Partly because it is wrong; partly because it simply doesn't work.

It is proper to support allies, but the help should go above-board to the foreign government, not to the political party that gives the best anti-communist speeches. The harsh reality is that governments, not parties, set policies and make the policies that determine whether they satisfy their constituents so they don't want a radical shift.

And if those people do want a change, trying to prop up friends with cash gifts under the table accomplishes little more than making them richer, not wiser. It is like splashing gasoline on the fires of nationalism, discontent and anti-Americanism.

The Morning Star

Rockford, Ill., January 9, 1976

Tragic as the collapse of another Italian government may be for the stability of that country, even more tragic is the U.S. intervention with $6 million to pay off politicians whom the CIA deemed worthy.

Have we learned nothing? Has Secretary of State Henry Kissinger learned nothing?

The payoffs are directly the result of Kissinger foreign policy and his unrest over Italy turning Communist. The Vatican is concerned that Italy is going Communist, too. And it is campaigning against the trend.

Fine. The Vatican is part of Italy.

But the United States, in Italy, is a foreign power. What right have we, however loathsome communism may be to us, to peddle $6 million to seek a dubious political advantage?

Having paid once, when does the next installment fall due? And at what cost?

No wonder Italian newspapers are full of CIA stories and accounts of American dollars in the pockets of Italian politicos favored by the CIA!

President Ford is angry because the news of the payoffs leaked. Too bad. He has to bear responsibility for this ridiculous caper. Will he also take responsibility for the fall of Italy's government?

If ever an incident merited congressional investigation, the rampant stupidity if not illegality demonstrated here needs public scrutiny.

Why can this country not resolve to conduct a positive foreign policy which would carry more influence than any dollars paid under the table? We have markets to share, defense experts and materials to share — all with long-run advantages for Italy as well as this country.

We have just been through a whole series of federal investigations into American companies with payola policies in foreign countries, including Italy.

Now the feds themselves have paid the price of admission to the same dance and the ticket-takers have stamped "payola" on their palms.

Whatever happened to the word, "integrity," which most of us still associate with the American flag? When will we erase any doubt about their association?

ARGUS-LEADER

Sioux Falls, S.D., January 8, 1976

Americans who support Republican or Democratic candidates for president are urged to show their backing by contributing money to their favorite's campaign.

Anyone who runs for Congress or for governor or other high office in South Dakota has friends who provide money to help him along.

So what's wrong with the United States funneling money into the hands of anti-Communist politicians in Italy, to help them beat the Communists in elections in that country?

According to The Associated Press, authoritative sources in Washington say the Central Intelligence Agency (CIA), is funneling $6 million to anti-Communist politicians in Italy. This represents a dramatic increase in CIA funding of centrist elements to head off what Secretary of State Henry Kissinger calls alarming advances by the Communist Party in Europe. One small Italian party—the Republican Party—denies that it has ever received funds from the CIA. Washington sources say the money is going directly to members of the Christian Democratic and Socialist parties.

We're not wise enough to say flatly that the United States should never help its friends in political elections overseas. There'd be an uproar of gigantic proportions in this country, if it were discovered that the intelligence agencies of friends or adversaries alike were funding either the Republicans or Democrats.

Which American party could survive handouts from British intelligence, or the Russians' spy agency, or from Fidel Castro's operatives? Neither party. Likely, the publicity about the American help for Italians opposing Communists will have the effect of helping the Reds and tarnishing friendships nurtured by Yankee dollars.

This country couldn't buy victory in Vietnam. We doubt if it can purchase political peace-of-mind in any country. There must be more effective ways for the United States to wage diplomacy than having the CIA peddle attache cases full of local currency to foreign politicians.

St. Petersburg Times

St. Petersburg, Fla., January 8, 1976

If faced with that choice, most Americans no doubt would rather see the CIA trying to buy other people's elections than fighting their wars. Outside of Washington, D.C., though, it may be hard to sell the idea that our government should be engaged in either kind of this extra-curricular effort.

Congress, in an accurate reflection of public opinion, already has sent a go-slow signal to the Administration on this country's covert involvement in the civil war in Angola. It very likely will order an end to CIA participation in this proxy battle unless President Ford calls a halt first.

NOW IT COMES out, though, that the CIA has been, and is, pumping millions of U.S. tax dollars into the political process in Italy, hoping to curb continued electoral gains by the Communist Party. So far Congress hasn't raised much cain about that.

Behind closed doors, key members were told at least $6-million has been secretly funneled since early December to leaders of Italy's non-Communist political groups. The payments reportedly were approved by President Ford in response to outside support for Italian Communist parties and after the Communists won about a third of the popular vote in last June's local elections.

Some of the lawmakers were said to have questioned the action, apparently mostly on the ground these unreported, non-accountable funds probably would be siphoned off into somebody's Swiss bank account. That, indeed, might be a reasonable basis on which to shut off the flow.

But more basic objections than that can be raised. An obvious one is that Italians are entitled to run their own elections. And another is that the business of secretly influencing other people's commitments to freedom isn't likely to work anymore, if it ever did.

Harry Truman may have been right when he first tried it in the Italian elections of 1948. That was a critical period in the postwar recovery of Europe, in which the U.S. played a dominant role. Non-Communist forces then needed all the help they could get.

BUT TIMES have changed.

So have Italian governments, incidentally. With and without the covert political aid that has flowed from the U.S., off and on, ever since, they have repeatedly fallen, and as often pulled themselves together through new coalitions of minority parties. It has been hard to keep count, but the current Italian government (we think) is the country's 37th in 32 years.

And only yesterday Socialist Party leaders decided to withdraw their support from the incumbent regime, raising the prospect of yet another parliamentary election in which the Communists (who no doubt get all kinds of help from the Soviet Union) probably will make further gains.

That will be sad. But is it still the business of Americans to attempt to influence Italian elections? If Italians are so unwise now as to vote for Communist candidates, is there really any way we can stop them?

✓ ✓ ✓

WE FIND THIS secret financing of Italian political parties especially ironic right now, when the U.S. is so diligently engaged in cleaning up its own election process.

Political financing in this country under a new law must be out in the open. Contributions and spending are limited. Income and outgo in support of each candidate must be publicly reported.

What the U.S. government is doing in Italy now not only would be a crime here if the Italian government were attempting the same thing in reverse. It also would be a signal for popular outrage, and the sure defeat of any candidate caught taking the money. Can the reaction in Italy be very different?

THE ROANOKE TIMES

Roanoke, Va., January 14, 1976

Published reports that the Central Intelligence Agency is channeling $6 million into Italy to aid non-Communist political parties prompt some reflection on the usefulness of campaign funds abroad.

We will not attempt to dredge up and either apologize for or condemn the past. Without doubt, the CIA has spent tens, if not hundreds, of millions of dollars in attempts to influence Western Europe's elections since World War II. Doubtless the Soviet Union has been active on a comparable scale. U.S. activities in Europe during the past 30 years—which included not just money for politicians but also billions for economic and military aid, plus the presence of American troops and weapons—played probably the decisive role in steering war-impoverished nations away from communism and toward the prosperity and freedom they enjoy today.

U.S. economic aid and military presence, however, count for much less today. The threat of armed Communist takeover does not energize Europe any more; nor is there the same worry about gradualist communism. Changing countries like Portugal and Italy are trying to work out their futures without reacting to bugaboos. They may be mistaken in writing off the Communist or Socialist threat; but there is little point any more in our trying to raise the same alarms.

There also appear to be diminishing prospects in underwriting certain political parties. For one thing, the word seems sure to leak out, as it did about Italy. For another, U.S. dollars won't bring stability. Since World War II Italy has had 32 governments; its once-dominant Christian Democratic party is a shadow of its former self; and no one can be sure of the eventual shape of Italy's politics or what blend of ideology may emerge. To put money into that looks like a bigger gamble than Las Vegas roulette.

One of the key complaints among Americans in postwar years has been about our inability to win friends with foreign aid; do politicians abroad stay bought? Let those campaign funds remain at home. We're cranking up a horse race here that will have a bigger impact on our future than elections in Italy.

The Charleston Gazette

Charleston, W. Va., January 9, 1976

When Gerald Ford assumed the office of the presidency he seemed anxious to dispel the aura of White House secrecy formed during the Nixon years. At the first Ford press conference, he vowed that his administration would be an "open" one, that under his stewardship the executive branch would put its card on the table in the presence of the people.

Of course, his predecessor had said the same thing. But in view of the scandals which accompanied Richard Nixon's flight from Washington, Mr. Ford's listeners were persuaded to believe what he said. Editorials, including one in this newspaper, praised Mr. Ford's commendable resolution to let the people know what their government was doing.

Mr. Ford's promise was kept no longer than Richard Nixon's. The President has kept up a running battle with select congressional committees in a desperate effort to prevent disclosures about the CIA and the FBI. Only when backed into a corner was he willing to admit the financial presence of the United States in Angola. Now he is keeping his mouth closed when asked to confirm or deny the story that the CIA has funneled $6 million into Italy in an attempt to influence elections there. But he is opening his mouth often and vigorously to deplore the allegations of the CIA's Italian operation.

By doing so, the President creates a credibility gap of considerable proportions at the White House. If the CIA didn't interfere in Italian internal affairs, all Mr. Ford need do is say so. By refusing to confirm or deny the story, while at the same time denouncing "disclosures," Mr. Ford is displaying the near-psychopathic mistrust of the American people that afflicted both Lyndon Johnson and Richard Nixon and led them to say, in essence, that the less the people know, the better.

As to whether the stories are true, we have little doubt of their accuracy, and predict that Mr. Ford will confirm them eventually. Doubtless he will defend the expenditure of $6 million of your tax money with brave remarks about the necessity to confront communism.

But in Italy, where one of four voters is a Communist, the elections are as free as our own. Meddling in free elections strikes us as being the worst possible way to fight communism, but we doubt that the irony will strike Mr. Ford. In the meantime, Uncle Sam's "image" problem in the world community will have been worsened by the latest CIA grotesquerie.

If curbs aren't soon applied, the CIA may succeed in turning the rest of the planet against America, with President Ford standing by silently.

Newsday

Garden City, N.Y., January 8, 1976

What would happen if the Italian government slipped $6 million to the campaign of some American presidential candidate?

- American voters would wonder—with good reason—who the candidate would be working for if they elected him.
- The candidate who received the money would be liable for a $25,000 fine and a five-year prison term.
- So would the contributor.

But of course Italy is not the United States, and evidently the Ford administration believes it can do in Rome what the Italians could be jailed for doing in Washington. In the past month the Central Intelligence Agency has funneled $6 million to Italian politicians—mostly to the Christian Democrats who headed Italy's governing coalition. This in the name of preventing the Communists, Italy's second largest party, from increasing their strength enough to demand a place in the government. A lot of good it seems to have accomplished; Premier Aldo Moro's coalition collapsed yesterday. If anything, the CIA slush fund has now made Communist gains more likely, not less.

The usual justification for this kind of under-the-table funding is that the Russians are doing it—which they undoubtedly are—so we have to. But the Soviet Union does a good many things the U.S. government shouldn't stoop to, and covert meddling in the electoral politics of a democratic nation is one of them. It was a different matter when the Christian Democrats got U.S. help in the wreckage of Mussolini's fascist state. But Italian democracy has been stable—if not stagnant—for nearly three decades. CIA political spending there now is an insult to the integrity of the Italian people.

Sooner or later—if not in Italy, then somewhere else—Communists are going to come to power by the electoral process in a country that has traditionally been friendly to the U.S. The Ford administration's reaction to that possibility in Italy bears a strong resemblance to sheer panic.

Minneapolis Tribune

Minneapolis, Minn., January 8, 1976

Two months ago Secretary of State Henry Kissinger told the House International Relations Committee that the administration was disturbed by gains made by the Italian Communist Party during last June's elections. That was a reasonable expression of concern, to which Kissinger added this cautionary footnote: "Basically, the United States cannot determine the domestic structure of Italy; basically, the future of Italy is not an American foreign-policy problem."

Basically, that seems not to have been an entirely accurate portrayal of Ford administration views. Two U.S. newspapers this week reported the secret payment of at least $6 million to anti-Communist Italian political leaders in December, a month after Kissinger's testimony, in an effort to strengthen non-Communist political parties. One American official familiar with the large amounts spent by Italian political parties characterized the U.S. contribution — apparently a "black bag" payment by the CIA — as "peanuts" by comparison. According to New York Times sources, a member of the House oversight subcommittee criticized CIA director William Colby, when Colby explained the transaction, on grounds that much of the money would be used by the recipients to swell their own bank accounts.

Those observations say as much about the matter as does the transaction itself. The relative size of the contribution is not, in our view, the main issue; neither is the possibility of the funds' being used for personal purposes. The issue is whether the United States should be officially, even if covertly, aiding political factions in foreign countries or, for that matter, undercutting them. The secretary of state answered that question forthrightly, at least in terms of recent history, during an NBC television interview Monday night. Kissinger said that American support for parties opposed to the late Chilean president, Salvador Allende, was for the purpose of preserving freedom.

We see the question differently. To answer it in terms of pragmatism, of results, one should look first to Chile. We need not recite the dreary history of how Allende — an elected president — was overthrown by a military clique whose subsequent rule has earned it a reputation as one of the most oppressive on the current scene. We need only ask whether U.S. support for the anti-Allende factions brought more or fewer benefits of freedom to Chileans. As to Italy, the best thing that can be said of the $6 million is that it probably was not responsible for this week's break-up of the fragile non-Communist coalition that formed the latest government.

To argue, as we do, against meddling in other countries' internal politics is not to be complacent about communism, which in the form most often found is totalitarianism. Democracy is a result of self-determination, which means freedom of choice. That assumes competition among political parties for votes and assumes further that non-Communist parties will have stronger appeal. In our view, the assumption that the United States should presume to select which political parties to support in another country — whether Italy, Chile or (remember?) Vietnam — contradicts the principles of self-determination that are supposed to guide American foreign policy.

The Des Moines Register

Des Moines, Iowa, January 10, 1976

Just about everybody concerned is angry about the reported $6 million in secret funding of two Italian political parties by the U.S. Central Intelligence Agency.

President Ford and the CIA are angry because the secret got out, presumably through congressmen informed under the law.

Many in Congress and elsewhere are angry that the CIA should do such a thing (or contemplate doing it), after the furor which developed over similar subsidies in the 1948-67 period.

The Italian parties named in the report — the large Christian Democratic Party and the tiny Social Democratic Party — denied receiving such funds recently, and CIA Director William Colby denied giving them — yet. Italians in general are angry at U.S. interference in their domestic politics — though less indignant than Americans would be because of differing laws, traditions and practices.

The wisdom of the subsidy is extremely dubious. The Christian Democrats should be able to support their own activities by now, and if the Social Democrats cannot, they are probably hopeless. A subsidy to large and fractious groups is bound to become public, and to work in reverse when it does.

A covert campaign contribution from a foreign government would be illegal and resented in the U.S. Should we do such things abroad?

A campaign contribution is much less objectionable than an attempt to "destabilize" a foreign government, to say nothing of subsidizing assassinations, coups and invasions. But Americans have good reason to regard the buying of foreign politicians as distasteful.

"Covert" operations cover a broad range of possible activity and are not all dirty. In some situations providing U.S. funds to political and non-political groups abroad might be justifiable.

Proposals are rife for (1) stricter congressional control of covert CIA operations, (2) abolition of covert operations, (3) separation of CIA information-gathering and covert operations.

Defining covert operations and drawing a line between permissible and impermissible activity will be among the toughest chores for Congress as it attempts to assert control over the CIA.

The Salt Lake Tribune

Salt Lake City, Utah, January 11, 1976

President Ford was said to have been "angry" that alleged Central Intelligence Agency (CIA) financing of anti-Communist politicians in Italy had been made public.

This reaction suggests that the President seriously believed that the CIA's reentry into Italian politics could be kept secret at a time when the intelligence agency is under intense scrutiny.

The President's attitude reflects inability to adjust to a current fact of national and international life: The days are gone when secret meddling in other nations' affairs could be carried out with small danger of being exposed.

To many, especially those directing foreign policy and charged with national security responsibility, this is a sad state of affairs. To others it represents a decided improvement, a move toward more enlightened international relations.

Be that as it may it is obvious enough that any President or Secretary of State who puts great faith in covert operations these days has little to complain about when the secret gets out and the country must absorb the inevitable damage that exposure brings.

In the case of Italy and of Angola it can be argued that there are better ways of pursuing U.S. goals than secretly putting millions of dollars in cash and equipment into the hands of local politicians and tribal leaders to use as they wish.

No doubt there are still a number of negotiations and other activities which must be conducted in secret and do, in fact, produce benefits for the United States. But in the present "open" atmosphere where secrecy is equated with evil intentions, covert operations must be carefully considered.

Foremost among such considerations should be the high risk that the project will ultimately be exposed. That being the case, Mr. Ford's anger was wasted emotion.

THE SACRAMENTO BEE

Sacramento, Calif., January 11, 1976

Covert attempts by the Central Intelligence Agency to manipulate and otherwise promote anti-Communist factions in Western Europe are now public knowledge. The morality of such practices could well be questioned, but even setting that thought aside, those practices should be ended simply on the basis such tactics rarely seem to work.

Rather, if the history of the past decade teaches anything, the result is to provide pro-Communist factions with the opportunity of calling their opposition stooges of the U.S., or to saddle this country with client governments made up of undemocratic reactionary hacks or generals.

This really does not advance our self-interest in aiding democratic movements in Western Europe and in other parts of the world.

It evidently hasn't been successful in Italy, an object of covert CIA political intervention for the past month. The Italian government has fallen despite these CIA machinations.

The emphasis in our objection to these commonly fruitless foreign involvements is to their secret disruptive or manipulative character. There is no objection to the CIA's essential intelligence-gathering. We need an effective intelligence apparatus.

Neither do we criticize the policy of aiding democratic factions in any country, whether Italy, say, or Portugal or Spain. But this should not be done by way of secret tactics of the CIA. They seem usually to backfire counterproductively.

We would do better to openly support, through diplomacy or other means, those pro-Western factions whose success is determined to be in our interest.

It seems useful to remember that the CIA's attempted covert manipulations are similar to those of the Russian KGB. The KGB hasn't been notably successful in its secret interventions. Most European Communist factions which have gained power have done so as a result of the actual or threatened might of the Red Army.

Considering the CIA's poor record in clandestine political manipulations, it is time to revise the National Security Act of 1947 to impose limits on its covert activities.

CHICAGO DAILY NEWS

Chicago, Ill., January 9, 1976

The collapse of yet another government in Italy — the 32d cabinet turnover since World War II — raises the distinct possibility that the Italian Communist Party may move into a position of power. Already the second largest party in Italy, the Communists won a third of the votes in the last election, and were kept out of the national government only by a coalition of the Christian Democrats and the third-ranking Democratic Socialist Party. When the Socialists withdrew their backing for Premier Aldo Moro, he had to resign.

At this stage, there's no predicting what the outcome of the new crisis will be in the rough-and-tumble of Italian politics. A new and probably unstable patchwork uniting the Christian Democrats and Socialists could result, or new elections could be called. In either case, the growing power of the Communists in a key nation of Western Europe is a proper cause for concern in the United States, the leader of the Western alliance.

But the question that now arises is how best that concern can be expressed. Almost at the same time the Moro government collapsed, it was revealed that $6 million had been set aside for the U.S. Central Intelligence Agency to give to members of the Christian Democratic and Democratic Socialist parties in Italy. Nobody was supposed to know about that, but a congressman still unidentified "leaked" the story after a secret briefing by the CIA, and once again the intelligence agency is in the soup.

Considering the amount of American aid that has been given openly to Western Europe in the postwar era, $6 million is a piddling sum. And a primary purpose of that aid, through the Marshall Plan and many other programs, was never disguised: It was to strengthen democracies and thwart the spread of communism.

The American people staunchly supported the help-Europe programs, and doubtless still would. Few in this country would rejoice to see Italy "go Communist" — or France or any other nation where the Communist parties have been gaining strength. There is no secret about Moscow's support for those parties, both overt and covert, even though Italian and French Communists may be a breed apart from the Moscow variety.

But what rankles is to discover that the U.S. government, via the CIA, is slipping money to Italian politicans under the table. The stench of bribery and corruption, and of meddling in the domestic political affairs of a friendly country, clings to the transaction. Using the CIA for such a purpose further blemishes the image of that organization and compromises its essential task of gathering intelligence.

If there is a case for supporting the democratic governments of Europe in their resistance to a Communist takeover — and we believe there is — let it be done openly, not under the table and not by the CIA. The surreptitious operations — certain to be found out in today's climate — can only help the Communists when they come to light, as they probably have helped already in this case.

The Washington Post

Washington, D.C., January 11, 1976

IN ITALY, as in Angola, current American operations seem as myopic in purpose as they are inept in management. The United States has been preparing to shovel $6 million into Italy's governing political parties, in the same manner in which a prudent gardner might dig fertilizer with his rose beds. The money was to be disbursed by the CIA, evidently at the behest of the State Department in its dogged but uninspired campaign to keep Communists out of the Italian cabinet. It is hard to think of any revelation that might do more harm to precisely those forces whom the State Department is trying to shore up.

This episode is another disquieting indication of misjudgment, on the Department's part, of the way things have changed both here and abroad. Aside from any more elevated consideration, the administration has had plenty of warning that the traditional procedures for keeping secrets have broken down. This latest revelation presumably comes from someone in Congress who opposes the subventions. Congress is not only sharply at odds with the administration but at odds with itself as well. Some members, isolated and frustrated, have learned to cast vetoes through leaks and public disclosure. But a government cannot really afford to embark on covert operations unless it can keep them covert. The Ford administration has been unable to work out the kind of understandings with Congress that protect the secrecy of these activities. Yet it keeps compulsively attempting to pursue them—even when they promise, at best, only trivial benefits.

It is not, after all, as though there were any great and urgent drought of political money in Italy. Money is a legitimate political weapon. The United States has apparently funneled some funds into Portugal, a country seized by economic collapse and political turbulence; it is entirely reasonable for the United States to provide, in a crisis, at least a partial counterweight to the aid that is flowing to the Portuguese Communists from the Soviet Union. By the same token, it was useful for this country to pump dollars into the Italian political system in the years after World War II. But since then there has been phenomenal economic growth in Italy; the standard of living is now in the same range as Britain's. The present generation of politicians is, if anything, too experienced; there are elaborate and well-established systems of patronage. If a party cannot raise adequate funds under these circumstances, it is a reflection on that party's competence. And here we come to the heart of the matter.

The Communists have been creeping upward in successive elections and polls for a wholly negative reason—the Italians' mounting exasperation with the other parties. The Christian Democrats have been dominant in every Italian government for more than 30 years; parties wear out, like the men who lead them and the ideas that inform them. The Christian Democrats have presided over the transformation of their country into a modern industrial state, but now they do not seem to know how to cope with the consequences. The most recent Cabinet fell this week. While the fall of a cabinet in a parliamentary system like Italy's is not necessarily very significant, the difficulty of patching together replacements has recently begun to rise sharply.

There is a pervasive sense in Italy that profound changes are coming—changes involving, one way or another, Communists in power—and each faction is trying to position itself to take advantage of this new fact. In recent months it had been generally assumed that little would happen until the middle of 1977, when the present parliamentary term expires. But the latest collapse may make elections necessary much sooner. It appears very possible that the Communists will get a bigger vote than the Christian Democrats and, to follow the most common line of speculation, that might result in a coalition cabinet. Certainly the Communists would not take over the government entirely; they are not likely to win an absolute majority and, in any case, they do not want to frighten the opposition. They have lately been saying very explicitly that they are committed to democracy and the traditional rules of the game. It is this sharing of power, with the Communists as the legitimate and accepted partner of a conservative and Catholic party, that the Ford administration is trying to forestall.

But the United States is going to have only a marginal influence over these events. It can quite properly point out to Italians that the arrival of Communists in the cabinet will probably make relations between our two countries less comfortable, and the military alliance less reliable. But the time is long since passed when Europeans were primarily concerned with Atlantic relations and defense. In Italy the main public preoccupations are social reforms, and the reorganization of obsolete and unresponsive public services.

Under these circumstances, the wisest course for the United States is to hold itself to the standard and conventional code of open diplomacy. That means making its interests and preferences clear to the world, but doing nothing that constitutes interference in Italy's internal politics. To go beyond this limit, as the affair of the $6 million suggests, can only push Italy toward the outcome that Mr. Kissinger wishes most strongly to avoid.

HOUSTON CHRONICLE

Houston, Tex., January 13, 1976

The proposed contribution of $6 million in U.S. funds to Italian political leaders would be a gross waste of tax dollars.

The fact that $6 million is proposed for politicians in Italy, where a coalition government just collapsed, sets one to wondering how many more millions of dollars have already gone the same route there and elsewhere.

There is small chance that even $6 million would prove decisive in the overall makeup of the Italian government, when many, many millions are employed in the political process there. There seems to be a large likelihood that a considerable portion of that $6 million would benefit different individuals rather than the cause of deterring communism.

And if $6 million doesn't turn out to be adequate, would $6 million more be pumped in? Or another $10 million?

President Ford is upset about the release of information on the proposed $6 million, and the fingers point to congressmen briefed on this operation. Leakage of information from committees is a serious problem and can pose threats to U.S. policies. It would be far better for the committees to exercise control without fanfare. However, it is easy to understand the indignation some congressmen must have over the idea of U.S. taxpayers contributing to Italian political parties.

Surely more positive ways can be found to spend $6 million.

LEDGER-STAR

Norfolk, Va., January 10, 1976

CIA Director William E. Colby says his agency hasn't "spent a nickel in Italy in the past few months," but when asked if the CIA is now starting to pour $6 million into the country to bolster anti-Communist politicians he went mum.

"I am not at liberty to discuss details," he said.

Well, the American people are entitled to a few details.

Keeping Italy non-Communist isn't so bad an idea. Despite problems of political instability, she is one of the world's industrial giants and her geographic position—stretching from the Alps deep into the Mediterranean toward Africa—makes her vital to the defense of Western civilization.

But you don't save a great country by slipping under-the-table payments to politicians. Italian politicians are not notably more honorable than their American counterparts, and who in his right mind would expect an American politician to accept secret payments, then spend them in a totally upright and honorable way?

If Mr. Colby would expect that, then he still believes in Easter bunnies and tooth fairies and the ultimate success of Vietnamization.

★ ★ ★ ★

In the first place, the United States has no business meddling in the internal politics of Italy or any other sovereign nation.

If there are exceptions to that rule, then it shouldn't be up to the CIA or the President or anyone other than Congress to write those exceptions. The American people are entitled to know when and under what circumstances their tax dollars are being used to influence the politics of other nations. And their elected representatives are entitled to say "no" to any proposal to use public funds for that purpose.

One government official, trying to downplay the importance of the reported $6 million infusion into Italian politics, was quoted as asking, "What can you buy for $6 million?

A lot of graft. A lot of ill will. And a good chunk of national dishonor.

NIXON CITES 'SOVEREIGN'S' RIGHTS, BACKS CIA INTERVENTION IN CHILE

Former President Nixon acknowledged, in sworn congressional testimony released March 11, authorizing secret efforts to undermine the presidency of the late Salvador Allende in Chile in 1970. He said, however, he did not recall specifically ordering a military coup or knowing that the Central Intelligence Agency had tried to stir up a military coup that year. The testimony was in answer to written interrogatories from the Senate Select Committee on Intelligence.

Nixon defended the intervention as being motivated by "the same national security interests" that prompted Presidents Kennedy and Johnson to authorize the CIA in the early 1960s to support Allende's political opponents financially. He also said, "It is quite obvious that there are certain inherently governmental actions which, if undertaken by the sovereign in protection of the interest of the nation's security, are lawful but which undertaken by private persons, are not."

The Miami Herald

Miami, Fla., March 13, 1976

WITH what we suppose is a straight face, Richard Nixon has defined the presidency as a "sovereign" power endowed with the right to break the law when, so he thinks, he is protecting national security.

Nixon

King Richard? This is an appallingly un-American statement by a man who, although legally trained, evidently is ignorant of the Constitution and the meaning of its doctrine of the separation of powers nearly 200 years old.

Almost as vicious in principle is the reaction of Henry Kissinger, who qualifies as the sovereign's First Minister, to criticisms of detente by presidential candidates (unnamed, but clearly Ronald Reagan and Henry Jackson) in the present campaign. He calls this an "orgy of recrimination" which is destroying the influence of the United States.

George Mason of Virginia feared that the proposed Constitution might be a "scheme for an elected monarchy." In his first weeks of office George Washington toyed with the idea of royal levies, and critics said his annual messages sounded like the British Speech from the Throne. But the country (and Washington) quickly put this aside.

How close did the United States come a couple of years ago to an authoritarian presidency? With the credentials to do so as a defender of Richard Nixon until he indicted himself, this newspaper shivers at the mere thought that the White House harbored a man who believed that he was a divinity sitting above the law.

We are not concerned with such trappings as Graustarkian uniforms for the White House police, although they were symptomatic, but rather with the effort to place the presidency over the Constitution.

The Founding Fathers were clear enough on this issue, and they had a modern spokesman just 50 years ago in Mr. Justice Brandeis. He said in Myers v. United States:

"The doctrine of the separation of powers was adopted by the Convention of 1787 not to promote efficiency but to preclude the exercise of arbitrary power. The purpose was not to avoid friction, but, by means of the inevitable friction incident to the distribution of the governmental powers among three departments, to save the people from autocracy."

Autocracy is implied also in the attitude of a Secretary of State who would squelch lawful debate on foreign policy with the full voice of his powerful office. Debate, that is to say, about his own policy.

If these two incredible utterances have any merit it is in reminding Americans on the 200th anniversary of their charter of freedom and the beginning of a system which has endured, unchanged, longer than any other, that their government belongs to the people, and not to any autocrats grasping for power.

THE SACRAMENTO BEE

Sacramento, Calif., March 13, 1976

Richard Nixon's statement likening the American president to a sovereign is both astonishing and repugnant.

Astonishing because it comes from a man trained in the law, who served in Congress, served as vice president and president — and who seemingly doesn't understand the basic tenets on which this country is founded.

Repugnant because the idea of a sovereign ruling from the White House is totally alien in a nation that declared its independence from the despotism of foreign royalty.

There is only one sovereign in the United States — and that is the people. This, said Daniel Webster in one of his orations, is the people's government, "made for the people, made by the people and answerable to the people."

By Nixon's interpretation, the president can exercise powers not granted by the Constitution no matter how you read it. As he put it, "There have been — and will be in the future — circumstances in which presidents may lawfully authorize actions in the interest and security of this country, which if undertaken by other persons, or even by the president under different circumstances, would be illegal."

And he made himself perfectly clear when asked whether "actions, otherwise illegal," could be undertaken: "It is quite obvious that there are certain inherently governmental actions which if undertaken by the sovereign in protection of the interest of the nation's security are lawful but which if undertaken by private persons are not."

Sen. Frank Church, D-Idaho, chairman of the Senate Intelligence Committee, rightly denounced this sovereign doctrine as "pernicious and dangerous." But perhaps this is Nixon's way of trying to justify the abuses that brought about the greatest scandal in American history and forced him to resign as president.

As so often before, Nixon waves the flag of "national security" to shield the secret orders he gave the CIA, for instance, or the host of clandestine operations assigned to the FBI for political benefit.

His words ring false and hollow. They fail utterly to vindicate Richard Nixon, to absolve him from responsibility for illegal acts performed under self-conferred powers like those of Rudyard Kipling's adventurers in "The Man Who Would Be King."

Time continues to prove how fortunate the people's government is that Nixon no longer occupies the office he was honored with — and disgraced.

THE ATLANTA CONSTITUTION

Atlanta, Ga., March 13, 1976

Every American should perhaps be grateful for the words of wisdom so graciously dispensed now and then from San Clemente, the modest home of former President Richard Nixon. But some of us aren't.

Nixon's latest contribution to political thought is to be found in his answers to questions put by the Senate Select Committee on Intelligence. Listen carefully:

"It is quite obvious that there are certain inherently governmental actions which, if undertaken by the sovereign in protection of the interest of the nation's security, are lawful but which, if undertaken by private persons, are not."

The *sovereign?*

Who's he? Not the President, surely, who is a constitutional official subject to the same laws as any other citizen.

The last sovereign we know of who ruled over these parts was King George III. We kicked him out 200 years ago. The American people kicked Nixon out too, mainly because he said he was not a crook when the facts indicated otherwise.

Sovereign means subject to no one. It is a word that used to apply to kings but now usually refers to a nation's independence. In the United States of America no individual is sovereign; not the President nor anybody else. This is "quite obvious" to nearly everybody but our former self-styled "sovereign."

Nixon's recent statements to courts of law, congressional committees and sympathetic audiences in China make it clear that, out of his experience, he has learned nothing and forgotten nothing. He is still peddling the same discredited line, and publishers and television producers who have invested heavily in his "memoirs" should be getting worried. Who will want to hear it all over again?

THE COMMERCIAL APPEAL

Memphis, Tenn., March 13, 1976

WHEN FORMER President Richard Nixon signed his resignation and retired to his seaside home in San Clemente, many of us thought he finally had come to realize a president of the United States is not a power unto himself and above the law.

It is clear now he did not realize it at that time. Nor does he understand it even yet. He is obviously a slow learner.

His lack of understanding and his lack of appreciation of the basic tenets of our democratic institutions show clearly in the answers he has given to the questions posed by the Senate Intelligence Committee.

He still says "that there are certain inherently governmental actions which, if undertaken by the *sovereign* in protection of . . . the nation's security, are lawful but which if undertaken by a private person are not. . ."

A *"sovereign"?*

Where in the United States Constitution does it say that the president of this nation shall be regarded by the citizens or by himself as a sovereign?

We fought a revolution to get away from the concept of an all-powerful sovereign, not to create our own.

And the Constitution states clearly that all presidents shall take an oath that they will "preserve, protect and defend the Constitution of the United States." It does not say that presidents are above or beyond that Constitution and no other president to our knowledge ever has claimed such exemption from it.

The former president's replies bring to mind the arrogant John Ehrlichman's testimony before the Watergate investigating committee in which he stated that the president of the United States has the power "to do anything."

Spare us any more of such arrogance.

Chicago Tribune

Chicago, Ill., March 15, 1976

In his reply to Interrogatory 34 from the Senate Intelligence Committee, former President Nixon used a word that puts most Americans on their guard. The word is "sovereign," in contrast to "private persons." Mr. Nixon said, "It is quite obvious that there are certain inherently governmental actions which, if undertaken by the sovereign in protection of the interest of the nation's security, are lawful but which, if undertaken by private persons, are not."

He cited as an example President Franklin Roosevelt's "relocation" from the Pacific Coast states, at the beginning of World War II, of persons of Japanese ancestry, including native-born citizens. As Mr. Nixon said, "Forceable removal of persons from their homes for the purpose of sequestering them in confined areas" is normally "kidnaping and unlawful imprisonment."

"Sovereign" is a somewhat equivocal word. It has two principal meanings: "one who has supremacy or rank above or authority over, others," and "the recognized supreme ruler of a people or country under monarchical government." The latter probably comes to mind more quickly than the former. A good many people, including Sen. Church, chairman of the Intelligence Committee, were quick to assume that Mr. Nixon was speaking of the President as the sovereign. The text of Mr. Nixon's responses does not support this. And any suggestion that the United States has a sovereign in this sense is repugnant.

We Americans prefer our Presidents to say, as Woodrow Wilson said in 1916, "If America stands for one thing more than another, it is for the sovereignty of self-governing people." But we also acknowledge that a President does have "rank above, or authority over, others."

The Constitution says very little about a President's powers. It says "the executive power shall be vested in a President." But it also says that the President "shall take care that the laws be faithfully executed." It does not say that the chief executive is above the law.

The Senate committee's questions to Mr. Nixon about events during his presidency concern a wide range of known or suspected covert operations, from interventions in Chilean politics to snooping without warrants on letters and phones here. People will no doubt always differ on how much of this covert activity was warranted, given the circumstances.

Mr. Nixon parenthetically raised another subject that makes most other issues look relatively unimportant. Speaking of the "tremendous power" held by "any President," Mr. Nixon said that power includes "the power to wage nuclear war." The lightning speed of modern military technology has in effect transferred the warmaking power from Congress, where the Founding Fathers thought they had placed it, to the President.

But Mr. Nixon does not claim unlimited power for the presidency. In answer to Interrogatory 34 he also said, "This is not to say, of course, that any action a President might authorize in the interest of national security would be lawful. The Supreme Court's disapproval of President Truman's seizure of the steel mills is an example." It is also an example of an action that could not be covert.

Thus Mr. Nixon himself confirms rather than contradicts the national rejection of an all-powerful executive whose every word supersedes any other law. In his recommendations to the Senate, he said, "Freedom without security produces anarchy. Security without freedom produces dictatorship. Maintaining the delicate balance between freedom and security has been the genius of the American democracy and the reason it has survived for 200 years."

No doubt at times freedom and security are in conflict. However, the "sovereignty of self-governing people" assumes that in general freedom and security supplement each other, rather than clash. Many countries have neither freedom nor security. The United States means to have both.

THE SAGINAW NEWS

Saginaw, Mich., March 14, 1976

Alas there is a twinge of pity for Richard Nixon.

It is sad that fully a year and a half after he and the nation were traumatized in the learning experience that no president is above the law, Mr. Nixon's perception of the presidency remains unchanged.

It is as if Mr. Nixon is secluded in another world, unaware of time, unwilling to acknowledge any errors, errors fatal to his presidency. This never happened. He was always right. There is no such thing as the Constitution and its meticulously cast checks and balances. There were no lies. Only the event is a lie — an aberration for the rest of us.

Mr. Nixon continues to see the presidency in terms of "sovereignty" with sovereign rights to disregard the law in the name of national security. And there we go again. Government by one-man decree. What a president may do, a private citizen may not do. One may break the laws with impunity, the other may not. Richard Nixon said it. We didn't. He is secure in the Divine Right.

Of course he has said all of this before. And it is simply an opinion. The ex-president has a right to it. There is nothing unlawful about that. Only this time he has reiterated his stance without niceties. No waiting for the Senate Intelligence Committee to tell the public what he has already told it in written replies to 77 questions put to him.

Yes he ordered CIA involvement in Chilean politics. Yes he decided when to call it off. Yes he ordered the FBI infiltration of dissident activists and sometimes violent dissent groups in this country. Yes he was surprised when even J. Edgar Hoover doubted the legality of some of what he wanted done. No he didn't have anything to do with the assassination of Chilean President Allende — who had won office over U.S.-supported and CIA-guided opponents.

And finally, of course, Congress has no right to inquire of the conduct of the office of the presidency. No it has no right to tamper with CIA operations. Yes he would do it all again.

Applying Mr. Nixon's formula, it is quite simple. American presidents can meddle in the affairs of foreign countries in any fashion, at any time — even if it does start a war.

Jerry Ford, for example, could simply have picked up the phone a month ago and ordered a full-scale American invasion of Angola. No need to talk to anybody, even less need to answer to Congress.

It is an insight into the man himself. It is Richard Nixon's view of the imperial presidency. It is nothing of a surprise.

Yet the obstinacy with which he clings to his defense makes it certain Mr. Nixon will remain forever unrepentent over anything that brought him down. Except, perhaps, for ever making tapes. He rages as a Macbeth.

The Washington Star

Washington, D.C., March 16, 1976

Richard Nixon's recent written response to "interrogatory 34" addressed to him by the Senate Select Committee on Intelligence Activities has raised a predictable howl. Asked by the committee whether Presidents may do things "otherwise illegal" for national security reasons, the former President delivered himself of a provocatively candid answer.

Obviously they may do things which if done by private persons would be illegal, says Mr. Nixon. "Certain inherently governmental actions . . . if undertaken *by the sovereign* (emphasis ours) in protection of . . . national security" are lawful. It is "naive" to suppose otherwise, continues Mr. Nixon; "circumstances" determine the legality or illegality of these ultimate presidential actions.

In support of this elastic view of presidential power, Mr. Nixon instances President Roosevelt's controversial detention of West Coast Japanese-Americans during World War II, as well as certain executive actions taken by Abraham Lincoln at the outset of the Civil War — such as paying troops from the federal treasury without specific congressional appropriation.

The pummeling Mr. Nixon has taken as a result of this reply was, as we say, predictable. He has been admonished most emphatically that the framers of the Constitution subscribed to the theory of *popular* sovereignty, not *presidential* sovereignty. As Gouverneur Morris put it, "the people are to be king."

In limited defense of Mr. Nixon — for this pernicious notion of presidential sovereignty does, indeed, invite firm contradiction — it must be said that he does not shrink from rationalizing certain extra-constitutional presidential behavior in which any number of his predecessors indulged without apology. Mr. Nixon, like the lamentable King James I of England, is ever a natural pedant when it comes to constitutional explanations. This trait contributed to his ultimate downfall.

The great question that Mr. Nixon fails to deal with, in his reply to the Senate committee, is whether crises short of war excuse or justify "otherwise illegal" presidential acts as the exigencies of war itself have been held to do. In the *Korematsu* case of 1944, the Supreme Court dealt tardily with the Japanese detention cases, and a majority of the court, led by Mr. Justice Black, endorsed that extraordinary assumption of presidential and legislative power. But at least three justices of that court, including Murphy and Stone, thought the detention of the Nisei flagrantly unconstitutional. And that most distinguished of constitutional scholars, Dr. Edward Corwin, labeled it "the most drastic invasion of the rights of citizens of the United States by their own government that had thus far occurred in the history of our nation." Neither then nor today, that is to say, are students of the Constitution at one on Mr. Roosevelt's exercise of "a broad war-powers delegation from Congress."

But Mr. Nixon's critics, in hurling the slogan of "popular sovereignty" in his teeth, miss an irony. That theory has not restrained the inflated presidency; if anything, it has encouraged Presidents to exceed the law. How many times have defenders of presidential "vigor" told us, in recent years, that since the President uniquely is "elected by all the people," he is mysteriously clothed with implicit popular assent to acts defiant of congressional or judicial check? The "plebiscitory presidency" has fed on popular sovereignty; popular sovereignty, by this alchemy, has been transmuted into presidential sovereignty of just the kind Mr. Nixon defends.

Instead of belaboring Mr. Nixon for so candidly stating the theory on which he and certain predecessors acted, perhaps we ought to thank him for underscoring the theoretical source of Oval Office lawlessness.

Of course, the best answer to Mr. Nixon and his critics is that both forms of "sovereignty," popular and presidential — both when they are effectively one and the same and when they are separate — can be equally mischievous. The real sovereign in our system is the law. It binds Presidents as well as private persons, excesses of majority will no less than constitutional evasions that originate in the White House. Popular sovereignty and presidential sovereignty are close kin, and both may at times be equally foreign to "a government of laws, not of men."

THE DALLAS TIMES HERALD

Dallas, Tex., March 14, 1976

THOUGH THE inference has long been plain that Richard M. Nixon considered himself, as President, above the law, that inference has now been confirmed as fact.

And the confirmation is more than a little frightening.

Defending his intelligence policies in written replies to questions by the Senate Intelligence Committee, the former President said:

"It is quite obvious that there are certain inherently governmental actions which, if undertaken by the sovereign in protection of . . . the nation's security, are lawful, but which if undertaken by private persons are not . . .

"In short, there have been—and will be in the future— circumstances in which presidents may lawfully authorize actions in the interests of security of this country which, if undertaken by other persons or even by the president under different circumstances, would be illegal."

That statement tells us is that the break-in at the Watergate was a most fortunate event for this country. For it set in motion the train of events which eventually revealed what Mr. Nixon has now flatly admitted — his philosophy concerning his right to abrogation of powers suitable, perhaps, to an absolute monarch or a dictator, but not to a president.

The Philadelphia Inquirer

Philadelphia, Pa., March 14, 1976

There is nothing to be gained in further attacks on Richard Nixon for his conduct of the presidency, but anything which helps us understand *why* that conduct was fatally flawed merits attention.

It is instructive, therefore, to read the former President's justification for authorizing covert CIA efforts to prevent the election of Salvador Allende to the presidency of Chile in 1970. In one of his written answers to a series of questions asked by the Senate Intelligence Committee, Mr. Nixon said:

"It is quite obvious that there are certain inherently governmental actions which, if undertaken by the sovereign in protection . . . of the nation's security, are lawful, but which if undertaken by private citizens are not."

The sovereign?

That, as committee Chairman Frank Church observes, is a "pernicious and dangerous" doctrine in defining the powers of the presidency. The President, Sen. Church correctly points out, is not a sovereign who is above the law. He is, on the contrary, the servant of the law and obligated to respect and obey it just like the rest of us.

Had Richard Nixon understood that, and acted accordingly, he would still be President today.

OREGON Journal
AN INDEPENDENT NEWSPAPER

Portland, Ore., March 20, 1976

The monarchial attitude of Richard Nixon was apparent long before he tumbled from grace. Even so his blunt use of the term "sovereign" to describe the presidency as he sees it and his defense of its regal privilege is a head-shaker.

Almost pathetic was Nixon's claim that one set of laws would apply to a king-like president and another set to common citizens.

What better could describe the tragedy of the Nixon administration?

The ex-president's comment on questions put to him by the Senate Intelligence Committee serves as a timely reminder in this election year that it is imperative that the nation re-establish its president as what he always was supposed to be — just the first citizen in a citizens' self-governing democracy.

The Salt Lake Tribune

Salt Lake City, Utah, March 15, 1976

Not many people have ever accused Richard M. Nixon, late the President of the United States, of being a seriously dedicated student of history. And judging from the statements contained in his just-released replies to the Senate Intelligence Committee, not many people ever will.

The former president told the committee that the President of the United States is like a "sovereign" and in that capacity he may break the laws to protect the national security.

Nixon has forgotten, if he every knew, that absolute sovereignty went out the window back in 1215 when the knights of the realm persuaded King John, during a little clambake at Runnymede, to sign the Magna Carta.

That document, generally considered the beginning of modern English constitutional law and, subsequently, one of the building stones of the United States Constitution, slapped some rather severe restrictions on King John's ideas about absolute sovereignity.

The Great Charter told old John his powers were being nipped and that before he took action in some areas he would first have to talk things over with the knights of the realm.

Well, in Mr. Nixon's view, things probably went from bad to worse in the intervening seven and a half centuries. The list of things that the "sovereign" couldn't do without consulting the "peers of the realm" kept growing until they included just about everything. Working even more havoc with notions about the absolute sovereignty, the ranks of the peers of the realm expanded to the point where every Tom, Dick and Harry, along with every Suzy, Sally and Mary, in the country is included.

Nixon's assertion that he was a "sovereign" again demonstrates the correctness of Georg Wilhelm Hegel's statement in the early days of the 19th Century:

"What experience and history teach is this — that people and governments never have learned anything from history, or acted on principles deduced from it."

Mr. Nixon certainly never did, and he amply demonstrated his lack of learning — In spades

The Standard-Times

New Bedford, Mass., March 20, 1976

"It is quite obvious that there are certain inherently governmental actions which, if undertaken by the sovereign in protection of . . . the nation's security, are lawful, but which if undertaken by private persons are not . . . In short, there have been — and will be in the future — circumstances in which presidents may lawfully authorize actions in the interests of the security of this country which, if undertaken by other persons, or even by the president under different circumstances, would be illegal . . ."

—Richard M. Nixon

Both dictionary and precedent may lend some substance to Mr. Nixon's use of the word "sovereign" for president and his contention that the presidential sovereign may break laws to protect national security. Yet in the wake of Watergate, in this 200th anniversary of our break from the "hat'd sovereign," George III of England, both the language and the logic grate upon the spirit.

In such a way as to evoke concern, they fly in the face of the thinking that lies at our roots. In 1628, Sir Edward Coke — whose defense of the supremacy of the common law against the claims of the royal prerogative had a major influence on the development of English law — drafted his bill of liberties that ultimately took the form of the Petition of Right. In his greatest parliamentary hour, he molded the ancient precepts, including Magna Carta, into a charter of liberty limiting the royal prerogative. During debate in the House of Commons on May 17 of that year, Coke declared, "Magna Carta is such a fellow that he will have no sovereign."

In 1798, Charles James Fox — in a toast for which his name was erased from the Privy Council — hailed, "Our sovereign, the people," a sentiment that moved our own Daniel Webster to observe more than four decades later, that ours was "The people's government, made for the people, made by the people, and answerable to the people."

Nixon's reference to the president as a sovereign and his justification of unlawful action in the name of the sovereign raises the hackles. Whether it is no more than insensitive language or simple arrogance, the concept implied would make Coke, Fox, and our Founding Fathers shake their heads and wonder whether somebody was trying to turn the clock back three and half centuries.

Long Island Press

Jamaica, N.Y., March 13, 1976

If there were any serious doubts about the cause of Richard Nixon's political downfall, it has been dispelled by no less an authority than the former president himself.

In a written deposition to the Senate Intelligence Committee that covered a wide variety of intelligence related issues, Mr. Nixon said:

"It is quite obvious that there are certain inherently governmental actions which, if undertaken by the sovereign in protection of the interest of the nation's security, are lawful, but which, undertaken by private persons, are not."

That's a revealing statement, particularly the reference to the President of the United States as a "sovereign" who, in the guise of national security, has rights denied to "private persons."

If this were true, then the uniquely American concept of a democratic society led by an elected president who is beholden to all the people would be meaningless.

In our 200-year-old system there can be no difference between public and private persons. Since George Washington was inaugurated as our first chief executive, we had, until Mr. Nixon took office, a long line of elected leaders who were presidents, not sovereigns. Some, like Abraham Lincoln and Franklin D. Roosevelt, assumed extraordinary powers during time of war, but these were temporary powers given freely by Congress with the consent of the people. When the emergencies were over, the balance of power was promptly and completely restored.

Fortunately for the republic, Mr. Nixon's flirtation with the "sovereign" right of presidents caused his downfall, not that of the system. It was this warped view of the presidency, not the actions of his political critics, that led to the Watergate scandal and that, in turn, forced him from office in disgrace.

Detroit Free Press

Detroit, Mich., March 14, 1976

RICHARD NIXON'S sworn testimony on wiretapping and on CIA involvement in Chile, released this week, reads like a Nixon press conference. There's the old defiance of congressional encroachment on a privileged presidency, the resurrection of ghosts of presidents past to support his views, the self-serving discourses that attempt always to justify, never to repent, the excesses of the Nixon administration.

The former president's monumental gall is capped by the list of recommendations he makes for congressional oversight of intelligence activities, as if the Senate select committee had asked him for his advice instead of an accounting of his activities. .

"Freedom without security produces anarchy," Mr. Nixon declares in presidential tones. "Security without freedom produces dictatorship."

While no one disputes Mr. Nixon's qualifications to speak about anarchy and dictatorship, it is a bit hard to swallow his depiction of the president as a "sovereign" who may do things that would be illegal for any ordinary person. President Ford, when asked for comment, dismissed the whole notion as "foreign to our society."

The Nixonian declarations on wiretapping and Chile also were typical for raising more questions than they answer. Among other things, they contradict the findings of the Senate committee last year and the previous sworn testimony of Secretary of State Henry Kissinger and former CIA Director Richard Helms.

Messrs. Kissinger and Helms had told the Senate committee, for example, that Mr. Nixon had personally ordered the CIA to organize a coup against the elected Chilean government of Marxist Salvador Allende in 1970. Mr. Nixon acknowledges the "direct expenditure of funds" to help Mr. Allende's enemies, but denies ordering a coup attempt.

Someone is lying.

In the matter of the wiretaps, Mr. Nixon contends it was Henry Kissinger who supplied the FBI with the names of potential wiretap targets. Mr. Kissinger, then Mr. Nixon's national security adviser, denies knowing the list was for wiretap purposes.

Someone is lying.

Mr. Nixon says wiretaps were terminated at Mr. Kissinger's recommendation. Mr. Kissinger says he "had no knowledge of when an individual tap was terminated."

Someone is lying.

The truth may be left to a jury to decide when the suit by Morton Halperin, former National Security Council staffer and one of the wiretap victims, goes to trial, possibly ths spring. Halperin attornyes plan to call both Mr. Nixon and Mr. Kissinger to testify.

Determining the truth of the Chilean affair may be somewhat harder, since at this point it's Mr. Nixon's word against that of his former colleagues.

What these statements by a disgraced former president reveal more than anything, however, is not the guilt or innocence of any of the participants in his administration's questionable doings. It is that the abuse of power, when it escapes legal punishment, never really disappears. It has a way of coming back, in one form or another, as a constant, painful, embarrassing reminder of a time when the rule of law in our society was subverted by a government of men.

The Chattanooga Times

Chattanooga, Tenn., March 15, 1976

Without a complete text of the questions asked as well as the answers given, former President Richard Nixon's reply to the Senate Intelligence Committee on the CIA's 1970 involvement in Chilean internal affairs will hold little meaning for the public in general.

His deposition will have to be cross-indexed with the sworn testimony of other participants in the covert planning and his account of actions placed in context of contemporary events to be judged as to their credibility.

It is already apparent, however, that Mr. Nixon's recollections differ sharply from those of Henry Kissinger, then national security adviser in the White House, and other top aides.

Without categorizing any of the several versions which have been given under oath, it is very apparent that they cannot all be totally truthful.

Mr. Nixon's frequent use of the qualifying phrase, "I cannot recall," does bring back his admonition to an aide headed for questioning about particulars on the White House handling of the Watergate scandal. "You can always say, 'I can't remember, or 'To the best of my recollection,' " was in effect the former Chief Executive's advice.

In any event, it is certain that Uncle Sam was up to his suspender buttons in secretive and illegal meddling in the internal affairs of a sovereign nation with which this country was at peace, in the efforts to prevent Dr. Salvador Allende Gossens from becoming president in 1970, and later to encourage a coup to get him out of office.

Mr. Nixon may deny giving specific orders to this effect, but the words of Richard Helms, then head of the CIA, carry a ring of truth on this point. Of a White House conference on the matter, Mr. Helms has said he came away with an "all-inclusive order." He added: "If I ever carried a marshal's baton in my knapsack out of the Oval Office, it was that day."

The allusion fits perfectly the allusion of the "imperial presidency" which existed in the minds of a great many high officials of the day.

ST. LOUIS POST-DISPATCH

St. Louis, Mo., March 12, 1976

When from a long distant past nothing subsists . . . the smell and taste of things remain poised a long time, like souls, ready to remind us . . .

—Marcel Proust

Words, too, and fragments of sentences have that same power to transport us backward in time, to force a fresh recollection of events and a reconsideration of their significance. That is the case with the sworn documents that former President Nixon has sent forth from San Clemente with the intent of dissociating himself from a number of the scandals that characterized his Administration.

"I do not recall," he said, "receiving information while President concerning plans for a military coup in Chile." "I do not remember learning, while President," he said, that the United States intercepted communications to a foreign embassy. "I do not remember being informed," he said, that the CIA opened the mail of American citizens.

These phrases come from an interrogatory furnished by Mr. Nixon to the Senate Intelligence Committee, and the moment they evoke can be dated quite precisely. It is April 30, 1974, when Mr. Nixon surrendered to the House Judiciary Committee a tape made on March 21 of the previous year. Americans then were becoming familiar with the characters—as they existed in the transcripts—of P (for President Nixon), H (for White House Chief of Staff H. R. Haldeman) and D (for White House Counsel John Dean). On that March 21, P, H and D were in the Oval Office discussing ways of thwarting a grand jury investigation of Watergate.

H. *You can say you have forgotten too can't you?*

D. *Sure but you are chancing a very high risk for perjury situation.*

P. *But you can say I don't remember. You can say I can't recall. I can't give you answer to that that I can recall.*

As the Watergate cover-up proceeded, the danger of perjury was never far from the minds of the principals. And perjury now remains the last threat to Mr. Nixon, whose pardon covers only his actions while President. A sworn interrogatory to a Senate committee is a piece of formal testimony to that body, and perjury charges can grow out of any false statements in it.

The words Mr. Nixon used in his interrogatory, however, evoke something more than a discrete moment in time. They recall, too, the mood of Watergate, whose drama consisted, in part, of the tension generated by the conflict of fiction and fact, of Administration statements slowly withering in the face of observable phenomena.

To be sure, this may not occur in the case of the interrogatories, which Mr. Nixon says are based "totally on my present recollection of events." Yet the elements in the present situation are not unfamiliar. Mr. Nixon says he knew nothing, for example, of plans for a coup in Chile. But the Senate committee reported "there is no question that the CIA received a direct instruction from the President in September 15th (1970) to attempt to foment a coup." Mr. Nixon says he did not remember learning "while President" of intercepts of embassy communications, yet those intercepts were publicly disclosed by a former government agent in 1972.

Two conclusions, we think, can be drawn from the foregoing. The first is the need by relevant authorities to scrutinize Mr. Nixon's new statements, which are sworn, in light of the historical record and the testimony of others involved in these events, and after this to take any action that may be indicated. The second is that Americans should be reminded anew of the profound folly of President Ford's pardon of Mr. Nixon, which effectively foreclosed any opportunity for a formal, systematic examination that would have rendered a definitive judgment on his conduct of the presidency.

The FBI's 'Dirty Tricks'

COINTELPRO

FBI campaign against Dr. King revealed. The Federal Bureau of Investigation attempted to discredit Dr. Martin Luther King Jr. in a concerted six-year campaign that included bugging of his hotel rooms and the mailing of a letter the late civil rights leader took to be a suggestion that he commit suicide, the Senate Select Committee on Intelligence revealed Nov. 18, 1975.

According to the committee, King received an anonymously sent tape recording and an accompanying note in November 1964, only 34 days before he was to accept the Nobel Peace Prize. The recording supposedly revealed instances of unsavory behavior King had engaged in. The accompanying, unsigned note read: "King, there is only one thing left for you to do. You know what it is. You have just 34 days in which to do (the exact number has been selected for a specific reason). It has definite practical significance. You are done. There is but one way out for you."

F. A. O. Schwarz 3rd, chief counsel to the committee, said that the panel's staff had established that the tape was produced with the aid of an electronic surveillance device placed by the FBI and that FBI officials had written the note. Moreover, in December 1964, the FBI mailed anonymously a second tape recording, possibly of the same incident, to King's wife, Corretta Scott King, Schwarz said.

Schwarz said staff investigators had discovered an FBI memorandum to the late FBI director, J. Edgar Hoover, from William Sullivan, then the bureau's chief of counterintelligence, recommending that the FBI discredit King by "knocking him off his pedestal." The FBI adopted the plan, Schwarz said.

Although the FBI instituted 16 separate wiretaps and bugged eight hotel rooms, Schwarz said, it never established that King was criminally suspect, a national security risk or an inciter of violence. Moreover, Hoover ordered other FBI officials to rewrite reports showing that King apparently was not a threat to the country.

Officials of the FBI acknowledged in testimony before the committee Nov. 19 that repeated attempts to discredit King and other targets of its counterintelligence program, COINTELPRO, were legally unjustified. James B. Adams, assistant deputy director of the bureau, told the committee that the approximately 25 separate "actions" taken against King in the 1960s had "no statutory basis or justification."

COINTELPRO activities described. In documents and testimony presented to the Senate Select Committee on Intelligence, various activities of the Federal Bureau of Investigation's COINTELPRO program were related. The COINTELPRO operation consisted of surveillance and disruption of groups and individuals considered radicals. Among the FBI's targets, according to information given the committee, were the Ku Klux Klan, the Vietnam Veterans Against the War, the Black Panther Party, and Jane Fonda.

Testimony concerning the KKK was given Dec. 2 by a former FBI informer, Gary Rowe. He testified that the FBI had instructed him to have sexual relations with the wives of as many Klan members as possible, in order to obtain information, and create discord. (An FBI official denied that such instructions had ever been given, although the bureau agent who had been Rowe's superior told the committee that Rowe "couldn't be an angel and be a good informant.") Rowe also accused the FBI of not acting on information he supplied in advance of intended Klan attacks on blacks and civil rights workers.

Another former FBI informer, Mary Jo Cook, gave testimony before the committee Dec. 2 describing her work in infiltrating the Vietnam Veterans Against the War. She said that the FBI told her to gain the confidence of emotionally unstable members of the VVAW by acting as a "big sister" for them.

According to a story in the Dec. 3 *Los Angeles Times,* the Senate committee possessed documents revealing an attempt by the FBI to cripple the Black Panther Party, by aggravating a conflict existing between the Panther Party and another black militant organization called US. FBI field officers were told, in orders sent out by then FBI Director J. Edgar Hoover, "to submit imaginative and hard-hitting counter-intelligence measures" to the head office in a biweekly letter which "should also contain accomplishments obtained during the previous two-week period."

These orders were issued two months before the Jan. 17, 1969 murder of two BPP members, for which two members of C
the US Party were convicted. The Committee also had nine cartoons—some critical of the Panthers, and others of the US Party—which committee sources said the FBI had circulated in an attempt to embitter relations between the two groups. However, an FBI official testified that "none of our programs have contemplated violence".

An article in the Dec. 15 *New York Times* described two FBI memos (in the D
possession of the Senate committee) relating to an attempt to discredit film actress Jane Fonda. The first memo (written by an FBI agent in Los Angeles on June 17, 1970) requested permission from the head office to send a letter to the gossip columnist of *Variety,* the entertainment business newspaper. The letter would say that Jane Fonda, when attending a Black Panther rally on June 13, 1970, encouraged the audience to give money for the purchase of guns by the E
Panthers, and led the audience in a chant containing the words "we will kill Richard Nixon". (Miss Fonda stated that she has never helped raise money for guns, or said that she wanted to kill Nixon.) The second memo contained Hoover's approval of the plan, on the condition that it could not be traced back to the FBI. However, the columnist to whom the letter was supposed to have been sent said that he had no memory of ever having received such a F
letter. The Senate committee lent copies of the two memos and the letter to Fonda for use in her suit against the FBI and other federal agencies.

The FBI also used a letter in an endeavor to discredit a professor of the University of Chicago in 1968, according to FBI documents obtained by the Senate committee Dec. 18. The letter was about Richard Flacks, an assistant professor of sociology who had become somewhat G
well-known by his opposition to the war in Vietnam, his support of the Students for a Democratic Society, and his involvement in student demonstrations. The letter, which was signed by "a concerned alumnus," was sent to the trustees of the university, in the hope that drawing their

attention to Flacks' activities might "discourage Flacks or even result in his ultimate removal from the University of Chicago." According to FBI records, the letter did not have any effect. On May 5, 1969, Flacks was attacked and severely beaten in his office at the University of Chicago. FBI documents given to the committee showed no evidence of complicity of the bureau in the beating.

ACLU scores clemency board report. American Civil Liberties Union officials in a news conference Jan. 6, 1976 contested the claim, made in the final report of the Presidential Clemency Board for Vietnam war resisters, that "history will regard this [presidential clemency] program as a success." The ACLU maintained that the clemency board report vastly under-rated the number of individuals exposed to legal sanctions for war resistance. Having done this, it arrived at a figure for the percentage of persons applying for clemency much higher than was correct, according to the ACLU.

Besides challenging the government figures, ACLU spokesmen accused the Federal Bureau of Investigation of harassing groups seeking amnesty by "gathering information ... without the slightest justification." An FBI spokesman stated that "the FBI did not conduct any investigations of any amnesty groups solely because they advocated amnesty."

Newspaper says FBI backed right-wing terrorist group. A story in the Jan. 11 *San Diego Union* said that the Federal Bureau of Investigation provided weapons and explosives for, and played a role in the formation of, a right-wing terrorist group in California called the Secret Army Organization. Clarence M. Kelley, director of the bureau, acknowledged Jan. 11 that the FBI had maintained an informant within the group, but denied that it had supported any terrorist activities.

The *San Diego Union* story was based on testimony given before a California court in July 1972. A report prepared in June 1975 by the American Civil Liberties Union for the Senate Committee on Intelligence also purported to describe an illegitimate involvement of the FBI with the group. [See Vol. I, pp. 196C2]

The Secret Army Organization operated in San Diego in the early 1970s. Its activities were directed against antiwar protesters and dissidents, and allegedly involved burglaries of homes and offices, bombings, and kidnapping and assassination plots.

FBI support for the terrorist group was set forth in testimony given to a California court by Howard B. Godfrey, a former FBI informant. According to the Jan. 11 account in the *New York Times* of the testimony, Godfrey described his actions as follows: Under instructions from the FBI, he said, he helped found the group. He obtained between $10,000 and $20,000 worth of weapons and explosives from the bureau for use by the group. And on Jan. 6, 1972 he went along in the car from which a member of the group other than himself fired a pistol in an attempt to murder Peter Bohmer, a San Diego professor and radical.

According to sources on the Senate Intelligence Committee, Godfrey took possession of the pistol, and turned it over to the FBI agent to whom he reported, Steven Christiansen. The sources said that Christiansen concealed the gun for half a year while the San Diego police were looking for evidence on the affair. Christiansen was disciplined for his management of the operation, and later resigned from the FBI, according to the committee sources quoted in the *Times'* article.

The ACLU report quoted another FBI informant, John Rasperry, as saying that the FBI had told him to kill Bohmer, but he had not.

FBI rules on the use of informants, according to the *New York Times'* Jan. 11 story, prohibited them from initiating a crime, but did permit them to lead and supply a violent group.

Official Federal Bureau of Investigation papers, released March 28, 1976, revealed that the FBI had burglarized the New York offices of the Socialist Workers Party at least 92 times between 1960 and 1966. The papers had been sought by the leftist party as evidence for its $27 million lawsuit against the FBI.

On most of the occasions, the FBI records showed, nothing had been taken from the SWP offices, but numerous papers had been photographed. The SWP papers photographed included correspondence, records of political contributions, minutes of party meetings and notes on legal strategy of party members facing federal prosecution.

According to the March 29 *New York Times,* the FBI had previously admitted to 238 surreptitious entries, known as "black-bag jobs," involving 14 organizations between 1942 and 1968. The *Times* reported that, according to sources on the Senate Intelligence Committee, the actions against the SWP were not included in the figure of 238.

The *Times* quoted an unidentified FBI source as saying that agents who undertook the burglaries received substantial bonuses. The agents, if arrested, would have had to take personal responsibility for the burglary, without naming the bureau.

Peter Camejo, the SWP candidate for President, March 28 charged that New York City police had afforded the FBI agents protection while they carried out the burglaries. As evidence, he quoted from the released FBI records requests for authorizations for the burglaries saying: "Full security assured," and, "Security set forth at the time of the original authorization remains the same."

FBI sources quoted in the March 29 *Times* story expressed doubt that the FBI would have informed the police in advance of burglaries.

Camejo took issue with FBI director Clarence M. Kelley's statement that the burglaries were undertaken for reasons of national security. He said the information obtained by the FBI had been used "to get SWP members fired from their jobs and to otherwise disrupt the legal political activities of the SWP."

Camejo and SWP congressional candidate Caterino Garza March 28 called for the arrest and prosecution of the individuals responsible for the burglaries. Garza also charged the New York police with "refusing to conduct a serious investigation" into what he said was an assassination attempt against him. Camejo said a rifle bullet had been fired through the window of his apartment building March 16.

The SWP March 29 named three other incidents that, it maintained, the New York police had not investigated thoroughly: bombings of SWP offices in 1973 and 1966, and the throwing of a live grenade at an office in 1969. According to the SWP, two persons were injured in the 1973 bombing.

COINTELPRO targets may be notified. Attorney General Edward H. Levi announced April 1 that he had formed a panel within the justice department to review the actions of the Federal Bureau of Investigation under its counter intelligence program and, in some cases, notify individuals who had been targets of the program.

Notification, Levi said, would be restricted to those individuals who had actually suffered injury as a result of improper FBI actions, and who were not already aware that they had been targets. Individuals notified could seek further information on their cases from the justice department.

Justice department officials estimated that a "few hundred people" would be notified under Levi's guidelines. The April 2 *New York Times* stated that the FBI had carried out 2,370 actions—many involving more than one person—from 1956 to 1972 in 12 separate Cointelpro programs.

In related news, Levi March 30 in a letter to the attorney of columnist Joseph Kraft said that the FBI files on Kraft would be destroyed. The files contained the results of electronic and physical surveillance of Kraft in 1969. According to court and Congressional records, the FBI surveillance had been carried out at the request of then White House counsel John D. Ehrlichman, who sought to determine the source of leaks from the National Security Council.

Black COINTELPRO policy described. Federal Bureau of Investigation documents released April 5, 1976, in reponse to a freedom of information suit, set forth the aims of the FBI in initiating a counterintelligence program directed specifically against black groups.

A letter dated Aug. 25, 1967, which FBI headquarters sent to field offices at the start of the program, said: "The purpose of this new counterintelligence endeavor is to expose, disrupt, misdirect, discredit or otherwise neutralize the activities of black nationalist, hate-type groups, their leadership, spokesmen, membership and supporters, and to counter their propensity for violence and civil disorder."

A telegram that followed the letter, named, among other black groups, the Student Nonviolent Coordinating Committee (SNCC) and the Southern Christian Leadership Conference as having "radical and violence-prone leaders, members and followers."

Security Index

FBI keeps list of security risks. The Federal Bureau of Investigation maintained a current list of U.S. residents it considered potential threats to national security, according to FBI documents released Oct. 22, 1975 by Rep. Robert W. Kastenmeier (D, Wis.), chairman of the Courts, Civil Liberties and Administration of Justice Subcommittee of the Judiciary Committee.

Among the documents made public was one from President Franklin Roosevelt to the late FBI director, J. Edgar Hoover, dated 1939, ordering the FBI to compile a "custodial detention" list of individuals with "Communistic, Fascist, Nazi and other nationalistic background" who were deemed national security risks.

Kastenmeier also released a memorandum from Clarence Kelley, current director of the FBI, stating that the detention list, renamed the "security index" in 1943, had been discontinued, as were "all plans for the apprehension of those listed," when Congress repealed the emergency detention provision of the Internal Security Act in 1971.

Kelley said that the FBI subsequently obtained Justice Department approval to establish a new list of suspected subversives. The new list was to be used by the bureau as an "administrative aid" in watching potential troublemakers during an emergency, "pending legal steps by the President to take further action." As of August, the new list contained the names of 1,294 persons, Kelley said.

The current index, Kelley said, "was reviewed continuously," with some names deleted and others added. Individuals were not included on the list solely because of their opposition to government policies or membership in allegedly subversive organizations, he said. To be placed on the list, Kelley explained, a person must have "exhibited a willingness or capacity of engaging in treason, rebellion, sedition, sabotage, espionage, assassination of government officials, terrorism, guerrilla warfare" or other acts threatening to disrupt operations of the government.

Kelley claimed that past indexes could not be reconstructed since no records had been kept of persons whose names had been entered or deleted. However, Kelley's latter statement was apparently superseded by a report in the *New York Times* Oct. 25 that the bureau had discovered "only within the last several days" an intact file containing most of the names of the 15,000 individuals once included on the defunct security index.

The FBI and the Presidency

Senate committee says FBI offered political services. The staff of the Senate Select Committee on Intelligence issued a report Dec. 3, 1975 accusing the Federal Bureau of Investigation of providing political services for presidents from Roosevelt to Truman.

According to the report, the FBI in 1940 ran "name checks" (checks of its files) and supplied reports on persons opposing the foreign policy of President Roosevelt. In 1949, an investigation by the FBI of the National Lawyers Guild was passed on to President Truman. And in 1956, when President Eisenhower asked for a report on racial tension from the FBI, the report contained information "not only of incidents of violence, but also on the activities of seven governors and congressmen in groups opposing integration, as well as the role of Communists in civil rights lobbying efforts and the N.A.A.C.P.'s [National Association for the Advancement of Colored People] plans to push legislation."

Under the Kennedy administration, the Senate committee report said, Attorney General Robert Kennedy authorized wiretaps on newsmen, as well as on government officials, two lobbyists, and a Congressional staff member.

President Johnson received information from the FBI on seven newsmen, on members of the staff of his 1964 presidential opponent, Barry Goldwater, and on persons opposing his foreign policy, according to the report. The report stated that the FBI also sent to the White House information drawn from wiretaps on civil rights leader Dr. Martin Luther King Jr., at the time of the Democratic National Convention in 1964.

President Nixon, according to the report, had the FBI carry out wiretaps of newsmen and White House officials.

The report left open in several cases the question of whether the activities described of the FBI had been motivated politically, or by a desire to preserve national security, or prevent violence.

Nixon wiretap deposition. In a court deposition released March 10, 1976, former President Richard M. Nixon testified under oath that he ordered telephone wiretaps of 17 government officials and newsmen in 1969 to locate news leaks but that Secretary of State Henry Kissinger, then Nixon's national security adviser, had the responsibility for selecting those to be tapped. The responsibility for carrying out the program lay with then FBI Director J. Edgar Hoover, Nixon said.

The deposition, taken Jan. 15 at Nixon's San Clemente, Calif. house, was filed in U.S. district court in the District of Columbia in a damage suit brought by Morton H. Halperin, a former National Security Council aide and one of the 17 persons tapped. An account of Nixon's testimony had appeared in the *New York Times* Jan. 18. [See Vol. I, pp. 258–261]

In a deposition in the same lawsuit, filed Jan. 12, Kissinger had testified that Nixon had authorized a general program but specifically ordered electronic sur- A veillance on Halperin "and certain others."

(The deposition disclosed Kissinger's practice of having his personal secretaries monitor business telephone calls from his White House office and make summaries of the conversations.)

In other testimony on the topic before the Senate Foreign Relations Committee in July 1973, Kissinger had said he "had no knowledge of when an individual tap B was terminated and I was not involved in termination decisions."

In his deposition, Nixon said, "I, of course, did not select the names myself because I did not know [them]. I told Dr. Kissinger that he should inform Mr. Hoover of any names that he considered to be prime suspects." Nixon explained that this included those who had access to the leaked information and those who "had previous records about being loose in C their talk."

"It was his [Kissinger's] responsibility not to control the program," Nixon testified, "but solely to furnish the information to Mr. Hoover."

Nixon further stated he had no recollection of Halperin's name "coming up" during the discussion in which the program was authorized.

In other points, Nixon said the final decision on removal of a tap was to be made D by himself or Hoover; the material gathered in the taps was shifted from Kissinger to the White House because of the burden of work already on the National Security Council; "there was no political use and no private use" made of the material, "none was intended" and even if there were any misuse of the material it would be difficult to determine whether it was done in "good faith" or not, "whether their motivation was political or E whether their motivation was basically the security of the nation."

In defending the program, Nixon said four previous administrations had engaged in such practices; he had been advised it was legal; a foreign policy mission might "take precedence" over an individual's right to privacy; "had we not been able to conduct our policy with some confidentiality, we could not have made the progress that we have made"; and leaked F information on the secret U.S. bombing in neutral Cambodia "was directly responsible for the deaths of thousands of Americans because it required the discontinuance of a policy that saved American lives."

Haldeman deposition—Another deposition in the same court case, from former Nixon chief of staff H. R. Haldeman, was filed March 11.

In the 1974 impeachment hearings, it G had been disclosed that Haldeman had learned from the Halperin tap that former Defense Secretary Clark M. Clifford was preparing an anti-Nixon article and had suggested a rebuttal.

Queried in the deposition about political use of information from a national security wiretap, Haldeman testified he found nothing improper in such practice and the question of legality had not occurred to him at the time.

Purchasing Probe

FBI accused of attempt to 'squelch' witness. The House Select Committee on Intelligence had requested Attorney General Edward Levi to determine the purpose of an interview which two agents of the Federal Bureau of Investigation conducted with a committee witness, the *Washington Post* reported Jan. 1. The witness, Martin L. Kaiser, had appeared before the committee in connection with an investigation of possible improprieties in FBI purchasing.

Kaiser testified Oct. 9, 1975, that wiretap equipment which he supplied to the FBI had been marked up an average of 30% by an intermediary company, the U.S. Recording Co. of Washington, D.C., through which he was required to deal. (Committee investigators found markups ranging from 12 to 80%.) An FBI spokesman said that the use of an intermediary was required in order to preserve the confidentiality of the transactions.

Committee investigators discovered that, in the words of committee staff director A. Searle Field, "a close relationship [existed] between the president of U.S. Recording and the FBI official in charge of purchasing until 1972."

Committee suspicions that the FBI may have sought to squelch Kaiser were raised by a statement which he made after a six-hour interview with two FBI agents on Dec. 23, 1975. In it he said that a statement which the committee had prepared for him on the basis of his testimony had been "grossly inaccurate,"

Subsequently, Kaiser gave the committee a deposition stating that he stood by his Oct. 9 testimony. The deposition contained a description of his interview by the FBI agents, in which he said that at the end of six hours, "I had the two of them standing behind me now, over my shoulder, and this was the close of the day, the close of the statement and they kept pressuring me."

An FBI spokesman Dec. 31 denied that there had been any attempt to "influence or coerce anyone."

FBI purchasing investigation renewed, expanded. The *New York Times,* citing senior justice department officials, reported March 20 and 23 that the justice department had rejected a Federal Bureau of Investigation internal investigation of its purchasing activities, and ordered the bureau to open a new investigation. The new probe, while still concentrating on retired FBI administrative head John P. Mohr and the U.S. Recording Co. (through which the FBI obtained electronic equipment), would be expanded to cover all FBI purchasing.

Foreign Penetration

Foreign intelligence activity in U.S. reported. The *New York Times* March 10, 1976 reported that, according to an unidentified former intelligence official, the Federal Bureau of Investigation had possibly been "penetrated" on at least three occasions since World War II.

The *Times'* source admitted the evidence was circumstantial and had not led to prosecution of any FBI employe. He maintained, however, that in one case there was extremely good reason to believe that an FBI agent had been working for Soviet intelligence.

In that case, the source said, the agent had been observed going through typical procedures for contacting a Soviet "control" agent. However, the agent had recognized one of the FBI men watching him; he had then, the source said, ended his putative relationship with the Soviet agents and further investigation proved fruitless.

(FBI Director Clarence M. Kelley, in an interview published in the April 5 *U.S. News and World Report* said, "Exhaustive investigation has never revealed that a hostile foreign intelligence service has ever successfully recruited or operated an employe of the FBI.")

The *Times* Feb. 27 reported that, according to unidentified "well-informed" sources, the FBI had over the past 10 years largely abandoned efforts to uncover foreign covert agents. The sources explained this as partly owing to former FBI Director J. Edgar Hoover's preference to use the bureau's resources for the investigation of domestic radical organizations.

The change in policy, one of the sources said, had made the U.S. a "happy hunting ground [for foreign spies] since 1967."

The FBI Feb. 27 contested the *Times'* report, maintaining that counterintelligence continued as "one of the FBI's highest priorities."

Senate FBI Report

Senate panel hits domestic spying, asks curbs. The Senate Select Committee on Intelligence charged April 28 that the FBI and other U.S. agencies had conducted investigations—often employing "illegal or improper" methods—of a vast number of Americans.

The committee urged that the activities of the intelligence agencies be governed by statutory rules, and offered 96 recommendations as a basis for legislation. The proposals—all dealing with domestic intelligence—were contained in the second volume of the committee's final report.

The domestic investigations, the report maintained, were sometimes justified on a "guilty until proven innocent" basis. It said that this resulted in the recording of intimate details of the lives of persons engaged merely in "legal and peaceful political activites."

The main proposals made by the committee were:

- That domestic intelligence investigations be limited to cases in which there were specific grounds to believe that terrorist or hostile espionage activities had been committed or were about to be committed. Political views or activities, the committee stressed, would not be grounds for an investigation. Continuation of a preliminary investigation beyond 30 days, or of a full investigation beyond a year would require approval by the Attorney General or his designee.
- That domestic intelligence investigations be conducted (with a few narrow exceptions) only by the FBI.
- That judicial warrants be required for use of electronic surveillance, mail-opening or unauthorized entry.

The committee also called for closer supervision and review of the FBI by the attorney general, vigorous oversight of the FBI and other agencies by a permanent Senate Intelligence Committee, and an eight-year maximum term for the head of the FBI.

The report maintained that abuses by the intelligence agencies stemmed from the failure of the "constitutional system of checks and balances." The executive branch, Congress and the courts all shared blame for abdicating their responsibilities, the report said.

The report's documentation of domestic intelligence activities covered the following areas:

Size of intelligence operations. The report said that FBI headquarters alone had opened more than 500,000 domestic intelligence files, and that additional files had been developed at FBI field offices. In one year—1972—the FBI had opened 65,000 files, the report said, noting that these files usually contained information on more than one individual or group.

Nearly a quarter of a million letters were opened in the U.S. by the Central Intelligence Agency between 1953 and 1973, the report said. From their contents, the CIA compiled an index of nearly 1.5 million names.

Under a secret agreement with three U.S. telegraph companies, the panel found, the National Security Agency obtained millions of telegrams sent to, from or through the U.S. And, it said, the Army developed files on an estimated 100,000 citizens between the mid 1960s and 1971.

The IRS, between 1969 and 1973, created intelligence files on more than 11,000 individuals or groups and initiated tax investigations for political reasons, the report said. It also noted that an FBI list of persons to be interned in the event of a "national emergency" at one time numbered at least 26,000 persons.

Targets of investigations. The report said that investigations had been conducted not only against individuals and political groups on the right and left but also against religious groups, establishment politicians, advocates of nonviolence and racial harmony and supporters of women's rights.

Specific targets named in the report included Dr. Martin Luther King Jr., the National Association for the Advancement of Colored People, the Socialist Workers Party, the John Birch Society, the Conservative American Christian Action Council, the late Adlai E. Stevenson, who was twice a Democratic nominee for president, and former Supreme Court Justice William O. Douglas. In 1970, the FBI had ordered investigations of every member of the Students for a Democratic Society, and of all black student groups "regardless of their past or present involvement in disorders," the report said.

Investigations had been continued for decades, the report found, even when no criminal acts were uncovered. Thus, the report noted, an investigation of the NAACP for possible connections with the Communist Party lasted for 25 years, even though an initial report determined that the organization had a "strong tendency" to avoid alignment with communist activities.

The report argued that the "guilty until proven innocent" theory had held sway in the case of an FBI investigation of an adviser to the Rev. Dr. King. In support of this contention, it quoted an FBI headquarters memo:

"The bureau does not agree with the expressed belief of the field office that ____ is not sympathetic to the [Communist] party cause. While there may not be any evidence that ____ is a Communist, neither is there any substantial evidence that ____ is anti-Communist."

The report further stated that administrations of presidents from Franklin D. Roosevelt to Richard M. Nixon had received information on political opponents, or other services, from the intelligence agencies.

Covert activity. The report detailed a number of activities—chiefly engaged in by the FBI under COINTELPRO [its counterintelligence program]—aimed at disrupting, discrediting or neutralizing groups and individuals. Some tactics employed by the FBI, the report said, were "indisputably degrading to a free society."

The report recounted material previously disclosed by the committee on the FBI's campaign against Dr. King. The FBI's policy was summarized as a campaign against "a nonviolent man [who] was to be secretly attacked and destroyed as insurance against his abandoning nonviolence." [See Vol. I, pp. 195, 200, 223, 225, 235, 257]

Among the FBI tactics noted in the report were:

- Anonymously attacking a target's political views in an attempt to have his employer fire him.
- Attempting to destroy marriages by mailing anonymous letters to the spouses of targets.
- Falsely and anonymously naming as government informers members of groups known to be violent. Expulsion from the group or physical harm for the person so labeled could result from the action, the report observed.
- Sending an anonymous letter to the captain of a Chicago street gang, intended to "intensify . . . animosity" between the gang and the Black Panther Party, and possibly provoke "retaliatory action."

The report stated that the FBI and the CIA, in collecting information, had often adopted "illegal and improper means." Both the FBI and the CIA had conducted warrantless break-ins the report said. In the 1960s, it said, hundreds of break-ins had been conducted, some to install microphones, others to steal documents.

The report noted also that government informants attached to violent groups sometimes themselves had to engage in violence. To illustrate this, the report cited the case of an FBI informer, placed in the Ku Klux Klan, who had participated in assaults on blacks.

Media and political uses of intelligence. Information gathered from intelligence investigations was used by the FBI in attempts to discredit target groups or individuals, the report said. FBI field offices, the report noted, were specifically asked to collect data on the "scurrilous and depraved nature of many of the characters, activities, habits and living conditions representative of New Left adherents" for prompt relay to the news media.

The report observed that the FBI also, through a relationship with the chairman of the board of a national magazine, had sought to influence articles relating to the FBI published in that magazine. One article, the report said, was "squelched," another was "postponed" and in the case of a third, publication was "forestalled."

Besides using the media to discredit particular targets, the report faulted the FBI for distorting data in its public statements in ways calculated to influence or justify government policy. The report cited two cases of this, both involving overstatement of communist influence. One case involved former director J. Edgar Hoover's congressional testimony on forces behind the civil rights movement; the other concerned the bureau's reports on Vietnam war demonstrators.

Responsibility for abuses. The report charged that senior officials in the executive branch, and particularly the attorney general, had "virtually abdicated their constitutional responsibility to oversee and set standards for intelligence activity." Congress also had often failed to exercise adequate oversight, the report said.

The report noted that oversight had failed in some instances, however, because the intelligence agencies had concealed, or only partially disclosed, the activities in which they were engaged.

It charged that pressure exerted on the intelligence agencies by executive officials for results on specific problems was itself responsible for excesses and improprieties. The report quoted testimony given to the committee by senior intelligence officials, to the effect that the intelligence agencies had been concerned only with the "flap potential" that exposure of their activities might have. The illegality or unconstitutionality of the activities had never been suggested as a reason for not doing them, according to the testimony. One committee witness explained that considerations of legality had been overridden by the perceptions of what was necessary for the "greater good, the national security."

Cost. Besides the number of persons affected, another yardstick of the excesses of the domestic intelligence programs was their dollar cost, the report said. It observed that the FBI had budgeted $7 million in fiscal 1976 for domestic security informants, more than twice the amount allocated to informants on organized crime. For the same period, the FBI total budget for domestic security and counterintelligence programs totalled at least $80 million, the report said.

The FBI domestic security programs were also extremely wasteful, the report argued, when measured by their court successes. The FBI, the report said, launched over half a million investigations between 1960 and 1974 of persons or groups deemed "subversive." The investigations, the report said, were primarily justified on the basis of federal laws outlawing planning or advocating action to overthrow the government. Yet, the report noted, not a single prosecution had been brought under those laws since 1957.

The report also cited a General Accounting Office study of 17,528 FBI domestic intelligence investigations in 1974. Only 1.3% of the investigations, the report said, resulted in convictions.

The basic lesson to be drawn from the report, the committee held, was that the FBI should restrict its actions "to investigating conduct rather than ideas or associations." By doing so, the agency could avoid the "wasteful dispersion of resources" that had plagued its past investigation, the report said. More importantly, such a change in policy was necessary to safeguard "the constitutional rights of Americans," the report argued.

Excerpts from the Senate Select Committee's Report on Domestic Intelligence

Conclusions

A The findings which have emerged from our investigation convince us that the government's domestic intelligence policies and practices require fundamental reform. We have attempted to set out the basic facts; now it is time for Congress to turn its attention to legislating restraints upon intelligence activities which may endanger the constitutional rights of Americans.

The committee's fundamental conclusion is that intelligence activities have undermined the constitutional rights of citizens and that they have done so primarily because checks and balances designed by the framers of the Constitution to assure accountability have not been applied. . . .

The three main departures in the intelligence field from the constitutional plan for controlling abuse of
B power have been:

(a) Excessive Executive Power. In a sense the growth of domestic intelligence activities mirrored the growth of presidential power generally. But more than any other activity, more even than exercise of the war power, intelligence activities have been left to the control of the executive.

For decades Congress and the courts as well as the press and the public have accepted the notion that the control of intelligence activities was the exclusive prerogative of the chief executive and his surrogates. The exercise of this power was not questioned or even inquired into by outsiders. Indeed, at times the power was seen as flowing not from the law, but as inherent in
C the presidency. Whatever the theory, the fact was that intelligence activities were essentially exempted from the normal system of checks and balances.

Such executive power, not founded in law or checked by Congress or the courts, contained the seeds of abuse and its growth was to be expected.

(b) Excessive Secrecy. Abuse thrives on secrecy. Obviously, public disclosure of matters such as the names of intelligence agents or the technological details of collection methods is inappropriate. But in the field of intelligence, secrecy has been extended to inhibit review of the basic programs and practices themselves.

Those within the executive branch and the Congress
D who would exercise their responsibilities widely must be fully informed. The American public, as well, should know enough about intelligence activities to be able to apply its good sense to the underlying issues of policy and morality.

Knowledge is the key to control. Secrecy should no longer be allowed to shield the existence of constitutional, legal and moral problems from the scrutiny of all three branches of government or from the American people themselves.

(c) Avoidance of the Rule of Law. Lawlessness by government breeds corrosive cynicism among the people and erodes the trust upon which government depends.

Here, there is no sovereign who stands above the
E law. Each of us, from presidents to the most disadvantaged citizen, must obey the law.

As intelligence operations developed, however, rationalizations were fashioned to immunize them from the restraints of the Bill of Rights and the specific prohibitions of the criminal code. The experience of our investigation leads us to conclude that such rationalizations are a dangerous delusion.

Although our recommendations are numerous and detailed, they flow naturally from our basic conclusion. Excessive intelligence activity which undermines individual rights must end. The system for controlling intelligence must be brought back within the constitutional scheme. . . .

F The constitutional amendments protecting speech and assembly and individual privacy seek to preserve values at the core of our heritage and vital to our future. The Bill of Rights, and the Supreme Court's decisions interpreting it suggest three principles which we have followed:

(1) Governmental action which directly infringes [upon] the rights of free speech and association must be prohibited. The First Amendment recognizes that even if useful to a proper end, certain governmental actions are simply too dangerous to permit at all. It commands that "Congress shall make *no* law" abridging freedom of speech or assembly.

(2) The Supreme Court, in interpreting that command, has required that any governmental action
G which has a collateral (rather than direct) impact upon the rights of speech and assembly is permissible only if it meets two tests. First, the action must be undertaken only to fulfill a compelling governmental need, and second, the government must use the least restrictive means to meet that need. . . .

(3) Procedural safeguards . . . must be adopted along with substantive restraints. For example, while the Fourth Amendment prohibits only "unreasonable" searches and seizures, it requires a procedural check for reasonableness—the obtaining of a judicial warrant upon probable cause from a neutral magistrate. Our proposed procedural checks range from judicial review of intelligence activity before or after the fact, to formal and high level executive branch approval, to greater disclosure and more effective congressional oversight.

The committee believes that its recommendations should be embodied in a comprehensive legislative charter defining and controlling the domestic security activities of the federal government. Accordingly, Part I of the recommendations provides that intelligence agencies must be made subject to the rule of law. In addition, Part I makes [it] clear that no theory, of "inherent constitutional authority" or otherwise, can justify the violation of any statute.

Starting from the conclusion, based upon our record, that the Constitution and our fundamental values require a substantial curtailment of the scope of domestic surveillance, we deal after Part I with five basic questions."

1. Which agencies should conduct domestic security investigations?

The FBI should be primarily responsible for such investigations. Under the minimization principle, and to facilitate the control of domestic intelligence operations, only one agency should be involved in investigative activities which, even when limited as we propose, could give rise to abuse. Accordingly, Part II of these recommendations reflects the committee's position that foreign intelligence agencies (the CIA, NSA, and the military agencies) should be precluded from domestic security activity in the U.S. Moreover, they should only become involved in matters involving the rights of Americans abroad where it is impractical to use the FBI, or where in the course of their lawful foreign intelligence operations they inadvertently collect information relevant to domestic security investigations. In Part III the committee recommends that non-intelligence agencies such as the Internal Revenue Service and the Post Office be required, in the course of any incidental involvement in domestic security investigations, to protect the privacy which citizens expect of first class mail and tax records entrusted to those agencies.

2. When should an American be the subject of an investigation at all; and when can particularly intrusive covert techniques, such as electronic surveillance or informants, be used?

In Part IV, which deals with the FBI, the committee's recommendations seek to prevent the excessively broad, ill-defined and open ended investigations shown to have been conducted over the past four decades. We attempt to change the focus of investigations from constitutionally protected advocacy and association to dangerous conduct. . . .

3. Who should be accountable within the executive branch for ensuring that intelligence agencies comply with the law and for the investigation of alleged abuses by employees of those agencies?

In Parts V and VI, the committee recommends that these responsibilities fall initially upon the agency heads, their general counsel and inspectors general, but ultimately upon the attorney general. The information necessary for control must be made available to those responsible for control, oversight and review; and their responsibilities must be made clear, formal, and fixed.

4. What is the appropriate role of the courts?

In Part VII, the committee recommends the enactment of a comprehensive civil remedy providing the courts with jurisdiction to entertain legitimate complaints by citizens injured by unconstitutional or illegal activities of intelligence agencies. Part VIII suggests that criminal penalties should attach in cases of gross abuse. In addition, Part IV provides for judicial warrants before certain intrusive techniques can be used.

5. What is the appropriate role of Congress?

In Part XII the committee reiterates its position that the Senate create a permanent intelligence oversight committee.

The recommendations deal with numerous ther issues such as the proposed repeal or amendment of the Smith Act, the proposed modernization of the Espionage Act to cover modern forms of espionage seriously detrimental to the national interest, the use of the GAO [General Accounting Office] to assist Congressional oversight of the intelligence community, and remedial measures for past victims of improper intelligence activity. . . .

Recommendations

Part I

Intelligence Agencies Are Subject to the Rule of Law

Establishing a legal framework for agencies engaged in domestic security investigations is the most fundamental reform needed to end a long history of violating and ignoring the law. . . . The legal framework can be created by a two-stage process of enabling legislation and administrative regulations promulgated to implement the legislation. . . Statutes enacted pursuant to these recommendations should provide the exclusive legal authority for domestic security activities.

1. There is no inherent constitutional authority for the president or any intelligence agency to violate the law.

2. It is the intent of the committee that statutes implementing these recommendations provide the exclusive legal authority for federal domestic security activities.

(a) No intelligence agency may engage in such activities unless authorized by statute, nor may it permit its employees, informants, or other covert human sources to engage in such activities. . .

(b) No executive director or order may be issued which would conflict with such statutes.

3. In authorizing intelligence agencies to engage in certain activities, it is not intended that such authority empower agencies, their informants, or covert human sources to violate any prohibition enacted pursuant to these recommendations or contained in the Constitution or in any other law.

Part II

United States Foreign and Military Agencies Should Be Precluded from Domestic Security Activities

Part IV of these recommendations centralizes domestic security investigations within the FBI. Past abuses also make it necessary that the Central Intelligence Agency, the National Security Agency, the Defense Intelligence Agency, and the military departments be precluded expressly, except as specifically provided herein, from investigative activity which is conducted within the U.S. Their activities abroad should also be controlled as provided herein to minimize their impact on the rights of Americans. . . .

The Central Intelligence Agency

4. To supplement the prohibitions in the 1947 National Security Act against the CIA exercising "police, subpoena, law enforcement powers or internal security functions," the CIA should be prohibited from conducting domestic security activities within the U.S. except as specifically permitted by these recommendations.

5. The director of central intelligence should be made responsible for "coordinating" the protection of sources and methods of the intelligence community. As head of the CIA, the director should also be responsible in the first instance for the security of CIA facilities, personnel, operations, and information. Neither function, however, authorizes the director . . . to violate any federal or state law. . . .

6. The CIA should not conduct electronic surveillance, unauthorized entry, or mail opening within the U.S. for any purpose.

7. The CIA should not employ physical surveillance, infiltration of groups or any other covert techniques against Americans within the U.S. except:

(a) Physical surveillance of persons on the grounds of CIA installations;

(b) Physical surveillance during a preliminary investigation of allegations an e nployee is a security risk for a limited period outside of CIA installations. Such surveillance should be conducted only upon written authorization of the director of central intelligence and should be limited to the subject of the investigation. . . ;

(c) Confidential inquiries, during a preliminary investigation of allegations an employee is a security risk, of outside sources concerning medical or financial information about the subject which is relevant to those allegations;

(d) The use of identification which does not reveal

CIA or government affiliation, in background and other security investigations permitted the CIA by these recommendations, and the conduct of checks, which do not reveal CIA or government affiliation for the purpose of judging the effectiveness of cover operations, upon the written authorization of the director of central intelligence;

(e) In exceptional cases, the placement or recruitment of agents within an unwitting domestic group solely for the purpose of preparing them for assignments abroad and only for as long as is necessary to accomplish that purpose. This should take place only if the director of central intelligence makes a written finding that it is essential for foreign intelligence collection of vital importance to the U.S., and the attorney general makes a written finding that the operation will be conducted under procedures designed to prevent misuse of the undisclosed participation or of any information obtained therefrom. In the case of any such action, no information received by CIA from the agent as a result of his position in the group should be disseminated outside the CIA unless it indicates felonious criminal conduct or threat of death or serious bodily harm, in which case dissemination should be permitted to an appropriate official agency if approved by the attorney general.

8. The CIA should not collect information within the U.S. concerning Americans except:

(a) Information concerning CIA employees, CIA contractors and their employes, or applicants for such employment or contracting;

(b) Information concerning individuals or organizations providing, or offering to provide, assistance to the CIA;

(c) Information concerning individuals or organizations being considered by the CIA as potential sources of information or assistance,

(d) Visitors to CIA facilities,

(e) Persons otherwise in the immediate vicinity of sensitive CIA sites; or

(f) Persons who give their informed written consent to such collection.

In (a), (b), and (c) above, information should be collected only if necessary for the purpose of determining the person's fitness for employment, contracting or assistance. If, in the course of such collection, information is obtained which indicates criminal activity, it should be transmitted to the FBI or other appropriate agency. When an American's relationship with the CIA is prospective, information should only be collected if there is a bona fide expectation the person might be used by the CIA.

9. The CIA should not collect information abroad concerning Americans except:

(a) Information concerning Americans which it is permitted to collect within the U.S.;

(b) At the request of the Justice Department as part of criminal investigations or an investigation of an American for suspected terrorist, or hostile foreign intelligence activities or security leak or security risk investigations which the FBI has opened pursuant to Part IV of those recommendations and which is conducted consistently with recommendations contained in Part IV.

10. The CIA should be able to transmit to the FBI or other appropriate agencies information concerning Americans acquired as the incidental byproduct of otherwise permissible foreign intelligence and counterintelligence operations, whenever such information indicates any activity in violation of American law.

11. The CIA may employ covert techniques abroad against Americans:

(a) Under circumstances in which the CIA could use covert techniques against Americans within the United States; or

(b) When collecting information as part of Justice Department investigation, in which case the CIA may use particular covert techniques under the standards and procedures and approvals applicable to its use against Americans within the U.S. by the FBI (see Part IV); or

(c) To the extent necessary to identify persons known or suspected to be Americans who come in contact with foreigners the CIA is investigating.

12. The CIA should not use in experimentation on human subjects, any drug, device or procedure which is designed or intended to harm, or is reasonably likely to harm, the physical or mental health of the human subject, except with the informed written consent, witnessed by a disinterested third party, of each human subject, and in accordance with the guidelines issued by the National Commission for the Protection of Human Subjects for Biomedical and Behavioral Research. The jurisdiction of the commission should be amended to include the Central Intelligence Agency and other intelligence agencies of the U.S. . . . .

13. Any CIA activity engaged in pursuant to recommendations 7, 8, 9, 10, or 11 should be subject to periodic review and certification of compliance with the Constitution, applicable statutes, agency regulations and executive orders by:

(a) The inspector general of the CIA;

(b) The general counsel of the CIA in coordination with the director of central intelligence;

(c) The attorney general; and

(d) The oversight committee recommended in Part XII.

All such certifications should be available for review by congressional oversight committees. . . .

The National Security Agency

14. NSA should not engage in domestic security activities. Its functions should be limited in a precisely drawn legislative charter to the collection of foreign intelligence from foreign communications.

15. NSA should take all practicable measures consistent with its foreign intelligence mission to eliminate or minimize the interception, selection, and monitoring of communications of Americans from the foreign communications.

16. NSA should not be permitted to select for monitoring any communication to, from, or about an American without his consent, except for the purpose of obtaining information about hostile foreign intelligence or terrorist activities, and then only if a warrant approving such monitoring is obtained in accordance with procedures similar to those contained in Title III of the Omnibus Crime Control and Safe Streets Act of 1968. . . .

17. Any personally identifiable information about an American which NSA incidentally acquires, other than pursuant to a warrant, should not be disseminated without the consent of the American, but should be destroyed as promptly as possible, unless it indicates:

(a) Hostile foreign intelligence or terrorist activities; or

(b) Felonious criminal conduct for which a warrant might be obtained pursuant to Title III of the Omnibus Crime Control and Safe Streets Act of 1968; or

(c) A threat of death or serious bodily harm.

If dissemination is permitted, by *(a)*, *(b)* and *(c)* above, it must only be made to an appropriate official and after approval by the attorney general. . . .

18. NSA should not request from any commercial carrier any communication which it could not otherwise obtain pursuant to these recommendations. . . .

19. The office of security at NSA should be permitted to collect background information on present or prospective employees or contractors of NSA, solely for the purpose of determining their fitness for employment. With respect to security risks or the security of its installations, NSA should be permitted to conduct physical surveillances, consistent with such surveillances as the CIA is permitted to conduct, in similar circumstances, by these recommendations. . . .

The Military Intelligence Agencies

20. Except as specifically provided herein, the Department of Defense should not engage in domestic security activities. Its functions, as they relate to the activities of the foreign intelligence community, should be limited in a precisely drawn legislative charter to the conduct of foreign intelligence and foreign counter-intelligence activities and tactical military intelligence activities abroad, and production, analysis, and dissemination of departmental intelligence.

21. In addition to its foreign intelligence responsibility, the Department of Defense has a responsibility to investigate its personnel in order to protect the security of its installations and property, to ensure order and discipline within its ranks, and to conduct other limited investigations once dispatched by the president to suppress a civil disorder. A legislative charter should define precisely—in a manner which is not inconsistent with these recommendations—the authorized scope and purpose of any investigations undertaken by the Department of Defense to satisfy these responsibilities.

22. No agency of the Department of Defense should conduct investigations of violations of criminal law or otherwise perform any law enforcement or domestic security functions within the U.S., except on military bases or concerning military personnel, to enforce the Uniform Code of Military Justice.

23. The Department of Defense should not be permitted to conduct investigations of Americans on the theory that the information derived therefrom might be useful in potential civil disorders. The Army should be permitted to gather information about geography, logistical matters, or the identity of local officials which is necessary to the positioning, support, and use of troops in an area where troops are likely to be deployed by the president in connection with a civil disturbance. The Army should be permitted to investigate Americans involved in such disturbances after troops have been deployed to the site of a civil disorder, (i) to the extent necessary to fulfill the military mission, and (ii) to the extent the information cannot be obtained from the FBI. . . .

A

24. Appropriate agencies of the Department of Defense should be permitted to collect background information on their present or prospective employees or contractors. With respect to security risks or the security of its installations, the Department of Defense should be permitted to conduct physical surveillance consistent with such surveillances as the CIA is permitted to conduct, in similar circumstances, by these recommendations.

25. Except as provided in 27 below, the Department of Defense should not direct any covert technique (e.g., electronic surveillance, informants, etc.) at American civilians.

B

26. The Department of Defense should be permitted to conduct abroad preventive intelligence investigations of unaffiliated Americans, as described in Part IV below, provided such investigations are first approved by the FBI. Such investigations by the Department of Defense, including the use of covert techniques, should ordinarily be conducted in a manner consistent with the recommendations pertaining to the FBI, contained in Part IV; however, in overseas locations, where U.S. military forces constitute the governing power, or where U.S. military forces are engaged in hostilities, circumstances may require greater latitude to conduct such investigations.

C

Part III

Non-Intelligence Agencies Should Be Barred from Domestic Security Activity

The Internal Revenue Service

27. The IRS should not, on behalf of any intelligence agency or for its own use, collect any information about the activities of Americans except for the purposes of enforcing the tax laws.

28. IRS should not select any person or group for tax investigation on the basis of political activity or for any other reason not relevant to enforcement of the tax laws.

D

29. Any program of intelligence investigation relating to domestic security in which targets are selected by both tax and non-tax criteria should only be initiated:

(a) Upon the written request of the attorney general or the secretary of the Treasury, specifying the nature of the requested program and the need therefore; and

(b) After the written certification by the commissioner of the IRS that procedures have been developed which are sufficient to prevent the infringement of the constitutional rights of Americans; and

(c) With congressional oversight committees being kept continually advised of the nature and extent of such programs. . . .

E

30. No intelligence agency should request from the Internal Revenue Service tax returns or tax-related information except under the statutes and regulations controlling such disclosures. . . .

31. All requests from an intelligence agency to the IRS for tax returns and tax-related information should be in writing, and signed by the head of the intelligence agency making the request, or his designee. Copies of such requests should be filed with the attorney general. Each request should include a clear statement of:

(a) The purpose for which disclosure is sought;

F

(b) Facts sufficient to establish that the requested information is needed by the requesting agency for the performance of an authorized and lawful function;

(c) The uses which the requesting agency intends to make of the information;

(d) The extent of the disclosures sought;

(e) Agreement by the requesting agency not to use the documents or information for any purpose other than that stated in the request; and

(f) Agreement by the requesting agency that the information will not be disclosed to any other agency or person except in accordance with the law.

G

32. IRS should not release tax returns or tax-related information to any intelligence agency unless it has received a request satisfying the requirements of recommendation 31, and the commissioner of internal revenue has approved the request in writing.

33. IRS should maintain a record of all such requests and responses thereto for a period of twenty years.

34. No intelligence agency should use the information supplied to it by the IRS pursuant to a request of the agency except as stated in a proper request for disclosure.

35. All requests for information sought by the FBI should be filed by the Department of Justice. Such requests should be signed by the attorney general or his designee, following a determination by the department that the request is proper under the applicable statutes and regulations. . . .

The Post Office

36. The Post Office should not permit the FBI or any intelligence agency to inspect markings or addresses on first class mail, nor should the Post Office itself inspect markings or addresses on behalf of the FBI or any intelligence agency, on first class mail, except upon the written approval of the attorney general or his designee. Where one of the correspondents is an American, the attorney general or his designee should only approve such inspection for domestic security purposes upon a written finding that it is necessary to a criminal investigation or a preventive intelligence investigation of terrorist activity or hostile foreign intelligence activity.

37. The Post Office should not transfer the custody of any first class mail to any agency except the Department of Justice. Such mail should not be transferred or opened except upon a judicial search warrant.

(a) In the case of mail where one of the correspondents is an American, the judge must find that there is probable cause to believe that the mail contains evidence of a crime.

(b) In the case of mail where both parties are foreigners:

(1) The judge must find that there is probable cause to believe that both parties to such correspondence are foreigners, and one of the correspondents is an officer, employee or conscious agent of a foreign power; and

(2) The attorney general must certify that the mail opening is likely to reveal information necessary either (i) to the protection of the nation against actual or potential attack or other hostile acts of force of a foreign power; (ii) to obtain foreign intelligence information deemed essential to the security of the U.S.; or (iii) to protect national security information against hostile foreign intelligence activity. . . .

Part IV

Federal Domestic Security Activities Should Be Limited and Controlled to Prevent Abuses Without Hampering Criminal Investigations or Investigations of Foreign Espionage

The recommendations contained in this part are designed to accomplish two principal objectives: (1) prohibit improper intelligence activities and (2) define the limited domestic security investigations which should be permitted. . . .

38. All domestic security investigative activity, including the use of covert techniques, should be centralized within the Federal Bureau of Investigation, except those investigations by the Secret Service designed to protect the life of the president or other Secret Service protectees. Such investigations and the use of covert techniques in those investigations should be centralized within the Secret Service.

39. All domestic security activities of the federal government and all other intelligence agency activities covered by the domestic intelligence recommendations should be subject to Justice Department oversight to assure compliance with the Constitution and laws of the U.S.

40. The FBI should be prohibited from engaging on its own or through informants or others, in any of the following activities directed at Americans:

(a) Disseminating any information to the White House, any other federal official, the news media, or any other person for a political or other improper purpose, such as discrediting an opponent of the administration or a critic of an intelligence or investigative agency.

(b) Interfering with lawful speech, publication, assembly, organizational activity, or association of Americans.

(c) Harassing individuals through unnecessary overt investigative techniques such as interviews or obvious physical surveillance for the purpose of intimidation.

41. The bureau should be prohibited from maintaining information on the political beliefs, political associations, or private lives of Americans except that which is clearly necessary for domestic security investigations. . . .

42. The FBI should be permitted to investigate a committed act which may violate a federal criminal statute pertaining to the domestic security to determine the identity of the perpetrator or to determine whether the act violates such a statute.

43. The FBI should be permitted to investigate an American or foreigner to obtain evidence of criminal activity where there is "reasonable suspicion" that the American or foreigner has committed, is committing, or is about to commit a specific act which violates a federal statute pertaining to the domestic security.

44. The FBI should be permitted to conduct a preliminary preventive intelligence investigation of an American or foreigner where it has a specific allegation or specific or substantiated information that the American or foreigner will soon engage in terrorist activity or hostile foreign intelligence activity. Such a preliminary investigation should not continue longer than thirty days from receipt of the information unless the attorney general or his designee finds that the information and any corroboration which has been obtained warrants investigation for an additional period which may not exceed 60 days. If, at the outset or at any time during the course of a preliminary investigation the bureau establishes "reasonable suspicion" that an American or foreigner will soon engage in terrorist activity or hostile foreign intelligence activity, it may conduct a full preventive intelligence investigation. Such full investigation should not continue longer than one year except upon a finding of compelling circumstances by the attorney general or his designee.

In no event should the FBI open a preliminary or full preventive intelligence investigation based upon information that an American is advocating political ideas or engaging in lawful political activities or is associating with others for the purpose of petitioning the government for redress of grievances or other such constitutionally protected purpose.

The second paragraph of recommendation 44 . . . would supplement the protection that would be afforded by limiting the FBI's intelligence investigations to terrorist and hostile foreign intelligence activities. It re-emphasizes the committee's intent that the investigations of peaceful protest groups and other lawful associations should not recur. It serves as a further reminder that advocacy of political ideas is not to be the basis for governmental surveillance. At the same time recommendation 44 permits the initiation of investigations where the bureau possesses information consisting of a "specific allegation or specific or substantiated information that [an] American or foreigner will soon engage in terrorist activity or hostile foreign intelligence activity."

This recommendation has been among the most difficult of the domestic intelligence recommendations to draft. It was difficult because it represents the committee's effort to draw the fine line between legitimate investigations of conduct and illegitimate investigations of advocacy and association. Originally the committee was of the view that a threshold of "reasonable suspicion" should apply to initiating even limited preliminary intelligence investigations of terrorist or hostile foreign intelligence activities. However, the committee was persuaded by the Department of Justice that, having narrowly defined terrorist and hostile foreign intelligence activities, a "reasonable suspicion" threshold might be unworkable at the preliminary stage. Such a threshold might prohibit the FBI from investigating an allegation of extremely dangerous activity made by an anonymous source or a source of unknown reliability. The "reasonable suspicion" standard requires that the investigator have confidence in the reliability of the individual providing the information and some corroboration of the information.

However, the committee is cautious in proposing a standard of "specific allegation or specific or substantiated information" because it permits initiation of a preliminary investigation which includes the use of physical surveillance and a survey of, but not targeting of existing confidential human sources. . . .

The ultimate goal which Congress should seek in enacting such legislation is the development of a standard for the initiation of intelligence investigations which permits investigations of credible allegations of conduct which if uninterrupted will soon result in terrorist activities or hostile foreign intelligence activities as we define them. It must not permit investigations of constitutionally protected activities as the committee described them in the last paragraph of recommendation 44. . . .

The committee has found serious abuses in past FBI investigations of groups. In the conduct of these investigations, the FBI often failed to distinguish between members who were engaged in criminal activity and those who were exercising their constitutional rights of association. The committee's recommendations would only permit investigation of a group in two situations: first, where the FBI receives information that the avowed purpose of the group is "soon to engage in terrorist activity or hostile foreign intelligence activity"; or second, where the FBI has information that unidentified members of a group are "soon to engage in terrorist activity or hostile foreign intelligence activity." In both cases the FBI may focus on the group to determine the identity of those members who plan soon to engage in such activity. However, in both cases the FBI should minimize the collection of information about law-abiding members of the group or any lawful activities of the group. . . .

The committee's recommendations would not permit investigation of mere association:

—The FBI could not investigate an allegation that a member of the Klan has lunch regularly with the mayor of a southern community.

—The FBI could not investigate the allegation that a U.S. senator attended a cocktail party at a foreign embassy where a foreign intelligence agent was present.

—However, when additional facts are added indicating conduct which might constitute terrorist activity or hostile foreign intelligence activity, investigation might be authorized:

—The FBI could initiate an investigation of a dynamite dealer who met with a member of the "action squad" described above.

—Likewise, the FBI could initiate an investigation of a member of the National Security Council staff who met clandestinely with a known foreign intelligence agent in an obscure Paris restaurant.

Investigations of contacts can become quite troublesome when the contact takes place within the context of political activities or association for the purpose of petitioning the government. Law-abiding American protest groups may share common goals with groups in other countries. The obvious example was the widespread opposition in the late 1960's, at home and abroad, to America's role in Vietnam.

Furthermore, Americans should be free to communicate about such issues with persons in other countries, to attend international conferences and to exchange views or information about planned protest activities with like-minded foreign groups. Such activity, in itself, would not be the basis for . . . [an] . . . investigation under these recommendations:

—The FBI could not open an investigation of an anti-war group because "known Communists" were also in attendance at a group meeting even if it had reason to believe that the Communists' instructions were to influence the group or that the group shared the goals of the Soviet Union on ending the war in Vietnam.

—The FBI could not open an investigation of an anti-war activist who attends an international peace conference in Oslo where foreign intelligence agents would be in attendance even if the FBI had reason to believe that they might attempt to recruit the activist. Of course, the CIA would not be prevented from surveillance of the foreign agent's activities.

However, if the bureau had additional information suggesting that the activities of the Americans in the above hypothetical cases were more than mere association to petition for redress of grievances, an investigation would be legitimate.

—Where the FBI had received information that the anti-war activist traveling to Oslo intended to meet with a person he knew to be a foreign intelligence agent to receive instructions to conduct espionage on behalf of a hostile foreign country, the FBI could open a preliminary investigation of the activist.

The committee cautions the Department of Justice and FBI that in opening investigations of conduct occurring in the context of political activities, it should endeavor to ensure that the allegation prompting the investigation is from a reliable source.

Certainly, however, where the FBI has received a specific allegation or specific or substantiated information that an American or foreigner will soon engage in hostile foreign intelligence activity or terrorist activity, it may conduct an investigation. . . .

45. The FBI should be permitted to collect information to assist federal, state, and local officials in connection with a civil disorder either—

(a) After the attorney general finds in writing that there is a clear and immediate threat of domestic violence or rioting which is likely to require implementation of 10 U.S.C. 332 or 333 (the use of federal troops for the enforcement of federal law or federal court orders), or likely to result in a request by the governor or legislature of a state pursuant to 10 U.S.C. 331 for the use of federal militia or other federal armed forces as a countermeasure; or

(b) After such troops have been introduced.

46. FBI assistance to federal, state, and local officials in connection with a civil disorder should be limited to collecting information necessary for

(a) the president in making decisions concerning the introduction of federal troops;

(b) military officials in positioning and supporting such troops; and

(c) state and local officials in coordinating their activities with such military officials.

47. The FBI should be permitted to participate in the federal government's program of background investigations of federal employees or employees of federal contractors. The authority to conduct such investigations should not, however, be used as the basis for conducting investigations of other persons. In addition, Congress should examine the standards of Executive Order 10450, which serves as the current authority for FBI background investigations, to determine whether additional legislation is necessary to:

(a) modify criteria based on political beliefs and associations unrelated to suitability for employment; such modification should make those criteria consistent with judicial decisions regarding privacy of political association; and

(b) restrict the dissemination of information from name checks of information related to suitability for employment.

48. Under regulations to be formulated by the attorney general, the FBI should be permitted to investigate a specific allegation that an individual within the executive branch with access to classified information is a security risk as described in Executive Order 10450. Such investigation should not continue longer than thirty days except upon written approval of the attorney general or his designee.

49. Under regulations to be formulated by the attorney general, the FBI should be permitted to investigate a specific allegation of the improper disclosure of classified information by employees or contractors of the executive branch. Such investigation should not continue longer than thirty days except upon written approval of the attorney general or his designee.

50. Overt techniques and name checks should be permitted in all of the authorized domestic security investigations described above, including preliminary and full preventive intelligence investigations.

51. All non-consensual electronic surveillance, mail-opening, and unauthorized entries should be conducted only upon authority of a judicial warrant.

52. All non-consensual electronic surveillance should be conducted pursuant to judicial warrants issued under authority of Title III of the Omnibus Crime Control and Safe Streets Act of 1968. . . .

53. Mail opening should be conducted only pursuant to a judicial warrant issued upon probable cause of criminal activity as described in recommendation 37.

54. Unauthorized entry should be conducted only upon judicial warrant issued on probable cause to believe that the place to be searched contains evidence of a crime, except unauthorized entry, including surreptitious entry, against foreigners who are officers, employees, or conscious agents of a foreign power should be permitted upon judicial warrant under the standards which apply to electronic surveillance described in recommendation 52.

55. Covert human sources may not be directed at an American except:

(a) In the course of a criminal investigation if necessary to the investigation *provided* that covert human sources should not be directed at an American as a part of an investigation of a committed act unless there is reasonable suspicion to believe that the American is responsible for the act and then only for the purpose of identifying the perpetrators of the act.

(b) If the American is the target of a full preventive intelligence investigation and the attorney general or his designee makes a written finding that (i) he has considered and rejected less intrusive techniques; and (ii) he believes that covert human sources are necessary to obtain information for the investigation.

56. Covert human sources which have been directed at an American in a full preventive intelligence investigation should not be used to collect information on the activities of the American for more than 90 days after the source is in place and capable of reporting, unless the attorney general or his designee finds in writing either that there are "compelling circumstances" in which case they may be used for an additional 60 days, or that there is probable cause that the American will soon engage in terrorist activities or hostile foreign intelligence activities.

57. All covert human sources used by the FBI should be reviewed by the attorney general or his designee as soon as practicable, and should be terminated unless the covert human source could be directed against an American in a criminal investigation or a full preventive intelligence investigation under these recommendations.

58. Mail surveillance and the review of tax returns and tax-related information should be conducted consistently with the recommendations contained in Part III. In addition to restrictions contained in Part III, the review of tax returns and tax-related information, as well as review of medical or social history records, confidential records of private institutions and confidential records of federal, state, and local government agencies other than intelligence or law enforcement agencies may not be used against an American except:

(a) In the course of a criminal investigation if necessary to the investigation;

(b) If the American is the target of a full preventive intelligence investigation and the attorney general or his designee makes a written finding that (i) he has considered and rejected less intrusive techniques; and (ii) he believes that the covert technique requested by the bureau is necessary to obtain information necessary to the investigation.

59. The use of physical surveillance and review of credit and telephone records and any records of governmental or private institutions other than those covered in recommendation 58 should be permitted to be used against an American, if necessary, in the course of either a criminal investigation or a preliminary or full preventive intelligence investigation.

60. Covert techniques should be permitted at the scene of a potential civil disorder in the course of preventive criminal intelligence and criminal investigations as described above. Non-warrant covert techniques may also be directed at an American during a civil disorder in which extensive acts of violence are occurring and federal troops have been introduced. This additional authority to direct such covert techniques at Americans during a civil disorder should be limited to circumstances where federal troops are actually in use and the technique is used only for the purpose of preventing further violence.

61. Covert techniques should not be directed at an American in the course of a background investigation without the informed written consent of the American.

62. If Congress enacts a statute attaching criminal sanctions to security leaks, covert techniques should be directed at Americans in the course of security leak investigations only if such techniques are consistent with recommendation 55(1), 58(1) or 59. With respect to security risks, Congress might consider authorizing covert techniques, other than those requiring a judicial warrant, to be directed at Americans in the course of security risk investigations, *but* only upon a written finding of the attorney general that (i) there is reasonable suspicion to believe that the individual is a security risk, (ii) he has considered and rejected less intrusive techniques, and (iii) he believes the technique requested is necessary to the investigation.

63. Except as limited elsewhere in these recommendations or in Title III of the Omnibus Crime Control and Safe Streets Act of 1968, information obtained incidentally through an authorized covert technique about an American or a foreigner who is not the target of the covert technique can be used as the basis for any authorized domestic security investigation. . . .

64. Information should not be maintained except where relevant to the purpose of an investigation.

65. Personally identifiable information on Americans obtained in the following kinds of investigations should be sealed or purged as follows (unless it appears on its face to be necessary for another authorized investigation):

(a) Preventive intelligence investigations of terrorist or hostile foreign intelligence activities—as soon as the investigation is terminated by the attorney general or his designee pursuant to recommendation 45 or 69.

(b) Civil disorder assistance—as soon as the assistance is terminated by the attorney general or his designee pursuant to recommendation 69, provided that where troops have been introduced such information need be sealed or purged only within a reasonable period after their withdrawal.

66. Information previously gained by the FBI or any other intelligence agency through illegal techniques should be sealed or purged as soon as practicable.

67. Personally identifiable information on Americans from domestic security investigations may be disseminated outside the Department of Justice as follows:

(a) Preventive intelligence investigations of terrorist activities—personally identifiable information on Americans from preventive criminal intelligence investigations of terrorist activities may be disseminated only to:

(i) A foreign or domestic law enforcement agency which has jurisdiction over the criminal activity to which the information relates; or

(ii) To a foreign intelligence or military agency of the U.S., if necessary for an activity permitted by these recommendations; or

(iii) To an appropriate federal official with authority to make personnel decisions about the subject of the information; or

(iv) To a foreign intelligence or military agency of a cooperating foreign power if necessary for an activity permitted by these recommendations to similar agencies of the U.S.; or

(v) Where necessary to warn state or local officials of terrorist activity likely to occur within their jurisdiction; or

(vi) Where necessary to warn any person of a threat to life or property from terrorist activity.

(b) Preventive intelligence investigations of hostile foreign intelligence activities—personally identifiable information on Americans from preventive criminal intelligence investigations of hostile intelligence activities may be disseminated only:

(i) To an appropriate federal official with authority to make personnel decisions about the subject of the information; or

(ii) To the National Security Council or the Department of State upon request or where appropriate to their administration of U.S. foreign policy; or

(iii) To a foreign intelligence or military agency of the U.S., if relevant to an activity permitted by these recommendations; or

(iv) To a foreign intelligence or military agency of a cooperating foreign power if relevant to an activity permitted by these recommendations to similar agencies of the U.S.

(c) Civil disorders assistance—personally identifiable information on Americans involved in an actual or potential disorder, collected in the course of civil disorders assistance, should not be disseminated outside the Department of Justice except to military officials and appropriate state and local officials at the scene of a civil disorder where federal troops are present.

(d) Background investigations—to the maximum extent feasible, the results of background investigations should be segregated within the FBI and only disseminated to officials outside the Department of Justice authorized to make personnel decisions with respect to the subject.

(e) All other authorized domestic security investigations—to governmental officials who are authorized to take action consistent with the purpose of an investigation or who have statutory duties which require the information.

68. Officers of the executive branch, who are made responsible by these recommendations for overseeing intelligence activities, and appropriate congressional committees should have access to all information necessary for their functions. The committees should adopt procedures to protect the privacy of subjects of files maintained by the FBI and other agencies affected by the domestic intelligence recommendations.

69. The attorney general should:

(a) Establish a program of routine and periodic review of FBI domestic security investigations to ensure that the FBI is complying with all of the foregoing recommendations; and

(b) Assure, with respect to the following investigations of Americans, that:

(i) Preventive intelligence investigations of terrorist activity or hostile foreign intelligence activity are terminated within one year, except that the attorney general or his designee may grant extensions upon a written finding of "compelling circumstances";

(ii) Covert techniques are used in preventive intelligence investigations of terrorist activity or hostile foreign intelligence activity only so long as necessary and not beyond time limits established by the attorney general except that the attorney general or his designee may grant extensions upon a written finding of "compelling circumstances";

(iii) Civil disorders assistance is terminated upon withdrawal of federal troops or, if troops were not introduced, within a reasonable time after the finding by the attorney general that troops are likely to be requested, except that the attorney general or his designee may grant extensions upon a written finding of "compelling circumstances."

Part V

The Responsibility and Authority of the Attorney General for Oversight of Federal Domestic Security Activities Must Be Clarified and General Counsels and Inspectors General of Intelligence Agencies Strengthened

The committee's recommendations give the attorney general broad oversight responsibility for federal domestic security activities. As the chief legal officer of the U.S., the attorney general is the most appropriate official to be charged with ensuring that the intelligence agencies of the U.S. conduct their activities in accordance with the law. The executive order, however, places primary responsibility for oversight of the intelligence agencies with the newly created oversight board. [See p. 308D2]

A *70.* The attorney general should review the internal regulations of the FBI and other intelligence agencies engaging in domestic security activities to ensure that such internal regulations are proper and adequate to protect the constitutional rights of Americans.

71. The attorney general or his designee (such as the office of legal counsel of the Department of Justice) should advise the general counsels of intelligence agencies on interpretations of statutes and regulations adopted pursuant to these recommendations and on such other legal questions as are described in b. below.

72. The attorney general should have ultimate responsibility for the investigation of alleged violations of law relating to the domestic intelligence recommendations.

B *73.* The attorney general should be notified of possible alleged violations of law through the office of professional responsibility (described . . . below) by agency heads, general counsel, or inspectors general of intelligence agencies as provided . . . below.

74. The heads of all intelligence agencies affected by these recommendations are responsible for the prevention and detection of alleged violations of the law by, or on behalf of, their respective agencies and for the reporting to the attorney general of all such alleged violations. Each such agency head should also assure his agency's cooperation with the attorney general in investigations of alleged violations.

75. To assist the attorney general and the agency
C heads in the functions described . . . above, the FBI and each other intelligence agency should have a general counsel, nominated by the president and confirmed by the Senate, and an inspector general appointed by the agency head.

76. Any individual having information on past, current, or proposed activities which appear to be illegal, improper, or in violation of agency policy should be required to report the matter immediately to the agency head, general counsel, or inspector general. If the matter is not initially reported to the general counsel, he should be notified by the agency head or inspector general. Each agency should regularly remind employes of their obligation to report such information.

77. As provided in recommendation 74, the heads of
D the FBI and of other intelligence agencies are responsible for reporting to the attorney general alleged violations of law. When such reports are made, the appropriate congressional committees should be notified.

78. The general counsel and inspector general of the FBI and of each other intelligence agency should have unrestricted access to all information in the possession of the agency and should have the authority to review all of the agency's activities. The attorney general, or the office of professional responsibility on his behalf, should have access to all information in the possession of an agency which, in the opinion of the attorney general, is necessary for an investigation of
E illegal activity.

79. The general counsel of the FBI and of each other intelligence agency should review all significant proposed agency activities to determine their legality and constitutionality.

80. The director of the FBI and the heads of each other intelligence agency should be required to report, at least annually, to the appropriate committee of the Congress, on the activities of the general counsel and the office of the inspector general.

81. The director of the FBI and the heads of each other intelligence agency should be required to report, at least annually, to the attorney general on all reports of activities which appear illegal, improper, outside the
F legislative charter, or in violation of agency regulations. Such reports should include the general counsel's findings concerning these activities, a summary of the inspector general's investigations of these activities, and the practices and procedures developed to discover activities that raise questions of legality or propriety.

82. The office of professional responsibility created by Attorney General [Edward H.] Levi should be recognized in statute. The director of the office, appointed by the attorney general, should report directly to the attorney general or the deputy attorney general. The functions of the office should include:

(a) Serving as a central repository of reports and notifications provided the attorney general; and

G *(b)* Investigation, if requested by the attorney general of alleged violations by intelligence agencies of statutes enacted or regulations promulgated pursuant to these recommendations.

83. The attorney general is responsible for all of the activities of the FBI, and the director of the FBI is responsible to, and should be under the supervision and control of, the attorney general.

84. The director of the FBI should be nominated by the president and confirmed by the Senate to serve at the pleasure of the president for a single term of not more than eight years.

85. The attorney general should consider exercising his power to appoint assistant directors of the FBI. A maximum term of years should be imposed on the tenure of the assistant director for the intelligence division.

Part VI

Administrative Rulemaking and Increased Disclosure Should Be Required

86. The attorney general should approve all administrative regulations required to implement statutes created pursuant to these recommendations.

87. Such regulations, except for regulations concerning investigations of hostile foreign intelligence activity or other matters which are properly classified, should be issued pursuant to the Administrative Procedures Act and should be subject to the approval of the attorney general.

88. The effective date of regulations pertaining to the following matters should be delayed ninety days, during which time Congress would have the opportunity to review such regulations:

(a) Any CIA activities against Americans, as permitted in II.a. above;

(b) Military activities at the time of a civil disorder;

(c) The authorized scope of domestic security investigations, authorized investigative techniques, maintenance and dissemination of information by the FBI; and

(d) The termination of investigations and covert techniques as described in Part IV.

89. Each year the FBI and other intelligence agencies affected by these recommendations should be required to seek annual statutory authorization for their programs.

90. The Freedom of Information Act (5 U.S.C. 552(b)) and the Federal Privacy Act (5 U.S.C. 552(a)) provide important mechanisms by which individuals can gain access to information on intelligence activity directed against them. The domestic intelligence recommendations assume that these statutes will continue to be vigorously enforced. In addition, the Department of Justice should notify all readily identifiable targets of past illegal surveillance techniques. . . .

Part VII

Civil Remedies Should Be Expanded

Recommendation 91 expresses the committee's concern for establishing a legislative scheme which will afford effective redress to people who are injured by improper federal intelligence activity. The recommended provisions for civil remedies are also intended to deter improper intelligence activity without restricting the sound exercise of discretion by intelligence officers at headquarters or in the field. . . .

. . . [The committee recommends] that where a government official—as opposed to the government itself—acted in good faith and with the reasonable belief that his conduct was lawful, he should have an affirmative defense to a suit for damages brought under the proposed statute. To tighten the system of accountability and control of domestic intelligence activity, the committee proposes that this defense be structured to encourage intelligence officers to obtain written authorization for questionable activities and to seek legal advice about them. . . .

91. Congress should enact a comprehensive civil remedies statute which would accomplish the following:

(a) Any American with a substantial and specific claim to an actual or threatened injury by a violation of the Constitution by federal intelligence officers or agents acting under color of law should have a federal cause of action against the government and the individual federal intelligence officer or agent responsible for the violation, without regard to the monetary amount in controversy. If actual injury is proven in court, the committee believes that the injured person should be entitled to equitable relief, actual, general, and punitive damages, and recovery of the costs of litigation. If threatened injury is proven in court, the committee believes that equitable relief and recovery of the costs of litigation should be available.

(b) Any American with a substantial and specific claim to actual or threatened injury by violation of the statutory charter for intelligence activity (as proposed by these domestic intelligence recommendations) should have a cause of action for relief as in (a) above.

(c) Because of the secrecy that surrounds intelligence programs, the committee believes that a plaintiff should have two years from the date upon which he discovers, or reasonably should have discovered, the facts which give rise to a cause of action for relief from a constitutional or statutory violation.

(d) Whatever statutory provision may be made to permit an individual defendant to raise an affirmative defense that he acted within the scope of his official duties, in good faith, and with a reasonable belief that the action he took was lawful, the committee believes that to ensure relief to persons injured by governmental intelligence activity, this defense should be available solely to individual defendants and should not extend to the government. Moreover, the defense should not be available to bar injunctions against individual defendants.

Part VIII

Criminal Penalties Should Be Enacted

92. The committee believes that criminal penalties should apply, where appropriate, to willful and knowing violations of statutes enacted pursuant to the domestic intelligence recommendations.

Part IX

The Smith Act and the Voorhis Act Should Either Be Repealed or Amended

93. Congress should either repeal the Smith Act (18 U.S.C. 2385) and the Voorhis Act (18 U.S.C. 2386), which on their face appear to authorize investigation of "mere advocacy" of a political ideology, or amend those statutes so that domestic security investigations are only directed at conduct which might serve as the basis for a constitutional criminal prosecution, under Supreme Court decisions interpreting these and related statutes.

Part X

The Espionage Statute Should be Modernized

The committee agrees with the attorney general that there may be serious deficiencies in the federal espionage statute. The basic prohibitions of that statute have not been amended since 1917 and do not encompass certain forms of industrial, technological or economic espionage.

94. The appropriate committees of the Congress should review the Espionage Act of 1917 to determine whether it should be amended to cover modern forms of foreign espionage, including industrial, technological or economic espionage.

Part XI

Broader Access to Intelligence Agency Files Should be Provided to GAO, as an Investigative Arm of the Congress

95. The appropriate congressional oversight committees of the Congress should, from time to time, request the comptroller general of the U.S. to conduct audits and reviews of the intelligence activities of any department or agency of the U.S. affected by the domestic intelligence recommendations. For such purpose, the comptroller general, or any of his duly authorized representatives, should have access to, and the right to examine, all necessary materials of any such department or agency.

Part XII

Congressional Oversight Should Be Intensified

96. The committee reendorses the concept of vigorous Senate oversight to review the conduct of domestic security activities through a new permanent intelligence oversight committee.

Senate staff reports detail FBI misdeeds. The staff of the Senate Select Intelligence Committee, in a number of follow-up studies to the committee's official report, added more particulars to the documentation of FBI abuses and excesses in the field of domestic intelligence.

Studies were issued on:

Persecution of Dr. King—The report on the FBI campaign against Dr. Martin Luther King, released May 5, charged that the FBI effort had been "marked by extreme personal vindictiveness," particularly by J. Edgar Hoover, then FBI director.

Hoover, the report noted, had as early as February 1962 jotted the remark, "King is no good," on a memo that had come to him. By May 1962, the FBI had included King on a list of persons to be interned in the event of a national emergency.

The FBI did not begin its investigation of alleged communist influence on King or his church organization, the Southern Christian Leadership Conference, until October 1962.

The report did not say whether former Attorney General Robert F. Kennedy had known of the FBI's persistent bugging of King's hotel rooms. No evidence had been found, the report said, to show that Kennedy had been "expressly informed." However, the report noted that a Dec. 15, 1966 FBI memo had stated that Kennedy in 1964 had received an 8-page account of King's activities based on wiretap material. The 1966 memo said that the report to Kennedy had been "couched in such a manner that it is obvious that a microphone was the source."

The FBI continued its anti-King posture even after the civil rights leader was assassinated, the report said. In April 1969, the agency's Atlanta bureau formulated a plan for "counterintelligence action" against King's widow, Coretta Scott King. However, the report said, Hoover decided against implementing the plan at that time.

The report also cited a March 18, 1969 FBI memo urging that the FBI meet with members of Congress who were then considering a bill to make King's birthday a national holiday. The memo, according to the report, said that the meeting could be used to convince the legislators that King "was a scoundrel" and that the holiday idea should be abandoned. The report did not say whether the meeting was held; Congress never voted on a birthday bill.

In a separate development, Attorney General Edward H. Levi announced April 29 that he had ordered a new investigation of the King case by the Justice Department's Office of Professional Responsibility. The probe would examine the FBI's actions in the agency's campaign against King to determine if there were grounds for criminal prosecution against the agency personnel involved. King's assassination also would be reexamined to see if there were any links to the FBI and to determine if the FBI's original investigation had been thorough.

In ordering the internal probe, Levi rejected a recommendation that an inquiry be undertaken by a group independent of the government to insure the credibility of its findings. That suggestion had been contained in a report, given to Levi April 9, describing a preliminary 5-month investigation of the King case conducted by lawyers in the Justice Department's civil rights division. That investigation, according to Levi's April 29 statement, had provisionally cleared the FBI of both King's assassination and failing to properly investigate it.

The Rev. Ralph David Abernathy, King's successor as head of the Southern Christian Leadership Conference, April 29 also called for an independent probe of King's death.

Harassment of the Black Panther Party—A staff study, issued May 6, added detail to reports that the FBI had attempted to destroy the Panthers by bringing them into conflict with other violence-prone groups. In San Diego in 1969, the report said, this policy had taken the form of circulating derogatory cartoons of party members. Although the cartoons had been originated by the FBI, they purported to be the work of an organization called United Slaves, the report noted. (In January 1969, two Panthers had been killed in a fight with United Slave members.) The report said that the local FBI office claimed, in a memo dated Sept. 19, 1969, that "shootings, beatings, and a high degree of unrest continues [sic] to prevail in the ghetto area of southeast San Diego." The memo was quoted further:

"Although no specific counterintelligence action can be credited with contributing to this overall situation, it is felt that a substantial amount of the unrest is directly attributable to this program."

In Chicago, the report said, the FBI and the city police both had maintained paid informants in the Panther party and had pooled the information gained. The report quoted an FBI memo which said that this collaboration had been "crucial to police" in conducting a raid on Panther member Fred Hampton's apartment. Hampton was killed during the raid.

The report also detailed FBI attempts to exacerbate, by sending forged letters, a split that had developed between two Panther factions, one led by Huey P. Newton, the other by Eldridge Cleaver.

Electronic surveillance—The staff report on FBI bugging, issued May 9, asserted that members of Congress had been recorded on wiretaps that were used to provide information for Presidents Lyndon B. Johnson and Richard M. Nixon. The congressmen had not themselves been targets of the wiretaps, the report said, but they had come under surveillance when they met with foreign-government representatives who were targets.

The report also listed several instances of FBI wiretaps that possibly were politically motivated. Among them:

- A Roosevelt-Administration wiretap on the Los Angeles Chamber of Commerce.
- A Truman-era wiretap on a former White House aide. The report did not name the aide, but the May 10 Washington Post said "reliable sources" had identified him as Washington lawyer Thomas G. Corcoran.
- Kennedy-Administration wiretaps that had been justified as pertaining to the investigation of a sugar lobby. The taps were removed after the Administration had won passage of a bill it had sought.

Kelley apologizes—On May 8, FBI Director Clarence M. Kelley responded to the recent disclosures of his agency's activities by making an apology to the American public. Kelley characterized some of the FBI activities as "clearly wrong and quite indefensible" and said that they must never be repeated.

The abuses, Kelley said, had chiefly beset the FBI in the "twilight" of Hoover's 48-year tenure as FBI director. Kelley called for a 10-year limit to the term of FBI directors.

Five days later, Kelley explained his apology, according to a *New York Times* report June 17. In a letter written May 13 to Ralph H. Jones, president of the Society of Former Special Agents of the FBI, Kelley said he hoped that his apology would deter tough new legislative controls on the bureau's operations. Jones received Kelley's letter in answer to his request for clarification of the May 8 speech, and distributed it to the several thousand members of the Society of Former Special Agents.

Kelley's letter to Jones:

Dear Ralph: there having been some apprehension expressed about my speech at Fulton, Missouri, May 8, 1976. I want to tell you about it.

"As well you know, the bureau has been receiving considerable attention by the Congress and the news media for several months. Lately the news accounts have been more frequent, more probative and most damaging to our position, because they imply we are unwilling to recognize and admit when we err. Congress continues to demonstrate an inclination to seriously consider legislation which would be restrictive to us. Frankly, our credibility is, in my estimation, in jeopardy.

"It might well be said this feeling does not reflect that of the rest of the country. That may be so but here is where Congress resides and it is here that their opinions are largely formed. We have friends in Congress and appreciate them. I only wish we had more.

"I therefore carefully reviewed the situation and decided the time had come to make certain admissions. They were not specific nor directed at any individuals. I think the issue has now been resolved. Of course, we all cannot agree on what can or should be said. Someone, however, must make a decision at such times. I made it because I believe this action might well prevent or at least somewhat retard the proliferation of highly restrictive legislation.

"I realize such a speech would invoke some criticism. I can only say I have tried to be fair at all times. Time will determine the wisdom of my action. I am sure you join me in the hope the future is a more pleasant one.

"I want to renew my pledge to all the ex-agents to do my best to maintain the position of pre-eminence for the bureau."

FBI Reforms

FBI gets test guidelines. The justice department March 10, 1976 issued provisional guidelines for the conduct of intelligence activities by the Federal Bureau of Investigation. Revelations before Congressional committees of FBI activities in its counter intelligence program (called COINTELPRO and directed against domestic radical and antiwar groups from the mid 1950s to the early 1970s) had prompted the demand for guidelines.

Activities prohibited to FBI men under
A the guidelines included inciting to riot, illegal entry and the anonymous circulation of information intended to hold "an individual up to scorn, ridicule or disgrace."

FBI agents would be allowed, in certain circumstances, with authorization from FBI headquarters, to infiltrate groups, use electronic surveillance, and check (without opening) suspects' mail.

Under the guidelines, groups in-
B volved—or those which "will" become involved—in violence or illegality intended to overthrow the government or interfere with foreign governments or their representatives could be investigated. Also, investigations could be undertaken of groups which were "substantially impairing—for the purpose of influencing the United States Government policies or decisions"—federal or state governments or interstate commerce.

C A provision in draft versions of the guidelines which would have allowed the FBI to take "preventive action" to forestall imminent violence was dropped from the guidelines because of Congressional opposition. Congressmen had voiced concern that the provision would open the way to a renewal of COINTELPRO abuses.

Attorney General Edward H. Levi said March 10 that the dropped provision was "never intended" nor would it have had
D the effect of "an affirmation or legitimization of COINTELPRO." It was dropped in response to the opposition expressed concerning it, Levi said.

The guidelines also provided that requests for investigations from the White House would have to be made in writing, and state precisely what was to be investigated. In addition, there would have to be a statement "signed by the subject of the investigation acknowledging that he has consented to the investigation."

E Some Congressmen objected that the guidelines would still allow the FBI too much leeway in choosing groups to investigate.

Justice department official Mary C. Lawton March 10 noted that the guidelines were in a trial stage, and that they would be reviewed after the FBI had had experience in working under them. In particular, she cited regulations on the
F use of informers as possibly "too restrictive." Under the guidelines, the FBI was barred from introducing informers into groups in preliminary or limited investigations.

FBI burglaries in '70s probed. The launching of a Justice Department investigation of illegal burglaries alleged to have been carried out by the FBI since 1971 was reported by the *New York Times* on
G June 24. FBI Director Clarence M. Kelley admitted June 30 that the bureau had carried out "a limited number" of break-ins in 1972 and 1973, targeted against radical groups.

Kelley, who had taken office in July 1973, said that he had never authorized any of the operations, nor had any of his subordinates told him of them. His previous Congressional testimony that "surreptitious entries in domestic security investigations terminated in 1966" had, Kelley said, been made with the "best knowledge that was furnished me at the time."

Evidence of the more recent FBI burglaries came to the attention of FBI headquarters, Kelley said, on March 17 when files from the FBI field office in New York City were examined in connection with a lawsuit lodged against the bureau by the Socialist Workers' Party. Kelley said that the FBI had immediately notified the Justice Department of the information.

The recent break-ins were reportedly made to photocopy records and install listening devices. The Justice Department probe, according to a *Los Angeles Times* report cited by the *New York Times* June 24, initially focused on 20 agents, most of whom had been based in New York. The department reportedly had begun telephoning the agents to inform them that they were subjects of a criminal investigation and should obtain legal counsel.

The *New York Times* June 27, citing unidentified sources, said that 28 FBI agents were under investigation and that some had been offered immunity from prosecution in return for testimony on the involvement of higher-level bureau officials. In an August 3 story, the *Times* reported that government sources had said the investigation had broadened to include about 50 more agents.

The Justice Department's Civil Rights Division, headed by Assistant Attorney General J. Stanley Pottinger, was conducting the investigation. In a June 30 statement, Pottinger denied press reports that Kelley had "been sealed off from all aspects of this investigation." Pottinger acknowledged, however, that Kelley had taken the "unusual step" of detaching a group of FBI agents to work with the Justice Department investigators on the affair; the agents, Pottinger said, reported only to the Justice Department investigative staff, not to their superiors in FBI channels.

The arrangement, Pottinger said, was devised to ensure that "the thoroughness and objectivity of this inquiry is preserved both in fact and appearance." He added that he and Kelley felt free to confer with each other on the investigation, but that any information shared with Kelley remained strictly with him, and was not "disseminated to other persons in the FBI or elsewhere."

Denver break-in investigated. The Justice Department announced July 27 that it would investigate a July 7 burglary of the Denver offices of the Socialist Workers' Party for possible links with the FBI. Timothy Redfearn, a paid FBI informant, had been tied to the burglary.

The *New York Times* reported July 30 that, according to sources close to the Denver investigation, Redfearn met with the FBI agent he worked under, John V. Almon, on the day of the robbery and showed him files he had taken from the SWP office. Almon reportedly did not take possession of any of the files.

On July 14, Redfearn was arrested by Denver police for another burglary. Later that day, the FBI informed the police that Redfearn might be connected with the SWP burglary.

The bureau's delay in informing police that Redfern possessed presumably stolen materials, was reported to be a central concern of the Justice Department in its inquiry. Also at issue was whether the FBI had actually received any of the documents. Almon said that he had refused to accept any of the documents shown him by Redfearn. However, the SWP, after examining Denver FBI office files obtained under court order, claimed July 31 that the files included documents stolen July 7.

(The SWP asserted June 26 that other FBI papers—also obtained by the party for preparation of its lawsuit against the FBI—revealed that the bureau had received stolen confidential SWP documents as late as May 1975. The FBI papers referred to the SWP documents as having been "removed" or "recovered" from party offices; they did not specify whether FBI agents or paid informers were used to obtain them, or whether they were gotten through forced entry.)

Other abuses reported. Other alleged domestic intelligence abuses were the subject of recent news reports. Among them:

■ A May 25 Associated Press story that the Secret Service had engaged in covert surveillance of the 1971 national convention in Houston of the Young Socialists' Alliance. YSA speakers had been photographed and tape recorded, according to government papers obtained by the SWP as part of its suit against the FBI and other agencies. (The YSA was a youth affiliate of the SWP.)

■ A June 25 *New York Times* report that an FBI source had said bureau agents had kidnapped a radical political activist within the past five years. According to the source cited, the kidnapping had been performed without authorization from the FBI hierarchy and in such a way that the victim would not know that the kidnappers were FBI agents. The object of the action, the source said, was to "disrupt" the individual's activities. The kidnapping victim was released without permanent injury, the *Times'* source said.

■ A July 11 *New York Times* disclosure that FBI agents had assaulted individuals and burned cars as part of a campaign against domestic radicals. The *Times'* unidentified sources said that the violence was not officially allowed by FBI field supervisors, but that the supervisors probably knew of its existence.

■ A July 29 *New York Times* disclosure that George P. Baxtrum Jr., an FBI agent, had testified in a deposition taken in New York in June that he had been involved in "between 50 and 90" burglaries of SWP offices in New York between 1958 and 1965. Baxtrum said all the break-ins were authorized by his section chief.

Baxtrum was one of the agents cited by the SWP in its damage suit. Also named were Arthur J. Green Jr. and John F. Malone, the special agent in charge of the FBI's New York office during the 1960s burglaries. (Malone's "personal folder" reportedly held the documents unearthed March 17 which pointed to the FBI break-ins during 1972 and 1973.) Another agent, Joseph Furrer, refused to testify July 14 about the burglaries, according to Cathy Perkus of the Political Rights Defense Fund. The Defense Fund was aided the SWP in its lawsuit. Perkus said that Furrer pleaded the Fifth Amendment about 80 times while an SWP lawyer was taking a deposition in the suit.

FBI restructured; Gray implicated in 1970s burglaries. Clarence M. Kelley, director of the Federal Bureau of Investigation, announced Aug. 11 that he had ordered extensive restructuring of the agency. One reform removed the responsibility for investigating domestic radical and terrorist groups from the FBI's intelligence division and transferred it to the agency's general investigations branch, which operated under more restrictive guidelines than the intelligence division.

Kelley's action followed disclosures that agents in the intelligence branch had conducted burglaries of domestic radical groups in the 1970s. The disclosures drew wide publicity because the bureau previously had said that break-ins had been terminated in 1966 by order of then FBI director, J. Edgar Hoover.

Evidence of the 1970s burglaries—reportedly targeted against the Weathermen—had emerged in connection with a suit filed in 1973 by the Socialist Workers Party against the bureau and other federal agencies

(The Weathermen were members of a radical organization called the Weather Underground, which had claimed responsibility for a number of bombings. The group—originally known as Weatherman—had started as a dissident faction of the Students for a Democratic Society.)

The Justice Department had begun a probe of the burglaries, which reportedly was focusing on low-level agents (chiefly in the New York field office) and attempting to establish the chain of authority behind the burglaries. The probe was first disclosed in June.

W. Mark Felt, a retired associate director of the FBI said Aug. 17 that the policy of allowing break-ins had been approved directly by L. Patrick Gray, acting director of the FBI from May 1972 to April 1973. Felt added the he himself had personally authorized two burglaries.

Felt admitted that his memory was "hazy" in regard to Gray's approval of a break-in policy. Gray, through his lawyer, Aug. 17 denied "condoning or approving, directly or indirectly, any illegal act" by the FBI. However, Felt's statement was supported Aug. 18 by Edward S. Miller, former chief of the bureau's intelligence division. Miller said that Gray had told him privately in August 1972 that he (Gray) had decided to permit "surreptitious entries." On Aug. 29, 1972, Gray met at FBI headquarters in Washington, D.C., with some of the agents in charge of the bureau's field offices and told them of his decision, Miller said. He said that Gray told the agents to "make damn sure that none of these [break-ins] are done without prior bureau authorization."

Other developments in the break-ins case, additional details of the bureau reorganization and the statements of Miller and Felt included:

The restructuring—Kelley, in his Aug. 11 announcement of the reforms, said that domestic intelligence investigations (which dealt with subversion and attempts to overthrow the government) were being moved to the general investigative division "for the express purpose that they be managed like all other criminal cases in that division." The guidelines covering the general investigative category generally confined bureau activity to probes of actual violations of law, rather than surveillance of those merely suspected of planning to break the law.

Kelley said that since he took office in 1973, the number of targets of domestic intelligence probes had fallen from 22,000 to 4,000. According to an unidentified FBI source cited in the Aug. 12 *Washington Post,* this reduction had been achieved by eliminating the "garbage cases—those where you opened a file on everybody who writes a letter to a Communist newspaper."

The intelligence division was still to handle cases in which foreign governments or groups were involved. These cases included espionage and terrorism.

The *New York Times,* quoting anonymous Justice Department sources, reported Aug. 16 that this arrangement meant that the FBI would continue its 38-year-surveillance of the Socialist Workers Party (SWP) because the activity was regarded as a counterintelligence—rather than domestic security—investigation.

(Counterintelligence probes presupposed that the group being investigated had a foreign link. The *Times* said that FBI's basis for presuming such a link involving the SWP was the party's involvement in the Fourth International, a worldwide Trotskyite organization. The SWP had resigned from the Fourth International in 1940, after the passage of legislation that hampered organizations maintaining such international affiliations. However, the SWP had sent observers to later meetings of the International. The *Times* further reported that FBI officials had admitted in testimony that SWP members had never engaged in espionage, and were "home-grown tomatoes.")

Kelley Aug. 16 repudiated the *Times'* story, saying that the SWP probe would be classed with the other 4,000 cases previously handled by the domestic security section of the intelligence division, all of which would be transferred to the general investigative division.

Other organizational reforms proclaimed Aug. 11 by Kelley included:

- Consolidation of the internal inspection service within the FBI's Office of Planning and Evaluation. The inspection service had been accused of laxity in investigating charges of kickbacks and financial misdealing within the bureau. A
- The establishment of a study group on the FBI's use of informants. Kelley had set up the review group after Timothy Redfearn, an FBI informant, stole documents from an SWP office in Denver in July. (At an Aug. 8 news conference, Kelley said, "If it's [an action] wrong to be done by the agent, it's wrong to be done by the informant." Kelley added that the bureau's liability for deeds performed by informants had been set forth in "regulations and admonitions" and noted that John Almon, the agent who had handled Redfearn, had been relieved of responsibility for supervising informants.) B
- The formation of an office of professional responsibility to investigate charges of misconduct by FBI personnel.
- The incorporation of the bureau's legal counsel division—prior to the reform an independent office—into the director's office. The move was intended to sharpen executive oversight and legal knowledge of bureau operations. C

Kelley also announced that Thomas J. Jenkins, deputy associate director for administration, was retiring Aug. 31. Kelley said Jenkin's retirement had no connection with the ongoing investigations of FBI activities. Kelley noted that when he found a successor for Jenkins, all of the positions at FBI headquarters with the rank of assistant director or above would have been filled by him personally. D

(On July 16, Kelley had fired Nicholas P. Callahan, an associate director. Kelley had declined to give any explanation for the action taken against the long-time Hoover protege, observing only that there were "continuing investigations" into allegations of misconduct by bureau officials. On July 20 Kelley named Richard G. Held, special agent in charge of the Chicago field office to replace Callahan. Held July 30 acknowledged that the FBI Minneapolis office had engaged in COINTELPRO activities while he headed it from 1962 to 1973, but maintained that no "illegal acts were committed or advocated by special agents" of the office during his tenure. E

Kelley conceded Aug. 11 that the morale of many individuals in the FBI had been "seriously affected by virtue of the possibility of either disciplinary or prosecutive action" emerging from the investigations that the bureau then had in progress. He gave notice, however, that the bureau would not return to "the good old days" of Hoover's directorship. "The sanctuary which we had in those days," Kelley said, "is no longer there." F

These remarks followed Kelley's statement on Aug. 8 that he had been "deceived" by aides into believing that the FBI policy of allowing break-ins had been ended permanently in 1966. He said that G he would "take some action" if he found those responsible for his deception.

Kelley Aug. 8, in response to a request for a "ballpark" figure on the number of FBI personnel who might be disciplined as a result of the ongoing investigations, gave an estimate of "three or four on up." When he was asked about reports that 30 or more agents had been notified they were under investigation, he said that such a figure would possibly "encompass . . . the situation involving surreptitious entries. Those [agents] might well be construed as not doing anything other than following the authority that they think stems from those higher up."

Kelley also said that he did not plan to submit a routine letter of resignation following the presidential election.

Felt's and Miller's accounts—The two break-ins that Felt recalled personally approving were at the Arab Information Center in Dallas—to obtain information about Palestinian terrorist activities—in 1972 and at the home of individuals in New York suspected of harboring Weathermen fugitives.

Felt said Aug. 17 that he was "convinced" that he had been acting with Gray's approval. "Gray's attitude was if you're going to do it, you've got to have top-level approval," Felt said.

He defended the break-ins as necessary measures, called for by the fact that "we [the FBI] were dealing with murderers, terrorists, people who were responsible for mass destruction." He said that he was proud of what he had done and believed that he had "observed the spirit and the letter of the Constitution."

Felt also argued that drawing a distinction between break-ins that were part of a domestic investigation and those that were "foreign-related" was "silly."

(The Justice Department investigation of the FBI burglaries reportedly was predicated on the understanding that, under the laws and court decisions in force at the time of the break-ins, warrantless "surreptitous entries" directed against foreign, or foreign-linked groups were not illegal, while those against domestic groups were.)

Felt charged that there were "political overtones to this [the Justice Department probe]—to show the Ford White House as a staunch defender of civil rights. . . .to offset Watergate and the Nixon pardon."

Miller, who, like Felt, made his remarks in telephone interviews with the *Washington Post* and the *New York Times*, was more positive in asserting Gray's authorization of the revival of the break-in policy. Miller said Aug. 18 that Gray had informed agents of the new policy at the Aug. 29, 1972 meeting in Washington and at a Sept. 15 meeting in Quantico, Va. for agents assigned to the Weathermen.

In his talks at both meetings, Gray had stressed that the break-ins had to be cleared in advance with Miller and Felt, Miller said. He said that he and Felt had approved as many as twelve break-ins in the New York area between Sept. 1972 and April 1973. He and Felt had ended the break-in policy in April 1973 when William D. Ruckelshaus replaced Gray as director of the bureau, Miller said.

Miller also noted that when he had informed one of his subordinates in the intelligence division, Robert L. Shackelford, of the decision to allow break-ins again, Shackelford replied, "That's good, because it's going on anyway." Shackelford said Aug. 18 that he had no recollection of having such a conversation with Miller.

Miller said that authorization for the New York break-ins had been requested verbally by Andrew J. Decker Jr., then agent in charge of the New York office. The only written records of break-in, requests, Miller said, were two-line memos that Miller sent to Felt noting his (Miller's) approval.

Miller said that Gray's decision to restore the break-in policy had been taken after consultations with many people in and out of the FBI, and that Gray had come to the decision "because he felt the burglaries were necessary to penetrate the communications of dangerous terrorist groups." Miller added that the impetus behind the resumption of break-ins had come from field agents, who had suffered from "tremendous frustration" in conducting their investigations under the limitation imposed by Hoover's 1966 ban on break-ins. FBI headquarters had never ordered a field agent to carry out a burglary, Miller said.

Miller concurred with Felt in seeing a political purpose behind the Justice Department probe of the burglaries. Miller and Felt were summoned to appear Aug. 26 before a federal grand jury in New York that was hearing evidence on the burglaries.

Socialist Workers Party

SWP's suit progresses. The SWP's three-year $37-million suit against the FBI and other federal agencies progressed through a number of hearings in U.S. District Court, Manhattan, in August, with Judge Thomas P. Griesa issuing these rulings:

■ The FBI was told Aug. 3 to turn over to the SWP by Aug. 17 all of its files on six alleged informants who had been identified by the SWP. Only the names of unidentified informants could be deleted from the files, the judge said. The file of Timothy Redfearn, an FBI informant who had been linked to the July burglary of the SWP's Denver office, already had been turned over to the SWP on July 30, the first such file to be released to the party. The judge deferred ruling on an SWP discovery motion seeking the files of 19 informants whom the government, in earlier disclosures, had admitted using but had not identified. The FBI opposed releasing information on informants who were not already known by name to the SWP.

■ A government motion seeking to dismiss the SWP's damage claim was rejected, at least temporarily, by Judge Griesa, the *New York Times* disclosed Aug. 15. The motion was based on the claim that the SWP had failed to comply with a federal law requiring that administrative claims for damages based on government misconduct be filed within two years of the plaintiff's learning of the alleged misconduct.

Griesa charged at an Aug. 3 hearing that the FBI had responded falsely to a question put to it by the SWP as part of the suit. The question had dealt with the source of information about the SWP obtained by an FBI informant. The bureau had replied that the information was publicly available. Subsequently it was learned that the informant was Redfearn and that some of the material had been obtained through burglaries.

The government acknowledged at the hearing that "discrepancies" existed between the initial FBI response and the later knowledge, but maintained that they were due to the "great haste" required of the bureau in answering the court's demands for information. Griesa rejected that explanation. He said that he could "draw no other conclusion than that the person making that answer intentionally omitted materials that were unfavorable to the government when he tried to summarize that file." Griesa noted that the finding cast doubt upon other responses prepared by the government for the trial, and possibly meant that only the original files would furnish the whole truth.

Motions in the SWP suit had produced the FBI papers that gave the first indications that the FBI had resumed its policy of break-ins in the 1970s. According to Leonard Boudin, a lawyer for the SWP who was quoted in the Aug. 8 *Washington Post*, the significance of the suit was not its connection with the SWP, but its "tremendous educational importance for Congress, the President and the FBI." If the SWP won the suit, Boudin said, then "no one [in the government] would be able to say he didn't know what he was doing by interfering in legitimate political activity."

The Justice Department Aug. 13 announced that it had persuaded "more than one FBI agent" to testify about the 1970s burglaries in return for immunity from prosecution. On Aug. 19, a special detachment of FBI agents, working under Justice Department orders, removed numerous files from the FBI Washington, D.C. headquarters and New York offices. The files were turned over to the government prosecutors investigating the burglaries. The bureau was given no advance notice of the files' seizure.

The *New York Times*, citing unidentified bureau sources, reported Aug. 20 that J. Walter LaPrade, an assistant director in charge of the FBI's Manhattan office, had authorized some of the burglaries. In addition to the break-ins, the Justice Department probe had uncovered evidence of thefts from the U.S. mail and illegal electronic surveillance by the FBI over the previous five years, the *Times* reported Aug. 22, citing sources close to the investigation.

Levi orders end to SWP investigation. Attorney General Edward H. Levi Sept. 10 ordered the end of the 38-year old FBI investigation of the Socialist Workers Party. The directive issued to the bureau was based on the recommendation of two Justice Department committees which had reported that the party's activities did not warrant FBI investigation under the March guidelines.

Peter Camejo, Socialist Workers candidate for President, called the ruling "an historic victory for democratic rights for all Americans." He said it was the "first step in bringing to a halt a Government program for political spying and harassment."

In its 38-year existence, the FBI probe had compiled eight million file entries. The bureau had committed an estimated 92 burglaries into SWP offices over six years, and had used its COINTELPRO activities to harass party members. No criminal charges have been brought against any party members. It was disclosed in August that the FBI had used 316 paid informers against the SWP since 1960. It also had "an army of some 1,300 free-floating informers who spy on the activities of members and a wide variety of groups."

Levi's directive appeared to override a statement made in mid-August by FBI Director Clarence M. Kelley that the FBI would continue to investigate the SWP, changing its jurisdiction from the intelligence division to the general crimes division.

Kelley's Gifts

Ford backs Kelley on favors, gifts. President Ford announced Sept. 4 that he would not fire FBI Director Clarence M. Kelley, who had admitted Aug. 31 that certain of his house furnishings had been provided by the FBI without charge and that he had received gifts from his top aides. Ford issued his statement after he had read a report on Kelley prepared by Attorney General Edward H. Levi. In the report Levi said that Kelley should be neither formally disciplined nor asked to resign. Ford, who Sept. 1 had asked for the report, said that he believed Kelley had "the capacity to meet the essentially high standards of the FBI."

Kelley, in response to a story published Aug. 31 in the *Washington Star,* admitted that day that FBI employes had installed some window fixtures in his apartment shortly after he took office in 1973. He said that it had been done "without [his] knowledge." (Kelley Sept. 2 gave the bureau a check for $335 to cover the cost of the labor and the fixtures.)

Bureau sources quoted in the Sept. 1 *Washington Post* recalled that when J. Edgar Hoover headed the FBI, it was common practice for the director and other top executives to receive special favors.

In light of this history, the bureau sources said, the fixtures might have been installed by overzealous employes without a request from Kelley.

Kelley also admitted Aug. 31 that at his request bureau employes had built a portable cabinet for his use at home. Kelley said, however, that he considered the cabinet to be FBI property and intended to return it when he left the bureau. The cabinet was used to house FBI stationery and related materials, Kelley said.

Kelley said that he was "prepared to make restitution" for the gifts he had received from his personal staff and from some executive aides if his acceptance of them violated federal regulations.

The day after Kelley's statement, Ford asked Levi for the report on Kelley. The *Washington Post* carried a story that day saying that a Justice Department investigator had recommended that Kelley be fired. The investigator's superior had toned that down to a recommendation that Kelley be publicly reprimanded, the *Post* said. The recommendation, which reportedly had been sent to Levi three weeks before the *Post* story, was made by officials in the Justice Department's Office of Professional Responsibility, the *Post* said. That office was investigating charges that FBI executives had abused their powers.

The Justice Department, in a Sept. 4 statement on the Kelley probe, said that gifts accepted by Kelley from his subordinates did not violate federal regulations. The statement said that the most expensive of the gifts—which included chair and a clock—cost $105. The statement noted that individuals had pooled their donations so that only "nominal" amounts—as required by federal regulations—had been given by any individual.

The window fixtures, the statement said, had not been requested by Kelley. The statement said that Kelley had offered to pay for the fixtures once he discovered they had been installed by the bureau. That offer had been rejected by bureau officials at the time, the statement said, on the grounds that the security of Kelley's apartment necessitated the installation of the fixtures by FBI personnel.

The Justice Department statement said that the security rationale was applicable to some of the "goods and services" afforded Kelley. It said that other such goods and services "were requested and provided to assist the director to work at home, particularly during the period of his wife's terminal illness."

The statement noted that there had been concern that unless Kelley were forced to resign there would be "an aura of special treatment because of his high position." It said that Kelley's conduct, however, was "different in kind" from that which deserved disciplinary action or prosecution.

"The caliber of government service [would not be] improved in situations such as this, where there is every evidence of an intention to be honest, by a reading of human conduct in its worst possible light," the statement said.

(On Aug. 13, John Dunphy, head of the exhibits section of the FBI, resigned from the bureau and pleaded guilty to a misdemeanor charge of using government lumber for a birdhouse at his home. Dunphy's action followed an agreement with Justice Department prosecutors that reportedly included a promise to give grand jury testimony on similar misuse of government property. The exhibits section A prepared models of crime scenes for use in trials.)

Would have ousted Kelley, but—Democratic presidential nominee Jimmy Carter told a reporter outside Brooklyn College Sept. 7 that, "knowing what I know now, I would have fired" FBI Director Clarence M. Kelley for accepting gifts and favors from his staff. Later, before a larger group of newsmen, Carter declined to say whether he would dismiss Kelley if elected B president. "I'll cross that bridge when I come to it," he said.

Carter had told his Brooklyn College audience that the record of the FBI was a "disgrace" when it "ought to be purer than Caesar's wife." In Philadelphia, he told his church audience that Kelley had been "caught having government employes using tax money decorate his home."

The President asked Attorney General Edward H. Levi to investigate, Carter C said, "and Mr. Levi said, 'Well, he did it' and Mr. Ford said, 'Well, I'll let him stay where he is.'"

"When big and little people," Carter continued, "see Richard Nixon lying, cheating and leaving the highest office in disgrace and the previous attorney general violating the law and admitting it, when you see the head of the FBI break a little law and stay there, it gives everybody the sense that crime must be OK. If the big shots in Washington can get away with it, D well, so can I."

Carter's remarks on Kelley scored—At a Sept. 8 news conference on the White House lawn, Ford assailed Carter's remarks on Kelley.

Carter, Ford said, "showed a lack of compassion" in saying Kelley should have been dismissed for accepting favors at a "very sad and difficult time," a reference E to the period when Kelley's wife had been ill with cancer and window valances were built in the Kelley apartment by FBI carpenters.

Ford said that he was "confused" by Carter's further remark that he was unsure whether he would retain Kelley at the FBI if he were elected president.

"So I am confused on the one hand by his flip-flop on this issue," Ford said, "and I am very disappointed at his lack of compassion on the other." F

The FBI vs. the Press

Tulley calls on 'warrior class.' Edward J. Tulley, who teaches at the FBI's Quantico, Va. headquarters, Aug. 12 called on Louisiana sheriffs to fight bureaucrats and the press, the *New York Times* reported Aug. 27. At a convention in Lake Charles, La., G Tulley complained that the FBI had become a victim "of bureaucrats who have been honing their knives for the FBI autopsy for the last 20 years." He called on the "warrior class" to "cry the battle alarm."

Tulley said the press reports of FBI misdeeds were inspired by a desire to "fill time between toothpaste commercials or sell papers" rather than by "any overriding social interest" on the part of the news organizations. The press, according to Tulley, "have set themselves up as judge and jury of us all," and the federal government has become "a captive of the press and special interest groups." Tulley claimed that the congressional investigations of the CIA were promoted "by politicians whose only interest lay in personal exposure on CBS News, hopeful of obtaining the necessary publicity that one needs to obtain higher office." He said that news reports of the investigations were written by journalists "who have allowed themselves to be prostituted by the hucksters of social change merely to fill the airways with what they call objective journalism." Tulley continued, "Objective journalism in 1976 is merely a thinly disguised and researched examination of unimportant issues which are then properly spaced to allow bathroom products to be commercially hawked throughout the land."

Scoring "the new intelligentsia," Tulley identified it as "persons who are educated beyond their capacity to learn" and who first emerged "to feed upon our nation in the middle 1950s." He said they "skillfully wormed their way into all levels of government bureaucracy," where they "fed themselves on the tax dollars of us all while they devised programs to cure all social ills."

Tulley called upon the law-enforcement community; "we are the ones who must make proper attitudes dominate." He said "we are the ones who must rout out from all levels of government those bureaucrats whose lack of understanding brought us to the point where we are today."

Kelley ordered to soften speech. FBI Director Clarence Kelley was ordered to soften the speech he was going to give Oct. 15 to the New Mexico Press Association in Albuquerque, the Associated Press reported Oct. 16. He allegedly threatened to end FBI cooperation with the news reporters he found hostile. A Department of Justice statement was issued Oct. 15, in which Kelley said he was abandoning that speech because it "appears to give the wrong impression and does not truly reflect my feelings about the press."

The *Washington Post* said that President Ford's counsel Philip W. Buchen initiated the action. Kelley was about to take off on a commercial flight from Washington, with a stop in Chicago, when the pilot was ordered to return to the airport because Attorney General Edward Levi wanted to speak to Kelley. The *Post* reported that Levi, following Ford's advice, told Kelley to use less harsh terms.

Kelley's actual speech was preceded by his remarks that he was "casting aside most of the prepared text." He said he would "speak from the heart but without what I now recognize could be misinterpreted." Kelley said he had intended in the speech "to point out the need for an understanding of our problems and the need to explore methods whereby we could join together in an effort to raise the FBI to a higher level of productivity." Referring to news coverage, Kelley said, "Past activities have been spotlighted, and rightfully so. We seek not to blame others for our plight, but to enlist their help in our renaissance." That, he said, might have "unduly intruded upon our reason and gave rise to rhetoric which too harshly assessed the blame on the press."

According to the Associated Press, the original text included and accusation that some members of the "national news media" had reported FBI misdeeds unfairly. Kelley allegedly wrote, "We will not continue to throw open the doors for those who invariably dash us with scalding water." He added, "In some instances when we opened our doors and extended every consideration to certain representatives of the news media, we were nailed to the barn door. We are journalistically bludgeoned, not by full exposure of all the facts, but by systematic selection and emphasis of facts with some heavy-handed 'interpretations' thrown in."

Security Investigations

Kelley reports drop in FBI investigations. FBI Director Clarence M. Kelley announced Sept. 22 that the FBI investigations of political groups had dropped from 21,414 to 626 over the 1973–76 period. Kelley attributed the 97 percent decline to the end of the Vietnam War and to special directives from the Justice Department.

Because of the war's end, "a major cause for divisiveness in this country" was ended, according to Kelley. He said the FBI "began closing thousands of investigations" when the armistice eliminated "the potential for violence" among antiwar groups.

After the Justice Department issued its guidelines in March, the FBI ended other investigations. The Socialist Workers Party probe had been ended by a special review by the department.

Kelley told the Senate Select Committee on Intelligence that the reductions had been made "largely because we have discontinued investigations of rank and file members" of organizations. Rather, he said, the FBI would investigate the activities of the groups and focus upon those members who have indicated their desire "to use force or violence in violation of federal law." The 626 current cases could be divided into probes of 78 organizations and 548 persons.

FBI'S HARASSING OF KING REVEALED; NO GUILT PROVED AFTER SIX YEARS

The Federal Bureau of Investigation attempted to discredit Dr. Martin Luther King Jr. in a concerted six-year campaign that included bugging of his hotel rooms and the mailing of a letter suggesting that he commit suicide, the Senate Select Committee on Intelligence revealed Nov. 18.

According to the committee, King received an anonymously sent tape recording and an accompanying note in November 1964, only 34 days before he was to accept the Nobel Peace Prize. The recording supposedly revealed instances of unsavory behavior King had engaged in. The accompanying, unsigned note read: "King, there is only one thing left for you to do. You know what it is. You have just 34 days in which to do (the exact number has been selected for a specific reason). It has definite practical significance. You are done. There is but one way out for you."

F. A. O. Schwarz 3rd, chief counsel to the committee, said that the panel's staff had established that the tape was produced with the aid of an electronic surveillance device placed by the FBI and that FBI officials had written the note. In December 1964, the FBI mailed anonymously a second tape recording, possibly of the same incident, to King's wife, Coretta Scott King. Schwarz said staff investigators had discovered an FBI memorandum to the late FBI director, J. Edgar Hoover, from William Sullivan, then the bureau's chief of counterintelligence, recommending that the FBI discredit King by "knocking him off his pedestal." Although the FBI instituted 16 separate wiretaps and bugged eight hotel rooms to implement the plan, Schwarz said it never established that King was criminally suspect or a national security risk.

Officials of the FBI acknowledged in testimony before the committee Nov. 19 that repeated attempts to discredit King and other targets of its counterintelligence program, Cointelpro, were legally unjustified. James B. Adams, assistant deputy director of the bureau, told the committee that the approximately 25 separate "actions" taken against King in the 1960s had "no statutory basis or justification."

THE ATLANTA CONSTITUTION

Atlanta, Ga., November 20, 1975

There was some controversy in Atlanta about the late Dr. Martin Luther King Jr. in late 1964, almost exactly 11 years ago.

King had been awarded the Nobel Peace Prize, and a number of prominent Atlantans were determined to honor King in an appropriate fashion. Among them were former Mayor Ivan Allen Jr. and the late Mayor Bill Hartsfield and Archbishop Paul J. Hallinan and Dr. Benjamin Mays and the late Rabbi Jacob Rothschild.

There was controversy inevitably because King himself was controversial, the best known American civil rights leader. Yet as Rabbi Rothschild put it at the time: "This Atlanta tradition of appropriateness, of courtesy, of acknowledging achievement whether in the field of sports, music, art, literature or other areas, is a part of the fabric of the city. And now another honor has been added to Atlanta's long list: the highest international award has been given for the second time to a Southerner and this time to an Atlantan. In recognition of this highly coveted award, Atlanta citizens are honoring Dr. King, an Atlantan, in the traditional Atlanta way."

The dinner was a great success. More than 1,500 people attended the dinner in the old Dinkler Plaza Hotel.

Why go through that old story in review? Only one reason. We now know that in that same period of time just 11 years ago the Federal Bureau of Investigation sent an anonymous letter to King, seeming to suggest that he commit suicide rather than accept the Nobel Peace Prize and saying that he would face disgrace on undisclosed allegations unless he took such action.

It is incredible. But that is the story revealed this week at Senate Intelligence Committee hearings in Washington.

The FBI has a proud record in many ways, but this shabby, almost unbelievable incident marks a shameful episode indeed in the FBI's history.

BUFFALO EVENING NEWS

Buffalo, N.Y., November 21, 1975

Testimony and documents submitted to the Senate Select Committee on Intelligence strongly suggest that for six years the FBI wrongly spied upon and harassed the late civil rights leader, the Rev. Dr. Martin Luther King.

The governing motive for this prolonged campaign to smear and discredit Dr. King is not entirely clear. But there is little doubt that the FBI strayed far beyond any legitimate authority in persistently bugging Dr. King's quarters and apparently even writing him an anonymous note in late 1964 which he interpreted as an effort to drive him to suicide.

Such tactics, whether used against him or against other leaders in black militant or white-supremacist groups, are contemptible.

The Senate committee's staff testified they could discover no valid reason for the extensive and prolonged surveillance of Dr. King, concluding it evolved from his criticism of the FBI itself. But there are other possible reasons, too, as News columnist Charles Bartlett, a close friend of former President John Kennedy, notes in his column on this page today.

"The Kennedy brothers were initially puzzled over King's intentions," Mr. Bartlett writes. "He appeared to have links that reached into both the Rockefeller and Communist camps. Uncertain whether he was conspiring to overthrow the country or the Kennedy administration, they readily assented to Hoover's plans for close scrutiny." In 1962, of course, Nelson Rockefeller was the one Republican who seemed to be the greatest threat to President Kennedy's reelection.

But the Senate committee and its chairman, Sen. Frank Church (D., Ida.) appeared to show no interest whatever in digging into the Kennedy brothers' apparently more-than-casual support for the FBI's close scrutiny of Martin Luther King. Sen. Church seemed appalled by the extent of Mr. Hoover's six-year surveillance and harassment operation, but even after hearing testimony that the two Kennedys had discussed "their concern of Communist influence with Dr. King," he indicated little interest in digging deeper into either the Kennedy administration's or the later Johnson administration's possible political motivations for wanting Dr. King watched, embarrassed or discredited.

The foremost danger here is that of a powerful national police agency abusing an American citizen merely because it either objects to his opinions and judgments, or it wants to secretly keep tabs on his connections with potential political rivals.

The FBI has legitimate and important surveillance functions in the national security area. It is responsible for apprehending violators of federal law. But its authority should never involve the pursuit of groups or leaders whose only "offense" is their unpopularity with the administration in power or the FBI itself.

It should be noted, of course, that the cited misuses of power all occurred before the death of J. Edgar Hoover in May, 1972. There are signs that Clarence Kelley, the present FBI director, better appreciates the proper limits of his agency's authority. In any event, Congress should require prior court approval of any wiretap or electronic bug placed against American citizens by federal agencies. And if any doubt remains over the proper limits of the FBI's awesome police powers, then Congress should also legislate them in the plainest terms, as well as penalties for their violation.

The Charleston Gazette

Charleston, W. Va., November 28, 1975

It fell to James Adams, assistant deputy director of the FBI, to confess to a congressional investigating committee the agency's contemptible campaign to "get" Martin Luther King had no "statutory basis or justification."

To his credit, Adams held back nothing and gave his shameful testimony without excuses. As his unwholesome story of J. Edgar Hoover's poison pen letter and the falsification of reports by FBI agents unfolded, it became obvious that Congress must react strongly with measures to insure that such tactics cannot be repeated.

Adams asked the committee for guidelines. Congress should supply them. The first should be "Obey the law." Congress also should create the machinery for oversight and provide broad authority for periodic checks on an agency which has strayed far from decent conduct. And then Congress should make law limiting the term of the FBI director and making his office subject to continuing congressional review. We want no more J. Edgar Hoovers.

Neither the FBI nor the CIA should be permitted to run any longer beyond control. Their illegal and immoral acts are as much of a threat to the American way as the subversive elements they sometimes saw in imaginary numbers.

Chicago Daily Defender

Chicago, Ill., November 26, 1975

The excesses committed by U. S. intelligence agencies, especially the Federal Bureau of Investigation, in the dreadful days of Director J. Edgar Hoover, showed a dangerous erosion was leading the United States into the crucible of a police state.

We can see now in restrospect whence the late Wisconsin Senator Joseph McCarthy got his red paint with which he tried to smear good, loyal Americans who dissented from his extremism, when he saw a Communist under every bed of the people who disagreed with him.

Even Pres. Eisenhower and a number of Army Generals were suspected of harboring Red sympathy. The revelation that the FBI used all manner of clandestine means to smear and discredit Dr. Martin Luther King, Jr., was not surprising. Hoover hated him, because King criticized the Bureau for doing next to nothing to help apprehend the white racists who were shooting down black as well as white activists at the height of the civil rights revolution.

King had become too powerful a figure on the American scene. And he was gaining too many white converts to the cause of freedom and peace which King championed with matchless eloquence and fortitude. Such a man, in Hoover's demoniacal mind had to be destroyed at all costs.

It has long been hinted that the FBI had much to do with the rifle shot that ended King's meteoric career in Memphis in 1963. The investigation into the murder of the greatest apostle of peace and freedom in modern times was conspicuously perfunctory and inordinately brief.

Now 12 years later comes a post-mortem explanation by the Bureau that the decision to investigate Dr. King was based on the presumption that his civil rights movement was being infiltrated by members of the Communist Party. Obviously that was a subterfuge designed to furnish the rationale for FBI agents to get a foothold in a movement which operated under no political banner or slogan and advocated no use of force or violence to attain its objectives.

The letter to Dr. King was an attempt by the FBI to drive him to suicide and knock him off the pedestal of power and influence to which the masses had elevated him. Hoover was so saturated with the Jehovah complex he would have smeared Christ had the Savior disagreed with him. The FBI director was without the shadow of a doubt the most dangerous demagogue this nation has ever created. With him as a manipulative force behind the throne America was being transformed into a garrison state where rights and freedom would be trampled under foot.

We hope that those evil days are over.

The Ann Arbor News

Ann Arbor, Mich., November 24, 1975

AFTER ALL what has been unravelled about the FBI and CIA, it's a wonder there's any room left for shock value. But the latest disclosures about the activities of the FBI are shocking.

What's more, they're reprehensible. The campaign to discredit Dr. Martin Luther King had no justification whatever. And King wasn't the only target of the snoops and infiltrators.

A "tough, dirty and dangerous" campaign included efforts to destroy marriages through letters alleging infidelities. Black and anti-war groups and the women's movement were targets of infiltration and disruption.

Because Dr. King was perceived by FBI director J. Edgar Hoover as an irritant with suspected Communist ties, the civil rights leader was wiretapped and bugged. He even received an anonymous threatening letter strongly suggesting that he commit suicide as the only "way out."

That these dirty tricks would receive the permission of some the highest officers in governme ought to be unthinkable, but t abuses have become all too rea Now it is the FBI and other ins tutions which are discredited.

* * *

IT IS a shame too that such formerly topflight crimebusti agency like the FBI is us against ordinary citizens. Is it a wonder that many citizens ha grown cynical of government a politicians? To put the best pos ble face on these revelations, least the abuses have come public light and now we can beg to regain authority over la enforcement and intelligen gathering.

Ours is a nation grown weary the outrages committed by so of our most respected institutio Laws and the rights of citize have been trampled upon. N there must be a turnaround, Congress seeks to check the po er that corrupts. It has the so support of an angry public.

The Commercial Appeal

Memphis, Tenn., November 20, 1975

THE REVELATIONS about former FBI Director J. Edgar Hoover's obsession with Dr. Martin Luther King Jr. fall heavily in Memphis.

It was the FBI which took over the investigation of the assassination of Dr. King here after the April 4, 1968, tragedy. Details of the investigation learned later showed that it was a herculean effort which resulted, with an assist from Scotland Yard, in the arrest of James Earl Ray. At the time of King's death, however, suspicions of a conspiracy were rampant, especially among blacks.

The suspicions were fed by the standard retort of "no comment" to questions and the instant and total embargo on information by law enforcement agencies.

The evidence of an FBI campaign to destroy King's influence brought out in Senate Intelligence Committee hearings aggravates those lingering suspicions even though there has been no persuasive evidence of coverup or conspiracy.

EVIDENCE in the committee hearings shows that Hoover ordered reports that King was not a threat to the country rewritten to coincide with what must be considered his personal prejudice. Hoover's fixation against King is evident in the tawdry letter and tape recording sent anonymously by the FBI to King 34 days before he received the 1964 Nobel Peace Prize. The sender, after alleging knowledge of unsavory activities by the civil rights leader, said he had "only one way out." That way has been construed to mean suicide.

King did go on to accept the prize. And he went on, until his death in Memphis, to marshal efforts in the struggle against injustices to blacks and the poor. Despite the FBI's six-year effort to discredit him, neither his resolve nor his courage were shaken. Indeed, Hoover's failure can be regarded as particular corroboration of that resolve and that courage.

The FBI's campaign against K should not be taken as a general ind ment of the bureau. It should not incl the thousands of professionals within bureau who always have and continue do valuable service. And even though has become fashionable of late to critic Hoover, it should not be forgotten that was the man who seized control in 1920s from political hacks and hangers and built the FBI into what is still con ered the most efficient law enforcem agency in the world.

Hoover was a man who stayed on yond his time, secure in a power nurtu by self-appointed sycophants. His car despite contemporary criticism, was m admirable than not, but in the final ch ter he cast a shadow on that in which had so much pride.

A POLICE czar is contrary to ideals of this nation. Such power must be allowed for one man again. Acco ability must be demanded, even as it being demanded now.

In a recent speech, the present dir tor, Clarence Kelley concedes t "perhaps our operations will derive be fit from the unprecedented surge of m media and official interest in the FBI."

It is unlikely Hoover would h made such a concession.

But having said that, Kelley pointed out that "the threat posed by thal bands of revolutionaries, hate gro and extremists who openly espouse lence and hostility to our system of g ernment" still exists.

"Unchecked," he said, "these p dlers of death and destruction represen very genuine threat to the freedom tranquility of people like you — law-a ing and productive citizens throughout nation."

That fact should not be forgot even as the FBI is being held account for past sins and struggles to regain public confidence it needs if it is to effective.

The Courier-Journal

Louisville, Ky., November 20, 1975

NO SINGLE adjective will suffice to describe the massive snooping activities of the FBI, details of which are still being divulged by Senate intelligence committee investigators. Destructive intrusions into the private lives of thousands of people, from the well-known to the unknown, by a government police agency and for no valid reason, is unconstitutional, immoral and, ultimately, horrifying.

Yet it happened. Campaigns of harassment, including the mailing of anonymous letters, were directed at thousands of individuals whose only offense was to belong to groups in the sidestreams of American life, among them radical, civil rights and women's liberation movements. A deliberate and prolonged effort was made to destroy the late Martin Luther King as a national black leader by such despicable methods as an anonymous suggestion, following his award of the Nobel Peace Prize, that he commit suicide.

It's not enough, however, to register revulsion at such perversions of law enforcement. We must try hard to make certain that the opportunity can never recur. Setting a limit on the term a person may serve as FBI director is one obvious safeguard. The lifetime tenure of J. Edgar Hoover was clearly a factor in the gross misuse of FBI power.

The memory of current disclosures, of course, should afford protection for a time. Any attempt to twist legitimate inquiries to serve illegal ends or to pursue personal vendettas through the agency is now more likely to be reported by those officials who still have scruples.

But the next time the country goes through a tumultuous period — and there will be restless times ahead, even though they may not be carbon copies of the civil rights and war protests — this lesson could be forgotten if a preventive mechanism isn't built into the system now. And at such times, the persecution mania can quickly spread beyond the FBI, as is demonstrated in Richard Harris' current *New Yorker* series of articles on Alan and Margaret McSurely, the anti-poverty workers whose revolutionary ideas upset the Eastern Kentucky establishment and brought down the full power of unrestrained police and prosecutors in 1967.

Above all, what must be remembered is that it's not just radicals or even the politically active who are harassed unduly when law enforcement agents run amok. Ordinary citizens can easily be swept up into the net, too. When the privacy and the freedom of any individual, however extreme his views, is threatened by unwarranted government intrusion, then nobody's privacy and freedom are secure.

Chicago Tribune

Chicago, Ill., November 20, 1975

e latest evidence of extracurricular ıres by the FBI, presented Tuesday e Senate Select Committee on Intelce, tends to confirm previous res of its eagerness—more than a decago under the late J. Edgar Hoover discredit the Rev. Martin Luther Jr. Mr. King was later assassinatn 1968.

ıether or not the FBI was responsifor the anonymous letters threaten- Mr. King and embarrassing his ement that were cited before the mittee, there is enough evidence to that the FBI went far beyond its er responsibility in gathering dirt Ir. King. If Mr. King's image suffers, the FBI's image suffers even more.

Fortunately the FBI appears to have abandoned this sort of activity long ago. The importance of getting its past sins on the record lies not in smearing the FBI [tho this may be the purpose of some of its critics] but rather in the deterrent effect it will have on future excesses by the FBI and other intelligence agencies. The FBI's mission in this country is an essential one, and in general it has done its job well. There is nothing to gain by making it the whipping boy for past sins. But there is much to gain by alerting government in general to these sins and encouraging the resolution never to let them happen again.

THE SAGINAW NEWS

Saginaw, Mich., November 20, 1975

The FBI's orchestrated attack on Martin Luther King Jr. and other groups and individuals associated with civil rights and other reform movements throughout the 1960s further attests to the wayward ways of the government's intelligence community.

Possibly that's a thing of the past. It should be. Yet the latest evidence made public by the Senate Intelligence Committee raises macabre questions.

There is enough to at least suggest that Senate probers dig until a reasonable determination can be made on what role, if any, the government may have played in the King assassination. That is a chilling suggestion, to be sure. Yet it is hardly more chilling than testimony already a matter of record concerning alleged spy network involvement with organized crime in the field of international assassination.

The Senate panel has now heard testimony from one former high-ranking FBI official that the tactics used in the assault upon social activists were "rough, tough and dirty."

What the public is entitled to know is just how rough and tough they were. That is, if the public can stand it.

There is already a pretty good case made for how dirty it was.

The concerted six-year attack on Dr. King with the sole aim of bringing him down and destroying his effectiveness as a leading civil rights advocate reads like a horror story.

The trace is clear in official documents released by the Senate that Dr. King was a particular target of J. Edgar Hoover's dislike. They indictate the FBI's campaign against King was conducted for fully six years. And that each time the civil rights advocate rose in visibility the intensity of surreptitious attacks upon him intensified. That can hardly be coincidence.

It didn't stop at that. The word is now on the record that the Federal Bureau of Investigation resorted to raw psychological warfare that may well have destroyed homes and marriages. Part of this nifty little game was use of the mails to suggest to spouses of men and women involved in racial harmony programs that they had other motives.

No individual, no groups associated with any form of dissent against the government or any movement for reform were immune from such FBI-sponsored tactics.

What the Senate panel has in hand is enough to gag a maggot. There is new evidence that Rev. King was confronted by government blackmail taking the form of a subtle suggestion that he could commit suicide 34 days before he was to receive the Nobel Peace Prize in 1964. The subtlty is not missed. The FBI supposedly had enough on him to ruin his reputation — all of it gathered by the rankest invasions of privacy.

At the root of the mentality that commanded the minutest inspection of private lives was the suspicion that a Communist lurked in every closet. And beyond that, that sex was the root of all evil.

The incredible aspect from direct testimony is that when agents came back to report there was no evidence of subversive links, they were sent back repeatedly to look again.

Dr. King may have been uniquely singled out for character assassination, but he was not the only target of what appears to be a manic preoccupation with the grossest kind of dirt gathering. Other groups were thoroughly infiltrated. There is a litany of illegal bugging and breaking-in, of keeping dossiers on congressmen and their private habits and the investigations of newsmen and columnists.

The question before the Senate Intelligence Committee today is not whether Dr. Martin Luther King Jr. or thousands upon thousands of others were perfect human beings. It is whether their Constitutional rights were trampled left and right by what indeed became a rogue elephant on the loose.

It can only be presumed that the FBI has mended its ways since Clarence M. Kelley took over as bureau chief two years and some months ago, In light of the latest revelations, that responsibility devolves more heavily than ever upon Mr. Kelley.

On numerous occasions since taking office he has promised a fresh approach to FBI activities. Just as often he has been an apologist for sleazy operations conducted before he assumed command.

Always the excuse has been that what was done was done for "the good of the nation" and in the interest of national security. It is impossible to defend the latest documented actions on any such ground.

Mr. Kelley inherited a messy situation. Only he can see to it that past practices are never again resorted to.

Democrat and Chronicle

Rochester, N.Y., November 25, 1975

Revelation of a no-holds-barred FBI effort to discredit the late Martin Luther King is so shocking it's hard to know what to say.

The Federal Bureau of Investigation, supposedly in the business of protecting Americans, admittedly harassed the renowned civil rights leader with anonymous letters in the early 1960s. One was accompanied by a tape recording containing material embarrassing to Dr. King.

King interpreted the letter's warning that "... there is only one thing left for you to do ..." as an urging to commit suicide.

Whether or not that was the FBI's intent, the letter clearly constituted an attempt to blackmail King into withdrawing as a leader of the growing black movement. When law enforcement agencies commit crime in attempting to affect political leadership, American democracy is in danger from its own government.

Since some FBI officials welcome the revelations as a step in ushering out an era of which they did not approve, there is hope that such outrages are a thing of the past. The sad thing is that Dr. King is not alive to receive the apology due him from the FBI.

Portland, Ore., November 20, 1975

Columnist Jack Anderson has come up with appalling evidence of the extent to which the late J. Edgar Hoover would go to satisfy his obsession with destroying the career of the late Martin Luther King.

But none was so sickening as the material dredged up by the Senate investigating committee indicating that Hoover's FBI attempted to force the great civil rights leader to commit suicide.

So the once proud image of the founder of the FBI continues to crumble as shocking evidence mounts about the abuses undertaken at his direction by a powerful agency that had held the public's trust.

While King seemed to be a special target of Hoover, without cause, he was far from the only person harassed by the FBI.

Sen. Walter Mondale, D-Minn., a level-headed legislator not given to overstatement, was so alarmed by what his committee has seen that he called FBI activities under Hoover "a roadmap to the destruction of American democracy."

Offsetting such harsh judgment is the fact that eventually the institutions of American democracy did work to uncover the abuses and check them. That's what the Senate committee is up to right now.

And that brings up another vital point. It is urgent that the senators, in their just outrage over the wrongs they are finding, do not engage in the American habit of over-reacting and letting a pendulum that has swung too far one way go too far the other.

Despite the Hoover abuses, the FBI also did some very important work for the country, and the nation will continue to need its service in the future.

Hoover had been a faithful servant. Unfortunately he succumbed to the temptations to use the power he had amassed in evil ways.

It is important that no FBI director ever have so much power again, or achieve a position beyond accountability. But it is also important that the FBI not be dismantled or emasculated because of the sins of a former director who had placed himself above the law.

THE LINCOLN STAR

Lincoln, Neb., November 20, 1975

The story now unfolding of FBI harassment of American citizens, most notably the late Dr. Martin Luther King, is a grim reminder both of the abuse that can be suffered from entrenched power, in this instance in the imposing form of J. Edgar Hoover, and the paranoia of the Nixon years.

Hoover personally hated Dr. King, but beyond that, King represented to the FBI a disruptive, un-American threat from the left, a bad influence which could undermine the nation's strength. That Dr. King was leading a moral revolution using the rights given most Americans but long withheld from his people did not register with Mr. Hoover. Similarly, the dissent which swirled ominously outside what Nixon regarded as the mainstream of American thought was viewed by the disgraced former president with dark suspicion. Their reactions to what bedeviled them was in the tradition of all the dictators of the ages.

In the case of the Nobel Peace Prize laureate Dr. King, the FBI, we are learning, tailed him, bugged him, discredited him, lied about him, harassed him and s[ent] him anonymous letters suggesting that [he] commit suicide before he was publi[cly] ruined. The latter tactic has got to be o[ne] of the sleaziest, and most embarrassi[ng,] disgusting and sophomoric in the annals [of] the FBI.

That the FBI is riding out the storm [of] these new revelations with relative grace [is] a healthy sign. The agency seems to [be] aware of the need for a public discussion [of] past abuses so that such tactics can [be] purged from the FBI's modus operandi.

The continuing review of abus[es] perpetrated by authority in the past may [be] depressing, it may make us feel uncomf[or]table and it may seem to be vaguely [un]patriotic. But what is happening now m[ost] assuredly is patriotic and necessa[ry] because these investigations will [re]emphasize the basic freedoms America[ns] tend to take for granted and they will h[elp] assure a future in which all America[ns] hopefully will be able to enjoy the rig[hts] and freedoms which to some have be[en] only empty promises written on paper.

Sentinel Star

Orlando, Fla., November 22, 1975

TWO CONCLUSIONS can be drawn from FBI testimony being spread across the news by Senate Intelligence Committee hearings: 1) The FBI has been doing its jobs and 2), it has been ruthlessly exceeding its authority.

There is truth in both conclusions, but the preponderance of evidence so far weighs heavily on the side of the bureau's vigilance against domestic subversion.

* * *

FBI MEMOS from the late 1960s through the early 1970s reveal orders for investigating student groups, antiwar groups, neighborhood antibusing groups, certain women's liberation organizations, violence-prone individuals and other specified organizations and people with a history of riotous opposition to the establishment, the status quo or whatever the target of their hate happened to be.

If investigation turned up nothing stronger than peaceful protest, continued FBI surveillance was ordered as a precaution.

Considering the student disturbances of the 1960s — the bombings, the street riots, the needless loss of innocent lives — the FBI, in our judgment, acted entirely within its jurisdiction by investigating suspect factions and keeping them under watch. Indeed, we sleep more soundly by knowing that subversives out to overthrow the government are known to the government, and we can't see what purpose, other than destructive, can be served [by] publicized probing.

* * *

TO PERFORM proficient[ly] any federally empowered inv[es]tigative bureau must oper[ate] with reasonable secrecy or [it] naturally converts to an ea[rly] warning system for criminals.

Unreasonable secrecy [is] another matter and could [be] applied to the "dirty trick[s"] ascribed to the FBI during t[he] tenure of Director J. Edg[ar] Hoover and to the anonymo[us] letter sent to the late Dr. Mar[tin] Luther King which seemed [to] suggest he commit suicide [or] face ruin.

* * *

IF THE charges prove tr[ue] they certainly illustrate t[he] excess of power that can accr[ue] to an individual or an organiz[a]tion over a long span of tim[e.] Like the FBI investigations [of] dissident groups, the bureau['s] scare tactics deserve simil[ar] scrutiny for the same reasor[s.]

The democratic system [of] checks and balances must [be] rigidly maintained within [all] branches of government if t[he] democracy is to survive.

Using the same yardstick, t[he] rights of individuals to peacef[ul] protest cannot be allowed [to] erupt into revolution. That is t[he] form of checks and balances t[he] FBI has, since its inception ar[ound] through war and peace, do[ne] with remarkable success.

If the time has come to tighte[n] its own operational check rei[ns,] the system provides the mean[s.]

It can and should be do[ne] without melodrama.

FBI DOCUMENTS REVEAL 92 BURGLARIES OF SOCIALIST WORKERS PARTY OFFICES

Official Federal Bureau of Investigation papers, released March 28, revealed that the FBI had burglarized the New York City offices of the Socialist Workers Party (SWP) at least 92 times between 1960 and 1966. The papers had been sought by the leftist party as evidence for its $27 million lawsuit against the FBI. On most of the occasions, the FBI records showed, nothing had been taken from the SWP offices, but numerous papers had been photographed. The SWP papers photographed included correspondence, records of political contributions, minutes of party meetings and notes on legal strategy of party members facing federal prosecution.

According to the March 29 *New York Times*, the FBI had previously admitted to 238 surreptitious entries, known as "black-bag jobs," involving 14 organizations between 1942 and 1968. The *Times* reported that, according to sources on the Senate Intelligence Committee, the actions against the SWP were not included in the figure of 238. The *Times* quoted an unidentified FBI source as saying that agents who undertook the burglaries received substantial bonuses. The agents, if arrested, would have had to take personal responsibility for the burglary, without naming the bureau.

Peter Camejo, the SWP candidate for President, March 28 charged that New York City police had afforded the FBI agents protection while they carried out the burglaries. As evidence, he quoted from the released FBI records requests for authorizations for the burglaries saying: "Full security assured," and, "Security set forth at the time of the original authorization remains the same." FBI sources quoted in the March 29 *Times* story expressed doubt that the FBI would have informed the police in advance of burglaries. Camejo took issue with FBI director Clarence M. Kelley's statement that the burglaries were undertaken for reasons of national security. He said the information obtained by the FBI had been used "to get SWP members fired from their jobs and to otherwise disrupt the legal political activities of the SWP."

The Miami Herald

Miami, Fla., March 30, 1976

WHEN a break-in was discovered at the Watergate offices of the national Democratic Party — and a Republican administration tried to cover it up — the reverberations shook this constitutional republic to its foundations.

It will be interesting, therefore, to see what kind of reaction, if any, follows the disclosure that not one but a series of 92 break-ins and burglaries occurred between 1960 and 1966 at the New York offices of the Socialist Workers Party.

Those misdeeds took place during a period overlapping the administrations of Dwight Eisenhower, John Kennedy and Lyndon Johnson. The Federal Bureau of Investigation did the dirty work, usually in the middle of the night using specially trained agents. New York City police apparently cooperated.

Details of the FBI operations against the SWP were made available only after a court ordered an end to the long FBI coverup. The party had to engage in a long series of lawsuits to pry the information loose from a reluctant federal government.

Unfortunately, the coverup continued for so long that the passage of time and the public's weariness with "Watergates" will probably temper whatever predisposition may have existed to be outraged by the FBI's activities in this case.

Nevertheless, the subject should not be passed over too lightly. A break-in at the offices of the Socialist Workers Party is just as alien to the American system of constitutional law as a break-in at the offices of one of the major parties.

The acts are not made any less abhorrent by the fact that they took place during the administrations of presidents other than Richard Nixon. Neither can the actions be rationalized away because they occurred during the reign of the late J. Edgar Hoover, who is no longer in charge of the FBI but whose policies still haunt it.

While nobody would suggest that the SWP incidents could or should be magnified to a national ordeal of Watergate proportions, there must at least be a complete and open airing of the federal government's unconstitutional activities against a legitimate political party, with fair recompense for any damages done.

THE ATLANTA CONSTITUTION

Atlanta, Ga., March 31, 1976

William C. Sullivan, a former high official in the FBI, calls them "black bag jobs" and, in a 1966 internal memo, reminded his associates that "such technique involves trespass and is clearly illegal."

Nevertheless, recent disclosures tell us, FBI agents were among the most active burglars in the country for 28 years ending in 1968. They racked up 238 black bag jobs, including 92 at the New York offices of the Socialist Workers Party and the Young Socialist Alliance. This was not a matter of ferreting out spies; it was political harrassment pure and simple.

No wonder people have lost faith in and respect for institutions like the FBI and others. When an agency that is supposed to uphold and enforce the law makes a regular routine of breaking it, sooner or later the public wises up.

"We know there has been a loss of credibility," says the FBI's new director, Clarence Kelley, "but we're now at the turn of the road and we're coming back."

All Americans hope that's true.

The Charleston Gazette

Charleston, West Va., March 31, 1976

FBI burglaries of the offices of the Socialist Workers party aren't quite the same as the burglary of Democratic headquarters by hoods from Richard Nixon's campaign committee.

It's worse.

The Watergate burglary, at least, wasn't pulled off by policemen sworn to uphold the law, not break it.

The regular raids by the FBI on the Socialist Workers party apparently were undertaken in the belief that any organization with the word "socialist" in it is a threat to America.

That may be the case. But there are Americans who believe Republicans are a threat to America, and there are Americans who believe Democrats are a threat to America.

What people, including policemen, believe about Republicans, Democrats, and Socialist Workers is beside the point. The point is that all three of these parties are legitimate organizations protected by the Constitution.

A Socialist Worker has the same constitutional rights as the Republican county chairman, and neither should be harassed by policemen because of what their ideology is perceived to be.

A good policeman knows that he is employed to protect rights, not trample on them. And a good policeman cannot assume that unpopular opinion is the same as unlawful opinion.

THE KNICKERBOCKER NEWS

··· UNION-STAR ···

Albany, N.Y., March 30, 1976

The Federal Bureau of Investigation has admitted burglarizing the New York City offices of the Socialist Workers Party no fewer than 92 times during a six year period in the 1960s. Any reasonable man might wonder whether those 92 burglaries were included in the bureau's annual compilation of crime statistics for those years. If so, it might help explain the ever-rising crime rate.

The Providence Journal

Providence, R.I., March 31, 1976

There seems no end to the trail of snooping that federal agents have been willing to carry out in defiance of the law. Mail intercepted, phones tapped, legitimate groups harassed — all for the most specious reasons. Disclosures of the past couple of years have given Americans widening grounds for fearing that the Bill of Rights is more fragile than was known.

The latest disclosure in the series, of course, is that agents of the Federal Bureau of Investigation conducted at least 92 burglaries of the offices of the leftist Socialist Workers Party in the years from 1960 to 1966. In what the bureau likes to call "surreptitious entries," agents broke into the offices at night and photographed, over the six-and-a-half-year time period, thousands of documents and correspondence. Much of the FBI's haul had nothing at all to do with national security or foreign intelligence, the only areas in which the FBI might even possibly have had an interest.

These disclosures, although their shock value is diminished by the weight of similar evidence that has been accumulating for months, must be seen for what they mean: that a long-running and wholly unwarranted campaign of governmental lawbreaking was waged by an FBI that for years operated immune from nearly all restraint.

The disclosures demonstrate anew how easy it is for a secret police agency to trample on the constitutional rights of any individual or group whose views do not fall within the scope of conduct officially deemed acceptable. It is this frightening simplicity with which official subversion can be undertaken, and the danger that it could apply to any citizen, any organization, that makes the news of the FBI's string of burglaries so damning.

The Socialist Workers Party, as it itself has insisted for years and as the FBI has conceded, is a nonviolent Marxist organization, operating entirely within the scope of America's laws. There was, and is, no justification whatsoever for any agency of government to arrogate to itself authority to act the thief and to flout the rights of peacable citizens. The fact that the late J. Edgar Hoover halted the FBI's practice of break-ins in 1966 is no assurance that such excesses may not recur.

Mr. most of Mr. Hoover's long tenure as FBI Director, he ruled his empire as one virtually unassailable by any critic, including the string of Presidents he ostensibly served. This isolation and secrecy bred into the Bureau an air of invulnerability and invincibility, a climate that encouraged excess. Secrecy, even more than concentration of power, fosters corruption and tends to blind leaders to basic principles of law, ethics and just plain good sense.

Since Mr. Hoover's passing, the Department of Justice has taken a few steps — some of them sound — to bring the former rogue FBI under tighter departmental jurisdiction. The disclosures of the FBI's "black-bag jobs" make this control absolutely imperative. No FBI director, it should go without saying, can be suffered to gain the kind of autocratic sway that typified the Hoover years.

Beyond this, the FBI burglaries make it especially crucial that Congress set up a permanent committee to keep track of what U.S. intelligence agencies are doing. And the Hoover example makes it important that Congress give final approval to the bill providing that no FBI director can serve more than a single 10-year term. This bill passed the Senate a year ago by a vote of 85 to 0. The House should act in accord.

THE PLAIN DEALER

Cleveland, Ohio, March 30, 1976

A burglary committed by an FBI agent is just as much a crime as any other burglary. Dirty tricks and "black bag" tactics are a discredit to the FBI and the federal government.

Ninety-two times, once every three weeks over a 6½-year period, FBI gumshoe operators burglarized the Socialist Workers party headquarters in New York City. They made thousands of photographs of documents, letters and membership lists.

Never, so far as the records show, was a search warrant obtained. The night break-ins were never, so far as has come out, interfered with by city police.

These facts, mainly from the FBI's own reports, show a seamy side to the FBI's work of protecting the United States from subversives.

One evil spawns others. The Justice Department had asserted that the Socialist Workers were not one of the targets of federal agents. Now that has been proved a lie.

The FBI has acknowledged that it made 238 illegal entries against 14 "target" organizations, plus some other "domestic subversive targets" between 1942 and 1968.

What is to prevent the FBI from declaring subversive some other political party or club, some labor organization or civil rights group? Then the offices of that organization, and the home of its leader, as with the Socialist Workers party, would be considered a proper target for breaking and entering in the night season.

Some limit must be put on these doings. FBI sneaky tricks should require at least search warrant scrutiny in advance and responsible checkups by some other branch of government.

THE COMMERCIAL APPEAL

Memphis, Tenn., March 30, 1976

ONE OF THE BIG problems in fighting crime today is that the FBI, once the paragon of integrity in law enforcement, has lost much of its credibility.

The disclosure of scores of burglaries of Socialist Workers Party offices by FBI agents back in the early 1960s contradicts Justice Department statements denying such activity. Coming amid so many other revelations of strange and sometimes unethical conduct in FBI operations of the past, this is one more raveling of a once-proud past.

But once again it underlines the great task of rebuilding the Federal Bureau of Investigation's image. No one is more acutely aware of this need than Clarence Kelley, the candid former Kansas City police chief who is now director of the nation's foremost investigative agency.

KELLEY, WE ARE glad to note, wastes no time making apologies for the embarrassing, improper and illegal activities which have surfaced since the empire of J. Edgar Hoover cracked with his death in May, 1972.

Kelley does spend a lot of time trying to convince the public that none of those abuses has been swept under the rug. And he keeps repeating that the present FBI is being run strictly according to what is legal and what is right.

While the director rightly says that performance is the best way to restore public confidence, he admits he spends much time being "a salesman for the FBI."

Kelley is aware of the pitfalls there. He agrees that the FBI was "oversold" in Hoover's day. "I think this attention on the spectacular gave an aura of mystery and mystique to the FBI, when there was none," says Kelley. "It's a hard, laborious type of activity — knocking on doors, going through the investigative process. The aura was aided, to a great extent, by the movies and the press."

The "guilty" pleas to that will be many. The hero worship in himself which Hoover encouraged, and the cover he built for FBI excesses and imperfections all succeeded because so many image makers were willing to be led — or misled.

SOMETHING HAS BEEN learned. Congress, the Justice Department, the executive branch and the public know what to avoid and what recourse to take to keep the FBI both honest and efficient.

We need the bureau. It is the model for all police agencies in America. It is the ultimate in law-enforcement training. It sets the tone and character that filter down through local police and sheriff departments.

That is why it is particularly important for the FBI to clean its house, to restore confidence, to rekindle respect for law.

At the same time, respect for the constitutional rights of private citizens will be a determining factor in how fast the FBI travels back up the road to credibility.

FORT WORTH STAR-TELEGRAM

Fort Worth, Tex., March 31, 1976

In the light of new information about the "surreptitious" activities of the Federal Bureau of Investigation in the past, it becomes more urgent than ever that the FBI's intelligence gathering activities be brought under strict control and careful supervision.

The new facts reveal that the FBI burglarized the New York offices of the Socialist Workers party and the Young Socialist Alliance twice a month from 1960 to 1966.

Being staunch free enterprisers, we hold no brief for the political aims of the socialists. But that's beside the point.

The surveillance-by-burglary activities were, according to as eminent an authority as former FBI intelligence official William C. Sullivan, "clearly illegal." Disclosure of the office burglaries suggests that the FBI may have engaged in more such activity than it indicated when it admitted to 238 burglaries before a Senate committee last September.

Whether one or a million, however, the principle remains the same. An FBI official told the Star-Telegram editorial board repeatedly during a recent interview that, yes, the FBI had broken the law. He insisted that this lawbreaking by the nation's No. 1 law-enforcement agency was justified in defending the nation's security against internal enemies.

Assuming all present members of the FBI have only the preservation of our constitutional freedoms and the safety of our innocent citizens at heart, however, such law-breaking would be dangerous both to individual and national liberties.

Today, the targets of surreptitious acts by the FBI may be "radical" groups about whose rights the general public feels little concern.

But who defines the term "radical" for the FBI? And who will the term include tomorrow, or next year, or 10 years from now? Labor unions? Jews? Methodists and Baptists? Masons?

It can't happen here, you say. Maybe not. But why take a chance? We're highly cognizant of the FBI's vital role in safeguarding America's freedoms. What we're saying is simply that the Constitution could best be protected by an agency operating under terms of the Constitution.

Los Angeles Times

Los Angeles, Calif., March 30, 1976

Only Salvador Dali in his prime would be capable of capturing in all its refulgent nuances the late J. Edgar Hoover's surrealistic vision of the tiny Socialist Workers Party as a threat to the national security of the United States.

In an era when fact often surpasses fantasy, the FBI has scored again. The nation's top law-enforcement agency broke into the office of the party and its youth affiliate as often as twice a month for a total of 92 postmidnight raids in the early 1960s.

Documents pried from the FBI under a court order showed that the industrious FBI agents photographed at least 8,700 pages of party files, including personal letters.

The party is suing the FBI and other government agencies, charging unconstitutional harassment of legal political activities. The defense to be offered by the government should be as interesting, if not more so, than the disclosure of the burglaries.

New York Post

New York, N.Y., March 30, 1976

Secret spying operations within the continental U. S. by skilled agents. Predawn burglaries by these operatives, not just once or twice but scores of times. Meticulous descriptions of burglarized premises. Photographing of thousands of documents, outright theft of others. All of it subversive, illegal and an affront to the U. S. Constitution.

An urgent case for the FBI? In a way; the trouble is that the spies were special agents of the FBI who, between 1960 and 1966, repeatedly entered and robbed the offices of the Socialist Workers Party. There is no dispute about what happened. Despite an earlier assertion by the Justice Dept. denying such activity, what amounts to a full FBI confession has now been made.

The confession was scarcely voluntary. Rather the G-men have provided the records under legal compulsion of an SWP federal lawsuit. As a result, a number of consequential legal decisions are now pending. None of them involves the "national security"; despite its relentless criminal activity, the FBI was wholly unable to produce any evidence to incriminate the SWP.

Will the proposed new Justice controls on FBI intelligence operations restrict such routine abuse of the most basic citizens' rights?

According to one official source, official Washington did not have any records of the SWP spying; the records were retained, it is said, by the FBI here. If that is so, if headquarters were really ignorant of the operation, how many other local "black bag" jobs were carried out? And how does Washington propose to regulate them?

The Justice "guidelines," as described so far, would, in fact, appear to authorize another series of burglaries of the SWP, a small, marginal, leftist sect that plainly presents no clear and present danger to the republic. One original justification for the break-ins was that the party members might turn to violence. The new guideline permits investigations of groups that "will" break the law—except, of course, the FBI.

FBI'S 'ILLEGAL' METHODS REVEALED; KELLEY APOLOGIZES TO U.S. PUBLIC

The Senate Select Committee on Intelligence charged April 28 that the FBI and other U.S. agencies had conducted investigations—often employing "illegal or improper" methods—of a vast number of Americans. The committee urged that the activities of the intelligence agencies be governed by statutory rules, and offered 96 recommendations as a basis for legislation. The proposals—all dealing with domestic intelligence—were contained in the second volume of the committee's final report.

The main proposals made by the committee were:

■ That domestic intelligence investigations be limited to cases in which there were specific grounds to believe that terrorist or hostile espionage activities had been committed or were about to be committed. Political views or activities, the committee stressed, would not be grounds for an investigation. Continuation of a preliminary investigation beyond 30 days, or of a full investigation beyond a year would require approval by the Attorney General or his designee.

■ That domestic intelligence investigations be conducted (with a few narrow exceptions) only by the FBI.

■ That judicial warrants be required for use of electronic surveillance, mail-opening or unauthorized entry.

The committee also called for closer supervision and review of the FBI by the attorney general, vigorous oversight of the FBI and other agencies by a permanent Senate Intelligence Committee, and an eight-year maximum term for the head of the FBI.

The report maintained that abuses by the intelligence agencies stemmed from the failure of the "constitutional system of checks and balances." The executive branch, Congress and the courts all shared blame for abdicating their responsibilities, the report said.

The staff of the Senate Select Intelligence Committee May 5 issued a follow-up study to the committee's official report, which charged that the FBI campaign against Dr. Martin Luther King had been "marked by extreme personal vindictiveness," particularly by J. Edgar Hoover, then FBI director. The six-year campaign that included bugging King's hotel room and mailing him a letter suggesting he commit suicide was first revealed by the Senate committee in November 1975.

FBI Director Clarence M. Kelley responded May 8 to the recent disclosures of his agency's activities by making an apology to the American public. Kelley characterized some of the FBI activities as "clearly wrong and quite indefensible" and said that they must never be repeated. The abuses, Kelley said, had chiefly beset the FBI in the "twilight" of Hoover's 48-year tenure as FBI director.

The Philadelphia Inquirer

Philadelphia, Pa., May 8, 1976

You don't have to be a fan of some of the organizations the FBI played dirty—and illegal—tricks on to feel a sense of outrage at the dirty tricks. The Senate Select Committee on Intelligence has now released another report providing new details on that 15-year counter-intelligence program, known as Cointelpro. The report makes fascinating, if hardly enjoyable, reading.

In the Cointelpro operation, the FBI, says the report, went after "a staggering range of targets." Those included not only the Communist Party and the Ku Klux Klan but anything which, in the FBI's view, came under the heading of "black nationalist" groups, ranging from the Black Panthers to the Southern Christian Leadership Conference.

The report describes the effort to destroy the late Dr. Martin Luther King as "marked by extreme personal vindictiveness," especially on the part of FBI Director J. Edgar Hoover. And that effort did not end with Dr. King's death by murder; the FBI continued trying to discredit his memory.

One quotation from an FBI memo is particularly edifying, in an ironic way. Two students who had participated in a free-speech demonstration were also put on the target list because of their "obvious disregard for decency and established morality."

For it was, of course, the FBI itself which, in disrupting groups and discrediting citizens who did not enjoy Mr. Hoover's seal of approval, was not only showing an "obvious disregard for decent and established morality" but for the Constitution and laws of the United States.

Now that the facts are known, what is to be done about them? Publicity poses problems; it does not solve them. True, J. Edgar Hoover is no longer around, and there is a new attorney general, a new FBI director, and new department guidelines for the FBI.

Yet the central lessons of it all cannot be brushed off. Police agencies cannot be relied upon to police themselves; nor can the executive branch be relied upon to oversee itself. The checks and balances of our system do not work automatically. It is Congress's responsibility to put the guidelines in the form of legislation and to maintain careful and continuous oversight to make sure that power is not abused again.

The Washington Post

Washington, D.C., May 3, 1976

BACK WHEN PRESIDENT NIXON'S impeachment was being debated, his champions tried to ›unter the charges of abuse of presidential power y raising, among other things, the "everybody does " defense. According to this theory, the enemies sts, the 17 wiretaps and the like could be excused beuse Democratic Presidents, notably John F. Kenedy and Lyndon Johnson, had also misused the IRS nd FBI. Mr. Nixon's defenders split among themlves on whether such conduct could be justified; eir point was that, however obnoxious, it was not nique to the Nixon presidency, and Mr. Nixon ould not be singled out for punishment.

The Senate select committee's report on domestic telligence has borne out part of this contention–but nly part. The Kennedy administration did launch nproper IRS investigations of right-wing (and, later, ft-wing) groups. President Kennedy or Attorney eneral Robert Kennedy did use FBI wiretaps to gain olitical intelligence on lobbying for sugar quotas, nd to investigate at least two leaks to journalists. resident Johnson employed FBI surveillance at the 64 Democratic convention. He and his aides also sed the bureau extensively to probe the activities d views of anti-war critics, including U.S. senators. oreover, it was the Johnson administration's anxiees about civil disorders and dissent that sparked the st expansion of surveillance of law-abiding citizens the CIA, the Army and other agencies in the mid-60s.

Such uses of power are neither decent nor defensie. They stopped far short, however, of the offenses at primarily caused Mr. Nixon's departure in disace: wholesale obstruction of justice, systematic ing about crimes and withholding evidence, and tting up a private, secret spying operation in the hite House—which was unknown to Congress and, erefore, not even potentially subject to the kind of ersight that the Congress could have exercised er such authorized agencies as the CIA and FBI if it d had the sense and the will to do so. Once the full agnitude of these uniquely Nixonian deeds had en disclosed, even Mr. Nixon's staunchest supports largely abandoned the feeble claim that he had en the victim of a relentless partisan attack.

However, a complementary notion does persist, d is generally justified. This is that the illiberal acts the Kennedy and Johnson administrations have en treated too lightly or excused too fast. Legally eaking, little punishment can now be meted out. t that does not dispose of the matter, for people seously concerned about restraining government and hancing civil liberties do have at minimum an oblition to acknowledge the misdeeds of Presidents nom they regarded generally as friends. Beyond at, the forces and fears behind these abuses of wer should be more widely understood, because ose impulses were not unique to any one adminisation or period of history.

Without embarking on a dissertation on the perils power, we would note a few troubling tendencies at are amply illustrated by the domestic spying of e Kennedy and, even more, the Johnson years. One the tendency of Presidents and their aides to use natever tools may be helpful and at hand. The FBI as capable, so it was given many chores. NSA knew how to intercept international phone calls, so the "watch lists" were drawn up. And so on.

Second, there is the tendency toward righteousness in high places, the elitist conviction that those entrusted with great power are somehow vested with special perceptions of what is right and necessary for America. This can be a bureaucratic conceit as well as a presidential one; J. Edgar Hoover's FBI, the Senate report observed, "saw itself as the guardian of the public order." Such attitudes may stem from arrogance or insecurity. In either case they become doubly dangerous in seasons of public discontent, because opposition tends to stir up a volatile mix of belligerence and bewilderment. One senior aide to President Johnson testified that when the anti-war protests erupted, top officials could not believe that "a cause that is so clearly right for the country, as they perceived it, would be so widely attacked if there were not some (foreign) force behind it."

This points to the third tendency, one of the darker themes throughout American history: the tendency to search for alien influences as an explanation of dissent–or as a scapegoat for official failures. The FBI, CIA and Army intelligence reports of the 1960s are permeated with suspicion and hostility; the "new left," so sprawling and fragmented, was seen as even more sinister than the domestic "Communist threat" of the late 1940s and early 1950s. With the rising public protest against the war, and the simultaneous eruption of urban riots, the government felt itself under siege–so much so that these misplaced protective efforts, as distinct from its genuine responsibility to maintain order, seemed imperative. Indeed, given the temperament of the President and the temper of the times, future historians may marvel that repressive operations were not even more extreme.

None of these attitudes is novel. They were not secrets at the time. Instead, they were widely shared and more widely tolerated, especially among politicians who were reluctant to challenge or alienate an aggressive President or agencies as entrenched and ingenious as the FBI. And so suspicions multiplied. The real sources of public disaffection were not examined carefully. The truly violent forces were not focused on. And a war justified as a fight for freedom overseas caused the erosion of the very liberties at home that are the basis of true democratic security.

In this perspective, Watergate becomes even more exceptional and much more ominous. The more one learns about the secret side of government in the 1960s, the more one sees how crude and offensive the misdeeds of Mr. Nixon and his men had to become, and what fortuitous influences of journalistic persistence and judicial pressure were required, before the country and Congress became aroused. Just before the House committee's impeachment vote, Rep. James Mann (D-S.C.) warned that "Next time, there may be no watchman in the night." There was none in the 1960s, and the nation was sorely hurt. The question now is what Americans will learn from that tragic experience. The remedy does not lie solely in new laws or stronger institutional checks and balances. The real safeguard is something even harder to sustain: a basic spirit of liberality that not only tolerates diversity and peaceful dissent, but welcomes them, especially in times of stress–and accordingly disciplines the exercise of power.

FORT WORTH STAR-TELEGRAM

Fort Worth, Tex., May 11, 1976

When the FBI allocates more money for domestic security informants than it earmarks for payment for information against organized crime, it's time to reassess some priorities.

That is one of the startling facts recently underscored by the U. S. Senate Select Committee on Intelligence.

The committee pointed out that for 1976 the FBI has budgeted $7 million for domestic security informants, an amount that is double what it spends for organized crime informants.

It is obvious that a serious intelligence effort is needed to combat the activities of underground terrorists and subversive elements in this country with foreign ties. But it is questionable whether the threat posed by those elements is greater than damage being done in this society by ever increasing crime.

Much of the crime that plagues this nation that is not directly attributable to organized crime has a traceable indirect connection. One has only to ponder the robberies, muggings and burglaries that are carried out for the purpose of obtaining money for narcotics.

The Senate Select Committee has detailed an alarming list of seemingly unjustifiable spying upon and harassment of American citizens by the FBI and other agencies for political purposes. It would be difficult to justify such activities. But one could rationalize them on the grounds that most of them took place during the hectic sixties. Such a rationalization, of course, would involve a political bias which the agencies carrying out such activities are not supposed to have.

The committee's report, therefore, lays the foundation for a good case for establishing a workable vehicle for overseeing the activities of those agencies.

The heavier emphasis on domestic security spying today, as indicated by the FBI's intelligence spending plan, suggests that the same kind of thinking that prevailed in the sixties is still around today. And that suspicion bodes ill for the preservation of the civil liberties most Americans cherish.

It adds force to the arguments of those calling for legislative surveillance of our intelligence gathering agencies.

Arkansas Gazette.

Little Rock, Ark., May 12, 1976

The Senate Intelligence Committee's published report of abuses by the Federal Bureau of Investigation is, in some ways, more bone-chilling than its documented record of appalling excesses by the Central Intelligence Agency. For the FBI is at work right here among us, as it turns out, with a layman spy network (it could be your friendly banker or landlord) which should give every citizen pause to consider whence we have drifted in the 100th birth year of our liberties.

Of course the more sensational part of the report, which is coming out in 13 volumes, deals with the era of "dirty tricks" against organizations (the FBI Cointelpro operations) which started roughly in 1956 and is supposed to have ended in 1971. During this period FBI headquarters, we learn, approved some 2,300 actions in a "rough, tough and dirty" campaign to disrupt and discredit a wide variety of U.S. organizations, ranging from the Black Panthers, to Antioch College in Ohio, to the Southern Christian Leadership Conference. The most intense and bizarre of these activities came during the civil-rights movement and then the Vietnam war, involving in some cases, as the Senate panel says, "dangerous, degrading or blatantly unconstitutional techniques" in which the FBI "appears to have become less restrained with each subsequent program."

Much of this has been revealed before, and the more frightening aspect is that in some of the worst instances the bureau was not judging what was legal but rather what was *moral* in its view. Or rather, we expect, what fit the standards of proper citizen conduct as set by the late Director J. Edgar Hoover, who to all practical purposes was above the law, and acted accordingly.

So we have some students, according to an FBI memo, investigated for "disregard for decency and established morality." We have the bureau initiating anonymous letters that accused spouses of infidelity, and encouraging warfare between rival groups (these are not *foreign* groups, mind you, but United States citizens). We have a letter to school officials trying to get a school teacher fired because of membership in a group disapproved by the bureau. We have the anonymous letter to Dr. Martin Luther King Jr.'s wife, taken to indicate he should commit suicide.

This is, as we say, "old stuff" now, though the Senate committee has done good work in showing the extent of it, if indeed it really was able to show the full extent. Now we shall see if Congress and the Justice Department can find the nerve to act on what has been revealed: The committee says the activities "may have violated specific criminal statutes," including those against mail fraud and extortion, and this suggestion needs to be pursued vigorously. But more importantly, Congress needs to steel itself to pass legislation which will place the FBI within a clearly defined perimeter of law and accountability, beyond which it can step only at its own peril.

In fact the Senate investigators say they have not been able to determine with "precision the extent to which Cointelpro may be continuing." They find that "attitudes within and without the bureau demonstrate a continued belief by some that covert action against American citizens is permissible if the need for it is strong enough." Furthermore, "Whether the attorney general can control the bureau still is an open question."

These questions ought to be closed this year, with a resounding bang, by Congress. Even lawmakers who are normally tremulous when confronted by the patriotic mystique and vast power of the bureau should be moved by some of these reminders from the not-too-distant past: of its "targeting" of some candidates for elective office, for example, because it did not think they should be elected, and slipping information to judges, covertly, to prejudice cases in ways it desired, these being some of the extremes unreeled by the Senate panel.

And something which is *not* old stuff is its disclosure that the FBI pays some $7 million a year to 1,500 citizen informants out among us who report on virtually everything they consider suspicious. And in addition it relies on more than 1,200 "confidential sources" such as "bankers, telephone company employes and landlords" who feed in information they come across in their daily work. Through the network of informants it has received reports on groups ranging from the Ku Klux Klan to the women's liberation movement, demonstrating, in the latter instance, how far the fantasies can reach. Surveillance has been kept on people who were simply concerned about the size of defense spending.

And *since* the issuance of the committee report there is one highly disturbing development: the allegation that a woman copy editor for Tennessee's eminent morning newspaper, The Tennesseean, has been an FBI informant inside the paper. In fact the publisher of The Tennesseean fired her last week end because of "past and recent conversations" with FBI agents. One must wonder if the bureau has made a serious attempt to infiltrate the press in this country, and with what success.

When bombs are being set off in government buildings, and the like, there is good reason for surveillance of suspects. But like many bureaucracies the FBI went beyond the legitimate objectives to far-fetched lengths, acquiring a grossly inflated sense of its mission in America.

And this is dangerous. People who now gladly support the growth of such an apparatus, which inquires secretly into a wide range of our civilian life, could be its targets in some other year henceforth. The dictum that absolute power corrupts absolutely is vindicated again as one considers the later career of J. Edgar Hoover, who was virtually unchallengeable in Washington, and whose imprint still is heavy upon the bureau. He passed through a parade of cheers from conventional America, for his patriotic effusions and his bulldog anti-Communism. But the cold irony in this citizen spy network is its resemblance to the Communist method, in which thousands of ordinary citizens are recruited to watch everyone, including each other, and tell the secret police what people say, what rumors are circulating about whom.

The bureau has thousands of high-principled workers who would be repelled at any notion of undermining our freedoms or abusing the public with secret powers. But we have been shown, most convincingly, how accumulating power itself has grave perils, and Congress should not hesitate to pass the recommended reform legislation, setting a firm eight-year term for the FBI director, and providing strict limitations and congressional oversight for this mammoth and pervasive intelligence bureaucracy we have created—and not been able to control. At the very least we should be able to keep it from breaking the law itself, which we have not done. Now is the time, if ever, for Congress to stop being timorous.

THE ATLANTA CONSTITUTION

Atlanta, Ga., May 1, 1976

This is a presidential election year and the Bicentennial year and we all ought to be thinking a little more seriously than usual about America, where it has been, where it is now, where it is going.

The history books tell us where America has been, and it is mostly an inspiring story. Not only native-born Americans but people everywhere else have seen ours as the land of the free and the home of the brave, as the massive immigrations of the 19th and 20th centuries confirm. And up until and for a while after World War II that belief held firm. But in recent decades a loss of faith in the American dream has been widely noted and commented on. That loss of faith occurred because our leaders and our institutions let us down.

No American institution was more revered and admired through much of this century than the FBI. An incorruptible, scientific law enforcement agency dedicated to upholding the law and protecting the people from crime and outside subversion, the FBI was the good guys. Now we find, after a long and painful Senate investigation, that the FBI and other agencies for many years were breaking the law routinely, violating the constitutional rights of innocent citizens, and doing so with the apparent tacit consent of every President from Roosevelt to Nixon.

There is no need to catalogue the very long and discouraging list of abuses cited by the Senate Select Committee on Intelligence Activities in its just-released report on domestic intelligence operations. It is there for all to read in the pages of this and other newspapers. The FBI's operations against Dr. Martin Luther King, now part of the dismal historical record, were the tactics of a police state at its worst. The excuse in this, as in so many other instances, was fear of Communist infiltration. But the tactics employed against Dr. King personally went far beyond any concern for Communist infiltration; it was directed against a citizen who happened to stir the hatred of the FBI's leadership. This sort of thing must be prevented from ever happening again. Otherwise our laws and constitutional guarantees are mockeries.

Many of these sordid and deeply discouraging revelations have been coming out for a year and more. That does not diminish the impact of the committee's findings not only about the FBI and CIA, but about the Internal Revenue Service and the armed service intelligence branches. On the contrary it does, or it should, reemphasize the committee's conclusion that a "fundamental reform" of the domestic intelligence community is "urgently needed." Those who were sworn to uphold the law and the Constitution in the past were pretty much expected to do that. Now, sadly, it is clear they cannot be trusted to do it on their own.

"The condition upon which God hath given liberty to man is eternal vigilance." That remark is commonly attributed to Jefferson or other famous persons, but it was said by John Philpot Curran, an obscure statesman of our founding period who lives by those words along. They were not new in his day. Diogenes, 350 years before Christ, said: "There is one safeguard known to the wise, which is an advantage and security to all, but especially to democracies as against despots. What is it? Distrust." A cynical view, perhaps, but an inescapabale one.

The Boston Globe

Boston, Mass., April 30, 1976

In its review of the domestic side of the country's intelligence operations, the Senate's report has confirmed in detail the fears that covert techniques used elsewhere have been applied to American citizens at home. In doing so, the report has formulated a comprehensive, often sensible list of suggestions for preventing repetition of the worst abuses without proposing insuperable roadblocks for an intelligence gathering system or for Federal law enforcement activities.

The report stresses the need for concentrating Federal action on actual breaking of the law — overt acts — rather than on trying to figure out where the law may be broken by some political group in the future. It would place new limitations on the practice of infiltrating political groups that the FBI thought dangerous.

Second, it would curtail "fishing trip" investigations — using one phony probe as the pretext for conducting another, building up large files on persons who were never the proper subject of criminal investigation.

Third, it outlines stringent control procedures for the exceptional cases in which genuine national security might justify the use of unconventional techniques for gathering information.The report emphasized the need for explicit descriptions of the reasons for such unusual practices, time limits on their use without court approval and much tighter supervision, before and after the fact, by the Attorney General.

The report, in calling for improved rights for persons who feel they have been wronged by the intelligence gathering process, puts pressure on the bureaucracy to avoid inflicting those wrongs in the first place.

But the Senate Committee also seemed to lean over backward in trying to retain as much flexibility as possible for law enforcement agencies. In the process it may have opened an enormous escape hatch.

"The FBI should be permitted to investigate an American or foreigner to obtain evidence of criminal activity where there is 'reasonable suspicion' that the American or foreigner has committed, is committing or is about to commit a specific act which violates a Federal statute pertaining to the domestic security."

That paragraph's impact depends entirely on the way it would be interpreted in every single case by those who sanctioned action under its terms. The courts, the Attorney General, administrative boards would all be tempted to stretch that meaning to suit the political temper of the times. The presumption must be, or course, that judges and officials are honest. But they are often also zealous and that zeal could warp their judgment in the future, as it did in the past, to allow extreme police action.

There can be no question that protection of domestic security requires some flexibility for Federal agencies. The Senate report tries with partial success to preserve that flexibility while sealing the worst of the legal loopholes through which abuses had crept. But Congress, the administration and the courts still have not found the way totally to immunize the political process from protection of national security.

Pittsburgh Post-Gazette

Pittsburgh, Pa., May 5, 1976

IN AMERICA as elsewhere are some citizens who seem habitually to find more that's wrong than right with their country. Surely they'll be as delighted with the domestic abuses detailed in the second part of the Senate Select Committee intelligence report as they were with the foreign abuses by U. S. spy agencies dealt with in the first part.

That doesn't prevent our also being appreciative of the committee's revelations and with many of its corrective recommendations. What the FBI, CIA, IRS and military-intelligence agencies did to thousands of Americans since, in some cases, as early as the 1940s deserves comprehensive congressional exposure.

Not only does it allow the citizens and the government an opportunity to find corrective measures, but it also indicates that as bad as the transgressions of law and personal rights have been, they haven't come even close to making America a closed society or a police state.

The ugliest tactics of the domestic spies were in the aggregate, in fact, remarkably ineffectual. For example, in spite of the scurrilous Hoover-led FBI attempts to dupe the news media into attacking Martin Luther King Jr., the late civil-rights leader never fell from preeminence.

Offering to newsmen tape recordings supposedly about Dr. King's sex life was so stupid in concept and purpose as to make a sensible person wonder if the FBI was using a stupidity-quotient test for hiring or if its employes just naturally suffered a decline in intelligence through propinquity to the late Mr. Hoover and his chosen lieutenants.

Nor did the FBI have spectacular success in using its friends in the news media to discredit the antiwar movement, the new or old left or the far right. For one thing, the more inane or violent fringe-politics types usually succeeded in discrediting themselves. For another, there are too many reporters and editors in print and broadcast journalism across the land who make their own judgments about news and purported facts for any intelligence agency to achieve the monolithic distortion it may desire.

The FBI and other Bill of Rights abusers are simply too puny to misshape a society so intellectually diverse and ideationally competitive as ours.

Doubtless, the lives of some Americans have been harmed or even wrecked by such tactics as the secret passing of derogatory information to employers or potential employers. Really, that sort of thing must be stopped. So must the CIA's meddling in the domestic spy business.

The U. S. needs a good foreign intelligence network and a good domestic one. Good ones won't have to resort to planning assassinations abroad and planting agents provocateurs at home. Good ones won't rely routinely on law breaking to be effective. And just to be sure, the Congress should exercise reasonable oversight.

Structural reform and oversight, however, may not be enough. To minimize abuses, the appointed heads of this nation's intelligence operations must have a greater respect for law than did their predecessors. They must have also a more balanced judgment on national security versus personal liberty. The value of the former is cheapened by the diminution of the latter.

The Knickerbocker News

··· UNION-STAR ···

Albany, N.Y., May 3, 1976

Aided, abetted and encouraged by persons as prominent as presidents, intelligence agencies generally and the Federal Bureau of Investigation particularly adopted "tactics unworthy of a democracy, and occasionaly reminiscent of the tactics of totalitarian regime."

So says a report of the Senate Intelligence Committee.

You had better believe it.

Time was when the only criticism of the FBI came from what appeared to many to be the "lunatic fringe". Even if it did, it must be acknowledged that the seemingly lunactic fringe had coherent days.

That Senate committee has filed a volume of charges against the FBI including illegal wire-taps, buggings, mail opening and even burglaries . It said:

"Unsavory and vicious tactics have been employed — including anonymous attempts to break up marriages, disrupt meetings, ostracize persons from their professions, and provoke target groups into rivalries that might result in deaths."

It must be emphasized that the charges against the FBI are based on that agency's activities during the reign (no other word will do) of the late J. Edgar Hoover. While presenting himself as the epitome of patriotism, Mr. Hoover was using tactics "unworthy of a democracy", to use words of the committee, even though those words were not aimed quite so directly at the former director.

Even as former presidents used the FBI to fulfill private and political whims, they feared Hoover for the hold he had on the American people and segments of Congress and for his files. Hoover had something on everyone.

The Senate committee found 96 recommendations were necessary to insure against continued excesses by intelligence agencies. One of the most important of those 96 limit the term of office of any FBI director to eight years.

That federal agency must never again be permitted to become any person's political fiefdom.

WORCESTER TELEGRAM.

Worcester, Mass., May 11, 1976

Director Clarence Kelley's apologies for the past misdeeds of the FBI should help clear the air. It is important that the current leadership of the organization acknowledge that the FBI in the last few years of J. Edgar Hoover strayed far afield from what it was supposed to be doing.

The FBI, after all, is a federal law enforcement agency, not an agent provocateur. It is not supposed to indulge in illegal burglaries, wiretaps and buggings. It should not get involved in domestic political issues and should not use its powers for the benefit of whoever happens to be in the White House. It is not the role of the FBI to decide what social and political movements and leaders are to be suppressed by fair means or foul.

Most important, the FBI should never again become the personalized vehicle of one dominant director, no matter how able. Under Hoover, it did become just that. For all of Hoover's achievements — and they were considerable — it is too bad that he did not retire earlier. Most of the abuses occurred during his last 10 years, when he had become a national institution. The old adage that power corrupts applied to Hoover as to everyone else.

There is no chance that any future director will serve 47 years. Kelley suggests that 10 years should be the maximum. The important thing now is not to dwell on the past, but to move toward the future, keeping in mind the lessons so painfully learned.

DESERET NEWS

Salt Lake City, Utah, May 11, 1976

One of the biggest threats to democratic government is for law-enforcement agencies to succumb to the temptation of ignoring the law or making their own interpretations of what the law should be.

That is why the FBI's admission of 238 illegal housebreakings between 1948 and 1966 is so abhorent.

The number, suggests columnist Jack Anderson, may be well above the FBI's own admission — perhaps more than 1,000.

These housebreakings were directed mainly against suspected spies, organized crime figures, foreign diplomats, and a few dangerous revolutionaries. All were done without obtaining warrants from the Justice Department, as required by law.

Granted, the nation was under many stresses during that period which do not seem so apparent today: The McCarthy witchhunt for Communists in government, unrest on the campuses, the urban riots, beginnings of the Vietnam war protests, and a scattered revolutionary movement which appeared much more ominous than it might look now.

Even so, the collective approach of society to these problems — as embodied in law — helps to prevent excesses of zeal which harm far more than they help. That process breaks down when an enforcement agency puts itself above the law.

To his credit, FBI Director Clarence Kelley has apologized publicly for the actions of his predecessor, J. Edgar Hoover, in sanctioning such actions. "We are truly sorry," he said last weekend in a speech at Fulton, Mo., "we were responsible for instances which now are subject to such criticism." Those mistakes must not be repeated, he added.

Respect for the law is so important it must begin at the top. That means not only the FBI, but Congress and the presidency as well. That simple lesson has gone unheeded far too often in recent years.

The Cleveland Press

Cleveland, Ohio, May 11, 1976

FBI Director Clarence Kelley was correct — though a bit late — to apologize to the nation for the bureau's abuses of power and lawless tactics.

In a carefully written weekend speech, Kelley said the FBI was "truly sorry" for its misdeeds and for the first time put the blame squarely on J. Edgar Hoover.

Kelley was referring to the FBI counterintelligence programs (Cointelpro) which from 1956 to 1971 tried to disrupt militant political groups such as the Communist Party, the Ku Klux Klan and the Black Panthers.

In its recent report the Senate Intelligence Committee criticized Cointelpro for making up derogatory information against its "targets" and sending it to their families and employers.

The committee cited several cases in which FBI misinformation led to violence between radical groups and even some killings. It also accused the FBI of smearing civil rights leader Martin Luther King Jr., urging him to commit suicide and disparaging his reputation even after his assassination.

Last year Attorney General Edward Levi called such Cointelpro activities "outrageous." Kelley, however, attempted to defend them. Now he is acknowledging that the FBI is not above the law and this is helpful.

As welcome as Kelley's conversion is, something more is needed. A secure democracy is based not on transient men but on laws. Congress has the imperative duty of passing laws that define just what the FBI and other intelligence can and cannot do.

At the same time Congress must overcome its inertia and set up a single powerful intelligence committee. What is demanded is one strong enough to see that the agencies respect their charters and discreet enough to keep secrets when national security is truly involved.

The time to act is now, when Hoover's persecution of King and the CIA's asinine assassination plots are fresh in the public mind. To delay will mean no reform and — inevitably — new abuses of power when the present furor is forgotten.

CHICAGO DAILY NEWS

Chicago, Ill., May 11, 1976

It isn't often that the American people get an apology like the one offered by Clarence M. Kelley, director of the Federal Bureau of Investigation. In a speech Saturday in Fulton, Mo., Kelley said the bureau is "truly sorry" for the abuses of its power that have been revealed.

Kelley was not apologizing for his own actions, but for those of his predecessor, the late J. Edgar Hoover. That made the admission of error easier. Yet it was a wholesome thing to do, and if it can't wipe the slate clean, it may at least provide needed reassurances that the FBI has learned from past mistakes and is on its way toward re-earning the public confidence it once enjoyed.

That confidence has undergone a severe jolt with the recent revelations that under Hoover the FBI ignored the law and morality and adopted a policy that the end justified any means. In its role as guardian of "national security," it ran roughshod over the individual rights of thousands of American citizens. Its counterintelligence program (COINTELPRO) stooped to burglaries, illegal spying and political sabotage.

Along with Kelley's public apology comes the promise that such tactics will never again be used, and that is the least the American people can expect. To ensure this, better congressional oversight must be established, and Congress has the recommendations of its investigative committees to guide it toward that end.

Kelley went a step further, and recommended that no director be allowed to remain at the helm of the FBI longer than 10 years. It was in the last years of Hoover's direction — in a span that covered 48 years as head of the bureau — that the worst abuses occurred. Toward the end, Hoover had amassed such power that he could intimidate congressmen, the attorneys general who were his nominal bosses and even Presidents.

A 10-year term might indeed militate against a repetition of such an accumulation of personal power. Yet it would be long enough to overlap presidential terms and in theory at least would provide some degree of independence from political pressure emanating from the White House.

The FBI has a vital role to play in the fight against organized crime, where it has been enormously effective, and it must also continue as a bulwark against any real threats to the nation's security by subversion from within. Reorganizing the agency and rebuilding its morale are items of high priority. And if we read Kelley right, he means to go beyond mere image-polishing and set the FBI on a course fully deserving of the public trust. In that endeavor, we wish him well.

THE KANSAS CITY STAR

Kansas City, Mo., May 14, 1976

It is easy to look back on targets of dubious FBI activities and say that this or that was not really a threat after all. But hindsight always is a simple matter, and the issue of improper law enforcement action is not whether the wrong individual or organization was illegally assaulted, but that they were assaulted at all.

Americans can generally agree that in times of war freedoms must be curtailed in varying degree, but even in cases that seem justified at the time there are usually doubts and almost always regrets. The wrongs done to Americans of Japanese ancestry in World War II were a clear example. The other day in Fulton, Mo., Clarence M. Kelley, FBI director, expressed his sorrow over excesses of the past. This is a refreshing departure from older days when the agency could do no wrong and to suggest that it could was to invite ferocious retaliation. Slowly but surely, Kelley is restoring the FBI to a different but better reputation han it had in grimmer times.

Whatever law enforcement agencies may have done to promote bloodshed and strife among such organizations as the Black Panthers and the Ku Klux Klan was wrong—not because the threat of the groups may have been exaggerated, but because the agencies were breaking the law they were created to uphold.

In a democracy the people must insist upon safeguards against legalized force. It always must be foremost in the public mind and in the rules of government that the police and the military are not ends unto themselves. They exist for one purpose only, and that is to protect the people and their liberties. Government is designed as a framework for those liberties, to facilitate their promotion and use. When the police power of government pursues what it thinks are justified ends through illegal means, then the whole system is perverted. A train of rationalization and corruption is set in motion and it can inflict tremendous destruction before it runs the course.

In law enforcement expedience and convenience are tempting. It takes truly unusual leadership of the Kelley quality to resist and see them for what they are—damaging in the long run to the sanctity of the law and the organizations created to enforce it.

Chicago Tribune

Chicago, Ill., May 11, 1976

FBI Director Clarence Kelley chose a particularly appropriate setting in which to apologize for the abuses of FBI power during "the twilight" of his predecessor J. Edgar Hoover's career. The apology came during a lecture at Westminster College, Fulton, Mo., on the responsibilities of power.

It is on college campuses that disillusionment with the so-called "power establishment" has been most conspicuous. For at least a generation, there has been a wholesome tendency on the campuses to question conventional values. The questioning turned to disillusionment and even hatred with the Viet Nam war, Watergate, and the recent disclosures of past abuses by the intelligence agencies.

It is also among the rising generation that institutions such as the FBI and the CIA must have understanding and support if the United States is to continue to hold its own in a world full of challenges — a world where spying and concealment and contempt for law are part of life, and where considerations of freedom and privacy are the exception rather than the rule.

The best way to seek this understanding and support is through candor — and that is what Mr. Kelley offered. He said he was "truly sorry that we were responsible" for some activities that "were clearly wrong and quite indefensible." He said that abuses of power "perhaps can be explained and possibly even excused, but only when the explanation is truthful, contrite, and accompanied by a well defined plan to prevent a recurrence."

Finally, it was at Westminster College just 30 years ago that Winston Churchill alerted the world to the challenging period it was then entering, and popularized the expression "iron curtain." The iron curtain still exists; it has been extended by the bamboo curtain and is being extended even further by an ivory curtain in Africa. The free world is dwindling. It needs the help of intelligence agencies. And if there is anything comforting about the abuses for which Mr. Kelley apologized, it is that they appear to have been purely political in nature and totally unnecessary to the protection of freedom and respect for law. They can be avoided — and must be avoided — without jeopardizing the ability of the agencies to do their proper job.

THE DALLAS TIMES HERALD

Dallas, Tex., May 11, 1976

THE ISSUE: Federal Bureau of Investigation Director Clarence Kelley acknowledges the FBI's past abuse of its power.

FBI DIRECTOR Clarence Kelley's candid admission that the late J. Edgar Hoover abused the agency's power should climax the purge of official wrongdoing in the FBI.

Mr. Kelley, in an address over the weekend, said for the first time that the FBI under Hoover, late in the 48-year reign of the FBI founder, made widespread use of illegal tactics to harrass and defame law-abiding American citizens.

Often times the target of the FBI abuses, as revealed by the Senate Committee on Intelligence, were activists in various civil rights movements or in other political causes.

In the motivation of those at the top of the FBI hierarchy and in the White House, there probably was much rationalization of illegal FBI activities against some activists. But, in fact, there seemed to be no distinction between illegal surveillance, for example, of the violence-prone Weathermen and certain members of Congress.

Journalists who received information about the workings of government were just as likely to be illegally wiretapped as spies for foreign governments.

The FBI, and much blame has to be placed on Mr. Hoover, confused the national security interest with the personal interests of presidents and the FBI director.

Mr. Kelley in his admittance of the FBI abuses also apologized. We believe his apology to be sincere and that he is trying to repair the badly tarnished image of the FBI.

But the FBI must purge root and branch any illegal activity from its mission, if it has not done so already.

We are mindful that it was not the FBI which undercovered and revealed its own abuses; but congressional investigators, journalists and others.

It is apparent that Congress and the President must exercise greater vigilance over the activities of the FBI and other federal law enforcement agencies. Mr. Kelley's suggestion that no FBI director serve more than ten years merits serious consideration.

This country must be very cautious about the expansion of governmental powers in order to protect the fragile liberties of all citizens.

A super agency such as the FBI with police powers can be a mighty force for preservation of our laws, or, it can be an equally mighty force for their destruction.

THE ROANOKE TIMES

Roanoke, Va., May 13, 1976

Some people are willing to excuse the excesses of the Central Intelligence Agency because that organization is supposed to operate in the foreign sector. If in the past it has sometimes strayed into the domestic field, imperiling Americans' civil liberties, some would write that off as over-zealousness or perhaps misuse of CIA powers by the executive branch.

Excuses are harder to make for the Federal Bureau of Investigation. This is the federal police and investigating force; by its very role it is a potential oppressor, an agency that should be kept under close watch.

Yet for decades, under the autocratic rule of J. Edgar Hoover, the FBI had virtual *carte blanche* to operate wherever it wanted within domestic polity. During a 48-year career, Mr. Hoover loomed so large that presidents dared not challenge or replace him even when he was greatly over age; his agency's image was so fiercely polished that to impugn it risked not only the public's suspicion but the bureau's own undercover wrath.

Late has the nation learned that the FBI, moved by Mr. Hoover's distorted view of the American scene, spent many years compiling dossiers on people the director feared or disliked, in some cases looking for (or fabricating) information that could defame them; and trying to infiltrate and disrupt groups such as the Communist party, Ku Klux Klan and Black Panthers. Meantime, organized crime flourished, Mr. Hoover refusing to admit that such a thing as the Mafia existed. An agency that was supposed only to fight crime became instead the political arm of one man.

Americans can devoutly hope that those days are forever gone. J. Edgar Hoover's successor, Clarence M. Kelley, acknowledged recently that "the superhuman image of the FBI, and the power and glory that accompanied it, has greatly diminished . . . . The FBI has descended from Mount Olympus. And, as it turns out, we are mere mortals, with human imperfections, and we always have been." He apologized for the agency's past abuses of power and—in the light of the Hoover experience—suggested that no man should again serve as FBI director for more than 10 years.

Mr. Kelley took a calculated risk in at last placing blame at the clay feet of a man who still is an idol to many, including a great number of FBI agents still on the job. But if the agency is to be rehabilitated, mistakes and abuses must be admitted and forsworn. Mr. Kelley has taken a painful but necessary step.

BUFFALO EVENING NEWS

Buffalo, N.Y., May 21, 1976

Clarence Kelley, the FBI director, inherited an almost impossible job. He must regain the confidence of millions of Americans for an agency whose previously superhuman public image has been shattered by revelations of sometimes ugly, lawless reality.

The lawlessness occurred before he became the director, yet he is saddled with its shadowed legacy. Mr. Kelley sought to cope with this burden in a recent speech frankly apologizing for "wrongful uses of power" by the FBI under the late J. Edgar Hoover.

"We are truly sorry we were responsible for instances which now are subject to such criticism . . . ," he said. "We need to make it clearly understood that we recognize errors and have learned from them."

Public apologies as straightforward as this one by high federal officials are as rare as they are remarkable. With us, the credibility of Mr. Kelley's impressive performance was enhanced by the tone of the address, by his personal pledge not to "abide incursions upon the liberties of the people" and by a sensible proposal that no director of the FBI serve longer than 10 years. These and other limitations are required to fully prevent gross mistakes of the past from recurring in the future. And those who want to reform rather than destroy the FBI have all the more reason to press for such limitations against abuse. Just as the FBI was unreasonably glorified in the past, moreover, as Mr. Kelley recognized, so it can be unreasonably scorned in the present.

Thus, we have no reason to doubt his admirable intentions in appealing for the opportunity to "permit the FBI to get on with its vital work, lest its credibility and effectiveness as an essential peace-keeper and guardian of liberties be permanently damaged."

For all of that, the public should also insist on imbedding the good intentions of lawful restraint in federal statutes. Certainly one lesson is not to unduly trust men with great power, but to circumscribe that power with effective safeguards, conforming law-enforcement techniques and missions with the U. S. Bill of Rights.

The Courier-Journal

Louisville, Ky., May 11, 1976

Enforcement of the law against those who violate it—that is, against those who impair the freedom of others—entails power. But power is always dangerous. It must be wielded by men; and men empowered to administer the law fall easily into the notion that they are empowered also to interpret and to shape it. Thus the power intended to prevent oppression by lawbreakers becomes, if not constrained and bounded, a means of oppressing the law-abiding. Power intended to preserve liberty may also imperil it.

—Alan Barth, The Price of Liberty, 1961

IT TOOK the breaking of the dam at Watergate to convince most Americans that the corruption of power had put their most basic freedoms in dire peril. But the seeds of this corruption had been sown many decades before.

That's the message of the final Senate committee report on domestic intelligence activities, and of the supplemental staff studies that are now appearing. Together they recount the history of how the United States government began wholesale spying on its citizens. Though many of the details had been made public earlier, they constitute shocking documentation of our gradual drift from the individual liberties and governmental checks and balances that are the linchpins of democracy. If these reports do nothing else, they should shock the American people into demanding swift congressional enactment of curbs on domestic intelligence gathering and steps to prevent a recurrence of its abuse by those in the highest offices of our government.

World War I, with its fears of anarchists and aliens, brought establishment of the first substantial domestic intelligence programs by the federal government. Many of these programs, conducted through the Justice Department's Bureau of Investigation, were later described by Attorney General Harlan Fiske Stone as "lawless, maintaining many activities which were without any authority in federal-state statutes and engaging in many practices which were brutal and tyrannical in the extreme."

Those words could have been uttered today, instead of 52 years ago.

That same year, in 1924, when Attorney General Stone appointed J. Edgar Hoover to head the Bureau (later re-established as the FBI), he charged Mr. Hoover to limit the agency's activities "strictly to investigations of violations of crime, under my direction or under the direction of an Assistant Attorney General. . . ." But no attempt was made to give this executive order the full weight of law. Nor was Congress involved when, during the 1930s, domestic intelligence gathering was reinstituted and expanded.

From then on, domestic spying was part of the governmental fabric. Mr. Hoover's 48-year reign as head of the FBI established him as one of the most powerful men in the country, beholden to no one and knowing enough secrets to perpetuate himself in office indefinitely. Many of the bureau's operations were unknown even to the White House; others were known, but ignored or condoned.

Meantime, presidents from Franklin Roosevelt on made use of FBI files and resources for their own political ends. The Johnson and Nixon years were different only in that the political spying increased markedly in response to the turbulence of the civil rights and Vietnam demonstrations.

The rapid development of technology over the past decade also made it much easier for the government to snoop on citizens without their knowledge. Further sophistication in the fields of interceptors and computers in future years makes the establishment of a tight rein on all governmental domestic intelligence work even more important.

It's not enough to assume that, with Mr. Hoover's death and the replacement of President Nixon by President Ford, the FBI's domestic surveillance will automatically flow back into acceptable, limited channels. One of last week's staff reports disclosed, for instance, that the FBI currently is spending $7 million yearly to maintain a network of 1,500 paid informants on the political activities of law-abiding citizens. That's twice what it is spending to gather information on organized crime.

FBI Director Clarence Kelly's weekend apology for the years of abuse is an encouraging sign. His admissions that Mr. Hoover remained in office far too long and that his long tenure was partly responsible for the abuses suggest a refreshing new willingness on the part of the bureau to pull the late director from his godlike pedestal and look at him as he really was. Without such a change of mood, FBI personnel will find it difficult to develop the respect for Americans' civil liberties that has been lacking all these years.

Mr. Kelly's recommendation that no FBI director be allowed to serve more than 10 years is an excellent one. But it needs to be embodied in law, not left to executive judgment. Similarly, the guidelines recently issued by Attorney General Edward Levi, though a useful start in themselves, should be followed up with legislative action. Executive orders alone can no longer suffice.

As history shows, once the memories have faded and new emergencies loom, the temptation to water down executive guidelines will be irresistible. Only prompt and radical action by Congress to cement strict controls into law will cut back the present cancerous growth and erect safeguards against future malignancies.

The Seattle Times

Seattle, Wash., May 11, 1976

"WE are truly sorry." With those words, Clarence M. Kelley, director of the Federal Bureau of Investigation, delivered an unprecedented apology to the American people for abuses of the FBI's investigative powers in past years.

It is to Kelley's credit that he has not tried to sidestep or gloss over the abuses brought to light in the post-Watergate congressional muckraking wave.

Kelley, as well as the Ford administration and Congress, is pledged to maintain firm standards for future FBI conduct.

For the foreseeable future, no President and no Congress is going to give the agency the kind of free rein it enjoyed in the pre-Watergate years. And the FBI, under Kelley, is certainly not asking for that kind of open-ended license.

In weighing the past, it is important to keep in mind that Congress for years made little or no attempt to exercise its oversight responsibilities, and that six Presidents, from Roosevelt to Nixon, not only condoned but encouraged questionable FBI behavior.

For at least a generation, occupants of the White House found it irresistible to fudge on the legitimate functions of the FBI and use that superbly trained and equipped agency for private spying.

It is not to whitewash past FBI excesses to observe that six Presidents as well as more than a dozen Congresses also have reason for apology.

TULSA DAILY WORLD

Tulsa, Okla., May 10, 1976

IT ISN'T often we hear an outright public apology from the head of any Government agency—much less the Director of the Federal Bureau of Investigation. But that is what came from director CLARENCE KELLEY Saturday.

KELLEY said the FBI is "truly sorry" for abuses of the Bureau's investigative power in the "twilight" of J. EDGAR HOOVER's years as its head.

"Some of those activities were clearly wrong and quite indefensible," said KELLEY. "We most certainly must never allow them to be repeated."

KELLEY has been reluctant, understandably, to make public apologies that would reflect on HOOVER. He and other FBI officials would have preferred to go on about their business and try to live down whatever sins have been committed in the past in the name of national security.

But so much hubbub has been raised over the alleged harassment and surveillance of many innocent Americans in the past that KELLEY apparently felt it would be best to clear the air. He made it clear that the "dirty tricks" used against some American dissidents, mostly in the late 1950s and the 1960s, will not be allowed to recur.

The Director's forthright acknowlegment of abuses and his apology for them should clear the way for the FBI now to get on with its assigned work and quiet its critics. If the anti-FBI barrage from Washington and elsewhere continues, it could damage an institution that has served the nation well through the years, in spite of the missteps KELLEY referred to.

Dwelling on past errors should not be allowed to cripple the bureau permanently. What's done should be noted and not repeated, but we still need the FBI that has served the nation in so many necessary and admirable ways.

The Times-Picayune

New Orleans, La., May 12, 1976

The Federal Bureau of Investigation, for so long a national squad of Untouchables but lately a national whipping boy, has at least now been rendered human by Director Clarence Kelley's public apology for the agency's history of abuses.

"We are truly sorry we were responsible for instances which are now subject to such criticism," Chief Kelley said of probers' revelations of FBI activities before he became director in 1973. "Some of those activities were clearly wrong and quite reprehensible. We most certainly must never allow them to be repeated."

Yet some were "good faith" efforts to protect life and property, he insisted, and he rightly noted that not only the late Director J. Edgar Hoover was involved in building the FBI's superhero image, but also the news media, Congress and a "grateful public." This is a useful reminder that often the liberties public officials and employes take with their authority are the result of feedback from the consensus operating in the national community at the time.

Justice Department guidelines and congressional watchfulness, Chief Kelley asserted, "will substantially assure the propriety of the FBI's operations now and in the future." This, of course is as it should have always been. It is a cornerstone of the American concept of justice — in theory and ideal, at least — that the law can be effectively enforced without breaking it, and that anyone's abusing the law makes everyone less secure.

But as in current efforts to "clean up" the Central Intelligence Agency, legislation to control the FBI and other domestic law enforcers must not only assure that the nation's policemen do not abuse their powers and the people's rights, but also take into realistic account the task enforcers face in protecting the law-abiding public's rights.

THE INDIANAPOLIS STAR

Indianapolis, Ind., May 9, 1976

The Federal Bureau of Investigation during the 1950s treated revolutionary guerrilla warfare outfits like revolutionary guerrilla warfare outfits, and the authors of a Senate Intelligence Committee report seem to think that's bad.

Gist of the committee's report on FBI "covert actions" is that the bureau set out to destroy a collection of hate-preaching, violence-practicing armies which had declared war on the United States government and society, and that the FBI pulled no punches in doing the job.

Officers of these guerrilla armies openly avowed that they were in a state of hostility with American society. In speeches and publications they urged the murder of police, officials and private citizens.

In Indianapolis the representative of one such outfit appeared on television and called for the assassination of the mayor and police chief.

No one can be certain how many murders of police and civilians, robberies, muggings, arson fires, bombings, beatings and other crimes were the direct responsibility of the urban warfare guerrillas whose actions, including cowardly attacks on the helpless and elderly, often were hailed in liberal publications as acts in a "war of liberation."

No one knows how many murders and other violent crimes even today are instigated by these guerrilla outfits and committed by their members. But there is no doubt at all that the revolutionary armies, many of which had nationwide organization, played a main role in the country's surging crime rate and the riots that racked U.S. cities in the 1960s.

The FBI is pledged to defend the United States "against all enemies foreign and domestic" as well as to investigate violations of and to enforce Federal laws.

By word and deed, the guerrilla armies were not only domestic enemies but were at war. The Marquis of Queensberry Rules do not apply in warfare.

FBI policy was set by the bureau's stern director, J. Edgar Hoover, not by pantywaists who fawn on murderers and demand solicitude for the human equivalent of mad dogs. The policy was tough.

The policy was in accord with the principle tnat the only justification for law is the protection of those who accept law and abide by it as opposed to those who reject it and break it. The maxim for this is: "If you will live among us obey our rules, or get out, or suffer the consequences."

A perverse new school of radical-liberal thought denies this principle, twists law to the single purpose of abetting the criminal and the revolutionary and even seeks to deprive the law-abiding members of society of the means of defending themselves.

The Senate Intelligence Committee's staff report smacks strongly of this brand of twisted thinking.

The Des Moines Register

Des Moines, Iowa, May 11, 1976

Senator Frank Church (Dem., Idaho), chairman of the Senate Intelligence Committee, has called for appointment of a special prosecutor to investigate the FBI's harassment of Dr. Martin Luther King, jr. Church voiced doubt that the Justice Department "can adequately conduct an investigation" of one of its own agencies.

Atty. Gen. Edward H. Levi decided to keep an investigation within the department although his top aide for civil rights matters recommended selection of an independent commission.

King's widow called Levi's decision "an absurdity." Coretta King added, "What is needed is a high-level, independent commission empowered and prepared to investigate, make hard judgments and recommendations, including punishments of wrongdoers at any level of involvement."

The appeals for an independent investigation take on added importance in view of the Senate committee's disclosure that an FBI supervisor involved in the campaign to discredit King still holds "a high position" in the agency. His identity was not revealed.

According to the report, the supervisor once suggested that the agency try to publicly link King to a foreign bank account "through friendly news sources, or the like, or we might turn the information over to the Internal Revenue Service for possible criminal prosecution."

The Senate committee report revealed that as long as a year after King was assassinated FBI officials talked of planning "counter-intelligence action" against his widow and moves to darken his memory.

A Justice Department investigation of this squalid affair would be viewed with skepticism by most Americans. Only an independent investigation could offer hope of providing an objective accounting of the FBI's undercover war against King.

St. Petersburg Times

St. Petersburg, Fla., May 12, 1976

In the eight years since Dr. Martin Luther King Jr. was shot to death nobody has explained satisfactorily how his assassin could have been at once as stupid and as wily as the record would have us believe.

THE FACT IS, the circumstances of King's assassination remain clouded because James Earl Ray was allowed to plead guilty, and so the case wasn't tried.

Ray, according to the official account, was a fumbling hoodlum who, after staking out King at a Memphis motel, picked him off with a rifle from a rooming house window nearby.

After the shooting he ran, dropping the gun, his binoculars, and two cans of beer in plain view on the street, all bearing his fingerprints. That was unbelievably witless, even for Ray.

Thereafter he successfully eluded for more than two months an FBI search that involved 3,000 agents and cost $1.4-million. That was unbelievably clever, especially for Ray.

FOR THESE AND other reasons we were disappointed that the 6th U.S. Circuit Court of Appeals Monday rejected Ray's request to withdraw his guilty plea and stand trial. Ray said he had been talked into the plea by his lawyers.

But the court said it found no evidence he hadn't volunteered his confession (which he retracted almost at once) and that therefore he couldn't be allowed now to repudiate it.

Legally, that probably makes sense. Practically, it leaves the case under clouds of suspicion which have darkened for eight years and which in the absence of a full hearing and trial aren't about to disperse.

Most people assume that Ray did fire the shot that killed King. And nobody, not even Ray, has claimed he didn't figure in the killing at least in some way, although he insists now he did not pull the trigger.

BUT CONSIDER SOME of the worrisome and unanswered questions, in addition to those raised above.

One is the FBI's role in harassing King in the years leading up to his killing, and the suspicion that J. Edgar Hoover, who hated King, may not have had his heart in the murder inquiry.

Then there is the fact — or at least it appears to be a fact — that for two weeks after the shooting the FBI never thought to run the Ray fingerprints — so handily left at the scene — through its criminal file, to get him identified.

HOW DID RAY after the shooting raise the thousands of dollars required to finance his flight through five countries? How did he acquire a Canadian passport issued in the name of a Canadian whom he resembled?

How did Ray know, in advance, where King would be staying? And besides all that, what was his motive in leaving his girl friend and a job offer in Los Angeles to drive across the country and assassinate Dr. King?

No doubt there are reasonable answers to all these questions. At a trial the questions at least might have been asked.

Ray's current attorneys say they will appeal the appeal court's ruling. We hope they do, and that the Supreme Court will be able to find legal grounds to support Ray's demand for a trial.

ASIDE FROM RAY'S interests — and they are considerable since he is serving 99 years in a Tennessee prison — the public interest will be served by getting all the available facts on the record.

ARGUS-LEADER

Sioux Falls, S.D., May 1, 1976

There's no evidence that the FBI's investigation of the assassination of Dr. Martin Luther King was faulty, according to Attorney General Edward H. Levi.

He said that nevertheless, he has ordered a continued review of all Justice Department records on the slain civil rights leader. An assistant in the department, J. Stanley Pottinger, said the continued investigation will be extensive and will include interviews with both FBI agents and others connected with the original investigation.

The Rev. Ralph Abernathy, who succeeded King as head of the Southern Christian Leadership Conference, criticized the FBI investigation and called for an independent probe.

There is nothing to be gained by impaneling a special committee to investigate the circumstances of the assassination in Memphis on April 4, 1968. The Justice Department's investigation of the original FBI probe should be sufficient.

The disclosures that the FBI had wiretapped and continually harassed the late Dr. King on the orders of the late FBI Director J. Edgar Hoover are upsetting. The action by Hoover was terrible and un-American, to say the least.

What action should be taken now is a determination that no man will ever again have lifetime tenure in the FBI. Specific terms with forced retirement at 65 should eliminate any recurrence. The nation does not need an imperial FBI ruler any more than it needs another imperial presidency.

Chicago Defender

Chicago, Ill., May 6, 1976

There are yet many cloudy facets of Martin Luther King's assassination to justify the belief that the recent search for evidence by the Federal Bureau of Investigation has only touched the tip of an iceberg of events. The malevolence and conspiratorial hatchings are deeper than what is now visible.

In view of this apparent possibility, it is difficult to understand Atty-General Edward Levi's refusal to accept the suggestion of his own assistant Attorney-General J. Stanley Pottinger that an independent commission of prominent citizens be appointed by Mr. Levi to review the full FBI record and that the examination be conducted along the lines of the commission under the late Chief Justice Earl Warren that investigated the assassination of President Kennedy.

There are some 200,000 files compiled by the FBI that have not yet been put to critical scrutiny. The Attorney General has agreed only to an internal review of these files. It would be far more reassuring were this review conducted by outside sources with unimpeachable integrity. The findings thereof would remove all lingering suspicions of any FBI complicity in Dr. King's murder.

For six long years, the FBI, at the direction of J. Edgar Hoover, was engaged in an unflagging program of harassment of Dr. King, tape recording his private activities, sending him an anonymous suggestion to commit suicide and trying to replace him in the civil rights movement.

Is it not conceivable that an agency that can go that far would not hesitate to contrive physical means to silence forever the man whom they feared and hated? A self-examination by the FBI is a charade that strains the credibility of the concerned public.

OKLAHOMA CITY TIMES

Oklahoma City, Okla., May 3, 1976

THE preliminary clearance given the Federal Bureau of Investigation in the Martin Luther King Jr. death—both the assassination and the inquiry into it—will bring a sense of relief to most Americans. Some people, especially among King's followers, will remain unconvinced, of course, and ugly rumors will not be stilled.

The Justice Department promises a full-scale review even while insisting the preliminary inquiry turned up no evidence that the original investigation of the April 4, 1968, shooting death was anything but honest and thorough.

Atty. Gen. Edward H. Levi is justified in ruling out a nongovernment, blue-ribbon approach to the review. In today's climate of skepticism it's not likely any rocks will be left unturned or skeletons uncovered in the Justice probe.

The present almost universal repugnance felt toward anything that smacks of governmental interference in private lives may cause many people to forget the prevailing mood of a decade or so ago. Some FBI activities now considered reprehensible, if not illegal, were once viewed as necessary and warranted.

It is in this light that the FBI's attitude—and particularly that of the late director, J. Edgar Hoover—toward Dr. King ought to be judged.

After his early success with the peaceful sit-in and freedom movements, King began to change his ideas of what constitutes true passive nonviolence. He embraced the potent weapon of civil disobedience. Indeed, he called for "mass violation of immoral laws." He seemed to depart from his earlier adherence to the Gandhi doctrine of passive disobedience, although he insisted the Indian leader would have approved the idea of "absolute refusal to obey unjust laws."

Like many others who adopted this stance, he never explained how there could be objective agreement on which laws are "unjust" and not to be obeyed.

Some critics felt that in his new militancy after 1960 Dr. King "jumped too far too soon." Later, as the Vietnam war heated up, his civil rights interests swung toward protesting the nation's Indochina policy.

Many people in those days worried about the effect of the radical fringe on the legitimate anti-war movement. It was easy in this atmosphere for some to impute nonpatriotic motives to King.

This does not excuse any obsession Hoover might have had that King was at least influenced by Communists or justify FBI harassment of the black leader—an activity now confirmed by J. Stanley Pottinger, assistant attorney general.

But, if we recall the grave concern with which many government officials, along with citizens, viewed the more extreme anti-war activists, it might be easier to understand the FBI's motivation for invoking the more unusual methods now in disrepute.

Detroit Free Press

Detroit, Mich., May 7, 1976

THE REPORT on the FBI's campaign to discredit the late Dr. Martin Luther King by the staff of the Senate Select Committee on Intelligence comes at a useful time and carries a useful message, emphasizing as it does the heavy hand of the Johnson and Kennedy administrations in that sorry effort.

For the message is that it is not merely the faceless bureaucrats who are to blame for the excesses of past years and that it was not merely the discredited Nixon administration that rode roughshod over the rights of citizens. The Kennedy and Johnson administrations played the dirty game, and against a man with whom they were supposedly making common cause.

The staff report does not reveal all that much that is totally new, but it does underscore the extent to which executive decisions were involved in some of the mean and dirty stuff that was directed against Dr. King. We had not only lost control of agencies such as the CIA and the FBI; we had lost control of our highest elected officials as well.

Is it any wonder, then, that there is a widespread revulsion against the leadership that we have had in recent years from Washington? Is it any wonder that ideology seems now less important and that the desire for a fundamental change in direction seems to cut across the political spectrum?

We must find a framework for all of that feeling, of course, or we shall wind up throwing out the valuable and good with the bad. The civil rights revolution that Lyndon Johnson helped to carry through must, for instance, be laid side-by-side with the shabby use of the FBI by his and the Kennedy administrations. The importance of the opening to China by former President Nixon must not be obscured by the sordidness of much of what happened under his tutelage.

Yet even with the danger of throwing out some good with the bad, it is about time we were fighting to regain control over such agencies as the CIA and the FBI and over our presidents and our congressmen. It is about time that we, conservatives and liberals alike, Republicans and Democrats alike, made it clear that we don't want to have business as usual any more, that we mean to be done with the corner-cutting and the rights-abusing and that public officials had better understand what we're saying.

Again, there is a danger that we will go to extremes and, in trying to cure old evils, create or compound new ones. It is a time for subtleties as well as standards.

But the people mean to have standards, and those standards do not include shabby attempts to destroy men who, whatever the human frailties they shared with the rest of us, were challenging the U.S. to be true to its best ideals. The clumsy and callous attempts to discredit Dr. King are a source of shame to all of us, and we must try now to rise above them to build a country more in keeping with the aims we profess.

The Washington Star

Washington, D.C., May 11, 1976

There was a refreshing humility in the apology put on the record over the weekend by Clarence M. Kelley, director of the Federal Bureau of Investigation. Mr. Kelley used the podium of Westminster College in Fulton, Missouri, scene of Winston Churchill's denunciation of the Iron Curtain 30 years ago, to herald the FBI's descent from Mount Olympus and Mr. Kelley's own lack of aspiration to climb that godly height. Amid a flow of detail from the Senate Intelligence Committee about FBI misdeeds of the past, the words were appropriate. They hold out hope of a future FBI performance more scrupulously governed by law and good sense.

"We are truly sorry we were responsible for instances which now are subject to such criticism," Mr. Kelley said in an unprecedented admission of fallibility. "Some of those activities were clearly wrong and quite indefensible. We most certainly must never allow them to be repeated."

Mr. Kelley's act of contrition, it must be noted, was not for personal wrongdoing but for abuses "chiefly during the twilight" of J. Edgar Hoover's long reign as the first FBI director. In one way, that may have made it easier for Mr. Kelley, who was the Kansas City police chief before being named to the FBI post three years ago, to confess the institution's sins. But as a relative outsider he has been wary, for reasons of bureau morale and also as the leader of many longtime FBI operatives, about sounding overly critical of the agency's past excesses. His frankness indicates increased confidence that the FBI can be weaned of habits that led it repeatedly to disregard the laws and Constitution.

The public may find it hard to get worked up over the new outpouring from congressional investigators. There is value in being reminded of how far the FBI strayed from its mandate — so far, for instance, as to plot violent confrontations between rival black nationalists. It is useful to be shown that FBI malpractice was not particularly Nixonian, but had the complicity of a succession of Presidents and attorneys general, going back to the Franklin Roosevelt administration.

Mr. Kelley sought to spread blame for the successful image-building that made the FBI practically immune from questioning — Mr. Hoover "was enthusiastically abetted by the news media, willingly indulged by Congress and warmly embraced by a grateful public." True, but what a marvelous con job it was.

Mr. Kelley bemoans the passing of more certain moral values, of a time when good guys were clearly distinguishable from bad guys. "Today," he said, "it often seems some elements of our society are pursuing the posse while the outlaws are shooting up the saloon." That has come about partly because of revelations that in too many cases it was the posse that was shooting up the saloon while some people in black hats were peaceably drinking.

Mr. Kelley's apology — together with the awareness shown in the Ford White House and the Attorney General's Office and on Capitol Hill — gives added promise that a Hoover-like cult will not soon reappear to shelter the federal agency from reasonable oversight.

JUSTICE DEPARTMENT PROMULGATES PROVISIONAL GUIDELINES FOR FBI

The justice department March 10 issued provisional guidelines for the conduct of intelligence activities by the Federal Bureau of Investigation. Revelations before congressional committees of FBI activities in its counter intelligence program (called Cointelpro and directed against domestic radical and antiwar groups from the mid 1950s to the early 1970s) had prompted the demand for guidelines. [See p. 42A1; 1975, p. 1005D2]

Activities prohibited to FBI men under the guidelines included inciting to riot, illegal entry and the anonymous circulation of information intended to hold "an individual up to scorn, ridicule or disgrace." FBI agents would be allowed in certain circumstances, with authorization from FBI headquarters, to infiltrate groups, use electronic surveillance, and check (without opening) suspects' mail.

Under the guidelines, groups involved—or those which "will" become involved—in violence or illegality intended to overthrow the government or interfere with foreign governments or their representatives could be investigated. Also, investigations could be undertaken of groups which were "substantially impairing—for the purpose of influencing the United States Government policies or decisions"—federal or state governments or interstate commerce.

The guidelines also provided that requests for investigations from the White House would have to be made in writing, and state precisely what was to be investigated. In addition, there would have to be a statement "signed by the subject of the investigation acknowledging that he has consented to the investigation."

Some Congressmen objected that the guidelines would still allow the FBI too much leeway in choosing groups to investigate. Justice department official Mary C. Lawton March 10 noted that the guidelines were in a trial stage, and that they would be reviewed after the FBI had had experience in working under them.

THE ATLANTA CONSTITUTION

Atlanta, Ga., March 10, 1976

The Senate Select Committee on Intelligence has just released a report casting more aspersions on the FBI.

The report adds to what is already known—that the FBI went to extreme lengths in attempting to "expose, disrupt, misdirect, discredit and otherwise neutralize" extremist groups on both the Left and the Right. Director J. Edgar Hoover either circumvented orders to curb questionable covert operations by the FBI or kept the Justice Department uninformed on what he was doing.

Two major conclusions seem now inescapable. The FBI for a long time did abuse its role and its power, and, for the most part, this was the result of having a director who was answerable to no one, even presidents.

The nation ought to make sure that no official in a key post such as that held by Hoover is allowed to become a law unto himself. It should also make sure that the FBI and other agencies charged with enforcing the law do not themselves make a mockery of the law.

Attorney General Levi, appointed by President Ford while the FBI and other agencies, including the Justice Department itself, were under severe criticism, has informed Congress that he will impose guidelines on the FBI in areas such as domestic security, civil disorder and White House employment. A controversial guideline permitting "preventive action" is out—at least for the time being.

Most Americans continue to admire the FBI for its outstanding role as a law enforcement agency. But no American who understands the basic laws of our nation wants to see them ignored or abused by the FBI or any other agency, no matter how respected. To be specific: episodes such as the disgraceful harassment of Dr. Martin Luther King Jr. cannot be condoned by anybody who understands what America is all about.

The nation needs just such an agency as the FBI was understood to be for many decades. It doesn't need a national police agency that indulges in the methods of the totalitarian regimes that are the enemies of free people. All Americans may hope that the period of intense criticism of the FBI and other agencies, and the efforts to curb abuses, will restore tarnished reputations and strengthen our country.

Detroit Free Press

Detroit, Mich., March 10, 1976

REFORM is not an easy task. That is especially so when the institutions of government that need reforming are the Federal Bureau of Investigation and the Central Intelligence Agency.

Each has been insulated from proper control and oversight for years. Each has been involved in excessive abuses of power and function.

And yet, each has a legitimate and necessary role to play.

The difficult task for the country is to bring about reform without doing great harm to the legitimate and useful roles both the CIA and the FBI can perform in the gathering of intelligence abroad and the fight against crime here at home.

The CIA engaged in assassination plots and other misdeeds overseas. But where both the CIA and the FBI went astray here in America was in their attempts to control the ideology—the political beliefs—of individual citizens.

Now the reform movement has begun. President Ford has announced measures designed to restrain further domestic abuses by the CIA; Attorney General Edward Levi has put forth new guidelines intended to rein in the FBI.

The question facing the country is whether the reforms go far enough. And, how far can reform go before it weakens the necessary functions of these two agencies? And can reform take place without weakening the flow of information?

The FBI's efforts to harass black radicals, white radicals and other political dissidents were a major invasion of individual rights. So, too, were the CIA's surveillance of Americans, telephone taps, and the illegal opening of mail.

Mr. Levi's new guidelines for the FBI—if one could be assured they would be followed—would go a long way toward putting the agency back into its legitimate role. To a degree, harassment would be prohibited, even in cases where it might prevent violence. Investigations of individuals would be permitted if they are involved in violent crime, or can be expected to become so involved, or are involved in breaking the law with the intent of overthrowing or hampering the government.

Several congressmen have already said the guidelines will not be sufficient, noting that the only way Congress can insure compliance with whatever reforms it believes are needed is through new laws and not Justice Department guidelines.

In the case of the CIA, the proposals put forth by the president would go too far in protecting the agency from the oversight it obviously needs from Congress. Other CIA proposals from Mr. Ford would restrict the free flow of information about the government to an unwarranted degree.

In the case of the FBI, Congress must carefully examine Mr. Levi's guidelines to make certain they will curb the agency to the extent necessary.

In both cases, reform and regaining firm control of two powerful instruments of government that had become laws unto themselves are essential. The country must look to Congress to make the final decisions on the course of reform. And those decisions must be framed in such a way that neither abuse of individual rights is permitted nor the destruction of the proper roles for the CIA and the FBI.

New York Post

New York, N.Y., March 22, 1976

Attorney General Levi has set a notable precedent in refusing to accept the findings of an FBI investigation of alleged corruption within the agency conducted by the bureau itself.

The inquiry was originally provoked by the testimony of an electronics manufacturer before the House Intelligence Committee. He asserted in essence that past and present FBI officials had received "kickbacks" in arranging for the purchase of equipment.

In accordance with ancient FBI practice, the matter was reviewed internally by the FBI, at the behest of director Clarence Kelley. An official who is reportedly familiar with the case contends the result was a "whitewash."

Dissatisfied by the report, Levi is now disclosed to have called on the Justice Dept.'s criminal division to stage a full-scale probe on its own. Indictment of some former and current FBI functionaries is described as a real possibility.

The full facts are still to be unfolded. But the sequence of events offers hopeful indication that the era of FBI immunity from the scrutiny to which other units of government are subjected is drawing to a close.

ST. LOUIS POST-DISPATCH

St. Louis, Mo., March 14, 1976

Representative Robert Drinan and other members of Congress are, for understandable reasons, dissatisfied with Attorney General Edward Levi's proposed guidelines supposedly designed to prevent further abuses by the Federal Bureau of Investigation. As Father Drinan put it, the guidelines, rather than halting abuses by the FBI, would formalize "many of the bureau's questionable activities."

The reasons for the Representative's skepticism are obvious. For example, the guidelines permit investigations of individuals and groups, not only when they are involved in violence and illegal acts but also if they "will" become involved in violence or law-breaking. This rule would give the FBI elastic authorization to investigate anyone it says might engage in violence. Another guideline permits investigations of groups which are substantially impairing federal or state governments or interstate commerce for the purpose of influencing U.S. policies or decisions. This fuzzy mandate is so unspecific that it would allow the agency to snoop on almost any group it chooses.

These guidelines are so broad, in the opinion of Representative Herman Badillo, that they would permit inquiries into almost any sort of political or social demonstration. As in the past, the FBI could investigate and keep files on people merely because of their unorthodox political views— which is not the FBI's business. Given the FBI's record of political surveillance and its apparent inability to understand that its mission is not to police political activity, the best way for Congress to respond to Mr. Levi's proposals would be to enact laws prohibiting FBI investigation and intelligence methods that go beyond the point of tracking down those who have actually violated federal laws.

The Charleston Gazette

Charleston, W. Va., March 24, 1976

One of Atty. Gen. Edward Levi's proposed guidelines for preventing further abuses by the FBI permits the investigation of individuals and groups not only when they are actually involved in illegal acts but also if they "will" become involved in legal acts.

Another of Levi's guidelines permits investigation of groups "which substantially impair federal or state governments for the purpose of influencing U.S. policies or decisions."

The first gives elastic authorization to the FBI to move against a citizen who has done nothing but who might do something. The second is fuzzy and unspecific enough to permit the FBI to do pretty much what it wants to do toward inhibiting the activity of a legal but unpopular group.

As Rep. Robert Drinan, D-Mass., puts it, the guidelines, rather than halting abuses by the FBI, would formalize many of the bureau's questionable activities.

We are as skeptical as Fr. Drinan. The guidelines might have been ordered up by the FBI to justify the very acts which brought the bureau into disrepute.

Unorthodox political views aren't against the law, yet, in this republic. But Levi's guidelines would permit the FBI to continue to keep files on American citizens for no other reason than that they express unpopular political viewpoints.

Expression of unpopular viewpoints has helped maintain our free society. Just why Edward Levi and grim young agents of the FBI should want to restrict that exercise in democracy escapes us.

The FBI is supposed to be a criminal investigation agency. It should be authorized to investigate the activities of those who violate federal law. It shouldn't be allowed to determine what ideology is suitable for Americans.

The Houston Post

Houston, Tex., March 9, 1976

Atty. Gen. Edward Levi, under congressional pressure, is reportedly reassessing his guidelines authorizing the FBI to use measures beyond arrest and search to prevent imminent acts of force and violence. Levi has already revised the original guidelines, approved last December, to ban some of the tactics used in the FBI's Cointelpro counterintelligence program to disrupt dissident groups. These include such techniques as writing poison pen letters, inciting violence and releasing defamatory information about organizations.

In defense of his "preventive action" guidelines, Levi has cited cases where "probable cause" existed of an immediate threat to life or property. Under his guidelines, the attorney general would decide when preventive measures were employed. Even Sen. Walter Mondale, D-Minn., chairman of the Senate intelligence committee's domestic subcommittee and a critic of extra-legal activity by the FBI, says he is "not willing to reject all nonviolent actions in extreme situations."

It is obviously impossible to precisely define an "extreme situation" or to determine in advance what constitutes "probable cause." Each situation must be judged on its own circumstances. Furthermore, definitions and criteria limit the bureau's flexibility to respond in an emergency. Yet limitations must be imposed to prevent the kind of abuses perpetrated for nearly 20 years under the old Cointelpro program. These same limitations, properly drawn and enforced, can also protect the FBI from being used as a weapon of personal or political vendetta.

It would be naive to believe that we do not need a federal law enforcement agency vigilant against elements in our society bent on violence and destruction. But in its efforts to protect us, that agency should not abridge the laws and principles that are the foundation of the society. The attorney general has an unenviable task. But when the final version of his guidelines is issued in the next few weeks, it should contain strong safeguards against infringement on citizen rights—rights that have been violated with impunity in the past.

TULSA DAILY WORLD

Tulsa, Okla., March 15, 1976

LEANING over backwards, the JUSTICE DEPARTMENT is trying to wash the FBI's hands clean of all hints of "dirty tricks" or anything that might give new ammunition to its critics. The result may be something less than beneficial to the nation.

The latest draft of guidelines defining the Bureau's proper role in domestic investigations is so cautious that it seems to stop short of true security.

The guidelines, for example, wouldn't give the FBI authority to take "preventive action" to prevent rioting or violence threatened by terrorist groups. The new restriction says:

"Information shall be collected and reported . . . for the limited purpose of assisting the PRESIDENT in determining whether Federal troops are required and determining how a decision to commit troops shall be implemented."

Note the expression "limited purpose." The FBI, once glorified for its aggressive role in fighting both crime and threats to national security, now will have to fill out an application form to interfere with domestic violence . . . only when troops are called for.

Is this really the role the people of America want for their once proud G-men? Has it been determined that because some smudges have been found in the FBI Story, the agency must be placed in a kind of protective custody to keep it from wrongdoing? Or is it possible that Congress and the JUSTICE DEPARTMENT are overreacting . . . in a way that will lessen this police force's ability to protect against subversives and terrorists?

The FBI should not be given a blank check to do whatever its whims dictate, for it is a servant of the public, not its master. But it would be equally damaging to bind it so tightly that it cannot move freely against our present and future enemies who labor under no such restraints.

DAYTON DAILY NEWS

Dayton, Ohio, March 10, 1976

As far as they go — which is not far enough — the regulations U.S. Attorney General Edward Levi has in mind for keeping the FBI in check are an improvement over his earlier version.

That included a provision that would have allowed the FBI to take "preventive action" against groups it decided might act violently or in any other way lawlessly, a loophole you could drive a police state through. In his revised regulations, Mr. Levi has closed it.

Even so, the rules, which the attorney general can promulgate and enforce administratively, still are so broadly drawn that they provide no real protection against the kind of abuses that congressional hearings have shown the bureau fell into in the past. Generously and vaguely worded, the regulations still could be interpreted to permit the FBI pretty much a blank check for investigating and spying on dissidents who present no violent threat to anyone.

In this, Mr. Levi seems to be acting out of a confidence, which there is no reason to question, that he, at least, never would permit the kinds of civil-liberty violations and outright provocations that the FBI committed over the last 15 or so years.

Alas, as Americans now know from recent sad experience, they cannot always count on the attorney general, the President and the FBI director being as sensible as the current lot is. Laws have to be written to lean against evil motives as well as to accommodate decent ones. Congress is going to have to back up Mr. Levi's internal regulations with firm, clear law.

San Francisco Chronicle

San Francisco, Calif., March 22, 1976

OVER THE PAST months, the various U.S. intelligence agencies have pleaded before Congress their case for secrecy from prying eyes focused from home or abroad, and they have intimated that recent revelations of agencies' occasional misdeeds have chastised them into models of propriety.

Attorney General Edward Levi held this view when he gave the FBI the charge of conducting an investigation into possible financial wrongdoings within the FBI itself. It was the perfect opportunity for the FBI to rebuild the image it has long had as a professional, efficient and trustworthy agency.

In Levi's view, however, the resultant report was unsatisfactory and he kicked it back to the FBI, asking that it be expanded in scope. The Los Angeles Times says that the original report raised more questions than it answered and may have been conducted in an "old-boy" atmosphere that left its findings softer than they should have been.

THE INVESTIGATION WAS charged with determining if past and present top FBI officials had improper financial dealings with an electronics firm which sold equipment to the FBI — the transmitting olive in the martini glass? — at an alleged 30 per cent markup. The original investigation was conducted by an assistant director who had worked under two of the officials in question. The new investigation will not be so hampered.

Under the circumstances, Levi's decision to let the FBI try again is commendable and proper, at one extreme, and absolutely ridiculous at the other. We trust that the final result will show the decision to be somewhere toward the middle of the scale of reasonableness, and suggest that a third chance at internal policing be considered simply out of the question.

The Philadelphia Inquirer

Philadelphia, Pa., March 30, 1976

Attorney General Edward H. Levi has prepared a set of guidelines to control the FBI, and the first thing to be said about them is that some guidelines are better than none at all. The second thing, though, is that these are not entirely satisfactory to cope with the kind of abuses that 18 months of congressional investigations have uncovered.

Consider, for example, what we have just learned about the FBI's harassment of a minuscule, nonviolent sect of Trotskyites called the Socialist Workers Party.

According to 354 pages of FBI documents produced in compliance with a court order, specially trained teams of FBI operatives on at least 92 occasions conducted "black bag" jobs, that is, burglaries, of the New York City offices of the party and two affiliated groups. In addition, FBI men burglarized the home of the party's national chairman and the home of a party member during that period.

It is not known how many such operations may have been conducted before 1960 against the Socialist Workers, but the FBI has previously admitted to at least 248 illegal entries against 14 groups between 1942 and 1968 and "numerous entries" against three others between 1952 and 1966.

The guidelines prohibit illegal entries. Fine. So does the U. S. Constitution. Yet the guidelines would still permit the FBI to conduct investigations of groups which are "substantially impairing—for the purpose of influencing the United States Government policies or decisions"—the Federal Government, state governments or interstate commerce.

That would, of course, depend on a subjective judgment. What is "impairing?" As New York Democratic Rep. Herman Badillo, a member of the House subcommittee, declared, "If you followed these guidelines, the Southern Christian Leadership Conference and the Rev. Martin Luther King would still be subject to FBI investigation. We're right where we were before."

Well, not quite where we were. Certainly we have learned a great deal about the abuses and misuses of the FBI—in particular, as the Senate Intelligence Committee has put it, the inability of those inside or outside the bureau "to tell the difference between legitimate national security or law enforcement information and purely political intelligence."

And it is a little too convenient to put all the blame, deserved as so much of it is, on the late J. Edgar Hoover. True enough, the former director, obsessed as he was with subversion and himself unable to tell the difference between subversion and dissent, felt justified in subverting the Constitution in order to protect it, with such tactics as illegal buggings, break-ins, blackmail, fomenting violence, provoking crimes, and the like.

Yet Presidents and attorneys general bear their share of the blame, and Mr. Nixon wasn't the only one, nor was John N. Mitchell.

The main lesson we should have learned from all this, however, is that no agency, no department, no branch of government, can be trusted to control itself. Justice Department guidelines may be useful, but attorneys general come and go, as do Presidents. Guidelines are no substitute for law, and even law is no substitute for consistent, meticulous congressional oversight. The checks and balances of our system are built in but do not operate automatically. That lesson is as old as the Republic.

:ELLEY PLANS FBI REORGANIZATION 'O RESTRICT PROBES OF RADICALS

Clarence M. Kelley, director of the Federal Bureau of Inves- jation, announced Aug. 11 that he had ordered extensive structuring of the agency. One reform removed the responsi- lity for investigating domestic radical and terrorist groups om the FBI's intelligence division and transferred it to the jency's general investigations branch, which operated under ore restrictive guidelines than the intelligence division. elley's action followed disclosures that agents in the intelli- ence branch had conducted burglaries of domestic radical 'oups in the 1970s. The disclosures drew wide publicity be- use the bureau previously had said that break-ins had been rminated in 1966 by order of then FBI director, J. Edgar oover.

Evidence of the 1970s burglaries—reportedly targeted jainst the Weathermen—had emerged in connection with a it filed in 1973 by the Socialist Workers Party against the ıreau and other federal agencies. (The Weathermen were embers of a radical organization called the Weather Under- 'ound, which had claimed responsibility for a number of ombings. The group—originally known as Weatherman—had arted as a dissident faction of the Students for a Democratic ociety.)

W. Mark Felt, a retired associate director of the FBI said ıg. 17 that the policy of allowing break-ins had been ap- oved directly by L. Patrick Gray, acting director of the FBI om May 1972 to April 1973. Felt added that he himself had rsonally authorized two burglaries. Felt admitted that his emory was "hazy" in regard to Gray's approval of a break-in licy. Gray, through his lawyer, Aug. 17 denied "condoning or oproving, directly or indirectly, any illegal act" by the FBI. owever, Felt's statement was supported Aug. 18 by Edward Miller, former chief of the bureau's intelligence division. iller said that Gray had told him privately in August 1972 at he (Gray) had decided to permit "surreptitious entries."

Kelley, in his Aug. 11 announcement of the reforms, said at domestic intelligence investigations (which dealt with sub- rsion and attempts to overthrow the government) were being oved to the general investigative division "for the express ırpose that they be managed like all other criminal cases in at division." The guidelines covering the general investiga- e category generally confined bureau activity to probes of tual violations of law, rather than surveillance of those erely suspected of planning to break the law.

Other organizational reforms proclaimed Aug. 11 by Kelley cluded:

Consolidation of the internal inspection service within the I's Office of Planning and Evaluation. The inspection service d been accused of laxity in investigating charges of kick- cks and financial misdealing within the bureau.

The establishment of a study group on the FBI's use of formants. Kelley had set up the review group after Timothy dfearn, an FBI informant, stole documents from an SWP fice in Denver in July.

The formation of an office of professional responsibility to vestigate charges of misconduct by FBI personnel.

The incorporation of the bureau's legal counsel division— ior to the reform an independent office—into the director's fice. The move was intended to sharpen executive oversight.

BUFFALO EVENING NEWS

Buffalo, N.Y.. August 13, 1976

When FBI director Clarence Kelley admits that he cannot flatly guarantee that no FBI agents are continuing to conduct illegal burglaries of homes and offices, he starkly defines the disturbing magnitude of a problem of internal discipline and management that obviously persists long after he had thought he had gotten on top of it.

A year ago Mr. Kelley said such illegal burglaries, the so-called "black bag jobs," ceased in 1966. But evidence coming to light since then suggests they continued into the early 1970s, and Mr. Kelley now says he was "lied to" by aides covering up this misconduct.

Disturbing as this certainly is, the attitude and corrective actions taken by Mr. Kelley impress us as honest and promising in their single-minded purpose: to clean up rather than cover up past mistakes.

Several weeks ago he publicly apologized for the bureau's past errors and he fingered the legendary J. Edgar Hoover for part of the responsibility for them. Now his candid admission of the possibility that some black bag jobs may still be going on in defiance of his orders, while disturbing, can only be the honest judgment of a cautious man. He plainly isn't covering up, evading or ignoring the problem. Significantly, a top aide was dismissed recently, and this week another Hoover holdover in the agency hierarchy resigned. A Justice Department investigation is, as it certainly should be, under way to determine if there are indictable criminal offenses involved.

Beyond that, Mr. Kelley has just announced not only changes in personnel but a realignment of some major responsibilities within the FBI. He has dissolved as a separate unit the group assigned to investigate terrorist and radical activities, a source of civil liberty problems, merging this into general investigations. He plans to create a new, special section of the bureau to examine alleged misconduct by FBI employes.

Thus, the director's attitudes and reforms all seem designed to reach four imperative objectives: To get the FBI firmly under his control as its top administrator; to end illegal actions and abuses of individuals by its agents; to insist on professional standards in the future by creating established internal mechanisms to probe wrongdoing; and, by all these means, to restore to the FBI its once-high internal morale and the great respect and confidence the public had in it.

There is no doubt that the FBI remains an agency in trouble, turmoil and transition. But Mr. Kelley, rather than either sticking his head in the sand and ignoring those needs or seeking to sugar-coat the agency's problems to the American people, is confronting them and forcing corrections.

In doing this, he deserves the enthusiastic support of Atty. Gen. Edward Levi, his immediate superior, and President Ford. He also deserves the unstinting support of the FBI establishment itself.

THE COMMERCIAL APPEAL

Memphis, Tenn., August 13, 1976

THE ONE THING FBI Director Clarence M. Kelley has going for him these days is his humbling candor.

It hurts to talk with the taste of gall in your mouth, but Kelley twice this year has gone to the public confessional to tell the American people that the Federal Bureau of Investigation is not all that the late J. Edgar Hoover made it out to be.

Last May 8 he made a public apology for past FBI wrongdoings after a thick report by the Senate Select Committee on Intelligence had cited chilling excesses over many years.

This week, Kelley said he would like to say categorically that the FBI is no longer "black bagging" (i.e., burglarizing) homes and offices of American citizens but that unhappily he cannot. Last year, Kelley went out on a limb of confidence in assuring the people there had been no burglaries against domestic targets since 1966. He has since learned that burglaries continued at least until 1973. So on Wednesday Kelley had to say, "I was lied to."

Lied to by whom? Not by enemies of America but by other high persons in the FBI. Why would they lie to Kelley? A good guess is to protect themselves.

KELLEY ORDERED one internal investigation of various high administration personnel and gave them a clean bill. The Justice Department ordered him to take another look. Since then there have been charges of misuse of funds. On July 16 Kelley fired his No. 2 man, Nicholas Callahan, who was vaguely accused of abuse of power. To fill the vacancy Kelley brought in a field agent, Richard G. Held. Two weeks later Held admitted that indirectly he was involved in some of the "dirty tricks" tactics used against black and militant groups between 1968 and 1970.

It has been hard for Kelley to have a "good week." The past keeps come coming back to haunt the FBI.

To be sure, the misconduct that has been brought out all predates Kelley's appointment in 1973.

The trouble is that the FBI chief has been led to believe he was getting the facts about the past from subordinates, only to find that he has been flim-flammed the same way Congress and the public have been.

It took a freedom-of-information suit to pry out some of the documents which revealed the FBI's embarrassing hare ment and disruption of black organizations.

PAINFUL AS ALL this is to the country, and bad as it is for the morale of loyal FBI agents, Kelley's confessions are essential if the agency is to be cleaned up and if public confidence is to be rebuilt.

Since Hoover's death and the tawdry Watergate episode involving his successor, Pat Gray, confidence in the FBI has gone downhill. Navy man Gray was to the bureau what Captain Queeg was to the Caine. But his burning of documents was an isolated thing. What has come out in congressional hearings shows a misuse of power that permeates the entire structure of the FBI.

If Hoover had been as open as Kelley this might not have been possible.

Kelley knows one answer to the problem. He has urged that no director ever be allowed to serve more than 10 years. Hoover was in office 48 years.

Until the inner structure of the FBI is rebuilt from the top down, citizens are not going to be any more willing than Kelley to believe that the deceptions are over.

Kelley has promised to "take action" if he finds any more "dirty linen." Relying on his personal record so far, he's as good as his word on that.

THE STATES-ITEM

New Orleans, La., August 16, 1976

Clarence M. Kelley, director of the Federal Bureau of Investigation, finds himself in the embarrassing position of having to confess that he cannot be absolutely sure that FBI agents or informers are not continuing to burglarize the homes and offices of American citizens.

Mr. Kelley cannot be sure because of another embarrassing revelation: Unnamed FBI officials lied to him, causing him to assure the nation more than a year ago that FBI burglaries in this country had stopped in 1966. The FBI director has since learned that FBI burglaries occurred as recently as 1973 and possibly even last month.

Mr. Kelley is pressing several interdepartmental investigations of the burglaries and possible misuse of agency finances.

The FBI director is concerned, as he should be, that these troubles are hurting department morale. Of broader concern, is the effect the continued revelations of FBI wrongdoing is having on the morale of U.S. citizens.

Director Kelley's forthrightness is commendable. He evokes sympathy. The former director for half a century, J. Edgar Hoover, is a tough act to follow, and Mr. Kelley increasingly is uninhibited in his blame of Mr. Hoover for the bureau's troubles today. It is imperative, however, that Mr. Kelley finds himself soon able to reassure the nation that the FBI liars and confidence-breakers have been identified and dismissed. Only then will the once-proud FBI deserve renewed public confidence. That confidence will take care of the FBI's internal morale problem.

Mr. Kelley obviously faces a timetable of his own. The FBI's problems deservedly are an issue in the presidential campaign. Restoring confidence in the agency is a top national priority.

St. Louis Globe-Democrat

St. Louis, Mo., August 10, 1976

Starting his fourth year as head of the Federal Bureau of Investigation, Director Clarence M. Kelley has applied a firm hand to correct abuses within the FBI which he believes cannot be denied or be allowed to continue.

Kelley has announced an extensive reorganization of the bureau and the creation of a new unit to conduct any future investigations of alleged wrongdoing by FBI agents or top officials.

In his effort to stop criticism of the FBI, Kelley has come under attack from some who feel he has not been loyal to the memory of J. Edgar Hoover, who served as director for 48 years.

Kelley responds to the new critics by deploring what he calls "an arrogant belief at high levels in the infallibility and appropriateness of all FBI activities." He expands his thoughts this way: "These human failings developed over many years and they were permitted to develop by Congress, the news media and others, including ourselves, through indifference or through unquestioning belief in a perfect image."

The FBI director is pained because he cannot say flatly that agents are no longer conducting illegal burglaries. He says he was deceived on this matter in the past and will no longer make categorical denials.

For many months Kelley has attempted to make it clear that he considers it paramount for the public to have confidence in the integrity of the FBI. Less than a month ago the bureau was shaken when Kelley fired his No. 2 man in the wake of Justice Department investigations into illegal burglaries and alleged financial kickbacks. This week Kelley announced the retirement of another top official, but cautioned against linking this departure with any suggestion of wrongdoing.

Kelley now is in position where every headquarters official with the rank of assistant director or higher will be one of his own appointees. Thus he will have a top team of his own choosing, fully accountable to him. And Kelley in turn will be justly answerable for the performance of all his aids.

It is discouraging that the FBI director should have had to spend so much of the last three years fighting off unfair attacks with one hand and in correcting internal abuses with the other.

Kelley needs to be able to approach his tremendous job with the sure hand he is capable of showing. In the past he has stood up effectively to meddlers in Congress who would undercut the FBI in its mission of combating subversion and other threats to national security.

The few FBI agents who may have performed poorly or excessively are a discredit to themselves. It is clear that no one ever abused authority on orders of Director Kelley.

THE EMPORIA GAZETTE

Emporia, Kans., August 13, 1976

THERE was something sad, almost pathetic, in the words of FBI Director Clarence Kelley as he responded to questions from reporters this week.

Our impression of Mr. Kelley, after hearing him speak to two newspaper groups, is that he is an open, straightforward lawman who has a great respect for the rules. He seemed to radiate the same kind of stern dignity when he was chief of police at Kansas City.

Now he is caught in the web of lies spun by his predecessors at the FBI.

The FBI Director was asked by a Kansas City Star reporter if he can flatly deny that FBI agents and informers are continuing to burglarize the homes and offices of Americans.

"I wish I could say categorically, unquestionably, that this is not going on. I will say, however, that I feel it is not being done. I can also say if I determine it's being done now, I will take action."

What a frightful admission! Mr. Kelley's answer proves that he still is not in full control of the FBI's activities.

To his eternal credit, he is man enough to admit the truth publicly. Even better, Mr. Kelley is trying to regain control by weeding out insubordinates and completely reorganizing the bureau. His three years as FBI director have been a "time of travail" and he longs to start afresh. "A cloud seems to have settled over us. I'm anxious to be lifted from this area of constantly explaining. I think we should clear up all these things and start afresh."

—

The American people agree. But Mr. Kelley cannot do the job alone. He has replaced all of J. Edgar Hoover's cronies at the top of the bureau. Of the regular agents, 7,000 worked under Hoover and 1,500 have been appointed by Mr. Kelley. It is a start.

The President, the Attorney General and members of the Congress must overcome their fear of guilt by association with the FBI and lend a hand with the reorganization. Dependable safeguards must be devised to stop abuses and restore faith in the bureau.

Otherwise, this investigative arm of the federal government will become an untrusted agency that will be unable to win public support of its fight against crime and espionage. — R.C.

The Dispatch

Columbus, Ohio, August 17, 1976

FBI DIRECTOR Clarence Kelley can be forgiven if he has been more concerned about vise than vice in recent months.

For it is a fact Director Kelley has found himself in a vise with pressure being applied by congressmen or the Department of Justice.

FORTUNATELY, no investigations by Justice or any congressional agency have tinted Mr. Kelley.

But there would have been a problem for anyone to be the successor to the late, legendary J. Edgar Hoover.

Many federal lawmakers, who now feel free to criticize the operations of the FBI under Director Hoover, ignored the opportunity to do so when he lived.

Director Kelley is not another Hoover any more than Secretary of State Henry Kissinger is another Dean Rusk or John Foster Dulles.

EACH IS and was his own man and history will record the individual accomplishments. One cannot be held responsible for the decisions or administrations of others.

So it is time to acknowledge Director Kelley as present FBI chief, responsible for current operation and future planning and not belabor him with ghosts of the past.

The FBI chief admits he has initiated a review of policies he feels may require updating such as the role of the informer in surveillances.

CONGRESS should be cautious in establishing guidelines for the FBI, such as one proposal that a court warrant would be required prior to use of an informer on an investigation.

Certainly, harassment by the FBI ought to be eliminated just as the harassment by some congressmen of the FBI ought to stop.

Atty. Gen. Edward H. Levi has confidence in Director Kelley and points out no one has challenged the latter's integrity.

CONGRESS should take the FBI director out of the vise and allow him to set up his own organization without placing him under the yoke of stringent guidelines and negating the purpose of the FBI.

Let Director Kelley be his own man.

Arkansas Gazette.

Little Rock, Ark., August 18, 1976

One cannot help but feel compassion for Clarence M. Kelley as he goes about the task of trying to reform the Federal Bureau of Investigation—or at least get control of it. Apparently he is frustrated at every turn in this. He meets the ghost of J. Edgar Hoover at every corner, or more specifically, he meeets the FBI personnel who are still loyal to the image of Mr. Hoover and the modes he originated, which have given the bureau such a black eye.

From all indications, Mr. Kelley is quite a long way from changing the bureau to the extent demanded by all those revelations of misdeeds since we learned that L. Patrick Gray III, as director, had destroyed files wanted by the Watergate investigators. We have no doubt that Mr. Kelley's directorship is devoted to cleaning up the FBI's soiled image and its methods as well. The upshot at this point is, however, that he still cannot give unqualified assurance, as director, that the bureau is not breaking the law somewhere in the country, by illegal breaking and entering or some other extraordinary means for which it has gained a dingy fame in the last few years.

But one thing can be said for Mr. Kelley: He has introduced a degree of candor and apparent earnestness into the bureau which it never has seen before. To admit, as he did in effect in recent interviews, that he really has not gained complete control over his agency, that he cannot give a flat-out personal pledge that the FBI isn't into something illegal right now, required a high sense of honesty.

Of course, he has been burned very badly in recent weeks. For he *did* say, earlier, that the FBI had conducted no burglaries against domestic subjects since 1966, only to learn, as he now admits, that he had been deceived within the bureau. Apparently some burglaries have been carried out fairly recently by FBI people. One allegedly was done just last month by a bureau informer. From all appearances it has been going on right along under his tenure, without his knowledge, and on top of this there are charges that some top FBI officials earlier engaged in financial wrongdoing with public funds.

And a worrisome aspect is that Mr. Kelley says he still doesn't know *who* deceived him, though he's hunting the guilty party or parties. Until the several investigations now underway turn up something, "I can no longer make categorical, sweeping statements" about the absence of misdeeds in the bureau. For, "I know that I was lied to because some of those who conducted these [burglaries] very definitely knew about them having been there . . . I was out making statements that there were none, while they knew that there were."

Well, there is much pathos in this—that the FBI hasn't been able to find its own internal deceivers. We have the impression that Mr. Kelley is trying hard, or he wouldn't have rolled all this out in the daylight. It does not reflect well on his administrative grasp, but he has a lot to untangle. Upon taking over, he said, he found some personnel devoted to the "authoritarian" traditions of Mr. Hoover, and he thinks this has been changed for the most part. But implicit in his remarks was that not all of the "old boy" crowd from the Hoover days has changed its notions, which may include the notion that in "special" cases the ends justify the means.

Mr. Kelley has broken ground toward reform, but it may be that his successor will have to finish the job. He doesn't plan to submit a formal offer to resign as director if Jimmy Carter is elected President. Nor does he think that if he's displaced, someone from outside the bureau should succeed him. But he should, we think, offer to step aside if a new administration comes in next January. His service has been devoted but not spectacular, and he may have, with these embarrassments he has had to endure, exhausted his capabilities by then.

If he declines to resign, a new President should replace him with someone from outside the FBI who is dedicated, in fact mandated, to sweep out with a stiff broom the dust and deplorable habits of the old Hoover days. This ought to be someone who is able in a very short time to say, unequivocally, that nothing illegal is going on in the bureau.

CHICAGO DAILY NEWS

Chicago, Ill., August 13, 1976

The Federal Bureau of Investigation is undergoing its most intensive shakeup since World War II, and on the testimony of its director, Clarence M. Kelley, the reorganization is long overdue. Even now, three years after he took over as director of the FBI, Kelley sadly admits that he has been deceived by some of his own agents, and that he can't be certain that illegal burglaries and other wrongdoings have been completely halted.

Kelley proposes to make certain that the agency stays within the law by dismantling the domestic intelligence division and transferring its duties to the general investigation branch. The effect should be closer supervision over the gathering of domestic intelligence, an important function of the FBI, but one that had clearly run out of control.

Recent disclosures have badly undermined public confidence in the FBI, and morale within the organization itself. The break-ins, the theft of private documents, the mailings of poison-pen letters designed to create chaos within dissident organizations — all these and more hardly fit the long-cherished image of the FBI as the clean-cut, square-shooting defender of public safety. Even if some of the organizations infiltrated easily qualify as "the bad guys," there is something terribly wrong when the good guys stoop to criminal methods in their pursuit.

Kelley clearly believed he had turned the intelligence division away from dirty tricks, and said so not long ago, at the same time apologizing for the misdeeds of the past. But further probes by the Justice Department and federal grand juries have turned up evidence to the contrary. It is entirely possible that some FBI agents will wind up in jail.

In the circumstances, a thorough housecleaning is essential. The public needs the FBI, but it needs an FBI it can fully trust. The hope must be that Kelley's moves will do their intended job.

The Virginian-Pilot

Norfolk, Va., August 13, 1976

Clarence M. Kelley deserves high marks as director of the Federal Bureau of Investigation.

He has one of the toughest tasks in Washington — cleaning up after the late J. Edgar Hoover.

Mr. Hoover ran the FBI for 48 years. He was kept on past retirement age because Presidents Kennedy, Johnson, and Nixon were afraid to fire him.

In his later years the activities of the FBI were focused upon the glorification of Mr. Hoover and fooling the public with the image he wanted.

Just how much the image distorted reality has been revealed since Mr. Hoover's death in 1972. Agents broke the law routinely. The FBI pursued political vendettas. Financial improprieties in the handling of funds are being investigated. As more and more misdeeds have been made public, the agency's morale has fallen lower and lower.

The extent of Mr. Kelley's problems was dramatized Wednesday when he said he couldn't guarantee that burglaries by the FBI have stopped, since he had been deceived by FBI officials in the past. "I can no longer make categorical, sweeping statements," he said.

But if there's more dirty linen, he promised, "we should clean it."

In announcing an extensive FBI reorganization at his press conference, Mr. Kelley minced no words. During the Hoover regime, he said, "there was a certain amount of arrogant belief at high levels in the infallibility and appropriateness of all FBI activities and policies."

Americans can find small satisfaction in the destruction of Mr. Hoover's reputation. What befell the FBI was the fault of a system tailored to one man's vanity. It became a bureaucracy of nitpickers.

As Arthur Murtaugh, an agent for many years, wrote in 1975, "Agents who had cut their teeth on lying about weight, overtime, hours in the office, and statistics were forced to refine their techniques.

"Many were well prepared for the task. They had entered the bureau as honest young men, strongly motivated to support justice. Years of rationalizing about what seemed to them trivia had broken down their moral fiber. Things were never black or white now; everything was gray. Loyalty took precedence over honesty; keeping Hoover mollified was more important than staying within the law. Preserving the bureau image and Hoover at its head was now a matter of self-interest for each agent and nothing was more important than self-interest. Those who excelled in the art of self-corruption had advanced to positions of power and authority where, a cadre of the gutless and unprincipled, they isolated Hoover from reality."

Many of those who transgressed while "keeping Hoover mollified" are fearful they may be prosecuted for their transgressions. And perhaps some will. External and internal investigations are proceeding.

Meanwhile, Mr. Kelley is going about the business of righting wrongs. He took an important step this week when he dismantled the bureau's domestic intelligence operations. Investigations of radicals and terrorists will be treated "like all other criminal cases," he said.

In other reforms, Mr. Kelley said that he is creating a group to review the FBI's use of informers, consolidating internal inspection procedures, and incorporating the legal counsel's office into the director's own operations. He deserves public support in his necessary — and painful — work.

HOUSTON CHRONICLE

Houston, Tex., August 11, 1976

Our respect for Clarence M. Kelley, director of the Federal Bureau of Investigation, continues to grow.

Kelley has headed the FBI for three years now, and even after that length of time is still battling the myths created by J. Edgar Hoover, who ruled the agency for 48 years.

Anyone who has ever had a promotion, whether it be to foreman or to the presidency of a company, knows how difficult assuming authority can be. A director of the FBI has those problems multiplied 48 times.

In the face of those difficulties, Kelley has held to a steadfast course. He has reported frequently to congressional committees. He has opened the FBI to outside scrutiny. He frequently answers questions from the press. He has acted firmly within the organization to provide new leadership.

In May of this year, he publicly apologized for FBI mistakes, particularly in connection with the Cointelpro activities to harass political radicals. Kelley has since learned that he was, to use his own word, deceived by aides concerning burglaries carried out by the FBI in recent years. Kelley says he will act to correct that situation.

Kelley sees his job as turning an agency that was an authoritarian one into an agency that operates with full respect for citizens' rights.

It looks more and more like he's the man who can do the job.

THE CHRISTIAN SCIENCE MONITOR

Boston, Mass., August 13, 1976

FBI director Clarence Kelley must be applauded for following up on his public apologies for the bureau's past abuses with internal reforms to prevent future ones. If he and the rest of his organization operate according to the spirit as well as the letter of the reforms, he should have no reason for further apologies.

The challenge of controlling the FBI's far-flung operatives is suggested by the fact that, even as he announced the reforms, Mr. Kelley could not say with certainty that no FBI burglaries were going on. He had the definite "feeling" that now they were actually stopped. But he knew he had said they had been stopped before – on the basis of what turned out to be false information from his associates. Clearly the task of restoring individual integrity and trust within the FBI must proceed along with the organizational safeguards against abuses.

Central to these safeguards is the formation of a professional responsibility group to investigate any wrongdoing within the agency.

Also, instead of counterintelligence harassing and fomenting turmoil in domestic political movements, the FBI will handle the investigation of them as in criminal cases. Guidelines specify such groups are not to be investigated unless believed to be actually violating federal law or – a controversial point with civil-rights advocates – about to violate the law.

Further reform could come through Mr. Kelley's announced review of the FBI's use of informants. One was reportedly involved in burglary as recently as last month.

Meanwhile, a Justice Department probe of the bureau continues. And FBI wiretapping remains under congressional investigation (though this is currently thwarted by a court injunction obtained by President Ford.)

But lasting improvement will have to come from within an FBI adhering to its own high stated standards. As Mr. Kelley said, "If there's linen to be cleaned in our household, we should clean it ourselves."

New York Post

New York, N.Y., August 9, 1976

FBI Director Clarence Kelley, appearing on CBS' Face the Nation yesterday, sounded sadly like a man operating in a world he never made. It was, alas, still the world of J. Edgar Hoover.

Thus Kelley conceded that he had been grossly "deceived" when he insisted not long ago that such FBI transgressions as rampant burglary belonged to the distant past. But when he was pressed to reveal whether he had yet been able to locate the men who lied to him, he was obliged to admit he had not.

On numerous other points Kelley's responses seemed to be those of a prisoner of the holdover Hoover apparatus rather than those of a man who has initiated a new era.

Kelley emphasized that he enjoys his job and hopes to retain it after November, even if Jimmy Carter is elected. He can hardly make a case for continued employment until or unless he decisively banishes Hoover's ghost from the FBI's corridors.

DAYTON DAILY NEWS

Dayton,Ohio, August 7, 1976

The big enchiladas are gone, but the odor of Watergate still lingers around the FBI.

Attorney General Edward Levi, a highly respected man, is busy spraying air deodorant around the bureau instead of throwing out the rotten corpses that are the source of the smell.

When J. Edgar Hoover took over the feds' law enforcement arm decades ago, he was faced with a similar situation. The agency was incompetent and had been used for political operations. He cleaned house. Hoover's proudest boast, and one that was apparently valid for many years, was that he got politics out of the FBI. Eventually, of course, Mr. Hoover himself brought politics back.

Mr. Levi and the bureau's faltering director Clarence Kelly ought to look over the record of Mr. Hoover's early years. There's a lesson there: those who are tainted by illegality and politics ought to go.

The Boston Globe

Boston, Mass., August 13, 1976

Director Clarence M. Kelley's plan to reorganize the FBI is a commendable start toward correcting two of the gravest problems the Bureau faces: corruption among officials on the inside, and illegal tactics against civilians on the outside.

Carried out with vigor and commitment, the shakeup could restore the Bureau's badly damaged credibility, and spare thousands of American citizens from the sort of harassment that has been only too well documented in recent months.

Regrettably, however, the action may have come too late in the day to spare Mr. Kelley himself. His statement the other day that he "can no longer make categorical sweeping statements" about FBI activities amounted to an admission that he has failed to gain full control in his three years as director.

Although we admire Mr. Kelley's candor, we cannot help but feel that his admission — and the administrative failure it implies — places him in an untenable position. The country will have little confidence in the director's reorganization plan if it perceives that the director lacks the will or the skill to carry out that plan.

Thus, with all due respect for Mr. Kelley's accomplishments as a career law enforcement officer — and perhaps even greater respect for his decent intentions — we feel compelled to urge that he offer his resignation when the chance routinely comes up after the presidential election in November. This would give the new President, whoever he may be, plenty of time to think about the choice of a reform-minded new director, and ensure continuity in the interim.

Although Mr. Kelley's immediate problems stem from disclosures of illegal FBI break-ins, and of financial indiscretions by some Bureau officials, it seems in retrospect that he was in a no-win position from the beginning.

Mr. Kelley was the police chief of Kansas City, Mo., when Richard Nixon chose him in 1973 to take over a drifting and demoralized FBI. The Bureau had been without a permanent director since the death of J. Edgar Hoover 14 months earlier, and its good-guy image already had been badly tarnished by Watergate.

As if taking on these problems were not enough, Mr. Kelley seemed to suffer from his own internal conflicts. He had been an FBI agent for 21 years prior to taking the Kansas City job, and had great respect for Hoover, if not for the Hoover style. Thus, on the one hand, he said he wanted to make the FBI a more responsive, open agency; but on the other, he kept on the payroll a great many Hoover-era administrators who stubbornly opposed — and apparently circumvented — changes in the status quo.

Mr. Kelley repeatedly was put into the position of defending past FBI abuses as having been justified by the mood of the times, while at the same time condemning them by the standards of current morality and accountability.

But finally, he has reached the point where he cannot have it both ways. His reorganization plan — which would take investigation of domestic radicals out of the hands of the Bureau's counterspy division, and set up an agency to deal with internal misconduct — is refreshing evidence that he recognizes the problem.

The plan has merit. But one wishes Mr. Kelley had initiated it before the damage had been done to his own status and reputation.

The Louisville Times

Louisville, Ky., August 17, 1976

When Clarence Kelley took over as director of the FBI three years ago, he was faced with the task of pulling the agency out of the morass of Watergate and freeing it from the pernicious legacy of the J. Edgar Hoover era.

His almost pathetic acknowledgment the other day that he can't be sure his subordinates are telling him the entire truth about bureau operations indicates that the job is proceeding at a depressingly slow pace.

Last year, Mr. Kelley assured the public that FBI agents had not illegally burglarized the homes and offices of American citizens since 1966. Later it turned out that the bureau's lawless approach to law enforcement had continued into the 1970s. Because FBI officials had concealed these facts from him, Mr. Kelley says he can not now say "categorically" that the burglaries have stopped.

Mr. Kelley has moved slowly, and perhaps wisely so, to overhaul an agency that had been calcified by decades of iron-handed, one-man rule.

The deliberate coverup of FBI misdeeds by lesser officials suggests, however, that the time has come for the director to move more forcefully.

Disciplinary action, and criminal prosecution, where appropriate, would certainly help to end abuses and set new standards of behavior for bureau employes. The Justice Department's investigation of the FBI's systematic harassment of radical political groups over the years and the current probe of internal corruption should go a long way toward clearing out the bad apples.

But deeply ingrained attitudes and work habits are slow to change, as the recent incident involving a break-in at the Denver headquarters of the Socialist Workers Party makes clear.

Indeed, the bureau's obsession with the Socialist Workers is disturbingly reminiscent of the Hoover days, when agents spent far too much of their time spying on aging and ineffectual Communists.

For 38 years, the Socialist Workers Party has been kept under surveillance on the theory that one of its goals is to overthrow the United States government by force. The party has been all but overrun with informers and has been the target of numerous unconstitutional FBI burglaries and other dirty tricks.

Yet the 2,000-member organization, though Trotskyite in its ideology, has not, so far as is known, used violence to accomplish its goals. Indeed, it has never been anything but a small and inconsequential political group.

FBI and other officials have said that the party is not controlled by a foreign government and does not engage in espionage. Nonetheless, the bureau says it wants to continue its investigation.

The bureau apparently still has trouble understanding that Trotskyites have the same right as other American citizens to meet, express their opinions and run for office.

While Mr. Kelley and Attorney General Levi have committed themselves to stricter supervision of the FBI and a crackdown on corruption, more fundamental changes are clearly needed.

The agency will regain the respect of the public only when its agents, from the top down, finally understand that the freedoms of all law-abiding American citizens are endangered when the freedoms of a few are trampled upon.

Newsday

Garden City, N.Y., August 15, 1976

The longer it takes the FBI to clean up its own operation, the less effective its law enforcement efforts will be. No one should know that better than director Clarence Kelley, who continues to be deceived by his own agents after three years in office. Last week Kelley had to admit that he couldn't say categorically that FBI agents weren't still violating the law.

Far from attempting a thorough housecleaning, however, Kelley seems so concerned over employee morale problems that he's unwilling to look .. far under the rug. He's moving slowly, he said Wednesday, because "there are many people whose morale has been seriously affected by the possibility of disciplinary action or prosecution."

But surely it should be obvious that the sooner Kelley rids the FBI barrel of its bad apples, the faster the bureau's morale will pick up.

Slow though he may be in dealing with wrongdoers, Kelley definitely seems determined to try to prevent future misdeeds. By transferring the agency's operations directed toward domestic radicals and terrorists from the intelligence division to the general investigations branch, Kelley hopes to curb some of the worst abuses that have come to light. Now domestic intelligence operations are to be handled like other criminal investigations.

In response to apparently widespread and covered-up corruption in the bureau's top echelons, Kelley announced he would form a professional responsibility section to conduct internal investigations. The present—and powerful—inspection division, which is presumptively at fault for not uncovering or seeking to correct past wrongdoings, will cease to exist as an independent entity.

Time and time again, Kelley has been in the embarrassing position of having to admit that he was wrong in stating that certain illegal practices such as burglaries were things of the past. As late as last month, an FBI informer allegedly showed documents stolen in a burglary of the Socialist Workers Party to an FBI agent in Denver. As a result, Kelley now says he will establish a panel to review FBI practices and relationships with informers. That step, too, is long overdue.

Trying to assume control of an agency that was as closely wedded to one man as the FBI was to the late J. Edgar Hoover is obviously not an easy task. But three years should be long enough for a new director to be certain his orders are being obeyed. If Kelley can't make his stick, maybe it's time to look for stronger leadership from someone else. The FBI is too important—and potentially too dangerous—to be allowed a life of its own without firm direction from above.

ST. LOUIS POST-DISPATCH

St. Louis, Mo., August 13, 1976

In some of his recent public statements, Clarence M. Kelley, director of the Federal Bureau of Investigation, has given the impression that the agency he heads is out of control. About two months ago he acknowledged that he had been wrong in saying previously that FBI burglaries of radical group offices had been halted in 1966. He implied that he had been deceived on the matter by subordinates, and said he was "truly sorry" for some of the agency's past activities. Just this week Mr. Kelley said he could not make a blanket statement that FBI agents are not still conducting illegal burglaries or engaging in other wrongdoing.

Obviously such public confessions of illegality and of uncertainty as to the present integrity of the nation's top law enforcement organization could not continue without assurances being given that drastic steps are being taken to bring the agency under control and to prevent future abuses. Mr. Kelley has now apparently taken such steps by instituting what has been called the most extensive internal reorganization of the FBI since the start of World War II.

Responsibility for investigations of so-called radical and terrorist organizations is being transferred from the intelligence division to the general investigations branch, where such investigations, Mr. Kelley said, will be treated "like all other criminal cases in that division." The intelligence division is the branch which through the years used burglaries, firebombings, unprovoked assaults, illegal wire taps, disruptive tactics, fraudulent letters and at least one kidnaping. The targets were often individuals and groups whose only offense was to espouse unorthodox political views. Although Mr. Kelley now says the number of persons subject to domestic intelligence investigations has been reduced from 22,000 to 4000, the question must still be asked whether all of the targeted individuals are suspected of criminal acts or whether some are merely placed on the list because of some political heresy.

Mr. Kelley also announced that the inspection division is being merged with the management-oriented office of planning and evaluation, and that he will create a professional responsibility section to conduct future investigations of alleged wrongdoing by FBI executives and agents. Clearly the inspection division has not served to check long-existing FBI abuses and it has recently come under criticism for not investigating thoroughly the possibility that FBI executives received kickbacks from bureau suppliers.

The final structural change announced by the director involves bringing the formerly independent legal staff under the aegis of the director's office in the hope of improving the quality of the bureau's legal advice. Mr. Kelley also announced an internal review of the FBI's use of paid and unpaid informers to gather information in criminal and domestic security cases. Whatever validity the use of informers may have, the employment of crooks and provocateurs in this capacity, as has happened in the past, can hardly be justified.

Apart from the reorganizations changes, the most important steps Mr. Kelley has taken may have been the removal of several long-time top level FBI officials, who apparently were involved in past abuses. Judging by the now evident deceit and illegal activities that continued after he assumed the directorship in 1973, Mr. Kelley needed his own appointees in top positions in order to be sure his intended housecleaning is being carried out. A necessary task still to be accomplished, however, is the prosecution of those officials and agents found to have violated the law.

The Providence Journal

Providence, R.I., August 13, 1976

The Federal Bureau of Investigation, under the late J. Edgar Hoover, mushroomed into a powerful national police agency that operated in secrecy and virtually immune from outside scrutiny. With Mr. Hoover's death, cracks began to appear in the bureau's iron facade. The FBI, it was learned, had engaged in tactics that were variously corrupt, abusive of civil liberties or outright illegal. Its excesses, directed mainly at probes of domestic dissidents, involved illegal wiretaps and burglaries.

Clarence M. Kelley, the FBI director for the past three years, has tiptoed rather gently through this field of disclosures. After first insisting that no more FBI burglaries were being conducted, he was forced to recant and to admit that high subordinates had "deceived" him. This lame explanation hardly gives Mr. Kelley a reputation as a firm executive committed to reform.

After nearly a year without a news conference, Mr. Kelley has spoken up on the FBI's future, and his sweeping reorganization marks a shakeup that is gravely overdue. He will require that the FBI henceforth treat probes of domestic terrorists as regular criminal investigations; that the once-powerful (and nearly autonomous) inspection division be merged with the FBI's planning office; and that the bureau set up a professional responsibility section to deal with potential future wrongdoing.

On paper, the reorganization holds some hope for a real house-cleaning. The FBI cannot be permitted to function as a collection of secret fiefdoms or as a politically malleable instrument, and if shuffling the organization chart around will provide more accountability, we're for it.

In the last analysis, however, it is the whole mind-set of the upper hierarchy — a mind-set that saw the bureau as ultra-power and invulnerable to law — that must be changed. At least two of the powerful bitter-enders from the Hoover era Mr. now are leaving, and this is healthy; more personnel changes are probably in order.

But Mr. Kelley still seems inclined to avoid rocking the boat — to avoid imposing just penalties on officials who condoned past illegalities. It is little short of a whitewash to suggest (as he did at his Wednesday news conference) that agents who carried out illegal actions may not be prosecuted because they were only following orders. Mr. Kelley is right to be concerned for the morale of the many conscientious FBI officials who have not stepped out of bounds. But this concern cannot be allowed to dilute the continuing investigation and tough corrective measures that appear necessary. So far, Mr. Kelley seems to be still functioning in awe of the Hoover legacy. His remedies for past wrongs are hesitant measures that just do not reach far enough.

Detroit Free Press

Detroit, Mich., August 13, 1976

BIT BY BIT, the sordid details continue to dribble out about the Federal Bureau of Investigation's campaign of harassment against Americans who had the temerity to support unpopular causes.

At one time or another, virtually every political organization that challenged the status quo in American society came under the unconstitutional scrutiny of the FBI.

But the most constant target of the bureau in recent years has been the Socialist Workers Party (SWP), a radical organization of modest size, which spent most of its time organizing peaceful anti-war rallies and running candidates in various elections.

Incredibly, the FBI has admitted to burglarizing the Manhattan offices of the SWP *more than 90 times* between 1960 and 1966. A single FBI agent, George P. Baxtrum Jr., has admitted that he personally burglarized the offices "between 50 and 90 times." Desks were searched, documents were photographed, and on some occasions bugging devices were planted.

It is now clear, moreover, that FBI Director Clarence Kelley has not been truthful in his public statements about the bureau's abuses of power.

When reports of the FBI's snooping first surfaced in the press last year, Mr. Kelley insisted that all harassment of radicals had ended in 1966. Soon afterward, evidence came to light indicating that the FBI had conducted illegal burglaries as recently as 1973. Mr. Kelley then admitted the accuracy of this new report, but asserted that he had ordered a halt to all such abuses.

The hollowness of that claim has been exposed by Timothy Redfearn, a paid FBI informer, who admitted that he burglarized the SWP's Denver office on July 7 of this year because he was "under pressure to produce" information for the bureau.

Mr. Kelley now attempts to explain his previous misstatements with the incredible assertion that he was "deceived" by aides about the scope of the burglaries. And he refuses to state categorically that such break-ins are not continuing at the present time.

Some plain truths need to be stated about this squalid record. The FBI's campaign of harassment has been blatantly illegal. The U.S. Constitution, in clear and unmistakable language, guarantees all Americans freedom of speech and of association, and freedom from unreasonable search and seizure. Those guarantees apply to everyone—those who champion radical ideas, as well as those in the mainstream.

In light of the FBI's record of gross disregard for these guarantees, Mr. Kelley's attempt to curb the excesses through an internal reorganization is woefully inadequate.

The U.S. Justice Department's civil rights divison is now conducting an investigation of FBI abuses to determine if indictments should be sought against agents who committed burglaries. This probe must move ahead vigorously.

Wherever the Justice Department can muster a strong enough case, the agents who did the dirty work—and their superiors who gave the orders for the break-ins—should be prosecuted to the full extent of the law. That, sadly, appears to be the only way of deterring further abuses in the future.

FORD WILL NOT FIRE FBI DIRECTOR AS KELLEY ADMITS RECEIVING GIFTS

President Ford announced Sept. 4 that he would not fire FBI Director Clarence M. Kelley, who had admitted Aug. 31 that certain of his house furnishings had been provided by the FBI without charge and that he had received gifts from his top aides. Ford issued his statement after he had read a report on Kelley prepared by Attorney General Edward H. Levi. In the report Levi said that Kelley should be neither formally disciplined nor asked to resign. Ford, who Sept. 1 had asked for the report, said that he believed Kelley had "the capacity to meet the essentially high standards of the FBI."

Kelley, in response to a story published Aug. 31 in the *Washington Star,* admitted that day that FBI employes had installed some window fixtures in his apartment shortly after he took office in 1973. He said that it had been done "without [his] knowledge." (Kelley Sept. 2 gave the bureau a check for $335 to cover the cost of the labor and the fixtures.) Bureau sources quoted in the Sept. 1 *Washington Post* recalled that when J. Edgar Hoover headed the FBI, it was common practice for the director and other top executives to receive special favors. Kelley said that he was "prepared to make restitution" for the gifts he had received from his personal staff and from some executive aides if his acceptance of them violated federal regulations.

The day after Kelley's statement, Ford asked Levi for the report on Kelley. The *Washington Post* carried a story that day saying that a Justice Department investigator had recommended that Kelley be fired. The investigator's superior had toned that down to a recommendation that Kelley be publicly reprimanded, the *Post* said. The recommendation, which reportedly had been sent to Levi three weeks before the *Post* story, was made by officials in the Justice Department's Office of Professional Responsibility, the *Post* said. That office was investigating charges that FBI executives had abused their powers.

Democratic presidential nominee Jimmy Carter told a reporter outside Brooklyn College Sept. 7 that, "knowing what I know now, I would have fired" Kelley for accepting gifts and favors from his staff. Later, before a larger group of newsmen, Carter declined to say whether he would dismiss Kelley if elected president. "I'll cross that bridge when I come to it," he said. Carter had told his Brooklyn College audience that the record of the FBI was a "disgrace" when it "ought to be purer than Caesar's wife." In Philadelphia, he told his church audience that Kelley had been "caught having government employes using tax money decorate his home."

At a Sept. 8 news conference, Ford said Carter "showed a lack of compassion" in saying Kelley should have been dismissed for accepting favors at a "very sad and difficult time," a reference to the period when Kelley's wife had been terminally ill with cancer and window valances were built in the Kelley apartment by FBI carpenters. Ford said that he was "confused" by Carter's uncertainty whether he would retain Kelley at the FBI if he were elected president. "So I am confused on the one hand by his flip-flop on this issue," Ford said, "and I am very disappointed at his lack of compassion on the other."

San Francisco Chronicle

San Francisco, Calif., September 2, 1976

FBI DIRECTOR Clarence M. Kelley has told FBI agents working with Justice Department investigators to "leave no stone unturned" in ferreting out corruption in the bureau. That's a praiseworthy sentiment, but, still, it seems as though some mighty small pebbles are being flipped over in the case of the director himself.

The case that's been making the front pages came up because Kelley received some gifts—a walnut table, a clock, an easy chair, that kind of thing—from his FBI confreres, and window valances were constructed in his apartment by carpenters from the bureau's exhibits section. Kelley had apparently commented to his driver that his late wife wanted the drapery frames and the driver passed the word along to the exhibits section.

THE EXHIBITS people, responding with knee-jerk alacrity as they had in the days of J. Edgar Hoover when a suggestion from that quarter constituted word from on high, whipped out the valances and installed them without Kelley's knowledge. Kelley said he intends to reimburse the bureau for labor and materials involved. He'll also make restitution for the gifts, if it turns out they violate federal regulations.

We're all in favor of the Justice Department looking into the misdeeds of the FBI, but here they're getting parlously close to nitpicking. It's excessive to call for Kelley's resignation over what amounts to some interior decoration; he shouldn't have had it done, but it's really "piddling stuff," as one Justice official put it. Kelley appears to be a fair-minded law-enforcement officer who is attempting, despite the potent and lingering influence of his predecessor, to build a new image for the FBI. Asking for his resignation in this case is unrealistic and will only weaken what positive influence he has so far had in the bureau.

The Evening Bulletin

Philadelphia, Pa., September 7, 1976

President Ford has agreeu with Attorney General Edward Levi that it is not necessary or desirable that Clarence M. Kelley, director of the Federal Bureau of Investigation be relieved of his post for what appear to have been small and unintentional mistakes.

What'd Mr. Kelley do?

He admitted taking some moderately expensive Christmas and anniversary gifts from his office staff and senior FBI officials. He himself had ordered in July that gift-giving to superiors be in strict conformity with the regulations. His own bosses concluded that his gifts were within those bounds.

Then there were the valances — decorative frames at the top of windows — that were installed in Mr. Kelley' apartment by the FBI's exhibits section. His wife, who was then ill, and has since died, had asked him to obtain valances. He didn't learn until later, he has said, that they were made in the exhibits section of the FBI. He's sent the bureau a check for $335 to cover the cost of materials and labor.

None of the items, about which Mr. Kelly appears to have been quite open, looks like any devious abuse of power on the part of a very busy man with a new and big job to do. At most it seems embarrassing that this occurred when he is in the midst of trying to clean up the bureau of an accumulation of offenses at the bureau.

The diversion of government property and manpower is improper at any level. We do not pooh-pooh any effort to see that this is not done by high officials or low. But certainly Mr. Kelley does not either: he has given every appearance of being dedicated to the restoration of the FBI's effectiveness and reputation. The President and Attorney General, we believe, have rightly judged their man.

CHICAGO DAILY NEWS

Chicago, Ill., September 3, 1976

For pity's sake, Clarence Kelley! Knowing that your job, foremost, was to take a scouring pad to the dirty pots and pans piled up at the FBI, how could you use such colossal poor judgment in your personal conduct?

Now it should be admitted that your improprieties — personal carpentry work in your apartment and acceptance of gifts purchased by a group of appreciative employes — hardly constitute grand larceny. Compared with some of the shenanigans indulged in by the late J. Edgar Hoover and his cronies, they were piddling. The point, of course, is that no FBI director has ever been on the line like you are. The President brought you back to the agency from a job in Kansas City to clean up the bureau and restore public confidence. The nation was grateful that an honest cop would take the job, and you have performed well, on the whole, amid such frustrations as having to admit that you couldn't be sure whether illegal FBI burglaries had stopped. You had the courage to acknowledge past FBI misdeeds and the guts to fire a top aide found to be misappropriating funds.

Now comes this stain on you, personally. What should you do?

Resign? The bureau cannot be subjected to a revolving door leadership. Your tenure has been one of building toward some stability, of ending the old cult of personality built up by Hoover.

We're not ready to give up on you yet. We doubt that the President is either, although you have put that man facing an election in a spot, don't you think?

A reprimand is in order, but you can stand it. It makes your job tougher, but if you can complete the job of cleaning up the FBI, that will be remembered long after your careless fiddling with the cookie jar is forgotten.

The Wichita Eagle and The Beacon

Wichita, Kans., September 4, 1976

Official investigations into illegal activities of the FBI, CIA and other intelligence agencies were valid and demanded by a public that rightfully resented invasion of privacy even in the name of law and order.

But we wonder if the zeal to uncover FBI corruption has not lost perspective when its director, Clarence Kelley, is attacked for what seem minor infractions — at least at this writing.

When a public official accepts free gifts and services, from employes or private enterprise, it may be said that he used poor judgment.

But "$35 to $40" drapery valances for his apartment and a chair, table and clock — each valued at about $250 — given to Kelley as Christmas and anniversary gifts by top aides do not rank with wiretappings, buggings, secret enemies lists and harassment of private citizens.

One situation involves a lack of discretion, the other breaking or severely bending laws.

With the Justice Department carrying out this investigation of questionable "loot," under the direct supervision of the attorney general and with the White House staff assessing the case, much ado about relatively little is certain to cost taxpayers a bundle.

Unless Kelley is accused of more substantial misconduct as the FBI's chief, further expense and wasted effort can be saved by filing the whole affair under "petty nonsense."

The Virginian-Pilot

Norfolk, Va., September 2, 1976

An honest person who moves into what used to be a disreputable house ought to eschew pink lampshades and player piano. That lesson unfortunately was ignored by Clarence P. Kelley when he became director of the Federal Bureau of Investigation in 1973.

He succeeded L. Pat Gray, who was tarnished by Watergate, in a period when J. Edgar Hoover's shortcomings, meanness, and law-flouting were crawling out of the woodwork.

Mr. Kelley nevertheless has had the poor judgment to accept for his Washington apartment some quite expensive gifts from subordinates and to allow it to be furnished with valances and a portable cabinet constructed by the FBI's special exhibits section. Now he is being investigated for the possible misuse of Government services and property and for exercising poor judgment in his staff relations.

In other years, Mr. Kelley's improprieties hardly would have been recognized as such, and in any event would have attracted little attention. They are less than shocking now.

The trouble, though, is that Mr. Kelley was charged with cleaning up the FBI and restoring it to the nation's confidence. He has been halting shady practices and culling out offending officials. Indeed, he collaborated with Attorney General Edward H. Levi in establishing the Justice Department-FBI task force that is putting the finger on him.

Mr. Kelley appears to have committed no outrage. But he's been inexcusably careless with his integrity.

DAILY NEWS

New York, N.Y., September 8, 1976

On the advice of Attorney General Edward Levi, President Gerald Ford has decided to retain Clarence Kelley as FBI director despite a flap over some work the agency did at Kelley's private digs.

Levi is satisfied that Kelley didn't solicit favors, and the government has been reimbursed the small sum involved. That, we trust, will write "finished" to an episode that has been blown up out of all proportion.

Sentinel Star

Orlando, Fla., September 5, 1976

FBI DIRECTOR Clarence M. Kelley, the tough Kansas City cop who promised to keep politics out of the bureau, is, it develops, not above dabbling in interoffice politics himself.

It is disappointing to learn he accepted more than $1,000 worth of gifts from his subordinates. But maybe the American people are getting accustomed to disappointment in public officials. The gifts Kelley accepted from employes whose salaries are smaller than his own, and the custom furnishings the bureau's carpentry shop made for his apartment seem almost trivial compared to certain other revelations of official misconduct.

But, as the saying goes, it isn't the gift, it's the thought behind it. And it doesn't take much imagination to read the thought behind a $250 clock an employe might give his boss.

Mr. Kelley's acceptance of expensive gifts clearly was out of order. And if, as he says, he didn't know the valances and kitchen cabinets for his Washington apartment came from the FBI workshop, he has less than a firm grasp on plant operations.

We don't want to see him replaced. As far as can be determined he has been an able law enforcement officer and the FBI has had enough turmoil without the strain of new and untried leadership.

Kelley should apologize publicly for his poor judgment, pay for the gifts as he has for the apartment furnishings and mend his ways.

THE CHRISTIAN SCIENCE MONITOR

Boston, Mass., September 2, 1976

We learn of Clarence Kelley's improprieties in office more in sorrow than in anger. It certainly was not greed or criminality that led the director of the FBI to accept minor services to improve his suburban apartment. The total cost of the window valances and the small cabinet built by the bureau, which he now offers to reimburse, is a relatively paltry sum. It hardly seems worth making a fuss about when there is so much genuinely malicious wrongdoing to go after.

Yet the incident cannot be ignored. For it is symptomatic of a widening trend in business as well as in government that ought to be firmly rooted out: the misuse of government or corporate positions for personal gain and justification of such action on grounds that "everyone does it."

It is a problem that extends also to petty pilferage of property by officials and subordinates alike. No one knows precisely how much is lost by corporate theft by employees – everything from furniture to stationery supplies – but it is costing the public hundreds of millions of dollars a year in higher prices. Similarly does the public pay when there is dishonesty in government.

It is not the cost alone that is important, however, but the whole moral tone of society that suffers as a consequence. And here executive officials, whether they are in the White House, in the Congress, in city halls, or in Lockheed, bear an enormous responsibility. When they themselves do not set an example of utmost honesty, they can hardly complain when their subordinates are caught with their fingers in the till. When they themselves do not demand the highest standards of integrity – in matters small and large – they encourage laxity all down the line.

In the wake of the Watergate experience, which greatly eroded Americans' confidence in government and business, much has been done to bring about reforms to prevent future such scandals. Mr. Kelley himself has courageously acknowledged the misdeeds of the FBI and led an extensive internal reorganization of the bureau as part of a cleansing process. Only a few weeks ago he dismissed his chief deputy for reportedly misappropriating bureau funds.

One would have expected Mr. Kelley to be especially careful about such things as gifts from his employees and menial personal services. Whether he should be fired for this obvious error of judgment is open to question. But in any event Attorney General Levi and President Ford should use the occasion to express the importance they place on high standards of conduct by all officials in the executive branch of government.

THE CINCINNATI ENQUIRER

Cincinnati, Ohio, September 9, 1976

PRESIDENT FORD'S decision last weekend not to press for the resignation of Clarence M. Kelley as director of the Federal Bureau of Investigation (FBI) ought to be interpreted as a signal to allow Mr. Kelley and the FBI to get on with their work.

There were two sets of infractions that led some in the Department of Justice to question Mr. Kelley's suitability for continued service.

One was that his home contained two drapery valances and a storage cabinet built by the FBI's carpentry shop. Once the facts became known, Mr. Kelley paid $335 to cover the materials and labor used in building the equipment.

The second was Mr. Kelley's apparent willingness to accept gifts from his subordinates.

Neither infraction amounted to a crippling disability. But if the Watergate era has taught official Washington nothing else, it should have taught the indispensability of avoiding even the appearances of impropriety.

Even if, as Mr. Kelley maintains, he was unaware that a pair of drapery valances had been built for him in the FBI's facilities, he must acknowledge that the valances constituted an appearance of misuse of authority.

And even if the gifts Mr. Kelley received from his subordinates had only a limited intrinsic value, he must acknowledge that the act of accepting them could easily have impaired his ability to exercise the evenhanded authority an FBI director must possess in dealing with his subordinates.

It is regrettable that these most recent allegations— along with other allegations about the FBI's misuse of power— have occupied an inordinate amount of Mr. Kelley's time and energy. Even more important, they have diminished the stature of the FBI.

But Mr. Kelley's time and energy and the damage to the FBI's reputation will not have been wasted if these incidents remind him—and all others in the public service—that the American people are entitled to the appearance as well as the substance of honest, detached, principled conduct on the part of their elected and appointed officials.

The FBI has enemies who rejoice in the kind of ammunition that Mr. Kelley's inattention or imprudence has provided. We may be certain that they will be unimpressed by his apologies or by the chastisement of his superiors. They will do their best to portray the FBI as permanently and irretrievably discredited.

Surely, with such foes, the FBI's official family needs to be more sensitive than ever to the dictates of prudence.

No arm of the federal government has a purpose more intimately related to the American public's safety than the FBI. We hope at long last that it will now get on with its work.

Arkansas Gazette.

Little Rock, Ark., September 5, 1976

The ordeal of Clarence M. Kelley grows worse by the day, and we wouldn't be surprised if the FBI director resigns rather soon under all the pressure. Indeed, a few days back, we suggested that he resign when a new national administration begins at the start of next year, or be displaced if he declines to quit the job.

The reasoning behind this was that, try as he may have, he simply hasn't gotten control of bureau, and by his own admission has been deceived from within it in recent weeks. Apparently the abuses which he swore had been ended under his directorship, including illegal breakins by FBI operatives, have continued without his knowledge. He has to contend with too many of the old hard-liners within the bureau, and obviously hasn't been able to, with much success, though we suspect that he has tried very hard. A new face is needed before long — one selected from outside the bureau.

But we doubt very much that Mr. Kelley deserves to be booted out, this close to the end of the year, on the basis of the latest allegations against him: that he accepted a number of Christmas and anniversary gifts from his office staff and senior FBI officials, and allowed the bureau's construction workers to install drapery valances in his apartment living room. This is penny-ante stuff, especially by Washington standards. He accepted a clock and a chair and some other minor items, and says he didn't even know the bureau people put up the valances. Some of these were joint gifts given by many employes, pooling their funds, and all together it amounts to less than $1,000 worth, from all indications. We doubt that this could buy any influence at all with this tough old cop, who is highly paid as FBI director and who, in his whole long career, has shown no signs of a lack of integrity.

He exercised poor judgment, perhaps, or was merely unthinking in this matter, but surely it measures up as trivial compared to the larger concerns and problems of the FBI. One Justice Department official is reported to have recommended that Mr. Kelley be fired on the grounds of these revelations, and another has urged that he be merely reprimanded. The latter certainly is preferable, we think, and it should not be too blistering a reprimand. An honorable career ought not be ended ignominiously for no more than this. Rather, he should step down after the election, or else be replaced for the only serious deficiency we have been able to discern — his lack of administrative grasp, which has rendered him unable to reform the bureau as it desperately needs to be reformed, for the good of all of us.

The Standard-Times

New Bedford, Mass., September 4, 1976

There is a distinct irony in the predicament in which FBI Director Clarence M. Kelley finds himself as a result of an internal investigation by the bureau.

It was just six weeks ago that Kelley fired the FBI's No. 2 man on grounds he had allowed public funds and material to be misappropriated for the benefit of other officials, but not for himself.

Three weeks ago, Kelley fired the head of the bureau's exhibits section after the latter admitted taking less than $100 worth of lumber for his personal use.

In the interim, the director ordered FBI agents working with Justice Department investigators "to leave no stone unturned" in seeking out corruption in the agency.

Apparently the agents took him literally. They learned that:

—Window valances were constructed in Kelley's apartment by bureau carpenters from the selfsame exhibits section. "Without my knowledge," says Kelley.

—The exhibits section built a portable cabinet in Kelley's apartment at his request. To hold "miscellaneous items, such as FBI stationery, pencils and pens, paper clips and memo pads," says the director.

—Kelley and his wife received expensive gifts from his office staff and top bureau officials.

The director now says he is "prepared to make restitution for any such gifts that are not clearly permitted by . . . the Code of Federal Regulations."

It is disturbing to be told the nation's top lawman learned about the origin of the valances three years ago, but made no effort to make restitution until bureau investigators uncovered the matter.

The same could be said of his ordering the cabinet to be made and of his accepting $200 clocks and $250 tables from those under his direct supervision — particularly since he fired subordinates for lesser lapses.

In light of his position and his extensive experience in the field of law enforcement, Kelley has displayed an astonishing lack of judgment that can only further erode confidence in the FBI, already beset by a series of scandals. He has greatly diminished his effectiveness by reducing his public image.

For the good of the bureau and the nation, Kelley should resign. And if he does not Attorney General Edward Levi should fire him, as Kelley fired his subordinates.

THE MILWAUKEE JOURNAL

Milwaukee, Wisc., September 4, 1976

FBI Director Kelley is a well intentioned man running out of time and stature.

His tough task in his three years as boss has been to clean up the house that J. Edgar Hoover built — eradicate pockets of corruption, end cronyism, restore the bureau's image. He has made gains, but slowly and often with grave setbacks.

Kelley got badly burned on the question of FBI burglaries. After saying that they had ended in 1966, he disclosed that he had been deceived by top aides. Actually, the break-ins had continued into 1972 and 1973, and Kelley could not flatly assure that they have not occurred since.

Meanwhile, amid criticism that he had not weeded out enough of Hoover's holdovers, Kelley blundered in picking a top deputy. The appointee, it turned out, had once headed an FBI dirty tricks operation.

Now, Kelley is in trouble over accepting expensive gifts from subordinates and using FBI services and property in his apartment. Although the extent of impropriety is unclear, Kelley has little margin for ethical error. He is supposed to brightly counter the example of Hoover, who often treated the FBI as private property. One especially wonders how Kelley can square his conduct with his recent ouster of a lesser official who took wood from the bureau's carpentry shop to build a birdhouse.

Recently, Kelley announced commendable changes designed to reduce secrecy, end illegal acts and rid the FBI of bad apples. The question today is whether he has enough prestige left to make reform stick.

Chicago Tribune

Chicago, Ill., September 3, 1976

It's sad that FBI Director Clarence M. Kelley let himself be trapped by what was apparently an old FBI custom—subordinates doing favors and giving personal gifts to the boss, sometime at FBI expense. The amount of money involved does not seem large—drapery valences in his house, some lumber, a $250 table, a $250 easy chair, an expensive clock. . . .

But Mr. Kelley was given his job in 1973 primarily on the basis of his reputation as an incorruptible law enforcement officer—12 years as police chief in Kansas City, Mo., where he cleaned up the scandal-plagued police force, and 21 years with the FBI. His task was to regain for the FBI the public esteem it lost in Watergate. And as unpleasant truths emerged about the activities of the late J. Edgar Hoover, the scope of the repair job expanded.

Mr. Kelley is a dedicated man and has done a great deal for the FBI. But the circumstances surrounding his appointment required him to be purer than Caesar's wife. In this he has failed. His indiscretion, however trivial, will embarrass the FBI and become a campaign issue.

President Ford will probably be reluctant to send Mr. Kelley, who will be 65 in October, back to Kansas City permanently. But he must—quickly and without fuss.

Known to be particularly hard on lying and corruption among police officers, Kelley once warned a class of police recruits in Kansas City that "errors of the heart [crookedness]" would be "severely judged." But "errors of the mind, mistakes in judgment . . . are in a different category." No one is suggesting Kelley is crooked. But the FBI—and President Ford—can't afford even this kind of a small mistake in judgment.

The Boston Globe

Boston, Mass., September 2, 1976

One depressing parallel among the Watergate, Wilbur Mills, Wayne Hays and now FBI scandals is that open abuses of the Constitution were tolerated for years — and petty thievery and minor misconduct at last brought down public wrath.

The latest to be caught is FBI director Clarence Kelly, who is trying to put across the unpersuasive story that the Bureau's exhibits section came to his apartment without his knowledge and had carpenters build a window valance, apparently with government materials and on government time. Kelly also knowingly had the Bureau carpenters build a cabinet for his home (to store FBI stationery and paper clips, he explains), and he concedes that when he took office he gathered in gifts from his subordinates.

Last month Kelly said he was unable to figure out which of his employees had been authorizing burglaries and lying to him about it, but that he would "take action" if and when he found the culprit. That plea for guiltlessness by reason of incompetence ranked with Richard Nixon's Watergate evasions, and moved this newspaper to call on Kelly to resign after the election.

Hardly anyone else, however, seemed to be upset by Kelly's remarks, even as the grand jury list of indictable FBI agents climbed into the dozens. Some of them opened mail, tapped telephones, broke into homes, stole property. Some joined J. Edgar Hoover in misappropriating FBI funds. Some helped Hoover attempt to harass Martin Luther King Jr. toward suicide.

Now a Justice Department official has caught Kelley in a trivial indiscretion, and has called on Atty. Gen. Edward Levi to force him to resign — which Kelley should, but not just for chiseling furniture. The FBI was once a source of national pride. It is now a humiliation. And the Constitution, not a cabinet and a window valance, is what should concern Mr. Levi.

The Washington Post

Washington, D.C., September 4, 1976

TO SOMEONE who reads only headlines, it may have seemed this week that FBI Director Clarence M. Kelley had been found guilty of some heinous crime. One Justice Department investigator recommended that the director be fired; another called for a public reprimand; the President asked the Attorney General for an immediate report. All this suggested that yet another shocking scandal had erupted at the FBI, and that the director who was supposed to clean up that agency had been found to have dirty hands himself.

And what was all the fuss about? One charge was that in 1973 the FBI's special exhibits section built a pair of window valances for Mr. Kelley's apartment, in violation of the law against private use of public property. This did have more than the usual import because last month Mr. Kelley fired the veteran director of the exhibits section, John P. Dunphy, who pleaded guilty to a misdemeanor charge of using government wood to build a birdhouse at his home. The two cases differ, however, in at least one crucial respect. Mr. Dunphy acknowledged deliberate wrongdoing. Mr. Kelley has said that the valances were made "without my knowledge" and has reimbursed the government for the $335 cost. Indeed, it is easy to see how one of Mr. Kelley's subordinates could have taken it on himself to order up the carpentry out of an eagerness to help the new director and his cancer-stricken wife get settled here. Mr. Kelley could easily have gotten too busy to inquire about just how the valances had been made.

The second charge is that the director accepted expensive gifts from his subordinates in violation of a federal rule. The gifts involved—including an $83.48 clock, a $105 easy chair and a walnut table—do sound substantial, until one learns that they were purchased by a group of FBI executives, each of whom chipped in $10 or $15, and were given to the boss at Christmas or an anniversary. The officials involved have told the Attorney General that they regarded the presents as nominal and permissible under the rules.

When these details are spelled out, the incidents are revealed as quite common and trivial, involving problems of judgment and sensitivity rather than criminal intent. These matters are worth reporting, but they hardly justify the huge headlines and front-page treatment which have been lavished on the Kelley case—and which have unfairly cast shadows over the director's integrity. At almost any other time, with almost any other agency, the story would have been kept in better perspective. But in the wake of Watergate, every hint of official misconduct is doubly suspect, especially when it involves the scandal-ridden FBI—and no reporter or editor wants to risk underplaying any story that might turn out to be a piece of something big. Thus normal news judgment and discrimination got suspended; the result was overkill. The only point that might have merited such coverage was the Justice Department investigator's recommendation that Mr. Kelley be fired. But that, too, stemmed from excessive zeal and undiscriminating righteousness. Attorney General Levi's more temperate reaction is far more mature and appropriate.

This is not to say that the case has no importance. Besides serving as a barometer of pressures on the media, the affair provides additional evidence on two important points about the FBI. The first is that the old habits of paying court to the director have persisted past J. Edgar Hoover's reign. Mr. Hoover demanded absolute obedience and deference for so long that such actions became reflexive and routine. The way to deal with the director, veterans at FBI headquarters learned, was to give him whatever he wanted, no matter how outrageous that might seem—and to anticipate his wishes and whims whenever possible. Although the new director was not autocratic in style, he was treated much the same way. He was given valances for his curtains, and an easy chair to rest his ailing back—and he was given firm assurances that illegal break-ins had been stopped, and was not told about other offenses that have gradually come to light.

That leads to the second, sad point. It is that Mr. Kelley has simply been unable to bring the bureau under control. He has asserted himself sporadically, as in firing Mr. Dunphy. He has reorganized the intelligence sections and tightened the retirement rules. But he has been too inconsistent, far too gentle, far too trusting, and not nearly sensitive enough to the impact of small matters like valances and clocks in the atmosphere of public mistrust that envelops the FBI. He is a good, sturdy police officer, but the mess at the Hoover building is simply too much for him.

Perhaps it took the compromising of Mr. Kelley to show beyond a doubt that compromise solutions are not enough. The FBI needs more vigorous corrective leadership and a thorough house-cleaning. This cannot be achieved in the middle of a presidential campaign. But it should be a matter of high priority for either Mr. Ford or Mr. Carter next year.

The Charleston Gazette

Charleston, W. Va., September 2, 1976

It shakes one's faith in the Federal Bureau of Investigation to read that the nation's No. 1 policeman, FBI Director Clarence M. Kelley, didn't notice that somebody had installed valances above some windows in his home.

Of course he could have noticed them and simply wasn't curious about how they got there. Anyway, he said they were put up without his knowledge. If you are able to believe this, perhaps you'd better look above your own windows to see if elves have been at work in your house.

It turned out that Kelley's valances — decorative devices which enhance the effect of draperies — were installed by FBI employes and constructed by FBI employes on FBI time from FBI materials.

In other words, Kelley accepted — unwittingly, he contends — gifts which became available directly through criminal misapplication of public funds.

Kelley acknowledged the mysterious presence of the valances in his home only after the *Washington Star* reported that Kelley had been questioned by Justice Department investigators.

Thus it is obvious that Kelley, far from being the shining knight bent on reforming the FBI, is merely following in the footsteps of the unlamented J. Edgar Hoover, who also helped himself to favors, at public expense, from the bureau.

A pair of window valances may be a small thing. But Kelley's unquestioning acceptance of them betrays him as just another cheap bureaucrat insensitive to moral implications.

We're weary of the "I didn't know anything about it but I'll pay for it" response of public officials when they get caught in some grubby little scheme to use their offices for private gain.

Kelley should, indeed, pay for it. He should pay for the valances, for the time involved in their construction, and for the materials. Then he should be asked to resign. So should the FBI employes who — if Kelley is telling the truth — took it entirely upon themselves to use your money to please the boss.

Newsday

Garden City, N.Y., September 3, 1976

The FBI, like the White House, had two urgent needs after Watergate: a new image and a new broom.

Most people would agree that FBI director Clarence Kelley, like Gerald Ford, brought the needed aura of trust and candor to his job. But the evidence mounts of failure in his parallel responsibility to clean the place out.

Various embarrassments have been emerging all summer. Now the director has had to admit that one of the more inscrutable abuses of the Hoover era, the use of FBI staffers for petty personal services (in this case, building window valances for Kelley's apartment) is still with us.

There's no suggestion in all this that Kelley is personally evil. But the FBI is simply too important to remain under such debilitating clouds as suspected corruption and perceived ineffectiveness.

Kelley has been FBI chief three years. Anyone familiar with the paramilitary discipline of a well-run police agency knows it shouldn't take that long to bring it under control.

Yet if Kelley has indeed fallen short at the FBI, then so has the President. He kept him in the job.

So Kelley's days at the FBI are probably numbered. In the event that the Justice Department's pending investigation does not require his replacement, electoral reality probably will; Henry Kissinger's recent treatment indicates the White House attitude toward political liabilities.

Kelley, a dedicated careerist in public service, is 63 and has been in and out of hospitals this summer with back trouble. The most compassionate option for him and the President at this point probably would be retirement for health reasons. His long service entitles him to that much.

ST. LOUIS POST-DISPATCH

St. Louis, Mo., September 8, 1976

President Ford has concluded that there is no justification for firing FBI Director Clarence M. Kelley because of gifts from subordinates. In response to reporters' questions, Jimmy Carter, the Democratic presidential candidate, said he would have dismissed Mr. Kelley but, lacking detailed information, did not call on Mr. Ford to take such action.

The gifts incident hardly amounts to a campaign issue, of course, but it illustrates the doubts created after disclosures that Mr. Kelley had accepted gifts from some FBI officials, and that FBI carpenters had installed valances in his apartment. Mr. Kelley said he was not aware of how the valances got there, and he has repaid the Government for them. Attorney General Levi told Mr. Ford that the gifts were allowable. The President's decision to support Mr. Kelley followed.

Yet the affair was unfortunate because Mr. Kelley is expected to restructure the FBI and abolish or curtail some of the practices that grew up under the late J. Edgar Hoover — the burglaries, illegal searches and wire taps, the widespread political surveillance. Mr. Kelley recently announced several internal structural changes intended to bring the FBI under closer legal supervision. He fired two top officials apparently involved in misuse of funds or property. But at least two dozen FBI agents are under grand jury investigation for possible illegal break-ins. After three years in office Mr. Kelley still faces an unfinished task of rebuilding public confidence in the FBI.

In the midst of this occurred the affair of the gifts — a practice Mr. Kelley also inherited from Mr. Hoover without giving much apparent thought to its implications. The implications are that gifts to Mr. Hoover were a form of homage to an autocracy that Mr. Kelley should wish to avoid. Mr. Kelley is undoubtedly a decent, well-intentioned man and his integrity is not in question. What remains questionable is his understanding of the scope of past agency abuses and his capacity for ending them.

Detroit Free Press

Detroit, Mich., September 5, 1976

THE FBI has had enough trouble to sort out and correct without its director, Clarence M. Kelley, getting caught with his hand in the cookie jar.

Mr. Kelley, it should be noted, apparently didn't take very many cookies—just a few gifts from his underlings and the construction at taxpayer expense of some valences and other furnishings in his Washington apartment.

His lack of good judgment, however, could not have come at a worse time.

The integrity of the FBI has been seriously damaged by the slipshod and often illegal manner in which the nation's chief law enforcement agency was run by the late J. Edgar Hoover and some of his subordinates.

In far too many cases, the FBI acted as a threat to the liberty of Americans, rather than as a protector of individual freedom. In recent weeks, the bureau's image has been shaken further by Mr. Kelley's own investigation of alleged misuse of government funds and the firing of one top official left over from the Hoover regime.

One source has been quoted as saying the Justice Department is focusing on "a massive case of fraud" involving a number of FBI officials and the personal use of FBI funds.

Mr. Kelley is supposed to be at the forefront of the efforts to clean up the agency and restore it to its proper role with the full integrity that role demands.

That is why his own admissions of accepting gifts and work in his apartment add to the damage already done, even though the amounts of money involved are not large. Mr. Kelley may have thought he was merely following in the tradition of Mr. Hoover, who annually accepted expensive gifts from his staff and who allowed the FBI to build a front porch on his home and a fish pond in his backyard.

No matter. Mr. Kelley acted improperly, and has seriously undercut whatever efforts he was making to bring the FBI out of a decade of darkness. President Ford is now waiting for a full report from Attorney General Edward Levi. In the interim, it is hard to escape the feeling that Mr. Kelley has jeopardized his position and that the pressing need to end all abuses and unethical behavior in the FBI will require a new director with a stronger commitment to total integrity.

The Pittsburgh Press

Pittsburgh, Pa., September 5, 1976

FBI Director Clarence Kelley, who has been caught up in a mini-scandal, has put President Ford behind the eight ball.

Overall, Mr. Kelley has done a good job of running the Federal Bureau of Investigation since taking over the agency in the wake of Watergate.

He has thus helped restore some of the luster the FBI lost when it was revealed how the bureau had been misused by J. Edgar Hoover during the latter part of his 48-year reign.

But now Mr. Kelley has allowed his own reputation to be sullied and his own usefulness to the country to be diminished by thoughtlessly or foolishly accepting gifts and favors from some FBI underlings.

Offhand, the Christmas and anniversary gifts he got don't seem like much — a walnut table, a clock, an easy chair, a jewelry box. And Mr. Kelley says some of the gifts he gave in return cost more. But there's a law against acceptance of gifts by government officials.

There's also a law against misuse of government property. Yet Mr. Kelley now admits that FBI carpenters built two wooden window valances and a portable cabinet in his suburban apartment shortly after he moved to Washington from Kansas City.

Mr. Kelley says he didn't ask them to do this work and didn't even know they were FBI employes until they had completed the job. He also has reimbursed the government for this with a $335 check.

There is no reason to doubt Mr. Kelley's word. However, an FBI director — and especially one with a clean-up mission — is expected to be above all suspicion, and this position he has now compromised.

Moreover, the revelations about Mr. Kelley's poor judgment come at an inopportune time. It's the political season, and one of President Ford's talking points is that he has restored honesty and integrity to the executive branch.

Stories about the FBI director's valances and clock, while fairly petty stuff, are embarrassing to Mr. Ford in the political homestretch, and may leave the President no choice but to ask for Mr. Kelley's resignation.

THE ROANOKE TIMES

Roanoke, Va., September 7, 1976

Since he took office in mid-1973, FBI Director Clarence M. Kelley has seemed determined not only to straighten out the bureau's operations, but also to avoid the kind of prideful error J. Edgar Hoover made: considering himself above principles that apply to ordinary men.

Alas, Mr. Kelley too appears to have feet of clay. He has admitted to a task force probing power abuses in the bureau that he accepted expensive gifts from other FBI officials, and that window valances and a cabinet were made for his apartment by FBI workers at government expense.

Even a school teacher is warned against accepting the legendary apple from a student because it might lead to bias, or accusations thereof. Mr. Kelley was oddly blind to the implications of taking presents worth $200 and more from subordinates. Rank may have its privileges, but in a democracy they shouldn't be that lordly.

Mr. Kelley says the cabinet in his apartment is FBI property and he'll return it when he leaves office (which could, in view of these revelations, be sooner than he had planned). He asserts that he didn't know the valances had been made for him by the bureau's special exhibits section, which suggests either (1) poor communication within the Kelley household or (2) that the FBI chief believes in benevolent elves.

The situation is a throwback to the Hoover days. For all his image of staunch integrity, the late Mr. FBI wasn't above accepting costly tribute from his agents and using the bureau's resources for his own convenience. He and his FBI sidekick Clyde Tolson allegedly called some of their vacation trips "inspection tours" and billed the taxpayers for expenses. A retired bureau official has testified that Mr. Hoover once had a large porch added to his Washington home, material and labor furnished by the FBI.

Mr. Kelley's public actions toward cleaning up the FBI have been impressive. But the fresh instances of unsanctioned wiretapping and break-ins, of questionable gifts and illicit carpentry are signs that within the bureau are people who consider Mr. Kelley's campaign to be window-dressing, behind which nothing has really changed. The FBI director is due at least a reprimand. And if he can't soon convince his people, by both words and actions, that he means business, then he ought to be told it's time to turn in his bureau-made cabinet.

LEVI ISSUES DIRECTIVE ENDING FBI'S 38-YEAR OLD SWP PROBE

Attorney General Edward H. Levi Sept. 10 ordered the end of the 38-year old FBI investigation of the Socialist Workers Party. The directive issued to the bureau was based on the recommendation of two Justice Department committees which had reported that the party's activities did not warrant FBI investigation under the March guidelines.

Peter Camejo, Socialist Workers candidate for President, called the ruling "an historic victory for democratic rights for all Americans." He said it was the "first step in bringing to a halt a Government program for political spying and harassment."

In its 38-year existence, the FBI probe had compiled eight million file entries. The bureau had committed an estimated 92 burglaries into SWP offices over six years, and had used its COINTELPRO activities to harass party members. No criminal charges have been brought against any party members. It was disclosed in August that the FBI used 316 paid informers against the SWP since 1960. It also had "an army of some 1,300 free-floating informers who spy on the activities of members and a wide variety of groups."

Levi's directive appeared to override a statement made in mid-August by FBI Director Clarence M. Kelley that the FBI would continue to investigate the SWP, changing its jurisdiction from the intelligence division to the general crimes division.

The Salt Lake Tribune

Salt City, Utah, September 22, 1976

In the mid 1930s Leon Trotsky gave up hope of reforming the Communist International. He called on his followers, in Russia and elsewhere, to establish their own revolutionary parties and form a Fourth International.

This movement, says the Encyclopedia Britannica, proved to be "little more than a shadow organization although a small founding conference was held in France in 1938."

The movement's branch in the United States was the Socialist Workers Party (SWP), also launched in 1938. Like its parent organization, the party never got off the ground. Out of nine pages of solid type in the Britannica about socialism it rates only two lines.

To the Federal Bureau of Investigation, however, the SWP—not to be confused with the Socialist Party of the late Norman Thomas—presented a tenacious threat to United States security.

For 38 years the FBI kept tabs on rag-tag members of the SWP. As far as is publicly known the bureau never turned up anything that had substantial bearing on United States security, internal or external.

The other day Atty. Gen. Edward M. Levi called off the SWP stakeout. In almost four decades of tailing the few thousand renegade Communists, the FBI amassed five million separate file entries and committed numerous illegal burglaries and other acts of harassment.

About the only positive thing to come out the dogged pursuit of domestic Trotskyites is the revelation that the bureau stooped to illegal activities. And remnants of the SWP are suing the government for that.

The bureau's mistake is not that it looked in on an organization that promoted revolution. That is accepted operating procedure. And this was especially true during many of those 38 years when Communist plots, even those hatched by Trotskyites, were taken more seriously.

The FBI's transgression is that it over-reacted. In so doing, it discredited itself while enhancing an otherwise puny collection of malcontents calling themselves a political party.

The Charleston Gazette

Charleston, W.Va., September 28, 1976

For decades the Federal Bureau of Investigation has taken it upon itself to determine which associations are proper for Americans and which should be discouraged.

This extraconstitutional role has been overlooked by a succession of presidents and congresses which sniveled and cowered in the presence of J. Edgar Hoover and babbled their praise of the FBI for its patriotism.

The FBI has been anything except patriotic. If the FBI were patriotic it would recognize the right of American citizens to participate in nonviolent political activity of their choosing.

When such activity is inhibited by a national police force — that is more than unpatriotic, un-American activity. It is activity so sinister that every freedom loving American should demand an end to it.

One of the FBI's most sinister assaults upon the American system was its systematic harassment of the Socialist Workers party, a tiny and perfectly legitimate political organization which opposes violence as a matter of stated doctrine.

Atty. Gen. Edward H. Levi on Sept. 14 ordered an end to the harassment. Prior to Levi's order, the SWP, composed of no more than 1,500 persons, forced the FBI to surrender documents which showed that 66 FBI informers were still posing as members of the party. That's one informer for every 23 Socialist Workers. The FBI also admitted to several burglaries of SWP offices.

The burglary of a Socialist Workers party office is a crime identical to the burglary of Democratic National Headquarters offices in the Watergate complex. The Watergate burglars went to jail. The FBI continued to badger the SWP, and thoughtful Americans surely wish the SWP well in its suit against the government. If a Socialist Worker can be harassed without cause by a national police force, so can a vegetarian, or a Methodist.

For those who wish to acquaint themselves with the organization that has managed to obsess past and present FBI leaders, *The Nation* will publish in its next issue an article in which SWP members provide historical background on their party and explain its ideological position.

We suggest that the article be read by FBI administrators and operatives who seemed to be afflicted by the crazed notion that only Democrats and Republicans can be Americans.

The Washington Post

Washington, D.C., September 27, 1976

IT WAS THE FIRST appearance of the director of the FBI before the new Senate Intelligence Committee, and Clarence Kelley's disclosures made the most of it. Mr. Kelley announced that the FBI's domestic intelligence caseload had been reduced by 97 per cent, from 21,414 investigations in 1973 to 626 cases currently. This was, Mr. Kelley said, in line with the bureau's new emphasis on "quality over quantity." It's not every day that an agency of government announces the virtual abolition of an activity, and the significance of Mr. Kelley's announcement cannot be overemphasized, for it represents further evidence that the FBI is emerging from the dark shadow of its past.

But it ought not to be forgotten that Mr. Kelley's announcement is also a stark indictment of that past. His very use of the words "quality over quantity" in describing the elimination of practically all domestic intelligence cases tends to confirm what many had suspected about the bureau's activities: that the FBI had become a bureaucracy in relentless pursuit of political groups that gave top FBI officials ideological or social offense.

And nothing better illustrates this point than the saga of the FBI and the Socialist Workers Party. It may never be known or understood what aroused the interest of J. Edgar Hoover's FBI in the SWP back in 1938. One might guess that it was the inevitable result of a time of great concern about communism, socialism and "isms" generally. Still, nothing can justify or excuse the infiltration, bugging and harassment of a legitimate political party in the manner of the FBI operation. That the FBI enterprise lasted for 38 years and was closed down by the Justice Department only two weeks ago defies all understanding.

To this day, the FBI's justification for this affront to the democratic process has not been made public. No particular crime was alleged, no violence on the part of the SWP was suggested, and no evidence of espionage was brought forward as far as we know. In short, none of the reasons a police agency should have for being interested in a political group appears to have played any part in the FBI's decision.

Nevertheless, the FBI had 1,600 informers in the SWP over those four decades, and 66 of them were still functioning in the party at the time the Justice Department finally decided enough was enough. The SWP has brought a $40 million lawsuit against the FBI and others associated with the campaign against the party. In one poignant paragraph, the lawsuit says that the party has been so thoroughly infiltrated that it is impossible for its leaders to tell when some aspects of the party's work might have been directed by FBI infiltrators.

Within the FBI, there appear to have been no brakes and no place where the effort was evaluated or where some rigorous standard was set for what constituted a proper use of agency manpower. Surely any such review at any point along the way in nearly 40 years might have suggested to someone at the top of the agency that perhaps it would do well to shut down the Socialist Workers desk.

Instead, something quite different appears to have happened: What was done to the SWP was done to others. By the mid-1960s, that kind of operation was standard operating procedure, and it even had a name of its own, COINTELPRO, standing for counterintelligence program. The program had as its major and enduring target the Communist Party, of course, but it soon came to include many others. The same slovenly standards for what should be a target of government attention applied to all—they needed only to have offended some FBI standard of conduct, or to have had the name "black" or "liberation" in their title. Some had shown violent tendencies, but many, if not most, had not.

Regardless, they were spied upon, had their mail covered, their phones tapped, their meetings bugged. They became the victims of government-sponsored pranks and dirty tricks, some quite deadly. As far as anyone can tell, the biggest intelligence yield from the FBI's labors in the Socialist Workers' vineyard was a great deal of intelligence, if we can use that word, on the sex lives of SWP members, stuff that is no business of the FBI.

As Mr. Kelley's Senate testimony suggests, there is a great struggle going on to clean up the FBI and make it a police agency again and not a malevolent busybody. That effort is laudable and necessary. But those files of dirty information about members of the SWP and other groups should have been destroyed long ago. An FBI task force at the Justice Department is now in the process of studying the accumulation of such files to determine their future disposition. Where the files contain information about the personal lives of individuals having no bearing on crimes and law enforcement, that material should be destroyed—period. This kind of information has a great potential for harm—and virtually no potential for good.

Others have obligations too. Those of us who were pleased to leave all the crime-busting and Red-chasing to the FBI without asking what they were doing can see now why citizens should continue to show an active interest in what government does in our name—and what Congress does on our behalf. The FBI had so many friends in Congress it never had to give any real account of itself. The bureau has said that it sent reports to the various Attorneys General over the years describing COINTELPRO. Practically all living former Attorneys General express surprise at that, claiming to have heard little or nothing of the sort of thing now coming out. That is not good enough. Those responsible in the executive branch should be put on notice that the public expects them to know what the government's police agencies are doing. Not knowing, in these situations, is not a matter of mere ignorance; it is a matter of gross negligence.

Rocky Mountain News

Denver, Colo., September 27, 1976

UNDER ORDERS from Atty. Gen. Edward H. Levi, the FBI will now bring to a close its 38-year inquiry into the Socialist Workers Party.

During that time, the FBI amassed some eight million file entries, hired an unknown number of informants and indulged in numerous illegal burglaries — 92 of them in the six-year period between 1960 and 1966.

The bureau has brought no criminal charges against any member of the party or its youth affiliate, the Young Socialist Alliance, since 1940, when 18 members were tried and convicted of violations of a law that since has been declared unconstitutional.

Director Clarence H. Kelley also has reported to the Senate Committee on Intelligence that the number of American citizens and organizations being investigated because of their political ideologies has dropped from 21,414 to 626. That's about 97 per cent.

IT IS DIFFICULT to know whether the drop is significant, since Kelley has switched from investigating both groups and their individual members to just the groups alone. But certainly dropping the Socialist Workers Party investigations was long overdue.

The FBI record in that case can only be called absurd. After watching the group for 40 years or more, they have come up with evidence of no crimes except the burglaries pulled off by the FBI and their paid informants.

John Ehrlichman, who was President Nixon's second in command at the White House, was convicted by a federal jury in Washington a few years ago for the burglary of the office of Daniel Ellsburg's psychiatrist. Ehrlichman contended that he was acting in the national interest.

However Judge Gerhard Gesell turned aside that argument. He stated in effect that burglary is burglary and a crime under the law. There can be no justification for government officials ordering felonies to be committed just because they think they are acting in the national interest.

With all that well-known history, and with all the public outcry about burglaries and other illegal acts by law enforcement agencies and spies, Timothy Redfearn, on the local FBI payroll, breaks into the Denver Socialist Workers Party headquarters. This wasn't done in the Ehrlichman days, but on July 7 of this year, 1976.

Redfearn has been indicted for the break-in but his old bosses have not.

"I've been indicted and who's guilty?" he said as he was taken off to be booked. Then he answered his own question: "The FBI."

RECENTLY WE CALLED for the resignation of Director Kelley, whose pledge to restore the bureau's tarnished image was made a bad joke by FBI subordinates who duped him into thinking agents' dirty tricks had been stopped. Kelley now admits he was lied to, but the subordinates who lied to him remain on the job, rotten apples still in the barrel.

Kelley should resign and make way for someone who will clean house. The FBI needs a new beginning.

The Des Moines Register

Des Moines, Iowa, September 19, 1976

It took an order by Atty. Gen. Edward Levi to end the 40 years of intensive investigation and harassment of the tiny Socialist Workers Party in the United States by the Federal Bureau of Investigation. The FBI acknowledged using some 1,600 informers against the party since 1960 alone.

The Socialist Workers Party was always so small that common sense should have raised questions whether that much effort was needed.

In spite of the party's extreme doctrines — it claimed originally to be more truly revolutionary than the Communists, from whom it split off over the Trotsky question — no criminal charges were filed as a result of the probing during the 40 years.

Now the party claims to oppose violence and to use only peaceful means, including the ballot. In 1972 the party got on the ballot in 25 states and attracted 97,256 votes out of more than 77 million cast. Some thousands of the party's 30,945 votes in Arizona were apparently cast for it by mistake.

No great danger to the republic.

THE KNICKERBOCKER NEWS
··· UNION-STAR ···

Albany, N.Y., September 16, 1976

If you brought in a dozen army tanks to kill a pesky mosquitoe, it wouldn't be much more ludicrous than the FBI's unrelenting and absolutely futile investigation of a bunch of harmless radicals for the past 38 years.

The object of the agency's intense, microscopic scrutiny has been the Socialist Workers Party. In one six-year period alone, the FBI committed 92 burglaries as part of its efforts to spy on these people. It has amassed 8,000,000 file entries on the party. Under their counter-intelligence program, the federal sleuths were guilty of hundreds of acts of harassment against the socialists.

Finally, this week, Attorney General Edward H. Levi told the FBI to cut it out. No more inquiries into the party. It is, to say the least, about time. The FBI should devote its energy to tracking down real criminals, not abusing the rights of American citizens and breaking the law in the process.

Los Angeles Times

Los Angeles, Calif., September 20, 1976

The long FBI investigation of the Socialist Workers Party and its youth affiliate, the Young Socialist Alliance, was, as it turned out, the bureau's equivalent of the leaf-raking projects of the old WPA. But the latter at least had the socially useful purpose of providing a minimum income to the jobless, while the former's objective, pursued for nearly 40 years, was something quite different.

The stated purpose of the investigation, begun 38 years ago, was to protect the national security—but from what? The SWP and the YSA, a spinoff of the Socialist Party, disavowed violence as a means of social change. They claim a membership of only 2,500. The FBI now admits that more than 10% of the membership of these minuscule organizations were bureau informers. In addition, the FBI had access to a reserve force of 1,300 free-lance agents who monitored the party, its affiliate and other organizations that attracted the attention of the federal police.

Never had so many been assigned to watch over so few for so long with such minimal results.

Information extracted from the bureau during the course of a current lawsuit against the government by the party and its affiliate reveals that the FBI used informers not only as informers but also as agents provocateurs. One document showed that the FBI instructed informant No. 1123 to "continue to question the loyalty of other members (of the alliance) at every opportunity," an obvious tactic to disrupt the organizations.

Atty. Gen. Edward H. Levi has now ordered the FBI to quit its investigation of the two groups, on the basis that they do not constitute a threat to the security of the United States and that an investigation is an unnecessary invasion of their privacy.

This order—somewhat tardy, yet welcome nevertheless—amounts to a confession that the FBI, stepping outside the law, acted for many years as a political policeman over a group of Americans who were exercising their rights of citizenship within the law.

THE BLADE

Toledo, Ohio, September 20, 1976

BOWING to a direct order by Attorney General Levi, the FBI has finally and reluctantly closed the book on its 38-year investigation of the Socialist Workers party. This is a classic instance in which the cliche — it's about time! — can be applied with total accuracy.

This futile and frequently illegal investigation consumed untold millions of dollars, resulted in 8 million file entries, employed thousands of agents and paid informers, included countless burglaries — 96 in one six-year period — and saw an unconscionable trampling of the legal rights of individuals all over the place.

The FBI has not even filed a charge against an SWP member of the past 36 years. Still, driven by the paranoia over this splinter group inspired by the late J. Edgar Hoover, the agency never let up in its dogged sleuthing. As late as last month, an FBI informer was revealed to have been stealing documents from a party office in Denver.

Granted, when the followers of Leon Trotsky were booted out of the Socialist party in the 1930s and formed the Socialist Workers party, it became a revolution-expounding band. But after nearly four decades of fruitless investigating during which the party never attracted more than 2,500 members at any given time, and during which the FBI could uncover no evidence of illegalities, someone somewhere along the line should have had the good sense to call a halt. This Mr. Levi has done, to his credit.

Just think where we might be today if for nearly 40 years the FBI had been devoting to the task of actually combating crime in this country all the enormous energy, time, talent, money, and resources that it wasted in an empty harassing of a handful of noisy revolutionaries. All the agency has to show for its work is a $40 million suit which the party has now filed against the U.S. Government for past injustices — and a dark page in its own annals.

DAYTON DAILY NEWS

Dayton, Ohio, September 17, 1976

The decison of the Justice Deparment to end the FBI's 38-year crime wave against the Socialist Workers Party comes just 38 years late. Imagine, this nonsense has been going on since 1938! The Big Band Era was just reaching its stride.

The FBI is believed to have conducted at least 92 illegal burglaries of SWP offices in just the last five years, at one period breaking in at an average rate of once every three weeks; agents must have put a revolving door on the safe. The bureau has paid at least 1,600 infiltrators to rat on SWP affairs, just since 1960. There are believed to be about 66 FBI submarines still submerged in the party's membership.

All of this without ever a single criminal charge being filed against the SWP, with no particular indication that the party plotted violence and against a "political threat" whose membership is never exceeded 2,500. Nation-wide.

To say that the FBI's obsession with the Socialist Workers Party was crazy is not to put the matter at all too strongly.

The FBI undertook lawless campaigns much more threatening to American principles and democratic institutions than the campaign against the SWP — its hate-and-harassment attack on Martin Luther King Jr., for example. The SWP never had a stood a chance of becoming a significant force in U.S. politics. The attack on it was wrong, of course, but really made no difference in the larger scheme of things.

But that is the point. Precisely because of its meaninglessness otherwise, the effort is a telling demonstration of how a bureaucratic operation, run in secret by one man whose tenure achieved a kind of unquestionable, secular divinity, can persist relentlessly in a bizarre error and, in the process, dig itself deeper and deeper into worse and worse trouble.

Maybe someone should have told the FBI that, according to legend, it is eternal vigilence that is the price of liberty. Not eternal surveillance.

ST. LOUIS POST-DISPATCH

St. Louis, Mo., September 20, 1976

After 38 years of investigating the Socialist Workers Party without ever bringing charges against any member of the organization, the Federal Bureau of Investigation has finally been ordered by Attorney General Edward Levi to cease its surveillance of the party. Apparently it took an order from higher up to make the FBI realize that its investigation was pointless, if not improper, since only last month word from the Justice Department indicated that the bureau expected to continue shadowing the party, whose only offense has been to voice radical rhetoric.

During nearly 40 years of activity against the SWP, the FBI has amassed 5,000,000 file entries, committed many illegal break-ins (92 in one six-year period) and hundreds of separate acts of harassment. Now that the investigation has been officially terminated, the party has justification for its demand that the Government remove all informants from the organization and surrender the names of past and present informants. Documents recently released under court order showed that the FBI has used 316 paid informers against the party since 1960.

In its damage suit against the Government and various officials, the Socialist Workers Party has served the public interest by forcing the disclosure of key documents revealing the wide extent of improper and illegal FBI activity. The revelations of vast expenditures of money and energy essentially to monitor legitimate, though unorthodox, political acitivity should drive home the lesson that the FBI should never again be allowed to become the free-wheeling agency that it was for years under its late director, J. Edgar Hoover.

THE ARIZONA REPUBLIC

Phoenix, Ariz., September 23, 1976

Hindsighters are busily raking the FBI over the coals for its 38-year investigation and infiltration of the Socialist Workers Party.

Foolish, the critics now call the intelligence operation. A threat to freedom. Non-productive.

Indeed, the tiresome probe was non-productive, as it turned out, and perhaps should have been ended long ere this.

But the FBI cannot be faulted for good intentions when it started the probe in 1938. After all, the mood of the country — including Congress — was one of deep suspicion.

The Third Reich, to reminisce, was gobbling up Europe. Americans were not yet at war themselves, but they were reminded constantly of the dangers of Fifth Column saboteurs, and subversives who would overthrow the American way.

The Socialist Workers Party, whose Marxist and Communist teachings were clear enough, was a visible threat to democracy in those days.

But just as morals and the length of skirts change, so too did the American public's tolerance for radicals and political subversion. The Communist Party, U.S.A. can now buy paid political advertising time on television, whereas 30 years ago its advocacy of violent revolution was considered a crime.

Now the country is faced with new levels of subversion and political violence. Croatian nationalists only recently hijacked an airplane, and planted a bomb in New York which killed police.

Puerto Rican nationalists randomly bomb business buildings. The Symbionese Liberation Army kidnaps, murders, bombs. Fugitives in the Weathermen Army still threaten violence.

Who in his right mind would now say that the FBI should not try penetrating these groups for information, and to break them up as threats to life and property?

The FBI has the right to do so, and, more important, the responsibility.

Yet, 30 years from now, perhaps the American people will have reached a new plateau in their tolerance of public behavior. Perhaps hijacking will be accepted as a form of political activism, and bombings will be tolerated as legitimate methods of protest and social change.

And then the hindsighters will yelp that spying on the Croatians and the SLA and the Puerto Rican nationalists was foolish.

THE TENNESSEAN

Nashville, Tenn., September 19, 1976

FINALLY, after 40 years, the Federal Bureau of Investigation has concluded that the Socialist Workers party no longer needs to be investigated.

Justice Department spokesmen said that U.S. Attorney General Edward Levi made the decision in accordance with new guidelines for intelligence gathering on domestic organizations.

The guidelines, which were established last spring, state that FBI headquarters officials must determine that a group presents a serious and immediate threat to the country before such investigations are permitted. The attorney general is to review these investigations annually.

The attorney general's decision was forwarded on Monday to the judge hearing the SWP's $40 million lawsuit against the FBI for its alleged harassment of and illegal spying on the SWP.

In hearings on that suit, FBI agents have admitted breaking into SWP headquarters. Despite these activities of the FBI, the agency's investigation has produced no criminal charges against the SWP.

The FBI's tactics have only brought shame and disrepute on the agency. What effect Mr. Levi's decision will have on the suit — in which a permanent injunction against FBI harassment was sought along with the $40 million in damages — remains to be seen.

Restoring the FBI's reputation and insuring that it is not politicized in the future are even more difficult tasks.

THE CHRISTIAN SCIENCE MONITOR

Boston, Mass., September 16, 1976

The Justice Department's new FBI guidelines have been dramatically observed in Attorney General Levi's order bringing to an end the long, fruitless, and in many instances illegal investigation of the Socialist Workers Party. We are as radically opposed to this small (2,500-member) group's revolutionary Trotskyist ideology as it is radically committed to purveying it. But such groups have a right to carry on lawful, nonviolent activities without governmental interference.

In the 1930s the Socialist Workers Party (SWP) was formed by Trotskyites expelled from the Socialist Party, which was left weakened as a party but strengthened in its anticommunist resolve by the situation. In the early '40s 18 members of the SWP were convicted under the Smith Act (later found unconstitutional) for advocating violent revolution and counseling insubordination in the armed forces.

But in all the subsequent years of FBI surveillance, break-ins, and Cointelpro (counterintelligence program) harassment, the bureau did not come up with the evidence to make a case of SWP law violation. Under the new guidelines domestic political groups are to be investigated only if believed to be violating or about to violate federal law. And any investigation is subject to periodic review – and termination if no evidence of wrongdoing is found.

Certainly almost 40 years is too long to continue on a false trail. Now the resolution of the SWP's damage suit against the government should be expedited. And let the FBI stop draining off for political crusades the resources that should be used in the fight against escalating crime.

Index

This index includes references to information in the news digest and in the editorials. Index entries referring to the news digest can be identified by a marginal letter identification, e.g. 195B2, page 195, section B, column 2. Editorial references have no identification other than the page number, e.g. 142, page 142. In both cases the date of the event is given when possible, e.g. 4-29-76, April 29, 1976.